P9-CKP-925

Scott Foresman

CALIFORNIA MATHEMATICS

Authors and Advisors

Jennie Bennett
Charles Calhoun
Mary Cavanagh
Lucille Croom
Stephen Krulik
Robert A. Laing
Donna J. Long
Stuart J. Murphy
Jesse A Rudnick
Clementine Sherman
Marian Small
William Tate

Randall I. Charles
Alma B. Ramirez
Jeanne F. Ramos

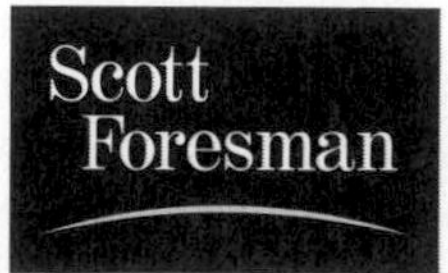

Editorial Offices: Glenview, Illinois • Parsippany, New Jersey • New York, New York
Sales Offices: Reading, Massachusetts • Duluth, Georgia • Glenview, Illinois
Carrollton, Texas • Ontario, California

ISBN: 0-328-00468-5

9 10-VH-07 06

Mathematician Content Reviewers

Roger Howe *Grades K–2*
Professor of Mathematics
Yale University
New Haven, Connecticut

Edward Barbeau *Grades 3–4*
Professor of Mathematics
University of Toronto
Toronto, Ontario, Canada

Gary Lippman *Grades 3–6*
Professor of Mathematics and
Computer Science
California State University Hayward
Hayward, California

David M. Bressoud *Grades 5–6*
DeWitt Wallace Professor of
Mathematics
Macalester College
Saint Paul, Minnesota

California Content Standard Reviewers

Damien Jacotin *Kindergarten*
Los Angeles, California

Jennifer Lozo *Kindergarten*
Lodi, California

Sharon Frost *Grade 1*
Burbank, California

Beth Gould-Golland *Grade 1*
Encinitas, California

Linda Newland *Grade 2*
Santa Clarita, California

Wendy York *Grade 2*
Merced, California

Shakeh Balmanoukian *Grade 3*
Glendale, California

Donna M. Kopenski *Grade 3*
Poway, California

Armine Aghajani *Grade 4*
Tujunga, California

Floyd Flack *Grade 4*
Westminster, California

Donna Crist *Grade 5*
Turlock, California

Jimmy C. Jordan *Grade 5*
La Crescenta, California

Felicia Clark *Grade 6*
Compton, California

Vahe Tcharkhoutian *Grade 6*
Pasadena, California

Contents

Place Value

Adding and Subtracting Whole Numbers and Money

Multiplication and Division Facts

Multiplying by One-Digit Numbers

Multiplying by Two-Digit Numbers

Dividing by One-Digit Divisors

Fraction Concepts and Probability

Adding and Subtracting Fractions and Mixed Numbers

Decimals

Data and Graphs

Geometry

Chapter 12 Measurement, Perimeter, and Area

California Mathematics Content Standards
Grade 4

By the end of grade four, students understand large numbers and addition, subtraction, multiplication, and division of whole numbers. They describe and compare simple fractions and decimals. They understand the properties of, and the relationships between, plane geometric figures. They collect, represent, and analyze data to answer questions.

Number Sense

1.0 Students understand the place value of whole numbers and decimals to two decimal places and how whole numbers and decimals relate to simple fractions. Students use the concepts of negative numbers:

1.1 (🔑) Read and write whole numbers in the millions.

1.2 (🔑) Order and compare whole numbers and decimals to two decimal places.

1.3 (🔑) Round whole numbers through the millions to the nearest ten, hundred, thousand, ten thousand, or hundred thousand.

1.4 (🔑) Decide when a rounded solution is called for and explain why such a solution may be appropriate.

1.5 Explain different interpretations of fractions, for example, parts of a whole, parts of a set, and division of whole numbers by whole numbers; explain equivalents of fractions (see Standard 4.0).

1.6 Write tenths and hundredths in decimal and fraction notations and know the fraction and decimal equivalents for halves and fourths (e.g., $\frac{1}{2} = 0.5$ or .50; $\frac{7}{4} = 1\frac{3}{4} = 1.75$).

1.7 Write the fraction represented by a drawing of parts of a figure; represent a given fraction by using drawings; and relate a fraction to a simple decimal on a number line.

1.8 (🔑) Use concepts of negative numbers (e.g., on a number line, in counting, in temperature, in "owing").

1.9 (🔑) Identify on a number line positive the relative position of fractions, positive mixed numbers, and positive decimals to two decimal places.

2.0 Students extend their use and understanding of whole numbers to the addition and subtraction of simple decimals:

2.1 Estimate and compute the sum or difference of whole numbers and positive decimals to two places.

2.2 Round two-place decimals to one decimal or the nearest whole number and judge the reasonableness of the rounded answer.

3.0 (🔑) Students solve problems involving addition, subtraction, multiplication, and division of whole numbers, and understand the relationships among the operations:

3.1 (🔑) Demonstrate an understanding of, and the ability to use, standard algorithms for the addition and subtraction of multidigit numbers.

3.2 (🔑) Demonstrate an understanding of, and the ability to use, standard algorithms for multiplying a multidigit number by a two-digit number and for dividing a multidigit number by a one-digit number; use relationships between them to simplify computations and to check results.

3.3 (🔑) Solve problems involving multiplication of multidigit numbers by two-digit numbers.

3.4 (🔑) Solve problems involving division of multidigit numbers by one-digit numbers.

4.0 Students know how to factor small whole numbers:

4.1 Understand that many whole numbers break down in different ways (e.g., $12 = 4 \times 3 = 2 \times 6 = 2 \times 2 \times 3$).

4.2 (🔑) Know that numbers such as 2, 3, 5, 7, and 11 do not have any factors except 1 and themselves and that such numbers are called prime numbers.

Algebra and Functions

1.0 Students use and interpret variables, mathematical symbols, and properties to write and simplify expressions and sentences:

1.1 Use letters, boxes, or other symbols to stand for any number in simple expressions or equations (e.g., demonstrate an understanding and the use of the concept of a variable).

1.2 (🔑) Interpret and evaluate mathematical expressions that now use parentheses.

1.3 (🔑) Use parentheses to indicate which operation to perform first when writing expressions containing more than two terms and different operations.

1.4 Use and interpret formulas (e.g., *area* = *length* × *width* or $A = lw$) to answer questions about quantities and their relationships.

1.5 (🔑) Understand that an equation such as $y = 3x + 5$ is a prescription for determining a second number when a first number is given.

2.0 (🔑) Students know how to manipulate equations:

2.1 (🔑) Know and understand that equals added to equals are equal.

2.2 (🔑) Know and understand that equals multiplied by equals are equal.

Measurement and Geometry

1.0 Students understand perimeter and area:

1.1 Measure the area of rectangular shapes by using appropriate units, such as square centimeter (cm^2), square meter (m^2), square kilometer (km^2), square inches (in^2), square yard (yd^2), or square mile (mi^2).

1.2 Recognize that rectangles that have the same area can have different perimeters.

Reproduced from the Mathematics Content Standards for California Public Schools. The symbol (🔑) indicates a key standard as designated by a green oval in the Mathematics Framework for California Public Schools.

1.3 Understand that rectangles that have the same perimeter can have different areas.

1.4 Understand and use formulas to solve problems involving perimeters and areas of rectangles and squares. Use those formulas to find the areas of more complex figures by dividing the figures into basic shapes.

2.0 (🔑) Students use two-dimensional coordinate grids to represent points and graph lines and simple figures:

2.1 (🔑) Draw the points corresponding to linear relationships on graph paper (e.g., draw 10 points on the graph of the equation $y = 3x$ and connect them by using a straight line).

2.2 (🔑) Understand that the length of a horizontal line segment equals the difference of the *x*-coordinates.

2.3 (🔑) Understand that the length of a vertical line segment equals the difference of the *y*-coordinates.

3.0 Students demonstrate an understanding of plane and solid geometric objects and use this knowledge to show relationships and solve problems:

3.1 Identify lines that are parallel and perpendicular.

3.2 Identify the radius and diameter of a circle.

3.3 Identify congruent figures.

3.4 Identify figures that have bilateral and rotational symmetry.

3.5 Know the definitions of a right angle, an acute angle, and an obtuse angle. Understand that 90°, 180°, 270°, and 360° are associated, respectively, with $\frac{1}{4}$, $\frac{1}{2}$, $\frac{3}{4}$, and full turns.

3.6 Visualize, describe, and make models of geometric solids (e.g., prisms, pyramids) in terms of the number and shape of faces, edges, and vertices; interpret two-dimensional representations of three-dimensional objects; and draw patterns (of faces) for a solid that, when cut and folded, will make a model of the solid.

3.7 Know the definitions of different triangles (e.g., equilateral, isosceles, scalene) and identify their attributes.

3.8 Know the definition of different quadrilaterals (e.g., rhombus, square, rectangle, parallelogram, trapezoid).

Statistics, Data Analysis, and Probability

1.0 Students organize, represent, and interpret numerical and categorical data and clearly communicate their findings:

1.1 Formulate survey questions; systematically collect and represent data on a number line; and coordinate graphs, tables, and charts.

1.2 Identify the mode(s) for sets of categorical data and the mode(s), median, and any apparent outliers for numerical data sets.

1.3 Interpret one- and two-variable data graphs to answer questions about a situation.

2.0 Students make predictions for simple probability situations:

2.1 Represent all possible outcomes for a simple probability situation in an organized way (e.g., tables, grids, tree diagrams).

2.2 Express outcomes of experimental probability situations verbally and numerically (e.g., 3 out of 4; $\frac{3}{4}$).

Mathematics Reasoning

1.0 Students make decisions about how to approach problems:

1.1 Analyze problems by identifying relationships, distinguishing relevant from irrelevant information, sequencing and prioritizing information, and observing patterns.

1.2 Determine when and how to break a problem into simpler parts.

2.0 Students use strategies, skills, and concepts in finding solutions:

2.1 Use estimation to verify the reasonableness of calculated results.

2.2 Apply strategies and results from simpler problems to more complex problems.

2.3 Use a variety of methods, such as words, numbers, symbols, charts, graphs, tables, diagrams, and models, to explain mathematical reasoning.

2.4 Express the solution clearly and logically by using the appropriate mathematical notation and terms and clear language; support solutions with evidence in both verbal and symbolic work.

2.5 Indicate the relative advantages of exact and approximate solutions to problems and give answers to a specified degree of accuracy.

2.6 Make precise calculations and check the validity of the results from the context of the problem.

3.0 Students move beyond a particular problem by generalizing to other situations:

3.1 Evaluate the reasonableness of the solution in the context of the original situation.

3.2 Note the method of deriving the solution and demonstrate a conceptual understanding of the derivation by solving similar problems.

3.3 Develop generalizations of the results obtained and apply them in other circumstances.

Place Value

Diagnosing Readiness

In Chapter 1, you will use these skills:

Ⓐ Place Value Through Hundred Thousands

(Grade 3)

Give the value of the underlined digit.

1. $1,\underline{3}08$ **2.** $5\underline{4}$

3. $4\underline{7}6$ **4.** $3\underline{8}6,450$

5. $\underline{6}78,009$ **6.** $5\underline{9},034$

Ⓑ Reading and Writing Numbers

(Grade 3)

Write each number in expanded form.

7. 30,468

8. 731,150

9. The Congo River in Africa is about two thousand, nine hundred miles long. Write this number in standard form.

10. Tutenado, Colombia, also known as the wettest spot on Earth, has an average annual rainfall of 1,177 cm. Write this number in expanded form.

C Rounding to the Nearest Ten and Hundred

(Grade 3)

Round to the nearest ten.

11. 17 **12.** 52

13. 93 **14.** 68

Round to the nearest hundred.

15. 435 **16.** 661

17. 258 **18.** 948

D Comparing and Ordering Numbers

(Grade 3)

Use $>$ or $<$ for each ●.

19. 85 ● 91

20. 342 ● 340

21. 6,489 ● 6,498

Order the numbers from least to greatest.

22. 63, 36, 92, 14, 54

23. 1,451; 309; 1,199; 903

E Adding

(Grade 3)

24. $\begin{array}{r} 41 \\ +\ 17 \\ \hline \end{array}$ **25.** $\begin{array}{r} 75 \\ +\ 24 \\ \hline \end{array}$

26. $\begin{array}{r} 39 \\ +\ 14 \\ \hline \end{array}$ **27.** $\begin{array}{r} 68 \\ +\ 25 \\ \hline \end{array}$

28. Randall bought a soccer ball for $25.00, a basketball for $18.50, and a tennis racket for $49.00. How much did he pay for the two balls?

29. Beatrice makes $6.00 per hour. One week, she worked 5 hours each day for 3 days. How much money did Beatrice earn that week?

F Finding a Pattern

(Grade 3)

Fill in the missing numbers.

30. 4, 7, 10, 13, ■, ■, ■

31. 7, 14, ■, 28, ■, ■

32. 9, 14, ■, ■, 29, ■

33. 75, 125, ■, 225, ■, ■

To the Family and Student

Looking Back	Chapter 1	Looking Ahead
In Grade 3, students learned place value, rounding, and ordering whole numbers through thousands.	**Place Value** In this chapter, students will learn place value, rounding, and ordering whole numbers through millions.	In Grade 5, students will learn place value, rounding, and ordering whole numbers through billions.

Math and Everyday Living

Opportunities to apply the concepts of Chapter 1 abound in everyday situations. During the chapter, think about how place value, rounding, and ordering whole numbers can be used to solve a variety of real-world problems. The following examples suggest just several of the many situations that could launch a discussion about place value, rounding, and ordering whole numbers.

Math and Architecture
Some of the tallest buildings in the world are more than 1,000 feet tall. List the buildings in the table in order from tallest to shortest.

Building	Height (ft)
Town Center	1,285
Misty Hall	1,307
City Building	1,298

Math and Time There are 2,419,200 seconds in 28 days. How many seconds is that rounded to the nearest hundred thousand?

Math and Real Estate
Three different homes in the same neighborhood are for sale. Their costs are \$317,000, \$298,500, and \$320,900. List them in order from least to greatest.

Math and Banking
Suppose you withdraw \$25 from your bank account. Which number represents the change in your account balance, 25 or $^{-}25$?

Math and Business
Suppose you sell newspapers. The first week you sell 10, the second week you sell 20, and the third week you sell 30 newspapers. If the pattern continues, how many newspapers will you sell in the fifth week?

Math at the Library
Suppose there are 1,747,429 books in your local library. About how many million books is this?

Math and Transportation
Your family is car shopping. The car you like costs \$25,246. The car your brother likes costs \$24,986. Which car is more expensive?

Math and Climate The average temperature in one city in January is $^{-}10$°F. In February the average temperature is $^{-}5$°F. Which month is warmer?

 California Content Standards in Chapter 1 Lessons*

Number Sense	Teach and Practice	Practice
1.1 (🔑) Read and write whole numbers in the millions.	1-1	
1.2 (🔑) Order and compare whole numbers	1-3	
1.3 (🔑) Round whole numbers through the millions to the nearest ten, hundred, thousand, ten thousand, or hundred thousand.	1-5	
1.8 (🔑) Use concepts of negative numbers (e.g., on a number line, in counting, in temperature, in "owing".)	1-6, 1-7	

Mathematical Reasoning	Teach and Practice	Practice
1.1 Analyze problems by . . . observing patterns.	1-4	
2.0 Students use strategies, skills, and concepts in finding solutions.		1-2, 1-4, 1-7
2.3 Use a variety of methods, such as words, numbers, symbols, charts, graphs, tables, diagrams, and models, to explain mathematical reasoning.		1-4
2.4 Express the solution clearly and logically by using the appropriate mathematical notation and terms and clear language; support solutions with evidence in both verbal and symbolic work.		1-4
2.5 Indicate the relative advantages of exact and approximate solutions to problems and give answers to a specified degree of accuracy.	1-2	
3.2 Note the method of deriving the solution and demonstrate a conceptual understanding of the derivation by solving similar problems.		1-4

* The symbol (🔑) indicates a key standard as designated in Mathematics Framework for California Public Schools. Full statements of the California Content Standards are found at the beginning of this book following the Table of Contents.

Place Value Through Millions

 **California Content Standard** *Number Sense 1.1(🔑); Read and write whole numbers in the millions.*

Math Link You know how to read and write numbers through hundred thousands. Now you will learn how to read and write numbers through millions.

Warm-Up Review

Give the value of the 2 in each number.

1. 299
2. 502
3. 2,685
4. 5,625
5. Tim is riding in a bike-a-thon. The trail is 10 miles long, and there are 2 rest stops along the way. Tim has ridden 7 miles. How many more miles does he need to ride?

A place-value chart, like the one at the right, can be used to help you read and write numbers. The number shown can be written in four different ways.

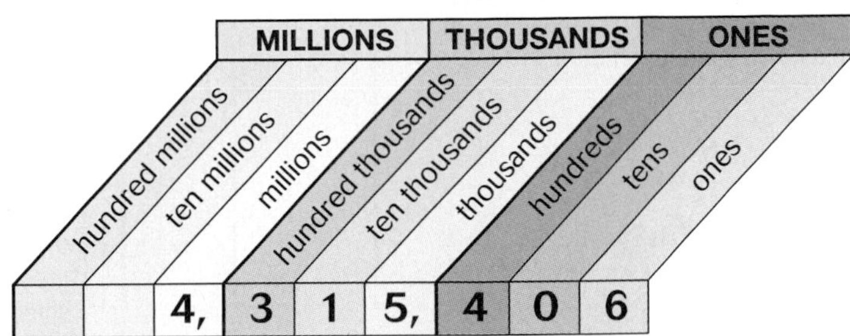

Each group of three numbers is called a **period.**

Standard form: 4,315,406
Word form: four million, three hundred fifteen thousand, four hundred six
Short word form: 4 million, 315 thousand, 406
Expanded form: 4,000,000 + 300,000 + 10,000 + 5,000 + 400 + 6

Example 1

Write 18,652,300 in word form and expanded form.

Word form: Eighteen million, six hundred fifty-two thousand, three hundred
Expanded form: 10,000,000 + 8,000,000 + 600,000 + 50,000 + 2,000 + 300

Example 2

Write four hundred twenty-nine million, five hundred eighteen thousand in standard form.

Standard form: 429,518,000

Word Bank

period
standard form
word form
short word form
expanded form

Example 3

Write the value of the underlined digit in 2<u>8</u>7,415,084.

The underlined digit is in the ten millions place, so the value of the underlined digit is 80,000,000.

Guided Practice *For another example, see Set A on p. 26.*

Write each number in word form and short word form.

1. 1,461,900 **2.** 5,603,000 **3.** 18,300,150 **4.** 125,370,210

Write the value of the underlined digit.

5. 5,410,463 **6.** 7,625,321 **7.** 98,224,000 **8.** 750,409,100

9. Australia has 261,931,000 acres of forest. Write this number in expanded form.

Independent Practice *For more practice, see Set A on p. 28.*

Write each number in word form and short word form.

10. 3,729,000 **11.** 9,500,379 **12.** 56,440,102 **13.** 834,700,000

Write the value of the underlined digit.

14. 8,185,600 **15.** 12,933,528 **16.** 85,984,630 **17.** 192,774,013

18. Mercury is the closest planet to the sun. The diagram at the right shows the distance of the Earth and Mercury from the sun. Write the value of the digit 3 in each number.

Mixed Review

19. Mrs. Walters bought 2 cartons of eggs for $1.19 each, detergent for $6.89, and bread for $1.50. How much did she spend in all?

20. $\begin{array}{r} 85 \\ +\ 14 \\ \hline \end{array}$ **21.** $\begin{array}{r} 68 \\ -\ 23 \\ \hline \end{array}$ **22.** $\begin{array}{r} 861 \\ +\ 345 \\ \hline \end{array}$ **23.** $\begin{array}{r} 589 \\ -\ 163 \\ \hline \end{array}$

Write the value of each underlined digit.

24. 899 **25.** 4,256 **26.** 650,900 **27.** 28,107,428

 **Test Prep** **Choose the correct letter for each answer.**

28. (Gr. 3) Identify the number in expanded form: 3,000 + 600 + 2.

A 3,622 **C** 3,602

B 3,620 **D** 362

29. (Gr. 3) There are 6 groups of students. Each group has 4 students. How many students are there in all?

F 10 students **H** 24 students

G 12 students **J** 28 students

Problem-Solving Skill:

Recognizing Exact Numbers or Estimates

Warm-Up Review

1. 25 + 9
2. 32 − 8
3. 6 × 4
4. 28 ÷ 4
5. Mark read 28 books in June, 19 books in July, and 23 books in August. How many more books did he read in August than in July?

California Content Standard *Mathematical Reasoning 2.5: Indicate the relative advantages of exact and approximate solutions to problems and give answers to a specified degree of accuracy.*

Read for Understanding

Mount Rushmore National Memorial, in South Dakota, was started in 1927. It was finished 14 years later and cost almost $1,000,000 to make! Mount Rushmore is over 5,500 feet high. Each head is about 60 feet tall.

Name	President
George Washington	1st
Thomas Jefferson	3rd
Theodore Roosevelt	26th
Abraham Lincoln	16th

1. In what year was the sculpture started?
2. How tall is each president's head?
3. How many presidents are on Mount Rushmore?

Think and Discuss

Exact Numbers or Estimates

Estimates are not exact numbers. To identify estimates, look for numbers that have been rounded, or look for word clues such as *almost, over,* or *about.*

Reread the paragraph at the top of the page.

4. Is the year 1927 an exact number or an estimate? How do you know?
5. Is it correct to say that the sculpture cost exactly $1,000,000 to make? Why or why not?
6. In what year was the sculpture completed? Is your answer an exact number or an estimate?
7. Why is it important to be able to know if numbers are exact or if they are estimates?

Additional Standard: Mathematical Reasoning 2.0 (See p. 3.)

Guided Practice

Mount Rushmore National Memorial is off Highway 244 and is about 25 miles from Rapid City, South Dakota. The memorial is open 24 hours a day. Each year, more than 2,500,000 people come to view the sculpture.

1. Which number below is used as an estimate?

a. 2,500,000 visitors

b. Highway 244

c. 24 hours a day

2. Which number below is used as an exact number?

a. 2,500,000 visitors

b. 25 miles

c. 24 hours a day

3. How many miles is Mount Rushmore from Rapid City?

a. exactly 25 miles

b. about 25 miles

c. 244 miles

4. Which of the following is true?

a. The memorial is closed at night.

b. The memorial is never closed.

c. The memorial is open only during the day.

Independent Practice

About 17 miles south of Mount Rushmore is the Crazy Horse Memorial. Crazy Horse was a Lakota chief who led and won two famous battles in 1876 for the Lakota homeland. *Crazy,* in the Lakota language, means "spirited." When completed, the memorial will be more than 600 feet long and over 500 feet tall.

5. Which number below is used as an exact number?

a. 600 feet

b. 500 feet

c. 1876

6. How many miles is the Crazy Horse Memorial from Mount Rushmore?

a. exactly 17 miles

b. about 17 miles

c. at least 17 miles

7. Which number below best describes the height of the memorial?

a. less than 500 feet

b. exactly 500 feet

c. more than 500 feet

8. How many famous battles did Crazy Horse win in 1876?

a. one

b. two

c. more than two

Use Homework Workbook 1-2.

Comparing and Ordering Numbers

California Content Standard *Number Sense 1.2(🔑); Order and compare whole numbers . . ..*

Warm-Up Review

Use $>$ or $<$ for each ●.

1. 38 ● 27 **2.** 41 ● 59

3. 156 ● 142

4. 2,367 ● 2,376

5. There are 6 rows of desks in a classroom. Each row has 5 desks. All but 2 desks are filled. How many desks are filled?

Math Link You know how to compare and order whole numbers to 10,000. Now you will learn how to compare and order numbers through millions.

Example 1

Compare 459,285 and 458,600 using $<$ or $>$.
Remember, $<$ means *is less than* and $>$ means *is greater than.*

Step 1 Line up the numbers to compare the digits.

459,285
458,600

same different

The hundred thousands and ten thousands are the same. The thousands are different.

Step 2 Compare the thousands.

9 is greater than 8, so 459,285 is greater than 458,600.

You can write $459{,}285 > 458{,}600$, or $458{,}600 < 459{,}285$.

Example 2

Order the numbers from greatest to least.

21,603,500 3,480,150 35,892,400 3,875,350

Compare two numbers at a time. Begin with the numbers that have the same number of digits.

Step 1 Start at the left. Compare digits in the same place.

21,603,500
35,892,400

$3 > 2$, so 35,892,400 is the greater number.

Step 2 When two digits are the same, compare the digits to the right.

3,875,350
3,480,150

$8 > 4$, so $3{,}875{,}350 > 3{,}480{,}150$.

Step 3 Write the numbers in order from greatest to least.

35,892,400
21,603,500
3,875,350
3,480,150

You can write $35{,}892{,}400 > 21{,}603{,}500 > 3{,}875{,}350 > 3{,}480{,}150$.

Guided Practice *For another example, see Set B on p. 26.*

Compare. Use $>$ or $<$ for each ●.

1. 59,480 ● 85,450

2. 6,109,558 ● 6,129,599

3. Order the numbers from greatest to least: 745,900; 6,202,300; 639,500; 6,190,220.

Independent Practice *For more practice, see Set B on p. 28.*

Compare. Use $>$ or $<$ for each ●.

4. 68,902 ● 68,209

5. 1,570,800 ● 1,565,800

6. 6,750,491 ● 7,651,133

7. 18,520,324 ● 17,924,339

8. 34,000,625 ● 34,120,625

9. 291,032 ● 298,132

Order the numbers from greatest to least.

10. 144,494; 99,633; 106,780; 152,980

11. 41,253,000; 53,700,000; 41,080,000; 41,360,000

Use the table at the right for Exercises 12 and 13.

12. Which park is larger, Katmai or Glacier Bay?

13. List the parks in order from smallest to largest.

14. Math Reasoning Use the digits 8, 5, 2, 3, 7, and 4 to write the greatest and least possible 6-digit numbers. Each digit must be used exactly once.

National Parks in Alaska

Park	Number of Acres
Denali	4,741,910
Gates of the Arctic	7,523,888
Glacier Bay	3,225,284
Katmai	3,674,541
Kenai Fjords	670,643
Kobuk Valley	1,750,737
Lake Clark	2,636,839

Mixed Review

15. Write forty-two million, five hundred eight thousand, three hundred sixty-four in standard form.

Test Prep **Choose the correct letter for each answer.**

16. (Gr. 3) What is the difference between 138 and 246?

A 118 **C** 108
B 109 **D** 98

17. Algebra (Gr. 3) $7 \times \blacksquare = 28$

F 3 **J** 6
G 4 **K** NH
H 5

Understand
Plan
Solve
Look Back

Problem-Solving Strategy:
Find a Pattern

California Content Standard *Mathematical Reasoning 1.1: Analyze problems by . . . observing patterns.*

Warm-Up Review

Fill in the missing numbers.

1. 3, 6, 9, 12, ■, ■, ■
2. 8, 16, ■, 32, ■, ■
3. 70, 60, ■, ■, 30, ■
4. 100, 200, 300, ■, ■
5. Tina bought a blue sweater for $19.50, a white sweater for $25.00, and a scarf for $10.00. How much did she pay for the two sweaters?

Example

A fluffy chick grows from a single cell in a chicken egg. The cell divides into two cells. The two cells divide into four cells. The four cells divide into eight cells and so on. How many cells are there after eight divisions?

Start
1 cell

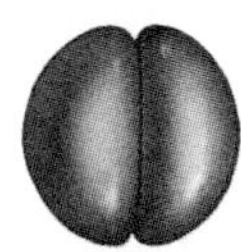

1st Division
2 cells

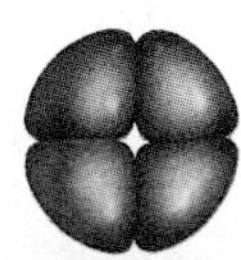

2nd Division
4 cells

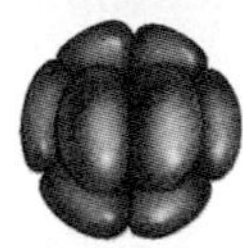

3rd Division
8 cells

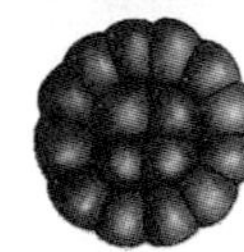

4th Division
16 cells

Understand

What do you need to find?

You need to find the total number of cells after eight cell divisions.

Plan

How can you solve the problem?

You can **find a pattern.** Look at the number of cells there are each time the cells divide.

Solve

Look at the numbers in the pattern.

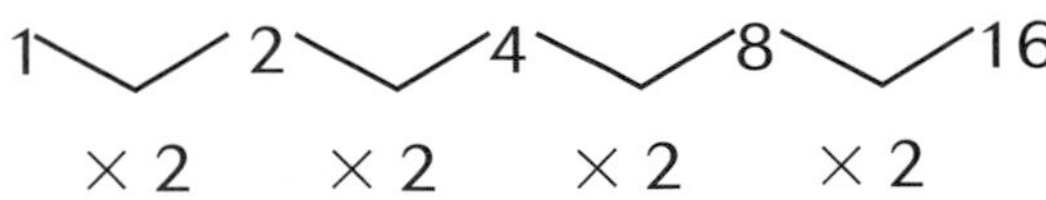

The cells double each time there is a cell division. So the pattern for eight divisions will look like this.

1 2 4 8 16 32 64 128 **256**

After 8 cell divisions, there will be 256 cells.

Look Back

Is there another way to describe the pattern above?

Additional Standards: Mathematical Reasoning 2.0, 2.3, 2.4, 3.2 *(See p. 3.)*

Guided Practice

Find a pattern to help you solve each problem.

1. Martha's number pattern begins with 1, 3, 6, 10, 15. What are the next four numbers in her pattern?

2. Each house on one side of a street has an odd number address. The first house number is 1; the second number is 3; the third is 5; and so on. What is the address of tenth house?

Independent Practice

Find a pattern to help you solve each problem.

3. Suppose the pattern in the wall at the right continues. How many bricks will be in the fifth layer?

4. Suppose you save $1.00 in January, $2.00 in February, and $3.00 in March. If you continue this pattern, how much money will you have saved in a year?

5. Pat has 28 shells. How many rows can she make if she continues the pattern shown at the right?

6. Lidia is making a necklace using beads of different colors. She places the beads on a string in the following order: red, red, yellow, green, red, red, yellow, green. If she continues the pattern, what will be the color of the 20th bead?

Mixed Review

Try these or other strategies to solve each problem. Tell which strategy you used.

Problem-Solving Strategies

- *Draw a Picture*
- *Find a Pattern*
- *Use Logical Reasoning*
- *Write a Number Sentence*

7. Together, Jill and Keesha have 17 rings. Jill has 5 more rings than Keesha. How many rings does each girl own?

8. Ted makes a square array with 4 rows and 4 columns of rocks. What is the least number of rocks he could take away and still have a square array?

Use Homework Workbook 1-4.

Diagnostic Checkpoint

Write each number in word form and short word form.

1. 2,400,210 (1-1) **2.** 12,290,124 (1-1) **3.** 23,110,000 (1-1) **4.** 125,000,000 (1-1)

Write the value of the underlined digit.

5. $\underline{1}$48,750 (1-5) **6.** 3,6$\underline{5}$1,000 (1-1) **7.** 1$\underline{9}$,146,013 (1-1) **8.** $\underline{6}$8,300,406 (1-1)

Compare. Use > or < for each ●.

9. 88,452 ● 88,542 (1-3)

10. 3,405,699 ● 3,450,699 (1-3)

11. 114,524 ● 14,678 (1-3)

12. 314,607,819 ● 314,706,819 (1-3)

Order the numbers from greatest to least.

13. 399,364; 155,640; 500,933; 99,300 (1-3)

14. 54,370,000; 54,703,000; 5,473,000; 54,337,000 (1-3)

Find a pattern to help you solve each problem.

15. (1-4) Remy writes these numbers: 22,453; 23,453; 24,453. Find the next three numbers if he continues the pattern.

16. (1-4) Suppose Catherine received $1.00 for her first birthday, $2.00 for her second, $4.00 for her third birthday, and $8.00 on her fourth birthday. If this pattern continues, how much will she receive on her eighth birthday?

Read the paragraph below. Answer each question.

Lunar eclipses occur when the moon passes into Earth's shadow. A total lunar eclipse occurred on January 20, 2000. The next total lunar eclipse will be in about six months.

17. (1-2) Is the day January 20, 2000, an exact number or an estimate? How do you know?

18. (1-2) Which number is used as an estimate?

Multiple-Choice Cumulative Review

Choose the correct letter for each answer.

1. Which shaded region represents $\frac{1}{3}$?

A 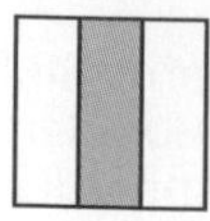

C 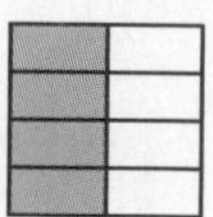

B 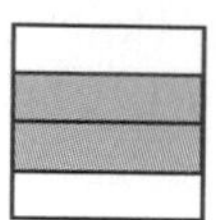

D 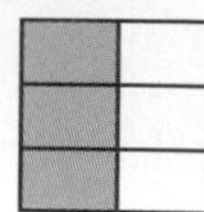

2. What is 343,762 rounded to the nearest ten thousand?

F 340,000
G 343,000
H 343,700
J 344,000

3. Ian left school at 3:10 P.M. It took him 12 minutes to get home. At what time did Ian get home?

A 3:12 P.M.
B 3:17 P.M.
C 3:22 P.M.
D 3:25 P.M.

4. If 3 times a number is 27, which expression could be used to find the number?

F 3×27
G $27 \div 3$
H $3 + 27$
J $27 - 3$

5. What is the missing number in this number pattern?

3, 6, 9, 12, ■, 18, 21

A 13
B 15
C 16
D 23

6. Look at the thermometer. What is the temperature?

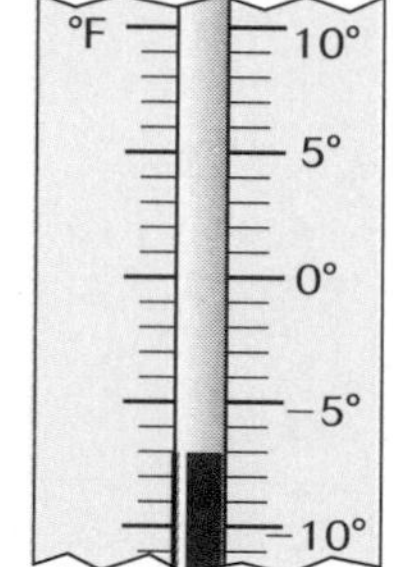

F $^{-}2$°F
G $^{-}5$°F
H $^{-}7$°F
J $^{-}9$°F

7. Al works 3 hours every day. How many hours does he work in 5 days?

A 18 hours
B 15 hours
C 12 hours
D 8 hours

8. Tina has a poster that is 1 foot 8 inches tall. How many *inches* tall is that? (Hint: 1 foot equals 12 inches.)

F 12 in.
G 18 in.
H 20 in.
J 24 in.

Rounding Numbers

California Content Standard *Number Sense 1.3(🔑); Round whole numbers through the millions to the nearest ten, hundred, thousand, ten thousand, or hundred thousand.*

Warm-Up Review

Round to the nearest ten.

1. 32 **2.** 59

3. 88 **4.** 21

Round to the nearest hundred.

5. 875 **6.** 241

7. 381 **8.** 577

9. Sally earns $6.00 per hour babysitting. This week she will work 4 hours a day for 3 days. How much will she earn in all?

Math Link You know how to round numbers through the thousands. In this lesson you will learn how to round numbers through the millions.

Example 1

The projected populations of several California counties in the year 2040 are given in the table below. Round the projected population of Lassen County to the nearest ten thousand.

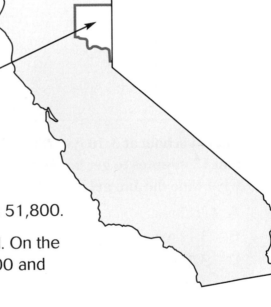

Projected Populations of California Counties

County	2040 Population
Fresno	2,497,700
Glenn	69,800
Lassen	51,800
Monterey	773,300
Ventura	1,319,100

The projected population of Lassen County is 51,800.

You can use a number line to help you round. On the number line below, 51,800 is between 50,000 and 60,000. The halfway number is 55,000.

51,800 is closer to 50,000 than to 60,000. 51,800 rounds down to 50,000.

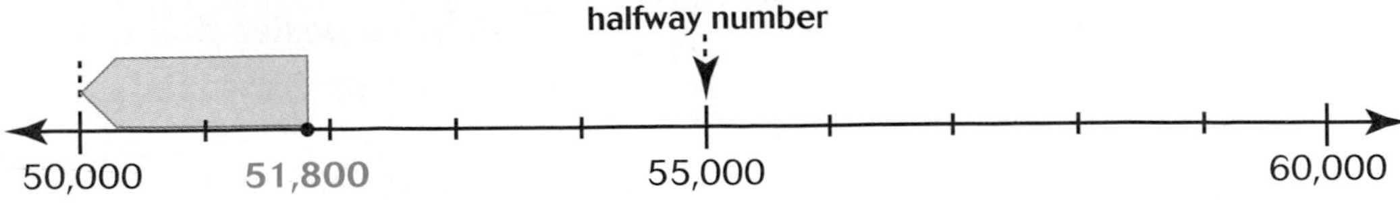

When the number to be rounded is less than the halfway number, round down.

To the nearest ten thousand, 51,800 rounds to 50,000.

Example 2

Round 2,934,500 to the nearest ten thousand.

Step 1 Find the ten thousands place.

2,934,500

Step 2 Look at the first digit to the right.

2,934,500

Step 3 If the digit to the right is less than 5, round down. If the digit is 5 or greater, round up.

2,934,500 rounds to 2,930,000.

Since 4 < 5, keep the digit in the ten thousands place the same.

Example 3

Round 16,468,135 to the underlined place.

Step 1 The underlined digit is in the hundred thousands place.

16,468,135

Step 2 Look at the first digit to the right.

16,468,135

Step 3 If the digit to the right is less than 5, round down. If the digit is 5 or greater, round up.

16,468,135 rounds to 16,500,000.

Since 6 > 5, the digit in the hundred thousands place increases by 1.

Guided Practice *For another example, see Set C on p. 27.*

Round each number to the nearest ten, hundred, thousand, ten thousand, and hundred thousand.

1. 376,480 **2.** 2,845,207 **3.** 43,129,599 **4.** 22,386,063

Round each number to the underlined place.

5. 48,433 **6.** 929,813 **7.** 8,715,990 **8.** 31,545,026

9. The diameter of the Sun is 864,730 miles. Round this number to the nearest ten thousand.

Independent Practice *For more practice, see Set C on p. 29.*

Round each number to the nearest ten, hundred, thousand, ten thousand, and hundred thousand.

10. 11,658 **11.** 419,613 **12.** 1,810,398 **13.** 50,600,145

14. 582,611 **15.** 1,985,000 **16.** 52,609,012 **17.** 417,250,385

Round each number to the underlined place.

18. 48,235 **19.** 860,724 **20.** 4,346,132 **21.** 38,579,725

Use the table at the right for Exercises 22–24.

22. Round each of the numbers to the nearest hundred thousand.

23. Which locations, if any, have the same number of yearly visitors, when rounded to the nearest hundred thousand?

24. List the locations in order from most popular to least popular, based on the number of visitors.

Place	Number of Visitors Per Year
Historic Monument	670,457
National Park	3,274,403
State Beach	1,299,846
State Park	839,162
State Recreation Area	1,327,102

25. Math Reasoning Write a number with a 5 in the hundreds place that rounds to 20,000 when rounded to the nearest thousand.

Mixed Review

26. A new stereo costs $299. Steven has already saved $105. How much more money does he need to save?

27. Mental Math Find the sum of 124 and 59.

28. Use the table on page 14. Which county has the greatest projected population for the year 2040? Which county has the least?

Test Prep **Choose the correct letter for each answer.**

29. (1–4) The houses on Oak Street are numbered 5706, 5710, 5714, 5718, and so on. If 5706 is the first house, what is the address of the eighth house?

A 5720 **B** 5724 **C** 5728 **D** 5734

30. (1–1) Write five million, one hundred two thousand in standard form.

F 5,102 **G** 5,102,000 **H** 5,120,000 **J** 51,200,000

 Use Homework Workbook 1-5.

Positive and Negative Numbers

Warm-Up Review

Order the numbers from least to greatest.

1. 77, 23, 88, 92, 19
2. 2,385 648 1,997 812
3. Sue has collected 38 marbles. She wants to collect 90 by the end of the year. If there are 2 months left in the year, how many more marbles does she need to collect?

California Content Standard *Number Sense 1.8: Use concepts of negative numbers (e.g., on a number line, in counting, in temperature, in "owing").*

Math Link You have learned about numbers greater than zero. Now you will learn about numbers less than zero.

Word Bank

negative number
positive number

Thermometers show temperatures above and below 0°. Numbers above zero are greater than 0°. Numbers below zero are less than 0° and are written with a negative sign. The thermometer at the right shows a temperature of ⁻5°F.

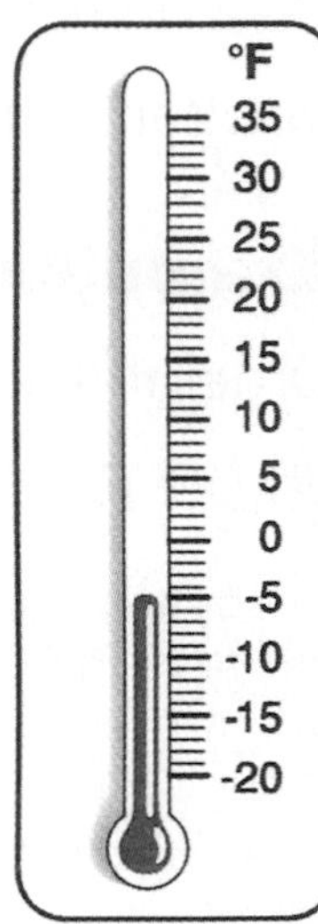

Count the degrees on each thermometer to find each temperature.

If the temperature rises 9°F, find the new temperature

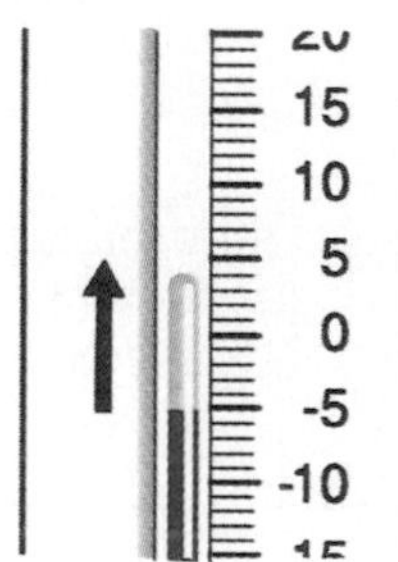

The new temperature is 4°F.

If the temperature falls 6°F, find the new temperature.

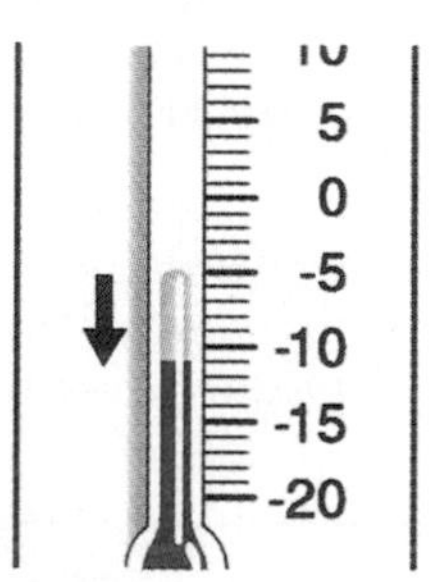

The new temperature is ⁻11°F.

You can use a number line to show negative and positive numbers. **Negative numbers** are less than 0 and are to the left of 0. **Positive numbers** are greater than 0 and are to the right of 0. The number 0 is neither positive nor negative.

Numbers increase as you move to the right.

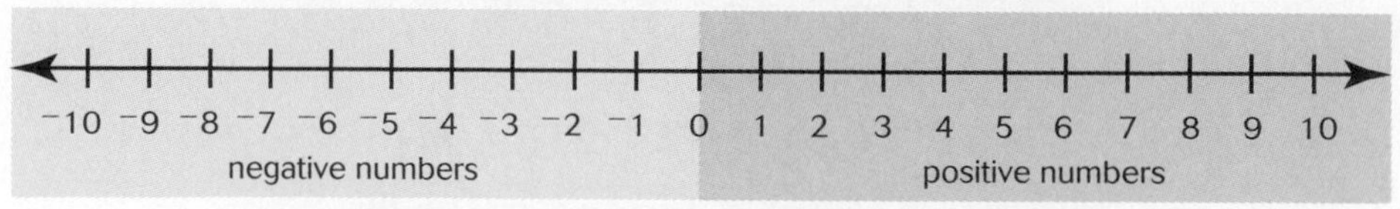

Numbers decrease as you move to the left.

Example 1

Fill in the missing numbers.

$^{-}11$, $^{-}9$, $^{-}7$, ■, $^{-}3$, ■, 1, 3, ■

You can use the number line on page 17. Notice the numbers increase by 2 at each step. The missing numbers are **$^{-}5$, $^{-}1$,** and **5**.

Example 2

Compare 7 and $^{-}10$. Use $>$ or $<$.

On a number line, $^{-}10$ is to the left of 7, so $^{-}10$ is **less than** 7.

You can write $^{-}10 < 7$ or $7 > {}^{-}10$.

Example 3

Compare $^{-}8$ and $^{-}3$. Use $>$ or $<$.

On a number line, $^{-}8$ is to the left of $^{-}3$, so $^{-}8$ is **less than** $^{-}3$.

You can write $^{-}8 < {}^{-}3$ or $^{-}3 > {}^{-}8$.

Example 4

Order the numbers from least to greatest: 4, $^{-}5$, 1, $^{-}7$, $^{-}2$.

Locate the numbers on the number line.

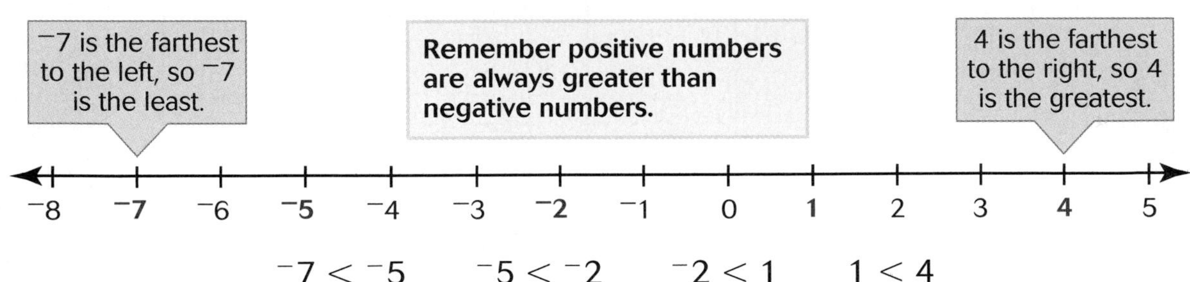

$^{-}7 < {}^{-}5$ $\quad$ $^{-}5 < {}^{-}2$ $\quad$ $^{-}2 < 1$ $\quad$ $1 < 4$

The numbers in order from least to greatest are $^{-}7$, $^{-}5$, $^{-}2$, 1, 4.

Guided Practice

For another example, see Set D on p. 27.

Fill in the missing numbers.

1. $^{-}8$, $^{-}7$, ■, $^{-}5$, ■

2. $^{-}12$, $^{-}9$, $^{-}6$, ■, ■, 3, 6

3. 10, 5, ■, $^{-}5$, $^{-}10$, ■, $^{-}20$

4. 4, 2, ■, $^{-}2$, $^{-}4$, ■

Compare using $>$ or $<$.

5. $^{-}15$ ● 15

6. 0 ● $^{-}3$

7. $^{-}9$ ● $^{-}4$

8. 25 ● $^{-}20$

9. The table at the right shows temperatures in Chicago during February. Which day was the coldest?

Day	Temperature
February 6	11°F
February 8	$^{-}2$°F
February 11	0°F
February 12	$^{-}6$°F

Independent Practice *For more practice, see Set D on p. 29.*

Fill in the missing numbers.

10. $^{-}25$, $^{-}24$, $^{-}23$, ■, ■, $^{-}20$

11. 8, 4, 0, ■, $^{-}8$, ■, $^{-}16$

Compare using > or <.

12. 22 ● $^{-}23$

13. $^{-}2$ ● 0

14. $^{-}29$ ● $^{-}13$

15. $^{-}18$ ● 15

The table at the right shows the low temperatures in five cities. Use the table for Exercises 16–18.

16. Is the temperature colder in Denver or Boston?

17. If the temperature in Boston rose 7°F, find the new temperature.

18. Order the temperatures from lowest to highest.

City	Low Temperature
Chicago	3°F
Minneapolis	$^{-}12$°F
Boston	$^{-}5$°F
Oakland	50°F
Denver	0°F

Mixed Review

19. On a hiking trip, Jenny and her two friends hiked 14 miles the first day, 9 miles the second day, and 5 miles the third day. How much farther did they hike on the first day than on the third day?

20. Round 625,000 to the nearest ten thousand and hundred thousand.

Compare using > or <.

21. 708,153 ● 709,152

22. 2,405,000 ● 2,205,000

23. Find the next three numbers in the pattern. 216, 236, 256, ■, ■, ■

Test Prep **Choose the correct letter for each answer.**

24. (1–1) What is the value of the digit 6 in 28,650,345?

A 60,000
B 600,000
C 6,000,000
D 60,000,000
E NH

25. (Gr. 3) Eric has 3 five-dollar bills, 2 quarters, 3 dimes, and 3 nickels. How much money does he have in all?

F $16.95
G $16.05
H $15.95
J $15.55

Problem-Solving Application:

Using Positive and Negative Numbers

Warm-Up Review

The temperature was $^{-}7$°C at 6:00 A.M. Find the new temperature if it:

1. rises 4°.
2. falls 3°.
3. falls 10°.
4. rises 7°.
5. rises 1°.
6. falls 1°.

 **California Content Standard** *Number Sense 1.8: Use concepts of negative numbers . . ..*

Example

Jack plays a game using the spinner shown below. He begins with zero points. Use the information at the right to find his score after spinning the spinner four times.

Understand

What do you need to find?

Jack's score after spinning the spinner four times.

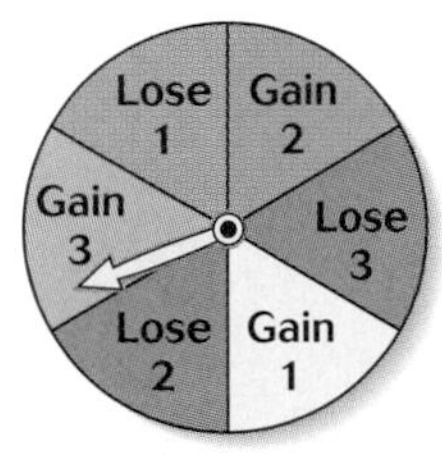

Jack's Four Spins	
Spin 1	Gain 2
Spin 2	Lose 3
Spin 3	Lose 2
Spin 4	Gain 1

Plan

How can you solve the problem?

Jack starts the game with zero points. You can find his score by using a number line to show each gain or loss.

Solve

Use the number line at the right to find Jack's score.

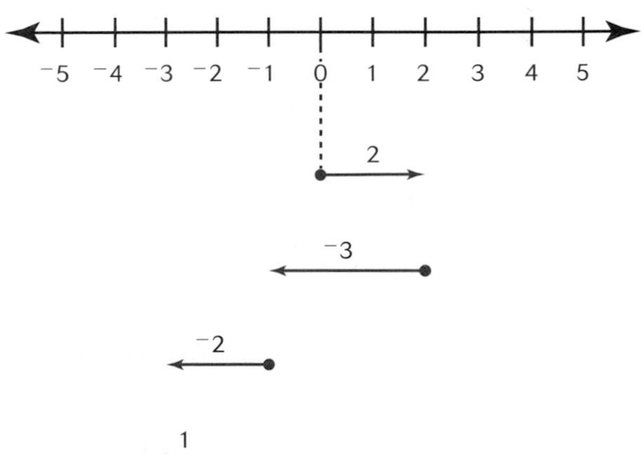

Spin	Points	Score
1	Gain 2	2
2	Lose 3	$^{-}1$
3	Lose 2	$^{-}3$
4	Gain 1	$^{-}2$

After these four spins, Jack's score is $^{-}2$.

Look Back

How are positive and negative numbers used to represent Jack's score after each spin?

Additional Standard: Mathematical Reasoning 2.0 (See p. 3.)

Guided Practice

1. On the 5th spin Jack lost 1 point. What was his score after 5 spins?

2. On the 6th spin Jack gained 3 points. What was his score after 6 spins?

Independent Practice

In Exercises 3–6, use a positive or negative number to represent each situation.

3. The director reported the company stock gained 5 points.

4. Ethanol freezes at 114°C below zero.

5. Emily made a deposit of $236 into her checking account.

6. On a new diet, Jesse had a weight loss of 15 pounds.

Elevations are given as above or below sea level. The elevation at sea level is 0. Use the table at the right for Exercises 7–9.

Place	Elevation
Dead Sea	1,312 feet below sea level
Mariana Trench	36,198 feet below sea level
Mount Everest	29,028 feet above sea level
Mount McKinley	20,320 feet above sea level
Mount Whitney	14,495 feet above sea level

7. Which elevation is the highest?

8. Which elevation is the lowest?

9. Write each elevation as a positive or negative number, then order from lowest to highest.

Mixed Review

10. There are 23 students in the computer lab. Eight more students enter the lab. Then 5 students leave. How many students are there in the computer lab now?

Use the table at the right for Exercises 11 and 12.

Today's Menu	
Spaghetti	$2.95
Burrito	$3.45
Turkey Sandwich	$3.15
Milk	$0.65
Juice	$0.80

11. Alice bought a turkey sandwich and milk for lunch. How much did she spend?

12. Jared decided to buy spaghetti and juice. If he paid with a five-dollar bill, how much change did he receive?

Use Homework Workbook 1-7.

Diagnostic Checkpoint

Complete. For Exercises 1–3, use the words from the Word Bank.

Word Bank
period
word form
short word form
standard form
expanded form
positive number
negative number

1. (1-6) On a number line, a number that is to the left of zero is a ________________.

2. (1-1) A group of three digits separated from other digits of a number by a comma is called a ________________.

3. (1-1) 500,000 + 40,000 + 300 + 80 is the ________________ of 540,380.

Round each number to the underlined place.

4. (1-5) 31$\underline{9}$,674 **5.** (1-5) 3,$\underline{4}$56,932 **6.** (1-5) 1,461,0$\underline{3}$8 **7.** (1-5) 18,$\underline{7}$32

8. (1-5) 29,64$\underline{4}$,964 **9.** (1-5) 91$\underline{0}$,488 **10.** (1-5) 10,$\underline{8}$12,000 **11.** (1-5) 44,9$\underline{0}$5,222

Compare using > or <.

12. (1-6) $^-12$ ● $^-16$ **13.** (1-6) 0 ● $^-6$ **14.** (1-6) $^-8$ ● $^-9$ **15.** (1-6) $^-49$ ● 38

Fill in the missing numbers.

16. (1-6) 2, 1, ■, ■, $^-2$ **17.** (1-6) $^-3$, $^-6$, ■, $^-12$, ■ **18.** (1-6) 8, ■, 0, $^-4$, ■

19. (1-6) $^-18$, $^-19$, ■, ■, $^-22$ **20.** (1-6) $^-15$, $^-5$, ■, 15, ■ **21.** (1-6) $^-6$, $^-12$, ■, ■, $^-30$

In Exercises 22–24, use a positive or negative number to represent each situation.

22. (1-7) Nathan is playing a game and loses 6 points.

23. (1-7) Clara made a withdrawal of $164 from her checking account.

24. (1-7) James went skiing when it was 23°F below zero.

25. (1-7) Badwater Basin in Death Valley is the lowest point in the United States. Its elevation is $^-282$ feet. Is Badwater Basin above or below sea level?

Chapter 1 Test

Write the value of the underlined digit.

1. $50,\underline{6}43,200$ **2.** $1\underline{3}6,889,045$ **3.** $\underline{4},416,319$

Write each number in word form.

4. 1,005,250 **5.** 30,000,490 **6.** 243,013

Order the numbers from greatest to least.

7. 136,310; 106,444; 63,999; 116,889

8. 1,099,110; 999,340; 1,901,999; 1,990,140

Round each number to the underlined place.

9. $4,264,2\underline{2}8$ **10.** $17,6\underline{1}7,690$ **11.** $5\underline{6},251,009$ **12.** $\underline{7}93,800$

Compare using > or <.

13. $^{-}36$ ● 35 **14.** 0 ● $^{-}3$ **15.** $^{-}18$ ● $^{-}7$ **16.** $^{-}4$ ● $^{-}12$

17. 49,500 ● 45,900 **18.** 632,000 ● 632,001 **19.** 3,768,003 ● 36,783

20. Fill in the missing numbers. $^{-}8$, $^{-}6$, ■, $^{-}2$, ■, 2, ■

21. Jeff is stacking cans at the grocery store. He stacks 64 cans in the first row, 32 cans in the second, and 16 cans in the third. How many cans will be stacked in the fifth row?

22. Beth has more than 200 stamps in her collection. She has 25 stamps from foreign countries and 48 animal stamps. She also has almost 90 flower stamps. Which numbers are exact and which are estimates?

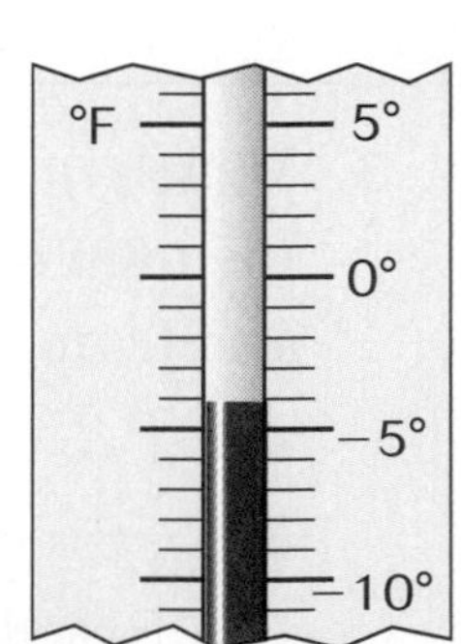

23. When Kevin woke up, the temperature outside was $^{-}4$°F. At noon, the temperature had increased by 9°F. What was the temperature at noon?

Use a positive or a negative number to represent each situation.

24. The elevation of Mount Whitney is 14,495 feet above sea level.

25. Mrs. Dobson lost 5 pounds by exercising.

Multiple-Choice Chapter 1 Test

Choose the correct letter for each answer.

1. What number is equal to thirty-nine million, four thousand, ten?

- **A** 3,940,010
- **B** 39,400,010
- **C** 39,004,010
- **D** 390,004,010
- **E** NH

Use the following paragraph for Questions 2 and 3.

Flora must leave at 6:45 A.M. to be on time for work. She drives over 50 miles each way and spends almost 2 hours each day commuting.

2. Which number is used as an exact number?

- **F** 2 hours
- **G** 50 miles
- **H** 6:45 A.M.
- **J** 100 miles

3. Which number below best describes the total distance Flora travels to and from work each day?

- **A** Less than 2 miles
- **B** Less than 100 miles
- **C** Exactly 100 miles
- **D** More than 100 miles

4. What is the value of the underlined digit in 9,<u>4</u>61,390?

- **F** 4,000
- **G** 40,000
- **H** 400,000
- **J** 4,000,000
- **K** NH

5. Which of the following numbers is less than 3,468,112?

- **A** 3,469,000
- **B** 3,468,125
- **C** 3,468,100
- **D** 3,470,000

Town	Population
Abbott	200,450
Beasley	240,510
Crowley	20,415
Davis	241,050

6. Order the populations from least to greatest.

- **F** Abbott, Beasley, Crowley, Davis
- **G** Crowley, Abbott, Beasley, Davis
- **H** Davis, Beasley, Abbott, Crowley
- **J** Davis, Crowley, Beasley, Abbott

7. **Randy is stacking colored blocks. He places the blocks one on top of another in this order: blue, red, yellow, blue, red, green, blue, red, yellow. If he continues the pattern, what will be the color of the 18th block?**

A Green
B Blue
C Red
D Yellow

---

8. **Which shows 384,200 in expanded form?**

F 3,000 + 800 + 42
G 30,000 + 8,000 + 400 + 20
H 300,000 + 8,000 + 400 + 20
J 300,000 + 80,000 + 4,000 + 200
K NH

---

9. **Round 18,965,000 to the nearest hundred thousand.**

A 18,800,000
B 18,900,000
C 18,970,000
D 19,000,000
E NH

---

10. **What is 4,315,990 rounded to the nearest ten thousand?**

F 4,300,000
G 4,310,000
H 4,316,000
J 4,320,000
K NH

Use the table below for Questions 11 and 12.

Average Daily Temperature In January	
Year	Temperature
1996	⁻4°F
1997	0°F
1998	⁻7°F
1999	5°F

11. **During what year was the average daily temperature in January the coldest?**

A 1996
B 1997
C 1998
D 1999

---

12. **Order the temperatures from lowest to highest.**

F ⁻4°F, ⁻7°F, 0°F, 5°F
G ⁻7°F, ⁻4°F, 0°F, 5°F
H 0°F, ⁻4°F, 5°F, ⁻7°F
J 5°F, 0°F, ⁻4°F, ⁻7°F

---

13. **Elena is playing a game. She begins with zero points. After two turns she has 4 points. On her third turn she loses 3 points. On her fourth turn she gains 2 points. On her fifth turn she loses 7 points. What is Elena's score after her fifth turn?**

A 2
B ⁻2
C 4
D ⁻4

Reteaching

Set A (pages 4–5)

Write 6,110,929 in four different ways.

Standard form: 6,110,929

Word form: six million, one hundred ten thousand, nine hundred twenty-nine

Short word form: 6 million, 110 thousand, 929

Expanded form: 6,000,000 + 100,000 + 10,000 + 900 + 20 + 9

Remember each group of three numbers is called a period. The numbers in a period are read together.

Write each number in word form and short word form.

1. 3,406,600 **2.** 27,006,301

3. 7,412,010 **4.** 110,344,612

5. 540,336,000 **6.** 19,400,350

Write the value of the underlined digit.

7. 8,<u>6</u>02,500 **8.** 9<u>6</u>4,112

9. 2<u>2</u>,400,337 **10.** 1,43<u>2</u>,531

Set B (pages 8–9)

Compare 3,348,624 and 3,349,100 using > or <.

Step 1 Line up the numbers to compare the digits.	**Step 2** Compare the thousands.
3,34 8 ,624 **3,34 9 ,100** **same different**	**8 is less than 9, so 3,348,624 is less than 3,349,100.** **You can write 3,348,624 < 3,349,100 or 3,349,100 > 3,348,624.**

Remember compare digits in the same place.

Compare. Use > or < for each ●.

1. 38,712 ● 38,217

2. 240,100 ● 140,100

3. 7,390,631 ● 6,790,633

4. 21,294,116 ● 20,429,116

5. 410,046,400 ● 410,460,100

6. 36,489,110 ● 3,648,911

Set C (pages 14–16)

Round 11,439,600 to the nearest ten thousand.

Step 1 Find the ten thousands place.
$11{,}4\underline{3}8{,}600$

Step 2 Look at the first digit to the right.
$11{,}4\underline{3}8{,}600$
↑

Step 3 Since $8 > 5$, the digit in the ten thousands place increases by 1. So, 11,438,600 rounds to 11,440,000.

Remember if the digit to the right is less than 5, round down. If the digit is 5 or greater, round up.

Round each number to the nearest hundred, thousand, ten thousand, and hundred thousand.

1. 436,720 **2.** 814,372

3. 2,635,108 **4.** 7,486,618

5. 54,118,677 **6.** 98,537,045

7. 21,360,883 **8.** 14,715,115

Round each number to the underlined place.

9. $54\underline{9}{,}612$ **10.** $24{,}\underline{0}97$

11. $7{,}\underline{3}50{,}200$ **12.** $37{,}6\underline{1}2{,}008$

Set D (pages 17–19)

Compare $^{-}4$ and $^{-}1$. Use > or <.

On a number line, $^{-}4$ is to the left of $^{-}1$, so $^{-}4$ is less than $^{-}1$.

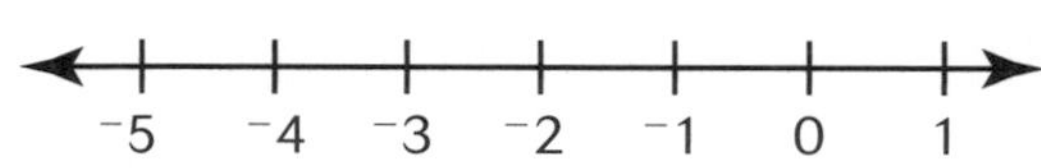

You can write $^{-}4 < {}^{-}1$ or $^{-}1 > {}^{-}4$.

Remember positive numbers are always greater than negative numbers.

Compare using > or <.

1. 18 ● $^{-}22$ **2.** $^{-}27$ ● $^{-}25$

3. $^{-}3$ ● 0 **4.** $^{-}15$ ● $^{-}17$

5. 10°F ● $^{-}10$°F **6.** $^{-}20$ ● 12

7. 3 ● $^{-}36$ **8.** $^{-}50$ ● $^{-}40$

9. $^{-}25$ ● $^{-}24$ **10.** 0 ● $^{-}6$

11. 5 ● $^{-}5$ **12.** $^{-}5$ ● $^{-}15$

13. $^{-}101$ ● 102 **14.** $^{-}101$ ● $^{-}102$

More Practice

Set A *(pages 4–5)*

Write each number in word form and short word form.

1. 75,410
2. 806,307
3. 125,015
4. 3,467,001
5. 9,301,899
6. 24,606,600
7. 36,412,332
8. 429,036,400

Write the value of the underlined digit.

9. 3,$\underline{4}$62,310
10. 6,8$\underline{1}$0,911
11. 5$\underline{4}$,372,009
12. 70,30$\underline{2}$,406
13. 1$\underline{2}$5,376,412
14. 23$\underline{4}$,712,050
15. 629,$\underline{3}$42,118
16. 909,7$\underline{6}$8,472
17. The area of the Pacific Ocean is about sixty-four million, one hundred seventy square miles. Write this number in standard form.
18. The population of California is about twenty-nine million, seven hundred sixty thousand. Write this number in standard form.

Set B *(pages 8–9)*

Compare. Use > or < for each ●.

1. 468,309 ● 648,999
2. 14,801 ● 124,108
3. 256,009 ● 206,590
4. 3,470,900 ● 3,475,880
5. 8,550,375 ● 8,750,990
6. 19,846,112 ● 9,846,102

Order the numbers from greatest to least.

7. 62,345,000; 62,180; 62,572,110; 62,099,400
8. 370,494,333; 393,444; 312,767; 372,100,746
9. The asteroid Juno is about 184,140,000 miles from the sun. The asteroid Hebe is about 179,490,000 miles from the sun. Which asteroid is farther from the sun?
10. The planet Mercury is about 57,900,000 kilometers from the sun and the planet Venus is about 108,200,000 kilometers from the sun. Which planet is closer to the sun?

Set C *(pages 14–16)*

Round each number to the nearest ten, hundred, thousand, ten thousand, and hundred thousand.

1. 486,112 **2.** 307,125 **3.** 670,982 **4.** 950,493

5. 1,217,157 **6.** 3,472,908 **7.** 6,192,347 **8.** 9,041,071

9. 11,071,394 **10.** 15,700,917 **11.** 20,378,956 **12.** 27,109,114

13. 37,400,908 **14.** 54,132,704 **15.** 65,119,099 **16.** 90,145,912

Use the table at the right for Exercises 17–18.

17. Which teams, if any, had the same attendance, when rounded to the nearest hundred thousand?

18. List the teams in order from greatest attendance to least attendance.

	Baseball Attendance
Team 1	493,348
Team 2	946,892
Team 3	857,119
Team 4	1,059,138
Team 5	1,004,917

Set D *(pages 17–19)*

Fill in the missing numbers.

1. $^{-}18$, $^{-}17$, $^{-}16$, ■, $^{-}14$, ■, ■

2. $^{-}9$, $^{-}5$, ■, ■, 7, ■

3. $^{-}12$, ■, $^{-}6$, $^{-}3$, ■, ■

4. $^{-}11$, $^{-}31$, ■, ■, $^{-}91$

5. $^{-}10$, $^{-}20$, ■, ■, $^{-}50$, ■

6. $^{-}76$, $^{-}56$, ■, ■, 4, ■

Compare using $>$ or $<$.

7. 15 ● $^{-}16$ **8.** 0 ● $^{-}9$ **9.** $^{-}14$ ● $^{-}28$

10. $^{-}12$ ● $^{-}11$ **11.** $^{-}12$ ● 4 **12.** $^{-}20$ ● 11

13. $^{-}9$ ● $^{-}25$ **14.** 8 ● $^{-}8$ **15.** $^{-}31$ ● 0

16. The actual temperature in New York is $^{-}15$°F. Due to the wind-chill factor, it feels like $^{-}37$°F. Which temperature is colder?

Problem Solving: Preparing for Tests

Choose the correct letter for each answer.

---

1. Kelly's town has about 25,000 people. Sue Ann's town has about twice as many people as Kelly's town. Which of these represents a reasonable number for the number of people in Sue Ann's town?

A 5,000
B 25,000
C 50,000
D 500,000

Tip
Sometimes you can eliminate some answer choices. Why can you eliminate Choices A and B in this problem?

---

2. Tim made ten tickets for a drawing. He numbered the first five tickets this way: 101, 121, 141, 161, 181. If he continues this pattern, what will be the numbers of the next three tickets?

F 201, 221, 241
G 191, 211, 221
H 191, 201, 211
J 182, 183, 184

Tip
You can use the *Find a Pattern* strategy to help you solve this problem.

---

3. Juan has collected 57 pictures of trains, 28 pictures of boats, and more than 100 pictures of airplanes. Which of these is reasonable for the total number of pictures Juan has collected?

A Less than 85 pictures
B Between 85 and 100 pictures
C Between 100 and 185 pictures
D More than 185 pictures

Tip
Words like *more than, almost,* and *about* tell you that numbers are estimated, not exact.

4. Paula has a collection of 58 blue marbles, 29 red marbles, and 12 green marbles. About how many marbles does she have in all?

F 90 marbles

G 100 marbles

H 110 marbles

J 120 marbles

---

5. Ruth is taller than Jake. Jake is shorter than Sally. Carlos is taller than Ruth. Which of the following is a reasonable conclusion?

A Ruth is the tallest.

B Carlos is taller than Jake.

C Sally is shorter than Jake.

D Carlos is the shortest.

---

6. Maria measured two ribbons. One ribbon was 620 cm long and the other was 260 cm long. Which number sentence can be used to find the difference in the lengths of the ribbons?

F 260 cm − 620 cm = ■

G 620 cm − 260 cm = ■

H 260 cm + 620 cm = ■

J 260 cm + 260 cm = ■

---

7. Lee's car travels about 39 miles on one gallon of gas. About how far can the car travel on 3 gallons of gas?

A 40 mi

B 80 mi

C 120 mi

D 140 mi

8. In a 500-piece jigsaw puzzle, 84 pieces are green and 129 pieces are blue. How many pieces are NOT blue?

F 213 pieces

G 287 pieces

H 371 pieces

J 381 pieces

Use the graph for Questions 9 and 10. This graph shows how students get to school each day.

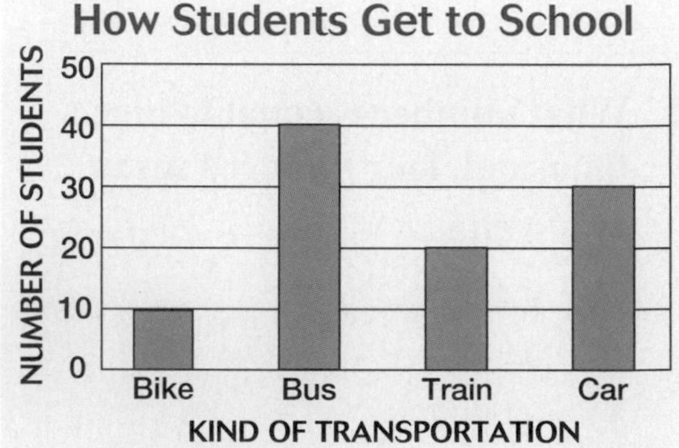

9. How many more students take a bus to school than ride bikes to school?

A 30 students

B 25 students

C 40 students

D 15 students

---

10. On rainy days, students who usually ride bikes to school come by car instead. How many students come to school by car on rainy days?

F 10 students

G 20 students

H 30 students

J 40 students

TEST PREP

Multiple-Choice Cumulative Review

Choose the correct letter for each answer.

Number Sense

1. What is the difference between 4,000 and 532?

   A 3,578
   B 3,568
   C 3,472
   D 3,468
   E NH

2. What number is equal to nine thousand, four hundred seven?

   F 9,407
   G 9,470
   H 94,070
   J 94,007
   K NH

3. What is the missing number?

Number of Birds	Number of Legs
1	2
2	4
3	6
4	■

   A 4
   B 7
   C 8
   D 10
   E NH

4. Which of the following numbers is between −21 and −18 on a number line?

   F ⁻11
   G ⁻15
   H ⁻19
   J ⁻23
   K NH

Use the graph for Questions 5 and 6.

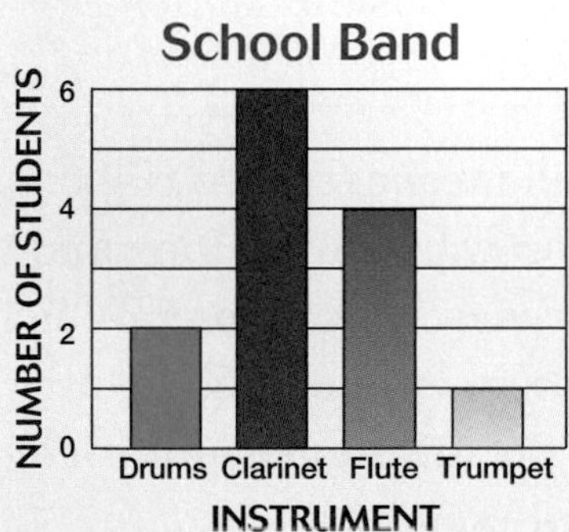

5. Which instrument is played by the most students?

   A Drums
   B Clarinet
   C Flute
   D Trumpet

6. How many more students play the flute than the drums?

   F 0 students
   G 1 student
   H 2 students
   J 4 students

Measurement and Geometry

7. What is the *area* of the shaded region?

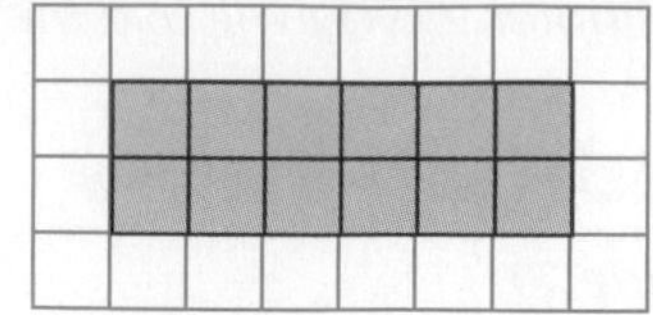

A 2 square units
B 6 square units
C 12 square units
D 16 square units
E NH

8. Which of the following is not a quadrilateral?

F square
G triangle
H rectangle
J parallelogram

9. Which of these units of measure would you use to measure the distance between two cities?

A liter
B kilometer
C gram
D centimeter

10. How many cups are in 2 quarts?

F 2
G 4
H 6
J 8
K NH

11. What is the perimeter of a square whose sides measure 6 inches?

6 in.

A 12 in.
B 18 in.
C 24 in.
D 36 in.
E NH

12. A triangle has 3 sides of equal length. What type of triangle is it?

F obtuse
G scalene
H equilateral
J isosceles

13. Use an inch ruler to measure the segment below. What is the length of the segment?

A 1 in.
B 2 in.
C 3 in.
D 4 in.
E NH

14. Look at the clock. What time will it be in 45 minutes?

F 12:55
G 1:00
H 12:45
J 12:50

Adding and Subtracting Whole Numbers and Money

Diagnosing Readiness

In Chapter 2, you will use these skills:

Ⓐ Addition Facts

(Grade 2)

1. 8 + 4 **2.** 3 + 4

3. 7 + 7 **4.** 6 + 7

5. 6 + 9 **6.** 7 + 8

7. 9 + 8 **8.** 7 + 6

9. Kenesha ran 6 miles one week and 8 miles the next. How many miles did she run in all?

Ⓑ Adding Two-Digit Numbers

(Grade 3)

10. $\begin{array}{r} 23 \\ +\,15 \\ \hline \end{array}$ **11.** $\begin{array}{r} 40 \\ +\,34 \\ \hline \end{array}$

12. $\begin{array}{r} 93 \\ +\,34 \\ \hline \end{array}$ **13.** $\begin{array}{r} 36 \\ +\,91 \\ \hline \end{array}$

14. $\begin{array}{r} 38 \\ +\,25 \\ \hline \end{array}$ **15.** $\begin{array}{r} 89 \\ +\,43 \\ \hline \end{array}$

16. Lily saved $98 during April, $70 during May, and $81 during July. How much money did she save in April and July?

C Subtraction Facts

(Grade 2)

17. 7 − 1

18. 10 − 4

19. 12 − 4

20. 18 − 9

21. 14 − 6

22. 15 − 8

23. 16 − 7

24. 17 − 9

25. At the end of a checkers game, you had captured all 12 of your opponent's pieces. Your opponent had captured 7 of your pieces. How many more pieces did you capture than your opponent?

D Subtracting Two-Digit Numbers

(Grade 3)

26. $\begin{array}{r} 48 \\ -\ 26 \\ \hline \end{array}$

27. $\begin{array}{r} 96 \\ -\ 35 \\ \hline \end{array}$

28. $\begin{array}{r} 52 \\ -\ 14 \\ \hline \end{array}$

29. $\begin{array}{r} 60 \\ -\ 21 \\ \hline \end{array}$

30. $\begin{array}{r} 93 \\ -\ 64 \\ \hline \end{array}$

31. $\begin{array}{r} 86 \\ -\ 49 \\ \hline \end{array}$

32. Maurice read 26 pages of his book one night and 35 pages the next night. How many more pages did he read the second night than the first?

E Rounding Numbers

(pages 14–16)

Round each number to the nearest hundred.

33. 426

34. 892

Round each number to the nearest thousand.

35. 6,793

36. 8,129

Round each number to the nearest ten thousand.

37. 17,027

38. 49,850

F Number Sentences with Addition and Subtraction

(Grade 3)

Find each missing number.

39. 4 + ■ = 9

40. 29 + 43 = ■

41. 25 + ■ = 37

42. 17 − ■ = 8

43. 46 − 23 = ■

44. 58 − ■ = 38

To the Family and Student

Looking Back	Chapter 2	Looking Ahead
In Grade 3, students learned how to add and subtract whole numbers and money with up to four digits. $12.95 + $26.84	**Adding and Subtracting Whole Numbers and Money** In this chapter, students will learn how to add and subtract whole numbers and money with up to five digits. 87,423 − 26,974	In Chapter 9, students will learn how to add and subtract decimals. 4.6 + 0.8

Math and Everyday Living

Opportunities to apply the concepts of Chapter 2 abound in everyday situations. During the chapter, think about how adding and subtracting whole numbers and money can be used to solve a variety of real-world problems. The following examples suggest just several of the many situations that could launch a discussion about adding and subtracting whole numbers and money.

Math at Play How much more is the cost of a game player and one game at Video World than at Super Mart?

VIDEO WORLD

Game Player $129.99

Games $49.50 each

SUPER MART

Video Games $ 45.99 each

Game Player $119.45

Math and Travel How far is it from San Francisco to San Diego, through Los Angeles?

Math and Transportation A new car your family likes costs $14,826. An options package costs $590. How much does the car cost with the options package and $924.96 sales tax?

Math and Shopping At the grocery store, you spend $33.83 on groceries. You use several coupons that total $2.55. The tax is $1.01. How much did you spend in all at the grocery store?

Math and Recreation Golden Gate National Recreation Area is 73,690 acres. Point Reyes National Seashore is 71,060 acres. How much bigger is Golden Gate National Recreation Area than Point Reyes National Seashore?

Math at the Library Your school library had 48,265 books last year. This year the school bought 87 new books for the library. How many books does the library have now?

California Content Standards in Chapter 2 Lessons*

	Teach and Practice	Practice
Number Sense		
1.4 (🔑) Decide when a rounded solution is called for and explain why such a solution may be appropriate.	2-2	
2.1 Estimate and compute the sum or difference of whole numbers and positive decimals to two places.	2-1	2-2, 2-3, 2-4, 2-7
3.1 (🔑) Demonstrate an understanding of, and the ability to use, standard algorithms for the addition and subtraction of multidigit numbers.	2-3, 2-4, 2-5, 2-6, 2-7, 2-9	
3.3 (Gr. 3) (🔑) Solve problems involving addition, subtraction . . . of money amounts in decimal notation	2-12	
Algebra and Functions		
1.0 Students use and interpret variables, mathematical symbols, and properties to write and simplify expressions and sentences.		2-10
1.1 Use letters, boxes, or other symbols to stand for any number in simple expressions or equations (e.g., demonstrate an understanding and the use of the concept of a variable.)	2-10, 2-11	
2.0 (🔑) Students know how to manipulate equations.	2-11	

	Teach and Practice	Practice
Mathematical Reasoning		
1.1 Analyze problems by identifying relationships, distinguishing relevant from irrelevant information, sequencing and prioritizing information, and observing patterns.		2-8
1.2 Determine when and how to break a problem into simpler parts.		2-8
2.0 Students use strategies, skills, and concepts in finding solutions.		2-2, 2-8, 2-12
2.1 Use estimation to verify the reasonableness of calculated results.	2-3, 2-4, 2-5, 2-6, 2-7	
2.2 Apply strategies and results from simpler problems to more complex problems.	2-8	
2.3 Use a variety of methods, such as words, numbers, symbols, . . . and models, to explain mathematical reasoning.		2-8
2.5 Indicate the relative advantages of exact and approximate solutions to problems	2-2	2-1
3.2 Note the method of deriving the solution and demonstrate a conceptual understanding of the derivation by solving similar problems.		2-8
3.3 Develop generalizations of the results obtained and apply them in other circumstances.		2-3

* The symbol (🔑) indicates a key standard as designated in the Mathematics Framework for California Public Schools. Full statements of the California Content Standards are found at the beginning of this book following the Table of Contents.

Estimating Sums and Differences

 **California Content Standard** *Number Sense 2.1: Estimate . . . the sum or difference of whole numbers and positive decimals to two places.*

Warm-Up Review

1. Round 78 to the nearest ten.
2. Round 506 to the nearest hundred.
3. Anthony received $10 for his birthday. He spent $5.30 for a paperback and $3.95 for a puzzle. How much did he spend altogether?

Math Link You have learned how to round numbers. You also know that an estimate is an approximate answer. Now you will estimate sums and differences of whole numbers and money.

Example 1

Estimate 82 + 28.

Round to the greatest place value to get numbers you can add easily.

82 + 28

rounds to — rounds to

80 + 30 = 110

82 + 28 is about 110.

To the nearest ten, 82 rounds to 80.

To the nearest ten, 28 rounds to 30.

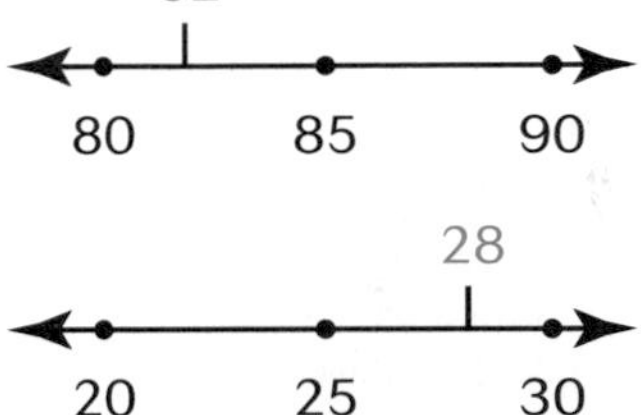

Example 2

Estimate $7.57 − $2.38.

$7.57 − $2.38

$8.00 − $2.00 = $6.00

$7.57 − $2.38 is about $6.00.

Round to the nearest dollar.

If you have 50¢ or more, round up to the next dollar.

If you have less than 50¢, keep the number of dollars the same.

Example 3

Estimate the sum.

$$\begin{array}{r} 516 \\ +\ 359 \\ \hline \end{array}$$

516 + 359

rounds to — rounds to

500 + 400 = 900

516 + 359 is about 900.

Guided Practice *For another example, see Set A on p. 72.*

Estimate each sum or difference.

1. 37 + 21 **2.** 52 − 37 **3.** 786 − 143 **4.** \$5.29 + 3.76 **5.** 763 − 254 **6.** 5,250 + 3,772

7. 89 − 48 **8.** 613 + 286 **9.** \$41.99 − \$22.05 **10.** 6,890 − 1,038

11. In a dart game, Jesse scored 52 points, and Nora scored 28 points. Estimate how many more points Jesse scored.

Independent Practice *For more practice, see Set A on p. 74.*

Estimate each sum or difference.

12. 83 − 29 **13.** 473 + 224 **14.** 631 + 567 **15.** \$6.17 + 1.75 **16.** 32,134 − 19,423 **17.** \$18.50 − 12.14

18. Jesse wants to buy a new dart board and a box of target balls, as shown at the right. Estimate what they will cost him altogether.

19. Math Reasoning Describe a situation where you might need only an estimated sum or difference. When might you need an exact sum or difference?

Mixed Review

20. Sean spent \$7.32 for a calendar and \$0.99 for a marker. How much did he spend altogether?

21. Round 45,610,205 to the nearest ten thousand and nearest million.

22. Compare: $^{-}4$ ● $^{-}2$

23. Compare: 8 ● $^{-}8$

24. Write 24,038,619 in word form.

25. Write 5,227,973 in expanded form.

 **Test Prep** **Choose the correct letter for each answer.**

26. What is the value of 2 in 624,790? (1-1)

A 200 **C** 20,000

B 2,000 **D** 200,000

27. Which number is greatest? (1-3)

F 14,966,333 **H** 9,899,699

G 14,976,300 **J** 13,995,000

Understand
Plan
Solve
Look Back

Problem-Solving Skill:
Is an Estimate Enough?

Warm-Up Review

Estimate each sum or difference.

1. 64 + 21 **2.** 566 + 703

In the following situations, which numbers are exact and which are estimates?

3. The Sears Tower is nearly 1,500 feet tall.

4. Reggie Hill received 3,468 votes.

California Content Standard *Mathematical Reasoning 2.5: Indicate the relative advantages of exact and approximate solutions to problems . . .. Also, Number Sense 1.4 (See p. 37.)*

Read for Understanding

Smith School held a board game tournament to raise money. Twenty-one teams played. Eighteen girls and 19 boys volunteered to help run the event. Eighty-nine students each paid to watch.

Tournament Fees

Competing teams:	$22.00 per team
Observers (non-volunteers):	$2.00 each

1. How many teams played in the tournament?

2. How much did each team pay to play in the tournament?

3. How many students paid to watch the event?

Think and Discuss

Is an Estimate Enough?

Sometimes you only need to estimate to solve a problem. If you are asked to find "about how much," or to decide "if there are enough," often you can estimate.

Reread the paragraph at the top of the page.

4. Would you estimate or find an exact answer to tell how much money the teams paid altogether to be in the tournament? Explain.

5. The school has 45 volunteer badges. Is that enough for all the volunteers? Can you estimate to solve this problem? Explain.

6. Why is it helpful to be able to solve a problem by using an estimate rather than an exact answer?

 Additional Standards: Number Sense 2.1; Mathematical Reasoning 2.0 (See p. 37.)

Guided Practice

One of the games at the tournament is a word game. Read the rules at the right. Yoshi picked 5 letters: *H*, *W*, *Y*, *E*, and *N*. She could make either of the words shown below the rules.

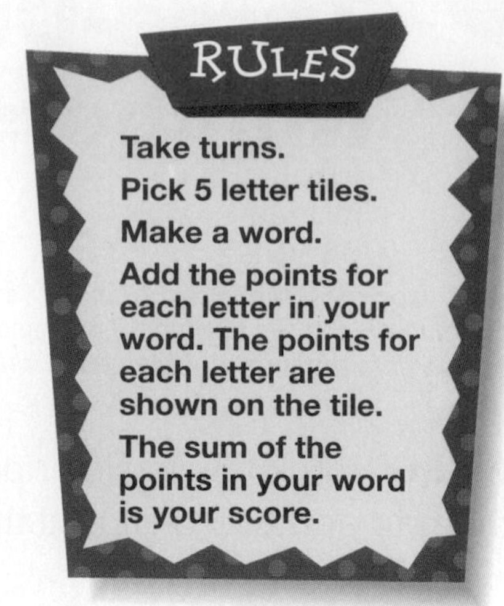

1. What is the best way for Yoshi to decide which word will give her the most points?
   - **a.** Round the points of each letter to the greatest place value. Then add the rounded points for each word.
   - **b.** Add the total number of points of all 5 letters that Yoshi picked.
   - **c.** Find the exact number of points for each word and compare.

2. Which of the following best shows how Yoshi should decide which word to make?
   - **a.** $20 + 10 + 10 + 10 = 20 + 10 + 20$
   - **b.** $23 + 8 + 5 + 14 < 23 + 8 + 24$
   - **c.** $23 + 8 + 5 + 14 + 24 = 74$

Independent Practice

At the tournament refreshment stand, a taco costs $2.75, and a drink costs $0.95. You want to buy 2 tacos and 2 drinks. You have $10.00. Do you have enough money?

3. What are you asked to find?
   - **a.** the cost of the tacos and drinks
   - **b.** if you have enough money to purchase the tacos and drinks
   - **c.** the change you will receive from the $10.00

4. What do you need to know?
   - **a.** about how much the tacos and drinks will cost
   - **b.** exactly how much money you will have left
   - **c.** how much more a taco costs than a drink

5. **Math Reasoning** Do you need to find an exact answer or an estimate to solve the problem? Explain.

Adding Two- and Three-Digit Numbers

Warm-Up Review

1. 4 + 7 **2.** 9 + 5

3. 8 + 6 **4.** 5 + 8

Estimate each sum.

5. 14 + 56 **6.** 720 + 250

7. Gil baked 2 loaves of cranberry bread, 3 loaves of banana bread, and 3 loaves of pumpkin bread. How many loaves did he bake in all?

California Content Standard *Number Sense 3.1. (🔑): Demonstrate an understanding of, and the ability to use, standard algorithms for the addition . . . of multidigit numbers. Also, Mathematical Reasoning 2.1 (See p. 37.)*

Math Link You know basic addition facts. Now you will use them to add two-digit and three-digit numbers.

Example 1

At the beginning of summer, Josh had 176 marbles. By the end of summer he had won 148 marbles. How many marbles did Josh have by the end of summer?

176	+	148	=	■
marbles at beginning of summer		**marbles won during summer**		**total marbles at end of summer**

Step 1 Add the ones. Regroup 14 ones as 1 ten 4 ones.	**Step 2** Add the tens. Regroup 12 tens as 1 hundred 2 tens.	**Step 3** Add 3 hundreds.
$\begin{array}{r} {\scriptstyle 1} \\ 176 \\ +\ 148 \\ \hline 4 \end{array}$	$\begin{array}{r} {\scriptstyle 1\,1\ } \\ 176 \\ +\ 148 \\ \hline 24 \end{array}$	$\begin{array}{r} {\scriptstyle 1\,1\ } \\ 176 \\ +\ 148 \\ \hline 324 \end{array}$

Josh had 324 marbles at the end of summer.

Check by estimating: 200 + 100 = 300. The answer is reasonable because 324 is close to 300.

More Examples

A. $\begin{array}{r} {\scriptstyle 1\ } \\ 74 \\ +\ 46 \\ \hline 120 \end{array}$

B. $\begin{array}{r} {\scriptstyle 1\,1\ } \\ 325 \\ 132 \\ +\ 74 \\ \hline 531 \end{array}$ ← **Be sure to line up the addends on the right side.**

C. $\begin{array}{r} {\scriptstyle 1\ \ } \\ \$1.25 \\ +\ 2.08 \\ \hline \$3.33 \end{array}$ ← **Remember to show dollars and cents in the answer.**

 Additional Standards: Number Sense 2.1; Mathematical Reasoning 3.3 (See p. 37.)

Guided Practice *For another example, see Set B on p. 72.*

1. $57 + 31$

2. $73 + 59$

3. $436 + 29$

4. $\$5.08 + 3.76$

5. $425 + 212 + 178$

6. How many children are competing in the marble contest altogether?

Marble Contest	
Boys	Girls
32	31

Independent Practice *For more practice, see Set B on p. 74.*

7. $23 + 26$

8. $58 + 37$

9. $\$0.34 + 0.29$

10. $\$3.41 + 2.35$

11. $314 + 72$

12. $465 + 226$

13. $529 + 345$

14. $38 + 27 + 19$

15. $54 + 49 + 3$

16. $325 + 243 + 157$

17. 49 + 21 + 5

18. 618 + 32 + 50

19. 29 + 712 + 165

20. Erica spent $4.19 for paints and $1.05 for paintbrushes. Estimate her total bill for these items. Then find the exact amount.

21. **Math Reasoning** If both addends are rounded up, is the estimated sum greater than or less than the actual sum? What if both addends are rounded down? What if one is rounded up and one is rounded down?

Mixed Review

22. Janine has 87 hard cover books and 91 paperback books. About how many books does she have in all?

23. Find the missing numbers; $^-4$, $^-3$, ■, ■, 0, 1, 2, ■, 4

24. Estimate the sum: 411 + 509

25. Estimate the difference: 75 − 43

 **Test Prep** **Choose the correct letter for the answer.**

26. Which number has five millions?
(2-1)
A 30,522,641
B 62,948,518
C 105,233,607
D 7,625,617

27. Which is the lowest temperature?
(1-6)
F $^-8$°F
G $^-10$°F
H 0°F
J 3°F

Use Homework Workbook 2-3.

Adding Greater Numbers

California Content Standard *Number Sense 3.1. (🔑): Demonstrate an understanding of, and the ability to use, standard algorithms for the addition . . . of multidigit numbers. Also, Mathematical Reasoning 2.1 (See p. 37.)*

Math Link In the last lesson you added two-digit and three-digit numbers. Now you will add four-digit and five-digit numbers.

Warm-Up Review

Estimate first. Then add.

1. 19 + 34
2. 76 + 11
3. 455 + 92
4. 555 + 617
5. $5.04 + $2.30
6. 517 + 913 + 710
7. Sheri has 23 hockey cards from one team and 53 cards from another. How many hockey cards does she have in all?

Example 1

Hector is playing a computer game in which points are earned for exploring different countries. While Hector explored China, he earned the points shown at the right. How many points did Hector score in all?

15,986	+	13,539	=	■
Game 1 points		**Game 2 points**		**total points**

Add each column. Regroup if necessary.

Step 1 Add the ones.	**Step 2** Add the tens.	**Step 3** Add the hundreds.	**Step 4** Add the thousands.	**Step 5** Add the ten thousands.
$\begin{array}{r} {}^{1}\\ 15{,}986 \\ +\ 13{,}539 \\ \hline 5 \end{array}$	$\begin{array}{r} {}^{1\,1}\\ 15{,}986 \\ +\ 13{,}539 \\ \hline 25 \end{array}$	$\begin{array}{r} {}^{1\ 1\,1}\\ 15{,}986 \\ +\ 13{,}539 \\ \hline 525 \end{array}$	$\begin{array}{r} {}^{1\ 1\,1}\\ 15{,}986 \\ +\ 13{,}539 \\ \hline 9{,}525 \end{array}$	$\begin{array}{r} {}^{1\ 1\,1}\\ 15{,}986 \\ +\ 13{,}539 \\ \hline 29{,}525 \end{array}$

Hector's total score was 29,525 points.

Check by estimating: 20,000 + 10,000 = 30,000. The answer is reasonable because 29,525 is close to 30,000.

Additional Standard: Number Sense 2.1 (See p. 37.)

More Examples

A.
```
   1 11
   3,564  ← 
 +   758  ←
   4,322
```
Be sure to line up the addends on the right side.

B.
```
   1 1 1
  $76.38
 + 38.79
 $115.17  ←
```
Remember to show dollars and cents in the answer.

C.
```
   1 21
   2,375
   4,680
 + 1,276
   8,331
```

Guided Practice
For another example, see Set C on p. 72.

1. 6,354 + 1,243

2. $56.72 + 38.56

3. 47,865 + 26,527

4. 315 + 7,106 + 2,423 + 3,201

5. 1,245 + 3,162 + 4,391 + 2,146

6. 8,803 + 7,296 **7.** 19,350 + 23,185 **8.** 93,215 + 4,022

9. The table at the right shows Hector's scores for six games. What was his combined score for Games 3, 4, and 5?

10. Suppose Hector plays a seventh game. He scores 9,036 more points than he did in Game 6. Find his score for Game 7.

Game Scores

Game	Score
Game 1	15,986
Game 2	13,539
Game 3	32,562
Game 4	41,376
Game 5	23,765
Game 6	31,450

Independent Practice
For more practice, see Set C on p. 74.

11. 5,345 + 2,284

12. 6,784 + 2,137

13. 25,461 + 32,327

14. $363.95 + 452.20

15. 68,125 + 46,596

16. 78,356 + 47,143

17. 25,214 + 36,170 + 2,456

18. $575.31 + 287.25 + 306.17

19. 37,607 + 12,513 + 4,051 + 25,638

20. 42,173 + 5,609 + 812 + 12,463

21. 3,602 + 9,081 **22.** 63,005 + 18,999 **23.** 5,220 + 37,643

24. 4,518 + 27,009 + 30,687 **25.** 42,111 + 13,758 + 28,514 + 8,662

26. Jeremy worked two jobs during the summer. He earned $453.92 in July and $385.09 in August. How much did he earn during those two months?

Air Distances		
From:	To:	Miles
Hong Kong	Port Said, Suez Canal, Egypt	4,950
Port Said, Suez Canal, Egypt	Capetown, South Africa	4,590
Capetown, South Africa	Zanzibar City, Tanzania	2,350
Zanzibar City, Tanzania	Istanbul, Turkey	3,310
Istanbul, Turkey	Calcutta, India	3,650
Calcutta, India	Hong Kong	1,530

Use the table for Exercises 27 and 28.

27. Yolanda is planning to fly from Calcutta, India, to Istanbul, Turkey, then to Zanzibar City, Tanzania, and then to Capetown, South Africa. Find the total air distance.

28. Estimate the total air distance of a trip from Hong Kong to Port Said, Egypt, then to Capetown, South Africa, then to Zanzibar City, Tanzania, then to Istanbul, Turkey, then to Calcutta, India, and then back to Hong Kong.

Mixed Review

29. Morgan is taking a 550-mile road trip. She packed two suitcases. One weighed 28 pounds and the other weighed 44 pounds. What was the total weight of her luggage?

30. Write in standard form: two million, nine hundred fourteen.

31. Refer to the table on page 45. What was Hector's highest game score?

32. Estimate 513 + 244.

33. Estimate 29 + 91.

34. 74 + 18

35. $2.38 + $9.01

36. 716 + 55

37. 8 + 16 + 753

Test Prep **Choose the correct letter for each answer.**

38. (1-3) Which number is less than 418,096?

A 418,098 **C** 418,079

B 418,104 **D** 420,002

39. (2-1) Choose the best estimate for 87 + 42.

F 50 **H** 130

G 120 **J** 140

 Use Homework Workbook 2-4.

Subtracting Two- and Three-Digit Numbers

Warm-Up Review

1. 6 − 2
2. 8 − 3
3. 17 − 8
4. 15 − 7
5. 22 + 39
6. 314 + 72

Estimate each difference.

7. 58 − 28
8. 413 − 170
9. Gerald scored 4 points and then 8 points. How many more points does he need to have a total of 15 points?

California Content Standard *Number Sense 3.1. (🔑): Demonstrate an understanding of, and the ability to use, standard algorithms for the . . . subtraction of multidigit numbers. Also, Mathematical Reasoning 2.1* *(See p. 37.)*

Math Link You know basic subtraction facts. In this lesson, you will use basic facts and regrouping to subtract two-digit and three-digit numbers.

Example 1

A sporting goods store sells jump ropes. How many more jump ropes did the store sell in June than in May?

Month	Number Sold
May	37
June	52
July	68
August	46

52	−	37	=	■
jump ropes sold in June		**jump ropes sold in May**		**difference in jump ropes sold**

Step 1 Subtract the ones. Regroup 1 ten as 10 ones.

$$\begin{array}{r} \overset{4}{\cancel{5}}\overset{12}{\cancel{2}} \\ -\ 37 \\ \hline 5 \end{array}$$

Step 2 Subtract the tens.

$$\begin{array}{r} \overset{4}{\cancel{5}}\overset{12}{\cancel{2}} \\ -\ 37 \\ \hline 15 \end{array}$$

The store sold 15 more jump ropes in June.

<u>*Check*</u> by estimating: 50 − 40 = 10. The answer is reasonable because 15 is close to 10.

You can also check by adding: 15 + 37= 52.

Example 2

Find 634 − 149.

Step 1 Subtract the ones. Regroup 1 ten as 10 ones.	Step 2 Subtract the tens. Regroup 1 hundred as 10 tens.	Step 3 Subtract the hundreds.
2 14 634 − 149 5	12 5 2 14 634 − 149 85	12 5 2 14 634 − 149 485

Check by estimating: 600 − 100 = 500. The answer is reasonable because 485 is close to 500.

You can also use addition to check your work: 485 + 149 = 634.

More Examples

A.

```
 510
 608
− 74
 534
```

Be sure to line up the addends on the right side.

B.

```
  4 12
 $5.23
− 4.51
 $0.72
```

Remember to show dollars and cents in the answer.

Guided Practice

For another example, see Set D on p. 72.

1. 47 − 27 **2.** 60 − 32 **3.** 568 − 85 **4.** $7.09 − 2.47 **5.** 523 − 146

6. 96 − 38 **7.** 82 − 29 **8.** 499 − 165 **9.** 758 − 46

10. How many more times did Jill jump in the Double Dutch Competition than did Adam?

Double Dutch Competition

Name	Jumps in 1 minute
Jill	221
Leesa	202
Adam	198

Independent Practice

For more practice, see Set D on p. 74.

11. 63 − 32 **12.** 78 − 5 **13.** 96 − 18 **14.** $4.68 − 1.46 **15.** $0.84 − 0.57

16. $\begin{array}{r} 812 \\ -\ 57 \\ \hline \end{array}$

17. $\begin{array}{r} 630 \\ -\ 325 \\ \hline \end{array}$

18. $\begin{array}{r} \$8.20 \\ -\ 3.47 \\ \hline \end{array}$

19. $\begin{array}{r} 534 \\ -\ 8 \\ \hline \end{array}$

20. $\begin{array}{r} \$5.31 \\ -\ 1.85 \\ \hline \end{array}$

21. 47 − 9 **22.** 335 − 327 **23.** 876 − 36 **24.** $3.94 − $0.37

25. At the Double Dutch Championships in South Carolina in June 1996, the winning team jumped 447 times in 2 minutes. Another team jumped 298 times in 2 minutes. How many more jumps did the winning team make?

26. The zoo has 197 birds. Of these, 29 are parrots. How many birds other than parrots are there?

27. Math Reasoning When do you need to regroup a ten for ones? a hundred for tens?

Mixed Review

28. Keesha read 51 pages and then 46 pages. Nigel read 63 pages and then 49 pages. About how many more pages did Nigel read then Keesha?

Refer to the number line below for Exercises 29 and 30. What number should be written at each point?

29. Point *A*

30. Point *B*

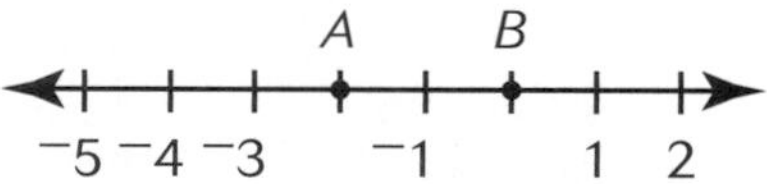

31. 54 + 17 **32.** 394 + 38 **33.** 4,166 + 2,083 **34.** $\begin{array}{r} 12{,}870 \\ +\ 2{,}940 \\ \hline \end{array}$

Test Prep **Choose the correct letter for each answer.**

35. (2-3) Alan started with 132 marbles. He bought 24 more. Then he won 23. Now how many marbles does he have?

A 47 **B** 155 **C** 156 **D** 169 **E** NH

36. (1-1) Which digit is in the hundred thousands place in 45,073,891?

F 0 **G** 5 **H** 7 **J** 8 **K** NH

Subtracting Greater Numbers

LESSON 2-6

California Content Standard *Number Sense 3.1. (🔑): Demonstrate an understanding of, and the ability to use, standard algorithms for the . . . subtraction of multidigit numbers. Also, Mathematical Reasoning 2.1* *(See p. 37.)*

Warm-Up Review

1. 15 − 6 **2.** 17 9

3. 91 − 53 **4.** 424 − 417

5. 4,508 + 2,473

Estimate each difference.

6. 27 − 14 **7.** 813 − 166

8. LouAnne scored 523 points in a game, while Kyle scored 438 points. How many more points did LouAnne score?

Math Link You have subtracted with two-digit and three-digit numbers. In this lesson you will subtract four-digit and five-digit numbers.

Example

In 2000, Logan Falls had a population of 36,248. In 1950, the population was 19,563. By how many people did the population increase in those 50 years?

36,248	−	19,563	=	■
population in 2000		**population in 1950**		**population increase**

Subtract each column. Regroup if necessary.

Step 1 Subtract the ones.	**Step 2** Subtract the tens.	**Step 3** Subtract the hundreds.	**Step 3** Subtract the thousands.	**Step 5** Subtract the ten thousands.
	1 14	5 11 14	2 15 5 11 14	2 15 5 11 14
36,248	36,248	36,248	36,248	36,248
− 19,563	− 19,563	− 19,563	− 19,563	− 19,563
5	85	685	6,685	16,685

From 1950 to 2000, the population increased by 16,685 people.

<u>Check</u> by adding:

36,248	16,685
− 19,563	+ 19,563
16,685	36,248

You can also check by estimating: 40,000 − 20,000 = 20,000.

The answer is reasonable because 16,685 is close to 20,000.

Guided Practice *For another example, see Set E on p. 73.*

1. 5,875 − 2,375
2. 8,026 − 4,753
3. 47,892 − 1,545
4. \$642.38 − 564.57
5. 85,036 − 37,564

6. How many years were there between the first airplane ride and the first landing on the moon?

7. How many years were there between Lindbergh's solo airplane flight from New York to Paris and the Wright Brothers' first airplane flight?

Notable Flights	
Year	**Flight**
1903	Wright Brothers' first airplane flight
1927	Lindbergh's solo airplane flight from New York to Paris
1961	First orbital flight
1969	Apollo-Saturn 11 landing on the moon

Independent Practice *For more practice, see Set E on p. 74.*

8. 5,641 − 2,375
9. 7,435 − 3,596
10. 6,753 − 3,568
11. 45,734 − 12,356
12. 62,539 − 27,645

13. 9,806 − 6,978
14. \$70.56 − \$60.79
15. 50,347 − 4,985

16. Refer to the table above. How many years were there between Charles Lindbergh's flight from New York to Paris and the first flight that orbited Earth?

17. In June, a small airline had 14,786 passengers. This was 1,417 more passengers than they had in May. How many passengers did the airline have in May?

Mixed Review

18. Jennifer has \$50.00. She spent \$23.47 for a sweatshirt and \$11.40 for a cap. How much did she spend in all?

19. Write in word form: 31,614,079
20. Compare: 77,266 ● 77,626

21. 89 − 36
22. 418 − 219
23. 31,087 + 34,251

Test Prep Choose the correct letter for each answer.

24. Find the next number in the pattern 91, 82, 73, 64, ■ (1-4)

A 56 C 52
B 55 D 45

25. 23,672 + 48,955 = (2-4)

F 61,527 H 72,627
G 71,627 J 72,717

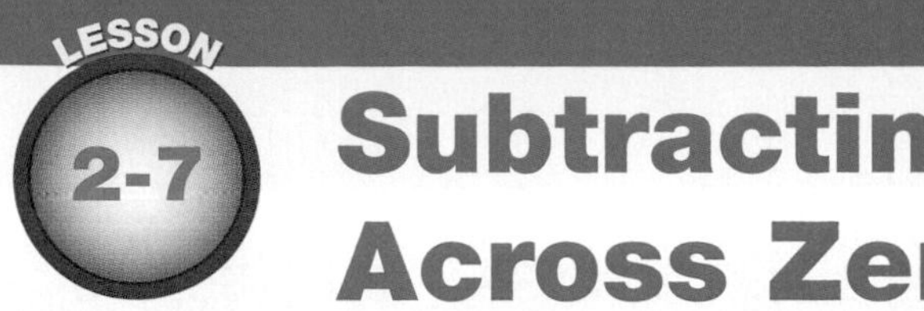

Subtracting Across Zeros

California Content Standard *Number Sense 3.1 (🔑): Demonstrate an understanding of, and the ability to use, standard algorithms for the . . . subtraction of multidigit numbers. Also, Mathematical Reasoning 2.1* *(See p. 37.)*

Warm-Up Review

1. 1 hundred = ■ tens
2. 1 ten = ■ ones
3. 852 − 576
4. \$543.12 − \$267.35
5. Estimate 5,129 − 1,866
6. There are 4,275 parking spaces in a parking lot. If 3,366 spaces are filled, how many are empty?

Math Link You know how to regroup to do some subtraction problems. Now you will learn to regroup to subtract with zeros.

Example

Amy's new jigsaw puzzle has a total of 3,000 pieces. So far, Amy has used 1,675 pieces. How many more pieces must she use to complete the puzzle?

3,000	−	1,675	=	■
total number of puzzle pieces		**puzzle pieces used so far**		**puzzle pieces still to be used**

There are no ones, tens, or hundreds. So these columns must be regrouped.

Step 1 Regroup 1 thousand as 10 hundreds.	**Step 2** Regroup 1 hundred as 10 tens.	**Step 3** Regroup 1 ten as 10 ones.	**Step 4** Subtract.
2 10 3,000 − 1,675	9 2 10 10 3,000 − 1,675	9 9 2 10 10 10 3,000 − 1,675	9 9 2 10 10 10 3,000 − 1,675 1,325

Amy has 1,325 more puzzle pieces to use.

Check by adding:

```
  3,000          1,325
− 1,675        + 1,675
  1,325          3,000
```

You can check to see if the answer is reasonable by estimating: 3,000 − 2,000 = 1,000. The answer is reasonable because 1,325 is close to 1,000.

Additional Standard: Number Sense 2.1 *(See p. 37.)*

Guided Practice *For another example, see Set F on p. 73.*

1. 800 − 479

2. 4,000 − 1,265

3. 8,000 − 472

4. 40,008 − 10,547

5. 70,907 − 56,746

6. A stadium in Chicago has 66,944 seats. A stadium in San Diego has 71,000 seats. How many more seats are there in the stadium in San Diego?

Independent Practice *For more practice, see Set F on p. 75.*

7. 300 − 120

8. 603 − 368

9. 800 − 509

10. 6,080 − 2,270

11. 90,900 − 32,790

12. 4,000 − 1,074

13. 78,000 − 57,892

14. 80,096 − 6,874

15. The Garcia family is working on completing the rain forest puzzle shown at the right. Marisa has joined 1,309 pieces to the puzzle. Her sister Susana has joined 975 pieces. Estimate how many more pieces they have to join to finish the puzzle.

16. Ms. Johnson's class is working on a 1,500-piece puzzle. Every week, each of her 28 students puts 10 pieces in the puzzle. How many pieces will be left after 3 weeks?

Mixed Review

17. A plane trip from Honolulu to Hong Kong is 5,540 miles. A plane trip from Honolulu to London is 7,230 miles. How much farther is the trip to London?

18. 2,457 − 1,266

19. \$3.12 − \$3.08

20. 893 − 645

21. 704 + 149

 **Test Prep** **Choose the correct letter for each answer.**

22. If rounded to the nearest thousand, which number does *not* round to 36,000? (1-5)

A 36,493

B 36,527

C 35,710

D 35,514

23. Brianne has 596 points. How many more points must she score to tie the top score of 872? (2-5)

F 1,468

G 322

H 286

J 276

Diagnostic Checkpoint

For Exercises 1–10, estimate each sum or difference.

1. (2-1) $71 + 18$

2. (2-1) $36 + 23$

3. (2-1) $89 - 32$

4. (2-1) $65 - 29$

5. (2-1) $735 + 198$

6. (2-1) $\$8.17 + 2.54$

7. (2-1) $5{,}724 + 3{,}672$

8. (2-1) $\$9.43 - 4.78$

9. (2-1) $7{,}642 - 2{,}413$

10. (2-1) $\$12.74 - 8.16$

11. (2-3) $56 + 31$

12. (2-3) $298 + 536$

13. (2-3) $\$6.74 + 2.98$

14. (2-4) $14{,}723 + 12{,}175$

15. (2-4) $47{,}286 + 35{,}437$

16. (2-4) $57{,}684 + 8{,}296 + 795 + 32{,}517$

17. (2-4) $\$36.75 + 27.36$

18. (2-3) $54 + 33 + 29$

19. (2-3) $325 + 172 + 286$

20. (2-4) $\$38.42 + 67.83 + 51.70$

21. (2-5) $43 - 29$

22. (2-5) $70 - 54$

23. (2-5) $\$0.92 - 0.32$

24. (2-5) $86 - 17$

25. (2-5) $526 - 135$

26. (2-6) $3{,}479 - 1{,}254$

27. (2-7) $7{,}029 - 3{,}642$

28. (2-7) $8{,}000 - 5{,}461$

29. (2-7) $50{,}000 - 17{,}932$

30. (2-6) $79{,}765 - 4{,}893$

31. (2-7) You and a friend played a computer game. You scored 5,000 points. Your friend scored 3,765 points. How many more points did you score?

Use the following information for Exercises 32 and 33.

You want to buy two videotapes for $19.95 each and a music cassette for $12.65. Prices include tax. You have $60.00.

32. (2-2) Do you need to find an exact answer or an estimate to determine whether or not you have enough money? Explain.

33. (2-2) You gave the cashier $55 and your change was $2.45. Do you need to find an exact answer or an estimate to determine whether or not you got the correct change back?

TEST PREP

Multiple-Choice Cumulative Review

Choose the correct letter for each answer.

1. Which number makes this number sentence true?

   16 ÷ ■ = 4

   A 20
   B 12
   C 6
   D 4

2. Which shows a line of symmetry?

   F 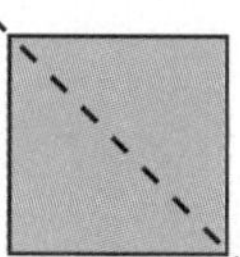

   G 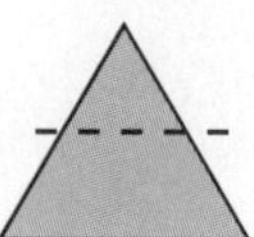

   H 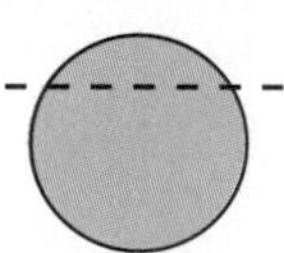

   J 

3. What is 14,865 rounded to the nearest hundred?

   A 14,800
   B 14,870
   C 14,900
   D 15,000

4. Look at the thermometer. What is the temperature?

   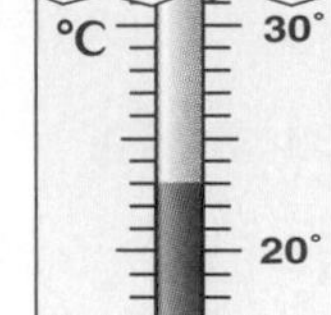

   F 23°C
   G 24°C
   H 25°C
   J 27°C

5. What is the value of the digit 3 in 23,247,985?

   A 3,000
   B 30,000
   C 300,000
   D 3,000,000

6. Find 7,632 – 3,967.

   F 3,565
   G 3,655
   H 3,667
   J 4,335
   K NH

7. A stereo receiver costs $124.32, and a pair of speakers costs $83.91. Find the cost of the complete system (receiver and speakers).

   A $40.41
   B $108.23
   C $201.23
   D $208.23

Problem-Solving Strategy:

Solve a Simpler Problem

Warm-Up Review

1. 7 × 4
2. 30 ÷ 5

What are the next three numbers in each pattern?

3. 80, 70, 75, 65, 70, 60, 65, 55, 60, ■, ■, ■
4. 5, 7, 10, 12, 15, 17, 20, 22, 25, ■, ■, ■
5. Jenny read for 25 minutes. She started at 10:15 A.M. When did she finish?

California Content Standard *Mathematical Reasoning 2.2: Apply strategies and results from simpler problems to more complex problems.*

Example

Sixty-four students play in pairs in a Mancala tournament. If players lose, they are out of the tournament. If players win, they play another game. Winners play until one winner is left. How many games must be played before there is a single winner?

Understand

What do you need to find?

You need to find the number of games that must be played to find a single winner.

Plan

How can you solve the problem?

First **solve a simpler problem.** How many games would be played if there were 2 players? If there were 3 players? 4 players?

Solve

2 players would need to play 1 game.
3 players would need to play 2 games.
4 players would need to play 3 games.
5 players would need to play 4 games.
6 players would need to play 5 games.
⋮ ⋮
64 players would need to play 63 games.

Think About 4 Players

Game 1

Game 2

Game 3

WINNER!

Look Back

How did solving a simpler problem make solving this problem easier?

  *Additional Standards: Mathematical Reasoning 1.1, 1.2, 2.0, 2.3, 3.2 (See p. 37.)*

Guided Practice

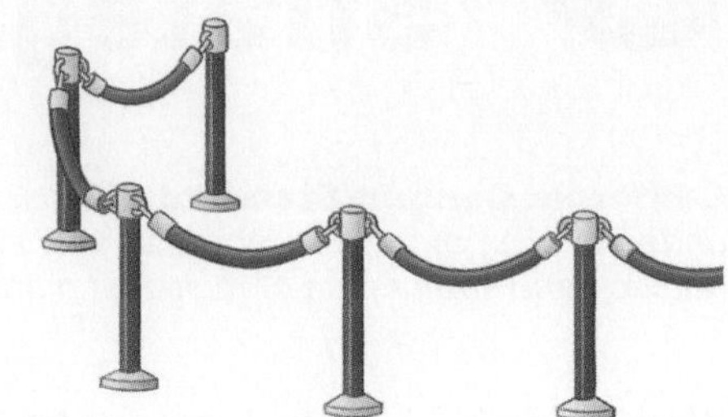

1. The tournament is set up in the school gym. Several games are played at once. A rope barrier separates different playing areas. To make the barrier, the rope is cut into 15 equal pieces. How many cuts are made?

2. The pieces of rope are hooked to posts as shown at the right. How many posts are needed for the 15 pieces of rope?

Independent Practice

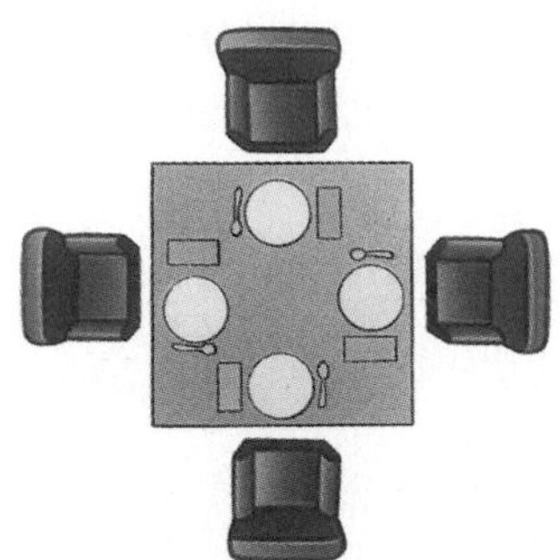

3. The students involved in the tournament are served lunch at long tables. These tables are made by placing 16 tables like the one shown at the right end to end. How many students can sit at one long table?

4. A local bakery is donating dessert for the tournament. The organizers want to be sure that everyone has enough, so they order 5 desserts for every 3 players. How many desserts are needed for 15 players?

5. After the games are over, each judge shakes hands with each of the other judges. How many handshakes will be exchanged if there are 6 judges?

Mixed Review

Try these or other strategies to solve each problem. Tell which strategy you used.

Problem-Solving Strategies

- *Make a List*
- *Solve a Simpler Problem*
- *Find a Pattern*
- *Write a Number Sentence*

6. At the Mancala tournament, 3 games are played at each table. How many tables are needed for 20 games?

7. Round 1 of the tournament began at 9:00 A.M., Round 2 at 9:45 A.M., and Round 3 at 10:30 A.M. At what time did Round 6 begin?

Use Homework Workbook 2-8.

Mental Math Strategies

California Content Standard *Number Sense 3.1 (🔑): Demonstrate an understanding of, and the ability to use, standard algorithms for the addition and subtraction of multidigit numbers.*

Warm-Up Review

Write in expanded form.

1. 57
2. 618
3. 855
4. 3,915

Add mentally.

5. 30 + 16
6. 400 + 235
7. Last summer 517 boys and 456 girls attended Camp Hurley. How many more boys were there?

Math Link You know how to add and subtract. Now you will learn how to use mental math to help you add and subtract.

Word Bank

breaking apart
compensation

There are a variety of ways to add and subtract mentally. Sometimes you can get the answer by **breaking apart** the numbers in the problem.

Example 1

Use breaking apart to find 48 + 26.

Think: 48 = 40 + **8** 26 = 20 + **6**

Start with the tens. Add 40 and 20.	Then add the ones.	Next, add the sums of the tens and ones.
$\begin{array}{r} 40 \\ +\ 20 \\ \hline 60 \end{array}$	$\begin{array}{r} 8 \\ +\ 6 \\ \hline 14 \end{array}$	$\begin{array}{r} 60 \\ +\ 14 \\ \hline 74 \end{array}$

Breaking apart also works for subtraction.

Example 2

Use breaking apart to find 57 − 34.

Think: 57 = 50 + **7** 34 = 30 + **4**

Subtract the tens.	Subtract the ones.	Add the differences of the tens and ones.
$\begin{array}{r} 50 \\ -\ 30 \\ \hline 20 \end{array}$	$\begin{array}{r} 7 \\ -\ 4 \\ \hline 3 \end{array}$	$\begin{array}{r} 20 \\ +\ 3 \\ \hline 23 \end{array}$

Example 3

Use breaking apart to find 214 + 138.

$$\begin{array}{r} 200 \\ +\ 100 \\ \hline 300 \end{array} + \begin{array}{r} 10 \\ +\ 30 \\ \hline 40 \end{array} + \begin{array}{r} 4 \\ +\ 8 \\ \hline 12 \end{array} = 352$$

Add the sums.

Example 4

Use breaking apart to find 545 − 323.

$$\begin{array}{r} 500 \\ -\ 300 \\ \hline 200 \end{array} + \begin{array}{r} 40 \\ -\ 20 \\ \hline 20 \end{array} + \begin{array}{r} 5 \\ -\ 3 \\ \hline 2 \end{array} = 222$$

Add the differences.

Compensation is another method you can use to add or subtract mentally.

Example 5

Use compensation to find 436 + 199.

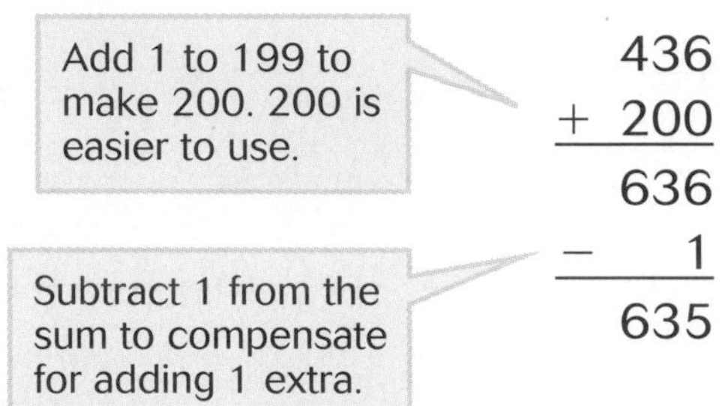

Add 1 to 199 to make 200. 200 is easier to use.
Subtract 1 from the sum to compensate for adding 1 extra.

$$\begin{array}{r} 436 \\ +\ 200 \\ \hline 636 \\ -\ \ \ 1 \\ \hline 635 \end{array}$$

Example 6

Use compensation to find 4,500 − 2,995.

Add 5 to 2,995 to make 3,000. 3,000 is easier to use.

Add 5 to the difference to compensate for subtracting 5 extra.

$$\begin{array}{r} 4{,}500 \\ -\ 3{,}000 \\ \hline 1{,}500 \\ +\ \ \ \ 5 \\ \hline 1{,}505 \end{array}$$

Guided Practice

For another example, see Set G on p. 73.

Add or subtract mentally. Use breaking apart.

1. 24 + 37 **2.** 97 − 24 **3.** 469 − 323 **4.** 2,335 + 1,442

Add or subtract mentally. Use compensation.

5. 38 + 17 **6.** 86 − 28 **7.** 698 + 123 **8.** 5,000 − 2,990

9. For the winter choral concert, 297 seats were filled in the auditorium. Use mental math to find how many seats were empty.

Independent Practice *For more practice, see Set G on p. 75.*

Add or subtract mentally. Use breaking apart.

10. 33 + 15 **11.** 74 − 31 **12.** 254 + 315 **13.** 437 + 114

14. 678 − 352 **15.** 3,479 − 363 **16.** 5,423 + 1,182

Add or subtract mentally. Use compensation.

17. 58 + 23 **18.** 61 − 29 **19.** 483 + 198 **20.** 548 − 196

21. 497 + 456 **22.** 2,678 − 398 **23.** 7,995 + 1,178

24. On Saturday, 2,415 people went to the circus. On Sunday, there were 2,124 people. Use mental math to find the total number of people who went to the circus on these two days.

Mixed Review

For Exercises 25 and 26, use the data at the right.

25. List the newspapers in order from the one with the greatest number of subscribers to the one with the least number of subscribers.

26. How many more people subscribe to *City Banner* than to *Today's Herald?*

Newspaper Subscribers	
Daily Journal	15,396
Today's Herald	12,613
City Banner	15,700
People's Press	12,630

27. Estimate 473 + 330. **28.** Round 2,043 to the nearest hundred.

29. 8,944 − 318 **30.** 42,678 − 31,598 **31.** 7,000 − 4,163

 **Test Prep** **Choose the correct letter for each answer.**

32. (2-4) Last year Ms. Silver flew 36,254 miles on business trips. This year she flew 40,168 miles. How many miles did she fly altogether?

A 76,322 **B** 76,412 **C** 76,422 **D** 77,422 **E** NH

33. (1-1) What number is four thousand, fifty-two?

F 452 **G** 4,052 **H** 40,052 **J** 40,520 **K** NH

 Use Homework Workbook 2-9.

Expressions with Addition and Subtraction

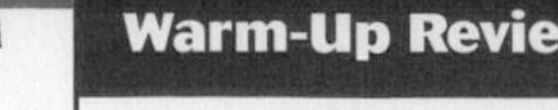

California Content Standard *Algebra and Functions 1.1. Use letters, boxes, or other symbols to stand for any number in simple expressions . . ..*

Warm-Up Review

Complete each table.

1.

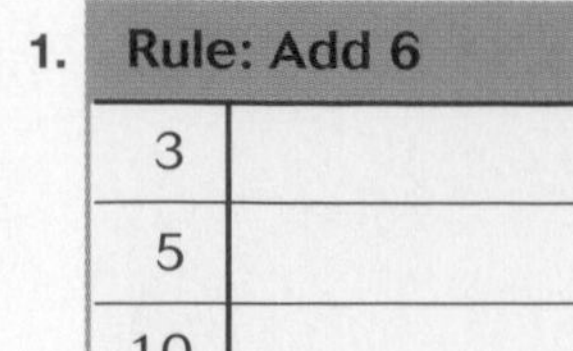

Rule: Add 6	
3	
5	
10	

2.

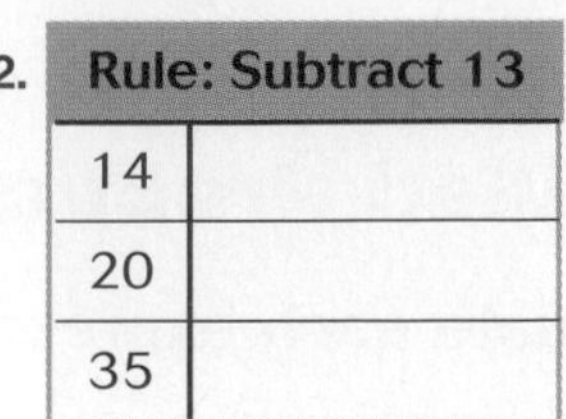

Rule: Subtract 13	
14	
20	
35	

3. Find the missing numbers in the pattern:

24, 22, 20, 18, ■, ■, ■

Word Bank

variable

algebraic expression

Math Link You have worked with numerical expressions, such as 14 + 30. In this lesson you will learn about algebraic expressions.

A **variable** is a symbol that stands for a number.

Each of these expressions contains a variable:

$10 + \Delta$ ■ − 32 $n + 17$

Expressions with variables are called **algebraic expressions.** The value of an algebraic expression depends on the number you substitute, or replace for the variable.

Example 1

Find the value of $n - 8$ when $n = 15$.

Substitute 15 for n. Then subtract.

$n - 8$

↓

$15 - 8 = 7$

Example 2

Evaluate $7 + \Delta$ for $\Delta = 4$.

Substitute 4 for Δ. Then add.

$7 + \Delta$

↓

$7 + 4 = 11$

Example 3

Find the missing number in the table.

Substitute 10 for x in the expression $x + 6$.

$x + 6$

↓

$10 + 6 = 16$

The missing number is 16.

x	$x + 6$
3	9
5	11
6	12
10	?

Additional Standard: Algebra and Functions 1.0 (See p. 37.)

More Examples

A. Find the value of $52 - y$ for $y = 25$.

$52 - y$

$52 - 25 = 27$

B. Evaluate $17 + u + 9$ for $u = 20$.

$17 + u + 9$

$17 + 20 + 9 = 46$

Guided Practice *For another example, see Set H on p. 73.*

Evaluate each expression for $n = 7$.

1. $9 + n$ **2.** $13 - n$ **3.** $24 - n$ **4.** $27 + n + 654$

5. What is the total length of the truck when $x = 8$?

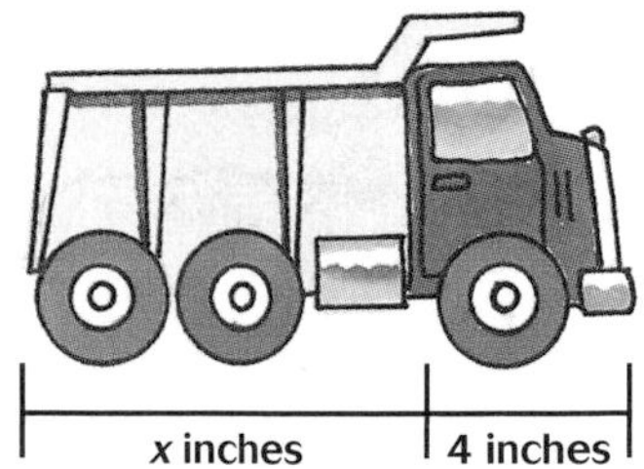

Independent Practice *For more practice, see Set H on p. 75.*

Evaluate each expression for $a = 3$.

6. $5 + a$ **7.** $16 - a$ **8.** $22 + a + 98$ **9.** $3 - a$

Evaluate each expression for $k = 24$.

10. $k + 8$ **11.** $21 + 14 + k$ **12.** $k - 18$ **13.** $153 - k$

Copy and complete each table.

14.

x	$x + 9$
4	13
8	
20	
31	

15.

d	$15 - d$
3	
5	
12	
15	

16.

m	$66 + m$
0	
8	
13	
28	

17.

w	$w - 20$
27	
34	
96	
109	

18. Evaluate $\Delta - 53$ for $\Delta = 300$.

19. Evaluate $741 + ■$ for $■ = 368$.

20. Find the total height of the plant and the pot shown at the right when $y = 13$.

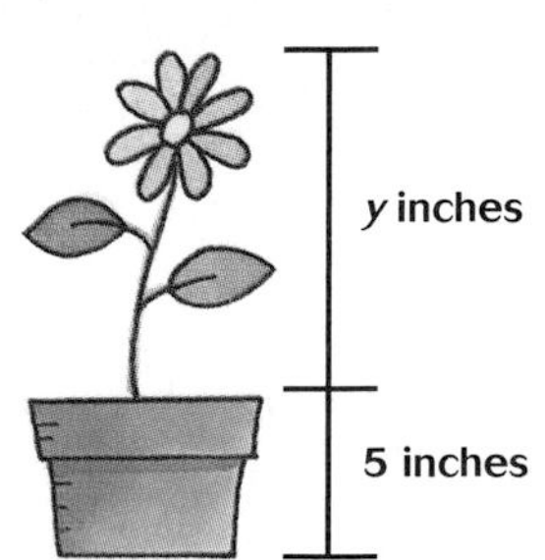

21. Beth feeds the goldfish when her neighbors are away. Each time she is paid, she spends only $2 and saves the rest. Copy and complete the table to show her savings.

Earnings (in dollars)	n	4	6	13	7
Savings (in dollars)	$n - 2$				

Mixed Review

22. Mental Math Angela had 19 collector dolls. She was given 14 more. How many does she have now?

23. Gina is arranging pennants at the county fair as shown at the right. If she starts with an orange pennant, what color will the 25th pennant be?

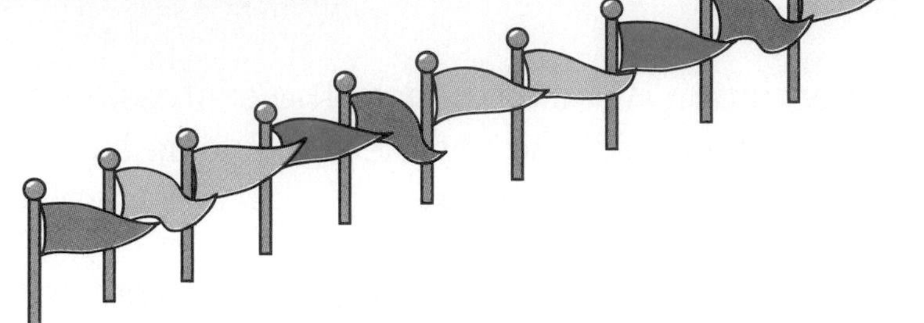

24. Mental Math Use compensation to find 7,500 − 5,998 mentally.

25. Mental Math Use breaking apart to find 254 + 123 mentally.

26. Estimate 369 + 510.

27. Estimate 719 − 85.

28. Algebra If $n = 32$, what is the value of $n - 19$?

29. Round 13,714,207 to the nearest hundred thousand.

30. $\begin{array}{r} 500 \\ -\ 351 \\ \hline \end{array}$

31. $\begin{array}{r} 2{,}716 \\ +\ 4{,}891 \\ \hline \end{array}$

32. $\begin{array}{r} 52{,}366 \\ -\ 17{,}248 \\ \hline \end{array}$

33. $\begin{array}{r} 30{,}100 \\ -\ 2{,}544 \\ \hline \end{array}$

34. $\begin{array}{r} \$17.33 \\ +\ 42.21 \\ \hline \end{array}$

Test Prep **Choose the correct letter for each answer.**

35. (2-4) In a recent election, 7,412 people voted for Candidate A, 605 people voted for Candidate B, and 2,194 people voted for Candidate C. How many people voted altogether?

A 9,211 **B** 10,201 **C** 10,211 **D** 15,656 **E** NH

36. (1-1) Last year a bagel shop sold eighty-four thousand, seven hundred six bagels. Which shows this number?

F 84,706 **G** 84,760 **H** 840,706 **J** 84,000,706 **K** NH

Equations

California Content Standard *Algebra and Functions 2.0.* (🔑): *Students know how to manipulate equations. Also, Algebra and Functions 1.1* *(See p. 37.)*

Warm-Up Review

Evaluate each expression for $u = 12$.

1. $16 - u$
2. $u + 4$
3. $u - 7$
4. $21 + u$
5. Complete the table.

x	$x + 8$
4	
9	
14	

Word Bank

equation
solution

Math Link In the last lesson, you learned about algebraic expressions. Now you will learn about equations.

An **equation** is like a balance. The expression on one side of the equal sign has the same value as the expression on the other side.

The equation $x + 3 = 10$ is pictured on the balance scale below.

When you solve an equation with a variable, you find the value of the variable that makes the two sides balance. In other words, the value of the variable is called a **solution** if it makes the equation true.

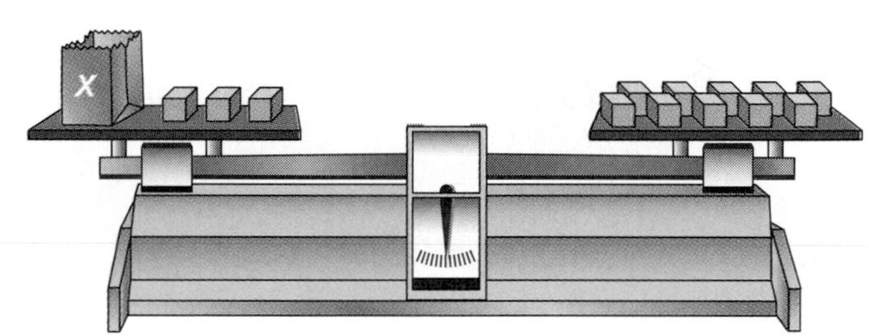

$x + 3 = 10$

Example 1

Solve the equation $x + 3 = 10$ by testing these values for x: 3, 6, 7, 9.

$x + 3 = 10$

Try $x = 3$: $3 + 3 = 6$

Try $x = 6$: $6 + 3 = 9$

Try $x = 7$: $7 + 3 = 10$

Try $x = 9$: $9 + 3 = 12$

The solution to the equation is $x = 7$.

Example 2

Solve the equation $23 - m = 8$ by testing values for m.

Try	$23 - m = 8$	Does $23 - m = 8$?
$m = 3$	$23 - 3 = 20$	No
$m = 18$	$23 - 18 = 5$	No
$m = 17$	$23 - 17 = 6$	No
$m = 15$	$23 - 15 = 8$	Yes

The solution to the equation is $m = 15$.

Guided Practice *For another example, see Set I on p. 73.*

Solve each equation by testing these values for x: 3, 4, 6, 12.

1. $x + 5 = 11$ **2.** $16 - x = 12$ **3.** $3 + x + 8 = 23$ **4.** $x - 3 = 9$

5. Write an equation for the balance scale shown at the right. Solve the equation by testing these values for b: 2, 5, 7, 9.

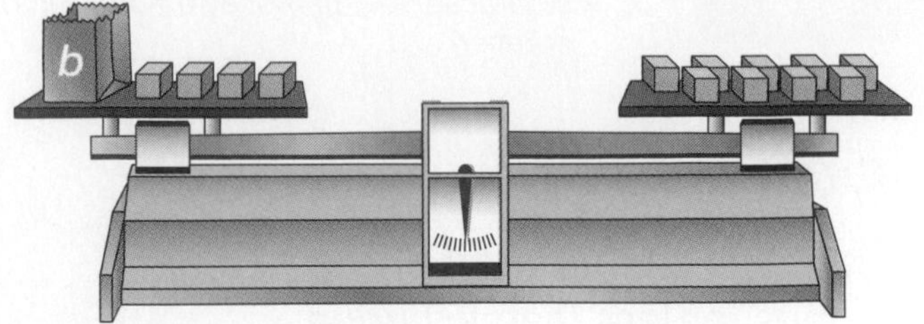

Independent Practice *For more practice, see Set I on p. 75.*

Solve each equation by testing these values for y: 0, 7, 9, 14.

6. $y + 6 = 13$ **7.** $18 - y = 18$ **8.** $5 + 10 + y = 24$ **9.** $20 - y = 6$

Solve each equation by testing values for the variable.

10. $30 + c = 45$ **11.** $k - 8 = 17$ **12.** $z + 9 = 21$ **13.** $89 - w = 65$

14. $x + 75 = 126$ **15.** $47 + y = 84$ **16.** $138 - a = 118$ **17.** $f - 27 = 63$

18. Math Reasoning Refer to the balance scale shown above. Suppose 2 blocks were removed from each side. Would the scale still balance? What if 3 blocks were added to each side? Explain your thinking.

Mixed Review

19. The principal at Reynolds School wants the children to read a total of 3,000 books. So far they have read 2,246 books. How many more books do they need to read?

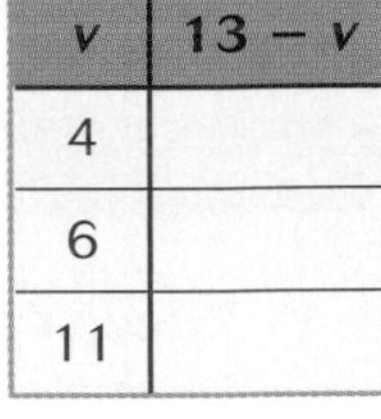

v	$13 - v$
4	
6	
11	

20. Algebra Copy and complete the table at the right.

21. Mental Math Find 302 + 466. **22. Mental Math** Find 2,143 + 3,251.

23. 17,231 + 24,799 **24.** 19,008 − 6,734 **25.** 388 + 216 + 107

Test Prep **Choose the correct letter for each answer.**

26. Give the place value of 4 in 24,296.
(1-1)

A ones **C** hundreds
B tens **D** thousands

27. Algebra If $d = 17$, then $38 + d =$
(2-10)

F 21 **H** 55
G 45 **J** 59

Problem-Solving Application:

Using Money

California Content Standard *Number Sense 3.3 (Gr. 3) (🔑): Solve problems involving addition, subtraction . . . of money amounts in decimal notation . . ..*

Warm-Up Review

1. $144.99 + $306.48
2. $24.07 − $13.68
3. $16.35 ● $16.53
4. $9.04 ● $8.79
5. Tyler had $9.50. He spent $5.24. How much does Tyler have now?

Example

Coupons can be used to buy games for less than full price. The amount on the coupon is subtracted from the game price. Game prices and coupons are shown at the right. Which of the games will cost less than $18.00 if bought with a coupon?

Boiling Point
$1.50
Discount

Understand

What do you need to find?

You need to find which games cost less than $18.00 when bought with a coupon.

Plan

How can you solve the problem?

You can subtract the amount on each coupon from each game price. Then you can compare the new price to $18.00.

Solve

Stepping Stones	Memory Lane	Boiling Point
$24.25	$19.95	$19.75
− 6.75	− 2.25	− 1.50
$17.50 $<$ $18.00	$17.70 $<$ $18.00	$18.25 $>$ $18.00

With a coupon, Stepping Stones and Memory Lane cost less than $18.00.

Look Back

How could you use addition to check your subtraction?

Additional Standard: Mathematical Reasoning 2.0 (See p. 37.)

Guided Practice

Use the information below for Exercises 1 and 2.

1. Is $15.00 enough to buy Mystery Mountain with a coupon? Explain.

2. Which game costs less with a coupon, Raceway or Leapin' Lizards?

Independent Practice

Use the table at the right for Exercises 3–6.

The price of each game sold is recorded at Goofy Games toy store. The sale price is then compared to the price paid to buy the game from a manufacturer. The difference between the prices is the money Goofy Games made by selling the game.

Game	Selling Price of the Game	Price Paid to Manufacturer	Money the Store Made
A	$19.95	$12.50	$7.45
B	$6.85	$4.75	?
C	$11.99	$7.15	?
D	$22.25	?	$6.40
E	?	$21.75	$9.15

3. How much money did the store make on Game B? on Game C?

4. What price did Goofy Games charge customers for Game E?

5. How much did the store pay the manufacturer for Game D?

6. Which game made the most money for the store?

Mixed Review

7. Robin bought a jewelry kit priced at $14.50. She gave the clerk $20.00. How much change did she receive?

8. A scuba diver spotted some sea turtles 55 feet below sea level. If sea level is 0 feet and altitude is the distance above sea level, how would you represent the altitude of the turtles?

Use Homework Workbook 2-12.

Diagnostic Checkpoint

Complete. For Exercises 1–4, use the words from the Word Bank.

Word Bank
algebraic expressions
breaking apart
compensation
equation
solution
variable

1. (2-9) If you add $58 + 34$ by thinking $60 + 34 = 94$, and $94 - 2 = 92$, then you are using a strategy called ______________.

2. (2-11) The value of the variable in an equation is called a ______________ if it makes the equation true.

3. (2-10) A ______________ is a symbol that stands for a number.

4. (2-10) Expressions with variables are called ______________.

Add or subtract mentally. Use breaking apart.

5. (2-9) $76 - 23$
6. (2-9) $78 + 17$
7. (2-9) $598 - 376$
8. (2-9) $7{,}841 + 1{,}103$

Add or subtract mentally. Use compensation.

9. (2-9) $57 + 39$
10. (2-9) $63 - 9$
11. (2-9) $798 + 137$
12. (2-9) $621 - 395$

Evaluate each expression for $n = 19$.

13. (2-10) $7 + n$
14. (2-10) $32 - n$
15. (2-10) $n + 11$
16. (2-10) $n - 5$

Solve each equation by testing values for the variable.

17. (2-11) $x + 9 = 15$
18. (2-11) $4 + 6 + p = 23$
19. (2-11) $30 - h = 24$
20. (2-11) $y - 11 = 15$

21. (2-8) Kate jogs 3 miles every 2 days. How many miles does she jog in 30 days?

22. (2-12) The Joyces set aside $200.00 for meals on their three-day vacation. Use the chart at the right to decide on which day they spent the most money.

Cost of Meals

Day	Breakfast	Lunch	Dinner
Fri.	$12.75	$18.00	$20.56
Sat.	$15.11	$16.48	$32.95
Sun.	$14.50	$21.35	$36.70

Chapter 2 Test

1. $47 + 36$
2. $574 + 368$
3. $\$3.57 + 4.86$
4. $4{,}564 + 2{,}671$
5. $26{,}072 + 45{,}184$
6. $83 - 49$
7. $702 - 356$
8. $\$6.63 - 3.95$
9. $8{,}000 - 4{,}637$
10. $57{,}536 - 12{,}784$
11. 32,578 + 17,986 + 5,243 + 28,504

Estimate each sum or difference.

12. $56 + 23$
13. $73 - 37$
14. $\$5.78 - 1.98$
15. $435 + 243$
16. $3{,}629 + 5{,}331$

Add or subtract mentally. Use breaking apart or compensation.

17. 43 − 19
18. 476 − 254
19. 198 + 137
20. 5,936 − 2,514

Evaluate each expression for $n = 25$.

21. $n + 16$
22. $4 + n + 19$
23. $n - 8$
24. $42 - n$
25. Solve $48 - z = 35$ by testing these values for z: 9, 11, 13, 14.
26. Solve $8 + k = 19$ by testing values for the variable.
27. The students in Grades 4, 5, and 6 are planning a boat trip. The table at the right shows how many students are in each grade. Should they request a boat that holds up to 150 passengers or one that holds up to 300 passengers? Can you estimate to solve this problem? Explain.

Grade	Number of Students
4	83
5	75
6	78

28. Eight students signed up to play doubles tennis. The coach wants to try all possible two-player teams to find the best combination. How many different teams are there?
29. Toy Town sells a building set for \$17.95 plus \$1.08 tax. Big Mart has the same set for \$18.29, but tax is only \$0.64 because Big Mart is in another state. At which store does the building set cost less?

TEST PREP

Multiple-Choice Chapter 2 Test

Choose the correct letter for each answer.

1. Pete has 42 marbles. Sally has 37. How many marbles do they have altogether?

A 5 marbles
B 79 marbles
C 85 marbles
D 89 marbles
E NH

2. Estimate 780 + 205.

F 700
G 800
H 1,000
J 1,100

3. Tina needs string for 6 balloons. The string for each balloon must be 32 inches long. String comes in rolls of 100 or 200 inches. What should Tina buy?

A a 100-inch roll of string
B a 200-inch roll of string
C a 100-inch roll and a 200-inch roll of string
D Two 200-inch rolls of string

4.

$$\begin{array}{r} 2{,}173 \\ 1{,}201 \\ 3{,}562 \\ +\ 1{,}010 \\ \hline \end{array}$$

F 7,846
G 7,946
H 8,846
J 8,946
K NH

5. A video store sells a computer game for $15.79. It sells another game for $9.98. What is the total price for both games?

A $25.67
B $25.77
C $2,567
D $2,577
E NH

6. The large piñata contains 235 treats. The small piñata holds 178 treats. How many more treats does the large piñata contain than the small one?

F 57
G 67
H 157
J 167
K NH

7. Find 9,321 − 6,784.

A 2,537
B 2,547
C 2,637
D 3,463
E NH

8. $\begin{array}{r} 5{,}000 \\ -\ 2{,}760 \\ \hline \end{array}$

F 3,760
G 3,340
H 2,340
J 2,240
K NH

9. **A square horse corral is 40 feet on a side. Fence posts are placed every 5 feet. How many posts are needed?**

A 8 posts
B 24 posts
C 30 posts
D 32 posts

10. **How can you find 471 − 195 mentally using compensation?**

F Subtract 400 − 100, 90 − 70, and 5 − 1. Then add the differences.
G Subtract 470 − 200 and then subtract 6 from the difference.
H Subtract 471 − 200 and then subtract 5 from the difference.
J Subtract 471 − 200 and then add 5 to the difference.

11. **If $h = 23$, then $51 - h =$**

A 18
B 28
C 34
D 74

12. **Solve the equation $x + 15 = 34$.**

F $x = 19$
G $x = 29$
H $x = 39$
J $x = 49$

Use the table for Questions 13 and 14.

Shoes	Regular Price	Discount
Loafers	$49.99	$12.50
Boots	$39.99	$11.00
Sandals	$34.99	$5.25
Sneakers	$45.49	$9.10

13. **How much do sneakers cost with the discount?**

A $27.99
B $29.74
C $36.39
D $37.49

14. **Which shoes cost the least with the discount?**

F Loafers
G Boots
H Sandals
J Sneakers

15. **Find 784 + 235.**

A 549
B 919
C 1,019
D 1,029
E NH

Reteaching

Set A (pages 38–39)

Estimate 478 + 235.

478 + 235

rounds to / rounds to

500 + 200 = 700

478 + 235 is about 700

Remember you can round to the greatest place value to get numbers you can add or subtract easily.

Estimate each sum or difference.

1. 42 + 17 **2.** 92 − 37

3. 615 + 386 **4.** $6.78 − $ 1.59

Set B (pages 42–43)

Find 329 + 285 + 62.

$$\begin{array}{r} {}^{1\,1} \\ 329 \\ 285 \\ +\ 62 \\ \hline 676 \end{array}$$

Be sure to line up the addends on the right side.

Remember to estimate the sum to be sure your answer makes sense.

1. $\begin{array}{r} 78 \\ +\ 17 \\ \hline \end{array}$ **2.** $\begin{array}{r} 417 \\ +\ 231 \\ \hline \end{array}$ **3.** $\begin{array}{r} \$5.28 \\ +\ 2.37 \\ \hline \end{array}$

4. 229 + 473 + 74

5. 183 + 542 + 95

Set C (pages 44-46)

Find 25,374 + 17,184.

$$\begin{array}{r} {}^{1\ \ \ 1} \\ 25{,}374 \\ +\ 17{,}184 \\ \hline 42{,}558 \end{array}$$

Remember to add each column, starting with ones, and regroup as necessary.

1. $\begin{array}{r} 6{,}789 \\ +\ 2{,}092 \\ \hline \end{array}$ **2.** $\begin{array}{r} 38{,}502 \\ +\ 12{,}351 \\ \hline \end{array}$ **3.** $\begin{array}{r} \$459.23 \\ +\ 235.91 \\ \hline \end{array}$

Set D (pages 47–49)

Find 435 − 271.

$$\begin{array}{r} 435 \\ -\ 271 \\ \hline 4 \end{array} \qquad \begin{array}{r} {}^{3\,13} \\ \not{4}\not{3}5 \\ -\ 271 \\ \hline 64 \end{array} \qquad \begin{array}{r} {}^{3\,13} \\ \not{4}\not{3}5 \\ -\ 271 \\ \hline 164 \end{array}$$

Remember you can regroup 1 ten as 10 ones or 1 hundred as 10 tens.

1. $\begin{array}{r} 96 \\ -79 \\ \hline \end{array}$ **2.** $\begin{array}{r} 692 \\ -378 \\ \hline \end{array}$ **3.** $\begin{array}{r} 723 \\ -465 \\ \hline \end{array}$

4. $\begin{array}{r} 520 \\ -\ 176 \\ \hline \end{array}$ **5.** $\begin{array}{r} 90 \\ -\ 47 \\ \hline \end{array}$ **6.** $\begin{array}{r} 352 \\ -\ 68 \\ \hline \end{array}$

Set E (pages 50–51)

Find 42,137 − 12,849.

```
  11 10 12
 3 1  0 2 17
 4 2,1 3 7
−1 2,8 4 9
 2 9,2 8 8
```

Remember to start with the ones column, subtract, and regroup as necessary.

1. 6,478 − 3,165 **2.** 8,927 − 4,768 **3.** 89,373 − 56,734

Set F (pages 52–53)

Find 6,004 − 2,438.

```
    9  9
 5 10 10 14
 6, 0  0  4
−2, 4  3  8
 3, 5  6  6
```

Remember that you can regroup several places at once when there are zeros.

1. 500 − 321 **2.** 8,000 − 5,376 **3.** 80,000 − 37,680

Set G (pages 58–60)

Use compensation to find 384 − 198.

```
 384
−200
 184
+  2
 186
```

Add 2 to 198 to make 200.

Add 2 to the difference to compensate for subtracting 2 extra.

Remember to use numbers that you can add or subtract mentally.

Add or subtract mentally. Use compensation.

1. 828 − 398 **2.** 475 + 198

Set H (pages 61–63)

Find the value of $n + 6$ when $n = 12$.

$n + 6$

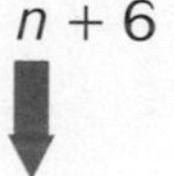

$12 + 6 = 18$

Remember that a variable is a symbol that stands for a number.

Evaluate each expression for $m = 9$.

1. $m + 7$ **2.** $m - 4$ **3.** $28 - m$

Set I (pages 64–65)

Solve the equation $15 - x = 8$ by testing these values for x: 5, 7, 9.

$15 - x = 8$

Try $x = 5$: $15 - 5 = 10$

Try $x = 7$: $15 - 7 = 8$

Try $x = 9$: $15 - 9 = 6$

The solution to the equation is $x = 7$.

Remember that the value of the variable is a solution if it makes the equation true.

Solve each equation by testing these values for x: 3, 5, 13, 15.

1. $x + 11 = 14$ **2.** $17 - x = 4$

More Practice

Set A (pages 38–39)

Estimate each sum or difference.

1. 59 + 33
2. 72 − 34
3. $5.28 + 2.76
4. 862 − 217
5. $11.13 − 2.74
6. The school's bake sale made $132 on Friday and $296 on Saturday. Estimate how much the event made altogether.

Set B (pages 42–43)

1. 76 + 23
2. 45 + 19
3. $0.47 + 0.29
4. 305 + 469
5. $6.73 + 1.09
6. You started with 132 marbles. You bought 24 more. Then you won 43. How many marbles do you have in all?

Set C (pages 44–46)

1. 6,715 + 1,263
2. 5,624 + 3,295
3. 32,750 + 17,625
4. 56,179 + 27,618
5. 41,758 + 36,593
6. Jill scored 12,345 points on a video game, and Linda scored 24,689 points. How many points did they score altogether?

Set D (pages 47–49)

1. 74 − 21
2. $0.53 − 0.17
3. 809 − 492
4. $6.52 − 3.85
5. 975 − 382
6. Dan walked 536 feet and Ron walked 398 feet. How much farther did Dan walk than Ron?

Set E (pages 50–51)

1. 5,407 − 1,862
2. 7,463 − 2,874
3. 9,876 − 697
4. 75,672 − 27,564
5. 87,673 − 8,524
6. Morton College has 21,317 students. This is 14,862 more students than Riverwood College has. How many students are at Riverwood?

Set F (pages 52–53)

1. $\begin{array}{r} 400 \\ -\ 128 \\ \hline \end{array}$ 2. $\begin{array}{r} 800 \\ -\ 609 \\ \hline \end{array}$ 3. $\begin{array}{r} 7{,}000 \\ -\ 2{,}076 \\ \hline \end{array}$ 4. $\begin{array}{r} 50{,}000 \\ -\ 26{,}781 \\ \hline \end{array}$ 5. $\begin{array}{r} 90{,}080 \\ -\ 40{,}986 \\ \hline \end{array}$

6. A jump-rope competition began with 600 contestants. There were 247 contestants eliminated after the first round. How many contestants were left?

Set G (pages 58–60)

Add or subtract mentally. Use breaking apart.

1. $32 + 64$ 2. $57 - 36$ 3. $483 + 221$ 4. $795 - 352$

Add or subtract mentally. Use compensation.

5. $87 - 26$ 6. $479 - 397$ 7. $198 + 72$ 8. $4{,}251 + 2{,}999$

9. You are playing a mental math game and you are given this problem: $498 + 362$. Explain how you would find the sum.

Set H (pages 61–63)

Evaluate each expression for $j = 16$.

1. $j + 15$ 2. $j - 8$ 3. $5 + 17 + j$ 4. $104 - j$

5. The base of a statue is 2 feet high. The total height of the statue with the base can be represented by $x + 2$. Find the total height when $x = 7$.

Set I (pages 64–65)

Solve each equation by testing these values for z: 5, 6, 8, 10, 12.

1. $z + 7 = 12$ 2. $21 - z = 9$ 3. $z + 5 + 6 = 17$ 4. $z - 5 = 3$

Solve each equation by testing values for the variable.

5. $h - 4 = 36$ 6. $x + 8 = 40$ 7. $3 + y + 2 = 12$ 8. $31 - a = 12$

9. Stan wants to collect 25 leaves for a leaf collection. He said he only needs 8 more leaves to reach his goal. Solve the equation $x + 8 = 25$ to find how many leaves Stan has.

Problem Solving: Preparing for Tests

Choose the correct letter for each answer.

---

1. Georgia uses 20 inches of wood around the edges of a rectangular frame. If the frame is 6 inches long, how wide is it?

A 4 inches

B 8 inches

C 12 inches

D 14 inches

> **Tip**
> Try drawing a picture to solve this problem.

---

2. A bird watcher counted 324 wrens and 465 sparrows. Which number sentence could be used to find how many more sparrows than wrens were counted?

F 324 + 465 = ■

G 465 + 465 = ■

H 324 − 465 = ■

J 465 − 324 = ■

> **Tip**
> Sometimes you can eliminate an answer choice. Why can you eliminate Choice H in this problem?

---

3. There are 4 people at a party. Each person shakes the hand of each of the other people once. How many handshakes are there?

A 4

B 6

C 7

D 8

> **Tip**
> You can use the *Draw a Picture* strategy to help you solve this problem.

4. **Jenny has 2 pets and Kyle has 7 pets. Nina has more pets than Jenny but fewer pets than Kyle. Which is reasonable for the number of pets Nina has?**

F 1 **H** 5

G 2 **J** 8

---

5. **Will played three dart games. His scores were 297, 186, and 302. Which is the best estimate of his total score for the three games?**

A 500

B 700

C 800

D 900

---

6. **Alice arranges boxes of greeting cards in a store window. She puts 8 boxes on the bottom row, 6 boxes on the next row, and so on. There are 2 boxes on top. How many boxes does Alice arrange in the display?**

F 16 boxes

G 20 boxes

H 21 boxes

J 36 boxes

---

7. **Bill has \$3.00. He wants to buy 2 tacos for 99¢ each and a drink for \$1.99. *About* how much more money does he need?**

A \$0.50

B \$1.00

C \$1.50

D \$4.00

---

8. **Victor bought apples, pears, and peaches at the market. He bought twice as many pears as apples. He bought 2 more peaches than apples. What other information is needed to determine the total number of fruits Victor bought?**

F The number of pears he bought

G The weight of the fruit

H The cost of the fruit

J The size of the apples

Use the graph for Questions 9 and 10.

This graph shows how some people learn about the news.

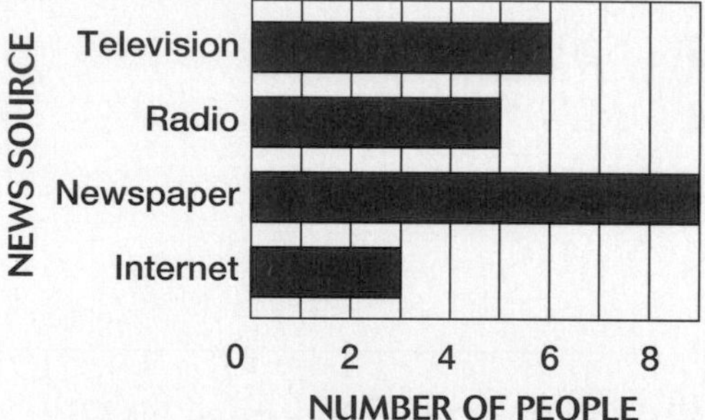

9. **Which is the most popular way to learn about the news?**

A Television

B Radio

C Newspaper

D Internet

---

10. **How many more of these people use television than the Internet to learn about the news?**

F 1 **H** 3

G 2 **J** 6

TEST PREP

Multiple-Choice Cumulative Review

Choose the correct letter for each answer.

Number Sense

1. What number is equal to seven million, forty-nine thousand, six hundred seventy?

   A 704,967
   B 7,049,670
   C 7,490,067
   D 7,490,607

2. What is 569 rounded to the nearest ten?

   F 500
   G 560
   H 570
   J 600
   K NH

3. Which shaded region does NOT represent $\frac{1}{2}$?

   A 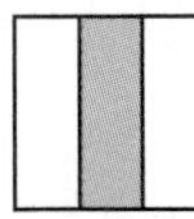
   C 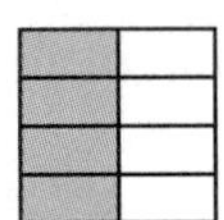
   B 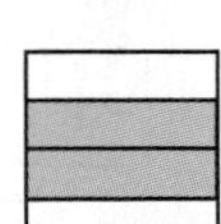
   D 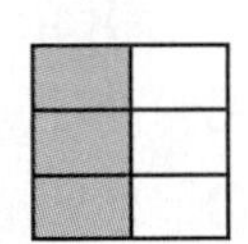

4. What is 5,854 rounded to the nearest hundred?

   F 6,000 H 5,800
   G 5,900 J 5,000

5. Martin has 4 quarters and 2 dimes. How much will he have left if he spends a quarter?

   A $0.42
   B $0.59
   C $0.95
   D $1.20

6. Marisa bought two boxes of crackers for 99¢ each and a pound of grapes for $1.29. *About* how much did she spend?

   F $1.00 H $2.00
   G $1.50 J $3.00

7. Sam practices the piano 2 hours every day. How many hours does he practice in 7 days?

   A 21 hours
   B 14 hours
   C 9 hours
   D 5 hours
   E NH

8. Fran read one book that had 188 pages and another that had 197 pages. *About* how many pages did she read in all?

   F 500 pages H 300 pages
   G 400 pages J 200 pages

Algebra and Functions

9. When $n = 18$, $n + 17 =$

   A 1
   B 34
   C 35
   D 36

10. Which number sentence is in the same family of facts as $35 \div 7 = 5$?

   F $20 + 15 = 35$
   G $5 \times 7 = 35$
   H $7 + 5 = 12$
   J $35 - 7 = 28$

11. Which number pair completes the last row of the table?

Number of Bikes	Number of Wheels
2	4
4	8
■	■

   A 8, 4
   B 6, 3
   C 5, 12
   D 6, 12

12. What is the missing number in the number pattern?

   63, 54, 45, ■, 27

   F 18
   G 32
   H 36
   J 40

Measurement and Geometry

13. How many sides does a quadrilateral have?

   A 3
   B 4
   C 5
   D 6

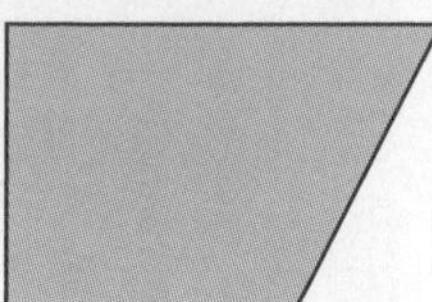

14. How many corners does a hexagon have?

   F 3
   G 4
   H 5
   J 6

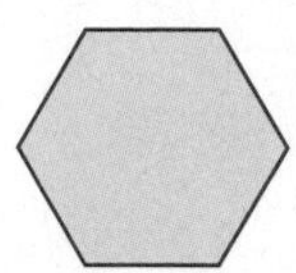

15. How many faces does a cube have?

   A 3
   B 4
   C 5
   D 6

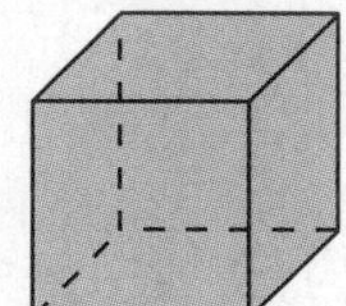

16. Tim left school at 3:05 P.M. It took him 17 minutes to get home. What time did Tim get home?

   F 3:12 P.M.
   G 3:17 P.M.
   H 3:22 P.M.
   J 3:25 P.M.

17. Tony has a toy robot that is 1 foot 6 inches tall. How many *inches* tall is that? (Hint: 1 foot = 12 inches.)

   A 12 inches
   B 18 inches
   C 20 inches
   D 24 inches

Multiplication and Division Facts

Diagnosing Readiness

In Chapter 3, you will use these skills:

Ⓐ Relating Multiplication and Addition

(Grade 3)

1. 3 + 3 + 3 **2.** 6 + 6 + 6

3. 9 + 9 + 9 + 9 **4.** 7 + 7

5. 8 + 8 + 8 + 8 + 8

6. 2 + 2 + 2 + 2 + 2 + 2

7. Betsy had 5 pencils and 3 erasers. She bought 5 more pencils. How many pencils does she have altogether?

Ⓑ Expressions with Addition and Subtraction

(pages 42–43, 47–49)

8. 36 + 15 **9.** 27 + 56

10. 73 + 24 **11.** 99 + 12

12. 54 − 21 **13.** 36 − 17

14. 62 − 25 **15.** 84 − 56

16. Carly had 156 points. Tanya finished with 97 points. By how many points did Carly win?

C Equations with Addition and Subtraction

(Grade 3)

Find each missing number.

17. $5 + ■ = 9$

18. $■ + 8 = 15$

19. $■ - 7 = 12$

20. $39 - ■ = 24$

21. $■ - 25 = 41$

22. Katrina has 26 books, 15 of which are fiction. Use the equation $15 + ■ = 26$ to find how many books are of other kinds.

D Properties of Addition

(Grade 3)

Find each missing number.

23. $9 + ■ = 4 + 9$

24. $6 + (4 + 3) = (■ + 4) + 3$

25. $7 + ■ = 7$

E Using Variables in Expressions with Addition and Subtraction

(pages 61–63)

Evaluate each expression for $x = 7$.

26. $12 + x$ **27.** $15 - x$

28. $x - 5$ **29.** $54 + x$

30. $9 - x$ **31.** $x + 72$

32. $2 + x$ **33.** $16 + x$

F Using Variables in Addition and Subtraction Equations

(pages 64–65)

Solve each equation by testing these values for x: 1, 5, 15, 30.

34. $3 + x = 8$ **35.** $9 - x = 4$

36. $x - 10 = 20$ **37.** $x + 12 = 17$

38. $24 + x = 39$ **39.** $42 - x = 41$

40. Patrick scored 124 points in the spring basketball season. This is 19 more points than he scored in the fall season. How many points did he score in the fall season?

To the Family and Student

Looking Back

In Grade 3, students learned multiplication and division facts through 10.

Chapter 3

Multiplication and Division Facts

In this chapter, students will practice multiplication and division facts. They will learn how to use variables in multiplication and division expressions and equations.

Looking Ahead

In Chapter 4, students will learn how to multiply two-digit and three-digit numbers by one-digit numbers.

Math and Everyday Living

Opportunities to apply the concepts of Chapter 3 abound in everyday situations. During the chapter, think about how multiplication and division can be used to solve a variety of real-world problems. The following examples suggest just several of the many situations that could launch a discussion about multiplication and division.

Math and Sports
A football team scored 3 touchdowns in the second half of the championship game. If each touchdown is worth 7 points, how many points did they score in the second half?

Math and Gardening
Mrs. Su wants to plant 4 rows of tomatoes in a small garden. She has 20 tomato plants. Each row has the same number of plants. How many plants are in each row?

Math and Recreation
Jessica walks 4 miles every day. How many miles does she walk in a week?

Math and Baking Gloria is baking muffins for her class. The muffin pan has 3 rows of 4 muffins. How many muffins does the muffin pan hold?

Math and Crafts You have $27 to buy some ceramic eggs to paint for a craft project. If each egg costs $3, how many eggs can you buy?

Math and Celebrations
Annie has 21 party favors that she wants to share among 7 friends. How many party favors does each friend get?

Math and Fundraising
Claire is raising money for a charity by walking. For every mile she walks, she can collect $5 from sponsors. If she walks 6 miles, how much money will she collect?

Math and Collecting Jake has 64 stamps in his stamp collection. He wants to put an equal number of stamps on each page of an 8-page album. How many stamps can he put on each page?

Math and Shopping
A florist sells roses for $3 each. If Bob spent $24 on roses, how many roses did he buy?

Math and Bicycles
The Johnson family owns 6 bicycles. Each bicycle has 2 wheels. How many wheels are there altogether?

California Content Standards in Chapter 3 Lessons*

	Teach and Practice	Practice
Number Sense		
2.2 (Grade 3) (🔑) Memorize to automaticity the multiplication table for numbers between 1 and 10.	3-1	
2.3 (Grade 3) (🔑) Use the inverse relationship of multiplication and dvision to compute and check results.	3-3	
2.6 (Grade 3) Understand the special properties of 0 and 1 in multiplication and division.	3-2, 3-4	
3.0 (🔑) Students solve problems involving addition, subtraction, multiplication, and division of whole numbers and understand the relationships among the operations.	3-5	
4.1 Understand that many whole numbers break down in different ways.		3-2
4.2 Know that numbers such as 2, 3, 5, 7, and 11 do not have any factors except 1 and themselves and that such numbers are called prime numbers.		3-2
Algebra and Functions		
1.1 Use letters, boxes, or other symbols to stand for any number in simple expressions or equations. (e.g., demonstrate an understanding and the use of the concept of a variable.)	3-1, 3-3, 3-4, 3-8, 3-9	3-2, 3-5, 3-6
1.2 (🔑) Interpret and evaluate mathematical expressions that now use parentheses.	3-6	3-2, 3-8, 3-10
1.3 (🔑) Use parentheses to indicate which operation to perform first when writing expressions containing more than two terms and different operations.	3-6	3-10
1.5 (Grade 3) Recognize and use the commutative and associative properties of multiplication (e.g., if 5 × 7 = 35, then what is 7 × 5? and if 5 × 7 × 3 = 105, then what is 7 × 3 × 5?).	3-2	
2.0 (🔑) Students know how to manipulate equations.	3-9	

	Teach and Practice	Practice
Statistics, Data Analysis, and Probability		
1.3 Interpret one- and two-variable data graphs to answer questions about a situation.	3-10	
Mathematical Reasoning		
1.1 Analyze problems by identifying relationships, distinguishing relevant from irrelevant information, sequencing and prioritizing information, and observing patterns.		3-5
1.2 Determine when and how to break a problem into simpler parts.		3-1
2.0 Students use strategies, skills, and concepts in finding solutions.		3-5, 3-7, 3-10
2.2 Apply strategies and results from simpler problems to more complex problems.		3-1, 3-6
2.3 Use a variety of methods, such as words, numbers, symbols, charts, graphs, tables, diagrams, and models to explain mathematical reasoning.	3-7	3-1, 3-2, 3-4, 3-9
2.4 Express the solution clearly and logically by using the appropriate mathematical notation and terms and clear language; support solutions with evidence in both verbal and symbolic work.		3-6
3.2 Note the method of deriving the solution and demonstrate a conceptual understanding of the derivation by solving similar problems.	3-7	3-6
3.3 Develop generalizations of results obtained and apply them in other circumstances.		3-2, 3-3

* The symbol (🔑) indicates a key standard as designated in the Mathematics Framework for California Public Schools. Full statements of the California Content Standards are found at the beginning of this book, following the Table of Contents.

Multiplication Facts

Warm-Up Review

1. $4 + 4 + 4$
2. $3 + 3 + 3 + 3 + 3$
3. $20 + 20$ **4.** $15 + 15$
5. Count by 2s to 30. Now by 5s. Now by 10s.
6. May has 6 bookmarks. She bought 6 more. Now how many does she have?

California Content Standards *Number Sense 2.2 (Grade 3) (key): Memorize to automaticity the multiplication table for numbers between 1 and 10. Also, Algebra and Functions 1.1* *(See p. 83.)*

Word Bank

factor
product
array

Math Link You know your addition and subtraction facts. In this lesson you will review and practice multiplication facts.

You can show multiplication using equal groups.

$2 + 2 + 2 + 2 + 2 = 10$

5	×	2	=	10
factor		**factor**		**product**

You can also show multiplication using an **array**, an arrangement of rows and columns. An array is used in Example 1.

Example 1

Josh stores his minicar collection in trays. The cars in each tray form an array, as shown. How many cars does each tray hold?

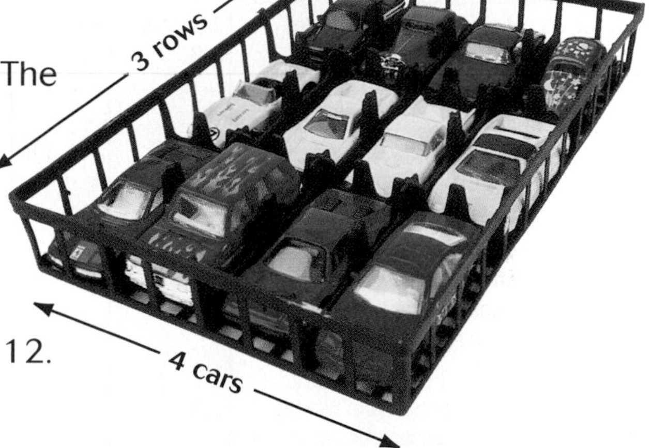

3	×	4	=	n
number of rows		**cars per row**		**number of cars in tray**

Complete the multiplication fact: $3 \times 4 = 12$.

Each tray holds 12 cars.

Sometimes you can use a strategy to help you remember a multiplication fact.

Example 2

Find 6×4.

Since 6 is the double of 3, you can use doubles.

$3 \times 4 = 12$

$6 \times 4 = 24$

Think: Since $3 \times 4 = 12$, $6 \times 4 = 12 + 12$.

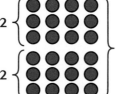

$3 \times 4 = 12$
$3 \times 4 = 12$
$6 \times 4 = 24$

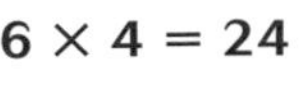

Additional Standards: Mathematical Reasoning 1.2, 2.2, 2.3 *(See p. 83.)*

More Examples

A. Find 4×10.

You can skip count by 10s.

$4 \times 10 = 40$

Think: 10, 20, 30, 40.

B. Find 7×4.

Add on with facts you already know.

$6 \times 4 = 24$

$7 \times 4 = 28$

Think: Add 4 more. $24 + 4 = 28$.

C. Find 9×3.

You can change the order of the factors.

$3 \times 9 = 27$

$9 \times 3 = 27$

Think: $9 \times 3 = 3 \times 9$.

D. Find the missing factor: $7 \times n = 42$.

7 times what number equals 42?

You know $7 \times 6 = 42$.

So, $n = 6$.

Guided Practice *For another example, see Set A on p. 116.*

1. 6×2 **2.** 3×5 **3.** 4×4 **4.** 8×6 **5.** 7×9

6. Algebra Find the missing factor: $4 \times n = 20$.

7. Crystal walks 5 miles every day. How many miles does she walk in a week?

Independent Practice *For more practice, see Set A on p. 118.*

8. 3×2 **9.** 8×3 **10.** 9×1 **11.** 8×8 **12.** 7×3

13. 10×3 **14.** 5×4 **15.** 8×2 **16.** 4×9 **17.** 0×6

18. $\begin{array}{r} 3 \\ \times\ 6 \\ \hline \end{array}$ **19.** $\begin{array}{r} 8 \\ \times\ 4 \\ \hline \end{array}$ **20.** $\begin{array}{r} 10 \\ \times\ 7 \\ \hline \end{array}$ **21.** $\begin{array}{r} 9 \\ \times\ 9 \\ \hline \end{array}$ **22.** $\begin{array}{r} 7 \\ \times\ 8 \\ \hline \end{array}$

Write a multiplication sentence for each diagram.

23. 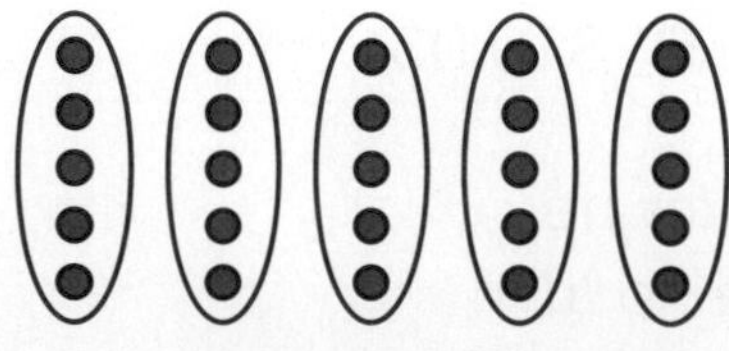

24.

Algebra **Find the missing number.**

25. $2 \times n = 12$ **26.** $8 \times 5 = a$ **27.** $m \times 3 = 24$ **28.** $9 \times n = 54$

29. Copy and complete the multiplication chart at the right.

×	0	1	2	3	4	5	6	7	8	9	10
0	0	0	0	0							
1	0	1	2	3							
2	0	2	4	6							
3											
4											
5											
6											
7											
8											
9											
10											

30. Write 9 + 9 + 9 + 9 + 9 + 9 as a multiplication expression.

31. Claudia put 5 flowers in each of 10 vases. How many flowers did she use in all?

32. Which costs more, 7 minicars at $2 a car or 5 minitrucks at $3 a truck?

Mixed Review

33. Algebra Solve the equation $x - 14 = 13$ by testing these values for x: 20, 23, 27, 30.

Algebra Evaluate each expression for $m = 19$.

34. $23 + m$ **35.** $82 - m$ **36.** $m - 5$ **37.** $44 + 32 + m$

38. $\begin{array}{r} 3{,}046 \\ +\ 2{,}945 \\ \hline \end{array}$ **39.** $\begin{array}{r} 21{,}792 \\ 15{,}688 \\ +\ 4{,}360 \\ \hline \end{array}$ **40.** $\begin{array}{r} 41{,}215 \\ -\ 12{,}236 \\ \hline \end{array}$ **41.** $\begin{array}{r} 8{,}000 \\ -\ 327 \\ \hline \end{array}$

 **Test Prep** **Choose the correct letter for each answer.**

42. (2-12) Bernice bought a roll of film priced at $5.19 and a photo album priced at $12.99. She used a coupon for $0.85 off the price of the film. How much did she spend altogether?

A $13.84 **B** $17.33 **C** $18.18 **D** $19.03

43. (2-5) Hank has been collecting comics for 6 months. So far he has collected 23 comics. How many more does he need in order to reach his goal of 50?

F 17 comics **G** 27 comics **H** 29 comics **J** 37 comics

Properties of Multiplication

California Content Standard *Number Sense 2.6 (Grade 3): Understand the special properties of 0 and 1 in multiplication. . .. Also, Algebra and Functions 1.5 (Grade 3)* *(See p. 83.)*

Warm-Up Review

1. 4×7
2. 8×8
3. $479 + 0$
4. $6 + 7 = \blacksquare + 6$
5. $(3 + 2) + 5 = 3 + (2 + \blacksquare)$
6. Seven children each bought 1 puzzle. How many puzzles did they buy in all? They each had \$0 left. How many dollars did they have left altogether?

Math Link You have learned multiplication facts. Now you will learn how multiplication properties can help you find products.

Commutative Property

The order in which factors are multiplied does not change the product.

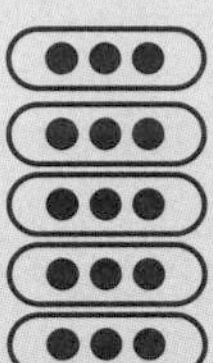

$5 \times 3 = 15$ $3 \times 5 = 15$

Associative Property

The way in which factors are grouped does not change the product.

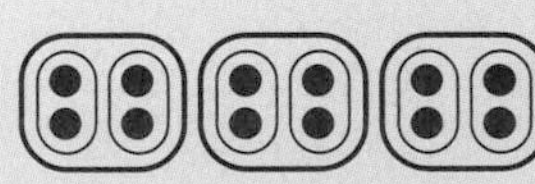

$(2 \times 2) \times 3 = 12$
$4 \times 3 = 12$

$2 \times (2 \times 3) = 12$
$2 \times 6 = 12$

Property of One

When you multiply any number by 1, the product is that number.

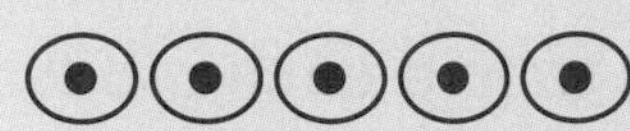

$5 \times 1 = 5$

Zero Property

When you multiply any number by 0, the product is 0.

$2 \times 0 = 0$

Additional Standards: Number Sense 4.1, 4.2; Algebra and Functions 1.1, 1.2 (key); Mathematical Reasoning 2.3, 3.3 *(See p. 83.)*

Example 1

Use a property to find the product of 164×1.

Use the property of one.

$164 \times 1 = 164$

Think: When you multiply any number by 1, the product is that number.

Example 2

Use a property to find the missing factor: $(4 \times 7) \times 3 = n \times (7 \times 3)$.

Group the factors the same way on each side of the equation. Then it's easy to see what number n represents.

$(4 \times 7) \times 3 = n \times (7 \times 3)$

Apply the Associative Property

$4 \times (7 \times 3) = n \times (7 \times 3)$

$n = 4$

Guided Practice *For another example, see Set B on p. 116.*

Use properties to find each product.

1. 0×6 **2.** 1×97 **3.** $2{,}589 \times 1$ **4.** $2{,}589 \times 0$

Find the missing factor. Name the property that helps you find each missing number.

5. $1 \times n = 8$ **6.** $8 \times m = 6 \times 8$ **7.** $0 \times 167 = b$ **8.** $n \times 54 = 54$

9. Write two multiplication sentences for the diagram at the right. What property is illustrated?

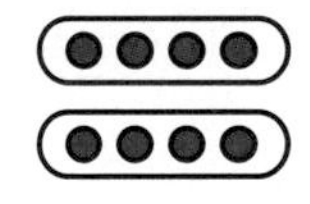

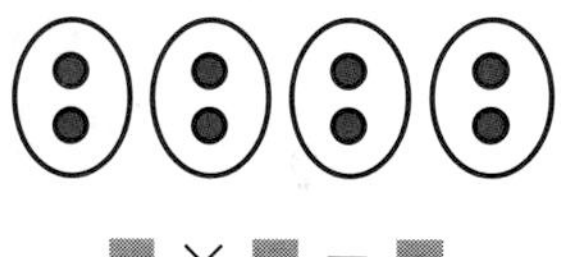

■ × ■ = ■ ■ × ■ = ■

Independent Practice *For more practice, see Set B on p. 118.*

Use properties to find each product.

10. 78×1 **11.** 0×42 **12.** 1×513 **13.** $11{,}046 \times 0$

Find the missing factor. Name the property that helps you find each missing number.

14. $10 \times 0 = n$ **15.** $4 \times 5 = n \times 4$ **16.** $(m \times 2) \times 7 = 8 \times (2 \times 7)$

17. $49 \times a = 0$ **18.** $83 \times w = 83$ **19.** $(1 \times n) \times 3 = 1 \times (5 \times 3)$

20. $b \times 6 = 6 \times 9$ 21. $n \times 736 = 736$ 22. $2 \times (r \times 1) = (2 \times 2) \times 1$

23. The product of two numbers is 0. Can you name one of the factors?

24. The product of two numbers is 17. What do you think the numbers are? Explain.

25. **Math Reasoning** Which multiplication properties are like the addition properties? Which are different? Give examples to explain your answers.

26. Megan and her mother are baking muffins. Megan said the muffin pan had six rows of three muffins. Her mother said it had three rows of six muffins. Write two different multiplication sentences to show how many muffins the muffin pan holds. What property does this illustrate?

Mixed Review

27. List the movies shown in the table from greatest attendance to least attendance.

28. In 1996, there were 79,091 public-school teachers in Georgia and 54,790 in Tennessee. How many more public-school teachers were there in Georgia?

Weekend Movie Attendance	
Danny Dolphin	4,089,453
Outer Space Rangers	4,216,377
Camp Wilderness	3,725,931
Ghost Ride	4,226,668

Algebra Solve each equation by testing these values for *y*: 4, 11, 13, 20.

29. $y + 19 = 32$ 30. $53 - y = 42$

31. $29 + 316 + 207$ 32. $762 - 547$ 33. \$15.85 + \$427.08

34. 8×3 35. 6×9 36. 7×7 37. 4×10

Test Prep **Choose the correct letter for each answer.**

38. Which number is between 41,632 and 41,657?
(1-3)

A 40,640
B 41,553
C 41,651
D 41,658

39. **Algebra** If $h = 52$, then $84 - h = ■$.
(2-10)

F 22
G 28
H 32
J 136

Use Homework Workbook 3-2.

Division Facts

Warm-Up Review

1. 7×7
2. 2×4
3. 3×6
4. 5×8
5. 1×9
6. 5×5
7. Find the missing number: $6 \times n = 54$.
8. Michael has a large trophy case with 7 shelves. He arranged 5 trophies on each shelf. How many trophies are in the case?

California Content Standards *Number Sense 2.3 (Grade 3). (🔑): Use the inverse relationship of multiplication and division to compute and check results. Also, Algebra and Functions 1.1* *(See p. 83.)*

Math Link You have learned multiplication facts. Now you will use them to help you learn division facts.

Susan is giving the 12 seashells she collected to her sisters. Here is how she divided them up.

Word Bank

dividend
divisor
quotient
fact family

12 shells divided into 3 groups of 4:

$$12 \div 3 = 4$$

We use division to show how many equal groups or how many items in each group. There are different ways to write a division number sentence. Here are two ways.

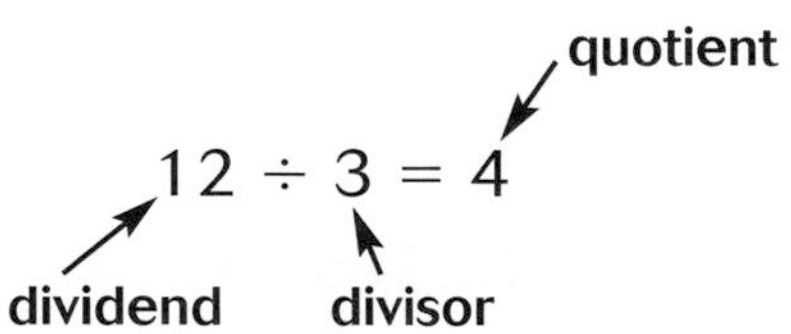

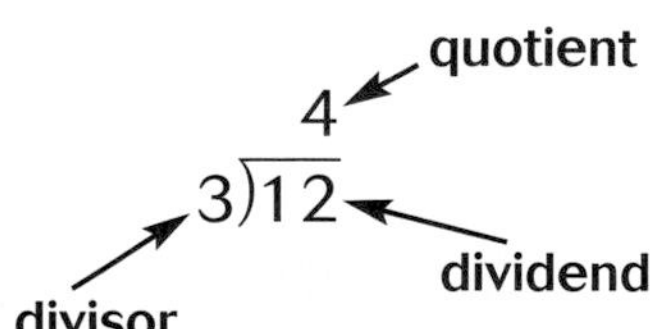

Every division fact has a related multiplication fact. Below is the multiplication fact for Susan's shell collection.

3 groups with 4 shells per group, 12 shells altogether:

$$3 \times 4 = 12$$

A **fact family** shows all the related multiplication and division facts for a set of numbers. This is the fact family for 3, 4, and 12.

$3 \times 4 = 12$ $\quad$ $4 \times 3 = 12$

$12 \div 3 = 4$ $\quad$ $12 \div 4 = 3$

Additional Standard: Mathematical Reasoning 3.3 *(See p. 83.)*

To help you remember division facts, think about the related multiplication facts.

Example 1

32 ÷ 4 = ■

Think: 4 × ■ = 32

4 × 8 = 32

So, 32 ÷ 4 = 8.

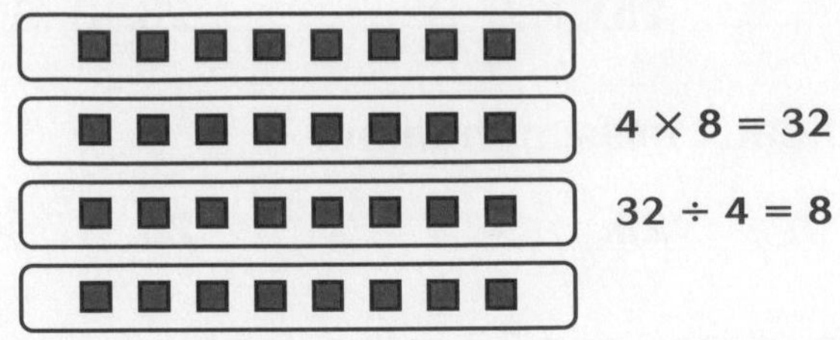

Example 2

Write the fact family for 3, 9, and 27.

Write the multiplication facts first. Then the related division facts are easy.

3 × 9 = 27
9 × 3 = 27
27 ÷ 3 = 9
27 ÷ 9 = 3

Example 3

Find the missing number: 18 ÷ *n* = 6.

Think: 18 divided by what number is 6?

You know 18 ÷ 3 = 6.

So, *n* = 3.

Guided Practice *For another example, see Set C on p. 116.*

1. 12 ÷ 6 **2.** 21 ÷ 3 **3.** 14 ÷ 2 **4.** 25 ÷ 5 **5.** 54 ÷ 9

6. Algebra Find the missing number: 24 ÷ *n* = 4.

7. Write the family of facts for 2, 8, and 16.

8. Stefano has 45 basketball cards to give away to 5 friends. How many cards does each friend get if they each get the same number?

Independent Practice *For more practice, see Set C on p. 118.*

9. 6 ÷ 3 **10.** 16 ÷ 4 **11.** 20 ÷ 10 **12.** 35 ÷ 7 **13.** 20 ÷ 5

14. 56 ÷ 8 **15.** 72 ÷ 9 **16.** 63 ÷ 7 **17.** 48 ÷ 6 **18.** 42 ÷ 7

19. $4\overline{)28}$ **20.** $3\overline{)24}$ **21.** $8\overline{)64}$ **22.** $9\overline{)81}$ **23.** $10\overline{)60}$

Write the family of facts for each set of numbers.

24. 2, 7, 14 **25.** 1, 8, 8 **26.** 8, 9, 72 **27.** 7, 7, 49

Algebra **Find each missing number.**

28. $15 \div 3 = n$ **29.** $m \times 3 = 21$ **30.** $10 \times a = 70$ **31.** $48 \div u = 6$

32. Nine is the divisor, and 63 is the dividend. What is the quotient?

33. Katie has 16 china figurines. She wants to divide the figurines equally and put them on two shelves. How many figurines can she put on each shelf?

34. Thom has 5 shelves he uses for his videotape collection described at the right. He wants to put the same number of videotapes on each shelf. How many should he put on each shelf?

Thom's Videotapes	
Comedy	12
Drama	6
Western	10
Science Fiction	12

35. Math Reasoning Why are there only 2 number sentences for Exercise 27? What is another fact family that has only 2 number sentences?

Mixed Review

36. For a fund-raiser, Erick collected $5 each from 6 different people. How much money did he collect?

37. Round 23,644 to the nearest thousand.

38. Estimate: $468 + 235$. **39.** Estimate: $1{,}211 + 733$.

40. 429×1 **41.** 7×6 **42.** 0×51 **43.** 8×8

Test Prep **Choose the correct letter for each answer.**

44. Algebra Which number is the solution to the equation $x + 34 = 60$? (2-11)

A 26 **C** 84
B 36 **D** 94

45. What is the place value of 5 in 85,296? (1-1)

F Ones **H** Hundreds
G Tens **J** Thousands

Diagnostic Checkpoint

1. 3×9 (3-1)
2. 6×7 (3-1)
3. 8×6 (3-1)
4. 7×4 (3-1)
5. 9×6 (3-1)
6. 8×7 (3-1)
7. $\begin{array}{r} 6 \\ \times\ 5 \\ \hline \end{array}$ (3-1)
8. $\begin{array}{r} 8 \\ \times\ 3 \\ \hline \end{array}$ (3-1)
9. $\begin{array}{r} 9 \\ \times\ 4 \\ \hline \end{array}$ (3-1)
10. $14 \div 2$ (3-3)
11. $45 \div 5$ (3-3)
12. $63 \div 7$ (3-3)
13. $8\overline{)40}$ (3-3)
14. $10\overline{)70}$ (3-3)
15. $8\overline{)72}$ (3-3)

Algebra Find the missing number.

16. $2 \times 4 = n$ (3-1)
17. $4 \times c = 32$ (3-1)
18. $r \times 7 = 49$ (3-1)
19. $72 \div 8 = t$ (3-3)
20. $k \div 7 = 5$ (3-3)
21. $27 \div g = 9$ (3-3)

Write the family of facts for each set of numbers.

22. 5, 8, 40 (3-3)
23. 3, 6, 18 (3-3)
24. 4, 7, 28 (3-3)

Algebra Find the missing number. Name the property that helps you find each missing number.

25. $6 \times n = 8 \times 6$ (3-2)
26. $0 \times 1 = m$ (3-2)
27. $1 \times 7 = r$ (3-2)
28. $(8 \times 0) \times 4 = a$ (3-2)
29. $w \times 7 = 7 \times 3$ (3-2)
30. $9 \times b = 7 \times 9$ (3-2)
31. (3-1) Adult tickets to a puppet show cost three times as much as a child's ticket. Write a number sentence to show how much an adult ticket costs.
32. (3-3) A family pays $24 for show tickets which include one adult ticket. How many children's tickets did they purchase?

33. (3-3) Toby scored 18 points in a basketball game. Each of his baskets was worth 2 points. How many baskets did Toby make during the game?

Rules of Division

California Content Standard *Number Sense 2.6 (Grade 3): Understand the special properties of 0 and 1 in multiplication and division. Also, Algebra and Functions 1.1* *(See p. 83.)*

Warm-Up Review

1. 4×0 2. 1×8
3. Compare. Use >, <, or =.
   6×1 ● 6×0
4. $7 \div 1$ 5. $7 \div 7$
6. Find the missing number: $1 \times n = 6$.
7. Terri had 6 postcards that she divided equally among 3 friends. How many postcards did each friend receive?

Math Link You have learned basic division facts. In this lesson you will learn division rules that apply to all division problems.

Kenny gave away some of his poster collection. He shared 4 posters equally among 4 friends. How many posters did each friend get?

You know we use division to find equal shares: $4 \div 4 = 1$. So, Kenny gave 1 poster to each friend.

These rules can help you divide with 0 and 1.

Division Rules

- When a number is divided by itself, the quotient is 1. — $4 \div 4 = 1$
- When a number is divided by 1, the quotient is the same as that number. — $4 \div 1 = 4$
- When 0 is divided by any number except 0, the quotient is 0. — $0 \div 4 = 0$
- You cannot divide a number by 0. — ~~$4 \div 0$~~

Example 1

Find the missing number: $3 \div 3 = n$.

$3 \div 3 = 1$ A number divided by itself equals 1.

So $n = 1$.

Example 2

Find the missing number: $m \div 8 = 0$.

$0 \div 8 = 0$ Zero divided by any other number equals 0.

So, $m = 0$.

Additional Standard: Mathematical Reasoning 2.3 *(See p. 83.)*

Guided Practice *For another example, see Set D on p. 116.*

Algebra **Use the division rules to find the missing numbers.**

1. $0 \div 9 = n$
2. $5 \div 5 = a$
3. $6 \div w = 1$
4. $u \div 1 = 67$

5. Adam had 7 videotapes, which he distributed evenly among his 7 friends. How many videotapes did each friend get?

Independent Practice *For more practice, see Set D on p. 119.*

Algebra **Use division rules to find each missing number. If it is not possible to divide, explain why.**

6. $m \div 8 = 0$
7. $9 \div 1 = h$
8. $7 \div n = 7$
9. $0 \div 26 = c$
10. $8 \div 0 = r$
11. $y \div 5 = 1$
12. $61 \div m = 1$
13. $0 \div 0 = w$

Compare. Use >, <, or = for ●.

14. $7 \div 1$ ● $7 \div 7$
15. $3 \div 1$ ● $6 \div 1$
16. $0 \div 6$ ● $0 \div 9$

17. How many travel posters can you buy with $8?

18. What is the greatest number of sports posters you can buy for $5?

19. **Math Reasoning** Use the relationship between multiplication and division to explain why the quotient must be 0 when 0 is divided by another number.

Mixed Review

20. There are 3 bones in each finger and 2 bones in each thumb. How many bones are in all your fingers and thumbs of two hands?

21. $18 \div 3$
22. $49 \div 7$
23. 154×1
24. 0×45

Test Prep **Choose the correct letter for each answer.**

25. Which number sentence is true?
(1-6)

A $7 > 8$ **B** $-5 < -6$ **C** $-5 > -6$ **D** $4 < -6$

26. $5{,}006 - 387$
(2-7)

F 5,393 **G** 5,389 **H** 4,629 **J** 4,619 **K** NH

Problem-Solving Skill:
Choose the Operation

Warm-Up Review

1. 4 × 2
2. 5 + 9
3. 12 − 9
4. 8 + 6
5. 14 ÷ 2
6. 8 + 9
7. 8 × 8
8. 72 ÷ 8
9. Toni has 35 seashells. Kirsten has 23. How many more seashells does Toni have?

 **California Content Standard** *Number Sense 3.0 (🔑): Students solve problems involving addition, subtraction, multiplication, and division of whole numbers and understand the relationships among the operations.*

Read For Understanding

Diana collects three different kinds of paperback books, as shown in the table.

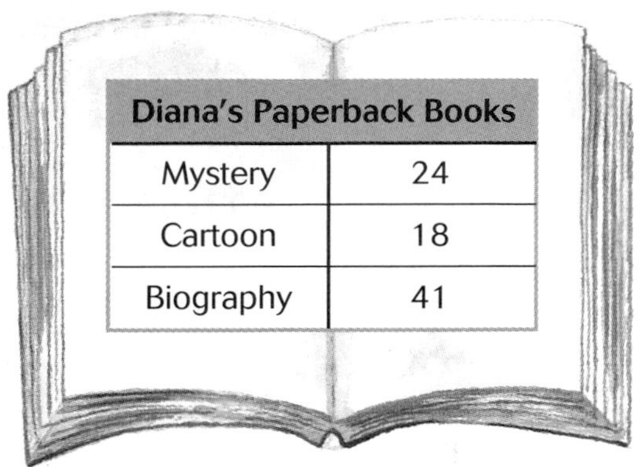

Diana's Paperback Books	
Mystery	24
Cartoon	18
Biography	41

1. How many kinds of books does Diana have?
2. How many of each kind of book does she have?

Think and Discuss

Choose the Operation

Addition, subtraction, multiplication, and division are operations you often use to solve problems. When you combine items, you add or multiply. When you want to find how many more of one thing you have than another, you subtract. When you find equal shares, you divide.

Reread the paragraph at the top of the page.

3. Suppose you want to know how many more biographies than cartoon books Diana has. Would you add or subtract to find out? Explain why.
4. Can Diana fit all her mystery and cartoon books on a shelf that holds 50 books? Explain what you need to do to solve this problem.
5. Make up a problem about Diana's books that requires multiplication. Make up another one that requires division.

Additional Standards: Algebra and Functions 1.1; Mathematical Reasoning 1.1, 2.0 (See p. 83.)

Guided Practice

Derrick has 24 space-exploration books, 33 joke books, and 18 mystery books. How many more joke books does Derrick have than space-exploration books?

1. Which operation could you use to solve the problem?
   - **a.** Subtraction
   - **b.** Division
   - **c.** Multiplication

2. Which number sentence could you use to solve the problem?
   - **a.** $18 \div 3 = \blacksquare$
   - **b.** $33 - 24 = \blacksquare$
   - **c.** $33 - 18 = \blacksquare$

3. How many books does Derrick have in all? What operation did you use to find out?

Independent Practice

Andy keeps all 20 of his biographies in one bookcase. He keeps all of his mystery books in another bookcase that has 4 shelves. He has 8 mystery books on each of the 4 shelves.

4. Which operation could you use to find how many mystery books Andy has?
   - **a.** Addition
   - **b.** Subtraction
   - **c.** Multiplication

5. Which number sentence shows how many mystery books Andy has?
   - **a.** $8 + 8 + 4 + 4 = \blacksquare$
   - **b.** $32 - 8 = \blacksquare$
   - **c.** $4 \times 8 = \blacksquare$

6. Andy wants to read all of his biographies during his 10-week summer vacation. He wants to read the same number of books each week. Which operation could you use to find how many he should read each week?
   - **a.** Multiplication
   - **b.** Division
   - **c.** Subtraction

7. Which number sentence shows how many biographies Andy should read each week?
   - **a.** $20 - 4 = \blacksquare$
   - **b.** $20 \div 10 = \blacksquare$
   - **c.** $4 \times 10 = \blacksquare$

8. **Math Reasoning** Look back at Exercise 5. What is another number sentence you could use to find how many mystery books Andy has?

Use Homework Workbook 3-5.

Using Parentheses with Computation

Warm-Up Review

1. 5×6
2. $8 + 7$
3. $16 \div 4$
4. $16 - 9$
5. $3 + 9 + 4$
6. Use the associative property to find the missing number.
   $(5 + n) + 3 = 5 + (6 + 3)$
7. Hugo spent $4.14 for a sandwich and $0.85 for milk. How much change did he get from $10.00?

California Content Standard *Algebra and Functions 1.2 (🔑): Interpret and evaluate expressions that now use parentheses. Also, Algebra and Functions 1.3 (🔑) (See p. 84.)*

Math Link You have done computations with the four basic operations: addition, subtraction, multiplication, and division. Now you will learn how to use parentheses when you are doing more than one computation.

When an expression contains more than one operation, **parentheses, ( ),** can be used to show which computation should be done first.

Example 1

Evaluate $5 \times (6 + 3)$.

$5 \times (6 + 3)$

$5 \times 9 = 45$

Do the computation inside the parentheses first.

Example 2

Evaluate $(5 \times 6) + 3$.

$(5 \times 6) + 3$

$30 + 3 = 33$

Do the computation inside the parentheses first.

Some expressions contain more than one set of parentheses. If one pair of parentheses is needed inside another pair, **brackets, [ ],** can be used. Parentheses and brackets are types of **grouping symbols** because they show which numbers and operations are grouped together.

Word Bank

parentheses
brackets
grouping

Example 3

Evaluate $(35 \div 5) - (4 + 2)$.

$(35 \div 5) - (4 + 2)$

$7 - 6 = 1$

Do the computation inside each pair of parentheses first.

Example 4

Evaluate $[72 \div (4 \times 2)] \times 3$.

$[72 \div (4 \times 2)] \times 3$

Work on the innermost grouping symbols first.

$[72 \div 8] \times 3$

Then work on the next grouping symbols.

$9 \times 3 = 27$

Additional Standards: Algebra and Functions 1.1; Mathematical Reasoning 2.2, 2.4, 3.2 (See p. 83.)

Example 5

Evaluate $52 - (14 + n)$ for $n = 3$.

$52 - (14 + n)$

Substitute 3 for n.

$52 - (14 + 3)$

Do the computation inside the parentheses first.

$52 - 17 = 35$

Guided Practice

For another example, see Set E on p. 117.

1. $63 \div (4 + 3)$
2. $(9 + 16) - (16 \div 8)$
3. $[(18 \div 6) + 4] \div 7$
4. Evaluate $54 \div (7 + n)$ for $n = 2$.
5. The table shows the puzzle books Ms. Phang purchased for her classroom. The price of each book was \$3. Write and then evaluate an expression with parentheses to show how much Ms. Phang paid for her books.

Puzzle-Book Purchases	
Word Searches	5
Crossword Puzzles	4

Independent Practice

For more practice, see Set E on p. 119.

6. $15 \div (9 - 6)$
7. $(9 \div 1) + 7$
8. $(4 + 2) \times (8 - 2)$
9. $81 \div (3 + 2 + 4)$
10. $(20 - 3) - (6 + 7)$
11. $[(3 + 5) \times 5] \div 10$
12. $4 \times [18 - (6 \times 2)]$
13. $83 - (34 - 13)$
14. $(411 + 384) - 217$

Rewrite with parentheses to make the statement true.

15. $21 + 14 \div 7 = 5$
16. $15 - 2 + 4 = 9$
17. $36 \div 12 \div 3 = 9$

Evaluate each expression for $m = 18$.

18. $(25 - m) + 9$
19. $13 - (22 - m)$
20. $m - (7 - 1)$
21. Evaluate $([(20 + 8) \div 4] + 3) \div 2$. What steps did you use to find the answer?

Math Reasoning For each exercise, insert +, −, ×, or ÷ in each ● and a one-digit number in each ■. Then insert parentheses to make a true statement.

22. 12 ● ■ ● ■ = 36
23. 8 ● ■ ● ■ ● ■ = 16

Games $2 each	
Bowling	3
Tree Swing	2
Bounce	4

24. The table shows the games the Weisman family played at the arcade. Write and then evaluate an expression with parentheses to show how much they spent at the arcade.

25. Mental Math Sunanda was able to mentally compute $(68 \times 9) \times 0$ by first applying the associative property. Can you explain her thinking? How could you use the associative property to help you mentally compute $(76 + 97) + 3$?

26. Math Reasoning You have studied the associative property for addition and multiplication. Do you think the associative property works for subtraction and division? Test the examples in the table to help you decide.

Operation	Example	Does the associative property work?
Addition	$(3 + 2) + 4 = 3 + (2 + 4)$	Yes
Subtraction	Does $(12 - 7) - 2 = 12 - (7 - 2)$?	
Multiplication	$(4 \times 2) \times 6 = 4 \times (2 \times 6)$	Yes
Division	Does $(32 \div 8) \div 2 = 32 \div (8 \div 2)$?	

Mixed Review

27. Margaret wants to display 30 plates on 3 shelves. How many plates can she put equally on the shelves?

28. $18 \div 1$

29. $63 \div 7$

30. $48 \div 8$

31. $0 \div 5$

32. $413 + 220 + 178$

33. $4{,}845 + 2{,}137 + 6{,}099$

34. $429 - 372$

35. $61{,}345 - 3{,}746$

Test Prep Choose the correct letter for each answer.

36. (3-1) Richard has 3 shelves that can hold 9 paint cans each. How many paint cans can the shelves hold in all?

A 3 cans
B 6 cans
C 12 cans
D 24 cans
E NH

37. (2-8) How many pieces of ribbon will you have if you use 9 cuts to cut it into shorter pieces?

F 8 pieces
G 9 pieces
H 10 pieces
J 11 pieces

Use Homework Workbook 3-6.

Problem-Solving Strategy:
Draw a Picture

California Content Standards *Mathematical Reasoning 2.3: Use a variety of methods, such as words, numbers, symbols, . . . diagrams, and models, to explain mathematical reasoning. Also, Mathematical Reasoning 3.2* *(See p. 83.)*

Warm-Up Review

1. 5×7 **2.** 6×9

3. 2×10 **4.** 8×8

5. How many rows are there in the array? How many columns? How many triangles are there in all?

Example 1

Joe has entered a bike race. There are 9 racers in each row. There are 10 rows. Joe is in the sixth row. How many racers are ahead of Joe? How many are behind Joe?

Understand

What do you need to find?

You need to find how many racers are ahead of Joe and how many are behind Joe.

Plan

How can you solve the problem?

You can **draw a picture** of the racers. Write an A for each racer ahead of Joe, B for each racer behind Joe, and **J** for each racer in Joe's row.

Solve

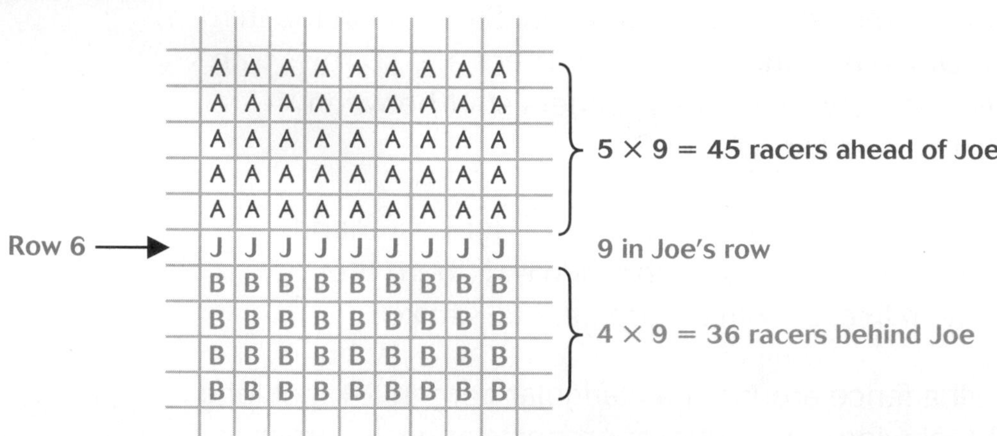

Look Back

How many racers are there in all? Explain at least two ways to find the answer.

Additional Standard: Mathematical Reasoning 2.0 *(See p. 83.)*

Example 2

Eleven sisters stand in a row for a group picture. The triplets are in the middle. How many sisters are on each side of the triplets?

Draw 11 dots in a row for the 11 sisters. Find the middle. Then mark the position of the triplets.

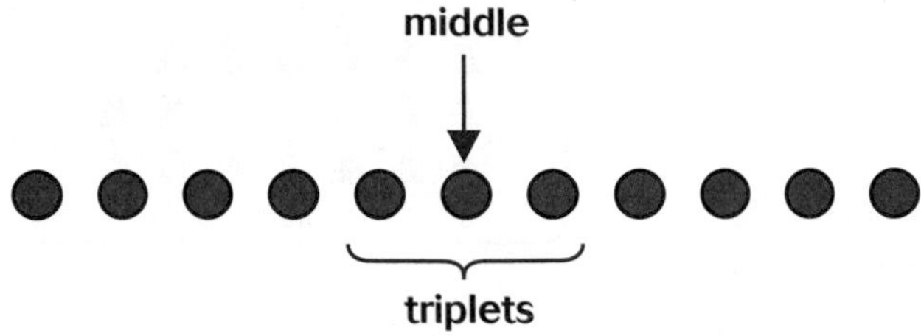

You can tell from the picture that there are 4 sisters on each side of the triplets.

Guided Practice

Draw a picture to solve Exercises 1–8.

1. Regina entered a bike race that has 7 rows of racers. There are 8 racers in each row. If Regina is in the second row, how many racers start behind Regina?

2. Gustav planted 13 flowers in a row. He had 5 white flowers, which he planted in the middle. How many flowers were there on each side of the white flowers?

Independent Practice

3. Steven and Dmitri entered a marathon. Steven is in the third row and Dmitri is in the eighth row. There are 10 rows with 6 runners per row. How many runners start between Steven's row and Dmitri's row?

4. Polly is in the middle of the lunch line. Her best friend, Kimiko, is the third person behind Polly. If there are 17 people in line, how many are behind Kimiko?

5. Gary built a fence around a rectangular garden 24 feet long and 12 feet wide. If he put support posts at each corner and additional posts every 6 feet, how many posts did he use?

6. Charlene is riding a roller coaster. There are 4 people in each car and 8 cars in all. Charlene is in the third car. How many people are in the cars ahead of Charlene? How many people are in the cars behind her?

7. Max lines up his baseball cards with the same number in each row. The card in the middle of the array has 4 cards to its left, 4 to its right, 4 above, and 4 below. How many cards are there in all?

8. Twenty-one folk dancers form a circle. There are 2 men on each side of every woman. How many men are there? How many women are there?

Mixed Review

Try these or other strategies to solve each problem. Tell what strategy you used.

Problem-Solving Strategies

- *Find a Pattern*
- *Solve a Simpler Problem*
- *Draw a Picture*
- *Write a Number Sentence*

9. Sal is playing a board game. The pattern of colors continues as shown at the right. He landed on the 17th square. What color is that square?

START

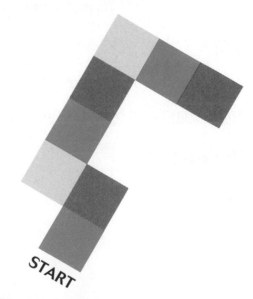

10. A worm is climbing up a well. Each day it climbs up 4 feet and slips down 1 foot. How far up the wall will it be after 10 days?

11. Kartik is collecting leap-year pennies. He has pennies from 1956, 1960, 1964, and 1968. Should he put a 1976 penny in his collection? Why or why not?

12. The Student Council ran a car wash to raise money for its Fun Fair. They washed 45 cars in the morning, 108 cars in the afternoon, and 18 cars in the evening. How many cars did they wash in all?

Use Homework Workbook 3-7.

Expressions with Multiplication and Division

Algebra

California Content Standard *Algebra and Functions 1.1: Use letters, boxes, or other symbols to stand for any number in simple expressions or equations.*

Warm-Up Review

Evaluate for $b = 16$.

1. $b - 12$
2. $73 + b$
3. Complete the table.

x	$15 + x$
5	
10	
27	

4. Karen has missed x days of school out of 180. How many days was she in school if $x = 6$?

Math Link You have learned how to evaluate algebraic expressions involving addition and subtraction. Now you will work with algebraic expressions that involve multiplication and division.

When a letter variable is used in a multiplication expression, the times sign is usually omitted. That is because the times sign could be confused with the letter x.

Example 1

Evaluate $6m$ for $m = 7$.

Substitute 7 for m. Then write the times sign and multiply.

$6m$

Think: $6m$ means 6 times m.

$6 \times 7 = 42$

A fraction bar is often used to show division. $\frac{15}{3}$ means the same thing as $15 \div 3$. Both expressions have the value of 5.

Example 2

Evaluate $\frac{21}{n}$ for $n = 3$.

Substitute 3 for n. Then divide.

$\frac{21}{n}$

Think: $\frac{21}{3}$ means $21 \div 3$.

$\frac{21}{3} = 7$

Additional Standard: Algebra and Functions 1.2 (key) *(See p. 83.)*

Some expressions may contain grouping symbols, such as parentheses.

Example 3

Evaluate $53 - (4x)$ for $x = 9$.

Substitute 9 for x. Then do the computations, starting inside the parentheses.

$53 - (4x)$ Remember that $4x$ means 4 times x.

$53 - (4 \times 9)$

$53 - 36 = 17$

Guided Practice For another example, see Set F on p. 117.

Evaluate each expression for $n = 8$.

1. $4n$ **2.** $\frac{n}{4}$ **3.** $(10n) + 14$ **4.** $12 - \left(\frac{40}{n}\right)$

5. Find the total number of marbles when $x = 8$.

Independent Practice For more practice, see Set F on p. 119.

Evaluate each expression for $x = 6$.

6. $4x$ **7.** $\frac{x}{2}$ **8.** $6x$ **9.** $\frac{54}{x}$

10. $x + 74$ **11.** $\frac{60}{x}$ **12.** $\left(\frac{x}{6}\right) + 18$ **13.** $67 - (3x)$

14. $\frac{x}{1}$ **15.** $37 - x$ **16.** $(3x) + \left(\frac{48}{x}\right)$ **17.** $\left[23 + \left(\frac{x}{3}\right)\right] \div 5$

18. What is the total number of paper clips in the envelopes if $x = 5$?

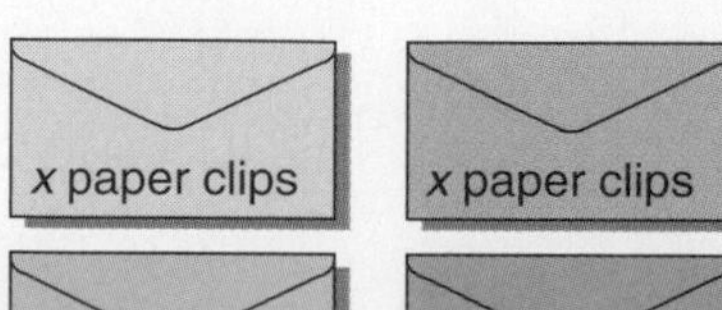

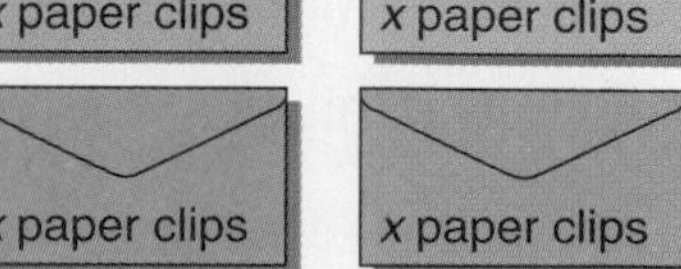

Copy and complete each table.

19.

x	$3x$
2	
7	
9	
10	

20.

w	$\frac{24}{w}$
3	
4	
6	
24	

21.

m	$81 - (7m)$
0	
1	
4	
9	

22. **Math Reasoning** When evaluated, which of the following expressions will always have the same value, no matter what value you choose for x? Explain.

$x + 3$ $\qquad \frac{x}{2}$ $\qquad 15 - x$ $\qquad 0x$

Mixed Review

23. Reggie had 49 red marbles and 28 blue marbles. He won 7 more blue marbles. How many more red marbles than blue marbles did Reggie have then?

24. Estimate \$6.21 + \$5.73.

25. **Mental Math** 804 + 136

Algebra **Evaluate each expression for $m = 114$.**

26. $532 - m$

27. $m + 239$

28. $5{,}804 + m$

29. $(9 \times 4) \div 6$

30. $18 \div 1$

31. $0 \div 93$

32. $47 + 32 + 918$

33. $(14 + 66) - (32 \div 8)$

34. $52 + [40 - (6 + 7)]$

35. $\begin{array}{r} 14{,}639 \\ +\ 28{,}090 \\ \hline \end{array}$

36. $\begin{array}{r} 63{,}924 \\ -\ 55{,}217 \\ \hline \end{array}$

37. $\begin{array}{r} 30{,}000 \\ -\ 12{,}148 \\ \hline \end{array}$

Test Prep **Choose the correct letter for each answer.**

38. (2-5) Pat drove 215 miles Monday and 346 miles Tuesday. How much farther did he drive on Tuesday?

A 131 miles

B 139 miles

C 551 miles

D 561 miles

39. (1-1) Which digit of 256,973 is in the ten thousands place?

F 2

G 5

H 6

J 7

TEST PREP

Multiple-Choice Cumulative Review

Choose the correct letter for each answer.

Use the bar graph for Questions 1–3.

The bar graph shows the types of birds seen on a field trip.

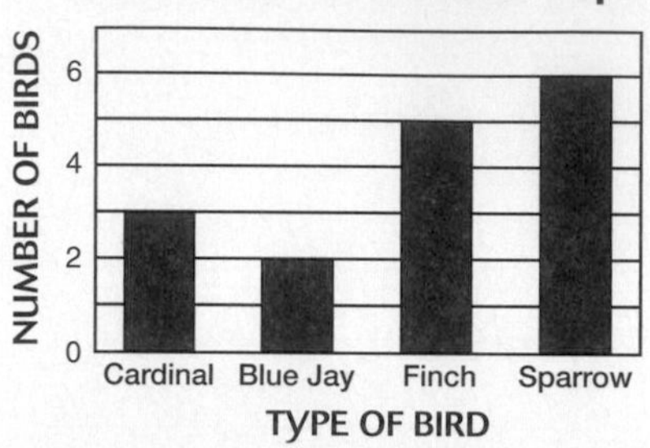

1. **What bird was seen the most?**

   A Cardinal
   B Blue jay
   C Finch
   D Sparrow

2. **How many more sparrows were seen than finches?**

   F 1
   G 2
   H 5
   J 6

3. **How many birds were seen on the trip?**

   A 16
   B 17
   C 18
   D 19

4. **The hat has the shape of a ______.**

   F Sphere
   G Cylinder
   H Pyramid
   J Cone

5. **Emily made 3 quarts of punch. How many cups is this?**

   A 4
   B 6
   C 9
   D 12

6. **Find the missing number.**

   $$49 \div \blacksquare = 7$$

   F 6
   G 7
   H 8
   J 9
   K NH

7. **Karen has 4 shelves that can hold 7 figurines each. How many figurines can Karen display?**

   A 4
   B 7
   C 21
   D 28

8. **Evaluate the expression for $y = 9$.**

   $$5 + y$$

   F 5
   G 9
   H 14
   J 45
   K NH

Equations

California Content Standards *Algebra and Functions 2.0 (🔑): Students know how to manipulate equations. Also, Algebra and Functions 1.1* *(See p. 83.)*

Warm-Up Review

1. 3×0
2. 5×6
3. $15 \div 5$
4. $49 \div 7$

Evaluate for $x = 9$.

5. $7x$
6. $\frac{36}{x}$
7. Solve $56 - n = 43$ by testing these values for n: 11, 13, 19.

Math Link You have worked with addition and subtraction equations. In this lesson you will learn about multiplication and division equations.

Example 1

Solve the equation $8x = 72$ by testing these values for x: 2, 5, 8, 9.

$8x = 72$

Try $x = 2$: $8 \times 2 = 16$

Try $x = 5$: $8 \times 5 = 40$

Try $x = 8$: $8 \times 8 = 64$

Try $x = 9$: $8 \times 9 = 72$

If you can solve the equation mentally, you do not have to test every value. Think: $8 \times 9 = 72$, so $x = 9$.

The solution to the equation is $x = 9$.

Example 2

Solve the equation $\frac{m}{6} = 7$ by testing values for m.

Try	$\frac{m}{6} = 7$	Does $\frac{m}{6} = 7$?
$m = 12$	$\frac{12}{6} = 2$	No
$m = 60$	$\frac{60}{6} = 10$	No
$m = 48$	$\frac{48}{6} = 8$	No
$m = 42$	$\frac{42}{6} = 7$	Yes

The solution to the equation is $m = 42$.

 Additional Standard: Mathematical Reasoning 2.3 *(See p. 83.)*

Guided Practice *For another example, see Set G on p. 117.*

Solve each equation by testing these values for the variable: 1, 4, 5, 8.

1. $3x = 15$ **2.** $\frac{40}{n} = 5$ **3.** $7w = 28$ **4.** $10m = 50$

5. Write an equation for the balance scale shown at the right. Solve the equation by testing these values for x: 2, 5, 6, 10.

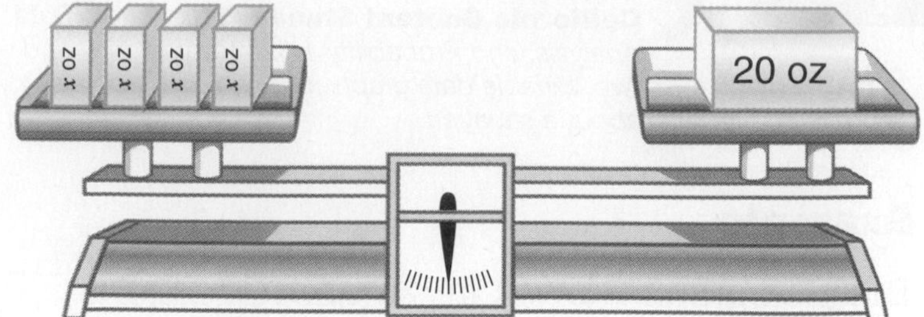

Independent Practice *For more practice, see Set G on p. 119.*

Solve each equation by testing these values for *m*: 2, 4, 5, 10.

6. $7m = 35$ **7.** $6m = 12$ **8.** $\frac{20}{m} = 5$ **9.** $10m = 100$

Solve each equation by testing values for *n*.

10. $\frac{n}{3} = 2$ **11.** $8n = 24$ **12.** $6n = 0$ **13.** $\frac{18}{n} = 2$

14. Math Reasoning Refer to the balance scale shown above. Suppose every weight on the scale is doubled. Would the scale still balance? Explain your thinking.

Mixed Review

15. Aaron is packing 8 boxes. He puts 6 packages in each box. How many packages is Aaron packing?

Algebra Evaluate each expression for $r = 8$.

16. $8r$ **17.** $\frac{72}{r}$ **18.** $\frac{r}{4}$ **19.** $3r$

Algebra Copy each expression and insert parentheses to get the greatest result.

20. $2 + 8 \times 2$ **21.** $10 - 2 \times 4$ **22.** $9 + 27 \div 9$

Test Prep Choose the correct letter for the answer.

23. Algebra Evaluate $32 - (x + 14)$ for $x = 5$.
(3-6)

A 13 **B** 23 **C** 41 **D** 51 **E** NH

Problem-Solving Application:

Using a Pictograph

 **California Content Standard** *Statistics, Data Analysis, and Probability 1.3: Interpret one- and two-variable data graphs to answer questions about a situation.*

Warm-Up Review

1. $9 \times (6 + 4)$
2. $(5 \times 5) + 17$
3. Phil washed 6 cars at \$3 each and 4 vans at \$5 each. How much did he earn?

Example

The pictograph shows Cindy's sport pin collection. How many pins does Cindy have in her collection?

Sport Pin Collection

Sport	Number of Pins
Soccer	◈ ◈ ◈ ◈ ◁
Basketball	◈ ◈ ◈ ◈ ◈ ◁
Hockey	◈ ◈ ◈ ◁
Football	◈ ◈ ◁

Each ◈ stands for 6 pins.

Understand

What do you need to find?

You need to find the total number of pins in the collection.

Plan

How can you solve the problem?

First, use the graph to find the number of pins for each sport. Then add to find the total number of pins.

Solve

Sport	◈ = 6 pins ◁ = 3 pins
Soccer	$(4 \times 6) + 3 = 24 + 3 = 27$
Basketball	$(5 \times 6) + 3 = 30 + 3 = 33$
Hockey	$(3 \times 6) + 3 = 18 + 3 = 21$
Football	$(2 \times 6) + 3 = 12 + 3 = 15$

Remember to work inside the parentheses first.

Add to find the total number of pins: $27 + 33 + 21 + 15 = 96$
There are 96 pins in Cindy's collection.

Look Back

Can you think of another way to find the answer?

 *Additional Standards: Algebra and Functions 1.2 (key), 1.3 (key); Mathematical Reasoning 2.0* *(See p. 83.)*

Guided Practice

Suppose you have a collection of sport caps. The pictograph at the right shows how many caps you have for each sport. Use the pictograph for Exercises 1–8.

Sport Cap Collection

Baseball | Basketball | Hockey | Football

Each stands for 4 caps.

1. For which sport do you have the least number of caps?

2. How many baseball caps do you have?

Independent Practice

3. List the types of caps you have in order from greatest to least.

4. Do you have more baseball caps or more football caps? How many more?

5. If you add 12 football caps to your collection, how many more will you draw? How many football caps will you have in your collection?

6. Is it true that you have twice as many basketball caps as hockey caps? Explain.

7. How many hockey caps would you need to add to your collection so that you would not have to show any half-cap symbols for hockey?

8. How could you show 29 basketball caps in your pictograph?

Mixed Review

9. Refer to the table of temperatures at the right. By how many degrees Fahrenheit did the temperature change between 8:00 A.M. and noon? Did it go up or down?

10. Margaret wants to buy a dress priced at $41.78 and a pair of shoes marked $23.79. Shoes are $2.50 off on Tuesdays. What would Margaret pay for the dress and shoes if she shops on Tuesday?

Time	Temperature
8:00 A.M.	−3°F
9:00 A.M.	−2°F
10:00 A.M.	0°F
11:00 A.M.	4°F
12:00 P.M.	5°F

Use Homework Workbook 3-10.

Diagnostic Checkpoint

Complete. For Exercises 1–3, use the words from the Word Bank.

Word Bank
Associative Property
Commutative Property
factor
product
Property of One
Zero Property

1. (3-1) You multiply numbers to find a ____________.

2. (3-1) A number you multiply is a ____________.

3. (3-2) The ____________ states that when you multiply any number by 0, the product is 0.

Algebra **Find each missing number.**

4. (3-4) $6 \div 6 = k$ **5.** (3-4) $0 \div 1 = t$ **6.** (3-4) $r \div 3 = 0$

Evaluate each expression.

7. (3-6) $36 \div (5 + 4)$ **8.** (3-6) $8 + (3 \times 0)$ **9.** (3-6) $12 \div (7 + 5)$

Algebra **Evaluate each expression for $b = 4$.**

10. (3-6) $(28 - b) \div 8$ **11.** (3-6) $(32 \div b) + 5$ **12.** (3-8) $28 \div b$ **13.** (3-8) $9b$

Algebra **Solve each equation by testing these values for n: 5, 6, 7, 8.**

14. (3-9) $6n = 42$ **15.** (3-9) $9n = 54$ **16.** (3-9) $\frac{n}{4} = 2$ **17.** (3-9) $\frac{24}{n} = 4$

18. (3-5) Andrea's picture album has 9 pages. Each page can hold 8 pictures. She has 54 pictures in the album. Which operation could you use to find how many pictures Andrea's album can hold in all?

19. (3-7) Sally is third in line. Her sister is last in line. If there are 15 people in line, how many are between Sally and her sister?

20. (3-10) Use the pictograph at the right. List the types of trees planted in order from greatest to least.

21. (3-10) How many trees were planted on Arbor Day?

Trees Planted on Arbor Day	
Elm	🌳🌳🌳🌳
Oak	🌳🌳🌳🌳🌳 ½
Fir	🌳🌳 ½
Maple	🌳🌳🌳 ½
Each 🌳 stands for 6 trees.	

Chapter 3 Test

1. 6×4
2. 7×5
3. 3×7
4. 8×8
5. $54 \div 9$
6. $40 \div 10$
7. $25 \div 5$
8. $42 \div 7$

Algebra **Find each missing number. Name the property that helps you find each missing number.**

9. $1 \times f = 7$
10. $y \times 3 = 3 \times 7$
11. $(6 \times 2) \times 4 = 6 \times (w \times 4)$

12. When 0 is divided by any number except 0, what is the quotient?

13. Write the fact family for 4, 5, and 20.

14. Evaluate $(3 \times 4) + 8$.

15. Evaluate $(5 - 1) + (15 \div 3)$.

Algebra **Evaluate each expression for $y = 4$.**

16. $9y$
17. $\frac{32}{y}$
18. $24 \div (2y)$

Algebra **Solve each equation by testing these values for x: 3, 6, 9, 12.**

19. $4x = 12$
20. $x \div 6 = 2$
21. $\frac{x}{3} = 3$

22. Colored pencils cost 7 cents each. Plain pencils cost 5 cents each. What operation could you use to find the number of colored pencils you can buy with 63 cents?

23. There are 15 students in line. The first and last students are boys, there are 3 boys in the middle, and all the other students are girls. How many girls are standing between the first boy and the boys in the middle?

Use the pictograph for Questions 24 and 25.

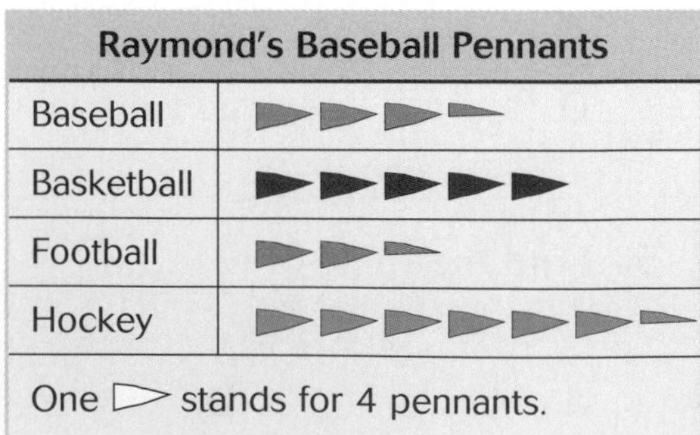

24. List the types of pennants Raymond has in order from greatest to least.

25. If Raymond adds 12 more pennants to his collection, how many more ▷ will he draw?

TEST PREP

Multiple-Choice Chapter 3 Test

Choose the correct letter for each answer.

1. Jordan has baseball pennants hanging on all 4 walls of his bedroom. There are 9 pennants on each wall. How many pennants is this?

A 9
B 32
C 36
D 49
E NH

2. Find the missing number.

$$6 \times q = 42$$

F 6
G 7
H 8
J 9

3. Mrs. Beaugh had 9 stickers left to hand out. She distributed them equally to 9 students. How many stickers did each student get?

A 1
B 2
C 5
D 9

4. Find the value of *m*.

$$(3 \times m) \times 2 = 3 \times (6 \times 2)$$

F $m = 2$
G $m = 3$
H $m = 4$
J $m = 6$

5. Find the value of *y*.

$$32 \div 4 = y$$

A $y = 6$
B $y = 7$
C $y = 8$
D $y = 9$
E NH

6. Suppose Felice has 45 books. She decides to put them in 9 equal stacks. How many books are in each stack?

F 4
G 5
H 7
J 9

Kirsten's Comic Books	
Action	36
Comedy	15
Super Hero	22

7. Which operation could you use to find how many comic books Kirsten has in all?

A Addition
B Subtraction
C Multiplication
D Division

8. Which of the following facts is *not* in the fact family of 3, 6, 18?

F $3 \times 6 = 18$
G $18 \div 6 = 3$
H $6 \times 3 = 18$
J $6 \div 3 = 2$

9. **When a number is divided by itself, the quotient is *always***

A 0.
B 1.
C 2.
D 5.

---

10. **Find the value of $\frac{z}{6}$ when $z = 30$.**

F 5
G 36
H 50
J 180

---

11. **Evaluate $36 \div (3 + 3)$.**

A 3
B 6
C 7
D 12

---

12. **Solve $\frac{36}{x} = 9$.**

F $x = 2$
G $x = 4$
H $x = 27$
J $x = 45$

---

13. **Katie and William spent a total of \$10 for lunch. Katie spent \$2 more for her lunch than William. How much did William spend?**

A \$2
B \$4
C \$6
D \$10

---

14. **Evaluate $4y$ for $y = 7$.**

F 4
G 7
H 11
J 26
K NH

---

15. **Drew wants to hang 20 posters on a wall in t equal rows. Which expression shows how many posters he can put in each row?**

A $20 \div t$
B $t \div 20$
C $20t$
D $t \times 20$

---

16. **Which property of multiplication is used?**

$$9 \times 4 = 4 \times 9$$

F Commutative Property
G Associative Property
H Property of One
J Zero Property

---

17. **Solve $9m = 63$.**

A $m = 0$
B $m = 1$
C $m = 7$
D $m = 9$
E NH

Use the pictograph for Question 18.

T-Shirts	
Blue	
Red	
Green	
Yellow	
One stands for 8 T-shirts.	

18. **How many more yellow T-shirts are there than blue T-shirts?**

F 12
G 16
H 24
J 36

Reteaching

Set A (pages 84–86)

Find 4 × 5.

$5 + 5 + 5 + 5 = 20$

$\underbrace{4 \times 5}_{\text{factors}} = \underset{\uparrow \text{ product}}{20}$

factors product

Remember you can change the order of the factors when you multiply.

1. 3×4 **2.** 5×8 **3.** 9×7

4. 6×6 **5.** 4×4 **6.** 6×5

Set B (pages 87–89)

Use properties to find the product of 0 × 5.

Zero Property:
When you multiply any number by 0, the product is 0.

So, $0 \times 5 = 0$.

Remember when you multiply any number by 1, the product is that number.

Use properties to find each product.

1. 6×0 **2.** 1×7 **3.** 5×1

4. 0×3 **5.** 9×0 **6.** 1×8

Set C (pages 90–92)

Find 21 ÷ 7.

You can write a fact family.

$3 \times 7 = 21$ $7 \times 3 = 21$

$21 \div 3 = 7$ $21 \div 7 = 3$

So, $21 \div 7 = 3$.

Remember if you know a related multiplication fact, you can use it to solve a division problem.

1. $18 \div 9$ **2.** $25 \div 5$ **3.** $32 \div 4$

4. $42 \div 7$ **5.** $54 \div 6$ **6.** $40 \div 8$

Set D (pages 94–95)

Find the missing number:
$5 \div 5 = w$

When a number is divided by itself, the quotient is 1.

$5 \div 5 = 1$.

So, $w = 1$.

Remember when 0 is divided by any number except 0, the quotient is 0.

Use the division rules to find each missing number.

1. $3 \div 3 = m$ **2.** $6 \div y = 1$

3. $k \div 1 = 5$ **4.** $0 \div 4 = t$

5. $9 \div s = 9$ **6.** $0 \div 8 = q$

Set E (pages 98–100)

Evaluate the expression.
$2 \times (5 + 3)$

The parentheses are used to show which computation should be done first.

$2 \times (5 + 3)$

$2 \times 8 = 16$

Remember to do whatever is in parentheses first.

Evaluate each expression.

1. $(1 + 8) \times 2$
2. $12 \div (4 + 2)$
3. $32 \div (6 + 2)$
4. $22 - (6 + 4)$
5. $42 \div (12 \div 2)$
6. $(9 - 4) \times 8$
7. $5 \times (4 + 1)$
8. $(10 \div 2) + 8$

Set F (pages 104–106)

Evaluate $4t$ for $t = 3$.

$4t$ means 4 times t.
Substitute 3 for t.
Then write the times sign and multiply.

$4t$

$4 \times 3 = 12$

Remember the letter variable in the expression represents a number.

Evaluate each expression for $y = 4$.

1. $5y$
2. $\frac{16}{y}$
3. $\frac{24}{y}$
4. $4y$
5. $\frac{36}{y}$
6. $9y$
7. $8y$
8. $\frac{y}{2}$

Set G (pages 108–109)

Solve the equation $\frac{m}{4} = 7$ by testing values for m.

Try $m = 24$: $\frac{24}{4} = 6$

Try $m = 36$: $\frac{36}{4} = 9$

Try $m = 28$: $\frac{28}{4} = 7$

The solution to the equation is $m = 28$.

Remember that the solution of an equation is a value of the variable that makes the equation true.

Solve each equation by testing values for t.

1. $\frac{t}{3} = 6$
2. $\frac{t}{6} = 5$
3. $8t = 40$
4. $5t = 45$
5. $\frac{t}{9} = 0$
6. $\frac{t}{7} = 7$

More Practice

Set A *(pages 84–86)*

1. 4×4 **2.** 5×3 **3.** 7×8 **4.** 9×3

5. 3×3 **6.** 2×7 **7.** 5×5 **8.** 8×4

Find each missing number.

9. $4 \times p = 36$ **10.** $9 \times 6 = y$ **11.** $1 \times y = 10$ **12.** $6 \times 7 = y$

13. A textbook weighs about 2 pounds. The books are packaged in boxes of 8. About how much does each box weigh?

Set B *(pages 87–89)*

Use properties to find each product.

1. 6×0 **2.** 1×7 **3.** 0×4 **4.** 8×1 **5.** 5×1

Algebra **Find the missing number. Name the property that helps you find each missing number.**

6. $4 \times 6 = 6 \times n$ **7.** $3 \times b = 5 \times 3$

8. $(4 \times 2) \times 3 = 4 \times (2 \times y)$ **9.** $(1 \times 6) \times 4 = t$

10. $(2 \times 3) \times 6 = d \times (3 \times 6)$ **11.** $(0 \times 3) \times 6 = k$

12. Carter has 2 shelves of model airplanes. There are 6 airplanes on each shelf. How many model airplanes does Carter have?

Set C *(pages 90–92)*

1. $16 \div 4$ **2.** $21 \div 7$ **3.** $15 \div 5$ **4.** $24 \div 6$

5. $36 \div 9$ **6.** $40 \div 8$ **7.** $48 \div 6$ **8.** $54 \div 9$

Find each missing number.

9. $63 \div 7 = n$ **10.** $72 \div s = 9$ **11.** $80 \div 10 = v$ **12.** $35 \div c = 7$

13. Markers come in boxes of 8. If you need 48 markers, how many boxes should you buy?

Set D (pages 94–95)

Use division rules to find each missing number.

1. $6 \div c = 1$ **2.** $6 \div d = 6$ **3.** $8 \div s = 1$ **4.** $0 \div 6 = m$

5. $3 \div 3 = f$ **6.** $7 \div r = 7$ **7.** $0 \div 9 = w$ **8.** $5 \div g = 1$

9. Kevin had 6 cans of tennis balls, which he distributed evenly among 6 tennis players. How many cans of tennis balls did each player get?

Set E (pages 98–100)

Evaluate each expression.

1. $24 \div (9 - 5)$ **2.** $(7 \div 7) + 7$ **3.** $[(5 + 7) \div 3] + 2$

Rewrite with parentheses to make the statement true.

4. $6 + 4 \times 9 = 42$ **5.** $12 - 7 \times 5 = 25$ **6.** $16 - 8 \div 2 = 12$

7. Zack bought 3 jazz tapes and 4 classical tapes. Each tape cost $8. Write and then evaluate an expression with parentheses to show how much Zack paid for the tapes.

Set F (pages 104–106)

Evaluate each expression for $y = 9$.

1. $\frac{y}{9}$ **2.** $3y$ **3.** $\frac{54}{y}$ **4.** $30 - 2y$

5. Mrs. Hanson asked her 30 students to work in small groups. There were x students in each group. How many groups were there?

Set G (pages 108–109)

Solve each equation by testing values for n.

1. $4n = 20$ **2.** $\frac{n}{5} = 3$ **3.** $6n = 42$ **4.** $\frac{n}{5} = 8$

5. Greg bought 3 sets of model cars for $12. There are 2 cars in each set. How much did he pay for each car?

Problem Solving: Preparing for Tests

Choose the correct letter for each answer.

1. **There are more than 8 boxes of candles on a shelf at a store. Each box holds 4 candles. Which of these is reasonable for the total number of candles?**

A Less than 12

B Between 12 and 30

C Between 30 and 32

D More than 32

Tip

Words like *more than* can tell you that numbers are estimated, not exact. Which number in this problem is estimated?

2. **Mrs. Anato has 42 sheets of craft paper to divide equally among 6 students. When she is finished, how many sheets of paper will each student have?**

F 1 sheet

G 2 sheets

H 7 sheets

J 38 sheets

Tip

You can use *The Draw a Diagram* strategy to help you solve this problem.

3. **Alex has 6 empty juice cans. He needs 4 times that many cans to win a prize in the recycling program at school. How many more cans does Alex need to win a prize?**

A 18 cans

B 20 cans

C 24 cans

D 28 cans

Tip

When more than one step is needed to solve a problem you must decide both *what* to do and in what *order* to do it.

4. **Sheila has 7 coins. Some are quarters and some are nickels. Their total value is 95¢. Which of these is a reasonable number of nickels for Sheila to have?**

F 4 nickels

G 5 nickels

H 6 nickels

J 7 nickels

5. **Brendan finds some colored markers on sale. There are a total of 36 markers in 3 boxes. How many markers are there in 2 boxes?**

A 12

B 24

C 33

D 39

6. **Mark and 3 friends want to share 24 marbles. How can you find the number of marbles each of them will get?**

F Add 3 to 24.

G Multiply 24 times 3.

H Divide 24 by 3.

J Divide 24 by 4.

7. **There were 89 children and 48 adults who signed up for a trip to the science museum. Which is the best estimate of the number of people going to the museum?**

A 60

B 130

C 140

D 200

8. **Shawna has 8 boxes of golf balls. Each box holds 3 balls. Which number sentence could be used to show how many golf balls Shawna has?**

F $8 \times 3 = ■$

G $8 \div 3 = ■$

H $8 + 3 = ■$

J $8 - 3 = ■$

9. **Tim, Jake, Penny, and Nan are in line to pay for a movie. Jake is second. Penny is behind Nan. Which shows the order of the four friends from first to last?**

A Nan, Tim, Jake, Penny

B Penny, Jake, Tim, Nan

C Tim, Jake, Nan, Penny

D Tim, Jake, Penny, Nan

The graph below shows the number of animals seen on a nature trip.

Animals Seen on a Nature Trip

Deer	🐾🐾
Squirrels	🐾🐾🐾🐾🐾 and part of a 🐾
Chipmunks	🐾🐾🐾
Raccoons	🐾🐾 and part of a 🐾

Each 🐾 stands for 4 animals.

10. **How many more squirrels were seen than raccoons?**

F 3

G 8

H 10

J 12

TEST PREP

Multiple-Choice Cumulative Review

Choose the correct letter for each answer.

Number Sense

1. $435 + 396 + 43 =$

A 764
B 774
C 874
D 8,614
E NH

2. Roberto weighs 114 pounds. His older brother Carlos weighs 185 pounds. What is the best estimate of their total weight?

F 200 lb
G 300 lb
H 350 lb
J 400 lb

3. Kristina put 36 beads into 6 equal groups. Which number sentence would you use to find how many beads are in each group?

A $36 \times 6 = ■$
B $6 \div 36 = ■$
C $36 - 6 = ■$
D $36 \div 6 = ■$

4. Judy takes 27 fruit bars to practice to share with her team. If each person gets 3 fruit bars, how many people are on Judy's team?

F 6 people
G 9 people
H 24 people
J 30 people

5. Evaluate $(16 \div 8) - 2$.

A 0
B 2
C 4
D 8
E NH

6. How many pieces of ribbon will you have if you cut a piece of ribbon 7 times?

F 6 pieces
G 7 pieces
H 8 pieces
J 9 pieces
K NH

7. Which number is between 4,840 and 4,907?

A 4,805
B 4,839
C 4,889
D 4,991

8. Find the missing number.

$$(6 \times 5) \times ■ = 6 \times (5 \times 2)$$

F 0
G 1
H 2
J 3

Algebra and Functions

9. Which number makes this sentence true?

$$72 \div \blacksquare = 9$$

A 7
B 8
C 9
D 12

---

10. One pencil costs 9¢. Two pencils cost 18¢. Three pencils cost 27¢. How much would 9 pencils cost?

F 45¢
G 54¢
H 81¢
J 90¢

---

11. Point *C* represents what number?

A B C D
6 8 12

A 11
B 10
C 9
D 8

---

12. If 4 plus a number is 18, which expression could be used to find the number?

F $4 + 18$
G 4×18
H $18 \div 4$
J $18 - 4$

Measurement and Geometry

13. How many more sides does a rectangle have than a triangle?

A 1
B 2
C 3
D 4

---

14. How many ounces are in 1 pound?

F 16 ounces
G 24 ounces
H 30 ounces
J 48 ounces

---

15. Truman has soccer practice from 5:00 P.M. to 6:30 P.M. How long does soccer practice last?

A 30 min
B 1 hour
C 1 hour 30 min
D 2 hours 30 min

---

16. Which statement is *not* true?

F 12 inches = 1 foot
G 1 yard = 36 inches
H 4 feet $<$ 1 yard
J 1 mile $>$ 5 yards

---

17. Sue is 3 feet tall. Tim is 6 inches taller than Sue. How tall is Tim?

A 36 inches
B 42 inches
C 48 inches
D 54 inches

Multiplying by One-Digit Numbers

4-1 **Mental Math: Multiplying Multiples of 10, 100, and 1,000**

4-2 **Problem-Solving Skill: Multistep Problems**

4-3 **Estimating Products**

4-4 **Multiplying Two- and Three-Digit Numbers**

4-5 **Problem-Solving Strategy: Make a Table**

4-6 **Multiplying Greater Numbers**

4-7 **Multiplying with Money**

4-8 **Problem-Solving Application: Using Money**

Diagnosing Readiness

In Chapter 4, you will use these skills:

Ⓐ Multiplication Facts

(pages 84–85)

1. 6×7 **2.** 5×9 **3.** 10×4

4. $\begin{array}{r} 8 \\ \times\ 3 \\ \hline \end{array}$ **5.** $\begin{array}{r} 6 \\ \times\ 0 \\ \hline \end{array}$ **6.** $\begin{array}{r} 7 \\ \times\ 9 \\ \hline \end{array}$

7. 8×7 **8.** 10×9 **9.** 2×5

10. A parking lot has 8 spaces in each row. How many spaces are in 6 rows?

Ⓑ Rounding

(pages 14–16)

Round each number to the underlined place.

11. $3\underline{8}6$ **12.** $1{,}\underline{4}38$

13. $1\underline{8}{,}704$ **14.** $24{,}\underline{0}51$

15. $\underline{3}63{,}941$ **16.** $60\underline{5}{,}722$

17. $1{,}\underline{7}45{,}382$ **18.** $1{,}745{,}\underline{3}82$

19. Mt. Kilimanjaro is about 19,340 feet above sea level. Round this to the nearest ten thousand feet.

C Adding Greater Numbers

(pages 44–46)

20. 364 + 937

21. 1,410 + 856

22. 3,847 + 602

23. 1,674 + 1,039

24. 36,402 + 3,697

25. 98,412 + 9,364

26. The attendance totals for 2 baseball games are 27,466 and 19,402. What is the total attendance for both games?

D Using Money

(pages 66–67)

27. \$64.95 + 15.32

28. \$148.13 + 96.45

29. \$336.10 − 54.99

30. \$500.00 − 122.33

31. Betsy wants to buy 2 yards of fabric that costs \$4.99 per yard, and 4 yards of lace that costs \$0.79 per yard. How much money will she need?

E Using Arrays

(pages 84–85)

Write a multiplication sentence for each array.

32.  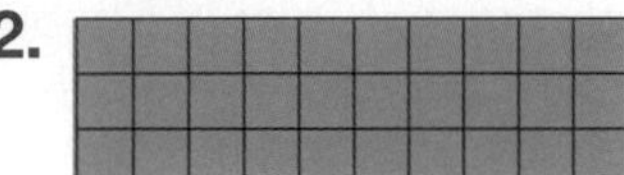

33. ● ● ● ● ● ●
● ● ● ● ● ●

34. At a coffeeshop, bags of coffee are arranged on shelves. There are 5 bags of coffee on each of 5 shelves. How many bags of coffee are there?

F Algebra

(pages 61–65)

Evaluate each expression for $x = 8$.

35. $53 - x$

36. $12 + x + 7$

37. $9x$

38. $\frac{48}{x}$

Solve each equation by testing these values for *n*: 35, 46, 52.

39. $46 + n = 81$

40. $n - 14 = 38$

To the Family and Student

Looking Back	Chapter 4	Looking Ahead
In Chapter 3, students learned multiplication facts through 10.	**Multiplying by One-Digit Numbers** In this chapter, students will learn how to multiply by one-digit numbers.	In Chapter 5, students will learn how to multiply by two-digit numbers.

Math and Everyday Living

Opportunities to apply the concepts of Chapter 4 abound in everyday situations. During the chapter, think about how multiplying by one-digit numbers can be used to solve a variety of real-world problems. The following examples suggest just a few of the many situations that could launch a discussion about multiplying by one-digit numbers.

Math and Shopping There are 800 items on each shelf of a supermarket. There are 4 shelves in one aisle. How many items are in that aisle?

Math and Art Seven cartoon artists are working together on a cartoon movie. If each cartoon artist draws 64 frames per day, how many frames are completed in 1 day?

Math and Work Stephanie does yard work on Saturdays to earn extra money. Each weekend, she earns $16.50. How much does she earn in 8 weeks?

Math and Crafts You want to buy some buttons for a club craft project. Buttons are sold by the pound at a craft store. There are about 400 buttons in each pound. You buy 3 pounds. About how many buttons is this?

Math and Publishing
A newspaper column can have 72 lines of text. How many lines of text are on a page of newspaper that has 4 columns?

Math and Work
Brian delivers 75 newspapers each day. How many newspapers does he deliver each week?

Math and Cars There are 9 rows of cars at a car dealership. Each row has 75 cars in it. How many cars are in all 9 rows?

Math and Medicine A hospital schedules 3 shifts of nurses each day. If 87 nurses work during each shift, how many nurses work each day at the hospital?

Math and Travel Mr. Dema gets 2 frequent-flier points for every mile that he travels. If he travels 37,410 miles in 1 year, how many frequent-flier points is that?

Math and Transportation
A commuter train has 4 cars that each seat 92 people. How many people can the train seat altogether?

California Content Standards in Chapter 4 Lessons*

	Teach and Practice	Practice
Number Sense		
2.4 (Grade 3) (🔑) Solve simple problems involving multiplication of multidigit numbers by one-digit numbers (3,671 × 3 = ___).	4-1, 4-4, 4-6	
3.3 (Grade 3) (🔑) Solve problems involving . . . multiplication . . . of money amounts in decimal notation and multiply . . . money amounts in decimal notation by using whole-number multipliers	4-7, 4-8	
Algebra and Functions		
1.1 Use letters, or other symbols to stand for any number in simple expressions or equations.		4-1, 4-3, 4-4, 4-6

	Teach and Practice	Practice
Mathematical Reasoning		
1.0 Students make decisions about how to approach problems.	4-2, 4-8	
1.1 Analyze problems by identifying relationships, distinguishing relevant from irrelevant information, sequencing and prioritizing information, and observing patterns.		4-1, 4-2, 4-5
1.2 Determine when and how to break a problem into simpler parts.		4-2, 4-8
2.0 Students use strategies, skills, and concepts in finding solutions.		4-2, 4-5, 4-8
2.1 Use estimation to verify the reasonableness of calculated results.	4-3, 4-4, 4-6, 4-7	
2.3 Use tables . . . to explain mathematical reasoning.	4-5	
2.4 Express the solution clearly and logically by using the appropriate mathematical notation and terms and clear language; support solutions with evidence in both verbal and symbolic work.		4-2, 4-4, 4-6
2.5 Indicate the relative advantages of exact and approximate solutions to problems and give answers to a specified degree of accuracy.		4-3
3.2 Note the method of deriving the solution and demonstrate a conceptual understanding of the derivation by solving similar problems.		4-5

* The symbol (🔑) indicates a key standard as designated in the Mathematics Framework for California Public Schools. Full statements of the California Content Standards are found at the beginning of this book following the Table of Contents.

Mental Math: Multiplying Multiples of 10, 100, and 1,000

Warm-Up Review

1. 7 × 8
2. 6 × 5
3. 4 × 5
4. 2 × 0
5. 12 + 8
6. 11 − 7
7. Mike has 6 boxes of markers. He needs four times as many boxes to pass out to all his classmates. How many more boxes of markers does Mike need?

California Content Standard *Number Sense 2.4 (Gr. 3) (key) Solve simple problems involving multiplication of multi-digit numbers by one-digit numbers . . ..*

Math Link You know how to find products with basic facts. Now you will learn how to find products of multiples of 10, 100, and 1,000.

Example 1

Find 200 × 4.

First look at some products when one of the factors is 10, 100, or 1,000.

10 × 4 = 4 × 10 = 4 tens = 40
100 × 4 = 4 × 100 = 4 hundreds = 400
1,000 × 4 = 4 × 1,000 = 4 thousands = 4,000

Now use a basic fact and a pattern with zeros to find 200 × 4 mentally.

2 × 4 = 4 × 2 = 4 × 2 ones = 8 ones = 8
20 × 4 = 4 × 20 = 4 × 2 tens = 8 tens = 80
200 × 4 = 4 × 200 = 4 × 2 hundreds = 8 hundreds = 800

The number of zeros in the factor equals the number of zeros in the product.

Here's WHY It Works

200 × 4 = (100 × 2) × 4
= 100 × (2 × 4)
= 100 × 8
= 800

Use the associative property of multiplication.

Example 2

Find 500 × 6.

5 × 6 = 30
50 × 6 = 300
500 × 6 = 3,000

When the product of a basic fact includes a zero, that zero is not part of the pattern.

Additional Standards: Algebra and Functions 1.1; Mathematical Reasoning 1.1 *(See p. 127.)*

Guided Practice *For another example, see Set A on p. 150.*

1. 80×6 **2.** 4×400 **3.** 900×7 **4.** $8 \times 5{,}000$ **5.** $3{,}000 \times 4$

6. There are 700 calculators on each shelf in an office supply warehouse. The calculators are stored on 4 shelves. How many calculators are there in all?

Independent Practice *For more practice, see Set A on p. 152.*

7. 90×8 **8.** 7×80 **9.** 600×4 **10.** 3×800

11. 900×5 **12.** $7{,}000 \times 8$ **13.** $5 \times 5{,}000$ **14.** $4{,}000 \times 2$

15. Sarah wants to rent an apartment that costs $600 a month. How much will it cost her to rent the apartment for 6 months?

16. Algebra Find the value of $6n$ if n is 9,000.

17. Math Reasoning What pattern do you notice about the products for pairs like 300×9 and 900×3, and $4{,}000 \times 7$ and $7{,}000 \times 4$?

18. Math Reasoning What happens to the product of 200×3 if both factors are doubled?

Mixed Review

19. Kevin drinks 3 glasses of milk each day. How many glasses of milk does he drink in a week?

20. Algebra Find the value of n when $5n = 35$.

21. Algebra Evaluate $4n$ when $n = 9$.

Compare. Use > or < for ●.

22. 379 ● 397 **23.** 5,675 ● 5,450 **24.** 49,999 ● 49,099

Test Prep **Choose the correct letter for each answer.**

25. (1-1) What is the value of the underlined digit in 3,6<u>2</u>4,100?

A 2,000 **C** 200,000

B 20,000 **D** 2,000,000

26. (2-4) A band on tour made trips of 538 miles, 718 miles, 325 miles, 1,302 miles, and 488 miles. How many miles did the band travel?

F 2,371 miles **H** 3,371 miles

G 3,071 miles **J** 3,434 miles

Problem-Solving Skill:
Multistep Problems

Warm-Up Review

1. 3×400 2. $6 \times 3{,}000$
3. $450 - 280$
4. $299 + 312$
5. $(3 \times 6) + (4 \times 5)$
6. In his art kit, Louis has 6 boxes of crayons and 3 boxes of colored pencils. There are 8 crayons in a box. How many crayons does Louis have in all?

California Content Standard *Mathematical Reasoning 1.0: Students make decisions about how to approach problems.*

Read for Understanding

Maria and her class planted a garden with marigolds, impatiens, and geraniums. The table at the right shows the number of rows and the number of seeds in each row of the three types of flowers they planted. How many more marigolds did they plant than geraniums?

Type of Flower	Number of Rows	Number of Seeds in Each Row
Marigolds	4	90
Impatiens	2	100
Geraniums	5	50

1. How many marigolds were planted in each row?
2. How many geraniums were planted in each row?

Think and Discuss

Multistep Problems

Sometimes it takes more than one step to solve a problem. You need to decide what the steps are, and in what order you should perform them.

Reread the paragraph at the top of the page.

3. How can you find the total number of marigolds and the total number of geraniums Maria's class planted? Explain.
4. How many more marigolds were planted than geraniums? What steps do you need to do to solve the problem?
5. Is there a different way to solve Exercise 4?

 Additional Standards: Mathematical Reasoning 1.1, 1.2, 2.0, 2.4 *(See p. 127.)*

Guided Practice

Jake wants to take his three cats to the veterinarian on Saturday. The costs of the veterinary services are given in the table at the right. Jake will be charged for a single office visit. In addition, he will pay for a rabies injection and a respiratory infection vaccine for each cat. Find the total cost of Jake's visit to the veterinarian.

Veterinary Services	Cost
Office visit	\$40
Rabies injection	\$20
Respiratory infection vaccine	\$30

1. What operations do you need to perform in order to solve the problem?

a. Addition and subtraction

b. Multiplication and addition

c. Multiplication and subtraction

2. Which number sentence could you use to find the total cost for Jake's 3 cats to have a rabies injection?

a. 3 × \$20 = \$60

b. 3 × \$30 = \$90

c. 3 × \$40 = \$120

3. Which number sentence could you use to find the total cost for Jake's three cats to have a respiratory infection vaccine?

a. 3 × \$20 = \$60

b. 3 × \$30 = \$90

c. 3 × \$40 = \$120

4. Which number sentence could you use to find the total Jake would have to pay?

a. \$60 + \$90 + \$40 = \$190

b. \$20 + \$90 + \$120 = \$230

c. \$60 + \$30 + \$120 = \$210

Independent Practice

In Mrs. Glennon's math class there are 6 tests worth 100 points each and 20 homework assignments worth 5 points each. What is the total amount of points possible in Mrs. Glennon's class?

5. Which number sentence could you use to find the total number of points possible for the six tests?

a. 6 + 100 = 106

b. 6 × 100 = 600

c. 20 × 100 = 2,000

6. Which number sentence could you use to find the total number of points possible for the 20 homework assignments?

a. 20 × 5 = 120

b. 20 × 100 = 2,000

c. 20 × 5 = 100

7. Math Reasoning What steps do you need to complete in order to find the total number of possible points in Mrs. Glennon's class? Explain.

Lesson 4-3 Estimating Products

California Content Standard *Mathematical Reasoning 2.1: Use estimation to verify the reasonableness of calculated results.*

Warm-Up Review

Round to the nearest hundred.

1. 3,865 **2.** 84,136

Round to the nearest thousand.

3. 5,284 **4.** 189,712

5. Mr. Conrad's grocery bill totaled $25.76. How much will he have to pay if he uses a 45¢ coupon and a 75¢ coupon?

Math Link You know how to multiply a one-digit number by a multiple of ten. In this lesson you will learn how to estimate a product mentally.

Example 1

Estimate 235 × 6.

Round 235 to the nearest hundred. Then multiply mentally.

235 × 6

200 × 6 = 1,200

To the nearest hundred, 235 rounds to 200.

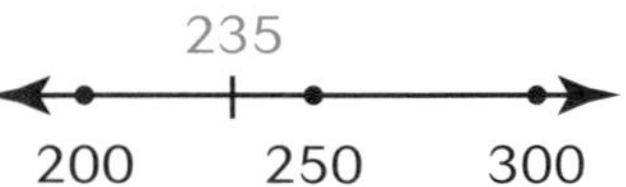

235 × 6 is about 1,200.

Example 2

Is 13,925 a reasonable answer for 2,785 × 5? Estimate by finding a range.

3,000 × 5 = 15,000 Round 2,785 up to 3,000.

2,785 × 5

2,000 × 5 = 10,000 Round 2,785 down to 2,000.
The exact answer is between 10,000 and 15,000

The answer is reasonable because 13,925 is between 10,000 and 15,000.

More Examples

A. Estimate 6,439 × 8.

6,439 × 8

6,000 × 8 = 48,000
6,439 × 8 is about 48,000.

B. Estimate $8.89 × 7.

$8.89 × 7

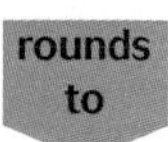

Round $8.89 to the nearest dollar.

$9.00 × 7 = $63.00
$8.89 × 7 is about $63.00.

Additional Standards: Algebra and Functions 1.1, Mathematical Reasoning 2.5 *(See p. 127.)*

Guided Practice *For another example, see Set B on p. 150.*

Round so you can estimate each product mentally.

1. 37 × 8 **2.** 4 × 473 **3.** $2.39 × 7 **4.** 7,984 × 8

5. Is 5,166 a reasonable answer for 574 × 9? Estimate by finding a range.

Independent Practice *For more practice, see Set B on p. 152.*

Round so you can estimate each product mentally.

6. 85 × 4 **7.** 98 × 7 **8.** 803 × 9 **9.** 5 × 767

10. $6.65 × 8 **11.** $19.72 × 4 **12.** 2 × 2,792 **13.** 5,308 × 6

14. Is 56,816 a reasonable answer for 8,352 × 8? Estimate by finding a range.

15. Algebra If the estimated product of n and 998 is 5,000, find a reasonable value for n.

Use the information in the table for Exercises 16 and 17.

16. The Lewis family makes about the same number of calls each month. About how many calls will they make in 3 months?

17. Math Reasoning Estimate how many more calls the Chan family made than the Rodriguez family in two months.

Calls Made per Month

Family	Number of Calls
Lewis	123
Rodríguez	99
Chan	191
Bartley	168

Mixed Review

18. Erica works in a building that has 8 floors. If there are 60 offices on each floor, how many offices are there on the 8 floors?

19. Algebra Solve 31 + x = 45 by testing these values for x: 8, 14, 24.

Test Prep **Choose the correct letter for each answer.**

20. 62,005 − 11,003 =
(2-7)

A 50,002 **C** 53,002

B 50,996 **D** 71,002

E NH

21. Give the next three numbers in this pattern: 2, 6, 10, 14, ■, ■, ■.
(1-4)

F 15, 16, 17 **H** 18, 22, 26

G 16, 18, 20 **J** 18, 24, 28

Multiplying Two- and Three-Digit Numbers

Warm-Up Review

1. 5 × 7
2. 8 × 3
3. 6 × 90
4. 5,000 × 9
5. 800 × 4
6. 5 × 3,000
7. Jen has 5 pencils and 8 pens. Mark has 8 times as many pencils as Jen. How many pencils does Mark have?

California Content Standard *Number Sense 2.4 (Gr. 3) (🔑): Solve simple problems involving multiplication of multidigit numbers by one-digit numbers . . .. Also, Mathematical Reasoning 2.1 (See p. 127.)*

Math Link You know how to multiply one-digit numbers by numbers like 30 and 400. Now you will learn to multiply one-digit numbers by any two- or three-digit number.

Susan's Pen Pals

Name	Country
Friedrich	Germany
Kiyoko	Japan
Manuela	Spain
Araba	Ghana
Dimitri	Greece
Estela	Puerto Rico

Example 1

Susan has pen pals from countries all around the world. Last year, each pen pal sent Susan 24 postcards. How many postcards did she receive in all?

24	×	6	=	n
postcards		pen pals		postcards in all

First use an array to show 24 × 6. Since each row contains 24 squares, there are 24 + 24 + 24 + 24 + 24 + 24, or 144 squares in all. So 24 × 6 = 144.

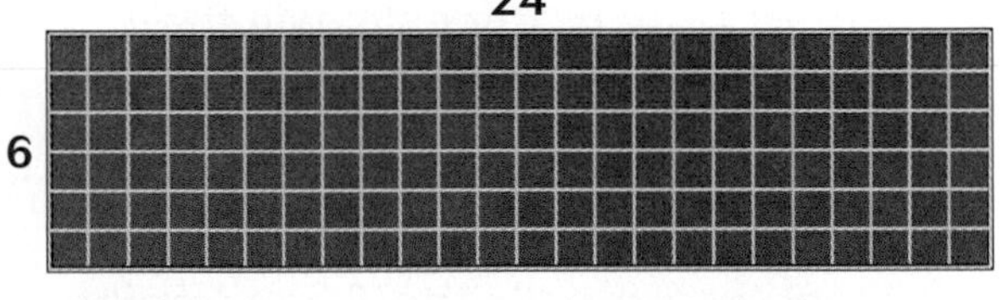

Here's a way to record your work.

Step 1 Multiply the ones.

$$\begin{array}{r} 24 \\ \times\ 6 \\ \hline \end{array}$$

6 × 4 ones = 24 ones

Step 2 Regroup if you can.

$$\begin{array}{r} \scriptstyle 2 \\ 24 \\ \times\ 6 \\ \hline 4 \end{array}$$

24 ones = 2 tens + 4 ones

Step 3 Multiply the tens. Add the regrouped tens.

$$\begin{array}{r} \scriptstyle 2 \\ 24 \\ \times\ 6 \\ \hline 144 \end{array}$$

6 × 2 tens = 12 tens
12 tens + 2 tens = 14 tens

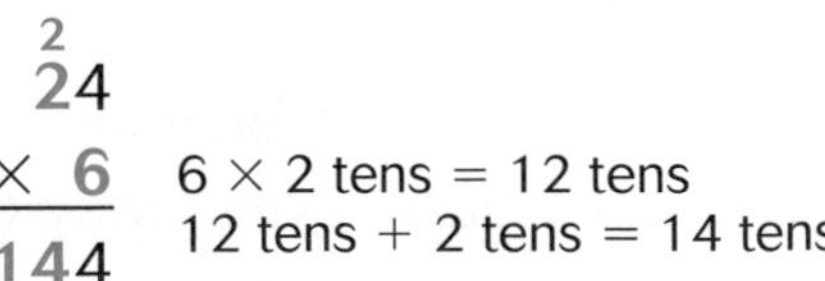

Here's WHY It Works

$$\begin{aligned} 24 \times 6 &= (20 + 4) \times 6 \\ &= (20 \times 6) + (4 \times 6) \\ &= 120 + 24 \\ &= 144 \end{aligned}$$

<u>Check</u> by estimating. 20 × 6 = 120. The answer is reasonable because 144 is close to 120.

Additional Standards: Algebra and Functions 1.1, Mathematical Reasoning 2.4 (See p. 127.)

Example 2

Find 387 × 4.

Step 1 Multiply the ones. Regroup if you can.	Step 2 Multiply the tens. Add the regrouped tens. Regroup as needed.	Step 3 Multiply the hundreds. Add the regrouped hundreds.
$\begin{array}{r} {}^{2} \\ 387 \\ \times\ \ 4 \\ \hline 8 \end{array}$	$\begin{array}{r} {}^{3\,2} \\ 387 \\ \times\ \ 4 \\ \hline 48 \end{array}$	$\begin{array}{r} {}^{3\,2} \\ 387 \\ \times\ \ 4 \\ \hline 1{,}548 \end{array}$

Here's WHY It Works

$$\begin{aligned} 387 \times 4 &= (300 + 80 + 7) \times 4 \\ &= (300 \times 4) + (80 \times 4) + (7 \times 4) \\ &= 1{,}200 + 320 + 28 \\ &= 1{,}548 \end{aligned}$$

Check by estimating. 400 × 4 = 1,600. The answer is reasonable because 1,548 is close to 1,600.

More Examples

A. $\begin{array}{r} {}^{2} \\ 49 \\ \times\ 3 \\ \hline 147 \end{array}$ **B.** $\begin{array}{r} {}^{7\,1} \\ 192 \\ \times\ \ 8 \\ \hline 1{,}536 \end{array}$ **C.** $\begin{array}{r} {}^{3} \\ 507 \\ \times\ \ 5 \\ \hline 2{,}535 \end{array}$

Guided Practice For another example, see Set C on p. 150.

1. $\begin{array}{r} 22 \\ \times\ 9 \\ \hline \end{array}$ **2.** $\begin{array}{r} 891 \\ \times\ \ 3 \\ \hline \end{array}$ **3.** $\begin{array}{r} 508 \\ \times\ \ 4 \\ \hline \end{array}$ **4.** 8 × 53 **5.** 674 × 7

6. There are 164 apartments in a building. Each apartment has 3 bedrooms. How many bedrooms are there in all?

Independent Practice For more practice, see Set C on p. 152.

7. $\begin{array}{r} 41 \\ \times\ 9 \\ \hline \end{array}$ **8.** $\begin{array}{r} 64 \\ \times\ 7 \\ \hline \end{array}$ **9.** $\begin{array}{r} 58 \\ \times\ 6 \\ \hline \end{array}$ **10.** $\begin{array}{r} 402 \\ \times\ \ 5 \\ \hline \end{array}$ **11.** $\begin{array}{r} 981 \\ \times\ \ 3 \\ \hline \end{array}$

12. 93 × 8 **13.** 4 × 96 **14.** 315 × 6 **15.** 3 × 877 **16.** 742 × 2

17. Eric can type 68 words in a minute. How many words can he type in 5 minutes?

18. Mental Math Explain how you would find 4 × 52 mentally.

19. **Algebra** Find the value of $316n$ when $n = 5$.

20. Louise has to read a book that has 157 pages. If she reads 15 pages a night, will she finish the book in a week? Explain.

21. **Math Reasoning** What happens to the product of 25×3 if both factors are doubled?

Mixed Review

22. Amy's team collects soup labels for a school contest. If the team collects 400 labels a week for 6 weeks, will it reach the goal of 2,500? Explain.

23. Roberto cut a 96-inch board into 5 pieces. Four of the pieces were each 18 inches long. How long was the fifth piece?

24. Is 35,888 a reasonable answer for $4{,}486 \times 8$? Estimate by finding a range.

25. Order the numbers from least to greatest:
$4, {}^{-}2, 7, {}^{-}5, 1, {}^{-}8, 6$.

26. $9 \div 9$ 27. $0 \div 5$ 28. 5×1 29. 8×0

30. 5×400 31. 80×7 32. $7{,}000 \times 8$ 33. $6 \times 3{,}000$

Round so you can estimate each product mentally.

34. 6×357 35. $5{,}073 \times 9$ 36. 95×7

Test Prep **Choose the correct letter for each answer.**

37. (3-5) Dan has 7 cans of tennis balls. If each can holds 3 balls, which number sentence shows how many tennis balls Dan has in all?

A $7 \times 3 = ■$

B $7 + 3 = ■$

C $7 \div 3 = ■$

D $7 - 3 = ■$

38. (3-3) There are 12 slices of pizza. Maria and 3 friends will share the pizza equally. How many slices will each person get?

F 3 slices

G 4 slices

H 15 slices

J 36 slices

Diagnostic Checkpoint

1. 50 × 9 (4-1)
2. 80 × 9 (4-1)
3. 3 × 600 (4-1)
4. 8,000 × 4 (4-1)
5. 800 × 2 (4-1)
6. 4 × 4,000 (4-1)
7. 20 × 6 (4-1)
8. 50 × 2 (4-1)
9. 3 × 8,000 (4-1)
10. 200 × 8 (4-1)
11. 6,000 × 8 (4-1)
12. 2 × 9,000 (4-1)
13. (4-4) $\begin{array}{r} 83 \\ \times\ 2 \\ \hline \end{array}$
14. (4-4) $\begin{array}{r} 24 \\ \times\ 5 \\ \hline \end{array}$
15. (4-4) $\begin{array}{r} 64 \\ \times\ 3 \\ \hline \end{array}$
16. (4-4) $\begin{array}{r} 72 \\ \times\ 8 \\ \hline \end{array}$
17. (4-4) $\begin{array}{r} 47 \\ \times\ 3 \\ \hline \end{array}$
18. (4-4) $\begin{array}{r} 314 \\ \times\ \ 4 \\ \hline \end{array}$
19. (4-4) $\begin{array}{r} 560 \\ \times\ \ 9 \\ \hline \end{array}$
20. (4-4) $\begin{array}{r} 413 \\ \times\ \ 5 \\ \hline \end{array}$
21. (4-4) $\begin{array}{r} 321 \\ \times\ \ 8 \\ \hline \end{array}$
22. (4-4) $\begin{array}{r} 546 \\ \times\ \ 3 \\ \hline \end{array}$
23. 21 × 7 (4-4)
24. 47 × 5 (4-4)
25. 306 × 8 (4-4)
26. 123 × 4 (4-4)
27. 681 × 2 (4-4)

Round so you can estimate each product mentally.

28. 59 × 5 (4-3)
29. 4 × 29 (4-3)
30. 7 × 82 (4-3)
31. 85 × 5 (4-3)
32. 659 × 2 (4-3)
33. 1,935 × 5 (4-3)
34. 172 × 5 (4-3)
35. 8 × 4,022 (4-3)
36. 2 × $3.97 (4-3)
37. $4.87 × 9 (4-3)
38. $2.15 × 5 (4-3)
39. $1.25 × 8 (4-3)

Use the sign at the right for Exercises 40–43.

40. (4-2) To find how much 5 paperback books and two hardback books cost, what operation should you do first?

41. (4-2) Anthony bought four calendars. Write a number sentence you could use to find the amount he paid.

42. (4-2) Rob, Luis, and Karen each bought a hardback book and an art book. Write a number sentence you could use to find the total amount they paid.

43. (4-2) Thomas bought 4 paperback books, 2 bookmarks, and 2 calendars. How much did he spend in all?

Book Sale

Item	Price
Art Books	$40
Hardback Books	$20
Paperback Books	$4
Bookmarks	$1
Calendars	$10

Problem-Solving Strategy: Make a Table

California Content Standard *Mathematical Reasoning 2.3: Use . . . tables . . . to explain mathematical reasoning.*

Warm-Up Review

1. 3 × 25
2. 5 × 24
3. 25 + 47
4. 125 + 36
5. 45 − 12
6. 276 − 38
7. 42 ÷ 6
8. 48 ÷ 8
9. There are 32 rocks in Peter's collection. He wants to store them on 4 shelves. How many rocks will be on each shelf?

Example

You are in charge of filling a column in your school newsletter. You are asked to put 72 lines in the column. You need to use the same number of articles and ads. All articles are 15 lines long, and all ads are 9 lines long. How many articles and ads should you use?

Understand

What do you need to find?

You need to find the same number of articles and ads that will fit exactly in a 72-line column.

Newsletter Page

Number of Each	Number of Article Lines	Number of Ad Lines
1	15	9
2	30	18
3	45	27
4	60	36
5	75	45

Plan

How can you solve the problem?

You can make a table. Then you can find the row in your table that tells you how many ads and articles will fit on 72 lines.

Solve

Make a table like the one shown. Look across the rows to see how many lines the articles and ads will fill. Find the row where the sum of the article lines and ad lines will be 72 lines.

45 + 27 = 72

So, you should use 3 articles and 3 ads to fill your column.

Look Back

Why is using a table helpful?

 Additional Standards: Mathematical Reasoning 1.1, 2.0, 3.2 *(See p. 127.)*

Guided Practice

Use the table on page 138 for Exercises 1–2.

1. How many ads fill the same number of lines as 3 articles?

2. Suppose you can fit 80 lines in your column. If you have only articles, how many articles will fit?

Independent Practice

3. Cara spends 15 minutes more each week than the week before working in her garden. If she works 45 minutes the first week, how long will she work the fourth week?

4. It costs $4 for 5 tubes of oil paint. If your art class needs 40 tubes for a project, how much will the paint cost?

5. Each day Joshua saves twice as many pennies as he saved the day before. On the first day he saved 3 pennies. How many pennies did he save on the fifth day?

Mixed Review

Try these or other strategies to solve each problem. Tell which strategy you used.

Problem-Solving Strategies

- *Find a Pattern*
- *Draw a Picture*
- *Solve a Simpler Problem*
- *Work Backward*

6. Joe fills a section in a newsletter with ads. Each ad is 1 inch square in size. If Joe fills an area 4 inches across and 3 inches down, how many ads can he fit on the page?

7. Nicole arranges 15 rocks in a pattern. She puts one in the first row, two in the second row, and three in the third row. If she continues this pattern, how many rocks are in the last row?

8. Beth attends a community meeting every other month. She went to her fourth meeting in October. In what month did she go to her first meeting?

Use Homework Workbook 4-5.

Multiplying Greater Numbers

California Content Standard *Number Sense 2.4 (Gr. 3) (🔑): Solve simple problems involving multiplication of multidigit numbers by one-digit numbers (3,671 × 3 = ____). Also, Mathematical Reasoning 2.1* *(See p. 127.)*

Warm-Up Review

1. 30 × 5
2. 8 + 63
3. 600 × 9
4. 512 − 3
5. 804 × 4
6. 7 × 9,000
7. At the first game of a baseball doubleheader, the attendance was 56,221. Before the second game, 1,927 people left. How many fans stayed for the second game?

Math Link You know how to multiply one-digit numbers by two- and three-digit numbers. Now you will learn to multiply one-digt numbers by greater numbers.

Example 1

Find 1,225 × 6.

Step 1 Multiply the ones. Regroup if necessary.	**Step 2** Multiply the tens. Add the regrouped tens. Regroup if necessary.	**Step 3** Multiply the hundreds. Add the regrouped hundreds. Regroup if necessary.	**Step 4** Multiply the thousands. Add the regrouped thousands.
regrouped: 3 1,225 × 6 0	regrouped: 1 3 1,225 × 6 50	regrouped: 1 1 3 1,225 × 6 350	regrouped: 1 1 3 1,225 × 6 7,350

Check by finding a range. 1,000 × 6 = 6,000; 2,000 × 6 = 12,000. The answer is reasonable because 7,350 is between 6,000 and 12,000.

Example 2

Find 19,872 × 4.

Step 1 Multiply the ones. Regroup if necessary.	**Step 2** Multiply the tens. There are no regrouped tens to add. Regroup if necessary.	**Step 3** Multiply the hundreds. Add the regrouped hundreds. Regroup if necessary.	**Step 4** Multiply the thousands. Add the regrouped thousands. Regroup if you can.	**Step 5** Multiply the ten thousands. Add the regrouped ten thousands.
19,872 × 4 8	regrouped: 2 19,872 × 4 88	regrouped: 3 2 19,872 × 4 488	regrouped: 3 3 2 19,872 × 4 9,488	regrouped: 3 2 2 19,872 × 4 79,488

Check by estimating. 20,000 × 4 = 80,000. The answer is reasonable because 79,488 is close to 80,000.

Additional Standards: Algebra and Functions 1.1; Mathematical Reasoning 2.4 *(See p. 127.)*

Guided Practice *For another example, see Set D on p. 151.*

1. 2,347 × 5

2. 37,901 × 7

3. 6 × 3,980

4. 41,846 × 2

5. A hardware store buys boxes of nails. If there are 1,485 nails in a box, how many nails are there in 3 boxes?

Independent Practice *For more practice, see Set D on p.153.*

6. 4,897 × 4

7. 8,095 × 9

8. 56,484 × 6

9. 23,507 × 3

10. 7 × 2,560

11. 5,312 × 2

12. 5 × 40,218

13. 18,362 × 8

Use the pictograph at the right for Exercises 14 and 15.

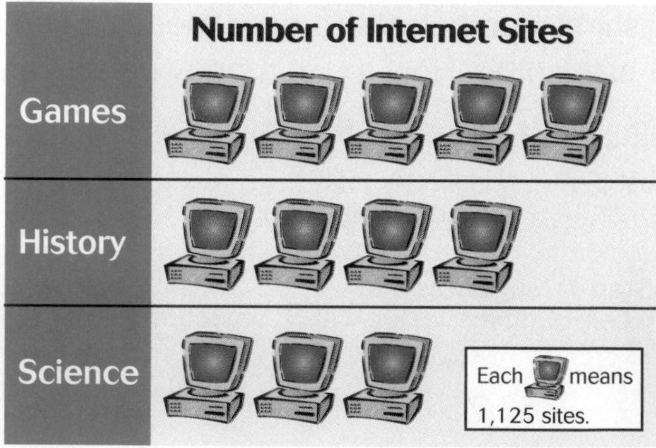

14. How many History sites are on the Internet?

15. How many more Games sites are there than Science sites?

16. Algebra Find the value of $5x$ when x is 10,354.

17. Math Reasoning Suppose you multiplied 8,562 × 7 and you got 5,992. How could you tell that this is not the right answer?

Mixed Review

18. Nathan delivers 275 newspapers each day. Estimate how many newspapers he delivers in a week.

19. Round 3,798 to the nearest thousand.

Test Prep Choose the correct letter for each answer.

20. 154 × 7 =
(4-4)

A 978 **B** 1,058 **C** 1,078 **D** 1,178 **E** NH

21. Mount Everest has an elevation of 29,028 feet. Mount McKinley has an elevation of 20,320 feet. How much higher is Mount Everest?
(2-6)

F 8,608 feet **G** 8,708 feet **H** 9,608 feet **J** 9,708 feet

Multiplying with Money

California Content Standard *Number Sense 3.3 (Gr. 3) (key): Solve problems involving . . . multiplication . . . of money amounts in decimal notation and multiply . . . money amounts in decimal notation by using whole-number multipliers . . .. Also, Mathematical Reasoning 2.1* *(See p. 127.)*

Warm-Up Review

1. 125 × 4 2. 6 × 2,375
3. \$4.75 + \$12.20
4. \$0.75 + \$1.45 + \$5.60
5. The school library has 5,090 books. Last week, 598 books were checked out and 312 books were returned. How many books were left in the library?

Math Link You know how to multiply multidigit numbers. Now you will do multiplication problems involving money.

School Band Fundraiser

Item	Cost
Hat	\$2.75
T-shirt	\$12.50
Button	\$0.95

Example 1

The members of the school band are selling hats, T-shirts, and buttons to raise money. Steven sold 6 hats so far. How much money did he raise?

\$2.75 × 6 = *n*

cost per hat · number of hats · total raised

Step 1 Multiply as with whole numbers.

$$\begin{array}{r} \$2.75 \\ \times\quad 6 \\ \hline \end{array}$$

Step 2 Regroup as needed.

$$\begin{array}{r} {\scriptstyle 4\ 3} \\ \$2.75 \\ \times\quad 6 \\ \hline 16\ 50 \end{array}$$

Step 3 Show dollars and cents in the product.

$$\begin{array}{r} \$2.75 \\ \times\quad 6 \\ \hline \$16.50 \end{array}$$

Steven raised \$16.50.

<u>Check</u> by estimating. \$3.00 × 6 = \$18.00. The answer is reasonable because \$16.50 is close to \$18.00.

Example 2

Find \$78.34 × 8.

Step 1 Multiply as with whole numbers.

$$\begin{array}{r} \$78.34 \\ \times\quad 8 \\ \hline \end{array}$$

Step 2 Regroup as needed.

$$\begin{array}{r} {\scriptstyle 6\ 2\ 3} \\ \$78.34 \\ \times\quad 8 \\ \hline 626\ 72 \end{array}$$

Step 3 Show dollars and cents in the product.

$$\begin{array}{r} \$78.34 \\ \times\quad 8 \\ \hline \$626.72 \end{array}$$

<u>Check</u> by estimating. \$80.00 × 8 = \$640.00. The answer is reasonable because \$626.72 is close to \$640.00.

Guided Practice *For another example, see Set E on p. 151.*

1. $8.31 × 2
2. $0.45 × 3
3. $12.80 × 7
4. 9 × $44.65
5. $19.98 × 4
6. Andy bought 4 CDs at a music store. Each CD cost $14.95. How much did he spend in all?

Independent Practice *For more practice, see Set E on p. 153.*

7. $14.59 × 4
8. $89.90 × 6
9. $0.79 × 9
10. $99.99 × 2
11. $7.55 × 7
12. $122.37 × 8
13. $10.89 × 3
14. $7.29 × 5
15. $0.55 × 7
16. $1.72 × 6
17. 4 × $33.93
18. $4.81 × 6
19. $0.09 × 5
20. 3 × $100.02

Use the pictures at the right for Exercises 21–23.

21. At a souvenir shop, Gary bought 3 animal figurines and 6 postcards. How much did he spend in all?

22. Ed bought 4 key chains. How much change did he receive from a $20 bill?
23. Monica had $45. She bought 5 animal figurines and 2 key chains. How much money did she have left?

Mixed Review

24. In the summer as many as 475 visitors tour a museum each hour. How many visitors can see the museum in 8 hours?
25. Find the product of 6 and 29,853.

Test Prep **Choose the correct letter for each answer.**

26. (2-1) Estimate the difference: 2,785 − 1,299
    - **A** 4,000
    - **B** 3,000
    - **C** 2,000
    - **D** 1,000
    - **E** NH

27. (3-6) (7 × 11) − (27 ÷ 3) =
    - **F** 86
    - **G** 77
    - **H** 69
    - **J** 67
    - **K** NH

Problem-Solving Application:

Using Money

California Content Standard *Mathematical Reasoning 1.0: Students make decisions about how to approach problems. Also, Number Sense 3.3 (Gr. 3) (🔑) (See p. 127.)*

Warm-Up Review

1. 25 + 63
2. 5 × 17
3. 415 − 36
4. 50 × 6
5. $2.50 × 3
6. 4 × $1.50
7. Leslie earns $12 an hour at her weekend job. She worked 5 hours on Saturday and 3 hours on Sunday. How much did she earn in all?

The Publicity Committee needs to make 475 copies of a one-page flier to advertise the Rose City Festival. The costs of the paper are given at the right below. How much money will the committee save if it uses white paper instead of yellow paper?

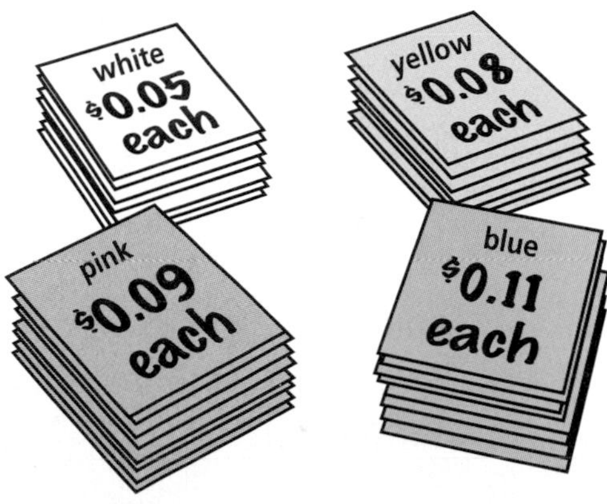

Understand

What do you need to know?

You need to know that yellow paper costs $0.08 a sheet and white paper costs $0.05 a sheet. You also need to know that the committee needs 475 sheets of paper.

Plan

How can you solve the problem?

Subtract to find the difference between the cost of a sheet of yellow paper and a sheet of white paper. Then multiply that difference by the number of copies.

Solve

Step 1 $0.08 − $0.05 = $0.03

Step 2 475 × $0.03 = $14.25

The committee will save $14.25.

Look Back

What is another way to solve the problem?

 Additional Standards: Mathematical Reasoning 1.2, 2.0 (See p. 127.)

Guided Practice

1. How much more would the committee spend if it used pink paper instead of yellow paper?

2. How much would it cost the committee to have 200 copies made on white paper and 275 copies made on yellow paper?

Independent Practice

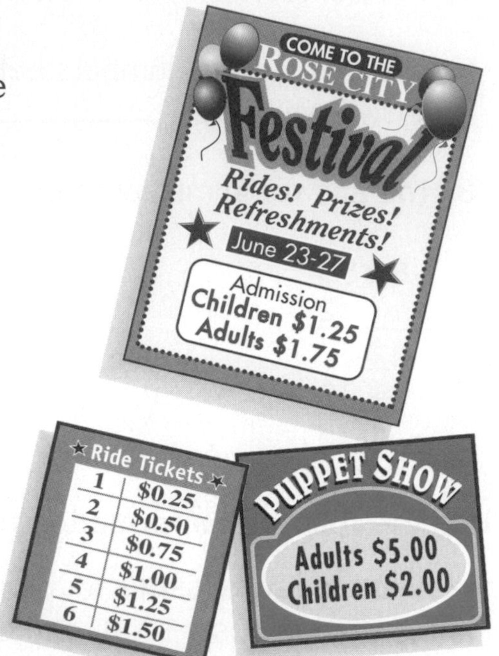

3. There are 4 children and 2 adults going to the festival. Is $10.00 enough to pay for their admissions? Why or why not?

4. How much will 5 children and 3 adults spend altogether on admission tickets?

5. Tickets for rides cost $0.25 each. If Keisha has $1.25, how many tickets can she buy?

6. Jenny sold $35.00 worth of puppet show tickets. She sold some $2.00 tickets and some $5.00 tickets. How many of each type of ticket might she have sold?

7. Rebecca pays for 2 children's tickets to the festival with $10.00. How much change should she get back?

Mixed Review

Use the pictograph for Exercises 8 and 9.

8. How many snow globes and wind-up toys did the shop sell combined?

9. How many more buttons than cookie cutters did the shop sell?

10. Badwater Basin in Death Valley is the lowest point in the United States. Its elevation is $^{-}282$ feet. Is Badwater Basin above or below sea level? Explain.

Sales at the Old Treasure Shop	
Cookie cutters	■ ■ ■ ■
Snow globes	■ ■ ■ ■ ■ ■ ■ ■
Fancy buttons	■ ■ ■ ■ ■ ■
Wind-up toys	■ ■ ■ ■ ■

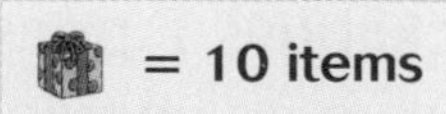

Diagnostic Checkpoint

Complete. For Exercises 1–3, use the words from the Word Bank.

Word Bank
array
estimate
factors
product

1. (3-1) The numbers that are multiplied are called ________.

2. (4-3) If you round the numbers before multiplying, your answer will be an ________.

3. (3-1) The answer in multiplication is called the ________.

4. (4-6) $8{,}350 \times 2$

5. (4-6) $6{,}701 \times 9$

6. (4-6) $6{,}402 \times 3$

7. (4-6) $32{,}836 \times 9$

8. (4-7) $\$9.23 \times 5$

9. (4-7) $\$4.92 \times 8$

10. (4-7) $\$10.45 \times 2$

11. (4-7) $\$32.36 \times 8$

Use the following information for Exercises 12 and 13.

You want to invite friends to a party. Each invitation costs $0.30 and each stamp costs $0.33.

Number of Friends	Cost of Invitations	Cost of Stamps	Total Cost
5	$1.50	$1.65	$3.15
6			
7			
8			
9			

12. (4-5) Copy and complete the table at the right.

13. (4-5) You have $5.00. Use the table to decide how many friends you can invite.

14. (4-6) Six libraries share books. Each library has 4,550 books. How many books do the libraries have altogether?

15. (4-8) Marbles cost $0.75 each. If Larry buys 5 marbles, how much will he pay?

16. (4-8) Pens cost $0.60 each. Vicki buys 7 pens and pays for them with a $5 bill. How much change should she get back?

Chapter 4 Test

1. $\begin{array}{r} 20 \\ \times\ 4 \\ \hline \end{array}$

2. $\begin{array}{r} 50 \\ \times\ 4 \\ \hline \end{array}$

3. $\begin{array}{r} 3{,}000 \\ \times\ 3 \\ \hline \end{array}$

4. $\begin{array}{r} 800 \\ \times\ 2 \\ \hline \end{array}$

5. $\begin{array}{r} 900 \\ \times\ 6 \\ \hline \end{array}$

6. $\begin{array}{r} 41 \\ \times\ 3 \\ \hline \end{array}$

7. $\begin{array}{r} 23 \\ \times\ 7 \\ \hline \end{array}$

8. $\begin{array}{r} 506 \\ \times\ 5 \\ \hline \end{array}$

9. $\begin{array}{r} 432 \\ \times\ 8 \\ \hline \end{array}$

10. $\begin{array}{r} 4{,}710 \\ \times\ 4 \\ \hline \end{array}$

11. $\begin{array}{r} 15{,}673 \\ \times\ 5 \\ \hline \end{array}$

12. $\begin{array}{r} 36{,}496 \\ \times\ 3 \\ \hline \end{array}$

13. $\begin{array}{r} \$2.55 \\ \times\ 6 \\ \hline \end{array}$

14. $\begin{array}{r} \$0.25 \\ \times\ 5 \\ \hline \end{array}$

15. $\begin{array}{r} \$20.05 \\ \times\ 4 \\ \hline \end{array}$

Round so you can estimate each product mentally.

16. 28×5 **17.** $\$5.18 \times 3$ **18.** 4×332 **19.** $8{,}760 \times 5$

20. Find the value of $8n$ if $n = 436$.

21. A toy shop has the same number of wagons as tricycles. If there are 42 wheels in all on these toys, how many wagons and tricycles are there?

22. A fruit salad costs $4.79 and a bottle of juice costs $1.29. Jesse bought 2 fruit salads and 3 bottles of juice. How much did he spend in all?

23. Angie noticed that each page of a phone book has 4 columns with 172 names per column. She concluded that there must be 1,088 names on a page. Is her answer reasonable? Estimate by finding a range.

24. Mr. Leonard has a cellular phone. He pays a monthly fee of $15 plus 30¢ a minute for each call he makes. Last month he used his cellular phone for 9 minutes. What was his total bill for last month?

25. There are 38 rooms on each floor at Westview Hospital. The hospital has six floors. How many rooms are there in all?

Multiple-Choice Chapter 4 Test

Choose the correct letter for each answer.

1. A jet plane travels at 450 miles per hour. It takes 6 hours to fly from Boston to San Francisco. What is the distance between the cities?

- **A** 2,706 miles
- **B** 2,700 miles
- **C** 2,400 miles
- **D** 1,400 miles

2. $3 \times 8{,}000 =$

- **F** 32,000
- **G** 24,000
- **H** 11,000
- **J** 2,400
- **K** NH

3. Estimate to the nearest dollar.

$$7 \times \$7.94$$

- **A** $49.00
- **B** $52.50
- **C** $56.00
- **D** $70.00
- **E** NH

4. Stacy types 72 words a minute. How many words can she type in 8 minutes?

- **F** 80 words
- **G** 476 words
- **H** 567 words
- **J** 578 words
- **K** NH

5. $$\begin{array}{r} 678 \\ \times \quad 4 \\ \hline \end{array}$$

- **A** 2,312
- **B** 2,412
- **C** 2,712
- **D** 3,390
- **E** NH

6. Find the value of n.

$$8 \times 300 = n$$

- **F** $n = 240$
- **G** $n = 2{,}400$
- **H** $n = 3{,}200$
- **J** $n = 11{,}000$
- **K** NH

7. Round so you can estimate the product.

$$\begin{array}{r} 3{,}915 \\ \times \quad 2 \\ \hline \end{array}$$

- **A** 9,000
- **B** 8,000
- **C** 7,000
- **D** 6,000
- **E** NH

8. Katie has $24. She plans to save twice as much of it as she spends. How much money will Katie save?

- **F** $8
- **G** $16
- **H** $20
- **J** $24

9. **A baseball team's season attendance was 89,412. If the team's attendance stayed the same for 4 years, what would the total attendance be?**

A 357,846 people
B 357,648 people
C 326,648 people
D 306,648 people

10. **Find $4.73 × 4.**

F $16.00
G $17.92
H $18.92
J $20.00
K NH

11. **Find 9 × 3,478.**

A 27,602
B 27,824
C 31,302
D 34,780
E NH

12. **There are 12 servings in a box of cereal. How many servings are in 9 boxes of cereal?**

F 21 servings
G 95 servings
H 108 servings
J 120 servings

13. **$14.05 × 6**

A $90.30
B $84.30
C $84.00
D $64.00
E NH

Use the table below for Questions 14 and 15.

Movie Admission	
Child (ages 2–5)	$3.25
Adult	$6.75
Student (over 5 years)	$4.50

14. **If 2 adults and 3 two-year-old children go to the movies, how much will they spend on tickets?**

F $23.25
G $26.75
H $27.00
J $29.25

15. **How much more do 3 student tickets cost than 3 child tickets?**

A $1.25
B $2.25
C $3.25
D $3.75

16. **Find 700 × 5.**

F 35
G 350
H 3,500
J 7,000
K NH

Reteaching

Set A (pages 128–129)

Find 500 × 8.
Use a basic fact and a pattern of zeros.

5 × 8 = 40
50 × 8 = 400
500 × 8 = 4,000

Remember that when the product of a basic fact contains a zero, that zero is not part of the pattern.

1. 40 × 3 **2.** 90 × 8 **3.** 7 × 60

4. 300 × 5 **5.** 4 × 800 **6.** 900 × 2

7. 6 × 5,000 **8.** 4,000 × 9

Set B (pages 132–133)

Estimate 342 × 7.

342 × 7

300 × 7 = 2,100

342 × 7 is about 2,100.

Remember to round 4-digit numbers to the nearest thousand, 3-digit numbers to the nearest hundred, and 2-digit numbers to the nearest ten.

Round so you can estimate each product mentally.

1. 75 × 6 **2.** 266 × 7 **3.** 824 × 4

4. 5 × 361 **5.** 470 × 2 **6.** 341 × 3

7. 3 × 8,652 **8.** $21.45 × 5

Set C (pages 134–136)

Find 285 × 3.

Step 1 Multiply the ones. Regroup if necessary.	**Step 2** Multiply the tens. Add any regrouped tens. Regroup if necessary.	**Step 3** Multiply the hundreds. Add any regrouped hundreds.
1 285 × 3 5	2 1 285 × 3 55	2 1 285 × 3 855

Check by estimating. 300 × 3 = 900.
So, 855 is a reasonable answer.

Remember that you can use an array to multiply smaller numbers.

1. 18 × 2 **2.** 28 × 4 **3.** 5 × 45

4. 28 × 3 **5.** 6 × 39 **6.** 33 × 5

7. 2 × 12 **8.** 19 × 3 **9.** 22 × 4

10. 239 × 4 **11.** 980 × 8 **12.** 758 × 9

Set D (pages 140–141)

Find 6,474 × 5.

Step 1 Multiply the ones. Regroup if necessary.

```
   2
6,474
×    5
     0
```

Step 2 Multiply the tens. Add the regrouped tens. Regroup if necessary.

```
  3 2
6,474
×    5
    70
```

Step 3 Multiply the hundreds. Add the regrouped hundreds. Regroup if necessary.

```
 2 3 2
6,474
×    5
   370
```

Step 4 Multiply the thousands. Add the regrouped thousands. Regroup if necessary.

```
 2 3 2
 6,474
×    5
32,370
```

Remember that you can estimate the product to check your answer.

1. 1,462 × 3
2. 2,845 × 5
3. 4,916 × 8
4. 7,839 × 6
5. 9,427 × 5
6. 8,628 × 9
7. 16,412 × 5
8. 10,789 × 8
9. 23,981 × 4
10. 36,048 × 6
11. 52,563 × 4
12. 87,375 × 3

Set E (pages 142–143)

Find 6 × $3.75.

Step 1 Multiply as with whole numbers.

```
$3.75
×    6
```

Step 2 Regroup as needed.

```
  4 3
$3.75
×    6
 2250
```

Step 3 Show dollars and cents in the product.

```
   4 3
 $3.75
×    6
$22.50
```

Remember to place the decimal point two places from the right.

1. $13.46 × 3
2. $84.99 × 5
3. $0.92 × 9
4. $30.05 × 8
5. $11.36 × 5
6. $3.14 × 4
7. $0.56 × 7
8. $8.19 × 6
9. $10.42 × 2
10. $114.36 × 4
11. $201.14 × 3

More Practice

Set A *(pages 128–129)*

1. 90×3
2. 200×9
3. 6×50
4. 700×5
5. 700×8
6. 9×400
7. 70×3
8. 900×9
9. 2×100
10. $8{,}000 \times 5$
11. 400×4
12. $7 \times 7{,}000$
13. 300×2
14. 400×3
15. 5×900
16. 700×2
17. $4 \times 6{,}000$
18. 500×7
19. $4{,}000 \times 5$
20. $7 \times 6{,}000$
21. If an actor spoke 70 words per minute for 3 minutes, how many words were spoken?

Set B *(pages 132–133)*

Round so you can estimate each product mentally.

1. 79×2
2. $5{,}462 \times 6$
3. 85×5
4. 23×4
5. $3 \times 4{,}307$
6. 28×2
7. $4 \times \$59.75$
8. 834×9
9. 611×3
10. $\$7.63 \times 5$
11. 946×6
12. $\$3.75 \times 4$
13. Two pen pals wrote letters to each other for 73 years. They exchanged 8 letters a year. About how many letters did they exchange?

Set C *(pages 134–136)*

1. 86×3
2. 47×9
3. 24×5
4. 36×4
5. 55×3
6. 42×6
7. 87×2
8. 39×7
9. 24×8
10. 67×9
11. 91×4
12. 59×6
13. 82×4
14. 600×8
15. 710×9
16. 164×2
17. 3×243
18. 160×5
19. 2×347
20. 5×482
21. On the Internet you have found 128 articles on pandas. If it takes 3 minutes to access and print each article, how many minutes will it take to access and print them all?

Set D *(pages 140–141)*

1. $5{,}124 \times 8$ 2. $6{,}739 \times 5$ 3. $2{,}009 \times 9$ 4. $8{,}092 \times 6$ 5. $3{,}407 \times 7$

6. $26{,}009 \times 8$ 7. $6{,}600 \times 3$ 8. $16{,}580 \times 5$ 9. $43{,}458 \times 4$ 10. $4{,}127 \times 4$

11. $3{,}046 \times 3$ 12. $17{,}394 \times 7$ 13. $18{,}260 \times 5$ 14. $24{,}930 \times 8$ 15. $98{,}765 \times 6$

16. 9 × 6,027 17. 6 × 3,648 18. 4 × 1,509 19. 2 × 9,999

20. 36,075 × 4 21. 4,379 × 8 22. 42,005 × 6 23. 18,475 × 5

24. If 2,380 cars are transported by ferry boat each day, how many cars are transported in 1 week?

Set E *(pages 142–143)*

1. \$1.36 × 8 2. \$0.73 × 4 3. \$2.99 × 3 4. \$18.45 × 5

5. \$42.69 × 6 6. \$5.05 × 7 7. \$0.18 × 9 8. \$10.55 × 2

9. \$2.15 × 7 10. \$3.25 × 5 11. \$1.87 × 6 12. \$4.09 × 9

13. \$130.89 × 4 14. \$21.50 × 7 15. \$10.99 × 3 16. \$1.39 × 8 17. \$11.25 × 6

18. \$22.02 × 9 19. \$35.47 × 3 20. \$121.04 × 8 21. \$43.21 × 2 22. \$79.09 × 9

23. \$63.20 × 9 24. \$42.06 × 1 25. \$17.42 × 5 26. \$253.75 × 3 27. \$562.78 × 7

28. T-shirts cost \$11.59 at T-Shirt Express. If Erin buys 4 T-shirts, how much will they cost?

29. Hoang bought 6 containers of juice for \$1.29 each. How much change did he receive from a \$10 bill?

Problem Solving: Preparing for Tests

Choose the correct letter for each answer.

---

1. Gina used 3 rolls of crepe paper to decorate for a party. Each roll was more than 8 feet long and less than 11 feet long. Which is reasonable for the amount of crepe paper Gina used?

A Less than 11 feet
B Between 20 feet and 24 feet
C Between 24 feet and 33 feet
D More than 33 feet

> **Tip**
> Start by finding the least possible product and the greatest possible product.

---

2. Paul had $27.00. He bought a baseball for $8.95. He gave the clerk $10.00. How much change should Paul get back?

F $1.05
G $2.05
H $18.05
J $18.95

> **Tip**
> Use estimation to eliminate one or more of the answer choices in this problem.

---

3. A student is arranging chairs for a school play. He puts 14 chairs in the first row, 17 in the second row, 20 in the third row, and 23 in the fourth row. If he continues this pattern, how many chairs will he put in the 10th row?

A 44 chairs
B 41 chairs
C 40 chairs
D 38 chairs

> **Tip**
> Use one of these strategies to solve the problem.
> - *Find a Pattern*
> - *Make a Table*
> - *Draw a Picture*

4. Kevin has 65¢. He wants to buy 8 pencils that cost 9¢ each. How much more money does he need?

F	7¢	H	56¢
G	13¢	J	72¢

5. Keesha has a CD tower that holds 48 CDs. Each shelf in the tower holds 8 CDs. Which shows how many shelves are in the tower?

A $48 - 8 = ■$

B $48 \div 8 = ■$

C $48 + 8 = ■$

D $48 \times 8 = ■$

6. During the first 3 months of the year, a toy store sold the following numbers of games: 879, 914, and 809. Which is the best estimate for the number of games sold in the 3 months?

F 2,500 games

G 2,600 games

H 2,800 games

J 3,000 games

7. Kay lives 3 miles from school. Kit lives 7 miles from school. Maisha lives farther from school than Kit. Which is reasonable for the distance from Maisha's home to school?

A Less than 3 miles

B Between 3 and 5 miles

C Between 5 and 7 miles

D More than 7 miles

8. Jack, Angie, and 3 of their friends each checked out 4 books from the library. Angie returned her books within a week. How many books had the group of friends not returned to the library?

F	7 books	H	14 books
G	12 books	J	16 books

Use the graph for Questions 9 and 10.

The graph below shows the number of people in different age groups who read the newspaper each day.

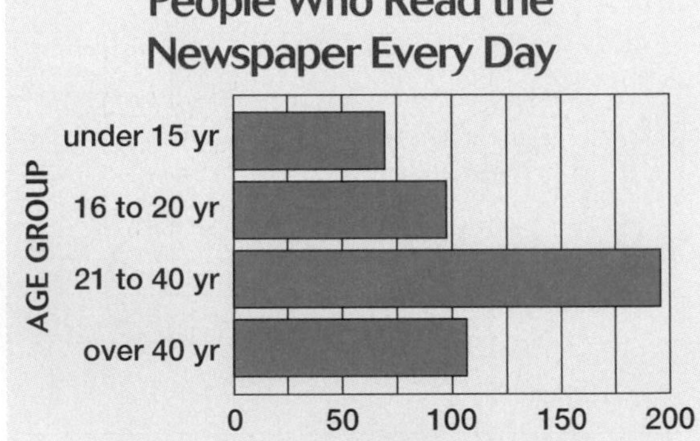

9. Which age group has the greatest number of people who read the newspaper every day?

A Over 40 years

B 21 to 40 years

C 16 to 20 years

D Under 15 years

10. About how many of the people who are 21 years old or older read the newspaper every day?

F About 150 people

G About 200 people

H About 300 people

J About 400 people

Multiple-Choice Cumulative Review

Choose the correct letter for each answer.

Number Sense

1. **What is the value of the 6 in 6,987,457?**

   A 6 thousand
   B 60 thousand
   C 600 thousand
   D 6 million
   E NH

2. **Which figure has more than $\frac{1}{2}$ shaded?**

   F 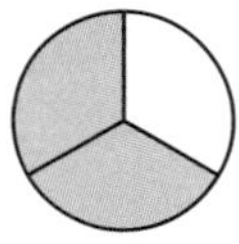
   H 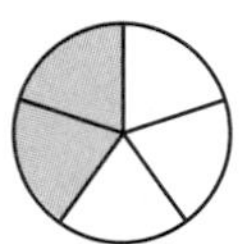
   G 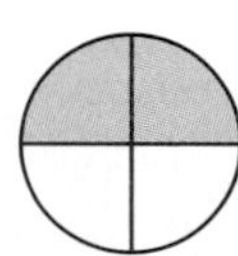
   J 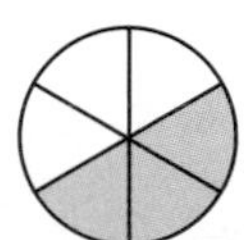

3. **Which set of numbers is in order from *least* to *greatest?***

   A 2,311 3,022 2,331 3,113
   B 2,311 2,331 3,022 3,113
   C 3,113 3,022 2,331 2,311
   D 2,331 2,311 3,022 3,113
   E NH

4. **Which number has a 3 in the ten thousands place and a 9 in the tens place?**

   F 291,532
   G 231,952
   H 231,592
   J 231,529
   K NH

5. **What is the product of 47 × 5?**

   A 9
   B 42
   C 52
   D 235
   E NH

6. **Perry spent $18 on colored markers. He bought 2 yellow markers, 3 pink markers, and 4 blue markers. If each marker cost the same amount, how much did each marker cost?**

   F $2.00
   G $3.00
   H $9.00
   J $22.00

7. **At a discount store you can buy 4 computer games for $36. What is the cost of each computer game?**

   A $154
   B $144
   C $32
   D $9

8. **Tia bought a CD for the regular price of $13.99 and a tape on sale for $5.49. The tape originally cost $7.89. How much money did Tia save?**

   F $2.40
   G $6.10
   H $13.38
   J $19.48

Algebra and Functions

9. Which expression could help you solve 6 × ■ = 42?

A 6 × 42
B 42 ÷ 6
C 42 × 6
D 42 − 6
E NH

10. Which number sentence is *not* in the same family of facts as 63 ÷ 7 = 9?

F 63 ÷ 9 = 7
G 9 × 7 = 63
H 9 × 3 = 27
J 7 × 9 = 63
K NH

11. The fourth-grade class had a read-a-thon. Ed read 2 chapters of a book in the first week. Each week after that, he read 2 more chapters than the week before. How many chapters did he read in the sixth week?

A 6 chapters
B 8 chapters
C 12 chapters
D 14 chapters

12. What is the missing number in this number pattern?

36, 32, 28, ■, 20, 16

F 18
G 22
H 24
J 26
K NH

Measurement and Geometry

13. A rectangular garden is 14 feet wide by 16 feet long. What is the perimeter of the garden?

A 30 feet
B 60 feet
C 120 feet
D 224 feet

14. The *perimeter* of a table is 14 feet. If the width is 3 feet, what is the length?

F 3 feet
G 4 feet
H 11 feet
J 17 feet

15. A car weighs 1,780 pounds. The driver weighs 210 pounds. There are ten 16-ounce packages in the back seat. What is the total weight of the car and the packages? (Hint: 16 ounces equals 1 pound.)

A 1,790 pounds
B 1,990 pounds
C 2,000 pounds
D 2,150 pounds

16. Chip started a 3-mile race at 3:30 P.M. He crossed the finish line at 4:05 P.M. How long did it take him to run the race?

F 25 minutes
G 35 minutes
H 45 minutes
J 75 minutes

Multiplying by Two-Digit Numbers

Diagnosing Readiness

In Chapter 5, you will use these skills:

Ⓐ Rounding

(pages 14–16)

Round to the nearest ten.

1. 63 **2.** 89

3. 85 **4.** 239

Round to the nearest hundred.

5. 212 **6.** 769

7. 350 **8.** 3,425

Round to the nearest thousand.

9. 3,214 **10.** 6,500

11. 7,815 **12.** 9,765

Ⓑ Multiplication Facts

(pages 84–86)

13. 7×5 **14.** 6×9

15. 8×8 **16.** 9×7

17. If Ann's weekly allowance is \$5, how much money will she have at the end of 4 weeks if she spends \$1 each week?

C Multiplying by Multiples of 10, 100, and 1,000

(pages 128–129)

18. 9 × 60

19. 5 × 700

20. 2 × 8,000

21. 8 × 300

22. A theater has 300 seats. If a play is performed twice a day for 5 days, how many people can see the play each day?

D Estimating Products

(pages 132–133)

Estimate each product.

23. 5 × 149

24. 7 × 352

25. 8 × 2,623

26. 2 × 4,198

27. In order for the Millers to arrive at their vacation resort on time, they plan to take 2 days to get there and drive at least 375 miles each day. Estimate their round-trip mileage.

E Adding

(pages 42–46)

28. $\begin{array}{r} 389 \\ +\ 57 \\ \hline \end{array}$

29. $\begin{array}{r} 672 \\ +\ 58 \\ \hline \end{array}$

30. $\begin{array}{r} 468 \\ +\ 346 \\ \hline \end{array}$

31. $\begin{array}{r} 8{,}905 \\ +\ 762 \\ \hline \end{array}$

F Multiplying by a One-Digit Number

(pages 134–136)

32. $\begin{array}{r} 78 \\ \times\ 8 \\ \hline \end{array}$

33. $\begin{array}{r} 47 \\ \times\ 6 \\ \hline \end{array}$

34. 7 × 322

35. 9 × 745

36. If a manufacturer can ship 475 cartons a day and each carton holds 60 items, how many cartons can be shipped in 5 days?

To the Family and Student

Looking Back

In Grade 3, students learned how to multiply by one-digit numbers. This is reviewed in Chapter 4 of this book.

5,284 × 3

Chapter 5

Multiplying by Two-Digit Numbers

In this chapter, students will learn how to multiply by two-digit numbers.

5,284 × 73

Looking Ahead

In Grade 5, students will learn how to multiply by three-digit numbers.

5,284 × 473

Math and Everyday Living

Opportunities to apply the concepts of Chapter 5 abound in everyday situations. During the chapter, think about how multiplication can be used to solve a variety of real-world problems. The following examples suggest just several of the many situations that could launch a discussion about multiplication.

Math at the Grocery Store At $1.09 per pound, what would your 22-pound Thanksgiving turkey cost?

Math at the Movie Theater You count 24 rows of seats with 28 seats in each row. How many seats are there in the theater?

Math at Home Last week your family collected 78 cans in the recycling bin. At that rate, how many would you collect in a year? (1 year = 52 weeks)

Math and Communication This month your family's telephone bill is $62.94. At that rate, how much would you pay for telephone service for the year?

Local service	44.92
Long distance	9.63
Information	2.25
Taxes	6.14
Total charges 3/14 to 4/13	**$62.94**

Math and Nutrition A single French-fried potato has about 15 calories. If you eat 20 French fries, how many calories are you consuming?

Math and Transportation You count 58 seats on your school bus and 13 buses in all. How many students can be transported at one time?

Math in the City You ride an elevator that states the maximum capacity is 16 people. Suppose each passenger weighs 170 pounds. What would be the weight in the elevator at full capacity?

Pershco Elevator Company

Maximum capacity 16 people

 California Content Standards in Chapter 5 Lessons*

	Teach and Practice	Practice
Number Sense		
3.0 (🔑) Students solve problems involving addition, subtraction, multiplication, and division of whole numbers and understand the relationship among the operations.	5-8	
3.2 (🔑) Demonstrate an understanding of, and the ability to use, standard algorithms for multiplying a multidigit number by a two-digit number	5-1, 5-2, 5-4, 5-5, 5-7	
3.3 (🔑) Solve problems involving multiplication of multidigit numbers by two-digit numbers.	5-4, 5-7	5-1, 5-5
Algebra and Functions		
1.0 Students use and interpret variables, mathematical symbols, and properties to write and simplify expressions and sentences.		5-1, 5-4
1.1 Use letters, boxes, or other symbols to stand for any number in simple expressions or equations (e.g., demonstrate an understanding and the use of the concept of a variable).		5-1, 5-2, 5-5, 5-7, 5-8
1.3 (🔑) Use parentheses to indicate which operation to perform first when writing expressions containing more than two terms and different operations.		5-5

	Teach and Practice	Practice
Mathematical Reasoning		
1.1 Analyze problems by identifying relationships, distinguishing relevant from irrelevant information	5-3	
1.2 Determine when and how to break a problem into simpler parts.		5-6
2.0 Students use strategies, skills, and concepts in finding solutions.		5-3, 5-6, 5-8
2.1 Use estimation to verify the reasonableness of calculated results.	5-2, 5-4, 5-5, 5-7	
2.2 Apply strategies and results from simpler problems to more complex problems.		5-6
2.3 Use a variety of methods, such as words, numbers, symbols, charts, graphs, tables, diagrams, and models, to explain mathematical reasoning.	5-6	
2.4 Express the solution clearly and logically by using the appropriate mathematical notation and terms and clear language; support solutions with evidence in both verbal and symbolic work.	5-6	5-5
2.5 Indicate the relative advantages of exact and approximate solutions to problems and give answers to a specified degree of accuracy.		5-2
3.2 Note the method of deriving the solution and demonstrate a conceptual understanding of the derivation by solving similar problems.		5-6
3.3 Develop generalizations of the results obtained and apply them in other circumstances.		5-4

* The symbol (🔑) indicates a key standard as designated in the Mathematics Framework for California Public Schools. Full statements of the California Content Standards are found at the beginning of this book following the Table of Contents.

Mental Math: Multiplying Multiples of Ten

Warm-Up Review

1. 5 × 6
2. 7 × 8
3. 6 × 7
4. 4 + 9
5. 5 × 60
6. 8 × 70
7. 6 × 700
8. 4 × 9,000
9. David earned $40 per day for 3 days and $50 per day for 2 days. How much did he earn in all?

California Content Standard *Number Sense 3.2: (🔑): Demonstrate an understanding of, and the ability to use, standard algorithms for multiplying a multidigit number by a two-digit number . . ..*

Math Link You know how to find 6 × 700. Now you will learn how to find products like 60 × 7,000.

Example 1

Find 40 × 300.

First look at some products when one or both factors are 10, 100, or 1,000.

10 × 10 = 10 tens = 100
10 × 100 = 10 hundreds = 1,000
10 × 1,000 = 10 thousands = 10,000
100 × 100 = 100 hundreds = 10,000

12 × 10 = 12 tens = 120
12 × 100 = 12 hundreds = 1,200
12 × 1,000 = 12 thousands = 12,000
30 × 1,000 = 30 thousands = 30,000

Now use a basic fact and a pattern with zeros to find 40 × 300 mentally.

4 × 3 = 12
4 × 30 = 120
40 × 30 = 1,200
40 × 300 = 12,000

The number of zeros in both factors equals the number of zeros in the product.

Here's WHY It Works

$$\begin{aligned} 40 \times 300 &= (4 \times 10) \times (3 \times 100) \\ &= (4 \times 3) \times (10 \times 100) \\ &= 12 \times 1{,}000 \\ &= 12{,}000 \end{aligned}$$

Use the associative and commutative properties of multiplication.

Example 2

Find 50 × 600.

5 × 6 = 30
5 × 60 = 300
50 × 60 = 3,000
50 × 600 = 30,000

When the product of a basic fact includes a zero, that zero is not part of the pattern.

 Additional Standards: Number Sense 3.3(🔑); Algebra and Functions 1.0, 1.1 *(See p. 161.)*

Guided Practice *For another example, see Set A on p. 188.*

1. 20 × 20 **2.** 40 × 700 **3.** 300 × 300 **4.** 6,000 × 70 **5.** 8,000 × 600

6. There are 900 people in a theater. The theater has 30 rows of seats with 60 seats in each row. How many seats are there in all?

Independent Practice *For more practice, see Set A on p. 190.*

7. 50 × 50 **8.** 90 × 400 **9.** 60 × 3,000 **10.** 40 × 9,000

11. 300 × 500 **12.** 4,000 × 600 **13.** 800 × 5,000 **14.** 2,000 × 5,000

15. Use the data in the table at the right. During breeding season, colonies of penguins form larger groups, called rookeries. How many penguins would be in a rookery made up of 20 colonies?

Animal Groups

Name	Number in group
Pod of whales	20
Mob of kangaroos	25
Colony of Penguins	300

16. Algebra Find the value of $40x - 50$ when x is 800.

Mixed Review

17. Round 675 to the nearest 10.

18. Round 8,955 to the nearest 100.

19. Algebra Evaluate (3 + 5) × 6.

20. Mental Math Find 9 × 20,000.

21. 9 × 2,315 **22.** 8 × $4.75 **23.** 7 × $12.43 **24.** 3 × 8,246

25. 9,000 × 6,000 **26.** 500 × 200 **27.** 80 × 5,000 **28.** 4,000 × 600

29. There are 1,200 students in an auditorium. The auditorium has 50 rows of seats with 40 seats in each row. How many seats are there in all?

Test Prep **Choose the correct letter for each answer.**

30. Algebra Find $n + 216$ when $n = 105$. (2-10)

A 111 C 221
B 211 D 321

31. Algebra Find $n - 375$ when $n = 600$. (2-10)

F 225 H 325
G 235 J 975

Estimating Products

California Content Standard *Mathematical Reasoning 2.1: Use estimation to verify the reasonableness of calculated results. Also, Number Sense 3.2 (🔑) (See p. 161.)*

Warm-Up Review

1. 6×7
2. 9×4
3. 10×40
4. 20×70
5. 50×900
6. $3{,}000 \times 60$
7. Terry bought 3 pins at \$3.75 each. She paid with a \$20 bill. How much change did she receive?

Math Link You can multiply multiples of ten. Now you will learn how to estimate a product by rounding.

Example 1

Estimate 19×24.

Round to get numbers you can multiply mentally.

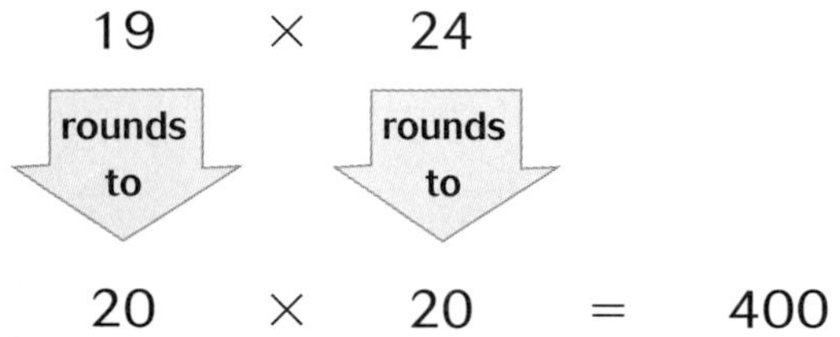

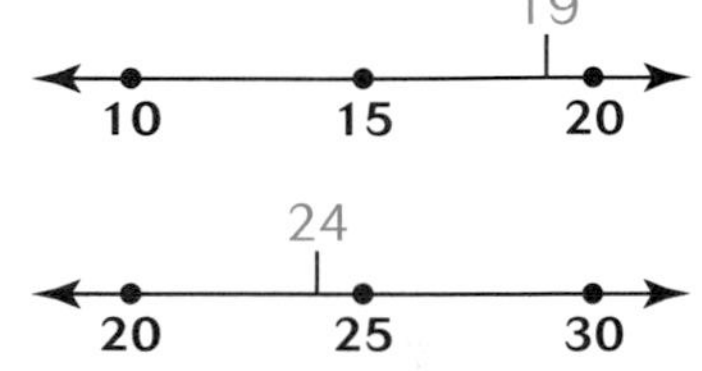

19×24 is about 400.

Example 2

Is 24,584 a reasonable answer for 439×56? Estimate by finding a range.

$$500 \times 60 = 30{,}000$$
$$\uparrow \quad \uparrow$$
$$439 \times 56$$
$$\downarrow \quad \downarrow$$
$$400 \times 50 = 20{,}000$$

Round both factors up.
Round both factors down.
The exact answer is between 20,000 and 30,000.

The answer is reasonable because 24,584 is between 20,000 and 30,000.

Guided Practice *For another example, see Set B on p. 188.*

Round each factor so that you can estimate the product mentally.

1. 56×28
2. 44×65
3. 920×33
4. $16 \times 9{,}723$
5. In one day, a museum had 832 visitors. Is it reasonable to say that the museum would have 25,792 visitors in 31 days? Estimate by finding a range.

 Additional Standards: Algebra and Functions 1.1; Mathematical Reasoning 2.5 (See p. 161.)

Independent Practice *For more practice, see Set B on p. 190.*

Round each factor so that you can estimate the product mentally.

6. 62×12 **7.** 87×36 **8.** 59×20 **9.** 66×43

10. 231×65 **11.** 128×34 **12.** 78×654 **13.** 456×24

14. $2{,}019 \times 23$ **15.** $6{,}089 \times 48$ **16.** $71 \times 3{,}909$ **17.** $87 \times 5{,}789$

18. Is 258,004 a reasonable answer for $4{,}389 \times 36$? Estimate by finding a range.

Use the table to solve Exercises 19 and 20.

19. If Bus 31 carries about 55 passengers each trip, estimate how many passengers it will carry in a week.

20. If Bus 15 carries about 46 passengers each trip, estimate how many passengers it will carry in a week.

Sweetwater City Buses	
Bus Number	**One-Way Trips per Week**
31	281
66	280
15	704
27	477

21. Algebra If the estimated product of n and 52 is 1,000, name at least two reasonable values for n.

Mixed Review

22. Algebra Evaluate the expression $n + 72$ for $n = 209$.

23. $\$3.09 \times 5$ **24.** $\$5.82 \times 7$ **25.** 70×400 **26.** $600 \times 9{,}000$

27. Estimate $19 \times 6{,}723$. **28.** Estimate $3{,}452 + 997$.

Test Prep **Choose the correct letter for each answer.**

29. (1-1) What is the value of the underlined digit in 67,1_2_3?

A 10 **C** 1,000

B 100 **D** 10,000

30. (4-4) $99 \times 7 =$

F 593 **H** 683

G 633 **J** 693

K NH

Problem-Solving Skill:

Too Much or Too Little Information

Warm-Up Review

1. 7 × 8
2. 80 × 9
3. 90 × 90
4. 600 + 90
5. $1.50 + $12
6. $1.50 + $2,000
7. At the school fair, 300 tickets were sold at $4 each. Another $550 was collected by selling food. How much money was collected in all?

California Content Standard *Mathematical Reasoning 1.1 Analyze problems by identifying relationships, distinguishing relevant from irrelevant information . . ..*

Read for Understanding

Sarah has worked at an animal shelter for 6 months. Each month she makes copies of a newsletter at the Super Fast Copy Center. Last month she made 80 copies. This month she needs to make 100 copies. She has $5.00 to spend.

Copy Costs	
Type of Page	**Cost per Page**
Black and White	4¢
Color	6¢

1. How many copies of the newsletter does Sarah need to make this month?
2. How much does Sarah have to spend?

Think and Discuss

Too Much or Too Little Information

Sometimes word problems contain too much or too little information. If there is too much, you need to choose what you need to solve the problem. If there is too little information, you cannot solve the problem.

Reread the paragraph at the top of the page.

3. Do you have enough information to find out how many more copies Sarah needs to make this month than she made last month? Explain.
4. Does Sarah have enough money to make 100 copies of the newletter? Does the paragraph give enough information? Explain.
5. Find the information in the paragraph that is needed to solve Exercise 4. Then identify any information that is not needed or that is missing.

 Additional Standard: Mathematical Reasoning 2.0 (See p. 161.)

Guided Practice

Leslie wants to sell bags of peanuts to earn money for "Friends of African Elephants." She will fill 25 bags and sell them for $1.00 a bag. She wants to put 50 peanuts in each bag. She spent $10 for 1,000 peanuts. Does Leslie have enough peanuts to fill the 25 bags?

1. What information do you need to solve the problem?

a. Leslie will charge $1.00 for each bag of peanuts.

b. Leslie wants to put 50 peanuts in each bag.

c. Leslie spent $10 on peanuts.

2. What other information do you need to solve the problem?

a. Each bag will sell for $1.00.

b. Leslie paid $10 for the peanuts.

c. Leslie has 1,000 peanuts.

3. Which number sentence tells how many peanuts she needs for 25 bags?

a. $25 \times 2 = 50$

b. $25 \times 50 = 1{,}250$

c. $25 \times 1{,}000 = 25{,}000$

Independent Practice

More than 2,000 of the world's plants and animals are endangered. In the United States alone, nearly 850 plants and animals are endangered. A group of concerned students posted photos of some endangered animals on their school's Web site. Each student posted 4 photos. How many photos did they post on the school's Web site?

4. What information is not needed to solve the problem?

a. Each student in the group posted 4 photos on the Web site.

b. Over 2,000 plants and animals in the world are endangered.

c. Both of the above.

5. What information do you need to solve the problem?

a. Nearly 850 plants and animals in the U.S. are endangered.

b. Each student posted 4 photos.

c. Both of the above.

6. Math Reasoning Is there enough information to find the total number of photos posted by the students? Explain your answer.

Use Homework Workbook 5-3.

Diagnostic Checkpoint

Use patterns with zeros to solve mentally.

1. 20 × 60 (5-1)
2. 40 × 40 (5-1)
3. 50 × 60 (5-1)
4. 90 × 700 (5-1)

5. 300 × 90 (5-1)
6. 800 × 200 (5-1)
7. 70 × 1,000 (5-1)
8. 3,000 × 400 (5-1)

Round each factor so that you can estimate the product mentally.

9. 46 × 29 (5-2)
10. 72 × 38 (5-2)
11. 64 × 131 (5-2)
12. 208 × 86 (5-2)

13. 406 × 842 (5-2)
14. 7,989 × 25 (5-2)
15. 8,125 × 100 (5-2)
16. 52 × 15,609 (5-2)

17. (5-2) Is 16,718 a reasonable estimate for 643 × 26? Estimate by finding a range.

Algebra Complete each table. Use patterns with zeros. (5-1)

Rule: Multiply by 30.

	Input	Output
18.	30	
19.	50	
20.	100	
21.	600	
22.	1,000	
23.	3,000	

Rule: Multiply by 400.

	Input	Output
24.	10	
25.	70	
26.	200	
27.	400	
28.	500	
29.	2,000	

Rule: Multiply by 6,000.

	Input	Output
30.	20	
31.	60	
32.	100	
33.	600	
34.	5,000	
35.	7,000	

36. (5-3) Each box in a shipping crate holds 8 baseballs. Each baseball sells for $9. There are 30 boxes in the crate. How many balls are in the crate?

37. (2-5) There were 350 people at Friday's performance of a play and 475 people at Saturday's performance. How many more people attended on Saturday than on Friday?

38. (5-2) Each club member needs to sell $62 worth of baked goods to meet the club's goal. There are 28 members in the club. Estimate how much they need to earn.

Multiple-Choice Cumulative Review

Choose the correct letter for each answer.

1. What is the value of the underlined digit in 3,6<u>8</u>7,200?

   A 800
   B 8,000
   C 80,000
   D 800,000
   E NH

2. Mrs. Jacobs had $988.46 in her savings account. Then she spent $214.38 for a plane ticket. How much did she have left in her savings account?

   F $774.08
   G $778.04
   H $874.08
   J $1,202.84

3. Which of the following has the greatest product?

   A 5×4
   B 3×9
   C 2×12
   D 6×3

4. Which number makes the number sentence true?

   $$48 \div n = 6$$

   F 9 **J** 6
   G 8 **K** NH
   H 7

5. The library lent 4,097 books during June, 3,963 books during July, and 3,802 books during August. About how many books were lent during the three months?

   A 10,000 **C** 12,000
   B 11,000 **D** 13,000

6. What is the value of $n - 7$ when $n = 51$?

   F 58 **J** 44
   G 54 **K** NH
   H 53

7. What is the missing number in the number pattern?

   144, 124, 104, *n*, 64

   A 98 **C** 84
   B 94 **D** 74

8. The table lists the low temperatures in four cities on a day in January. Which city was the coldest?

City	Low Temperature
Denver	⁻2°F
San Diego	52°F
Chicago	⁻15°F
New York	0°F

   F Denver **H** Chicago
   G San Diego **J** New York

Multiplying by a Multiple of Ten

California Content Standard *Number Sense 3.2 (🔑): Demonstrate an understanding of, and the ability to use, standard algorithms for multiplying a multidigit number by a two-digit number . . .. Also, Number Sense 3.3 (🔑); Mathematical Reasoning 2.1 (See p. 161.)*

Math Link You know how to multiply a number by 2, 3, 4, 5, 6, 7, 8, 9, or 10. Now you will learn how to multiply a number by 20, 30, 40, 50, 60, 70, 80, or 90.

Warm-Up Review

1. 7×8
2. 9×4
3. 73×5
4. 195×3
5. 96×10
6. 10×400
7. Use rounding to estimate 89×714.
8. Jo gets a total of $768 per week from 2 jobs. How much does she earn in 6 weeks?

Example 1

Endangered woolly spider monkeys live on reserves in Brazil.

Use the data at the right. What is the least number of monkeys living on reserves?

28	×	20	=	*n*
reserves		monkeys per reserve		monkeys in all

Step 1 Write a zero in the ones place.

$$\begin{array}{r} 28 \\ \times\ 20 \\ \hline 0 \end{array}$$

Write a zero.

Step 2 Multiply by the tens digit.

$$\begin{array}{r} \overset{1}{2}8 \\ \times\ 20 \\ \hline 560 \end{array}$$

2 tens × 28

Here's WHY It Works

$$\begin{aligned} 28 \times 20 &= 28 \times (2 \times 10) \\ &= (28 \times 2) \times 10 \\ &= 56 \times 10 \\ &= 560 \end{aligned}$$

Use the associative property of multiplication.

There are at least 560 woolly spider monkeys on reserves.

Check by estimating. $30 \times 20 = 600$. The answer is reasonable because 560 is close to 600.

Example 2

$$\begin{array}{r} 7{,}052 \\ \times\ 60 \\ \hline 0 \end{array} \leftarrow \text{Write a zero.}$$

$$\begin{array}{r} 7{,}\overset{3}{0}\overset{1}{5}2 \\ \times\ 60 \\ \hline 423{,}120 \end{array} \leftarrow \text{6 tens} \times 7{,}052$$

Additional Standard: Algebra and Functions 1.0; Mathematical Reasoning 3.3 (See p. 161.)

Guided Practice *For another example, see Set C on p. 188.*

1. 34×20
2. 872×50
3. $4{,}230 \times 20$
4. 62×30
5. 50×34

6. If a giant panda eats 80 pounds of bamboo per day, how many pounds of bamboo shoots will it eat in a year?

Independent Practice *For more practice, see Set C on p. 190.*

7. 18×20
8. 22×50
9. 172×60
10. $1{,}208 \times 80$
11. $2{,}316 \times 30$

12. 20×65
13. $70 \times 2{,}402$
14. 95×50
15. 45×40

16. 30×223
17. 744×90
18. 72×60
19. $1{,}180 \times 20$

Mental Math **How can you find each product mentally?**

20. 99×20
21. $2 \times 12 \times 5$

22. Dan worked 20 hours last week. He ordered 30 packages of paper cups with 48 cups in each package. How many cups did he order?

23. One year 19 monkeys were seen on 20 days. On how many of the 365 days were they not seen?

24. **Math Reasoning** What happens to the product of two numbers if both numbers are doubled?

Mixed Review

25. Round each factor and estimate the product of 82×389.

26. Find the next three numbers in the pattern.
355, 345, 335, ▬, ▬, ▬

27. $\$2.34 \times 9$
28. $915 - 76$
29. $3{,}198 + 4{,}657$
30. $872 - 160$
31. 700×80

Test Prep **Choose the correct letter for each answer.**

32. If $135 + n = 215$, then $n =$ (2-11)

A 350 **C** 90
B 340 **D** 80

33. If $n - 135 = 215$, then $n =$ (2-11)

F 350 **H** 90
G 340 **J** 80

Multiplying by Two-Digit Numbers

Warm-Up Review

1. 9×5
2. 40×70
3. 58×5
4. $744 + 35$
5. 76×20
6. 97×50
7. There are 8 sections of seats at the stadium. Each section has 400 seats, 200 are orange, and 200 are blue. How many seats does the stadium have?

California Content Standard *Number Sense 3.2 (🔑): Demonstrate an understanding of, and the ability to use, standard algorithms for multiplying a multidigit number by a two-digit number . . .. Also, Mathematical Reasoning 2.1 (See p. 161.)*

Math Link You can multiply by numbers like 20 and 30. Now you will learn to multiply any 2 two-digit numbers.

Example 1

Find 26×12.

First use an array to show 26×12. Then break the problem into two parts that you already know how to do.

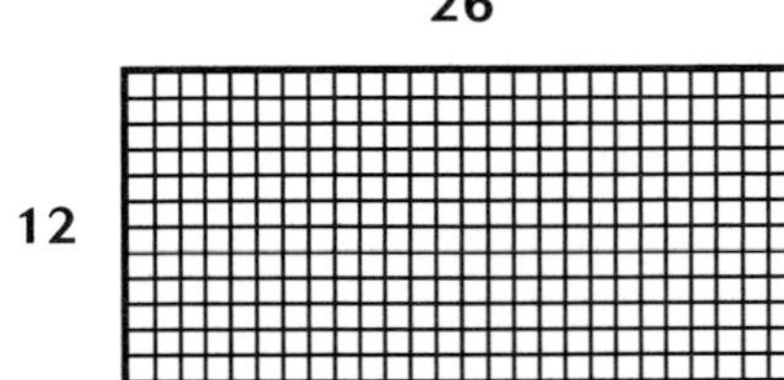

The total number of squares is 26×12.

Part A	Part B
26×2	26×10
52	260

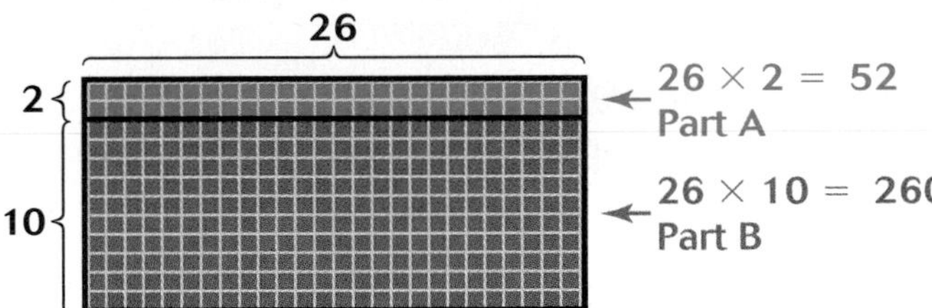

$26 \times 2 = 52$ Part A

$26 \times 10 = 260$ Part B

Add the two parts. $52 + 260 = 312$.
So $26 \times 12 = 312$.

Here's a way to record your work.

Step 1 Multiply by the ones. Regroup as needed.

$$\begin{array}{r} \overset{1}{2}6 \\ \times\ 12 \\ \hline 52 \end{array} \leftarrow 26 \times 2 \text{ Part A}$$

Step 2 Place a zero in the ones place. Multiply by the tens digit. Regroup as needed.

$$\begin{array}{r} \overset{1}{2}6 \\ \times\ 12 \\ \hline 52 \\ \underline{260} \end{array} \leftarrow 26 \times 10 \text{ Part B}$$

Step 3 Add the products.

$$\begin{array}{r} \overset{1}{2}6 \\ \times\ 12 \\ \hline 52 \\ +\ 260 \\ \hline 312 \end{array}$$

Here's WHY It Works

$$\begin{aligned} 26 \times 12 &= 26 \times (10 + 2) \\ &= (26 \times 10) + (26 \times 2) \\ &= 260 + 52 \\ &= 312 \end{aligned}$$

<u>Check</u> by estimating. $30 \times 10 = 300$. The answer is reasonable because 312 is close to 300.

Additional Standards: Number Sense 3.3 (🔑); Algebra and Functions 1.1, 1.3 (🔑); Mathematical Reasoning 2.4 (See p. 161.)

Example 2

Sometimes you need to regroup more than once.

Find 36×27.

Think of 27 in two parts, 7 and 20. Multiply each part by 36.

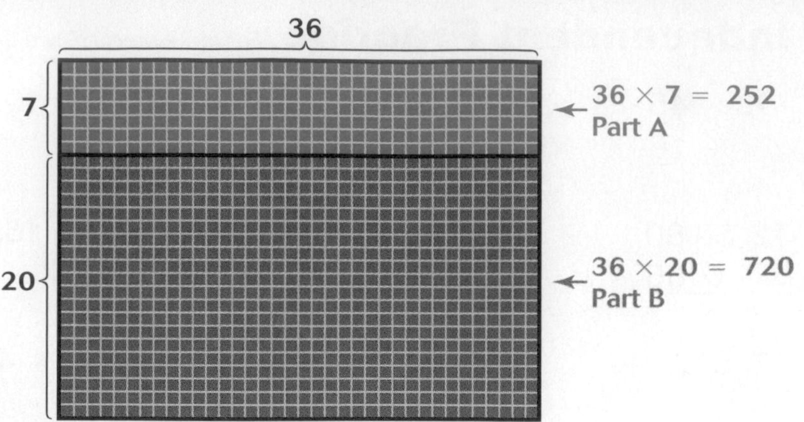

Step 1 Multiply by the ones. Regroup as needed.

```
  4
 36
× 27
 252 ← 36 × 7
       Part A
```

Step 2 Place a zero in the ones place. Multiply by the tens digit. Regroup as needed.

```
  1
  4
 36
× 27
 252
 720 ← 36 × 20
       Part B
```

Step 3 Add the products.

```
   1
   4
  36
×  27
  252
+ 720
  972
```

Here's WHY It Works

$$36 \times 27 = 36 \times (20 + 7)$$
$$= (36 \times 20) + (36 \times 7)$$
$$= 720 + 252$$
$$= 972$$

Check by estimating. $40 \times 30 = 1,200$. Since the factors 36 and 27 were rounded up, the exact answer will be less than the estimate. The answer is reasonable because 972 is less than 1,200.

More Examples

A.

```
   63          63       63
×  47        ×  7     × 40
  441 ←——— 441      2,520
 2520 ←————————————┘
2,961
```

B.

```
 $0.49         49       49
×   68        × 8     × 60
   392 ←——— 392      2,940
  2940 ←————————————┘
$33.32
```

Remember to show dollars and cents in the product.

Guided Practice

For another example, see Set D on p. 189

1. 33×14 **2.** 45×34 **3.** 62×35 **4.** 87×19 **5.** $\$0.28 \times 46$

6. How far can a car averaging 61 miles per hour travel in 14 hours?

Independent Practice For more practice, see Set D on p. 191.

7. 45×16
8. 36×52
9. 87×28
10. $\$0.63 \times 49$
11. 85×33

12. $\$0.80 \times 55$
13. 39×87
14. 86×25
15. 41×69
16. 98×91

17. 51 × 42 **18.** \$0.75 × 12 **19.** 64 × 46 **20.** 25 × \$0.99

21. 25 × 25 **22.** \$0.98 × 24 **23.** 38 × 43 **24.** 72 × 35

25. Mental Math How can you use mental math to find 25 × 99?

26. Algebra Find the value of $24n$ when $n = 68$.

27. Math Reasoning Look at Here's WHY It Works on page 172. Find 35 × 24 and show why it works.

28. Drew sent 15 letters. Each letter weighed between one and two ounces. How much did he spend on stamps?

29. The library has 52 bookshelves. Each shelf holds 28 books. Is there enough space for 1,000 books? Explain.

Stamps	
Letter (1st oz)	33¢
Each extra oz	22¢
Postcard	20¢

Mixed Review

30. Juanita earns \$12 an hour. Give an estimate of how much she earns if she works 32 hours in a week.

31. Zach earned \$128 in June, \$230 in July, and \$175 in August. How much more did he earn in July than in August?

32. \$0.63 + \$0.90 **33.** 2,485 − 520 **34.** 50 × 300 **35.** 60 × 834

Test Prep Choose the correct letter for the answer.

36. Which number is greatest?
(1-3)

A 9,000,900 **B** 999,999 **C** 9,900,999 **D** 8,999,999

37. A glass of lemonade costs \$1.75. How much does it cost for 4 glasses of lemonade?
(4-7)

F \$1.79 **G** \$4.00 **H** \$6.80 **J** \$7.00

Problem-Solving Strategy:
Make a List

California Content Standard *Mathematical Reasoning 2.4: Express the solution clearly and logically by using the appropriate mathematical notation and terms and clear language; support solutions with evidence in both verbal and symbolic work. Also, Mathematical Reasoning 2.3 (See p. 161.)*

Warm-Up Review

1. 4 × 9
2. 60 × 70
3. 138 × 7
4. 539 × 30
5. 80 × 37
6. 200 × 60
7. How many ways can you make 18¢?
8. For 4 days, 30 people worked 8 hours each day at $5 per hour. How much were they paid in all?

Example 1

A school group is doing volunteer work at a zoo. The volunteers wear special shirts and hats. The shirts are red or blue. The hats are purple, orange, or green. What are the different ways a volunteer could choose one shirt and one hat?

Understand

What do you need to find?

You need to find all the ways you can pick one shirt and one hat from a choice of two shirts and three hats.

Plan

How can you solve the problem?

You can **make a list** of all the choices by drawing a **tree diagram.** The branches farthest to the right list all the possible choices of shirts and hats.

Word Bank

tree diagram

Solve

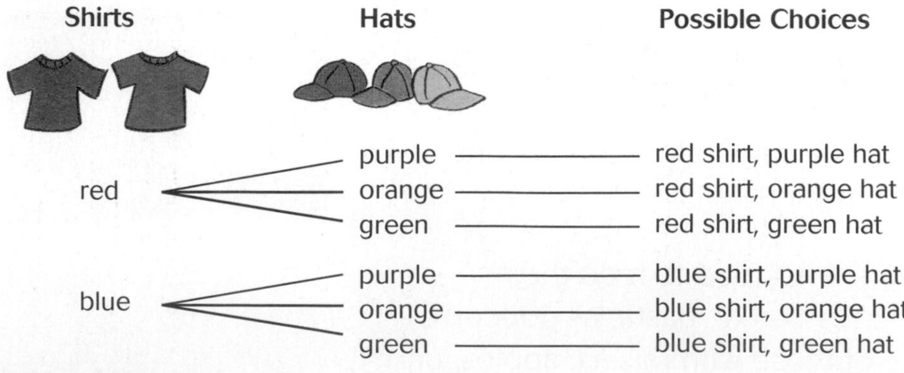

Look Back

Explain how you know that you have found all the choices.

Additional Standards: Mathematical Reasoning 1.2, 2.0, 2.2, 3.2 (See p. 161.)

Example 2

The volunteers are given a pin to wear on their cap. They can choose a giraffe, a lion, a bear, or a monkey pin. Each animal pin comes in gold, silver, or black. List all the possible choices of pins.

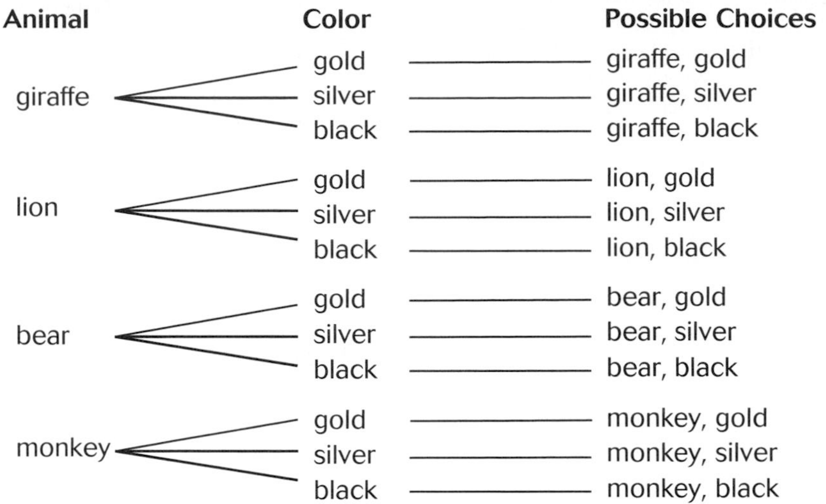

Guided Practice

Use a tree diagram to make a list to solve Exercises 1–8.

1. The purple, orange, and green hats worn by the volunteers come in three sizes: small, medium, and large. List all of the combinations of hats and sizes.

2. Angela can volunteer on Friday, Saturday, or Sunday. She can also pick either mornings or afternoons. Make a list of the days and times Angela can volunteer.

Independent Practice

3. Each volunteer gets a free lunch. The lunch choices are tacos or hamburgers. The dessert choices are fruit cup, applesauce, or yogurt. List all the possible choices for picking one lunch and one dessert.

4. Josh is mixing animal food to feed the monkeys. He uses cereal, pasta, or popcorn. He mixes one of those with raisins, apples, or dried bananas. What are the different combinations he can make?

5. Sam is buying a new sweater and a pair of slacks. The sweater comes in blue, white, yellow, or green. The slacks come in black, tan, or gray. List all the possible choices he can make.

6. At the class picnic, students can choose one meat and one vegetable from the list at the right. List all the possible meat and vegetable combinations.

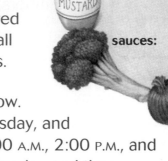

meats: chicken, hamburger
vegetables: broccoli, peppers, carrots, onions
sauces: ketchup, mustard

7. Ushers at the school play can wear either jeans or black pants. They can also choose one of four different-colored shirts: yellow, green, blue, or red. List all of the combinations of pants and shirts.

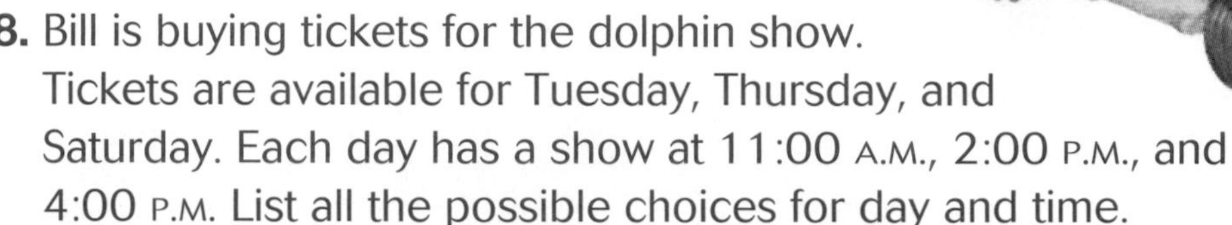

8. Bill is buying tickets for the dolphin show. Tickets are available for Tuesday, Thursday, and Saturday. Each day has a show at 11:00 A.M., 2:00 P.M., and 4:00 P.M. List all the possible choices for day and time.

Mixed Review

Try these or other strategies to solve each problem. Tell which strategy you used.

Problem-Solving Strategies

- *Make a List*
- *Work Backward*
- *Use Logical Reasoning*
- *Draw a Picture*

9. How much more did 6 bird key chains cost in 1999 than in 1995?

10. What was the cost of 3 fish key chains, 4 snake key chains, and 1 bird key chain in 1999?

Key Chains	1995 Price	1999 Price
Bird	\$2.39	\$2.75
Fish	\$1.98	\$2.29
Snake	\$2.59	\$3.00

11. Each locker has an even number and the lockers are numbered in order. If the number on the first locker is 2, what number is on the twenty-third locker?

12. A zookeeper gave 6 presentations about the care of lions. Each one lasted 15 minutes. By the end of the fourth presentation, how many minutes had the zookeeper talked?

Use Homework Workbook 5-6.

Multiplying Greater Numbers

California Content Standard *Number Sense 3.2 (🔑): Demonstrate an understanding of, and the ability to use, standard algorithms for multiplying a multidigit number by a two-digit number . . .. Also, Number Sense 3.3 (🔑); Mathematical Reasoning 2.1* *(See p. 161.)*

Warm-Up Review

1. 8×6
2. 2×3
3. 30×60
4. 400×60
5. 95×50
6. 38×52
7. Use rounding to estimate 89×35.
8. At $12 per hour, how much does it cost to rent a bike for 3 hours?

Math Link You know how to find 24 x 65. In this lesson you will learn how to multiply three-digit and four-digit numbers by two-digit numbers.

Example 1

Use the data at the right about how much a zoo elephant eats each day. How many carrots would the elephant eat in one year?

365	×	24	=	n
days per year		carrots per day		carrots in one year

You can use the same method you used in Lesson 5-5.

Step 1 Multiply by the ones. Regroup as needed.	**Step 2** Write a zero in the ones place. Multiply by the tens digit. Regroup as needed.	**Step 3** Add the products.
$\begin{array}{r} {}^{2\,2}\\ 365 \\ \times\ 24 \\ \hline 1{,}460 \end{array}$	$\begin{array}{r} {}^{1\,1}\\ {}^{2\,2}\\ 365 \\ \times\ 24 \\ \hline 1460 \\ 7300 \\ \hline \end{array}$	$\begin{array}{r} {}^{1\,1}\\ {}^{2\,2}\\ 365 \\ \times\ 24 \\ \hline 1460 \\ +\ 7300 \\ \hline 8{,}760 \end{array}$

Here's WHY It Works

$$\begin{aligned} 365 \times 24 &= 365 \times (20 + 4) \\ &= (365 \times 20) + (365 \times 4) \\ &= 7{,}300 + 1{,}460 \\ &= 8{,}760 \end{aligned}$$

The elephant would eat 8,760 carrots in one year.

<u>*Check*</u> by estimating. 400 *x* 20 = 8,000. The answer is reasonable because 8,760 is close to 8,000.

 Additional Standard: Algebra and Functions 1.1 *(See p. 161.)*

Example 2

Find 2,136 × 12.

Step 1 Multiply by the ones. Regroup as needed.	Step 2 Write a zero in the ones place. Multiply by the tens digit. Regroup as needed.	Step 3 Add the products.
$\begin{array}{r} \overset{1}{2,136} \\ \times\ 12 \\ \hline 4272 \end{array}$	$\begin{array}{r} 2,136 \\ \times\ 12 \\ \hline 4272 \\ 21360 \end{array}$	$\begin{array}{r} 2,136 \\ \times\ 12 \\ \hline 4272 \\ +\ 21360 \\ \hline 25,632 \end{array}$

Here's WHY It Works

$$\begin{aligned} 2,136 \times 12 &= 2,136 \times (10 + 2) \\ &= (2,136 \times 10) + (2,136 \times 2) \\ &= 21,360 + 4,272 \\ &= 25,632 \end{aligned}$$

Check by estimating. 2,000 × 10 = 20,000. Since both numbers were rounded down, the estimate will be less than the actual product. The answer is reasonable because 20,000 is close to 25,632 and also less than 25,632.

More Examples

A.
$$\begin{array}{r} 805 \\ \times\ 35 \\ \hline 4025 \\ 24150 \\ \hline 28,175 \end{array} \qquad \begin{array}{r} 805 \\ \times\ 5 \\ \hline 4,025 \end{array} \qquad \begin{array}{r} 805 \\ \times\ 30 \\ \hline 24,150 \end{array}$$

B.
$$\begin{array}{r} \$41.76 \\ \times\ 23 \\ \hline 12528 \\ 83520 \\ \hline \$960.48 \end{array} \qquad \begin{array}{r} 4176 \\ \times\ 3 \\ \hline 12,528 \end{array} \qquad \begin{array}{r} 4176 \\ \times\ 20 \\ \hline 83,520 \end{array}$$

Remember to show dollars and cents in the product.

Guided Practice

For another example, see Set E on p. 189.

1. $\begin{array}{r} 560 \\ \times\ 35 \\ \hline \end{array}$
2. $\begin{array}{r} 483 \\ \times\ 82 \\ \hline \end{array}$
3. $14.99 × 12
4. 23 × 3,409

5. Your dog eats 27 bags of dog food per year. If each bag costs $13.90, how much do you spend each year for dog food?

Independent Practice *For more practice, see Set E on p. 191.*

6. 624×13 **7.** 357×84 **8.** $4{,}341 \times 25$ **9.** $\$23.77 \times 16$

10. 215×63 **11.** 734×56 **12.** $3{,}687 \times 61$ **13.** $\$86.16 \times 28$

14. 268 × 34 **15.** 579 × 45 **16.** 62 × 743 **17.** 4,644 × 23

18. 81 × 2,226 **19.** $98.12 × 46 **20.** 51 × 2,072 **21.** 18,145 × 37

22. Use the data at the right. How much does it cost to rent the minivan for 14 days?

FAMILY RENT-A-CAR
SPECIAL
MINIVAN
7 DAYS
UNLIMITED MILEAGE
$ 291.30
See our friendly service representative for details.

23. Mental Math Is the product of 275 and 28 greater than or less than 10,000? Explain.

24. Algebra Solve $129x = 4{,}515$ by testing these values for x: 35, 45, 55.

Mixed Review

25. A bus makes 181 one-way trips per week. The bus seats 55 passengers. How many one-way trips does it make in one year? (1 year = 52 weeks)

26. Mental Math Compare: 58 × 20 ● 58 × 30

27. Algebra Evaluate $(25 \div 5) + n$ for $n = 31$.

28. Order from greatest to least: 1,062 1,261, 1,008

29. 81×40 **30.** 358×20 **31.** 95×18 **32.** 723×24

 **Test Prep** **Choose the correct letter for each answer.**

33. Write six million, four hundred seven thousand, twenty-five in standard form. (1-1)

A 64,725 **B** 6,400,725 **C** 6,407,025 **D** 6,470,025

34. Round 32,654 to the nearest thousand. (1-5)

F 33,000 **G** 32,000 **H** 31,000 **J** 30,000

 Use Homework Workbook 5-7.

LESSON 5-8

Understand
Plan
Solve
Look Back

Problem-Solving Application:

Using Operations

California Content Standard *Number Sense 3.0 (🔑) Students solve problems involving addition, subtraction, multiplication, and division of whole numbers and understand the relationship among the operations.*

Warm-Up Review

1. $53 + 27$
2. $298 - 49$
3. 8×7
4. 64×3
5. 72×50
6. 128×36
7. Last year, Jack earned $75 a month. He also was paid a $50 bonus at the end of the year. How much did Jack earn last year?

Example 1

The manatee is an endangered sea mammal. A mother manatee is pictured at the right. She is three times as long as her baby. How long is the baby manatee?

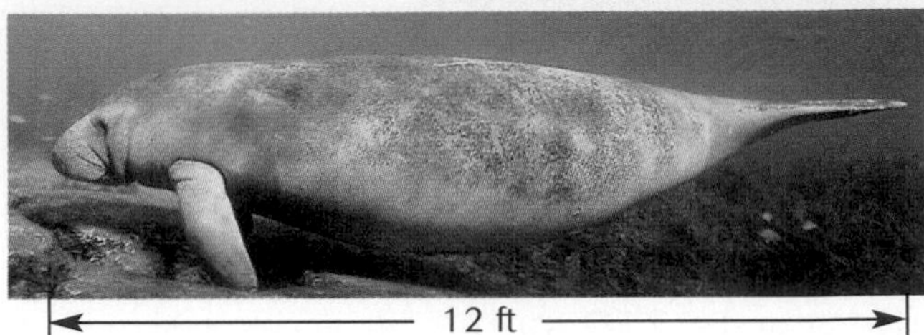

12 ft

Understand

What do you need to find?

You need to find the length of the baby manatee.

Plan

How can you solve the problem?

The problem suggests multiplication. You can **write a number sentence** to show the operation you will use.

Solve

Let n be the length in feet of the baby manatee.
Three times the baby's length is the mother's length.

$$3 \times \underset{\text{length of baby manatee}}{n} = \underset{\text{length of mother manatee}}{12}$$

$$n = 4$$

The baby manatee is 4 feet long.

Look Back

How could you check the answer?

Replace n with 4 in the number sentence. $3 \times 4 = 12$ checks. Then go back and reread the problem. Since the mother manatee is 12 feet long and $3 \times 4 = 12$, the answer is correct.

Additional Standards: Mathematical Reasoning 2.0; Algebra and Functions 1.1 *(See p. 161.)*

Example 2

Use the data at the right.

On the East Coast of Florida, how many more manatees were seen in 1992 than in 1991?

Find how many more manatees were seen in 1992.

manatees seen in 1992		manatees seen in 1991		difference in manatees
907	−	697	=	n

$$210 = n$$

There were 210 more manatees seen on the East Coast in 1992.

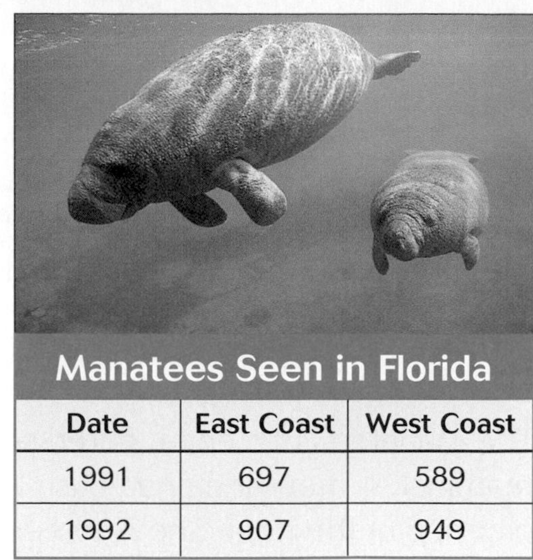

Manatees Seen in Florida

Date	East Coast	West Coast
1991	697	589
1992	907	949

Guided Practice

For Exercises 1–7, write a number sentence. Then solve.

1. A newborn manatee weighs 66 pounds. Its mother weighs 30 times as much. How much does the mother manatee weigh?

2. The typical life span of a lion is 15 years. This is 8 years longer than the life span of a kangaroo. How long does a kangaroo usually live?

Independent Practice

3. An adult manatee can eat 100 pounds of plants in one day. How many pounds can it eat in one week?

4. In a certain year, the Florida manatee population was only 2,019. Twenty years earlier there had been 2,481 more. What was the manatee population in Florida at the beginning of the 20-year period?

5. Fennecs, the smallest kind of foxes, are about 16 inches long. A red fox is about 25 inches long. What is the difference in length between a fennec and a red fox?

6. A wolf is one of the largest members of the dog family. The typical weight of a wolf is 90 pounds. A gray fox typically weighs 10 pounds. How much more does a wolf weigh than a gray fox?

7. Use the information in Exericse 6. The weight of a wolf is how many times the weight of the gray fox?

Mixed Review

Use the table at the right for Exercises 8 and 9.

8. The table shows the lowest elevations in four states. Write each as an integer. Then order the integers from least to greatest.

9. What is the difference in elevation between the highest and the lowest points in California?

State	Lowest Point	Highest Point
California	282 feet below sea level	14,495 feet above sea level
Colorado	3,350 feet above sea level	14,433 feet above sea level
Louisiana	5 feet below sea level	535 feet above sea level
Wyoming	3,100 feet above sea level	13,804 feet above sea level

10. The groceries Janice bought totaled \$37.32 and the tax was \$1.49. How much change should Janice receive from \$50.00?

11. Mr. Cooper bought a tube of toothpaste for \$2.50. The tax was \$0.15. If he used a coupon for \$0.55 off the price of the toothpaste, how much did he pay?

Use the pictograph for Exercises 12–14.

Distances Traveled to Warmer Climates	
Gray whale	● ● ● ● ● ●
White stork	● ● ● ● ● ● ● ●
Monarch butterfly	● ●
European eel	● ● ● ●

12. Which travels farther, the white stork or the gray whale?

13. How far does the European eel travel?

14. How much farther does a gray whale travel than a monarch butterfly?

Diagnostic Checkpoint

Complete. For Exercises 1–3, use the words from the Word Bank.

Word Bank
array
factors
product
tree diagram

1. The numbers you multiply are called __?__. (3-1)

2. The answer in multiplication is called the __?__. (3-1)

3. You can draw a(n) __?__ to help make a list. (5-6)

Find each answer.

4. (5-4) 25×10

5. (5-4) 74×60

6. (5-4) 251×80

7. (5-4) 325×60

8. (5-4) $5{,}560 \times 20$

9. (5-5) 34×12

10. (5-5) 22×53

11. (5-5) 76×38

12. (5-5) $\$0.95 \times 21$

13. (5-7) Find the product of 43 and 489.

14. (5-7) Find the product of 65 and 702.

15. (5-7) How many digits are there in the product of 1,352 and 18?

Algebra **Evaluate each expression for $m = 36$.**

16. (5-4) $20m$

17. (5-5) $18m$

18. (5-5) $91m$

19. (5-5) $521m$

20. (5-8) A video game costs $29. How much do 12 games cost?

21. (4-8) Admission to the fair is $5.25 for adults and $3.00 for children. Tia buys 2 adult tickets and 2 children's tickets with a $20 bill. How much change does she get back?

22. (5-6) Ann's mother tells her that she can choose one flower and one vase. The flower choices are roses, daisies, or lilies. The vases are either green or blue. What are the different ways Ann could choose one vase and one flower?

Chapter 5 Test

Use patterns with zeros to find each product.

1. 20 × 800 **2.** 700 × 700 **3** 50 × 6,000

Round each factor so that you can estimate the product mentally.

4. 72 × 35 **5.** 49 × 128 **6.** 506 × 64

7. 7,422 × 88 **8.** 367 × 99 **9.** 2,076 × 403

Find each product.

10. 24×20 **11.** 165×40 **12.** 88×60 **13.** $4,352 \times 70$ **14.** 709×30

15. $\$0.47 \times 23$ **16.** 200×65 **17.** $\$0.72 \times 47$ **18.** 65×82 **19.** 240×35

Solve.

20. A dog license costs $14. If a dog breeder buys 18 licenses, how much will she pay in all?

21. At the Belt Barn, men's belts come in sizes small, medium, large, and extra large. The colors are black or brown. List all possible choices.

22. To ensure they survive, people can adopt prairie dogs in name only, for $10 each. Suppose your school collects $4,500. Can it adopt 500 prairie dogs?

23. Nora bought a black Labrador puppy for $350 and a dog pen for $88. How much did she spend altogether?

24. Jim and Mary jog 12 miles a week. Is it reasonable to say that they jog 624 miles in a year? Estimate by finding a range.

25. There are 23 classrooms at Jefferson School. The principal ordered 25 new desks and 6 storage cabinets for each classroom. How many desks did the principal order?

TEST PREP

Multiple-Choice Chapter 5 Test

Choose the correct letter for each answer.

1. **Estimate 23 × 68.**

A 2,100
B 1,800
C 1,400
D 1,300

2. **Find the product of 30 × 55.**

F 1,550
G 1,650
H 1,660
J 16,500
K NH

3. **Which is the most reasonable estimate of 325 × 69?**

A 1,800
B 18,000
C 21,000
D 28,000

4. **Find the product of 20 × 800.**

F 160
G 1,600
H 16,000
J 160,000
K NH

5. **The drama club is making programs to sell at their performance of the variety show. It takes 10 sheets of paper to make each program. They want to make 85 programs. How many sheets of paper will they need?**

A 85,000 sheets
B 8,500 sheets
C 850 sheets
D 85 sheets
E NH

6. **A nursery has 45 rows of shrubs. Each row has 20 shrubs. How many shrubs are there in all?**

F 90 shrubs
G 245 shrubs
H 450 shrubs
J 900 shrubs
K NH

7. **Brandon read every day for 17 days. Each day he read 32 pages. How many pages did he read in all?**

A 544 pages
B 534 pages
C 424 pages
D 256 pages
E NH

8. **Find the product.**

$$\begin{array}{r} 84 \\ \times\ 36 \\ \hline \end{array}$$

F 3,024
G 3,018
H 3,014
J 756
K NH

---

9. **Mr. McGuire travels to his job 21 days a month. The total distance he travels each day is 53 miles. How many miles does he travel to his job in a month?**

A 813 miles
B 1,113 miles
C 1,120 miles
D 1,590 miles
E NH

---

10. **Find the product.**

$$\begin{array}{r} 4,286 \\ \times\ \ \ 17 \\ \hline \end{array}$$

F 34,288
G 72,862
H 72,876
J 75,262
K NH

---

11. **Which is the most reasonable estimate of 9,390 × 27?**

A 18,000
B 90,000
C 180,000
D 270,000

12.

Oak City Trains	
Train Number	Number of Trips per Month
1	258
2	311
3	609
4	472

If Train 3 carries 47 passengers each trip, how many passengers will it carry in a month?

F 28,576 passengers
G 28,623 passengers
H 28,693 passengers
J 28,923 passengers
K NH

---

13. **Mrs. Wong drives 78 miles each week for business. How many miles does she drive in one year? (Hint: There are 52 weeks in one year.)**

A 4,106 miles
B 4,056 miles
C 4,046 miles
D 130 miles
E NH

---

14. **Which will give a product with 6 digits?**

F 1,099 × 84
G 5,420 × 14
H 2,989 × 16
J 4,007 × 50
K NH

Reteaching

Set A (pages 162–163)

Find 60 × 400.

6 × 4 = 24
6 × 40 = 240
60 × 40 = 2,400
60 × 400 = 24,000

Find 50 × 800.

5 × 8 = 40
5 × 80 = 400
50 × 80 = 4,000
50 × 800 = 40,000

Remember that you can use basic facts and patterns with zeros to multiply multiples of ten.

1. 60 × 20 **2.** 40 × 400

3. 80 × 3,000 **4.** 300 × 5,000

5. 60 × 50 **6.** 20 × 900

7. 200 × 700 **8.** 3,000 × 90

9. 70 × 800 **10.** 30 × 4,000

Set B (pages 164–165)

Estimate the product of 586 and 32.

To the nearest hundred, 586 rounds to 600.

To the nearest ten, 32 rounds to 30.

586 × 32
(rounds to) (rounds to)
600 × 30 = 18,000

Remember to round 4-digit numbers to the nearest thousand, 3-digit numbers to the nearest hundred, and 2-digit numbers to the nearest ten.

Round each factor so that you can estimate the product mentally.

1. 53 × 29 **2.** 15 × 82

3. 426 × 38 **4.** 611 × 703

5. 817 × 5,501 **6.** 9,734 × 3,452

Set C (pages 170–171)

Find 827 × 30.

Step 1 Write a zero in the ones place.

$$\begin{array}{r} 827 \\ \times\ 30 \\ \hline 0 \end{array}$$

Step 2 Multiply by the tens digit.

$$\begin{array}{r} \scriptstyle 2 \\ 827 \\ \times\ 30 \\ \hline 24{,}810 \end{array}$$

Remember to estimate to check if the product is reasonable.

1. $\begin{array}{r} 55 \\ \times\ 30 \\ \hline \end{array}$ **2.** $\begin{array}{r} 38 \\ \times\ 70 \\ \hline \end{array}$

3. $\begin{array}{r} 712 \\ \times\ 60 \\ \hline \end{array}$ **4.** $\begin{array}{r} 1{,}699 \\ \times\ 20 \\ \hline \end{array}$

5. 64 × 50 **6.** 139 × 90

Set D *(pages 172–174)*

Find 49 × 26.

Think of 26 as 6 + 20.

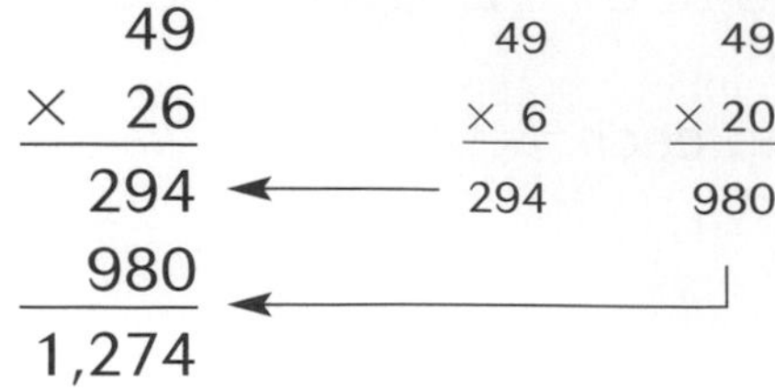

Remember to write the zero when you multiply by the tens digit.

1. 25×45
2. 19×32
3. 54×28
4. $\$0.53 \times 91$
5. 43×13
6. 37×44
7. $0.95 × 32
8. 46 × 62
9. 57 × 26
10. 78 × 39
11. 84 × 67
12. 92 × 51

Set E *(pages 178–180)*

Find 286 × 63.

Think of 63 as 3 + 60.

```
   286          286       286
 ×  63         × 3      ×  60
   858  <----   858    17,160
 17160  <------------------┘
18,018
```

Remember to show dollars and cents in the product when multiplying money.

1. 320×18
2. 776×42
3. $4{,}621 \times 35$
4. $6{,}085 \times 84$
5. $\$87.25 \times 19$
6. $13{,}624 \times 37$
7. 198 × 49
8. 93 × 704
9. $1.49 × 36
10. $9.20 × 14
11. 42 × $61.73
12. $42.21 × 87

More Practice

Set A *(pages 162–163)*

Find each product mentally.

1. 60×10 **2.** 9×20 **3.** 90×20 **4.** 20×900

5. 80×50 **6.** 800×50 **7.** 800×500 **8.** 5×40

9. 500×40 **10.** 700×70 **11.** $600 \times 10{,}000$ **12.** $5{,}000 \times 800$

13. If 39 students gathered 10 bags of acorns each, and each bag had 10 acorns, how many acorns did they find?

Set B *(pages 164–165)*

Round each factor so that you can estimate the product mentally.

1. 36×72 **2.** 41×17 **3.** 63×43 **4.** 37×109

5. 29×362 **6.** $3{,}010 \times 125$ **7.** $2{,}799 \times 45$ **8.** $39{,}000 \times 85$

9. At the science fair each grade displayed 135 projects. There were 6 grades. Estimate how many projects were displayed.

10. Is 31,192 a reasonable answer for 542×76? Estimate by finding a range.

Set C *(pages 170–171)*

1. 72×10 **2.** 29×20 **3.** 87×80 **4.** 38×60 **5.** 99×30

6. 577×40 **7.** 360×40 **8.** 298×50 **9.** 754×90 **10.** $2{,}922 \times 30$

11. 147×40 **12.** $\$326 \times 70$ **13.** 60×352 **14.** $90 \times 1{,}220$

15. Each of the 87 fourth graders earned $25.00 to donate to a wildlife organization. Estimate how much was earned by the fourth graders.

Set D (pages 172–174)

1. 76×32
2. 41×18
3. $\$0.92 \times 23$
4. 65×62
5. 37×43
6. 83×25
7. 745×56
8. $\$0.44 \times 97$
9. $\$0.26 \times 89$
10. $\$0.30 \times 67$

11. 36×18
12. 52×39
13. 55×75
14. $\$0.27 \times 37$

Algebra Evaluate each expression for $n = 53$.

15. $18n$
16. $62n$
17. $31n$
18. $76n$

19. The pet-store chain sold 48 pets a day for one 30-day month. Did they sell more or fewer than 1,500 pets that month?

Set E (pages 178–180)

1. 176×15
2. 295×65
3. 192×27
4. $3{,}005 \times 16$
5. $\$72.53 \times 65$
6. 541×51
7. $\$63.46 \times 89$
8. 964×38
9. 409×73
10. $3{,}706 \times 64$

11. 46×753
12. 561×18
13. $\$89.24 \times 42$
14. 47×209
15. 132×13
16. $3{,}900 \times 41$
17. 892×42
18. $47 \times 12{,}509$

19. **Algebra** Solve $201x = 6{,}432$ by testing these values for x: 24, 28, 32.

20. The fourth-grade class sold 550 animal booklets at the book fair. They charged 15 cents a booklet. Their goal was to make $100.00. Did they make their goal?

TEST PREP

Problem Solving: Preparing for Tests

Choose the correct letter for each answer.

---

1. Sally went to the store to buy supplies for school. She spent \$3.50 on pencils, \$4.25 on pens, and \$2.15 on note paper. How much money did Sally spend on pencils and pens?

A \$9.90

B \$7.75

C \$6.40

D \$5.75

> **Tip**
> Sometimes a problem gives information you don't need. Start by deciding what information in this problem you *do* need.

---

2. Kelley took a ride on a train that traveled 63 miles per hour. The train trip took exactly 11 hours. How can you find the distance Kelley traveled?

F Add 63 and 11.

G Subtract 11 from 63.

H Multiply 11 times 63.

J Divide 63 by 11.

> **Tip**
> Think about the action in the problem and then see which operation matches that action.

---

3. Patrick bought 16 tickets for a play. Each ticket cost \$18. Which number sentence could be used to find the change he got from \$300?

A $16 \times \$18 - \$300$

B $\$300 - 16$

C $\$300 - (16 \times \$18)$

D $\$300 - 16 - \$18$

> **Tip**
> When more than one step is needed to solve a problem, you must decide both *what* to do and in what *order* you should do it.

4. The cook at a restaurant bought 22 lb of spaghetti, 78 lb of oranges, 48 lb of grapes, and 34 lb of meat. About how many pounds of fruit did the cook buy?

F About 30 pounds
G About 130 pounds
H About 150 pounds
J About 180 pounds

5. Small cans of soup cost $1.08. Large cans of soup cost $2.99. About how much more does a large can cost than a small can?

A $4
B $3
C $2
D $1

6. A store has more puzzles than games, but fewer puzzles than books. There are 65 books. Which of the following is a reasonable conclusion?

F There are more books than games.
G There are more games than books.
H There are more than 65 games.
J There are more games than puzzles.

7. Shari earns $5.80 an hour for baby-sitting. Which shows how much money Shari will make if she baby-sits for 3 hours?

A $\$5.80 + \$5.80 = \blacksquare$
B $\$5.80 \times 3 = \blacksquare$
C $\$5.80 - \$3.00 = \blacksquare$
D $\$5.80 \div 3 = \blacksquare$

8. Terry is making a mural that is 15 feet wide. She uses a 1-foot strip of paper to divide the mural into 2 equal sections. How wide is each section of the mural?

F 4 ft
G 7 ft
H 12 ft
J 16 ft

9. Today Luanne has 45 magazines, 12 newspapers, and more than 85 books for sale in her shop. Which is reasonable for the number of items Luanne has in her shop today?

A Fewer than 120
B Between 120 and 130
C Between 130 and 140
D More than 140

10.

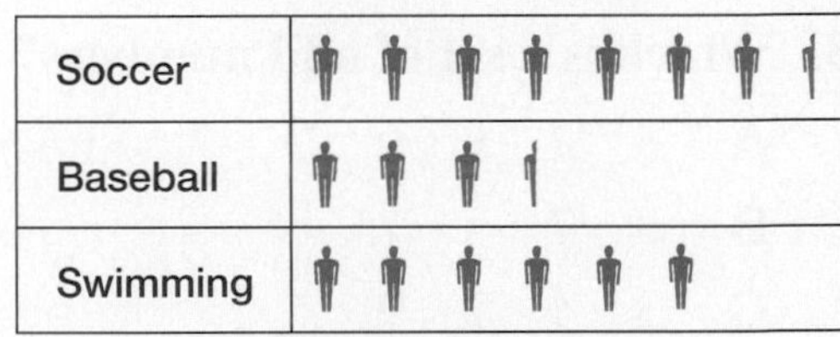

Look at the graph. How many more people picked soccer than swimming as their favorite sport?

F 20 more people
G 30 more people
H 60 more people
J 150 more people

Multiple-Choice Cumulative Review

Choose the correct letter for each answer.

Number Sense

1. What is 3,458 rounded to the nearest thousand?

A 3,000
B 3,400
C 3,500
D 4,000

2. Lauren wrote a number with a 2 in the ten thousands place and a 1 in the hundreds place. Which could be the number Lauren wrote?

F 4,231,334
G 4,233,134
H 4,323,134
J 4,324,314

3. Which is a set of odd numbers?

A 6 7 8 9
B 3 7 9 15
C 3 4 7 9
D 5 7 9 12

4. Which set of numbers is in order from *greatest* to *least?*

F 3,201 4,003 3,932 3,699
G 3,932 3,699 3,201 4,003
H 4,003 3,699 3,932 3,201
J 4,003 3,932 3,699 3,201

5. What is the quotient of 63 ÷ 7?

A 9
B 56
C 70
D 441
E NH

6. Annie read a 324-page book in one week. The next week she read a book about twice as long. *About* how many pages did she read in the 2 weeks?

F About 600 pages
G About 800 pages
H About 900 pages
J About 1,200 pages

7. Tina makes $11 a week on her paper route and $5 a week for baby-sitting. How much will Tina make in a year? (Hint: There are 52 weeks in a year.)

A $68.00
B $312.00
C $572.00
D $832.00

8. There are 27 girls and 18 boys camping at Camp Sunrise. Nine people can sleep in each cabin. How many cabins are needed for all the girls?

F 3 cabins
G 5 cabins
H 7 cabins
J 9 cabins

Algebra and Functions

9. What is the missing number in the number pattern?

2, 6, 18, 54, ■, 486

A 152 C 162
B 156 D 262

10. Which number line shows the graph of all whole numbers less than 9 and greater than 4?

F
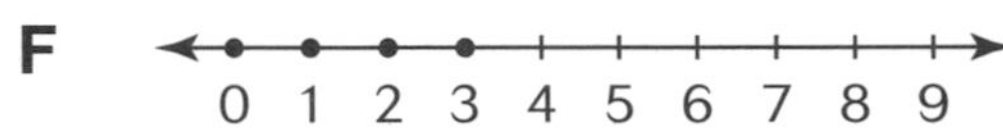

G
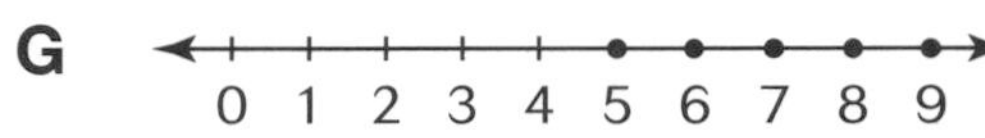

H
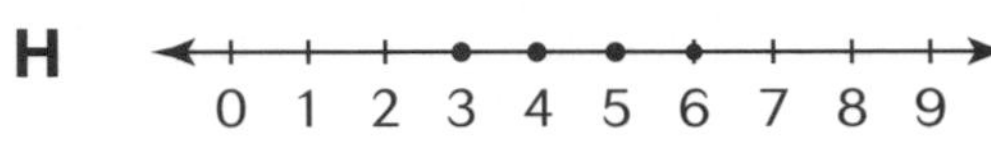

J
0 1 2 3 4 5 6 7 8 9

Use the table for Questions 11 and 12.

Number of Kites	Number of Sticks
1	2
2	4
3	6

11. How many sticks would you need to make 8 kites?

A 8 sticks C 12 sticks
B 10 sticks D 16 sticks

12. How many kites could you make with 20 sticks?

F 5 kites H 20 kites
G 10 kites J 40 kites

13. Find the value of $(7 \times n) - 19$ when $n = 35$.

A 264
B 226
C 112
D 23
E NH

14. If 98 of the 126 seats in a movie theater were filled, which number sentence could be used to find the number of empty seats?

F $126 \times 98 =$ ■
G ■ $- 98 = 126$
H $126 - 98 =$ ■
J $126 +$ ■ $= 98$

15. Evaluate the expression.

$$(2 \times 8) + (3 \times 9)$$

A 85
B 43
C 38
D 22
E NH

16. Which number makes this number sentence true?

9 ÷ ■ = 1

F 0
G 1
H 9
J 10

Dividing by One-Digit Divisors

Diagnosing Readiness

In Chapter 6, you will use these skills:

Ⓐ Adding Whole Numbers

(pages 42–46)

1. $36 + 9$
2. $49 + 23$
3. $103 + 88$
4. $255 + 317$
5. $4,809 + 375$
6. $8,064 + 1,243$

Ⓑ Subtracting Whole Numbers

(pages 47–53)

7. $48 - 25$
8. $63 - 37$
9. $146 - 89$
10. $214 - 176$
11. $795 - 288$
12. $403 - 124$
13. The auditorium at Harper School has 675 seats. If 148 seats were filled during a music concert, how many seats were empty?

C Multiplication Facts

(pages 84–86)

14. 5×7

15. 4×8

16. 6×9

17. 8×8

18. 3×7

19. 9×6

20. 8×5

21. 7×2

22. At a banquet there are 9 tables. Each table has a vase with 7 flowers. How many flowers are there?

D Division Facts

(pages 90–92)

23. $45 \div 9$

24. $56 \div 7$

25. $42 \div 6$

26. $32 \div 4$

27. $35 \div 5$

28. $72 \div 8$

29. $63 \div 7$

30. $36 \div 6$

31. $27 \div 9$

32. $12 \div 3$

33. Shari needs pieces of ribbon 3 inches long to make bows. She has 24 inches of ribbon. How many bows can she make?

E Estimating Products

(pages 132–133)

Estimate each product by rounding.

34. 2×439

35. 4×673

36. $1{,}249 \times 9$

37. $8{,}294 \times 3$

38. $6 \times 7{,}542$

39. About how many nails are in 4 boxes if each box contains 275 nails?

F Multiplying Whole Numbers

(pages 134–135)

40. $\begin{array}{r} 46 \\ \underline{\times 3} \end{array}$

41. $\begin{array}{r} 57 \\ \underline{\times 4} \end{array}$

42. $\begin{array}{r} 39 \\ \underline{\times 7} \end{array}$

43. $\begin{array}{r} 172 \\ \underline{\times \quad 5} \end{array}$

44. $\begin{array}{r} 342 \\ \underline{\times \quad 8} \end{array}$

45. $\begin{array}{r} 581 \\ \underline{\times \quad 9} \end{array}$

To the Family and Student

Looking Back	Chapter 6	Looking Ahead
In Chapter 3, students reviewed multiplication and division facts. $63 \div 9 = 7$	**Dividing One-Digit Divisors** In this chapter, students will learn how to divide multidigit numbers by one-digit numbers. $1{,}632 \div 4$	In Grade 5, students will learn how to divide by two-digit numbers. $2{,}347 \div 18$

Math and Everyday Living

Opportunities to apply the concepts of Chapter 6 abound in everyday situations. During the chapter, think about how dividing whole numbers can be used to solve a variety of real-world problems. The following examples suggest just several of the many situations that could launch a discussion about dividing whole numbers.

Math and Travel Your family is driving 225 miles to visit relatives. Without making any stops, can your family make the trip in 5 hours without breaking the speed limit?

Math at the Ball Park The baseball stadium in your city holds 48,000 people. The stadium has sections labeled A, B, C, D, E, F, G, and H. How many people can sit in each section if each section has the same number of seats?

Math and Gardening You want to plant tomatoes in your garden. You buy 4 flats with 6 tomato plants in each flat. Because of the size of your garden, you can only plant 5 tomato plants in each row. How many rows with 5 plants can you fill? How many plants will be in the last row?

Math and Shopping At a warehouse club, your family buys 24 cans of peas. Find all the ways you could arrange the cans on a shelf in equal rows.

Math and Sports The table shows the number of points you scored in the first 5 basketball games of the season. What is your average, or mean, number of points scored per game?

Game	Points
1	6
2	8
3	3
4	7
5	6

Math on a Picnic Your family buys a 6-foot submarine sandwich to eat at a picnic. Seven people need to share the sandwich equally. About how many inches long should you cut each piece? Remember, 1 foot = 12 inches.

California Content Standards in Chapter 6 Lessons*

	Teach and Practice	Practice
Number Sense		
1.4 (key) Decide when a rounded solution is called for and explain why such a solution may be appropriate.	6-4	
3.2 (key) Demonstrate an understanding of, and the ability to use, standard algorithms for . . . dividing a multidigit number by a one-digit number; use relationships between them to simplify computations and to check results.	6-1, 6-2, 6-3, 6-6, 6-7	6-5, 6-9
3.4 (key) Solve problems involving division of multidigit numbers by one-digit numbers.	6-2, 6-3, 6-6, 6-8, 6-10, 6-11	6-1, 6-4, 6-7
4.1 Understand that many whole numbers break down in different ways (e.g., $12 = 4 \times 3 = 2 \times 6 = 2 \times 2 \times 3$).	6-9	
4.2 (key) Know that numbers such as 2, 3, 5, 7, and 11 do not have any factors except 1 and themselves and that such numbers are called prime numbers.	6-9	
Algebra and Functions		
1.1 Use letters, boxes, or other symbols to stand for any number in simple expressions or equations (e.g., demonstrate an understanding and the use of the concept of a variable).		6-1, 6-2, 6-6, 6-12
2.0 (key) Students know how to manipulate equations.	6-12	
2.1 (key) Know and understand that equals added to equals are equal.	6-12	
2.2 (key) Know and understand that equals multiplied by equals are equal.	6-12	

	Teach and Practice	Practice
Statistics, Data Analysis, and Probability		
1.0 Students . . . interpret numerical and categorical data and clearly communicate their findings.		6-11
1.1 (Gr. 5) Know the concepts of mean	6-10, 6-11	
1.3 Interpret one- and two-variable data graphs to answer questions about a situation.		6-11
Mathematical Reasoning		
2.0 Students use strategies, skills, and concepts in finding solutions.		6-4, 6-8, 6-11
2.1 Use estimation to verify the reasonableness of calculated results.	6-5	
2.3 Use a variety of methods, such as words, numbers, symbols, charts, graphs, tables, diagrams, and models, to explain mathematical reasoning.		6-3, 6-7, 6-9
2.4 Express the solution clearly and logically by using the appropriate mathematical notation and terms and clear language; support solutions with evidence in both verbal and symbolic work.	6-8	
2.5 Indicate the relative advantages of exact and approximate solutions to problems and give answers to a specified degree of accuracy.	6-5	
2.6 Make precise calculations and check the validity of the results from the context of the problem.	6-4	
3.2 Note the method of deriving the solution and demonstrate a conceptual understanding of the derivation by solving similar problems.		6-8, 6-10
3.3 Develop generalizations of the results obtained and apply them in other circumstances.		6-5

* The symbol (key) indicates a key standard as designated in the Mathematics Framework for California Public Schools. Full statements of the California Content Standards are found at the beginning of this book following the Table of Contents.

Mental Math: Dividing Multiples of 10, 100, and 1,000

California Content Standard *Number Sense 3.2 (🔑): Demonstrate an understanding of, and the ability to use, standard algorithms for . . . dividing a multidigit number by a one-digit number; use relationships between them to simplify computations and to check results.*

Warm-Up Review

1. 6×2
2. 7×9
3. $12 \div 4$
4. $40 \div 8$
5. 6×30
6. 2×50
7. 7×900
8. $5 \times 6{,}000$
9. Applegate Theater sold 400 tickets at \$8 each and 200 tickets at \$5 each. How much money did the theater take in from ticket sales?

Math Link You know how to find $18 \div 6$. Now you will learn how to find quotients like $18{,}000 \div 6$.

Example 1

Find $18{,}000 \div 6$.

Use a basic fact and look for a pattern with zeros.

$$18 \div 6 = 3$$
$$180 \div 6 = 30$$
$$1{,}800 \div 6 = 300$$
$$18{,}000 \div 6 = 3{,}000$$

Here's WHY It Works

18 ÷ 6 = 3
180 ÷ 6 = 18 tens ÷ 6 = 3 tens = 30
1,800 ÷ 6 = 18 hundreds ÷ 6 = 3 hundreds = 300
18,000 ÷ 6 = 18 thousands ÷ 6 = 3 thousands = 3,000

18,000 (**dividend**) ÷ 6 (**divisor**) = 3,000 ← **quotient**

<u>Check</u> by using related multiplication sentences.

$3 \times 6 = 18 \rightarrow 18 \div 6 = 3$
$30 \times 6 = 180 \rightarrow 180 \div 6 = 30$
$300 \times 6 = 1{,}800 \rightarrow 1{,}800 \div 6 = 300$
$3{,}000 \times 6 = 18{,}000 \rightarrow 18{,}000 \div 6 = 3{,}000$

Example 2

Find $2{,}000 \div 5$.

$$20 \div 5 = 4$$
$$200 \div 5 = 40$$
$$2{,}000 \div 5 = 400$$

When the dividend of the basic fact includes a zero, that zero is not part of the pattern.

Additional Standards: Number Sense 3.4 (🔑); Algebra and Functions 1.1 *(See p. 199.)*

Guided Practice *For another example, see Set A on p. 238.*

1. 60 ÷ 3 **2.** 280 ÷ 4 **3.** 630 ÷ 7 **4.** 4,000 ÷ 8 **5.** 48,000 ÷ 6

6. A printer shipped 3,200 theater programs in 8 boxes. How many programs were in each box?

Independent Practice *For more practice, see Set A on p. 241.*

7. 80 ÷ 4 **8.** 900 ÷ 3 **9.** 560 ÷ 8 **10.** 300 ÷ 5

11. 6,000 ÷ 6 **12.** 1,800 ÷ 9 **13.** 40,000 ÷ 5 **14.** 64,000 ÷ 8

A movie studio stores its old costumes in boxes, 5 costumes to a box. Use the table at the right to solve Exercises 15 and 16.

Old Costumes	
Type of Movie	**Number**
Western	450
Science fiction	1,000
Musical	400
Historical	350

15. How many boxes are needed to pack the costumes from science fiction movies?

16. How many more boxes are needed for the costumes from westerns than for the costumes from musicals?

17. Algebra Find the value of $\frac{n}{9}$ when n is 7,200.

18. Math Reasoning If $28 \div n = 4$, what is the value of $2{,}800 \div n$?

Mixed Review

19. Marta spent $4.68 on office supplies. She bought 17 boxes of envelopes with 50 envelopes in each box. How many envelopes did she buy?

20. 7,820 + 2,944 **21.** 49 × 21 **22.** $1.57 × 4 **23.** $31.07 × 24

24. 674 × 35 **25.** 5,007 − 3,618 **26.** 52 × 38 **27.** 200 × 6,000

Test Prep **Choose the correct letter for each answer.**

28. (1-6) Find the missing number.
0, ⁻1, ⁻2, ■, ⁻4, ⁻5

A ⁻6 **C** ⁻3
B 3 **D** ⁻1

29. (3-8) **Algebra** Find the value of $6n$ when $n = 8$.

F 48 **H** 36
G 14 **J** 68

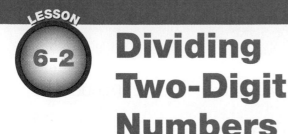

Dividing Two-Digit Numbers

California Content Standard *Number Sense 3.2 (🔑): Demonstrate an understanding of, and the ability to use, standard algorithms for . . . dividing a multidigit number by a one-digit number . . .. Also, Number Sense 3.4 (🔑)* *(See p. 199.)*

Math Link You can divide multiples of 10. In this lesson you will divide other 2-digit numbers.

Warm-Up Review

1. $8 - 5$
2. 9   7
3. 6×5
4. 34×7
5. $18 \div 2$
6. $480 \div 8$
7. 54 = ■ tens ■ ones
8. 1 ten 7 ones = ■ ones
9. There are 20 offices on the first floor of city hall. If 4 people work in each of these offices, how many people work in the offices on the first floor?

Example 1

During an ice show, a circle of 24 skaters separates into 2 rows. If each row has the same number of skaters, how many skaters are in each row?

24	÷	2	=	n
total number of skaters		number of rows		skaters per row

Step 1 Think about dividing 2 tens 4 ones into 2 equal groups.

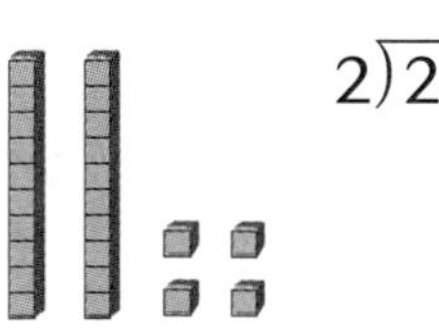

Step 2 Divide 2 tens into 2 equal groups. There are no tens left over.

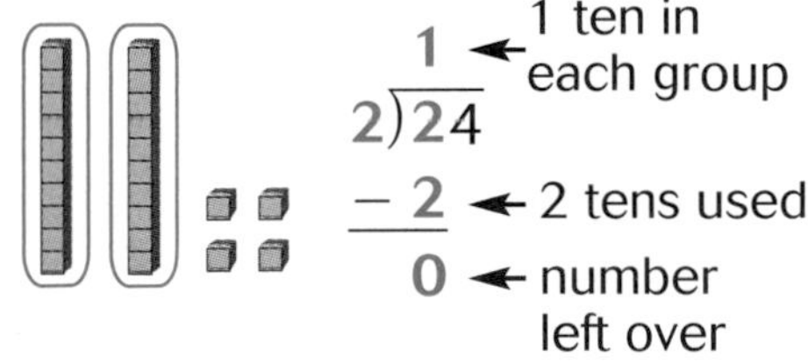

Step 3 Divide 4 ones equally among the 2 groups. There are no ones left over. So $24 \div 2 = 12$.

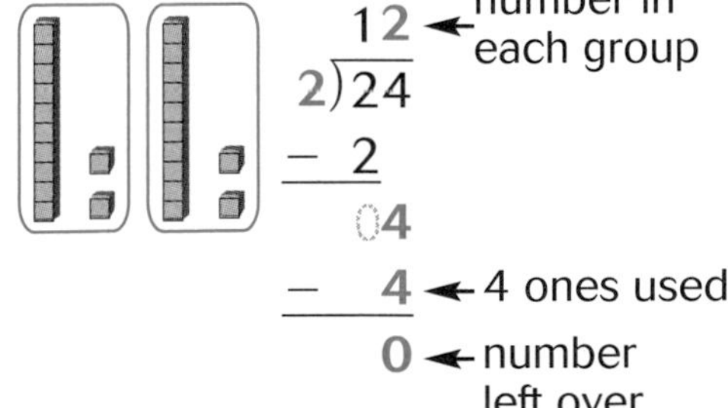

Here's WHY It Works

$$\begin{aligned} 24 \div 2 &= (20 + 4) \div 2 \\ &= (20 \div 2) + (4 \div 2) \\ &= 10 + 2 \\ &= 12 \end{aligned}$$

There are 12 skaters in each row.

Check the answer by multiplying the quotient by the divisor. Since $12 \times 2 = 24$, and the product is the dividend, the answer is correct.

Additional Standard: Algebra and Functions 1.1 *(See p. 199.)*

Example 2

Find $42 \div 3$.

Step 1 Think about dividing 4 tens 2 ones into 3 equal groups.

$3\overline{)42}$

Step 2 Divide 4 tens into 3 equal groups. There is 1 ten left over.

$$\begin{array}{r} 1 \\ 3\overline{)42} \\ -\ 3 \\ \hline 1 \end{array}$$

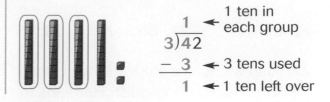

1 ten in each group; 3 tens used; 1 ten left over

Step 3 Regroup the 1 ten as 10 ones. Now there are 12 ones altogether.

$$\begin{array}{r} 1 \\ 3\overline{)42} \\ -\ 3\downarrow \\ \hline 12 \end{array}$$

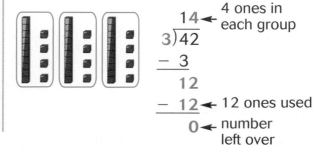

Step 4 Divide 12 ones equally among the 3 groups. There are no ones left over.

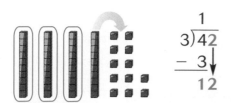

$$\begin{array}{r} 14 \\ 3\overline{)42} \\ -\ 3 \\ \hline 12 \\ -\ 12 \\ \hline 0 \end{array}$$

4 ones in each group; 12 ones used; number left over

Here's WHY It Works

$$\begin{aligned} 42 \div 3 &= (40 + 2) \div 3 \\ &= (30 + 12) \div 3 \\ &= (30 \div 3) + (12 \div 3) \\ &= 10 + 4 \\ &= 14 \end{aligned}$$

Check the answer by multiplying the quotient by the divisor. Since $14 \times 3 = 42$, and this equals the dividend, the answer is correct.

Guided Practice *For another example, see Set B on p. 238.*

1. $3\overline{)39}$ **2.** $4\overline{)96}$ **3.** $2\overline{)74}$ **4.** $88 \div 8$ **5.** $91 \div 7$

6. There are 47 men and 31 women going on a ski trip. The trip to the ski lodge is 85 miles. How many cars will be needed to transport the people if each car holds 6 people?

Independent Practice *For more practice, see Set B on p. 241.*

7. $2\overline{)28}$ **8.** $4\overline{)92}$ **9.** $3\overline{)48}$ **10.** $5\overline{)55}$ **11.** $2\overline{)36}$

12. $3\overline{)75}$ **13.** $5\overline{)75}$ **14.** $4\overline{)48}$ **15.** $7\overline{)84}$ **16.** $2\overline{)82}$

17. 51 ÷ 3 **18.** 70 ÷ 2 **19.** 87 ÷ 3 **20.** 99 ÷ 9 **21.** 60 ÷ 4

22. 81 ÷ 3 **23.** 86 ÷ 2 **24.** 90 ÷ 6 **25.** 68 ÷ 4 **26.** 96 ÷ 8

27. Julio will earn a trophy if he reads all 32 books on the library's Best Books list. He plans to read 2 books per week. How long will it take him to read all the books?

28. Last year there were 4 secretaries and 36 teachers at Harrison School. This year there are 40 teachers. How many more teachers are there this year?

29. Algebra Solve: $3x = 57$ by testing these values for x: 15, 19, 25.

Mixed Review

30. Order the game scores from least to greatest.

31. Round Rita's score to the nearest thousand.

Game Scores	
Player	**Score**
Glenn	22,050
Rita	19,800
Keoni	17,400
Lucille	18,800

32. Mr. Nathenson is planting rows of tomato plants. He has 160 plants. If there are 8 plants in each row, how many rows will he plant in all?

33. Write five million, one hundred twelve thousand in standard form.

34. 490 ÷ 7 **35.** 6,022 × 28 **36.** 75 × 347 **37.** 3,000 ÷ 5

38. Mental Math Find 3,400 − 1,998.

Test Prep Choose the correct letter for each answer.

39. What is the value of the underlined digit in 7<u>6</u>4,980?
(1-1)

A 6,000 **B** 700,000 **C** 10,000 **D** 60,000 **E** NH

40. Choose the best estimate for 6 × 718.
(4-3)

F 420 **G** 4,200 **H** 4,800 **J** 42,000 **K** NH

LESSON 6-3

Dividing Two-Digit Numbers with Remainders

Warm-Up Review

1. 12 − 7
2. 54 + 9
3. 70 − 63
4. 53 − 47
5. 5 × 4
6. 72 ÷ 8
7. 42 ÷ 6
8. 37 × 7
9. Which digit is in the tens place in 58?
10. If Ben puts 3 flowers in a vase, how many vases can he fill with 54 flowers?

California Content Standard *Number Sense 3.2 (🔑): Demonstrate an understanding of, and the ability to use, standard algorithms for . . . dividing a multidigit number by a one-digit number . . .. Also, Number Sense 3.4 (🔑)* *(See p. 199.)*

Math Link You have learned how to divide some numbers evenly. In this lesson you will learn what to do when there are some ones left over.

Example 1

There are 73 girls in the all-girls choir. How many trios can be formed? Will there be any girls left over?

Group	Number of Singers
Duet	2
Trio	3
Quartet	4
Quintet	5

Find 73 ÷ 3.

Step 1 Divide the tens. Write the first digit of the quotient above the tens place of the dividend.

```
  2 ← 2 tens in each group
3)73
```

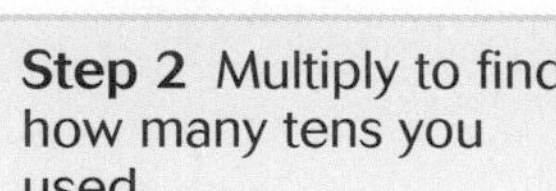

Step 2 Multiply to find how many tens you used.

```
  2
3)73
  6 ← 2 tens × 3
```

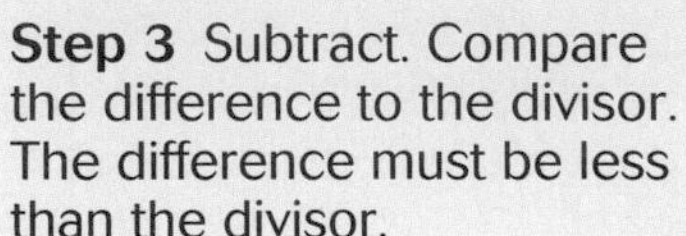

Step 3 Subtract. Compare the difference to the divisor. The difference must be less than the divisor.

```
  2
3)73
 −6
  1 ← 1 < 3
```

Step 4 Bring down the ones. Divide.

```
  24 ← 4 ones in each group
3)73
 −6↓
  13
```

Step 5 Multiply to find how many ones you used.

```
  24
3)73
 −6
  13
  12 ← 4 ones × 3
```

Step 6 Subtract and compare. There is 1 one left over. This is the remainder.

```
  24 R1 ← Remainder
3)73
 −6
  13
 −12
   1 ← 1 one left over
```

Twenty-four trios can be formed. There will be 1 girl left over.

Additional Standard: Mathematical Reasoning 2.3 *(See p. 199.)*

Check the answer by multiplying the quotient by the divisor and adding the remainder.

Original problem	Multiply the quotient by the divisor.	Then add the remainder.
$3\overline{)73}$ = 24 R1	$\overset{1}{24} \times 3 = 72$	$72 + 1 = 73$ ← If this matches the dividend, you divided correctly.

When you divide a two-digit number by a one-digit number, the quotient will have either one or two digits. In the first example, the quotient has two digits. In the next example, the quotient has one digit.

Example 2

Find 39 ÷ 5.

Step 1 There are not enough tens to divide into 5 groups. So regroup 3 tens 9 ones as 39 ones. Divide. Write the quotient above the ones place of the dividend.

7 ← 7 ones in each group
$5\overline{)39}$

Step 2 Multiply to find how many ones you used. Subtract and compare.

7
$5\overline{)39}$
− 35 ← 7 ones × 5
4 ← 4 ones left over

Step 2 Since there are no more digits in the divisor to bring down, you are done dividing. Write 4 as the remainder.

7 R4 ← Remainder
$5\overline{)39}$
− 35
4

Check the answer. 7 × 5 = 35, and 35 + 4 = 39. Since this result equals the dividend, the answer, 7 R4, is correct.

More Examples

A.

34 R1
$2\overline{)69}$
− 6
09
− 8
1

If there are enough tens to divide, write the first digit of the quotient over the tens place of the dividend.

Check by multiplying and adding.
34 × 2 = 68, and 68 + 1 = 69.

B.

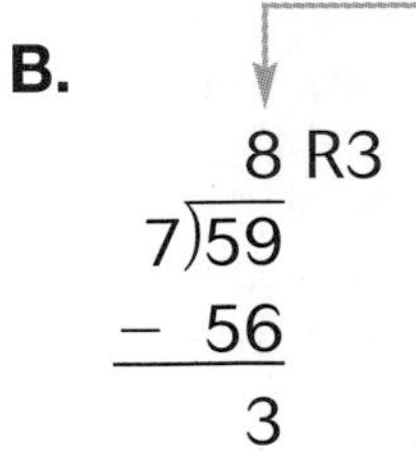

If there are not enough tens to divide, write the first digit of the quotient over the ones place of the dividend.

Check by multiplying and adding.
8 × 7 = 56, and 56 + 3 = 59.

Guided Practice

For another example, see Set C on p. 238.

1. $2\overline{)29}$ **2.** $3\overline{)83}$ **3.** $7\overline{)54}$ **4.** $4\overline{)87}$ **5.** $9\overline{)60}$

6. Mr. Kim collected 54 seashells and 19 pine cones. He wants to give the same number of seashells to each of his 4 children, and he wants to give away as many as possible. How many would each child get? How many would be left over?

Independent Practice

For more practice, see Set C on p. 241.

7. $4\overline{)51}$ **8.** $3\overline{)70}$ **9.** $2\overline{)53}$ **10.** $5\overline{)47}$ **11.** $4\overline{)34}$

12. $6\overline{)77}$ **13.** $5\overline{)74}$ **14.** $2\overline{)99}$ **15.** $8\overline{)27}$ **16.** $6\overline{)68}$

17. 78 ÷ 4 **18.** 93 ÷ 5 **19.** 20 ÷ 3 **20.** 69 ÷ 8 **21.** 38 ÷ 9

22. 31 ÷ 7 **23.** 88 ÷ 8 **24.** 50 ÷ 7 **25.** 87 ÷ 2 **26.** 78 ÷ 5

Use the table in Example 1 for Exercises 27 and 28.

27. The men's chorus has 29 members. How many quintets can be formed? How many singers will be left over?

28. Sixteen quartets sang at a music festival. How many singers were there in all?

29. Math Reasoning If you divide a number by 5, explain why the remainder cannot be 6.

Mixed Review

30. A painter uses 5 gallons of paint to paint the walls of a classroom and 1 gallon to paint the ceiling. How many gallons of paint are needed to paint 34 classrooms?

31. $6\overline{)84}$ **32.** 320 ÷ 8 **33.** 72 ÷ 2 **34.** $\begin{array}{r} \$14.62 \\ \times\ 27 \\ \hline \end{array}$ **35.** $\begin{array}{r} 561 \\ -\ 283 \\ \hline \end{array}$

Test Prep Choose the correct letter for each answer.

36. 3 × (4 + 6) =
(3-6)

A 13 **C** 30
B 18 **D** 72
E NH

37. Algebra If 56 + x = 94, then x =
(2-11)

F 150 **H** 48
G 140 **J** 38

Problem-Solving Skill:

Interpreting Remainders

Warm-Up Review

1. 4 × 7 **2.** 5 × 8

3. 24 ÷ 3 **4.** 81 ÷ 9

5. 31 ÷ 7 **6.** 89 ÷ 4

7. Laura has $14.87, Sandy has $5.09, and Tamara has $11.95. Together, do the girls have enough money to buy a boom box that costs $35?

California Content Standard *Number Sense 1.4 (🔑): Decide when a rounded solution is called for and explain why such a solution may be appropriate. Also, Mathematical Reasoning 2.6 (See p. 199.)*

Read For Understanding

Forty children are in a play at the New Star Theater. Straw hats are sold in boxes of 4 hats each, and no hat can be bought individually.

Props for Play	
Prop	**Quantity**
Wigs	36
Straw hats	23
Crown	1
Masks	10

1. How many straw hats are needed?
2. How many straw hats are sold in each box?
3. Would it be possible to buy just 3 straw hats? Explain why or why not.

Think and Discuss

Interpreting Remainders

When you divide to solve a problem, a remainder can affect the answer. Sometimes a remainder means the quotient should be rounded up to the next number. Sometimes a remainder is the solution. Sometimes a remainder should be ignored.

4. If you buy 5 boxes of straw hats, will there be enough hats for the show? Why or why not?
5. What is the least number of boxes of straw hats you could order and still have enough hats for the show? Write a division sentence to help you find the answer.
6. Look back at your solution to Exercise 5. Explain what you did with the remainder.

Additional Standards: Number Sense 3.4 (🔑); Mathematical Reasoning 2.0 (See p. 199.)

Guided Practice

Costume designers want to buy striped shirts for some of the actors. They have $40 to spend, and each shirt costs $7. They want to buy as many shirts as possible.

1. Which of the following statements is true?
   a. The shirt costs $40.
   b. There is enough money to buy more than one shirt.
   c. There is not enough money to buy any shirt.

2. Which of the following sentences could you use to find how many shirts can be bought?
   a. $40 \div 4 = \blacksquare$
   b. $40 \div 7 = \blacksquare$
   c. $7 \div 40 = \blacksquare$

3. How can the remainder from Exercise 2 help you to know how many shirts can be bought?
   a. Use it to round the quotient up.
   b. Add it to the quotient.
   c. Ignore it.

Independent Practice

Three yards of cloth are needed for each cape the children in the play will wear. The director of the play wants to make as many capes as possible from 14 yards of cloth. The leftover cloth will be used to make scarfs.

4. Which helps you find how many capes can be made?
   a. $14 \div 6 = 2$ R2
   b. $14 \div 5 = 2$ R4
   c. $14 \div 3 = 4$ R2

5. How many capes can be made?
   a. 3 capes
   b. 4 capes
   c. 5 capes

6. **Math Reasoning** What does the remainder in Exercise 4 stand for?

Juice for the cast party costs $4 per bottle. The director wants to buy as many bottles as possible for $35 and use the rest of the money for balloons.

7. Which helps you find how much money will be spent on balloons?
   a. $35 \div 8 = 4$ R3
   b. $35 \div 6 = 5$ R5
   c. $35 \div 4 = 8$ R3

8. How much money will be spent on balloons?
   a. $3
   b. $4
   c. $5

Diagnostic Checkpoint

1. 80 ÷ 4 (6-1)
2. 90 ÷ 3 (6-1)
3. 350 ÷ 7 (6-1)
4. 200 ÷ 5 (6-1)

5. 1,800 ÷ 2 (6-1)
6. 6,300 ÷ 7 (6-1)
7. 6,400 ÷ 8 (6-1)
8. 49,000 ÷ 7 (6-1)

9. $4\overline{)76}$ (6-2)
10. $3\overline{)57}$ (6-2)
11. $5\overline{)75}$ (6-2)
12. $4\overline{)68}$ (6-2)

13. $3\overline{)41}$ (6-3)
14. $8\overline{)67}$ (6-3)
15. $3\overline{)64}$ (6-3)
16. $7\overline{)81}$ (6-3)

17. 85 ÷ 6 (6-3)
18. 99 ÷ 4 (6-3)
19. 73 ÷ 8 (6-3)
20. 57 ÷ 9 (6-3)

21. (6-4) Steve and Ben are setting up chairs for a play. They have 75 chairs to put in rows of 8 each. How many chairs will be left over?

22. (6-2) A small symphony orchestra has 87 musicians.There are 45 people in the string section. Each of the three other sections has an equal number of musicians. How many musicians are in each of the other three sections of the orchestra?

23. (6-4) You can record 4 movies on a long-playing videotape. Will 14 videotapes be enough to record 58 movies? Why or why not?

24. (6-4) You have 24 gallons of lemonade for a family reunion picnic. How many 5-gallon containers can you fill?

25. (6-1) A manufacturer shipped 2,100 baseballs in 7 boxes. If each box had the same number of baseballs, how many baseballs were in each box?

26. (6-4) You have 26 feet of yarn. If you cut the yarn into 3 foot pieces, how many full three foot long pieces are there?

27. (6-4) You have $47 that you can use to buy games. Each game costs $9. How many games can you buy?

28. (6-4) How many dining tables are needed for 85 people, if 8 people can sit at each table?

Multiple-Choice Cumulative Review

Choose the correct letter for each answer.

1. Matthew's dog Tip weighed 13 pounds when Matthew got him. In the first year, Tip gained 45 pounds and grew 6 inches. In the second year he grew 3 more inches and gained 40 pounds. How much did Tip weigh then?

A 85 lb
B 98 lb
C 102 lb
D 106 lb

2. Which number sentence shows how you would divide 68 dancers into 4 equal groups?

F $68 + 4$
G $68 - 4$
H 4×68
J $68 \div 4$

3. How many more sides does an octagon have than a pentagon?

A 3
B 5
C 7
D 8

4. Find 2,028 − 354.

F 1,674
G 1,774
H 2,334
J 2,774
K NH

5. A small theater holds 75 people. There are 3 sold-out performances this weekend. How much money is collected if tickets cost $30 each?

A $225
B $675
C $2,250
D $6,750
E NH

6. Which is the best estimate of 4 × 379?

F 1,000
G 1,200
H 1,600
J 2,000

7. Which shows a line of symmetry?

A 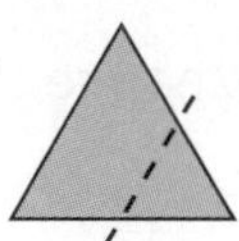
C 
B 
D 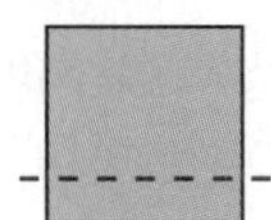

8. The movie started at 7:20 P.M. and ended at 9:15 P.M. How long did the movie last?

F 2 hours 5 minutes
G 1 hour 55 minutes
H 1 hour 50 minutes
J 1 hour 20 minutes

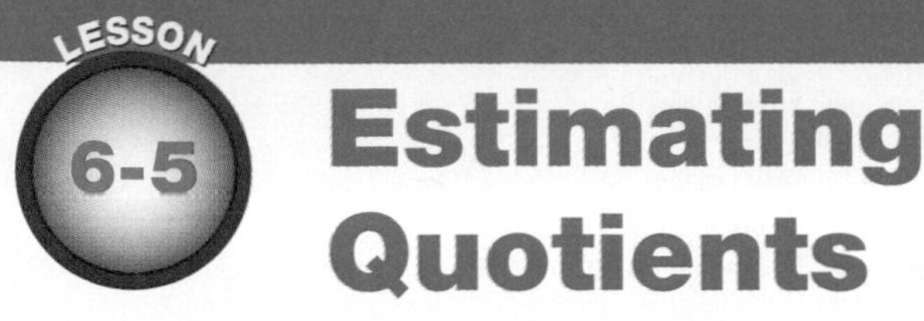

Lesson 6-5 Estimating Quotients

Warm-Up Review

1. 25 ÷ 5 **2.** 63 ÷ 9

3. 80 ÷ 4 **4.** 90 ÷ 3

5. 720 ÷ 8 **6.** 420 ÷ 6

7. A movie theater is giving away 450 free tickets to 3 schools. How many tickets does each school receive if each school receives the same number of tickets?

California Content Standard *Mathematical Reasoning 2.1 Use estimation to verify the reasonableness of calculated results. Also, Mathematical Reasoning 2.5 (See p. 199.)*

Math Link You have learned how to do division problems like 3,600 ÷ 9 and 75 ÷ 5. Now you will use these skills to estimate quotients.

Word Bank

compatible numbers

Example 1

Estimate 331 ÷ 8.

One way to estimate is to use **compatible numbers**. For division problems, compatible numbers are numbers that are easy to divide mentally.

Find a number close to the dividend that can be divided evenly by 8. Use basic facts to help you.

331 ÷ 8 ↓	Think: 32 ÷ 8 = 4, so 320 and 8 are compatible numbers.
320 ÷ 8 = 40	Change 331 to 320 and divide.

331 ÷ 8 is about 40.

Check by multiplying. 40 × 8 = 320, and 320 is close to the original dividend, 331. So, 40 is a reasonable estimate.

Example 2

Is 521 a reasonable answer for 2,084 ÷ 4? Estimate to decide. Find a number close to the dividend that can be divided evenly by 4.

2,084 ÷ 4 ↓	Think: 20 ÷ 4 = 5, so 2,000 and 4 are compatible numbers.
2,000 ÷ 4 = 500	Change 2,084 to 2,000 and divide.

The answer 521 is reasonable because 521 is close to the estimate, 500.

Additional Standards: Number Sense 3.2(🔑); Mathematical Reasoning 3.3 (See p. 199.)

Guided Practice *For another example, see Set D on p. 239.*

Estimate each quotient. Tell the numbers you used.

1. 23 ÷ 6 **2.** 55 ÷ 9 **3.** 281 ÷ 3 **4.** 389 ÷ 5 **5.** 2,934 ÷ 7

6. Mrs. Aran's factory canned 456 cases of apple juice in 8 hours. She recorded the hourly production as 43 cases per hour. Use estimation to decide if her report is reasonable.

Independent Practice *For more practice, see Set D on p. 242.*

Estimate each quotient. Tell the numbers you used.

7. 31 ÷ 4 **8.** 37 ÷ 8 **9.** 17 ÷ 2 **10.** 119 ÷ 3 **11.** 347 ÷ 6

12. 583 ÷ 7 **13.** 257 ÷ 9 **14.** 450 ÷ 6 **15.** 2,466 ÷ 8 **16.** 2,893 ÷ 5

17. Estimate the number of hours per month that sports programs are viewed.

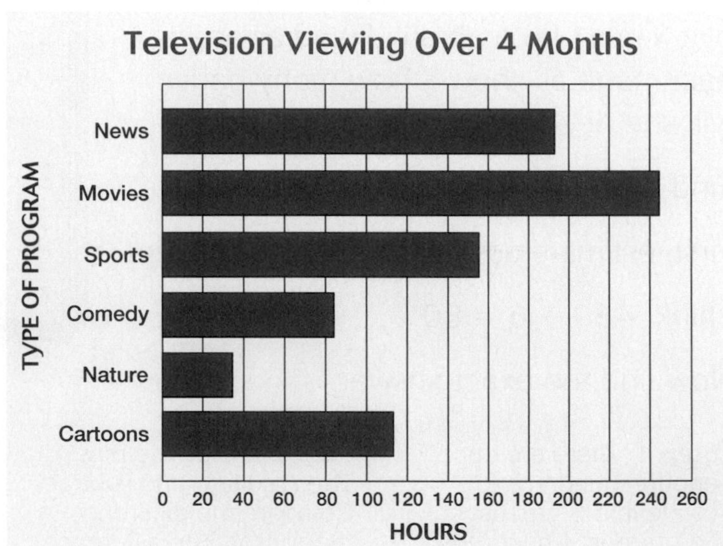

18. Jillian read that people watch 21 hours of comedies per month. According to the graph, is that reasonable?

19. Math Reasoning How can you tell if your estimate is greater than or less than the exact quotient?

Mixed Review

20. Algebra Evaluate the expression $n - 48$ for $n = 360$.

21. $5\overline{)22}$ **22.** 64 ÷ 4 **23.** 40 ÷ 6 **24.** $2\overline{)79}$

Test Prep **Choose the correct letter for the answer.**

25. 104,671 + 28,965 =
(2-4)

A 123,636 **B** 133,526 **C** 133,636 **D** 394,321 **E** NH

Dividing Multidigit Numbers

Warm-Up Review

1. 7×8 **2.** 4×5

3. $18 \div 3$ **4.** $54 \div 9$

5. 51×7 **6.** 813×3

7. $85 \div 5$ **8.** $70 \div 6$

9. Estimate $650 \div 8$.

10. Eunice has 34 pretzels to divide evenly among herself and 3 friends. How many pretzels will each person get? How many will be left over?

California Content Standard *Number Sense 3.2 (🔑): Demonstrate an understanding of, and the ability to use, standard algorithms for . . . dividing a multidigit number by a one-digit number . . .. Also, Number Sense 3.4 (🔑)* *(See p. 199.)*

Math Link You know how to divide two-digit numbers. In this lesson you will learn how to divide three-digit and four-digit numbers.

Example 1

Ms. Waterleaf has 474 snapshots to place in a photo album. If she arranges each page as shown, how many pages will she need?

Find $474 \div 6$.

First, estimate using compatible numbers.

Think: $480 \div 6 = 80$

Now find the exact answer.

Step 1 There are not enough hundreds to divide into 6 groups. So regroup 4 hundreds 7 tens as 47 tens.

```
6)474
```

Step 2 Divide the tens. Then multiply and subtract. Compare the difference to the divisor. The difference must be less than the divisor.

```
   7
6)474
 - 42 ← 7 tens × 6
    5 ← 5 < 6
```

Step 3 Bring down the ones. Divide. Then multiply and subtract. The remainder is 0.

```
   79
6)474
 - 42↓
    54
  - 54 ← 9 ones × 6
     0
```

Ms. Waterleaf will need 79 pages.

The answer, 79, is close to the estimate, so the answer is reasonable.

<u>Check</u> the answer by multiplying the quotient by the divisor. 79 x 6 = 474, the dividend, so the answer is correct.

Additional Standard: Algebra and Functions 1.1 *(See p. 199.)*

Example 2

Find 893 ÷ 5.

First, estimate using compatible numbers.

Think: 1,000 ÷ 5 = 200

Now find the exact answer.

Step 1 Divide the hundreds. Then multiply, subtract, and compare.

```
  1
5)893
- 5  ← 1 hundred × 5
  3  ← 3 < 5
```

Step 2 Bring down the tens. Divide. Then multiply, subtract, and compare.

```
  17
5)893
- 5↓
  39
- 35  ← 7 tens × 5
   4  ← 4 < 5
```

Step 3 Bring down the ones. Divide. Then multiply and subtract. The remainder is 3.

```
  178 R3
5)893
- 5
  39
- 35↓
   43
 - 40  ← 8 ones × 5
    3  ← Remainder
```

The answer, 178 R3, is close to the estimate, so the answer is reasonable.

Check the answer by multiplying the quotient by the divisor and adding the remainder. 178 × 5 = 890, and 890 + 3 = 893. Since this result equals the dividend, you divided correctly.

More Examples

A.

```
  2,429 R1
3)7,288
- 6
  12
- 12
   08
 - 6
    28
  - 27
     1
```

B.

```
   1,757 R6
8)14,062
- 8
  60
- 56
   46
 - 40
    62
  - 56
     6
```

C.

```
  $7.37
3)$22.11
 - 21
    11
  - 09
    21
  - 21
     0
```

Guided Practice *For another example, see Set E on p. 239.*

1. $7\overline{)527}$
2. 965 ÷ 4
3. \$74.65 ÷ 5
4. $6\overline{)31{,}039}$

5. Lucas takes a vitamin pill every day. How many weeks will a bottle of 175 vitamin pills last?

Independent Practice *For more practice, see Set E on p. 242.*

6. $4\overline{)187}$
7. $5\overline{)374}$
8. $9\overline{)801}$
9. $3\overline{)\$13.65}$

10. 9,712 ÷ 4
11. \$42.78 ÷ 6
12. 24,582 ÷ 7
13. 12,096 ÷ 9

Rule: Divide by 3

	Input	Output
14.	123	■
15.	204	■
16.	3,825	■

Rule: Divide by 9

	Input	Output
17.	54	■
18.	675	■
19.	8,037	■

Rule: Divide by 8

	Input	Output
20.	200	■
21.	4,464	■
22.	18,008	■

23. **Algebra** Solve $6x = 822$ by testing these values for x: 137, 157, 207.

24. A jazz group with 5 members needs new instruments. The cost will be \$1,175. If the band members share the cost equally, how much will each person pay?

25. The Cardenas family bought 5 sleeping bags at \$34.75 each and a tent for \$204.00. What was the total cost of the sleeping bags and tent?

Mixed Review

26. **Algebra** Use properties to help you find the missing factor: $(8 \times 5) \times 9 = 8 x (n \times 9)$.

27. Estimate 287 ÷ 6.

28. Estimate 15,027 ÷ 4.

29. $7\overline{)94}$
30. 72 ÷ (3 × 3)
31. $5\overline{)4{,}573}$
32. 14,219 − 1,864

Test Prep **Choose the correct letter for each answer.**

33. **Algebra** If $g = 44$, which expression has a value of 102? (2-10)
   - **A** $g + 68$
   - **B** $64 + g + 4$
   - **C** $146 - g$
   - **D** $58 - g$

34. Find the total weight of 14 boxes of tile if each one weighs 34 pounds. (5-5)
   - **F** 476 pounds
   - **G** 466 pounds
   - **H** 376 pounds
   - **J** 98 pounds

 Use Homework Workbook 6-6.

Zeros in the Quotient

LESSON 6-7

Warm-Up Review

1. 2×8
2. 6×6
3. 280×4
4. $4{,}607 \times 9$
5. Estimate $617 \div 7$.
6. Give the value of each digit in 6,704.
7. Write each number in expanded form:
   456 4,056

California Content Standard *Number Sense 3.2 (🔑): Demonstrate an understanding of, and the ability to use, standard algorithms for dividing a multidigit number by a one-digit number . . . .*

Math Link You have learned to divide multidigit numbers. In this lesson you will learn how to do division problems that have zeros in the quotient.

When you do a division problem, it is important to think about place value. Sometimes you must write a zero in the quotient.

Example 1

Find $619 \div 6$.

First, estimate using compatible numbers.

Think: $600 \div 6 = 100$

Now find the exact answer.

Step 1 There are enough hundreds to divide into 6 groups. Divide. Then multiply and subtract. Compare.

```
   1
6)619
 - 6  ← 1 hundred × 6
   0  ← 0 < 6
```

Step 2 Bring down the tens. There are not enough tens to divide into 6 groups. Write a 0 in the quotient.

```
   10 ← 0 tens in each group
6)619
 - 6↓
   01
```

One ten cannot be divided into 6 groups.

Step 3 Bring down the ones. Divide. Multiply and subtract. Write the remainder.

```
   103 R1
6)619
 - 6 ↓
   019
  - 18 ← 3 ones × 6
     1 ← Remainder
```

The answer, 103 R1, is close to the estimate, so the answer is reasonable.

Check the answer by multiplying the quotient by the divisor and adding the remainder. $103 \times 6 = 618$, and $618 + 1 = 619$. Since the result equals the dividend, the answer is correct.

Additional Standards: Number Sense 3.4 (🔑); Mathematical Reasoning 2.3 *(See p. 199.)*

More Examples

A.

```
   310 R2
 3)932
 − 9
   03
  − 3
    02
   − 0
     2
```

There are not enough ones to divide into 3 groups, so write 0 in the quotient.

B.

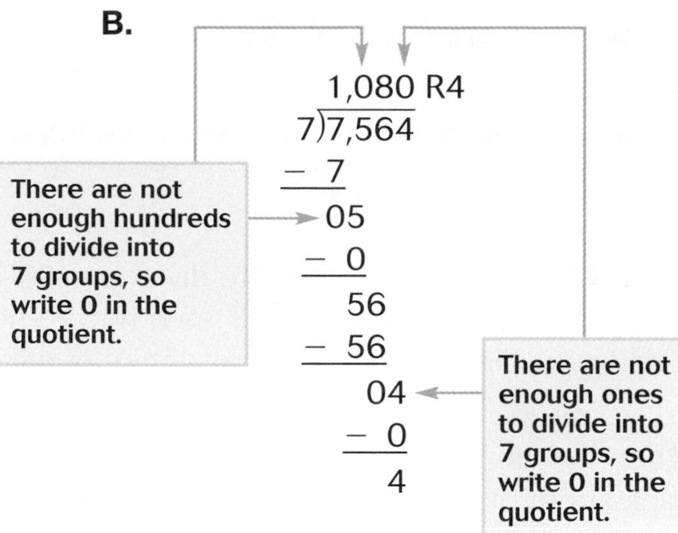

1,080 R4
7)7,564
− 7
05
− 0
56
− 56
04
− 0
4
There are not enough hundreds to divide into 7 groups, so write 0 in the quotient.
There are not enough ones to divide into 7 groups, so write 0 in the quotient.

Guided Practice *For another example, see Set F on p. 239.*

1. 7)75 **2.** 870 ÷ 8 **3.** 5,422 ÷ 5 **4.** 9)18,364

5. The student councils at four schools sold cheesecakes to raise money for software purchases. The distributor shipped them 6 to a box. Partially filled boxes were shipped so that each school received only the number of cheesecakes shown in the table. How many full boxes were delivered to Kennedy School?

Cheesecake Sales	
School	Number of Cheesecakes
Glen Oaks	804
Kennedy	619
Ridge North	698
Jackson	487

Independent Practice *For more practice, see Set F on p. 242.*

6. 4)43 **7.** 5)52 **8.** 9)98 **9.** 6)$6.24

10. 2)215 **11.** 9)997 **12.** 4)427 **13.** 8)880

14. 618 ÷ 3 **15.** 841 ÷ 4 **16.** 2,416 ÷ 6 **17.** 9,102 ÷ 9

18. 7,008 ÷ 7 **19.** $15.20 ÷ 5 **20.** 40,624 ÷ 5 **21.** 32,003 ÷ 8

22. Math Reasoning A student divided 713 by 7 and got 11 R6. Use estimation to explain why this quotient must be wrong. Then do the division and explain the mistake the student made.

23. Ms. Thalhammer drove 635 miles in 4 days. She drove the same number of miles on the first, second, and third days. Then on the fourth day she drove 95 miles. How many miles did she drive on the first day?

Use the data at the right for Exercises 24 and 25.

24. If a family rents the 2-bedroom cottage for 4 weeks, what is the cost per week?

25. The Franklins and the O'Hearns have reserved a 3-bedroom cottage at the 4-week rate. The manager is allowing the Franklins to use it for 3 weeks and the O'Hearns to use it for the last week. What would be a fair amount for the Franklins to pay?

Live by the Sea

Special 4-week Rates

Cottages	Rental Costs
•Efficiency	$2,980
•1-Bedroom	$3,220
•2-Bedroom	$3,620
•3-Bedroom	$4,200

Mixed Review

26. Mental Math Compare: 4,500 ÷ 9 ● 4,200 ÷ 7

27. Algebra Evaluate $456m$ for $m = 17$.

28. Mrs. Keats earned $2,325 in 3 weeks. Give an estimate of how much she earned per week.

29. Compare: 61,419 ● 60,599

30. Compare: 72 × 23 ● 81 × 17

31. 5,748 ÷ 7

32. $6\overline{)15{,}942}$

33. $3\overline{)4{,}217}$

34. $\begin{array}{r} \$0.47 \\ +\ 5.66 \\ \hline \end{array}$

Test Prep **Choose the correct letter for each answer.**

35. Algebra What number should be written at point *A*?
(1-6)

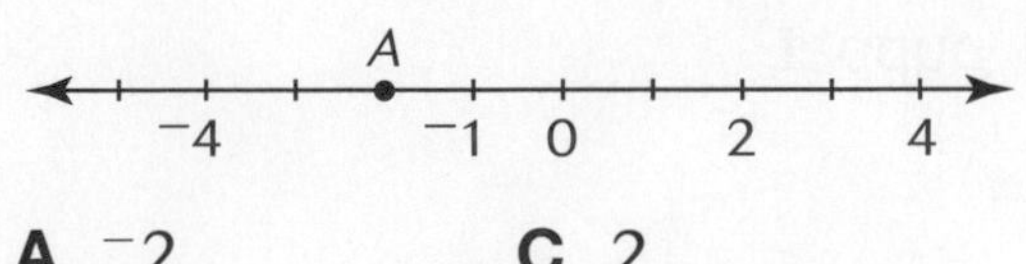

A $^-2$ **C** 2

B $^-6$ **D** $^-4$

36. Leonardo bought a cap for $12.45, a book for $8.99, and a calculator for $11.77. What was the total cost of the book and the calculator?
(2-13)

F $19.66 **H** $21.44

G $20.76 **J** $33.21

Problem-Solving Strategy:

Write a Number Sentence

Warm-Up Review

1. 16 ⟌ 59
2. \$53 + \$38
3. 8×94
4. 21×67
5. $762 \div 3$
6. $944 \div 5$
7. Tomas has 5 model cars. If he builds 2 more per day, how many will he have altogether after 3 weeks?

California Content Standard *Mathematical Reasoning 2.4: Express the solution clearly and logically by using the appropriate mathematical notation and terms and clear language; support solutions with evidence in both verbal and symbolic work. Also, Number Sense 3.4 (key) (See p. 199.)*

Example 1

Ha Si Phu spends 5 hours 20 minutes painting 4 water puppets. He spends the same amount of time painting each puppet. How many minutes does he spend painting one puppet?

Understand

What do you need to find?

You need to find the number of minutes it takes Ha Si Phu to paint one puppet.

Plan

How can you solve the problem?

Write number sentences to find the total number of minutes Ha Si Phu spends painting the puppets. Then write a number sentence to find how many minutes it takes him to paint one puppet.

Solve

Change 5 hours to minutes: 5×60 minutes = 300 minutes

Add 20 minutes: 300 minutes + 20 minutes = 320 minutes

Divide by the number of puppets painted:
320 minutes $\div$ 4 = 80 minutes

It takes Ha Si Phu 80 minutes to paint 1 puppet.

Remember:
1 hr = 60 min.

Look Back

Explain why it makes sense that it took Ha Si Phu between 1 and 2 hours to paint each puppet.

Additional Standards: Mathematical Reasoning 2.0, 3.2 (See p. 199.)

Example 2

Use the data given in the poster.

How much do tickets cost for 2 adults and 3 children?

Find the cost of the adults' tickets.

$$\$15 \times 2 = \$30$$

Find the cost of the children's tickets.

$$\$8 \times 3 = \$24$$

Add to find the total cost.

$$\$30 + \$24 = \$54$$

Tickets for 2 adults and 3 children cost $54.

Guided Practice

Write number sentences to help you solve each exercise. Show your work.

1. Lena has a piece of ribbon 7 feet 6 inches long. She is sewing 5 costumes and will use the same amount of ribbon for each. How many inches of ribbon will she use for each costume?

Remember: 1 ft = 12 in.

2. A dance troupe rented a theater for its performances. The rental cost was $175 per day plus $2 for each ticket sold. The dance troupe rented the theater for 6 days and sold a total of 1,311 tickets. How much did they pay to rent the theater?

Independent Practice

3. Mrs. Lucas is planning a talent show with her class. It will have 8 skits and 6 musical numbers. If each skit takes no more than 5 minutes and each musical number takes no more than 3 minutes, what is the longest the show might be?

4. A theater production is made up of 12 musicians and 14 actors. In addition there are half as many assistants as musicians. How many people work in the production?

5. A puppet show lasts 75 minutes, including a 10-minute intermission. There are 5 scenes in the show, and each scene lasts the same length of time. How long is each scene?

6. Kathleen wants to buy a digital camera for $170. She earns $8 for each lawn she mows. If she mows 16 lawns, how much more money will she need to buy the camera?

7. Three busloads of children attended a magic show at a children's theater. There were 42 children on each bus. The children sat in the left section of the theater where there are 9 seats per row. How many rows did the children fill?

Mixed Review

Try these or other strategies to solve each exercise. Tell which strategy you used.

Problem-Solving Strategies

- *Make a List*
- *Solve a Simpler Problem*
- *Make a Table*
- *Find a Pattern*

8. Kelly is wrapping a birthday present. She has a choice of striped paper, gold paper, flowered paper, or cartoon paper. She can trim it with either a red bow or a blue bow. List all the possible paper and bow combinations.

9. Derrick is making beaded necklaces using 16 beads per necklace. He is stringing on the beads as shown. If he continues the pattern, how many beads will be yellow?

10. There are 8 boys and 8 girls in a tennis tournament. Each boy plays each girl once. How many games are played?

11. There are 26 children in Mr. Garcia's 4th-grade classroom. There are 4 more boys than girls. How many girls are there?

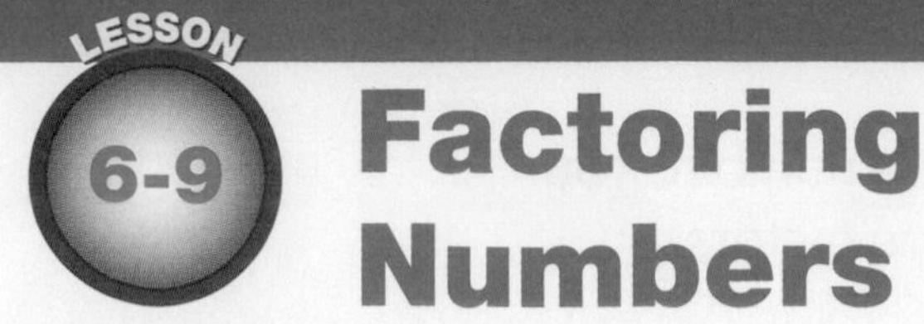

Lesson 6-9 Factoring Numbers

California Content Standard *Number Sense 4.2: (🔑): Know that numbers such as 2, 3, 5, 7, and 11 do not have any factors except 1 and themselves and that such numbers are called prime numbers. Also, Number Sense 4.1* *(See p. 199.)*

Warm-Up Review

1. 5 × 7
2. 36 ÷ 4
3. 2 × 4 × 6
4. 3 × 3 × 5
5. 82 ÷ 5
6. 90 ÷ 6
7. Write a multiplication sentence for this array.

• • • • • • •
• • • • • • •
• • • • • • •

Word Bank

composite number
prime number
divisible

Math Link You have learned how to multiply and divide numbers. Now you will learn about prime and composite numbers, as well as how to factor numbers.

A **composite number** is a whole number greater than 1 that has more than two different factors. 12 has six different factors, 1, 2, 3, 4, 6, and 12. So, 12 is a composite number.

A **prime number** is a whole number greater than 1 that has exactly two factors, the number itself and 1. Numbers such as 2, 3, 5, 7, and 11 are prime numbers.

Example 1

List all the factors of each number. Then tell if the number is prime or composite.

8	**Factors of 8: 1, 2, 4, 8**	8 is a composite number.
13	**Factors of 13: 1, 13**	13 is a prime number.
25	**Factors of 25: 1, 5, 25**	25 is a composite number.

Example 2

Is 4 a factor of 52?

Divide 52 by 4. If the remainder is 0, then 4 is a factor of 52.

$$\begin{array}{r} 13 \\ 4\overline{)52} \\ -\ 4 \\ \hline 12 \\ -\ 12 \\ \hline 0 \end{array}$$

4 is a factor of 52.

Example 3

Is 6 a factor of 39?

Divide 39 by 6. The remainder is not 0.

$$\begin{array}{r} 6\text{ R3} \\ 6\overline{)39} \\ -\ 36 \\ \hline 3 \end{array}$$

6 is not a factor of 39.

One number is **divisible** by another when the remainder is 0. Example 2 shows that 52 is divisible by 4.

Additional Standards: Number Sense 3.2 (🔑); Mathematical Reasoning 2.3 *(See p. 199.)*

Now that you know how to identify the factors of a number, you can write any number as a product of two or more factors.

Example 4

Write each number as a product of two or more factors in as many ways as possible.

11: 1×11

12: $1 \times 12, 2 \times 6, 3 \times 4, 3 \times 2 \times 2$

15: $1 \times 15, 3 \times 5$

28: $1 \times 28, 2 \times 14, 4 \times 7, 2 \times 2 \times 7$

Because of the commutative property, you don't need to list the turn-around products: $1 \times 11 = 11 \times 1$.

You can write any composite number as a product of prime numbers.

Example 5

Write 150 as a product of its prime factors.

$150 = 5 \times 30$ and $30 = 5 \times 6$, so $150 = 5 \times 5 \times 6$ which can be written as $5 \times 5 \times 3 \times 2$ or $2 \times 3 \times 5 \times 5$.

Example 6

Write 100 as a product of its prime factors.

$$100 = 10 \times 10$$
$$= 2 \times 5 \times 2 \times 5$$
$$= 2 \times 2 \times 5 \times 5$$

Write the prime factors from greatest to least or least to greatest.

Guided Practice *For another example, see Set G on p. 240.*

List all the factors of each number. Then tell if the number is prime or composite.

1. 6 **2.** 14 **3.** 23 **4.** 27 **5.** 32

6. Is 8 a factor of 68? **7.** Is 51 divisible by 3?

Write each number as a product of two or more factors in as many ways as possible.

8. 10 **9.** 16 **10.** 17 **11.** 18 **12.** 30

13. Write 90 as a product of its prime factors.

Independent Practice *For more practice, see Set G on p. 243.*

List all the factors of each number. Then tell if the number is prime or composite.

14. 9 **15.** 19 **16.** 21 **17.** 36 **18.** 40

19. Is 3 a factor of 72? **20.** Is 78 divisible by 4?

Write each number as a product of two or more factors in as many ways as possible.

21. 24 **22.** 29 **23.** 35 **24.** 42 **25.** 60

26. Mary has 20 snapshots she wants to display in a rectangular array. Draw all the different possible arrays and write a multiplication sentence for each.

Write each composite number as a product of its prime factors.

27. 48 **28.** 80 **29.** 125 **30.** 264

31. Math Reasoning List all of the prime numbers less than 50. Is 1 in your list? Is 2 in your list? Explain your thinking.

Mixed Review

32. The table at the right shows temperatures in a city during December. Which day was warmest? Which day was coldest?

Date	Temperature
Dec. 4	⁻3°F
Dec. 5	⁻5°F
Dec. 6	0°F
Dec. 7	⁻2°F

33. Estimate 12,219 + 28,445 by rounding to the greatest place value.

34. 418 ÷ 4 **35.** 12,907 ÷ 5 **36.** 26,907 × 8 **37.** 1,224 ÷ 6

Test Prep **Choose the correct letter for each answer.**

38. Algebra If $y - 713 = 188$, then $y =$
(2-11)

A 625 **C** 891
B 635 **D** 901
E NH

39. Which of the following does not round to 20,000 when rounded to the nearest ten thousand?
(1-5)

F 18,201 **H** 24,986
G 19,375 **J** 25,413

LESSON 6-10 Finding Averages

Warm-Up Review

1. 14 + 8 + 34 + 21
2. 4 × 7
3. 70 ÷ 3
4. 632 ÷ 2
5. 811 ÷ 8
6. Liz found 28 seashells, and Suzie found 51 seashells. If they share them equally, how many will each girl get?

California Content Standard *Statistics, Data Analysis, and Probability 1.1 (Grade 5) Know the concepts of mean. . . . Also, Number Sense 3.4 (key)* *(See p. 199.)*

Math Link You have learned how to divide numbers. Now you will apply those skills to find the average of a group of numbers.

Word Bank

average
mean

An **average,** or **mean,** is a way to describe a group of numbers. The average is a number that gives a general idea about the sizes of the numbers in the group.

Example 1

A musician had 6 weeks to practice for a concert. Her goal was to practice an average of 15 hours per week. According to her records in her music journal, did she practice at least 15 hours on the average?

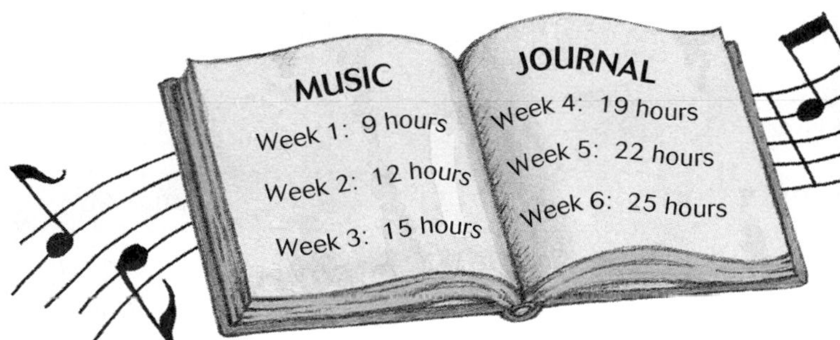

MUSIC
JOURNAL
Week 1: 9 hours
Week 2: 12 hours
Week 3: 15 hours
Week 4: 19 hours
Week 5: 22 hours
Week 6: 25 hours

▲ Christine Kwak has performed at Carnegie Hall in New York City.

Step 1 Add the numbers in the group.

$$\begin{array}{r} 9 \\ 12 \\ 15 \\ 19 \\ 22 \\ +\ 25 \\ \hline 102 \end{array}$$

Step 2 Divide the sum by the number of addends.

$$\begin{array}{r} 17 \\ 6\overline{)102} \\ -\ 6 \\ \hline 42 \\ -\ 42 \\ \hline 0 \end{array}$$

The musician practiced an average of 17 hours per week. This was more than her goal.

 Additional Standard: Mathematical Reasoning 3.2 *(See p. 199.)*

Example 2

Find the average, or mean of 88, 102, 97, and 97.

$88 + 102 + 97 + 97 = 384$ **Add the numbers in the group.**

$384 \div 4 = 96$ **Divide by the number of addends.**

Guided Practice *For another example, see Set H on p. 240.*

Find the average, or mean, of each group of numbers.

1. 4, 5, 1, 3, 2 **2.** 8, 18, 12, 18 **3.** 181, 154, 160

4. Keith read four books last month. They had 106 pages, 140 pages, 77 pages, and 81 pages. Find the average number of pages per book.

Independent Practice *For more practice, see Set H on p. 243.*

Find the average, or mean, of each group of numbers.

5. 9, 15, 12 **6.** 21, 22, 15, 14, 18 **7.** 12, 21, 32, 47

8. 8, 6, 4, 6, 5, 7, 6 **9.** 58, 90, 74 **10.** 210, 84, 129, 165

11. The table at the right shows the number of daily absences at Lincoln School during 4 weeks. Which week had the smallest average number of absences?

12. Math Reasoning The mean of a group of 3 numbers is 35. One of the numbers is 46. Another is 21. What is the third number?

Daily Absences

Week	Number of Absences
Nov. 4	16, 19, 24, 21, 15
Nov. 11	18, 20, 18, 19, 20
Nov. 18	22, 14, 18, 22, 14
Nov. 25	17, 25, 27

Mixed Review

13. Write 40 as a product of two or more factors in as many ways as possible.

14. $0 \times 4{,}029$ **15.** $25{,}612 \div 5$ **16.** $1{,}700 - 1{,}652$ **17.** $2{,}112 \div 3$

Test Prep **Choose the correct letter for each answer.**

18. (4-2) Glenn has 28 CDs. His brother has twice as many. How many CDs do the boys have in all?

A 30 CDs **B** 56 CDs **C** 84 CDs **D** 112 CDs

Understand
Plan
Solve
Look Back

Problem-Solving Application: Using Data

California Content Standard *Number Sense 3.4 (🔑): Solve problems involving division of multidigit numbers by one-digit numbers. Also, Statistics, Data Analysis, and Probability 1.1 (Grade 5) (See p. 199.)*

Warm-Up Review

1. 18 + 64 + 4 + 95 + 3
2. 25 ÷ 5
3. 78 ÷ 6
4. 176 ÷ 8
5. 508 ÷ 4
6. Read the bar graph on page 213. What does the graph tell you about comedies?

Example 1

The bar graph shows how many hours the Carlton Children's Choir practiced each week. What is the average, or mean, number of hours practiced each week?

Carlton Children's Choir Practice

HOURS OF PRACTICE: 0 1 2 3 4 5 6 7 8 9

WEEK: 1 2 3 4 5 6

WEEK	HOURS OF PRACTICE
1	2
2	2
3	2
4	4
5	6
6	8

Understand

What do you need to find?

You need to find the average number of hours the choir practiced each week.

Plan

How can you solve the problem?

First find the number of hours each bar stands for. Next add the hours together to find the total number of hours practiced. Then divide that number by the number of weeks.

Solve

Find the sum of the hours practiced.

2 + 2 + 2 + 4 + 6 + 8 = 24 hours

Then divide by the number of weeks of practice.

24 ÷ 6 = 4

The average number of hours practiced each week is 4 hours.

Look Back

The answer is reasonable because it is between the least and greatest number of hours practiced.

Additional Standards: Statistics, Data Analysis, and Probability 1.0, 1.3; Mathematical Reasoning 2.0 (See p. 199.)

Example 2

The recreation center ordered new skateboards. Their order form is shown at the right. Find the average price of the skateboards.

Skateboard Order			
Model	Length (in.)	Quantity	Price
Junior	25	1	$42
Blaster	31	2	$49
Arrowpath	29	1	$24
Spinout	31	4	$35

Find the sum of the prices.

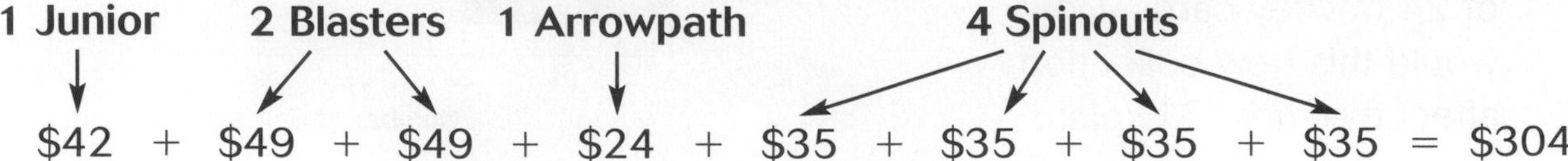

Then divide by the number of skateboards ordered.

$304 ÷ 8 = $38

The average price of the skateboards is $38.

Guided Practice

Use the data in the graph to solve Exercises 1–3.

1. What is the average age of the chorus members?

2. Explain how you know the answer is reasonable.

3. Suppose a new singer joins the chorus, but the average age of the chorus members does not change. How old must the new singer be? Explain.

Ages of Chorus Members	
9	
10	
11	
12	

Each stands for 1 member.

Independent Practice

Use the data in the skateboard order above for Exercises 4–6.

4. What is the mean length of the 8 skateboards?

5. What was the total cost of the skateboards?

6. Which cost more, the 4 Spinouts or the other 4 skateboards? How much more?

Use the graph for Exercises 7 and 8.

7. What is the mean number of cards Todd has for each sport?

8. Suppose Todd's brother gives Todd his collection of 24 hockey cards. How would this new collection affect the mean? Explain.

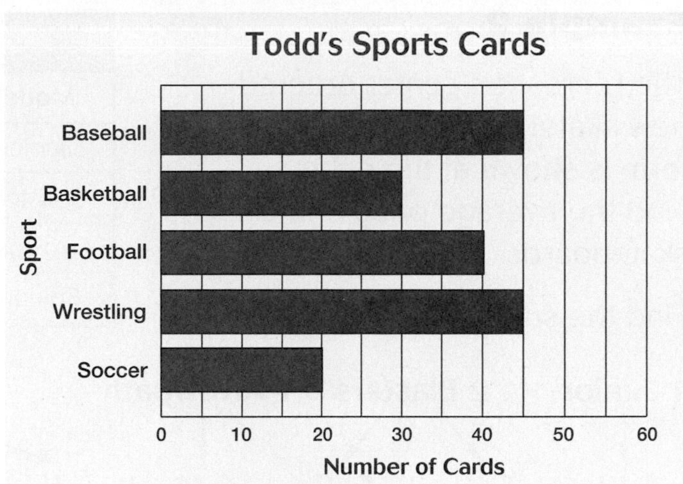

Mixed Review

9. Mrs. Miura bought a gallon of paint priced at $16.50 and a paintbrush priced at $5.99. She had a coupon for $3.25 off the price of the paint and another coupon for $0.75 off the price of the paintbrush. How much did she spend on the paint and paintbrush?

10. A scuba diver dove to a depth of 55 feet below sea level on her first dive, 65 feet below sea level on her second dive, and 62 feet below sea level on her third dive. Write each depth as an integer, and then order the integers from least to greatest.

11. Use the data at the right. In 1860 and 1861, the Pony Express delivered mail between St. Joseph, Missouri, and Sacramento, California. If a rider traveled for 10 hours a day at a speed of 15 miles per hour, could he make the trip in 2 weeks?

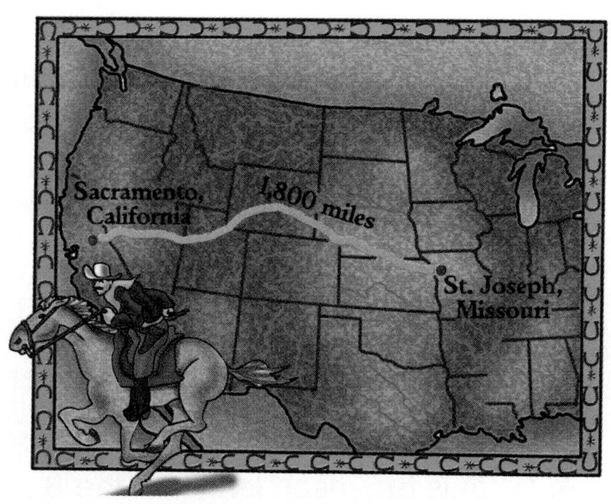

12. Kyle's dad gave him $20. Does he have enough money to buy a state park guide book for $6.50, 2 rolls of film at $4.55 a piece, and 14 rock samples at $0.45 each?

13. Jane is taking the following clothes on vacation: black slacks, blue slacks, white slacks, red shirt, green shirt, pink shirt. How many different slack and shirt outfits does she have?

 Use Homework Workbook 6-11.

Lesson 6-12 Properties of Equality

California Content Standard *Algebra and Functions 2.1: (Key): Know and understand that equals added to equals are equal. Also, Algebra and Functions 2.0(Key), 2.2(Key)* *(See p. 199.)*

Warm-Up Review

Evaluate each expression when $y = 18$.

1. $51 - y$
2. $(y - 5) \times 6$

Find each answer.

3. $(32 \div 8) + 4$
4. $(32 \div 8) \times 4$
5. $(3 \times 11) - 7$
6. $3 \times (11 - 7)$
7. Mr. Stewart bought a book for $19.95. The tax was $1.20. He gave the clerk $25.00. How much change did he receive?

Math Link You know the meaning of equality. Now you will learn about the properties of equality and equations.

When a scale is balanced, the weight on one side of the scale is equal to the weight on the other side. A scale can be used as a model for an equation. In an equation both sides are equal.

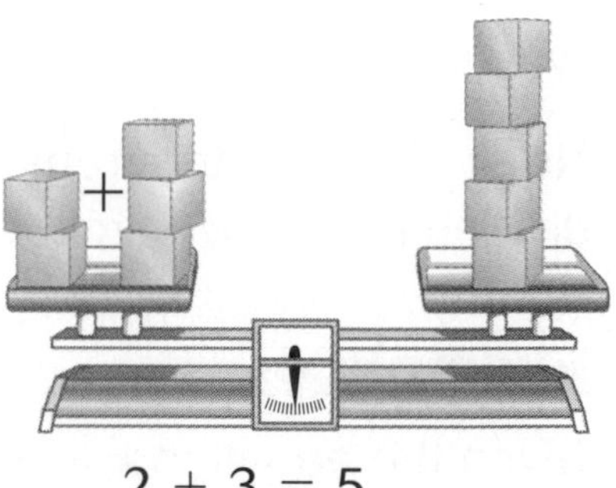

$2 + 3 = 5$

Whenever two quantities are equal to each other, you can add, subtract, multiply, or divide both quantities by the same number and the resulting quantities are still equal to each other. The table below lists the properties of equality for equations.

Properties of Equality

Property	Example
Equals added to equals are equal.	You know: $2 + 3 = 5$. Therefore, $2 + 3 + 8 = 5 + 8$.
Equals subtracted from equals are equal.	You know: $7 + 9 = 16$. Therefore, $(7 + 9) - 2 = 16 - 2$.
Equals multiplied by equals are equal.	You know: $3 \times 4 = 12$. Therefore, $3 \times 4 \times 2 = 12 \times 2$.
Equals divided by equals are equal.	You know: $8 + 10 = 18$. Therefore $(8 + 10) \div 3 = 18 \div 3$.

Additional Standard: Algebra and Functions 1.1 *(See p. 199.)*

Example 1

You know $5 + 9 = 14$. Does $5 + 9 + 12 = 14 + 12$?
Why or why not?

Yes. 12 is added to both sides. The property of equality is: equals added to equals are equal.

Example 2

You know $12 \times 2 = 24$. Does $12 \times 2 \times 5 = 24 + 5$?
Why or why not?

No. The left side is multiplied by 5, but 5 is added to the right side. The same thing is not done to both sides.

Example 3

Given the equation $5x = 40$, does $5x - 4 = 40 \div 4$?
Why or why not?

No. 4 is subtracted from the left side, but the right side is divided by 4. The same thing is not done to both sides.

Example 4

Given the equation $x + 7 = 12$, does $x + 7 - 7 = 12 - 7$?
Why or why not?

Yes. 7 is subtracted from both sides. The property of equality is: equals subtracted from equals are equal.

Guided Practice *For another example, see Set I on p. 240.*

Answer each question. Tell why or why not.

1. You know $80 \div 5 = 16$. Does $(80 \div 5) \times 3 = 16 \times 3$?

2. You know $9 \times 8 = 72$. Does $(9 \times 8) + 6 = 72 - 6$?

3. Given the equation $y - 9 = 86$, does $y - 9 + 9 = 86 + 9$?

4. Given the equation $11w = 132$, does $11w \times 2 = 132 \div 2$?

5. If you start with a balanced scale and add the same amount of weight to each side, what happens to the scale?

Independent Practice *For more practice, see Set I on p. 243.*

Answer each question. Tell why or why not.

You know:	Does:
6. $52 + 46 = 98$	$52 + 46 + 61 = 98 - 61$?
7. $68 \div 4 = 17$	$(68 \div 4) \times 5 = 17 \times 5$?
8. $10 \times 13 = 130$	$(10 \times 13) - 14 = 130 - 18$?
9. $24 - 9 = 15$	$(24 - 9) \div 3 = 15 \div 3$?
10. $18 + 23 = 41$	$18 + 23 + 4 = 41 + 4$?

Given the equation:	Does:
11. $y - 15 = 38$	$y - 15 + 15 = 38 + 15$?
12. $8x = 80$	$\frac{8x}{8} = \frac{80}{8}$?
13. $14 + y = 39$	$14 + y - 14 = 39 - 8$?
14. $16y = 48$	$16y + 4 = 48 \times 4$?
15. $w + 6 = 19$	$w + 6 - 6 = 19 - 6$?

16. Write an equation for the scale shown. If you want to get n all alone on the left side of the scale, what would you do to both sides of the balance scale?

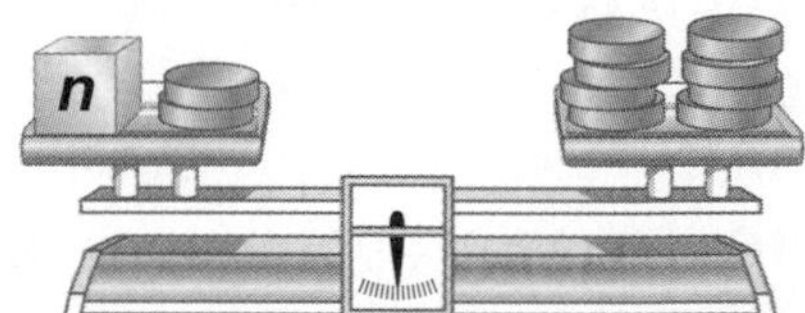

Mixed Review

17. Louise took 5 math tests last semester. Her scores were 85, 91, 80, 77, and 87. Find the average of her test scores.

18. $(24 \div 4) + 8$ **19.** $24 \div (4 + 8)$ **20.** $450 - (3 \times 6)$ **21.** $(450 - 3) \times 6$

22. Jeff baked 44 blueberry muffins. He shared as many as possible equally among 5 friends. How many muffins were left over?

Test Prep **Choose the correct letter for the answer.**

23. Which of the following is a composite number?
(6-9)

A 5 **B** 17 **C** 33 **D** 41

Diagnostic Checkpoint

Complete. For Exercises 1–3, use the words from the Word Bank.

Word Bank
average
composite number
divisible
mean
prime number

1. An ____________, or ____________, is a number that gives a general idea about the sizes of the numbers in the group. (6-10)

2. A ____________ is a whole number greater than 1 that has exactly two factors, the number itself and 1. (6-9)

3. 42 is ____________ by 6 because there is no remainder when you divide 42 by 6. (6-9)

In Exercises 4–7, estimate each quotient. Tell the numbers you used.

4. $83 \div 9$ (6-5)
5. $532 \div 5$ (6-5)
6. $400 \div 7$ (6-5)
7. $8{,}224 \div 9$ (6-5)
8. $6\overline{)734}$ (6-6)
9. $4\overline{)920}$ (6-7)
10. $8\overline{)17{,}637}$ (6-7)
11. $9\overline{)33{,}261}$ (6-6)

In Exercises 12–15, list all the factors of each number. Then tell if the number is prime or composite.

12. 8 (6-9)
13. 7 (6-9)
14. 15 (6-9)
15. 50 (6-9)

16. Find the average, or mean, of 384, 196, and 287. (6-10)

17. Ken recorded some songs on a 90-minute tape. Each song was 4 minutes long, and there were 14 minutes left over. How many songs did Ken record? (6-8)

18. The bar graph at the right shows the number of hours a pianist practiced each week. Find the average number of hours per week that the pianist practiced. (6-11)

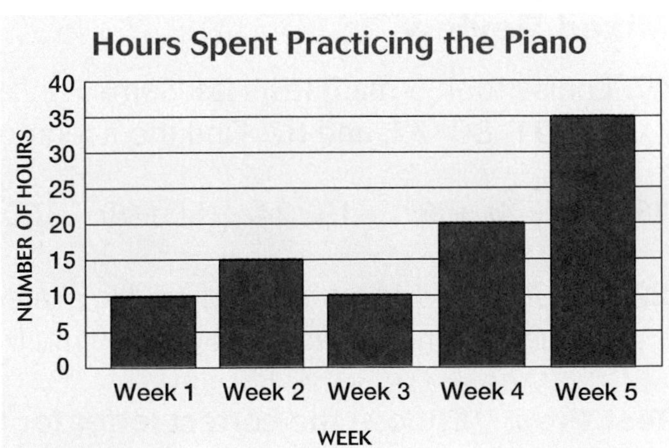

19. You know $14 + 19 = 33$. Does $(14 + 9) \times 2 = 33 \times 2$? Tell why or why not? (6-12)

Chapter 6 Test

1. $720 \div 9$
2. $5,600 \div 8$
3. $42,000 \div 6$
4. $46 \div 2$
5. $54 \div 3$
6. $78 \div 6$
7. $89 \div 8$
8. $80 \div 6$
9. $3\overline{)739}$
10. $6\overline{)5,542}$
11. $8\overline{)32,089}$
12. $3\overline{)911}$

In Exercises 13–16, estimate each quotient. Tell the numbers you used.

13. $68 \div 3$
14. $857 \div 4$
15. $786 \div 8$
16. $3,650 \div 7$

17. List all the factors of 33. Then tell if 33 is prime or composite.

Find the average, or mean, of each group of numbers.

18. 8, 6, 6, 7, 6, 8, 7, 8
19. 143, 150, 142, 157

For Exercises 20 and 21, answer each question. Tell why or why not.

20. You know $70 \div 5 = 14$. Does $(70 \div 5) - 7 = 14 + 7$?

21. Given the equation $8y = 88$, does $8y \div 8 = 88 \div 8$? Why or why not?

22. You need 108 hamburger buns for a picnic. The buns come in packages of 8. How many packages do you need to buy?

23. The school day at Bradford School is 6 hours and 30 minutes long. Lunch lasts 40 minutes. The rest of the time is divided into 7 equal periods. Write number sentences to find the length of each period. Remember there are 60 minutes in an hour.

24. The table shows the weights of 4 dogs. Find the average weight of the dogs.

Dog	Weight (pounds)
Spot	52
Ruff	40
KoKo	12
Speedy	36

Multiple-Choice Chapter 6 Test

Choose the correct letter for each answer.

1. **Find 5,400 ÷ 9.**
   - **A** 6
   - **B** 60
   - **C** 600
   - **D** 6,000
   - **E** NH

2. **A band with five musicians earns $800 one weekend. The band must pay their agent $275. How much should each of the musicians receive if the remaining money is divided equally?**
   - **F** $60
   - **G** $75
   - **H** $100
   - **J** $105
   - **K** NH

3. **A group of students is going to a museum in 7 buses. About how many students will be on each bus if there are 220 students in the group?**
   - **A** 20 students
   - **B** 30 students
   - **C** 40 students
   - **D** 50 students

4. **How many 4-member rowing teams can be formed from 57 students?**
   - **F** 13 teams with 3 students left over
   - **G** 14 teams with 1 student left over
   - **H** 14 teams with 3 students left over
   - **J** 15 teams
   - **K** NH

5. **How many $5 books can you buy with $23?**
   - **A** 3 books
   - **B** 4 books
   - **C** 5 books
   - **D** 6 books

6. **There are 5,280 feet in 1 mile. If four people run a mile relay race, how far will each person run?**
   - **F** 132 feet
   - **G** 1,032 feet
   - **H** 1,320 feet
   - **J** 1,400 feet
   - **K** NH

7. **Megan spent 4 hours 30 minutes painting 3 ceramic vases. She spent the same amount of time on each vase. Which number sentence could you use to find the number of minutes it takes Megan to paint one vase? Remember, 1 hour = 60 minutes.**
   - **A** $30 \div 3 = 10$
   - **B** $240 \div 3 = 80$
   - **C** $270 \times 3 = 810$
   - **D** $270 \div 3 = 90$

8. **Which is *not* a factor of 36?**

F 3
G 8
H 9
J 12

---

9. **Which shows 60 as the product of prime factors?**

A $2 \times 2 \times 3 \times 5$
B $4 \times 3 \times 5$
C $2 \times 3 \times 3 \times 5$
D $2 \times 2 \times 3 \times 3 \times 5$

---

10. **During the last 6 months, Paul's family spent these amounts going to the movies: $84, $114, $97, $151, $124, $90. What is the average amount they spent on movies per month?**

F $110
G $112
H $115
J $660

---

11. **Given the equation $4h = 12$, which is *not* true?**

A $4h \div 4 = 12 \div 4$
B $4h + 4 = 12 - 4$
C $4h \times 3 = 12 \times 3$
D $4h - 5 = 12 - 5$

---

12. **Find $76 \div 4$.**

F 14
G 17
H 18
J 20
K NH

---

13. **Find $612 \div 3$.**

A 24
B 203
C 204
D 214
E NH

Use the bar graph to answer Questions 14 and 15.

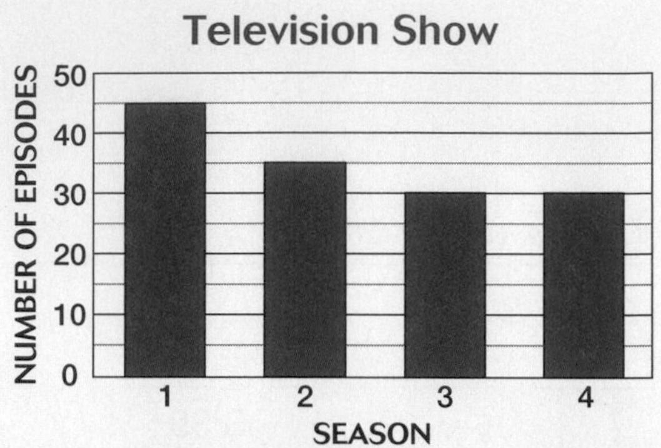

14. **What is the average number of episodes of the television show broadcast in the 4 years?**

F 33
G 34
H 35
J 36

---

15. **What is the average, or mean, number of episodes of the television show broadcast in the first 2 seasons?**

A 20
B 30
C 40
D 45

---

16. $8\overline{)18{,}265}$

F 2,149 R1
G 2,151 R7
H 2,282 R7
J 2,283 R1
K NH

Reteaching

Set A (pages 200–201)

Find 30,000 ÷ 6.

Use a basic fact and look for a pattern with zeros.

30 ÷ 6 = 5
300 ÷ 6 = 50
3,000 ÷ 6 = 500
30,000 ÷ 6 = 5,000

Remember that the first zero is not part of the pattern when the dividend of the basic fact includes a zero.

1. 400 ÷ 5 **2.** 270 ÷ 9

3. 350 ÷ 7 **4.** 180 ÷ 3

5. 1,600 ÷ 2 **6.** 2,800 ÷ 4

7. 4,000 ÷ 8 **8.** 10,000 ÷ 2

Set B (pages 202–204)

Find 39 ÷ 3.

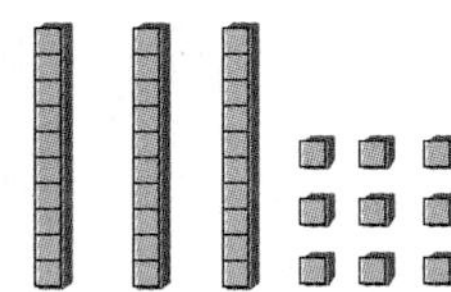

$$\begin{array}{r} 13 \\ 3\overline{)39} \\ \underline{-3}\downarrow \\ 09 \\ \underline{-9} \\ 0 \end{array}$$

Check the answer by multiplying the quotient by the divisor.
13 × 3 = 39

Remember you can check the answer by multiplying the quotient by the divisor.

1. $4\overline{)52}$ **2.** $3\overline{)93}$

3. $5\overline{)70}$ **4.** $8\overline{)96}$

5. $2\overline{)38}$ **6.** $4\overline{)76}$

7. $3\overline{)78}$ **8.** $7\overline{)91}$

Set C (pages 205–207)

Find 63 ÷ 4.

$$\begin{array}{r} 1 \\ 4\overline{)63} \\ \underline{-4} \\ 2 \end{array} \qquad \begin{array}{r} 1 \\ 4\overline{)63} \\ \underline{-4}\downarrow \\ 23 \end{array} \qquad \begin{array}{r} 15\text{ R3} \\ 4\overline{)63} \\ \underline{-4} \\ 23 \\ \underline{-20} \\ 3 \end{array}$$

Check by multiplying and adding.
15 × 4 = 60, and 60 + 3 = 63.

Remember you can check your answer by multiplying the quotient times the divisor and adding the remainder.

1. $4\overline{)39}$ **2.** $9\overline{)44}$

3. $7\overline{)83}$ **4.** $8\overline{)59}$

5. $3\overline{)97}$ **6.** $5\overline{)72}$

7. $6\overline{)71}$ **8.** $2\overline{)57}$

Set D (pages 212–213)

Estimate 473 ÷ 6.

473 ÷ 6
↓
480 ÷ 6 = 80
473 ÷ 6 is about 80

Think: 48 ÷ 6 = 8, so, 480 and 6 are compatible numbers.

Check by multiplying.
80 × 6 = 480, and 480 is close to 473.
So, 80 is a reasonable estimate.

Remember to use compatible numbers to estimate. For division problems, compatible numbers are numbers that are easy to divide mentally.

Estimate each quotient. Tell the numbers you used.

1. 152 ÷ 3 **2.** 277 ÷ 7

3. 397 ÷ 2 **4.** 3,964 ÷ 5

5. 1,115 ÷ 4 **6.** 7,287 ÷ 8

Set E (pages 214–216)

Find 1,674 ÷ 3.

```
   558
3)1,674
 -1 5
   17
  -15
    24
   -24
     0
```

There are not enough thousands to divide into 3 groups. So, regroup 1 thousand 6 hundreds as 16 hundreds.

Remember to start in the greatest place. You can estimate to see if your answer is reasonable.

1. 482 ÷ 5 **2.** $6.75 ÷ 9

3. 148 ÷ 7 **4.** 1,375 ÷ 4

5. $26.73 ÷ 3 **6.** 15,869 ÷ 8

Set F (pages 217–219)

Find 835 ÷ 4.

```
  208 R3
4)835
 -8
  03
 -0   <--
  35
 -32
   3
```

There are not enough tens to divide into 4 groups, so write a 0 in the quotient.

Remember to write zeros in the quotient when needed.

1. 6)723 **2.** 4)436

3. 9)927 **4.** 2)$6.16

5. 3)626 **6.** 2)614

7. 7)$35.42 **8.** 5)5,497

Reteaching (continued)

Set G (pages 223–225)

List all the factors of 18. Then tell if 18 is prime or composite.

Factors of 18: 1, 2, 3, 6, 9, 18

18 is a composite number because it has more factors than itself and 1.

Remember that prime numbers are whole numbers greater than 1 that have exactly two factors, the number itself and 1.

List all the factors of each number. Then tell if the number is prime or composite.

1. 5 **2.** 4 **3.** 12

4. 33 **5.** 42 **6.** 29

Set H (pages 226–227)

Find the average, or mean, of 57, 38, 43, and 46.

Add the numbers in the group.
57 + 38 + 43 + 46 = 184

Divide the sum by the number of addends.

```
   46
4)184
 -16
   24
  -24
    0
```

The average, or mean, is 46.

Remember that the average of a group of numbers cannot be greater than the largest number or smaller than the smallest number.

Find the average, or mean, of each group of numbers.

1. 7, 5, 4, 4, 2, 2

2. 176, 204, 184

3. 33, 35, 31, 36, 32, 31

Set I (pages 231–233)

Given the equation $7m = 42$, does $7m \times 3 = 42 \times 3$?

Yes. Both sides are multiplied by 3. The property of equality is: equals multiplied by equals are equal.

Remember that you can add, subtract, multiply, or divide both sides of an equation by the same number and the resulting sides will still be equal.

1. Given the equation $n - 3 = 9$, does $n - 3 + 3 = 9 + 3$? Why?

2. Given the equation $x + 2 = 6$, does $x + 2 - 2 = 6 \times 2$? Why?

More Practice

Set A *(pages 200–201)*

1. 40 ÷ 5
2. 180 ÷ 6
3. 4,500 ÷ 5
4. 1,200 ÷ 2
5. 7,200 ÷ 9
6. 4,200 ÷ 6
7. 40,000 ÷ 8
8. 540 ÷ 9
9. 150 ÷ 5
10. 240 ÷ 8
11. 3,000 ÷ 6
12. 49,000 ÷ 7
13. 4,800 ÷ 6
14. 160 ÷ 4
15. 1,500 ÷ 5
16. 420 ÷ 7
17. For a dance number in a musical, costumes for 8 dancers cost $2,400. How much will the costumes cost if the number of dancers is increased to 10?

Set B *(pages 202–204)*

1. $5\overline{)65}$
2. $4\overline{)92}$
3. $3\overline{)42}$
4. $8\overline{)88}$
5. $4\overline{)72}$
6. $7\overline{)91}$
7. $2\overline{)54}$
8. $5\overline{)70}$
9. 87 ÷ 3
10. 84 ÷ 7
11. 64 ÷ 4
12. 48 ÷ 3
13. 85 ÷ 5
14. 52 ÷ 4
15. 68 ÷ 4
16. 72 ÷ 3
17. During a three-week period, a total of 78 people rented a popular movie. On average, how many people rented the movie each week?

Set C *(pages 205–207)*

1. $5\overline{)37}$
2. $8\overline{)93}$
3. $2\overline{)71}$
4. $9\overline{)58}$
5. $5\overline{)83}$
6. $7\overline{)88}$
7. $4\overline{)65}$
8. $8\overline{)75}$
9. 45 ÷ 2
10. 68 ÷ 3
11. 78 ÷ 5
12. 76 ÷ 6
13. 38 ÷ 3
14. 59 ÷ 6
15. 68 ÷ 6
16. 94 ÷ 3
17. Tim has 3 dozen cartons of juice for his friends to share at his party. Seven friends come. How many cartons does each friend get if they share them equally? How many cartons of juice will be left over?

More Practice (continued)

Set D (pages 212–213)

Estimate each quotient. Tell the numbers you used.

1. 238 ÷ 6 **2.** 212 ÷ 3 **3.** 254 ÷ 5 **4.** 416 ÷ 7

5. 159 ÷ 2 **6.** 638 ÷ 8 **7.** 239 ÷ 4 **8.** 808 ÷ 9

9. 6,279 ÷ 9 **10.** 3,594 ÷ 4 **11.** 3,618 ÷ 6 **12.** 3,178 ÷ 8

13. A set of 8 CDs has a collection of 150 songs. Estimate the number of songs on each CD.

Set E (pages 214–216)

1. $3\overline{)193}$ **2.** $8\overline{)914}$ **3.** $5\overline{)\$7.45}$ **4.** $9\overline{)604}$

5. $4\overline{)573}$ **6.** $7\overline{)244}$ **7.** $2\overline{)473}$ **8.** $6\overline{)\$5.16}$

9. 1,907 ÷ 6 **10.** 762 ÷ 5 **11.** 2,564 ÷ 3 **12.** 8,492 ÷ 7

13. 10,824 ÷ 7 **14.** 18,997 ÷ 8 **15.** $78.76 ÷ 4 **16.** 21,466 ÷ 5

17. For a parade, 350 band members line up in rows of 6, starting with the front row. How many rows of 6 are there? How many musicians are in the last row?

Set F (pages 217–219)

1. $5\overline{)546}$ **2.** $7\overline{)845}$ **3.** $3\overline{)619}$ **4.** $8\overline{)\$8.16}$

5. $7\overline{)2,148}$ **6.** $6\overline{)3,842}$ **7.** $4\overline{)843}$ **8.** $9\overline{)5467}$

9. 730 ÷ 7 **10.** 925 ÷ 3 **11.** 851 ÷ 8 **12.** 638 ÷ 6

13. 763 ÷ 4 **14.** 940 ÷ 9 **15.** $18.50 ÷ 5 **16.** 1,813 ÷ 2

17. A movie theater sells 627 tickets for one show. There are 3 sections of seats in the theater, and the number of people in each section is the same. Find the number of people in each section.

Set G (pages 223–225)

In Exercises 1–4, list all the factors of each number. Then tell if the number is prime or composite.

1. 11
2. 20
3. 28
4. 22
5. Is 4 a factor of 76?
6. Is 48 divisible by 3?
7. Write 50 as a product of its prime factors.
8. Sally wants to arrange 24 buttons in a rectangular array. List all the different possible rectangular arrays she could use.

Set H (pages 226–227)

Find the average, or mean, of each group of numbers.

1. 23, 46, 87
2. 8, 6, 7, 2, 5, 8
3. 12, 15, 10, 11
4. 10, 9, 16, 7, 13
5. 384, 476
6. 236, 75, 187, 134
7. 109, 132, 125
8. 7, 12, 13, 8, 6, 9, 8
9. 91, 122, 116, 97, 124
10. The ages of the musicians in a band are 36, 42, 25, 56, 73, 39, 64, 49. What is the average age of the musicians in the band?

Set I (pages 231–233)

Answer each question. Tell why or why not.

1. You know $46 + 12 = 58$. Does $46 + 12 - 12 = 58 - 12$?
2. You know $8 \times 7 = 56$. Does $(8 \times 7) \times 3 = 56 \div 3$?
3. Given the equation $w - 4 = 12$, does $w - 4 + 4 = 12 + 4$?
4. Given the equation $5n = 35$, does $5n \div 5 = 35 \div 5$?
5. Given the equation $m + 6 = 19$, does $m + 6 - 6 = 19 + 6$?

Problem Solving: Preparing for Tests

Choose the correct letter for each answer.

1. **Paul has 2 strips of colored paper that are each 3 inches wide and 9 inches long. He puts one strip on top of the other to make a figure like a plus sign. What shape is formed where the strips overlap?**

   A a square 2 in. by 2 in.

   B a square 3 in. by 3 in.

   C a rectangle 2 in. by 3 in.

   D a rectangle 3 in. by 9 in.

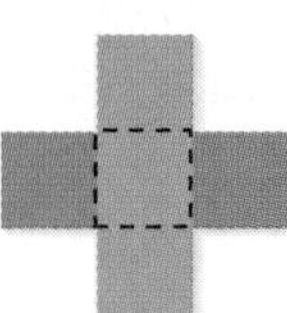

Tip

Use what you know about the length and width of the strips to figure out the length and width of the shape where they overlap.

2. **In 1998, Saryu and her family took a trip to the Grand Canyon. Fifteen years earlier, Saryu's grandmother had visited the Grand Canyon. Five years before that, Saryu's aunt visited the Grand Canyon. Which shows the year that Saryu's grandmother visited the Grand Canyon?**

   F 1998 − 15

   G 1998 − 20

   H 1998 − 30

   J 1998 + 15

Tip

Use one of these strategies to solve this problem.

- *Make a Table*
- *Draw a Picture*
- *Work Backward*
- *Write a Number Sentence*

3. **The T-shirts shown are on sale. How much would you pay for 8 T-shirts at this price?**

   A $30

   B $60

   C $120

   D $150

Tip

Try making a table to help you solve this problem. Write down the prices of 2, 4, 6, and 8 T-Shirts.

4. **Philip bought a game for $29 and a stuffed toy for $12. He gave the clerk $50. *About* how much change should Philip get back from the clerk?**

F	About $5	**H**	About $15
G	About $10	**J**	About $20

5. **In a swim race, Megan finished with a time of 45 seconds and Ana finished with a time of 48 seconds. Jen was the winner of the race. Which is a reasonable conclusion?**

A Jen's time was more than 48 seconds.

B Jen's time was less than 45 seconds.

C Megan finished last.

D Ana finished before Megan.

6. **There are 74 students and 10 adults going on a school trip. Each bus holds 35 people. How many buses are needed?**

F	1 bus	**H**	3 buses
G	2 buses	**J**	4 buses

7. **Tessa skated in an in-line skating race. It took her 19 minutes to skate the first half of the race and 32 minutes to skate the second half of the race. *About* how long did Tessa skate in all?**

A About 60 minutes

B About 50 minutes

C About 30 minutes

D About 20 minutes

Use the bar graph to answer Questions 8–11.

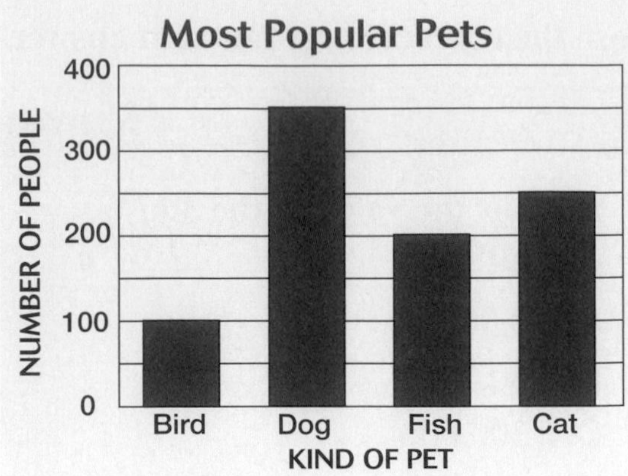

8. **How many more people like cats better than birds?**

F	100	**H**	200
G	150	**J**	250

9. **Which kind of pet is the most popular?**

A	Bird	**C**	Fish
B	Dog	**D**	Cat

10. **How many more people like fish better than birds?**

F	200	**H**	100
G	150	**J**	50

11. **What is the total number of people who participated in the survey on most popular pets?**

A 100 people

B 450 people

C 650 people

D 900 people

E NH

Multiple-Choice Cumulative Review

Choose the correct letter for each answer.

Number Sense

1. What is the value of the 3 in 4,321,078?

 A 3,000
 B 30,000
 C 300,000
 D 3,000,000

2. Which set of numbers is in order from *least* to *greatest?*

 F 4,401 4,312 4,276 4,295
 G 4,312 4,401 4,295 4,276
 H 4,312 4,295 4,401 4,276
 J 4,276 4,295 4,312 4,401

3. The models are shaded to show 2 equivalent fractions. Which fraction is equal to $\frac{1}{4}$?

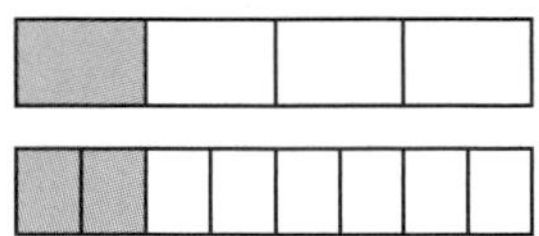

 A $\frac{2}{8}$ C $\frac{2}{4}$
 B $\frac{1}{3}$ D $\frac{4}{1}$

4. What is 3,627 rounded to the nearest thousand?

 F 2,000 H 3,500
 G 3,000 J 4,000

5. Carmen has 19 free passes to a concert. If she keeps one for herself and divides the rest equally among three friends, how many will each friend have?

 A 3 C 8
 B 6 D 18

6. It is Peter's turn to bring in the fourth-grade snack. There are 23 other students in his class. How many graham crackers should Peter bring so that he and his classmates each get 4 crackers?

 F 96 H 200
 G 108 J 204

7. A benefit raffle raised $382. *About* how many tickets were sold if each ticket cost $5?

 A About 40 C About 80
 B About 60 D About 100

8. An ad says, "Buy 3 pencils, get 1 pencil free." If you get 12 pencils total, how many of them are free?

 F 3 H 6
 G 4 J 12
  K NH

Algebra and Functions

9. Which number sentence completes the chart?

$6 \times 3 = 18$
$6 \times 30 = 180$
$6 \times 300 = 1{,}800$
■ × ■ = ■

A $3 \times 300 = 900$
B $6 \times 300 = 1{,}800$
C $6 \times 3{,}000 = 18{,}000$
D $6 \times 30{,}000 = 180{,}000$

10. Which number line shows the graph of all whole numbers less than 6 *and* greater than 2?

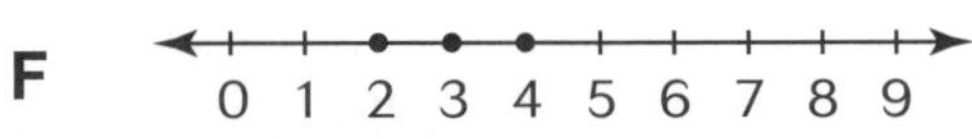

11. If 28 divided by a number is 4, which number sentence could be used to find the number?

A 4 × ■ = 28 **C** 28 − ■ = 4
B 28 + 4 = ■ **D** 28 × 4 = ■

12. What is the missing number in the number pattern?

12, 24, 36, 48, ■, 72

F 54 **H** 66
G 60 **J** 68

Measurement and Geometry

13. Which space figure would you use to draw the plane figure in the box?

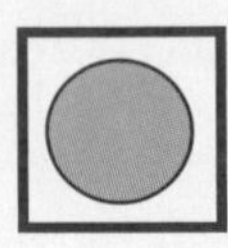

A 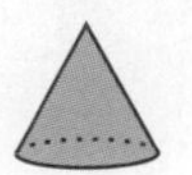 **C** 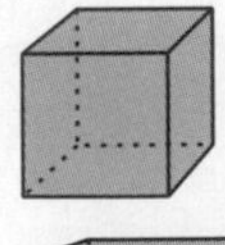

B 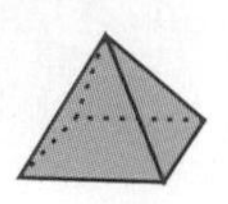 **D** 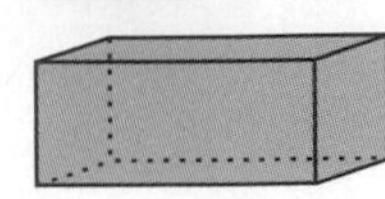

14. How many faces does a triangular prism have?

F 4
G 5
H 6
J 8

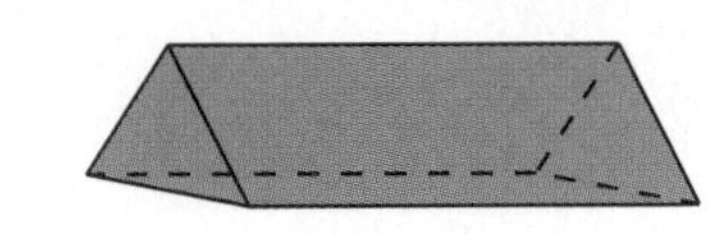

15. Which number has 2 lines of symmetry?

A 8 **C** 2
B 3 **D** 7

16. Which figure represents a pyramid?

F 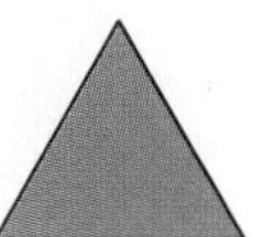 **H** 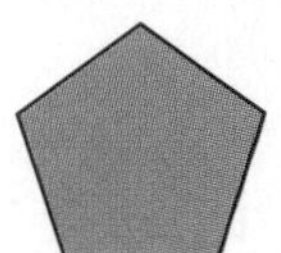

G 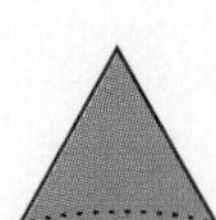 **J** 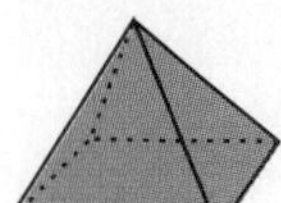

Fraction Concepts and Probability

Diagnosing Readiness

In Chapter 7, you will use these skills:

A Sets and Regions

(Grade 3)

Tell if each figure is divided into equal parts. Write yes or no.

1. 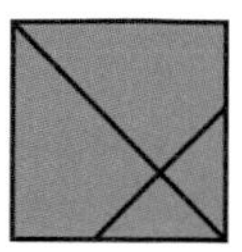

2. 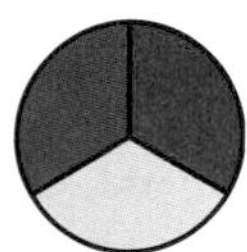

3.

4. 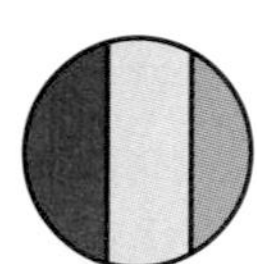

5. Divide the following set into 4 parts with equal numbers of shapes.

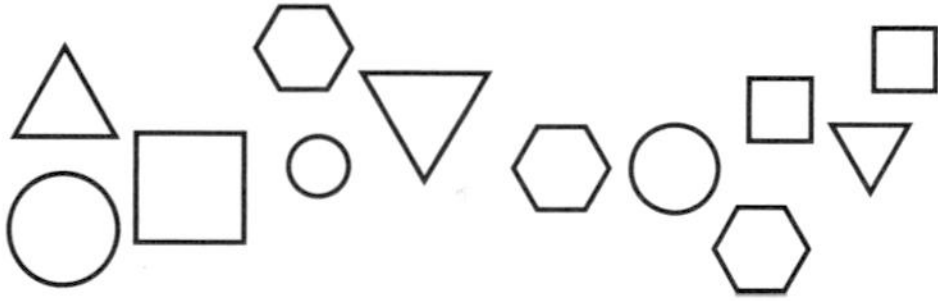

B Dividing

(pages 202–207)

6. 70 ÷ 9

7. $4\overline{)62}$

8. 81 ÷ 5

9. $3\overline{)67}$

10. 93 ÷ 7

11. $8\overline{)55}$

12. $7\overline{)210}$

13. $5\overline{)300}$

14. An audiotape can record 90 minutes of music. Jacob wants to record as many 6-minute songs onto one tape as he can. How may songs can he record?

C Using Parentheses with Computation

(pages 98–100)

15. $(3 \times 6) + 2$

16. $(45 \div 9) + 9$

17. $8 - (42 \div 7)$

18. $(5 \times 3) - 4$

19. $2 + (14 \div 7)$

20. $24 \div (3 + 3)$

21. $(6 + 3 + 11) \times 2$

22. $(3 \times 4) + (7 \times 2)$

D Factors

(pages 223–225)

List all the factors for each number.

23. 8

24. 12

25. 9

26. 7

27. 22

28. 18

29. Write the fact family for 3, 4, and 12.

E Comparing and Ordering Numbers

(pages 8–9)

Compare. Write $>$, $<$, or $=$ for each ●.

30. 107 ● 170

31. 11,348 ● 11,384

32. 364,410 ● 346,000

33. 1,645,314 ● 1,651,314

F Number Lines

(Grade 3)

Find each missing number.

34. 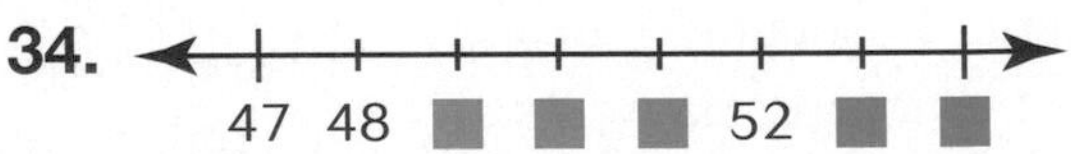

35. 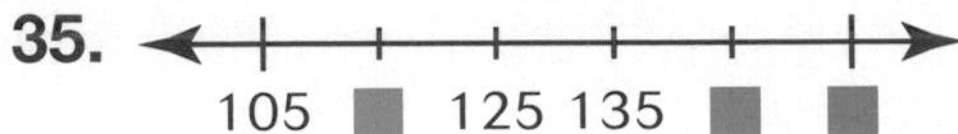

36. 3 ■ 7 9 ■ 13

37. 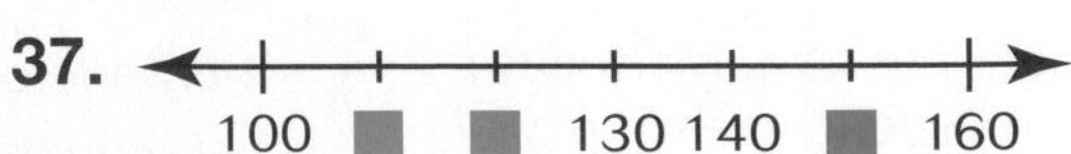

To the Family and Student

Looking Back	Chapter 7	Looking Ahead
In Grade 3, students learned how to identify fractional parts of a whole.	**Fraction Concepts and Probability** In this chapter, students will learn how to interpret fractions and find probability.	In Chapter 8, students will learn to add and subtract fractions and mixed numbers.

Math and Everyday Living

Opportunities to apply the concepts of Chapter 7 abound in everyday situations. During the chapter, think about how fraction concepts and probability can be used to solve a variety of real-world problems. The following examples suggest just several of the many situations that could launch a discussion about fraction concepts and probability.

Math at Home A recipe calls for $\frac{1}{2}$ cup of milk. Is this greater than $\frac{3}{4}$ cup or less than $\frac{3}{4}$ cup?

Math and Construction Nails come in different lengths. James is using three different lengths of nails to build a gazebo: $1\frac{1}{8}$ inches, $\frac{3}{4}$ inches, and $1\frac{3}{16}$ inches. He wants to order the nails by size. Write the nail sizes in order from least to greatest.

Math and Travel Your family is planning to visit 3 different cities in 12 days. You will spend $\frac{1}{3}$ of your visit in each city. How many days will you spend in each city?

Math at the Grocery Store Juice boxes come in packages of 3 boxes. If you have 20 juice boxes, how many packages do you have? Write the answer as an improper fraction and as a mixed number.

Math and Transportation A train carries various food crops across the country. If $\frac{1}{3}$ of the train's 72 cars carry corn, how many cars is this?

Math and Sewing You want to make a dress. You can choose between 2 dress patterns. One pattern requires $2\frac{5}{8}$ yards of fabric. The other requires $2\frac{3}{4}$ yards of fabric. If you want to make the dress that requires the least amount of fabric, which one should you make?

Math and Celebrations You invite 11 friends to your birthday party. You want to make sure you have enough pizza for everyone to have 3 slices. If a pizza has 12 slices, what fraction of the pizza is 3 slices? How many whole pizzas should you order for you and 11 friends?

Math and Games You and a friend are playing a game with a game spinner. The spinner has 6 equal spaces. Four of the spaces are green and 2 of the spaces are yellow. You need to spin yellow on your next turn. What is the probability that you will spin yellow?

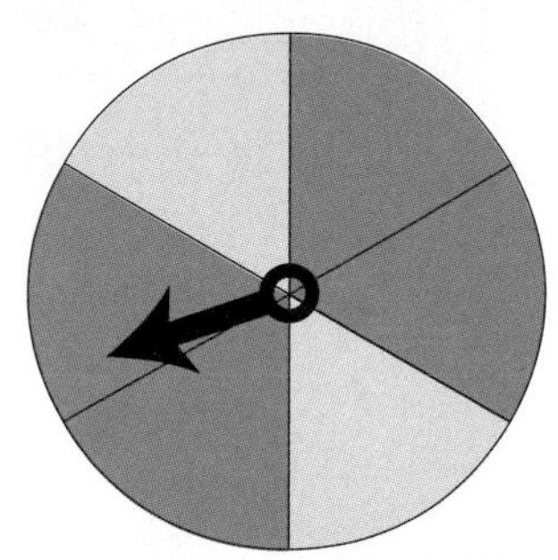

California Content Standards in Chapter 7 Lessons*

	Teach and Practice	Practice
Number Sense		
1.5 Explain different interpretations of fractions, for example, parts of a whole, parts of a set, and division of whole numbers by whole numbers; explain equivalents of fractions.	7-1, 7-2, 7-4, 7-5, 7-7, 7-8	7-3, 7-6
1.7 Write the fraction represented by a drawing of parts of a figure; represent a given fraction by using drawings; and relate a fraction to a simple decimal on a number line.	7-1, 7-2, 7-4, 7-5, 7-7	7-3
1.9 (🔑) Identify on a number line the relative position of positive fractions, positive mixed numbers, and positive decimals to two decimal places.	7-3, 7-4, 7-7	
4.1 Understand that many whole numbers break down in different ways. (e.g., $12 = 4 \times 3 = 2 \times 6 = 2 \times 2 \times 3$).		7-8
Statistics, Data Analysis, and Probability		
2.0 Students make predictions for simple probability situations.	7-10, 7-13	
2.1 Represent all possible outcomes for a simple probability situation in an organized way.	7-11	
2.2 Express outcomes of experimental probability situations verbally and numerically.	7-12	

	Teach and Practice	Practice
Mathematical Reasoning		
1.1 Analyze problems by identifying relationships, distinguishing relevant from irrelevant information, sequencing and prioritizing information, and observing patterns.	7-9	
1.2 Determine when and how to break a problem into simpler parts.		7-9
2.0 Students use strategies, skills, and concepts in finding solutions.		7-6, 7-9, 7-13
2.2 Apply strategies and results from simpler problems to more complex problems.		7-11
2.3 Use a variety of methods, such as words, numbers, symbols, charts, graphs, tables, diagrams, and models, to explain mathematical reasoning.		7-1, 7-2, 7-4, 7-10, 7-12
3.1 Evaluate the reasonableness of the solution in the context of the original situation.	7-6	
3.2 Note the method of deriving the solution and demonstrate a conceptual understanding of the derivation by solving similar problems.		7-9, 7-13
3.3 Develop generalizations of the results obtained and apply them in other circumstances.		7-3, 7-5, 7-8

* The symbol (🔑) indicates a key standard as designated in the Mathematics Framework for California Public Schools. Full statements of the California Content Standards are found at the beginning of this book following the Table of Contents.

Parts of a Region

California Content Standard *Number Sense 1.7: Write the fraction represented by a drawing of parts of a figure; represent a given fraction by using drawings. . . . Also, Number Sense 1.5 (See p. 251.)*

Warm-Up Review

Tell if each figure is divided into equal parts.

1. 
2. 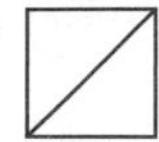
3. Draw a segment $\frac{3}{4}$ inch long.
4. If a granola bar is sliced into thirds, how many pieces are there?

Math Link You have learned to recognize equal parts of a region. Now you will write the fraction for those equal parts and draw your own pictures that represent fractions.

Example 1

Jocelyn and Spence decided to paint their treehouse floor four different colors. You can use a fraction to describe the part of the floor they have painted so far.

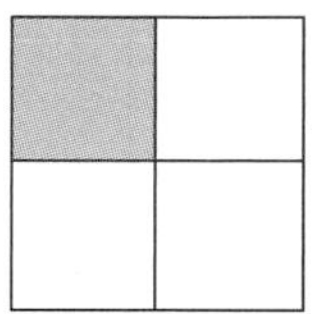

There are four equal parts, so the painted part is one-fourth, or $\frac{1}{4}$, of the floor.

number of equal parts painted ⟶ 1 ⟵ **numerator**
total number of equal parts ⟶ 4 ⟵ **denominator**

Four-fourths make up the whole floor. So we can write $\frac{4}{4} = 1$.

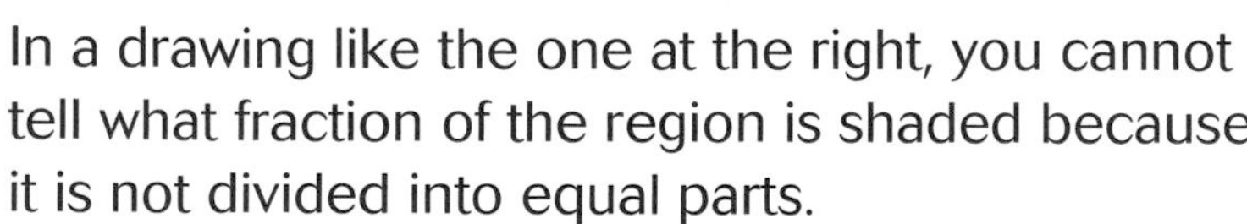

In a drawing like the one at the right, you cannot tell what fraction of the region is shaded because it is not divided into equal parts.

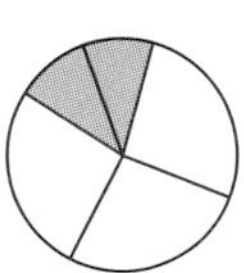

Example 2

Word Bank
numerator
denominator

Draw a picture to show $\frac{3}{8}$.

First draw a simple region and divide it into eight equal parts. Then shade any 3 of the parts.

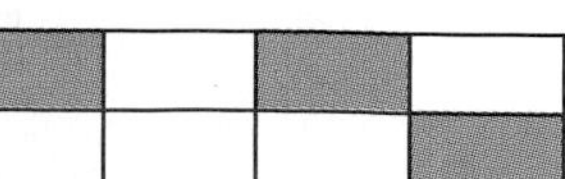

Think: number of equal parts shaded ⟶ 3
total number of equal parts ⟶ 8

 Additional Standard: Mathematical Reasoning 2.3 (See p. 251.)

Guided Practice *For another example, see Set A on p. 292.*

Write the fraction for the shaded parts of each region.

1. 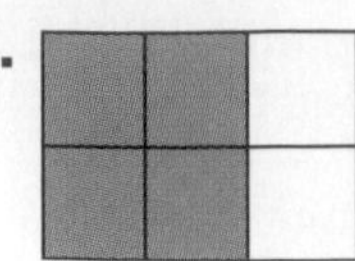 **2.** 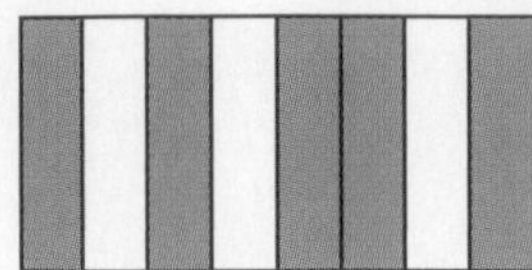 **3.** 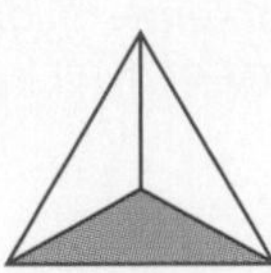 **4.** 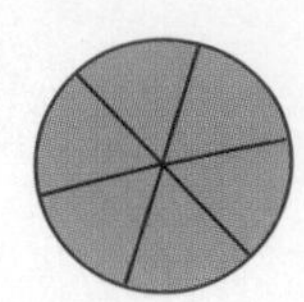

5. Gwen planted vegetables in $\frac{5}{6}$ of her garden. Draw a picture to show $\frac{5}{6}$.

Independent Practice *For more practice, see Set A on p. 295.*

Write the fraction for the shaded parts of each region.

6. 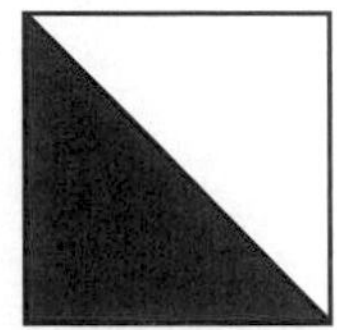 **7.**  **8.** 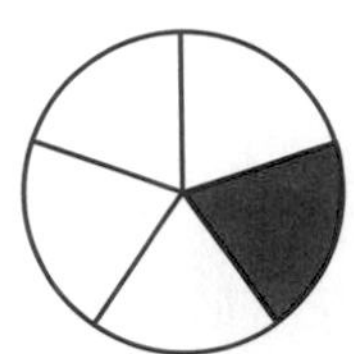 **9.** 

Draw a picture to show each fraction.

10. $\frac{1}{3}$ **11.** $\frac{2}{6}$ **12.** $\frac{1}{5}$ **13.** $\frac{1}{7}$ **14.** $\frac{2}{3}$ **15.** $\frac{5}{5}$

16. $\frac{3}{4}$ **17.** $\frac{5}{8}$ **18.** $\frac{8}{8}$ **19.** $\frac{3}{10}$ **20.** $\frac{7}{14}$ **21.** $\frac{7}{12}$

22. Math Reasoning Jocelyn made the flag shown at the right for the treehouse. Is it $\frac{3}{5}$ red? Explain why or why not.

Mixed Review

23. Denise's scores on three science tests were 71, 66, and 82. What is the mean score?

24. You know 15 + 21 = 36. Does 15 + 21 + 6 = 36 + 6? Explain.

25. 719 ÷ 7 **26.** 400 × 5,000 **27.** (8 + 11) × 13 **28.** 5)5,152

Test Prep Choose the correct letter for each answer.

29. $6.62 × 55 =
(5-7)

A $66.20 **B** $342.10 **C** $364.10 **D** $365.10 **E** NH

30. Algebra If *n* − 84 = 107, then *n* =
(2-11)

F 13 **G** 23 **H** 181 **J** 193 **K** NH

LESSON 7-2

Parts of a Set

California Content Standard *Number Sense 1.5: Explain different interpretations of fractions, for example, . . . parts of a set . . .. Also, Number Sense 1.7 (See p. 251.)*

Warm-Up Review

1. 24 ÷ 6
2. 49 ÷ 7
3. Write the fraction for the shaded parts of the region.

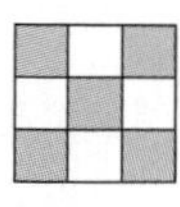

Draw a picture to show each fraction.

4. $\frac{4}{5}$
5. $\frac{1}{8}$

Math Link In the last lesson, you used fractions to name parts of a region. In this lesson, you will use fractions to describe parts of a set.

Example 1

What fraction of this train is made up of boxcars?

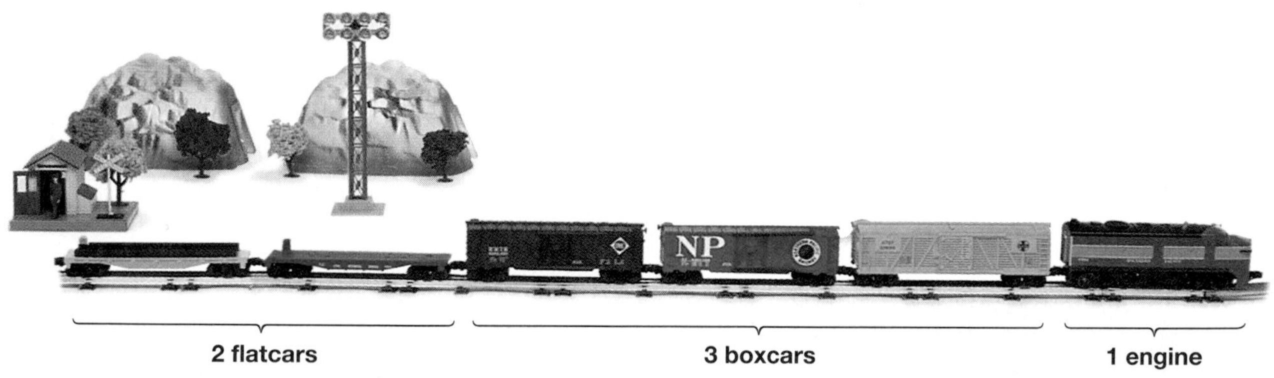

We can think about all the cars in the train as 1 whole set. We use a fraction to describe part of this whole set.

There are six cars in this train, and three of the cars are boxcars. So boxcars make up three-sixths, or $\frac{3}{6}$, of the train set.

number of boxcars ⟶ 3 ⟵ numerator

total parts of the train ⟶ 6 ⟵ denominator

Example 2

Find $\frac{1}{3}$ of 15.

Divide 15 into 3 equal parts.

$15 \div 3 = 5$

$\frac{1}{3}$ of $15 = 5$

Think of 15 as 1 whole set. If you divide the set into 3 equal parts, each part is $\frac{1}{3}$ of the whole set.

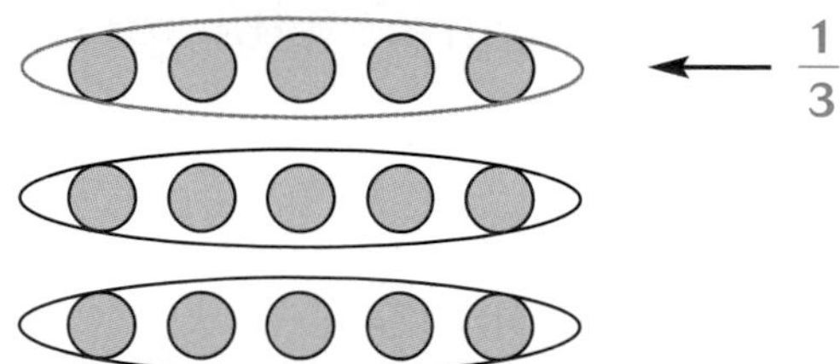

 Additional Standard: Mathematical Reasoning 2.3 (See p. 251.)

Example 3

Draw a picture with shaded shapes to show $\frac{4}{7}$.

First draw 7 simple shapes. Then shade 4 of them.

Think: number of shaded shapes ⟶ $\frac{4}{7}$ ⟵ total number of shapes

More Examples

A. What fraction of the squares are green?

number of green squares ⟶ $\frac{5}{8}$ ⟵ total number of squares

B. What is $\frac{1}{8}$ of 32?

$32 \div 8 = 4$

$\frac{1}{8}$ of $32 = 4$

Guided Practice *For another example, see Set B on p. 292.*

Write the fraction for the shaded parts of each set.

1.

2. 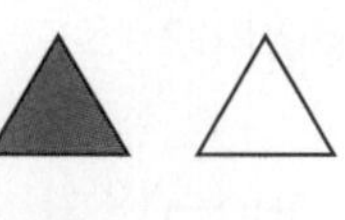

3. 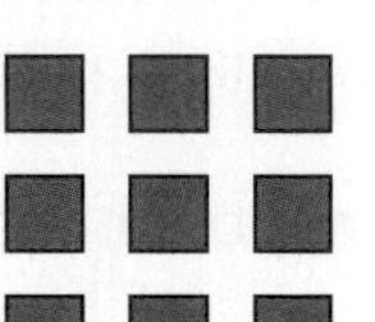

4. 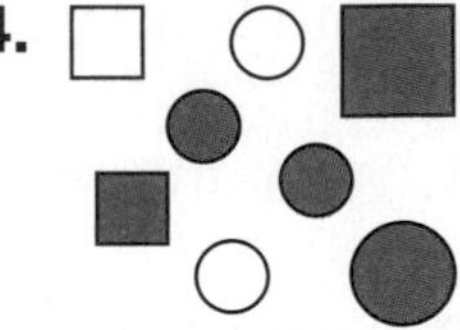

5. There are 20 train cars in a train set, and $\frac{1}{4}$ of the cars are tanker cars. How many tanker cars are in the set?

Independent Practice *For more practice, see Set B on p. 295.*

Write the fraction for the shaded parts of each set.

6.

7. 

8. 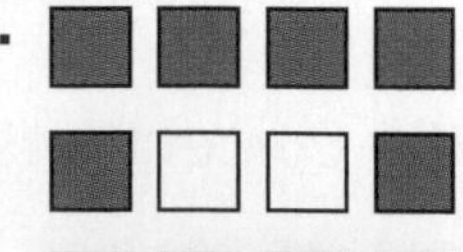

9. 

Draw a set of shapes and shade them to show each fraction.

10. $\frac{2}{3}$ **11.** $\frac{1}{5}$ **12.** $\frac{9}{12}$ **13.** $\frac{6}{6}$ **14.** $\frac{1}{10}$ **15.** $\frac{7}{8}$

Use the table at the right for Exercises 16–18.

Train Set Accessories	
Number	Accessories
2	Trestles
2	Bridges
7	Trees
4	Stoplights
4	Warning Lights
1	Train Station
1	Tunnel

16. What fraction of the train accessories are stoplights? Which fraction are bridges, trestles, and tunnels altogether?

17. What fraction would represent all the items in the set?

18. One-third of the accessories are made out of metal. How many accessories are made out of metal?

19. **Math Reasoning** What fraction of the stars are in the square? What fraction of the stars are in the circle? What fraction of the stars are in both the square and the circle at the same time?

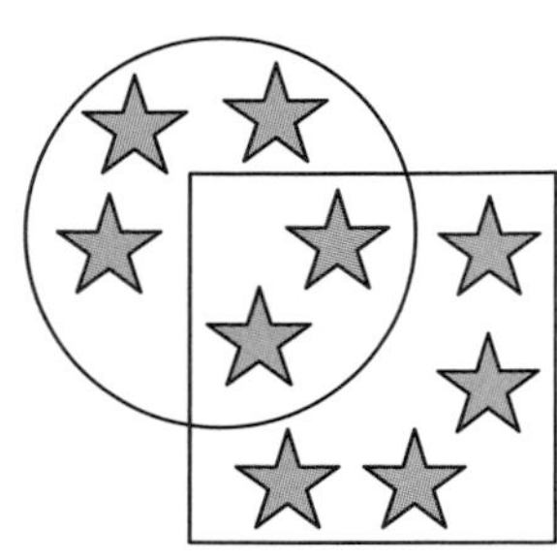

Mixed Review

20. The Bread Bakers baked 18 dozen buns. There are 12 buns to a dozen. If they place them on paper plates with 9 on a plate, how many plates will they fill?

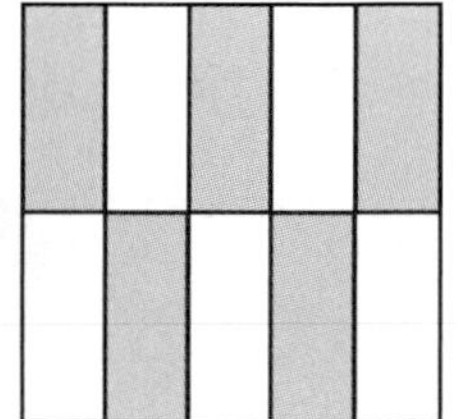

21. What fraction of the region at the right is shaded?

22. Given the equation $x + 12 = 33$, does $x + 12 - 12 = 33 \times 12$? Tell why or why not.

Rule: Divide by 6

	Input	Output
23.	642	■
24.	1,080	■
25.	1,218	■

Rule: Multiply by 4

	Input	Output
26.	63	■
27.	205	■
28.	1,419	■

Rule: Multiply by 27

	Input	Output
29.	124	■
30.	306	■
31.	815	■

Test Prep Choose the correct letter for each answer.

32. **Algebra** If $17n = 0$, then $n =$
(3-2)

A 0 B 17 C 18 D 34 E NH

33. $316.44 + $22.77 + $207.09 =
(2-4)

F $751.23 G $546.30 H $546.20 J $545.30 K NH

Fractions On a Number Line

Warm-Up Review

Write the fraction for the shaded part of each region.

1. 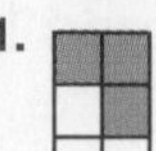

2. 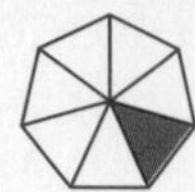

3. Draw a shaded region to show $\frac{3}{8}$.

4. Identify the missing numbers.

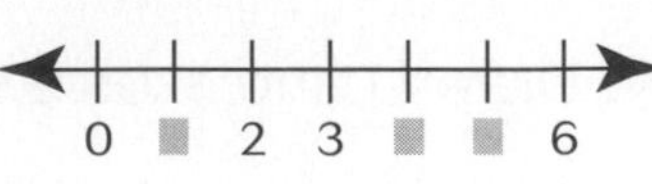

California Content Standard *Number Sense 1.9 (🔑): Identify on a number line the relative position of positive fractions . . ..*

Math Link You have learned how fractions are used to describe part of a whole. Now you will learn how to place fractions on a number line.

You can think of the distance from 0 to 1 on a number line as 1 whole.

If you divide this distance into equal parts, you can place fractions on the number line.

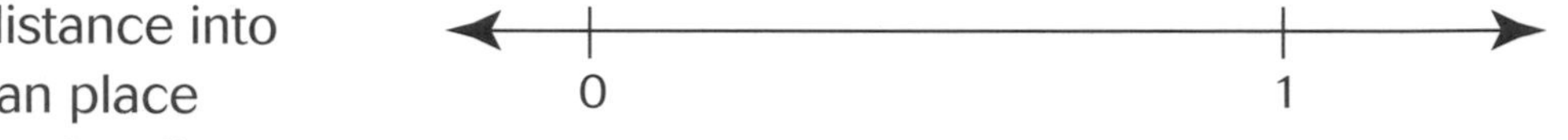

Example 1

Show $\frac{2}{3}$ on a number line.

Place 0 and 1 on a number line. Then divide the distance from 0 to 1 into 3 equal parts.

Label $\frac{1}{3}$ and $\frac{2}{3}$.

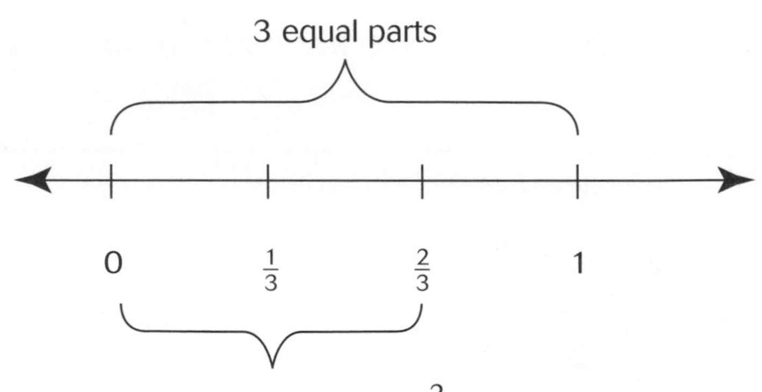

Example 2

What fraction should be written at point *A*?

There are 5 equal parts between 0 and 1. Point *A* shows 3 of the 5 equal parts.

So $\frac{3}{5}$ should be written at point *A*.

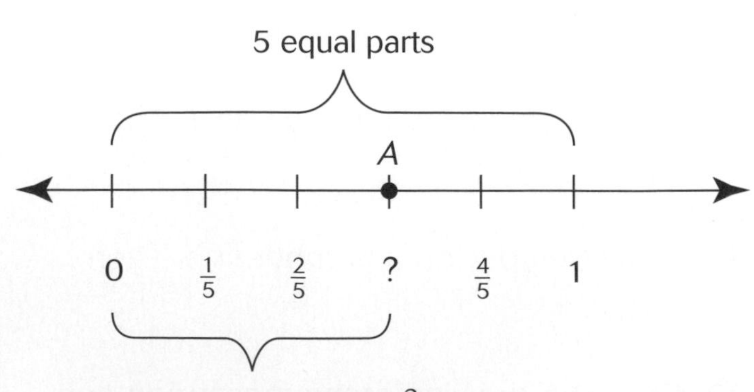

Additional Standards: Number Sense 1.5, 1.7; Mathematical Reasoning 3.3 *(See p. 251.)*

Guided Practice *For another example, see Set C on p. 292.*

What fraction should be written at each point?

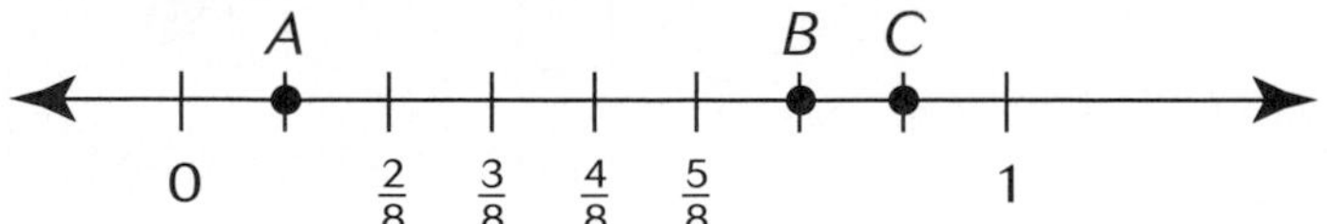

1. point *A**2.** point *B**3.** point *C*

4. Draw 0 and 1 on a number line. Then show $\frac{1}{6}$.

Independent Practice *For more practice, see Set C on p. 295.*

What fraction should be written at each point?

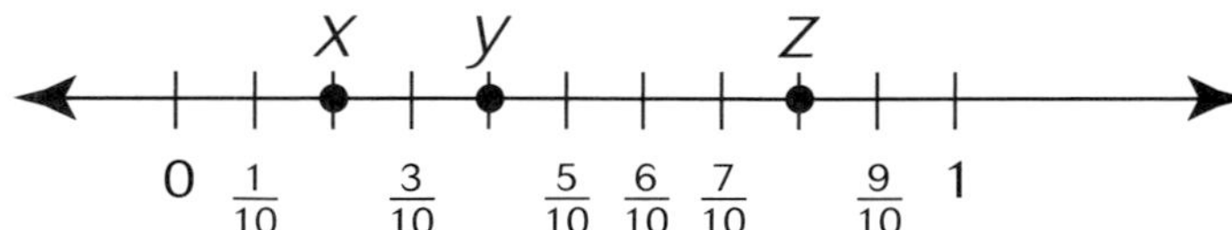

5. point *X**6.** point *Y**7.** point *Z*

In Exercises 8–10, give the missing fractions.

8. 

9. 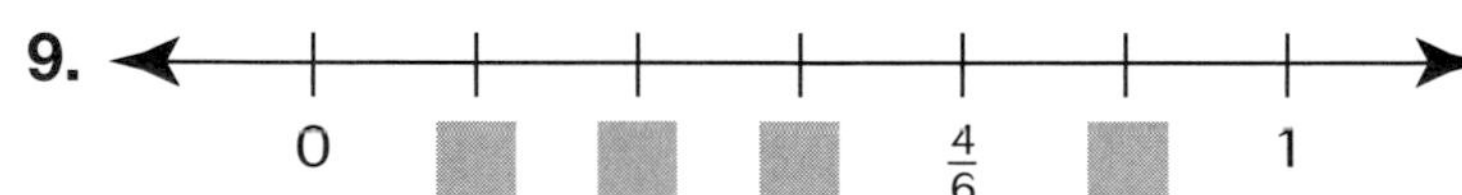

10. 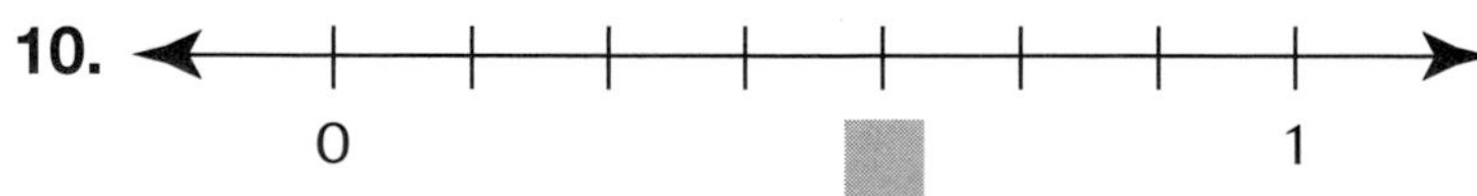

11. Draw 0 and 1 on a number line. Then show $\frac{1}{10}$ and $\frac{5}{10}$.

12. Draw 0 and 1 on a number line. Then show $\frac{7}{12}$.

13. Copy the drawing of the measuring cup. Write the missing measures.

Mixed Review

Use the schedule at the right for Exercises 14–16.

Escorted Canoe Trips	
Trip	**Times**
North Channel	7:00 A.M. to 11:00 A.M.
Henson's Valley	10:00 A.M. to 3:00 P.M.
East Branch	9:00 A.M. to 2:00 P.M.
Little River	10:00 A.M. to 1:00 P.M.
The Narrows	9:00 A.M. to 5:00 P.M.

14. Which canoe trip takes the least amount of time? Which canoe trip takes the greatest amount time?

15. Find the mean number of hours of the canoe trips.

16. On The Narrows canoe trip, $\frac{1}{4}$ of the time is spent hiking. How many hours are spent hiking?

17. Write a fraction for the shaded part of the region.

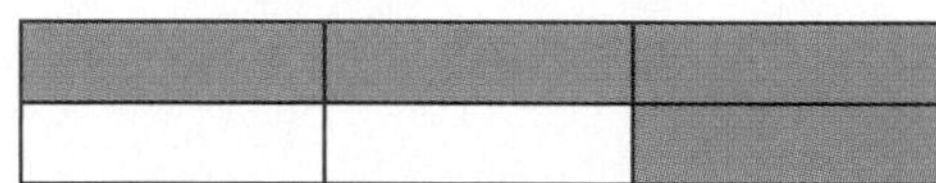

In Exercises 18–20, show $\frac{4}{5}$ using the type of picture described.

18. a set of shapes **19.** a region **20.** a number line

21. Write 36 as a product of two factors in as many ways as possible. Then, if possible, write 36 as a product of three factors, none of which is 1.

22. Estimate 76×32 by finding a range.

23. Estimate $552 \div 9$.

24. Find $\frac{1}{8}$ of 24.

25. Algebra Solve: $8x = 176$ by testing these values for x: 18, 22, 26, 32.

26. $^{-}7$ ⬤ $^{-}5$ **27.** $64{,}000 \div 8$ **28.** $59 \div 5$ **29.** $\begin{array}{r} 6{,}528 \\ \times \quad 41 \\ \hline \end{array}$

Test Prep **Choose the correct letter for each answer.**

30. Find the remainder: $7\overline{)86}$
(6-3)

A 12 **B** 7 **C** 3 **D** 2 **E** NH

31. There are 518 students at Harding School. The cafeteria baked 20 trays of biscuits with 24 biscuits per tray. How many biscuits were baked altogether?
(5-4)

F 1,036 **G** 998 **H** 240 **J** 48 **K** NH

Use Homework Workbook 7-3.

Mixed Numbers

California Content Standard *Number Sense 1.5: Explain different interpretations of fractions . . .. Also, Number Sense 1.7, 1.9 (🔑) (See p. 251.)*

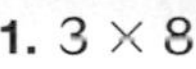

Warm-Up Review

1. 3×8 **2.** $21 \div 4$

3. $33 \div 6$ **4.** $27 \div 9$

5. $1 = \frac{■}{6}$ **6.** $1 = \frac{■}{8}$

7. Show $\frac{7}{10}$ on a number line, as part of a shaded region, and as part of a set.

Math Link You have been using fractions to describe quantities that are less than or equal to one. Now you will learn about fractions that describe quantities that are greater than or equal to one.

Example 1

A quilt is made up of many blocks like the one shown at the right. Each block is made up of small triangle pieces. How many blocks can be made with 13 triangle pieces?

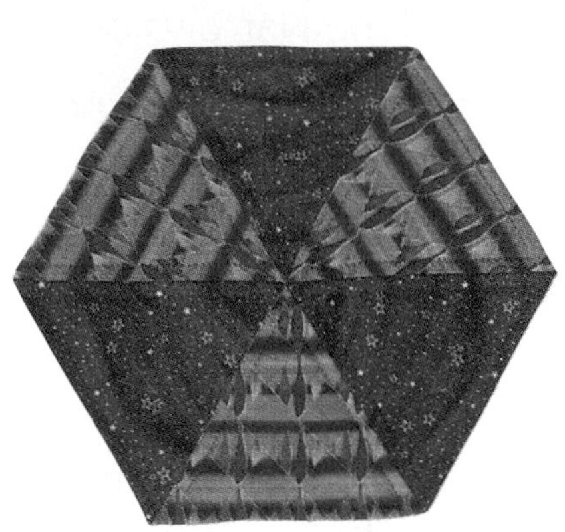

You can see that each triangle is $\frac{1}{6}$ of a whole block.

You have 13 one-sixth pieces, or $\frac{13}{6}$. By piecing them together, you can make $2\frac{1}{6}$ quilt blocks.

Word Bank

improper fraction
mixed number

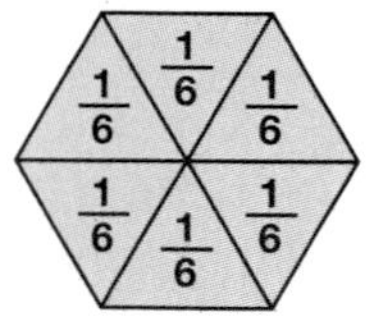

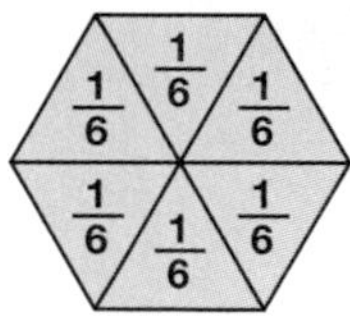

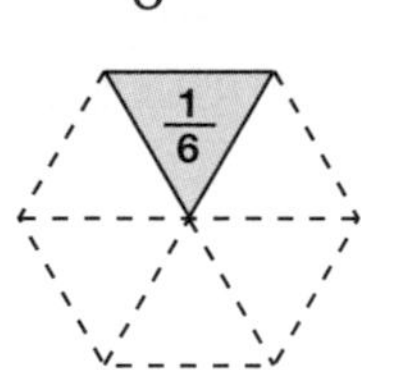

$$\frac{13}{6} = 2\frac{1}{6}$$

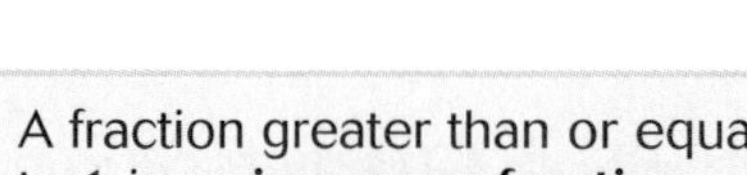

A fraction greater than or equal to 1 is an **improper fraction.**

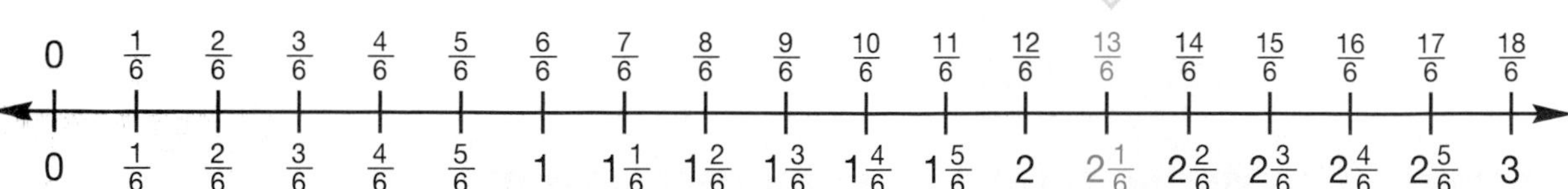

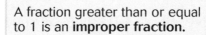

A number containing a whole number part and a fraction part is a **mixed number.**

Every whole number or mixed number can be written as an improper fraction. Similarly, every improper fraction can be written as a whole number or mixed number.

 Additional Standard: Mathematical Reasoning 2.3 (See p. 251.)

Example 2

Write $2\frac{1}{3}$ as an improper fraction.

Multiply the denominator by the whole number and add the numerator.

Write the result over the numerator.

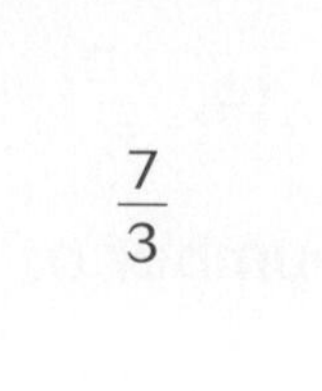

$\frac{7}{3}$

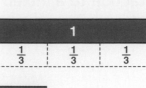

How many thirds are in 2 wholes?

3 thirds in each whole × 2 wholes = 6 thirds

Add another third.

6 thirds + 1 third = 7 thirds

Example 3

Write $\frac{17}{5}$ as a mixed number.

Divide the numerator by the denominator.

$$\begin{array}{r} 3\text{ R2} \\ 5\overline{)17} \\ -\ 15 \\ \hline 2 \end{array}$$

Write the quotient as the whole number. Write the remainder as the numerator of the fraction. Use the same denominator.

$3\frac{2}{5}$

How many wholes can you make with 17 fifths?

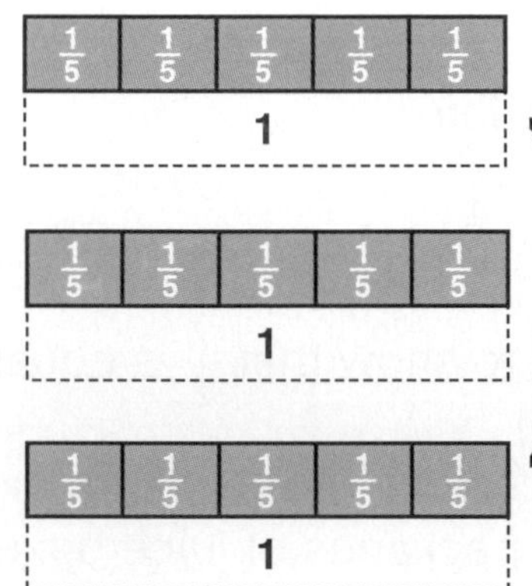

17 fifths ÷ 5 five in each whole = 3R2 wholes

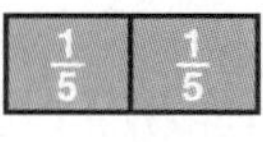

The R2 stands for two-fifths left over.

Guided Practice

For another example, see Set D on p. 292.

Change each improper fraction to a mixed number or whole number, and change each mixed number to an improper fraction.

1. $2\frac{1}{2}$ **2.** $\frac{9}{4}$ **3.** $1\frac{5}{6}$ **4.** $\frac{10}{5}$

5. There are 4 pudding cups in a package. Mrs. Quinn has 7 pudding cups in her pantry. Use a mixed number to tell how many packages this is.

Independent Practice *For more practice, see Set D on p. 290.*

Change each mixed number to an improper fraction.

6. $3\frac{2}{3}$ **7.** $5\frac{1}{2}$ **8.** $1\frac{1}{4}$ **9.** $1\frac{7}{8}$ **10.** $2\frac{4}{5}$

Change each improper fraction to a mixed number or whole number.

11. $\frac{5}{3}$ **12.** $\frac{7}{2}$ **13.** $\frac{8}{4}$ **14.** $\frac{20}{6}$ **15.** $\frac{13}{12}$

Write an improper fraction as well as a mixed number or whole number for each picture.

16. **17.**  **18.** 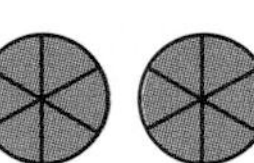 **19.** 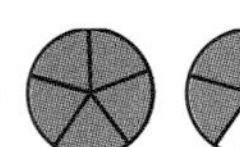

For Exercises 20–23, write the letter that locates each fraction or mixed number on the number line.

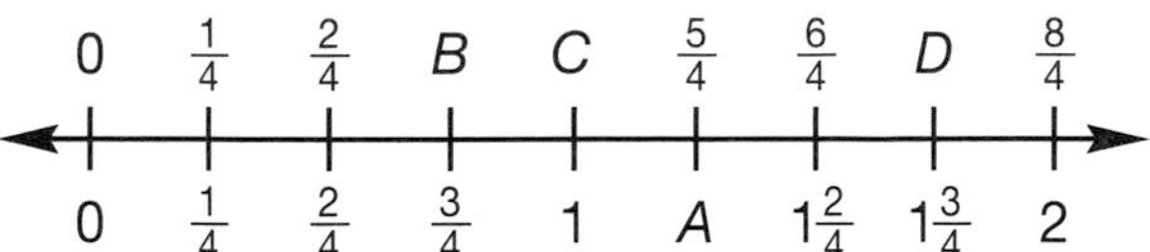

20. $1\frac{1}{4}$ **21.** $\frac{4}{4}$ **22.** $\frac{7}{4}$ **23.** $\frac{3}{4}$

24. Draw a number line to show that $\frac{7}{2}$ is equal to $3\frac{1}{2}$.

25. Write an improper fraction and a mixed number to describe how many packages of juice boxes are shown.

26. Math Reasoning Can the denominator of an improper fraction be greater than the numerator? Explain your answer.

Mixed Review

27. Draw 0 and 1 on a number line. Then show $\frac{3}{8}$, $\frac{6}{8}$, and $\frac{7}{8}$.

28. What fraction of the letters in HAMSTERS are vowels?

29. $4{,}166 + 8{,}553$ **30.** $600 - 247$ **31.** $\$3.62 \times 6$ **32.** $134 - (41 + 93)$

Test Prep **Choose the correct letter for each answer.**

33. (3-9) **Algebra** If $6m = 156$, then $m =$

A 18 **B** 26 **C** 27 **D** 29 **E** NH

34. (1-1) Which number has a 0 in the ten thousands place?

F 41,603 **G** 506,427 **H** 2,038,659 **J** 20,658,941 **K** NH

Fractions and Division

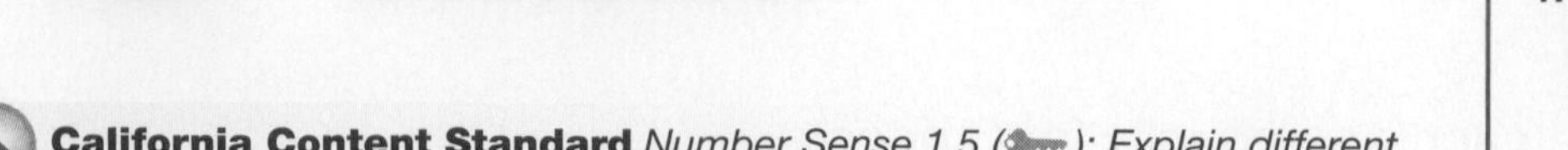

California Content Standard *Number Sense 1.5 (key): Explain different interpretations of fractions, for example, . . . division of whole numbers by whole numbers . . .. Also, Number Sense 1.7 (See p. 251.)*

Warm-Up Review

Write the fraction for the shaded part of each region.

1. 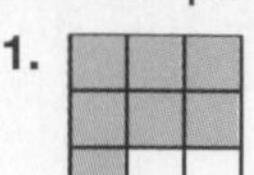

2. 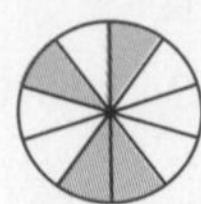

3. Draw a shaded region to show $\frac{1}{6}$.
4. Hillary has 24 dog biscuits to give to her 4 puppies. How many biscuits does each puppy get if they each get the same number?

Math Link You have used division to solve sharing problems with whole numbers. Now you will solve sharing problems that involve fractions.

Example 1

Max and Kate are sharing a vegetable pizza equally. How much does each child get?

Find 1 ÷ 2.

Draw a picture to show 1 pizza divided equally among 2 children.

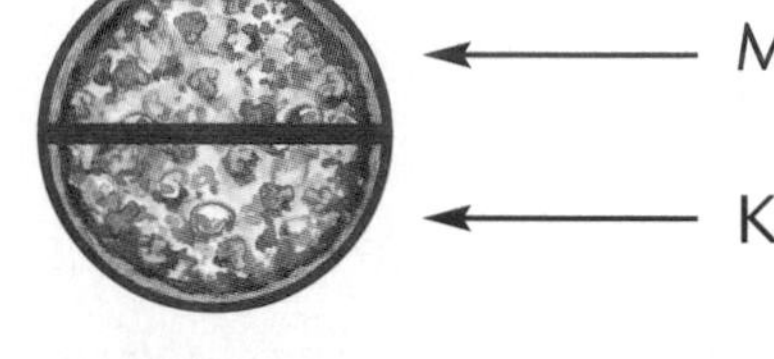

Each child gets $\frac{1}{2}$ pizza.

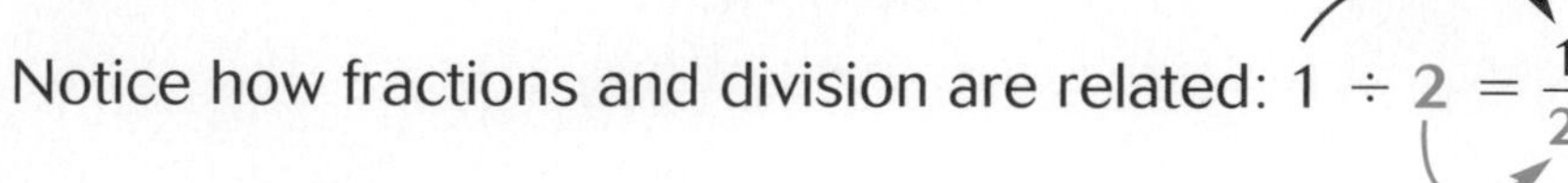

Notice how fractions and division are related: $1 \div 2 = \frac{1}{2}$

Example 2

Find 3 ÷ 5.

To find 3 ÷ 5, think about dividing 3 pizzas equally among 5 people. First divide each pizza into 5 equal parts.

Notice that each of the 5 people gets 1 slice from each pizza for a total of 3 slices. This is the same as $\frac{3}{5}$ of one pizza. →

So, $3 \div 5 = \frac{3}{5}$

  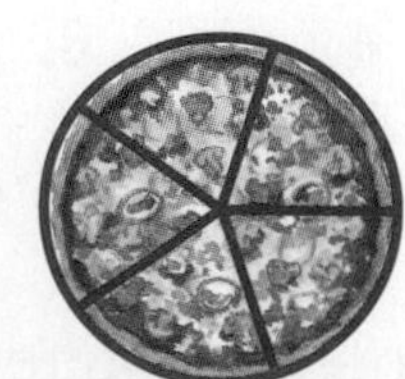

Additional Standard: Mathematical Reasoning 3.3 (See p. 251.)

Example 3

Find $4 \div 3$. Give the answer as a fraction, mixed number, or whole number.

Picture 4 pizzas. Divide each one equally for 3 people.

 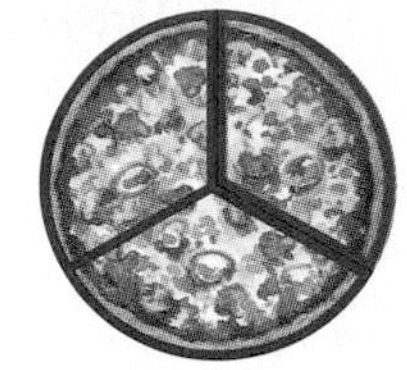 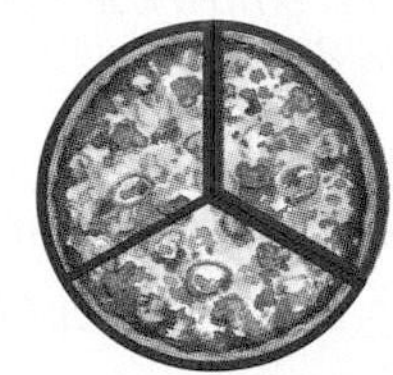 

Each person gets 1 slice of each pizza.

This is the same as $\frac{4}{3}$, or $1\frac{1}{3}$ pizzas. →

$4 \div 3 = \frac{4}{3}$, or $1\frac{1}{3}$

   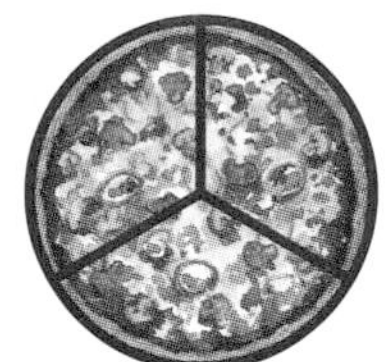

More Examples

A. Find $2 \div 8$. Give the answer as a fraction, mixed number, or whole number.

$2 \div 8 = \frac{2}{8}$

B. Find $10 \div 7$. Give the answer as a fraction, mixed number, or whole number.

$10 \div 7 = \frac{10}{7}$, or $1\frac{3}{7}$

Guided Practice *For another example, see Set E on p. 293.*

Give each answer as a fraction, mixed number, or whole number.

1. $1 \div 3$ **2.** $4 \div 5$ **3.** $3 \div 2$ **4.** $10 \div 4$ **5.** $8 \div 3$

6. Mrs. Berg ordered 3 pizzas to be shared equally by her family of 8. How much does each person get?

Independent Practice *For more practice, see Set E on p. 296.*

Give each answer as a fraction, mixed number, or whole number.

7. $1 \div 4$ **8.** $5 \div 6$ **9.** $7 \div 3$ **10.** $1 \div 9$ **11.** $7 \div 10$

12. $5 \div 2$ **13.** $9 \div 8$ **14.** $12 \div 4$ **15.** $3 \div 9$ **16.** $15 \div 7$

17. A pound of butter is divided equally into 4 sticks. What fraction of a pound does each stick weigh?

18. The table at the right shows the food Valerie bought for 4 gift baskets she made. Each basket was the same. Find the amount of each type of food that Valerie put in each basket.

Food	Amount
Cheddar cheese	2 pounds
California pistachio nuts	6 pounds
Canned juice	24 cans
Crackers	4 boxes

19. Juice boxes are sold in packages of 3. Ms. Lake has 11 juice boxes in the pantry. Use a mixed number to tell how many packages this is.

20. Math Reasoning Write a problem about friends sharing granola bars that could be pictured by the diagram at the right.

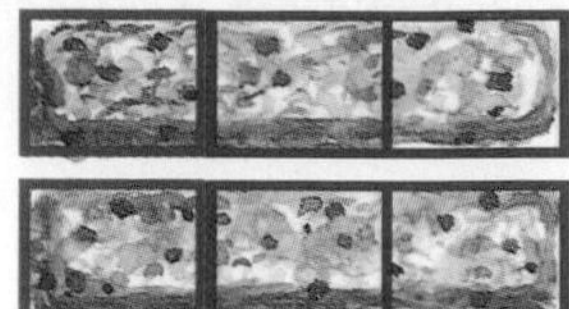

Mixed Review

21. Five children share 85 marbles equally. How many marbles does each child get?

22. There are 32 people at a picnic, and $\frac{1}{8}$ of them are babies. How many babies are at the picnic?

23. Give the missing numbers on the number line.

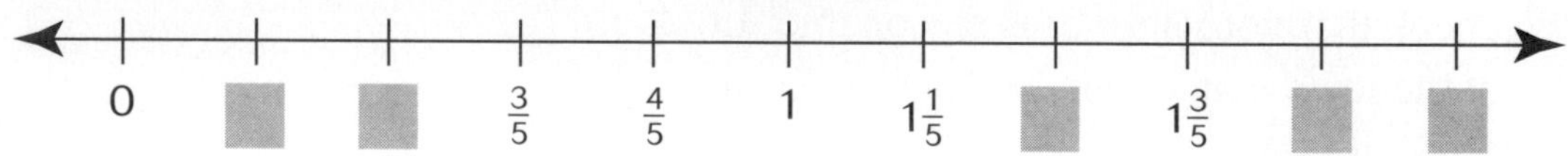

24. Algebra Evaluate $\frac{n}{6}$ for $n = 48$.

25. Write 48 as a product of three factors.

26. $\begin{array}{r} 947 \\ +\ 617 \\ \hline \end{array}$ **27.** $\begin{array}{r} 512 \\ \times\ 45 \\ \hline \end{array}$ **28.** $\begin{array}{r} 8{,}000 \\ -\ 458 \\ \hline \end{array}$ **29.** $777 \div 7$ **30.** $6\overline{)52{,}503}$

Test Prep Choose the correct letter for each answer.

31. (6-10) The daily high temperatures last week were 56°F, 54°F, 48°F, 54°F, 51°F, 44°F, and 43°. Find the mean high temperature.

A 70°F **C** 50°F

B 54°F **D** 5°F

32. (1-5) Round 53,618,357 to the nearest hundred thousand.

F 53,600,000 **H** 53,700,000

G 53,620,000 **J** 54,000,000

Use Homework Workbook 7-5.

Problem-Solving Skill:
Reasonable Answers

Warm-Up Review

1. $47 \div 5$ 2. $36 \div 7$

Write as a mixed number.

3. $\frac{16}{5}$ 4. $\frac{27}{4}$

5. $5 \div 8 = \frac{■}{■}$

6. $\frac{11}{3} = ■ \div 3$

7. Six friends equally share 30 baseball cards. How many cards does each friend get?

California Content Standard *Mathematical Reasoning 3.1: Evaluate the reasonableness of the solution in the context of the original situation.*

Read For Understanding

Mr. Ossmo bought a package of 10 model cars for Anders, Debbie, and Mark. How many cars does each child get if they share them equally?

1. How many cars are in the package?
2. How many children are sharing the cars?

Think and Discuss

Reasonable Answers

Whenever you solve a problem, you should check that your answer is reasonable. Look at the facts that are given. Then make sure your answer makes sense when compared to those facts.

Reread the paragraph at the top of the page.

3. Anders found each person's share by relating division and fractions. He said each child gets $3\frac{1}{3}$ cars. Is that reasonable?
4. Mark found each person's share by doing a division problem. He said each child gets 3 cars, and 1 car is left over. Is this reasonable?
5. Look back at Exercises 3 and 4. How did reading the paragraph at the top of the page help you decide if the answers were reasonable?

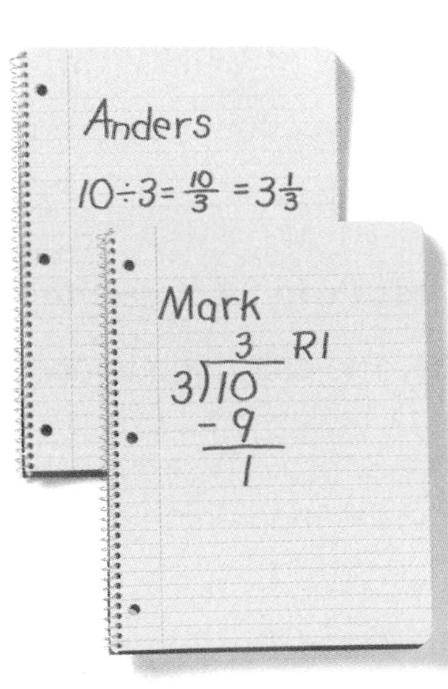

 Additional Standards: Number Sense 1.5; Mathematical Reasoning 2.0 (See p. 251.)

Two friends are sharing 5 burritos. If they divide them evenly, and each gets as much as possible, how much would each friend get?

Guided Practice

1. Which division sentence tells how the friends should share the burritos?
   - **a.** $5 \div 2 = 2$ R1
   - **b.** $5 \div 2 = \frac{5}{2} = 2\frac{1}{2}$
   - **c.** $2 \div 5 = \frac{2}{5}$

2. What is the most reasonable way to share the burritos?
   - **a.** Each friend gets 2 burritos, and 1 is left over.
   - **b.** Each friend gets $2\frac{1}{2}$ burritos.
   - **c.** Each friend gets 1 burrito and 3 are left over.

Independent Practice

Mrs. Cassini is planning party decorations for 4 tables. She has 18 balloons, 5 yards of ribbon, and 38 flowers. She wants the tables to look the same, and she wants to use as much of her decorations as possible.

3. Which division sentence tells how Mrs. Cassini should divide up the balloons?
   - **a.** $4 \div 18 = \frac{4}{18}$
   - **b.** $18 \div 4 = \frac{18}{4} = 4\frac{2}{4}$
   - **c.** $18 \div 4 = 4$ R2

4. How many balloons should she use for each table?
   - **a.** 2 balloons
   - **b.** $4\frac{2}{4}$ balloons
   - **c.** 4 balloons

5. Which division sentence tells how Mrs. Cassini should divide up the ribbon?
   - **a.** $5 \div 4 = 1$ R1
   - **b.** $5 \div 4 = \frac{5}{4} = 1\frac{1}{4}$
   - **c.** $4 \div 5 = \frac{4}{5}$

6. How much ribbon should she use for each table?
   - **a.** 1 yard
   - **b.** $1\frac{1}{4}$ yards
   - **c.** 5 yards

7. **Math Reasoning** Will Mrs. Cassini have any decorations left over? Explain.

Equivalent Fractions

California Content Standard *Number Sense 1.5: Explain different interpretations of fractions, for example, . . . explain equivalence of fractions. Also, Number Sense 1.7, 1.9* *(See p. 251.)*

Warm-Up Review

1. 2×6
2. 8×4
3. $20 \div 5$
4. $27 \div 3$

Show $\frac{3}{5}$ using each type of drawing.

5. number line
6. shaded region
7. set of shapes
8. Doreen has 14 T-shirts. Three of them are green. What fraction of Doreen's T-shirts are green?

Math Link You have learned how to use fractions to name parts of a region, name parts of a set, or identify points on a number line. Now you will learn how to find fractions that name the same amount.

Brett placed some fraction pieces on his desk. He noticed that 2 of the $\frac{1}{4}$ pieces show the same amount as a $\frac{1}{2}$ piece.

Since $\frac{1}{2}$ and $\frac{2}{4}$ name the same amount, they are called **equivalent fractions.**

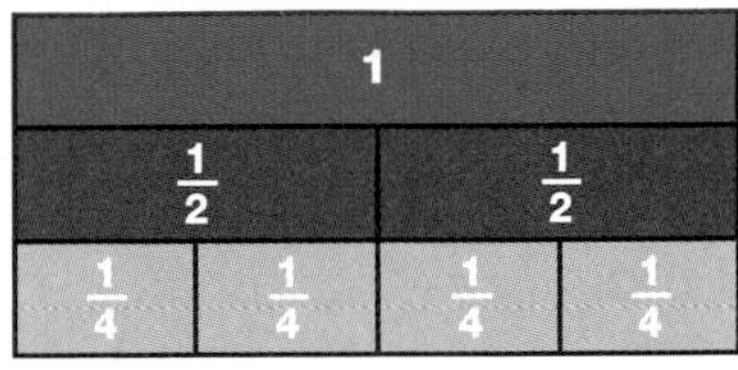

$$\frac{1}{2} = \frac{2}{4}$$

Word Bank

equivalent fractions

simplest form

You can also use number lines or sets to show equivalent fractions.

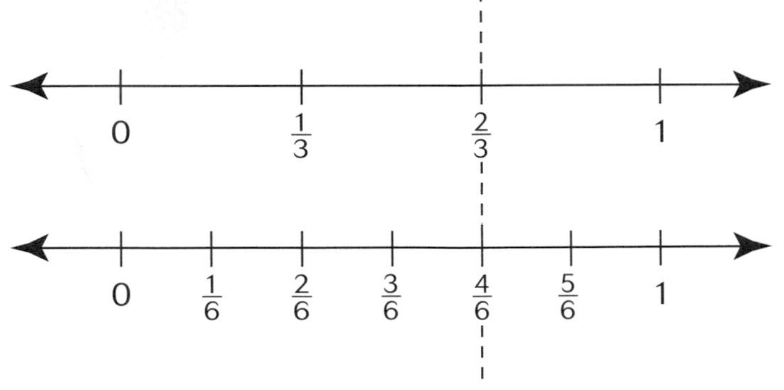

$$\frac{2}{3} = \frac{4}{6}$$

number of yellow flowers → $\frac{4}{10} = \frac{2}{5}$ ← containers with yellow flowers

total number of flowers → ← total number of containers

In the examples, you will learn how to use multiplication or division to find equivalent fractions.

Example 1

Use multiplication to find a fraction that is equivalent to $\frac{3}{4}$.

Multiply the numerator and denominator by the same number.

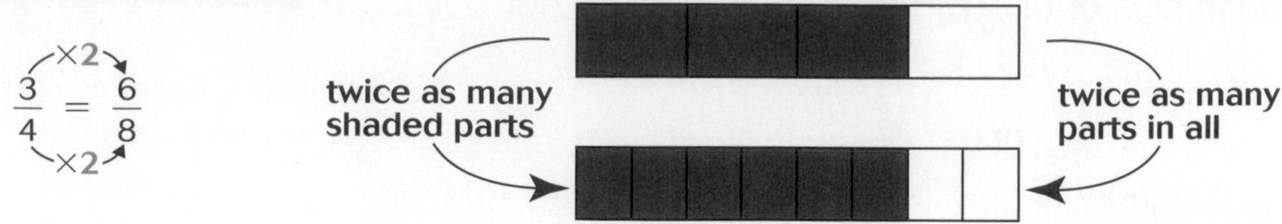

If you choose other numbers, you'll get other equivalent fractions. Do not use 0.

$\frac{3}{4} \overset{\times 3}{=} \frac{9}{12}$ $\qquad$ $\frac{3}{4} \overset{\times 5}{=} \frac{15}{20}$ $\qquad$ $\frac{3}{4} \overset{\times 10}{=} \frac{30}{40}$

$\frac{6}{8}$, $\frac{9}{12}$, $\frac{15}{20}$, and $\frac{30}{40}$ are all equivalent to $\frac{3}{4}$.

Example 2

Use division to write a fraction that is equivalent to $\frac{12}{18}$.

Think of a number that is a factor of both 12 and 18.

2 is a factor of both 12 and 18.

Divide the numerator and denominator by that factor.

$\frac{12}{18} \overset{\div 2}{=} \frac{6}{9}$

You can divide by other factors of both 12 and 18 to get other equivalent fractions.

If you continue to divide until 1 is the only number that is a factor of both the numerator and the denominator, you find the fraction in **simplest form.**

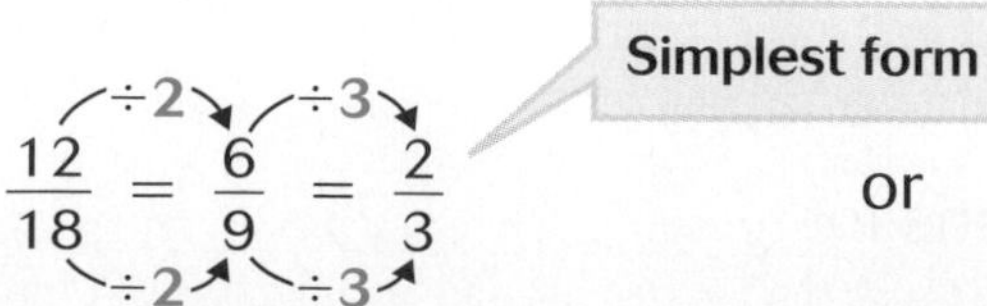

or

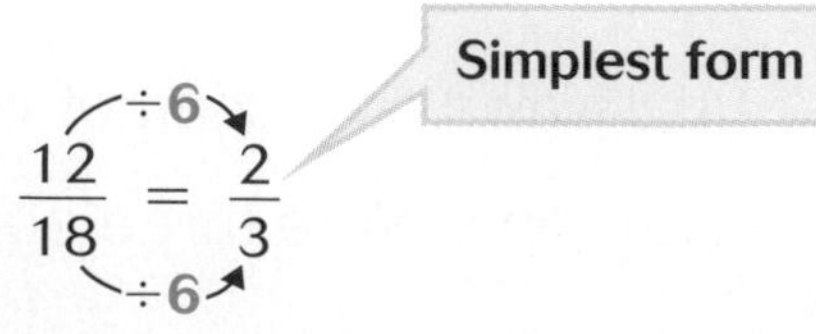

$\frac{6}{9}$ and $\frac{2}{3}$ are both equivalent to $\frac{12}{18}$. Only $\frac{2}{3}$ is in simplest form.

Example 3

Is $\frac{2}{3}$ equivalent to $\frac{4}{5}$?

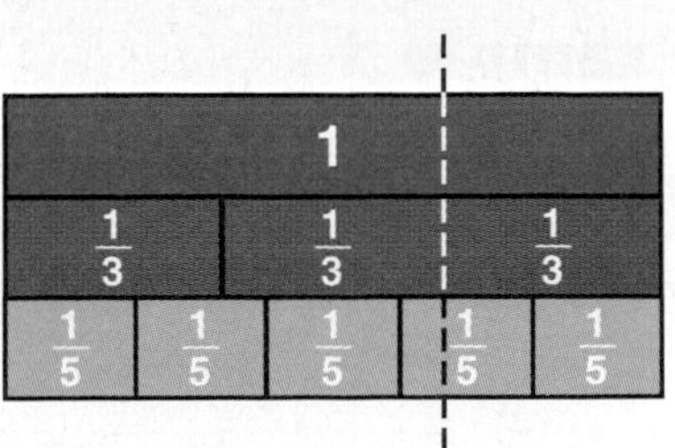

2 of the $\frac{1}{3}$ pieces do not show the same amount as 4 of the $\frac{1}{5}$ pieces.

Can you multiply or divide the numerator and denominator of $\frac{2}{3}$ by the same number to get $\frac{4}{5}$?

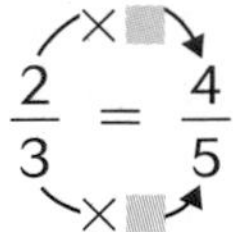

or

$\frac{2}{3} = \frac{4}{5}$ (÷■ numerator, ÷■ denominator)

There is no number that works.

$\frac{2}{3}$ is not equivalent to $\frac{4}{5}$.

More Examples

A. Find the missing number.

$\frac{3}{8} = \frac{■}{16}$

Think:

$\frac{3}{8} = \frac{■}{16}$ (×2 numerator, ×2 denominator) ➡ $\frac{3}{8} = \frac{6}{16}$

B. Find the missing number.

$5\frac{18}{24} = 5\frac{■}{4}$

Work with just the fraction part of the mixed number. The whole number stays the same.

Think:

$\frac{18}{24} = \frac{■}{4}$ (÷6 numerator, ÷6 denominator) ➡ $5\frac{18}{24} = 5\frac{3}{4}$

Guided Practice *For another example, see Set F on p. 293.*

1. $\frac{1}{2} = \frac{■}{10}$ **2.** $\frac{6}{8} = \frac{■}{4}$ **3.** $\frac{1}{3} = \frac{■}{12}$ **4.** $1\frac{12}{18} = 1\frac{■}{9}$

5. Write $2\frac{8}{12}$ in simplest form.

6. Is $\frac{1}{6}$ equivalent to $\frac{2}{12}$?

7. In Jillian's collection of videotapes, $\frac{3}{5}$ of the tapes are cartoons. Write three equivalent fractions for $\frac{3}{5}$.

Independent Practice *For more practice, see Set F on p. 296.*

8. $\frac{1}{3} = \frac{■}{9}$ **9.** $\frac{6}{12} = \frac{■}{2}$ **10.** $\frac{4}{7} = \frac{■}{14}$ **11.** $1\frac{12}{20} = 1\frac{■}{10}$ **12.** $\frac{5}{6} = \frac{■}{18}$

Write a pair of equivalent fractions for each picture.

13. 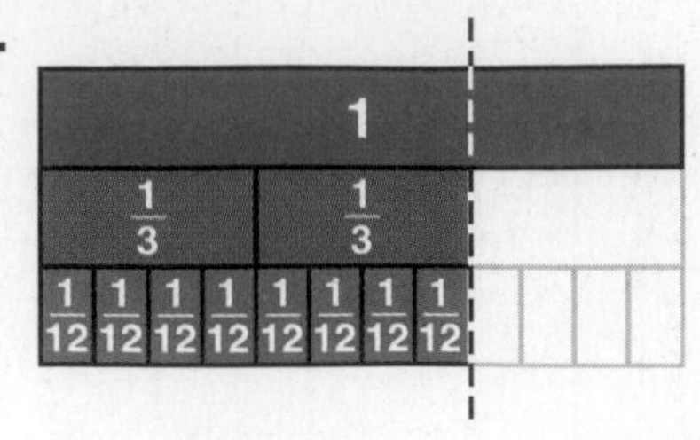

14. 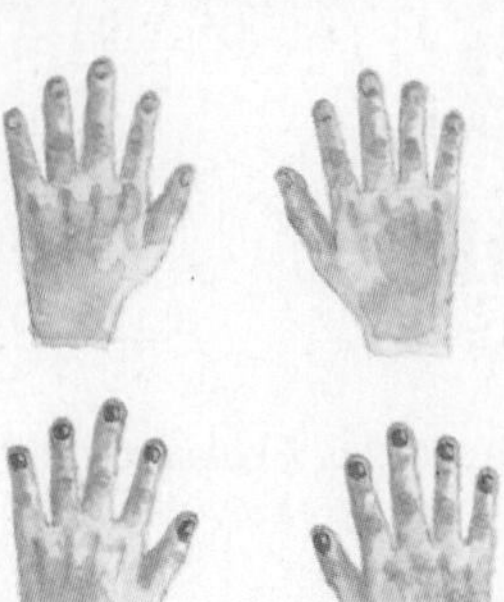

15. 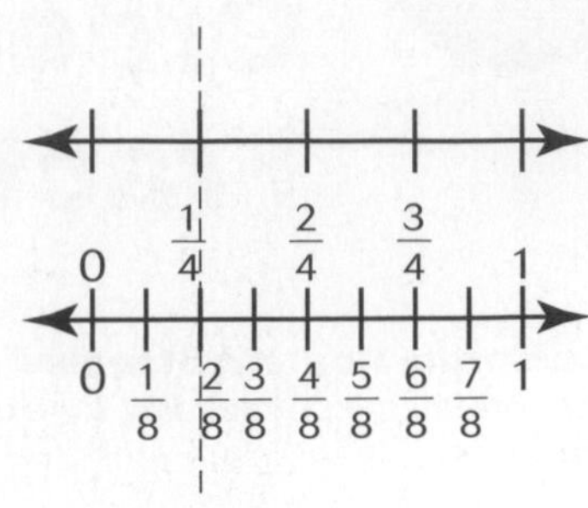

Write a fraction or mixed number equivalent to the fraction shown.

16. $\frac{1}{5}$ **17.** $\frac{4}{8}$ **18.** $\frac{2}{9}$ **19.** $5\frac{1}{8}$ **20.** $\frac{5}{7}$ **21.** $\frac{16}{20}$

Write each fraction or mixed number in simplest form.

22. $\frac{6}{8}$ **23.** $\frac{7}{14}$ **24.** $2\frac{4}{16}$ **25.** $\frac{8}{10}$ **26.** $\frac{7}{8}$ **27.** $\frac{5}{25}$

28. Is $\frac{4}{5}$ equivalent to $\frac{8}{10}$?

29. Is $\frac{1}{4}$ equivalent to $\frac{3}{10}$?

30. In the parking lot, $\frac{1}{6}$ of the cars are blue. Write three equivalent fractions for $\frac{1}{6}$.

Mixed Review

31. Three friends are sharing 2 submarine sandwiches equally. How much does each friend get?

32. $2\frac{3}{4} = \frac{■}{4}$

33. $\frac{17}{6} = ■\frac{■}{■}$

34. Algebra Solve $x - 102 = 17$ by testing these values for x: 139, 129, 119, 109.

35. Compare: $^-9$ ● $^-5$

36. Compare: 4 ● $^-14$

37. $7.66 × 8 **38.** 6,952 + 7,055 **39.** 83 × 56 **40.** 94 ÷ 4

Test Prep Choose the correct letter for each answer.

41. Which expression has the value of 5?
(3-6)

A 12 − (2 + 5) **B** (12 − 2) + 5 **C** (10 − 3) + 5 **D** 10 − (3 + 5)

42. Which product is greatest?
(4-1)

E 200 × 40 **F** 400 × 200 **G** 20 × 40 **H** 4,000 × 2

Use Homework Workbook 7-7.

LESSON 7-8

Comparing and Ordering Fractions

California Content Standard *Number Sense 1.5: Explain different interpretations of fractions, for example, . . . explain equivalence of fractions.*

Warm-Up Review

1. 3,194  3,914
2. Order from least to greatest:
   216 219 304 221

Give the factors of each.

3. 18
4. 24
5. $\frac{4}{5} = \frac{■}{20}$
6. $\frac{1}{3} = \frac{■}{12}$

Math Link You have learned about equivalent fractions. Now you will learn how to compare and order fractions.

Example 1

Compare $\frac{3}{4}$ and $\frac{1}{4}$.

To compare fractions that have the same denominator, simply compare their numerators.

You know that $3 > 1$, so $\frac{3}{4} > \frac{1}{4}$.

Three $\frac{1}{4}$ pieces are larger than one $\frac{1}{4}$ piece.

Example 2

Compare: $\frac{1}{2}$ and $\frac{5}{8}$.

Rewrite $\frac{1}{2}$ as an equivalent fraction with 8 in the denominator. Then you will have fractions with the same denominator.

$$\frac{1}{2} \overset{\times 4}{=} \frac{4}{8}$$

Compare the fractions using $\frac{4}{8}$ for $\frac{1}{2}$: $\frac{4}{8} < \frac{5}{8}$

Rewrite the comparison using the original fractions: $\frac{1}{2} < \frac{5}{8}$

One $\frac{1}{2}$ piece is smaller than five $\frac{1}{8}$ pieces.

Additional Standards: Number Sense 4.1; Mathematical Reasoning 3.3 *(See p. 251.)*

Example 3

Compare $\frac{3}{4}$ and $\frac{2}{3}$.

Rewrite the fractions using the same denominator.

$\frac{3}{4} = \frac{9}{12}$ (×3) $\frac{2}{3} = \frac{8}{12}$ (×4)

Think: What number has 3 and 4 as factors? 12
$\frac{3}{4} = \frac{■}{12}$ and $\frac{2}{3} = \frac{■}{12}$

Compare the new fractions: $\frac{9}{12} > \frac{8}{12}$

Write the comparison using the original fractions: $\frac{3}{4} > \frac{2}{3}$

You can choose a different number for the denominator as long as it has 4 and 3 as factors.

Example 4

Write $\frac{5}{6}$, $\frac{4}{9}$, and $\frac{1}{2}$ in order from least to greatest.

First rewrite the fractions using the same denominator.

$\frac{5}{6} = \frac{15}{18}$ (×3) $\frac{4}{9} = \frac{8}{18}$ (×2) $\frac{1}{2} = \frac{9}{18}$ (×9)

Think: What number has 6, 9, and 2 as factors? 18
$\frac{5}{6} = \frac{■}{18}$, $\frac{4}{9} = \frac{■}{18}$, and $\frac{1}{2} = \frac{■}{18}$

Write the new fractions in order from least to greatest: $\frac{8}{18}$ $\frac{9}{18}$ $\frac{15}{18}$

Then rewrite using the original fractions: $\frac{4}{9}$ $\frac{1}{2}$ $\frac{5}{6}$

Guided Practice

For another example, see Set G on p. 293.

Compare. Write >, <, or = for each ●.

1. $\frac{5}{6}$ ● $\frac{3}{6}$
2. $\frac{3}{10}$ ● $\frac{1}{2}$
3. $\frac{1}{3}$ ● $\frac{5}{15}$
4. $\frac{5}{8}$ ● $\frac{2}{3}$

5. Matt used three drill bits for a woodworking project. The drill bits were $\frac{7}{16}$ inch, $\frac{5}{8}$ inch, and $\frac{1}{4}$ inch. List the drill bits from smallest to largest.

Independent Practice *For more practice, see Set G on p. 296.*

Compare. Write >, <, or = for each ●.

6. $\frac{7}{10}$ ● $\frac{4}{10}$ **7.** $\frac{7}{8}$ ● $\frac{3}{4}$ **8.** $\frac{1}{2}$ ● $\frac{9}{16}$ **9.** $\frac{1}{3}$ ● $\frac{1}{4}$

10. $\frac{12}{18}$ ● $\frac{2}{3}$ **11.** $2\frac{1}{4}$ ● $2\frac{3}{20}$ **12.** $4\frac{1}{2}$ ● $3\frac{5}{7}$ **13.** $\frac{7}{9}$ ● $\frac{5}{6}$

Write each set of fractions in order from least to greatest.

14. $\frac{3}{8}, \frac{7}{8}, \frac{4}{8}$ **15.** $\frac{2}{3}, \frac{1}{2}, \frac{3}{4}$ **16.** $\frac{1}{6}, \frac{1}{3}, \frac{3}{8}$ **17.** $\frac{1}{2}, \frac{3}{10}, \frac{4}{5}$

18. Write these spices in order from the greatest amount to the least amount: turmeric, thyme, black pepper.

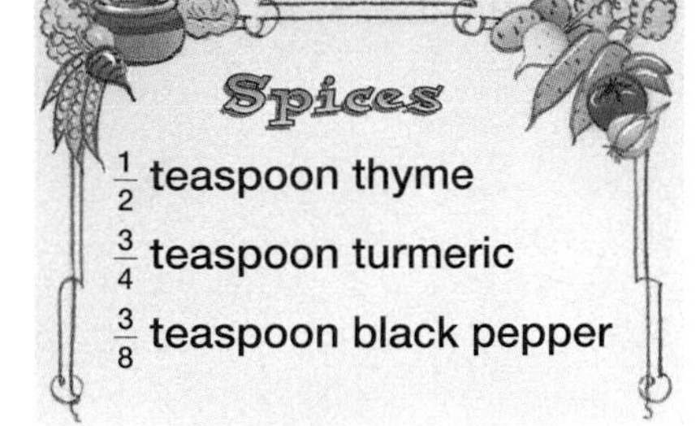

19. If black peppercorns cost $3.45 per jar, how much would 12 jars cost?

20. Math Reasoning Identify the fractions below that are less than $\frac{1}{2}$, those that are equal to $\frac{1}{2}$, and those that are greater than $\frac{1}{2}$.

$\frac{3}{10}$ $\frac{4}{8}$ $\frac{7}{11}$ $\frac{2}{3}$ $\frac{3}{6}$ $\frac{5}{8}$ $\frac{10}{20}$ $\frac{3}{8}$ $\frac{7}{12}$ $\frac{4}{9}$

21. In Exercise 20, can you tell quickly how a fraction compares to $\frac{1}{2}$? Explain.

Mixed Review

22. Write an equivalent fraction for each: $\frac{7}{21}, \frac{18}{24}, \frac{2}{5}$

23. Find 15 ÷ 4. Give the answer as a mixed number.

24. 38 × 84 **25.** 4,112 − 3,760 **26.** 48 + 62 + 736 **27.** 91 × 533

Test Prep **Choose the correct letter for each answer.**

28. Which fraction is not equivalent to $\frac{6}{8}$? (7-7)

A $\frac{3}{4}$ C $\frac{12}{24}$

B $\frac{24}{32}$ D $\frac{12}{16}$

29. Find the next number in the pattern: (1-4)
384, 415, 446, 477, ■

F 408 H 508

G 498 J 518

Diagnostic Checkpoint

Write the fraction for the shaded parts of each region or set.

1. (7-1) 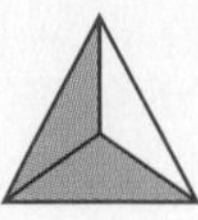

2. (7-1) 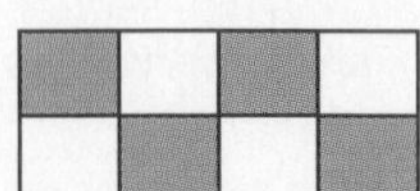

3. (7-2) 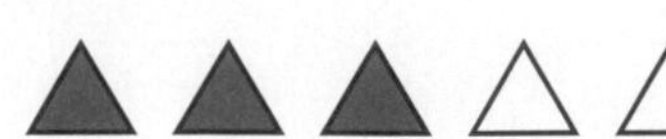

4. (7-2) 

What fraction should be written at each point?

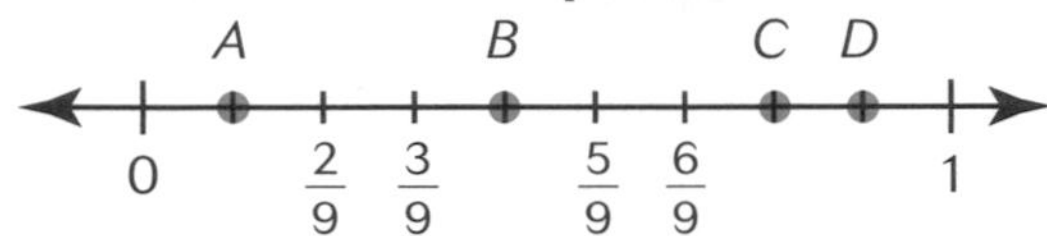

5. (7-3) point *A**   **6.** (7-3) point *B*   **7.** (7-3) point *D*

Write an improper fraction as well as a mixed number or whole number for each picture.

8. (7-4) 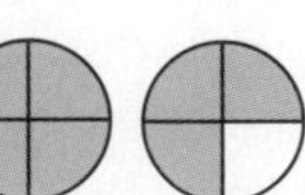

9. (7-4) 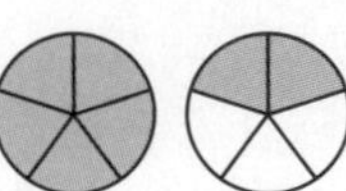

10. (7-4) 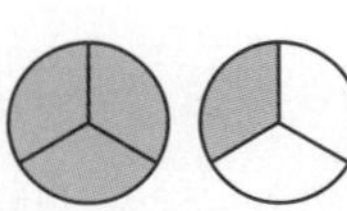

11. (7-4) 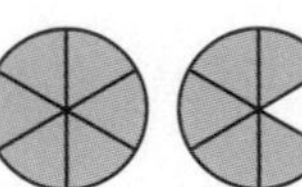

Give each answer as a fraction, mixed number, or whole number.

12. (7-5) $2 \div 1$ **13.** (7-5) $3 \div 4$ **14.** (7-5) $8 \div 5$ **15.** (7-5) $10 \div 3$

Find the missing number.

16. (7-7) $\frac{1}{8} = \frac{■}{16}$ **17.** (7-7) $3\frac{2}{3} = 3\frac{■}{6}$ **18.** (7-7) $\frac{15}{18} = \frac{■}{6}$ **19.** (7-7) $1\frac{5}{7} = 1\frac{■}{14}$

Compare. Write >, <, or = for each ●.

20. (7-8) $\frac{4}{7}$ ● $\frac{3}{7}$ **21.** (7-8) $\frac{2}{6}$ ● $\frac{5}{12}$ **22.** (7-8) $\frac{1}{4}$ ● $\frac{1}{6}$ **23.** (7-8) $\frac{3}{5}$ ● $\frac{7}{8}$

24. (7-6) Mario needs 8 paper triangles to make an ornament. He has 28 triangles. How many ornaments can he make?

25. (7-6) Cheryl has 34 ounces of lemonade to pour into 4 glasses. She puts the same amount of lemonade in each glass. How much lemonade is in one glass?

Problem-Solving Strategy:
Work Backward

California Content Standard *Mathematical Reasoning 1.1: Analyze problems by identifying relationships, distinguishing relevant information from irrelevant information, sequencing and prioritizing information, and observing patterns.*

Warm-Up Review

1. 13 × \$6.54
2. \$16.71 + \$4.93 + \$2.58
3. Abe cut a board into 4 equal pieces. He cut 4 inches off one of the pieces making it 18 inches long. How long was the original board?

Example

Mrs. Malewski sliced a pie into equal size pieces. Marty ate 2 slices. Then Carl ate 1 slice, which was $\frac{1}{4}$ of what Marty left for him. How many slices were there in the whole pie?

Understand

What do you need to find?

You need to find the number of slices in the whole pie.

Plan

How can you solve the problem?

Start with the slice Carl ate. Then work backward to find the number of slices in the whole pie.

Solve

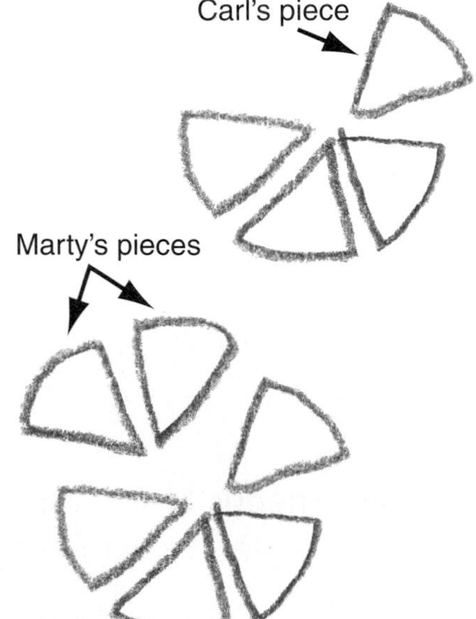

Start with the 1 slice Carl ate. This was $\frac{1}{4}$ of what Marty left for him. So there must have been 4 slices left for him.

Add the 2 slices Marty ate:
4 slices + 2 slices = 6 slices.

The whole pie had been cut into 6 slices.

Look Back

How can you work forward to check your work?

 Additional Standards: Mathematical Reasoning 1.2, 2.0, 3.2 (See p. 251.)

Guided Practice

1. Mr. Ramirez sliced a pan of lasagna into equal portions. He served 5 portions for supper. For lunch the next day, he ate 2 portions, which was $\frac{2}{3}$ of the leftovers. How many portions were there in the full pan?

2. The Nature Club spent Saturday washing cars as a fundraiser. They washed twice as many cars in the morning as in the afternoon. In the afternoon, they washed 71 cars. How many cars did the Nature Club wash altogether?

Independent Practice

3. Harriet bought some fabric to make costumes. She used half of it to make vests. Then she used 8 yards to make capes. She had 4 yards left over. How much fabric did Harriet buy?

4. Ron has half as many CDs as Felipa. Felipa has three times as many CDs as Lynn. Lynn has 6 CDs. How many CDs does Ron have?

5. Mr. Day gave Liz and Ted money to buy lunch. Ted spent $3.25 more than Liz. Liz bought a tuna sandwich and milk. The children gave Mr. Day $2.65 back in change. How much did Mr. Day originally give the children?

Lunch Menu

Hamburger	$3.55
Egg Salad	2.60
Tuna Sandwich	3.80
Spaghetti	3.40
Gyros	3.80
Juice	0.85
Milk	0.75
Iced Tea	0.95

Mixed Review

Try these or other strategies to solve each exercise. Tell which strategy you used.

Problem-Solving Strategies

- *Solve a Simpler Problem*
- *Work Backward*
- *Make a Table*
- *Write a Number Sentence*

6. Gale is saving $65 per month to buy a television for $450. After 6 months, how much more money will she need to buy the television?

7. Ginny has 5 blouses and 5 skirts. If she can pair up any blouse with any skirt, how many outfits can she make?

Use Homework Workbook 7-9.

Understanding Probability

California Content Standard *Statistics, Data Analysis, and Probability 2.0: Students make predictions for simple probability situations.*

Math Link You have learned how to compare fractions. Now you will learn how to compare how likely it is that an event will happen.

Warm-Up Review

What fraction of each region or set is orange?

1. 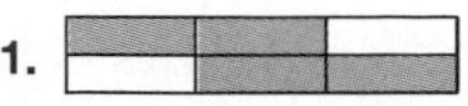

2. 

3. Give three fractions equivalent to $\frac{1}{2}$.

4. $\frac{3}{8}$ ● $\frac{7}{8}$ 5. $\frac{1}{2}$ ● $\frac{7}{10}$

6. Laura walked $\frac{2}{3}$ of a mile. Clare walked $\frac{1}{2}$ of a mile. Who walked farther?

Keoni and Mark are playing a game. It is Keoni's turn to spin the spinner shown below. Do you think it will land on yellow?

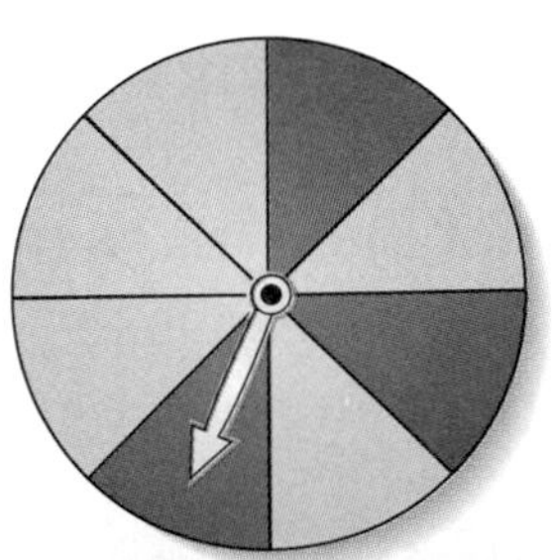

Probability tells the chance that an event will happen.

Word Bank

probability
more likely
less likely
equally likely
impossible
certain

Example 1

Is it **more likely** or **less likely** that the spinner will land on yellow?

Look at the spinner. More than $\frac{1}{2}$ of it is yellow. So it is more likely that the spinner will land on yellow.

Example 2

Suppose you reach into one of the bags shown below and pull out a marble without looking. For which bag is there an **equally likely** probability of pulling out a red marble as a blue marble?

Look at each bag. The chances are equally likely for Bag B because $\frac{1}{2}$ of the marbles are red and $\frac{1}{2}$ of them are blue.

Bag A

Bag B

 Additional Standard: Mathematical Reasoning 2.3 (See p. 251.)

Example 3

If you select a tile without looking, how likely is it to show a 1-digit number ? How likely is it to show an even number?

Selecting a 1-digit number is **certain,** since all the tiles show 1-digit numbers.

Selecting an even number is **impossible,** since there are no tiles that show an even number.

Guided Practice *For another example, see Set H on p. 294.*

For each bag, use the words below to describe how likely it is to select a green tile from the bag.

IMPOSSIBLE	LESS LIKELY	EQUALLY LIKELY	MORE LIKELY	CERTAIN

1.

2.

3.

4.

5. Claudia has a box that contains 5 red pencils and 7 blue pencils. If she selects one without looking, is it more likely that she will select a red pencil or a blue pencil?

Independent Practice *For more practice, see Set H on p. 297.*

For each spinner, use the words shown in the colored band above to describe how likely it is to spin blue.

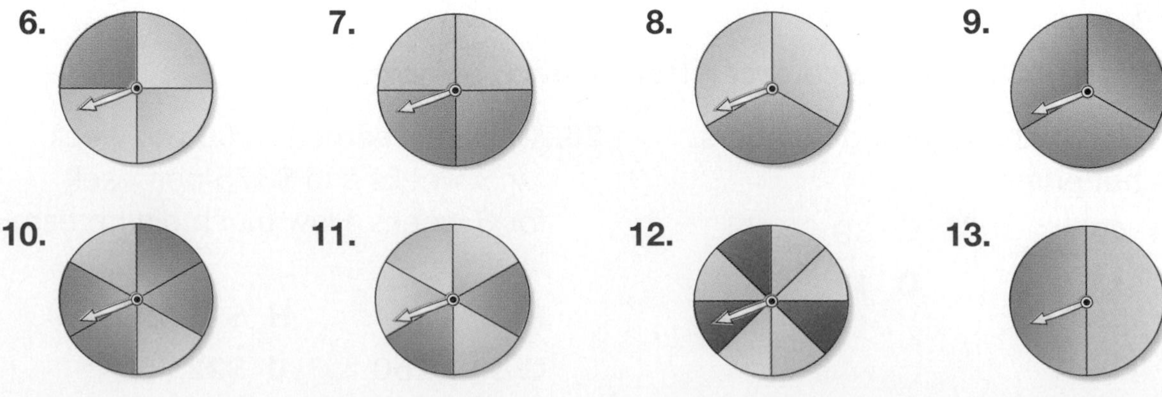

6. 7. 8. 9.

10. 11. 12. 13.

Use the cards shown for Exercises 14 and 15. Jim selects one of the cards without looking.

14. How likely is it that Jim's card shows a 3-digit number?

15. Is it more likely that Jim's card shows a prime number or a composite number?

16. Adam reaches into a bag that has 4 red markers and 6 yellow markers. Which color marker is he more likely to select? What color marker would it be impossible for Adam to select?

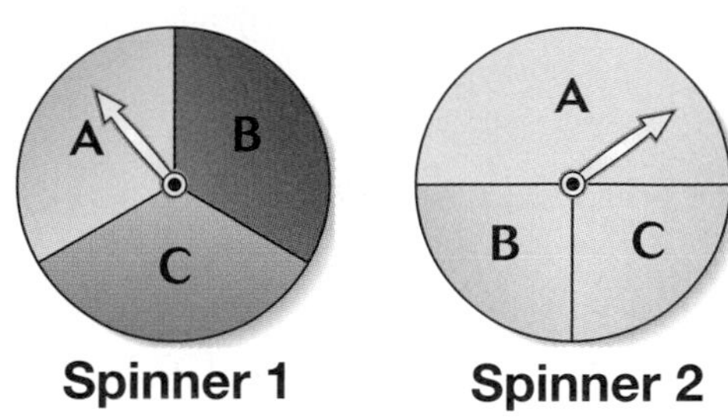

Spinner 1 **Spinner 2**

17. Math Reasoning In which spinner would spinning an A, spinning a B, or spinning a C all be equally likely? Explain.

Mixed Review

18. Peter is planting zinnias. He wants them to be all the same size and color. Make a tree diagram to show all the possible combinations.

Glorious Zinnias
$9.90 per flat

Colors: red, orange, yellow, hot pink, white

sizes: tall, dwarf

Compare. Use >, <, or =.

19. $\frac{7}{16}$ ● $\frac{3}{8}$ **20.** $\frac{3}{4}$ ● $\frac{7}{10}$

21. Mental Math 2,700 ÷ 9 ● 1,200 ÷ 4

22. Algebra Evaluate 918 − m for m = 77.

Write each fraction in lowest terms.

23. $\frac{15}{25}$ **24.** $\frac{9}{16}$

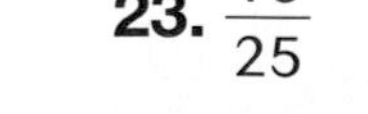

Test Prep Choose the correct letter for each answer.

25. (6-9) Which of the following numbers is not prime?

A 47 **C** 39

B 41 **D** 13

26. (4-2) Mr. Janus earned $750 per week for 8 weeks and $875 per week for 6 weeks. How much did he earn in all?

F $7,125 **H** $11,500

G $11,250 **J** $22,750

Multiple-Choice Cumulative Review

Choose the correct letter for each answer.

1. **Choose the picture that has $\frac{4}{5}$ shaded.**

   A 

   B 

   C 

   D 

2. **$8\overline{)50}$**

   F 5 R10
   G 6 R2
   H 7 R1
   J 8 R2
   K NH

3. **$\frac{20}{6} =$**

   A $1\frac{1}{4}$
   B $2\frac{1}{3}$
   C $3\frac{1}{3}$
   D $3\frac{3}{4}$
   E NH

Use the table below for Questions 4 and 5.

Place	Elevation
Mount Kilimanjaro	19,340 feet above sea level
Lake Assal	512 feet below sea level
Death Valley	282 feet below sea level
Vinson Massif	16,860 feet above sea level

4. **Put the elevations in order from lowest elevation to highest elevation.**

   F 19,340; 16,860; $^{-}$282; $^{-}$512
   G $^{-}$282; $^{-}$512; 16,860; 19,340
   H $^{-}$512; $^{-}$282; 16,860, 19,340
   J 16,860; 19,340; $^{-}$512; $^{-}$282

5. **If you descended 312 feet from the summit of Mt. Kilimanjaro, what would your new elevation be?**

   A 312 feet above sea level
   B 312 feet below sea level
   C 19,028 feet above sea level
   D 19,028 feet below sea level

6. **$1\frac{8}{14} = 1\frac{■}{7}$**

   F 1
   G 4
   H 8
   J 16
   K NH

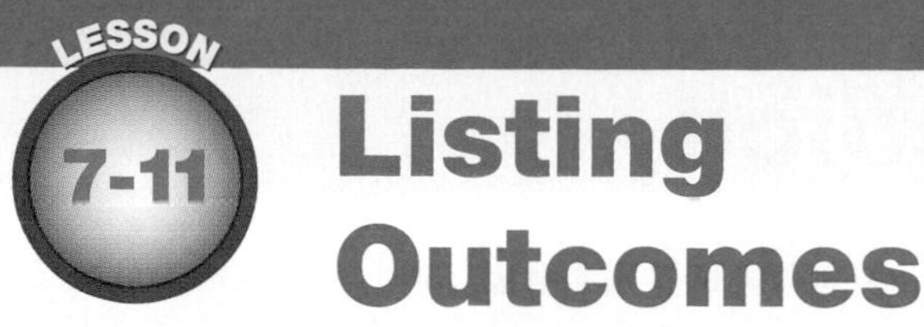

Lesson 7-11 Listing Outcomes

California Content Standard *Statistics, Data Analysis, and Probability 2.1: Represent all possible outcomes for a simple probability situation in an organized way (e.g., tables, grids, tree diagrams).*

Math Link You have been introduced to probability. Now you will learn how to record all the possible outcomes in a probability situation.

Warm-Up Review

1. Complete this multiplication chart.

×	7	8	9
4	28		
5			45
6			

2. A company makes beaded necklaces and bracelets in red, green, and blue. Make a tree diagram showing all the choices.

Word Bank

outcome

Example 1

Suppose you reach into the bag shown and select a slip of paper without looking. You can make a list of all possible results:

orange, yellow, blue, red, green

Each possible result is called an **outcome.**

Example 2

What are the possible outcomes for spinning both of the spinners at the right together?

Make a tree diagram.

Spinner 1	Spinner 2	Possible Outcomes
A	1	A, 1
	2	A, 2
	3	A, 3
B	1	B, 1
	2	B, 2
	3	B, 3

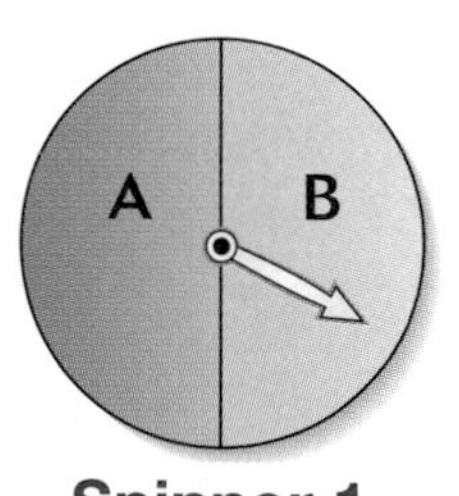

Spinner 1

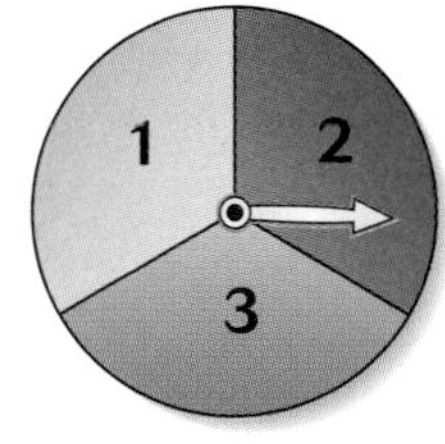

Spinner 2

You can also make a table to find the possible outcomes. Write the possible outcomes for Spinner 1 down the side of the table, and write the possible outcomes for Spinner 2 across the top. The shaded region shows the possible outcomes for spinning both spinners together.

	1	2	3
A	A, 1	A, 2	A, 3
B	B, 1	B, 2	B, 3

There are 6 possible outcomes: A, 1; A, 2; A, 3; B, 1; B, 2; and B, 3.

 Additional Standard: Mathematical Reasoning 2.2 (See p. 251.)

Guided Practice *For another example, see Set I on p. 294.*

List all possible outcomes for each situation.

1. 

2. 

3. 

4. 

5. Kenny spins the spinners in Exercises 1 and 3 together. Make a tree diagram or a table to show all possible outcomes.

Independent Practice *For more practice, see Set I on p. 297.*

List all possible outcomes for each situation.

6. 

7. 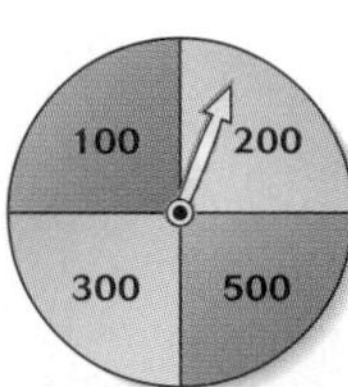

8. 

9. 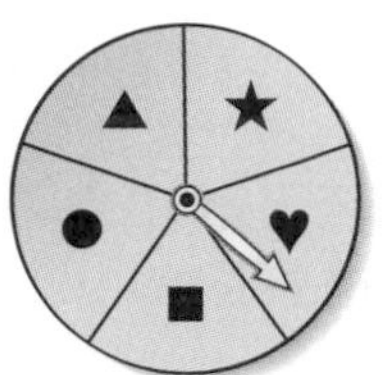

10. Yvette flips a coin and gets heads or tails. Suppose she flips a coin and draws a tile shown in Exercise 8. Make a tree diagram or a table to show all possible outcomes

Mixed Review

11. Algebra Suppose $b = 19$. Compare: $41b$ ● $730 + b$

12. In Exercise 1 above, describe a certain event and an impossible event.

13. $\frac{4}{9}$ ● $\frac{1}{6}$

14. $4\frac{3}{4}$ ● $4\frac{12}{16}$

15. $45{,}788 + 67{,}521$

16. $\$613.08 \times 74$

Test Prep Choose the correct letter for each answer.

17. $\frac{15}{36} =$ (7-7)

A $\frac{1}{12}$

B $\frac{1}{5}$

C $\frac{5}{12}$

D $\frac{7}{12}$

18. $5\frac{2}{3} =$ (7-4)

F $\frac{17}{5}$

G $\frac{13}{3}$

H $\frac{15}{3}$

J $\frac{17}{3}$

Finding Probability

California Content Standard *Statistics, Data Analysis, and Probability 2.2: Express outcomes of experimental probability situations verbally and numerically (e.g., 3 out of 4; $\frac{3}{4}$)*

Math Link You have learned how to describe the probability that an event will happen. Now you will use fractions to describe the probability more accurately.

Warm-Up Review

Write in simplest form.

1. $\frac{6}{12}$
2. $\frac{7}{9}$
3. $\frac{14}{21}$
4. $\frac{12}{20}$
5. Yuri wrote the names of the days of the weeks on separate slips of paper. He selects 1 slip. List all possible outcomes.

Example

What is the probability of tossing a 2 using a number cube labeled 1 through 6?

Count the possible outcomes. 1, 2, 3, 4, 5, 6
There are 6 possible outcomes.

Then count how many of those outcomes are a 2.
There is only 1 outcome that is a 2.

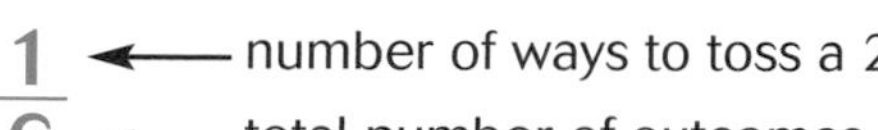
$\frac{1}{6}$ ← number of ways to toss a 2 / total number of outcomes

An impossible event has a probability of 0.
A certain event has a probability of 1.
Any other event has a probability between 0 and 1.

The probability of tossing a 2 is $\frac{1}{6}$.

We can also say that the probability of tossing a 2 is 1 out of 6.

More Examples

A. What is the probability of *not* tossing a 2 using a number cube labeled 1 through 6?

There are 6 possible outcomes: 1, 2, 3, 4, 5, 6.

There are 5 outcomes that are *not* a 2: 1, 3, 4, 5, 6.

$\frac{5}{6}$ ← number of ways *not* to toss a 2 / total number of outcomes

The probability of *not* tossing a 2 is $\frac{5}{6}$.

B. What is the probability of the spinner landing on a prime number?

There are 8 possible outcomes: 1, 2, 3, 4, 5, 6, 7, 8.

There are 4 outcomes that are prime numbers: 2, 3, 5, 7.

$\frac{4}{8}$ ← number of prime number / total number of outcomes

The probability of the spinner landing on a prime number is $\frac{4}{8}$, or $\frac{1}{2}$.

 Additional Standard: Mathematical Reasoning 2.3 (See p. 251.)

Guided Practice *For another example, see Set J on p. 294.*

Refer to the spinner in Example B. Write the probability of the spinner landing on:

1. 5 **2.** 10 **3.** a number less than 7

4. Corrinne is playing a game with a number cube labeled 1 through 6. What is the probability that she will toss an odd number?

Independent Practice *For more practice, see Set J on p. 297.*

Refer to the spinner in Example B. Write the probability of the spinner landing on:

5. 6 **6.** a 1-digit number **7.** a multiple of 3

Suppose you close your eyes and select one of these cards. What is the probability of drawing:

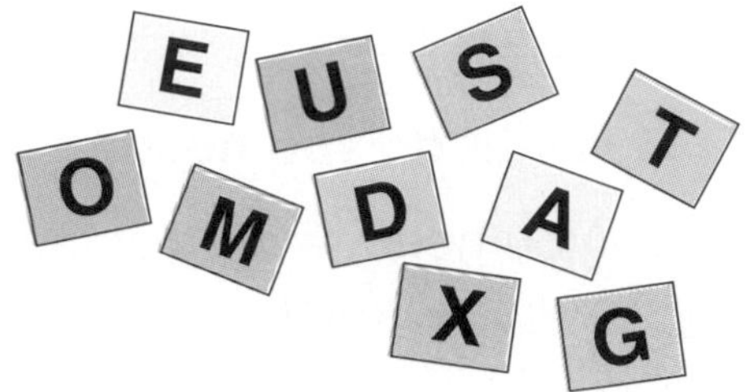

8. G **9.** a vowel

10. a letter that is not Z **11.** P

12. Math Reasoning Draw a spinner in which the probability of spinning a 3 is $\frac{1}{4}$. Explain how you know the probability is $\frac{1}{4}$.

Mixed Review

13. Refer to the spinner in Example B on page 284. Name two events that are equally likely.

14. Insert parentheses to make this a true sentence:
$16 - 8 + 2 + 3 = 9$

15. Casey tosses a coin and spins the spinner in Example B. Make a table or a tree diagram to show all possible outcomes.

16. Estimate 7,304 + 1,855. **17.** Estimate 3,148 ÷ 6.

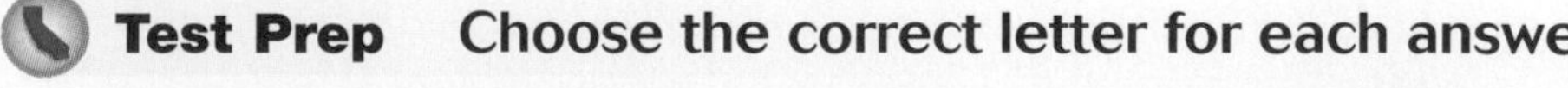

Test Prep **Choose the correct letter for each answer.**

18. Which fraction does *not* equal 1? *(7-1)*

A $\frac{9}{9}$ **C** $\frac{12}{12}$

B $\frac{1}{10}$ **D** $\frac{4}{4}$

19. Algebra If $a = 45$, then $\frac{a}{5} =$ *(3-8)*

F 225 **H** 40

G 50 **J** 9

Problem-Solving Application:

Making Predictions

Warm-Up Review

Write in simplest form.

1. $\frac{8}{32}$
2. $\frac{9}{18}$
3. A number cube with the numbers 1 through 6 is tossed. Find the probability of tossing a number greater than 4.
4. Lorita did $\frac{1}{4}$ of her 28 math problems. How many did she do?

California Content Standard *Statistics, Data Analysis, and Probability 2.0: Students make predictions for simple probability situations.*

Example 1

Suppose you spin the spinner 80 times. Predict how many times the spinner will land on A.

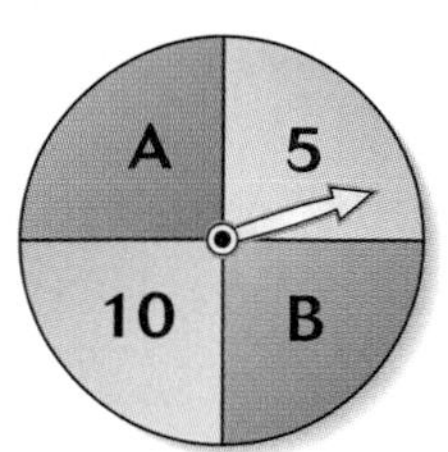

Understand

What do you need to do?

You need to predict the number of times the spinner will land on A.

Plan

How can you solve the problem?

First find the fraction that shows the probability that the spinner will land on A. Then find that fraction of 80 spins.

Solve

Find the probability that the spinner will land on A.

$\frac{1}{4}$ ← number of ways to land on A / total number of outcomes

Now find $\frac{1}{4}$ of 80.

$80 \div 4 = 20$

The spinner will probably land on A about 20 times.

Look Back

Do you think the spinner would land on A exactly 20 times?

 Additional Standards: Mathematical Reasoning 2.0, 3.2 (See p. 251.)

Guided Practice

1. Suppose you spin the spinner on page 286, 100 times. Predict how many times the spinner will land on A.

Suppose Mike tosses a number cube labeled 1 through 6, 60 times. Predict how many times he will get each outcome.

2. 3 **3.** 7 **4.** number less than 10

Independent Practice

In Exercises 5–7, suppose you select a tile from this box without looking. Then you return it, shake the box, and select again. If you make 80 selections, how many times would you expect to get each outcome?

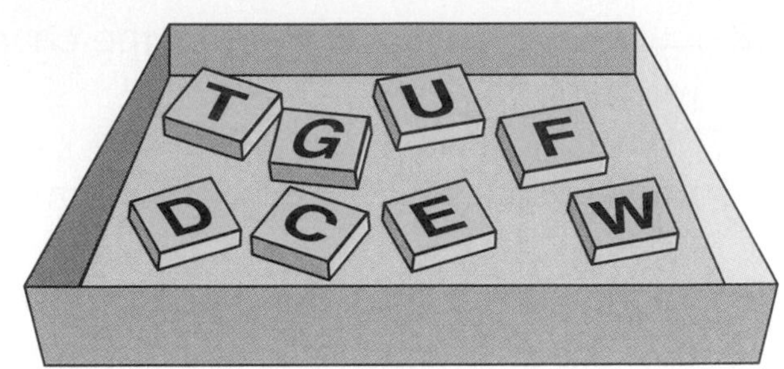

5. G **6.** vowel **7.** H

8. Math Reasoning Sandi predicted that in 50 spins, a spinner would land on a blue section 10 times. If Sandi's prediction is reasonable, what fraction of the spinner is blue?

9. In a survey, 50 students were asked which candidate they planned to vote for. The probability that someone will choose Bonnie as class president is $\frac{25}{50} = \frac{1}{2}$. Predict how many students out of 600 would choose Bonnie.

Candidates	Likely Votes
Jessica	4 votes
Bonnie	25 votes
Seth	6 votes
Tom	15 votes

Mixed Review

Use the pictograph for Exercises 10–12.

10. Which animal has the shortest life span?

11. How long is the grizzly bear's life span?

12. What is the mean life span of these animals?

Life Span	● = 10 years
Hippopotamus	● ● ● ●
White rhinoceros	● ●
Asian elephant	● ● ● ●
Grizzly bear	● ● ◖
Zebra	● ◖

13. Use a positive or negative number to represent this situation: Ethan owes $3,745 on a car loan.

Diagnostic Checkpoint

Complete. For Exercises 1–3, use the words from the Word Bank.

Word Bank
numerator
denominator
improper fractions
mixed number
equivalent fractions
impossible outcome
simplest form
probability
equally likely
certain

1. (7-1) The number below the fraction bar in a fraction is the ________________.

2. (7-10) ________________ tells us the chance an event will happen.

3. (7-12) A(n) ________________ event has a probability of 1.

For each spinner, use the words *impossible, less likely, equally likely, more likely,* or *certain* to describe how likely it is to spin green.

4. (7-10) 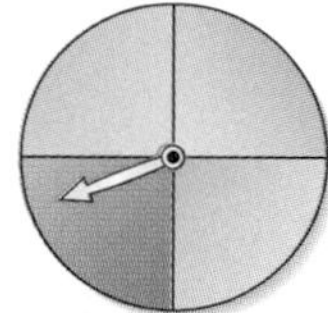

5. (7-10) 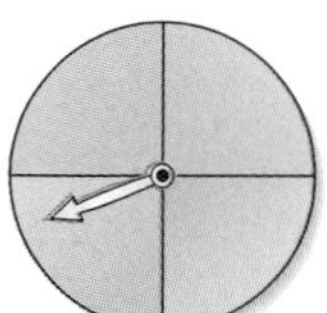

6. (7-10) 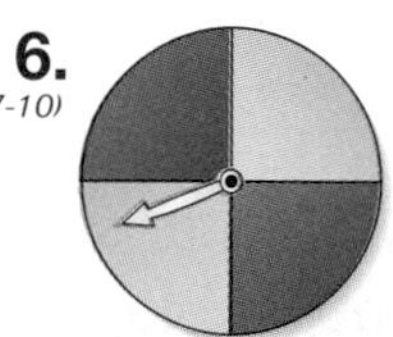

7. (7-10) 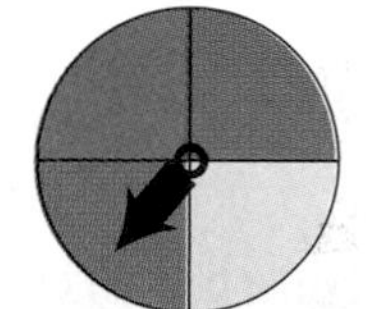

List all possible outcomes for each situation.

8. (7-11) 

9. (7-11) 

10. (7-11) 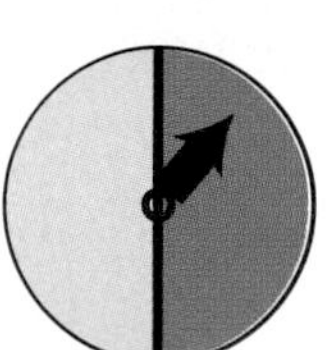

11. (7-11) 

For the spinner shown, write the probability of spinning:

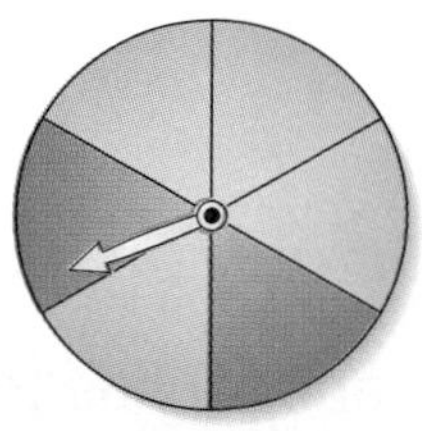

12. (7-12) green

13. (7-12) blue

14. (7-12) yellow

15. (7-12) blue or green

A number cube is labeled 1–6. Suppose Jerrod tosses it 60 times. Predict how many times he will get each outcome.

16. (7-13) 5

17. (7-13) an even number

18. (7-13) a number greater than 6

19. (7-9) Peter ordered a pizza for himself and some friends. Peter ate 2 pieces. Toby ate 2 more pieces, which was $\frac{1}{3}$ of what remained. If all the pieces of pizza were equal in size, how many pieces of pizza were there in the whole pizza?

Chapter 7 Test

Write the fraction for the shaded parts of each region or set.

1. 

2. 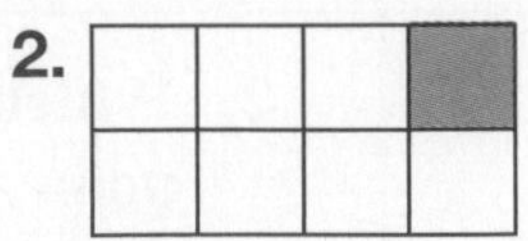

3. 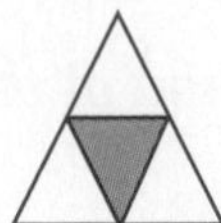

4. What fraction should be written at point *B*?

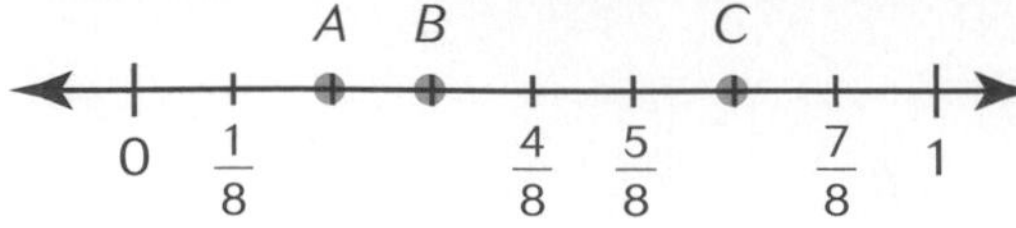

5. Write an improper fraction as well as a mixed number or whole number for the picture at the right.

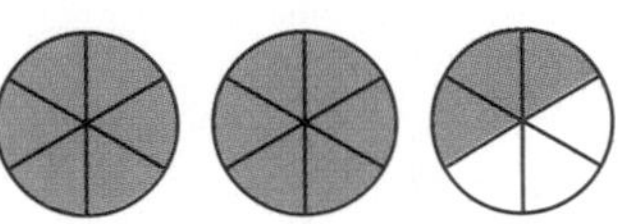

6. Divide 10 ÷ 9. Give your answer as a mixed number.

7. $\frac{5}{7} = \frac{■}{21}$ **8.** $\frac{25}{40} = \frac{■}{8}$ **9.** $5\frac{3}{4} = 5\frac{■}{20}$ **10.** $2\frac{5}{9} = 2\frac{■}{18}$

Write each set of fractions in order from least to greatest.

11. $\frac{5}{6}, \frac{2}{6}, \frac{4}{6}$ **12.** $\frac{2}{4}, \frac{2}{3}, \frac{2}{6}$ **13.** $\frac{1}{2}, \frac{7}{10}, \frac{3}{5}$

Use the spinner at the right for Exercises 14–17.

14. Is it *more likely* or *less likely* that the spinner will fall on an odd number?

15. List all the possible outcomes.

16. What is the probability of spinning an even number?

17. Suppose you spin the spinner 50 times. Predict how many times the spinner will land on 6.

18. Four friends are sharing 6 sandwiches. If they divide them evenly, how much would each friend get? Write a division sentence to help you solve the problem.

19. Mia baked half as many loaves of bread as Bob. Bob baked four times as many loaves as Sam. Sam baked 2 loaves of bread. How many loaves of bread did Mia bake?

Multiple-Choice Chapter 7 Test

Choose the correct letter for each answer.

1. What fraction of this region is shaded?

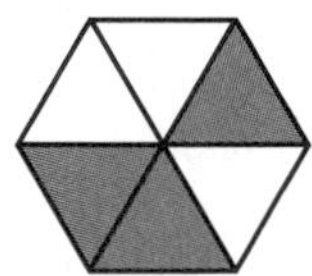

A $\frac{3}{3}$ C $\frac{6}{6}$

B $\frac{3}{6}$ D $\frac{1}{3}$

2. Which is equal to $3\frac{1}{4}$?

F $\frac{13}{3}$ H $\frac{8}{4}$

G $\frac{7}{4}$ J $\frac{13}{4}$

3. What fraction of the set are squares?

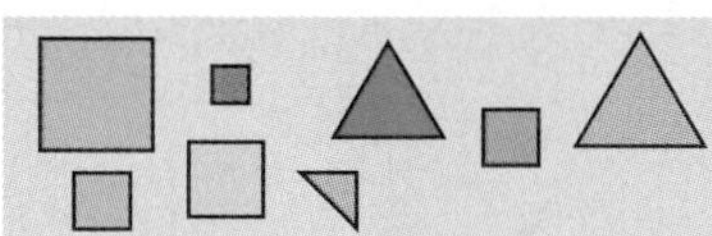

A $\frac{3}{8}$ C $\frac{5}{8}$

B $\frac{5}{5}$ D $\frac{5}{10}$

4. What is the probability of spinning an even number on the spinner below?

F $\frac{1}{5}$ H 1

G $\frac{2}{5}$ J $\frac{3}{5}$

5. Which fraction would be written at point *A*?

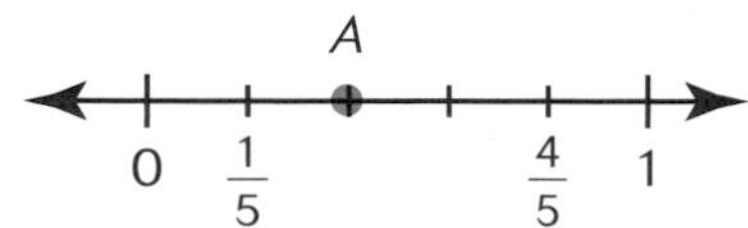

A $\frac{2}{5}$ C $\frac{2}{10}$

B $\frac{3}{5}$ D $\frac{5}{2}$

6. Mrs. Slough is making omelettes. She uses 3 eggs for each. She has 10 eggs. How many whole omelettes can she make?

F 1 H 3

G 2 J 4

7. $16 \div 5$

A $\frac{5}{16}$

B $3\frac{1}{5}$

C $2\frac{1}{5}$

D $3\frac{1}{16}$

8. Which fraction is NOT equivalent to $\frac{4}{10}$?

F $\frac{2}{5}$

G $\frac{4}{5}$

H $\frac{8}{20}$

J $\frac{16}{40}$

9. **Which set of fractions is in order from least to greatest?**

A $\frac{1}{2}, \frac{3}{10}, \frac{4}{5}$

B $\frac{2}{3}, \frac{2}{4}, \frac{2}{5}$

C $\frac{2}{3}, \frac{2}{6}, \frac{3}{9}$

D $\frac{1}{2}, \frac{3}{4}, \frac{7}{8}$

10. **Corinne's father gave her some money to spend at the mall. She spent $4.23 on a sandwich and a drink. She bought a purple skirt for $18.45. Corinne returned home with $2.32. How much money did her father give her?**

F $18.45 H $25.00
G $22.68 J $30.00

11. **How likely would it be to spin yellow?**

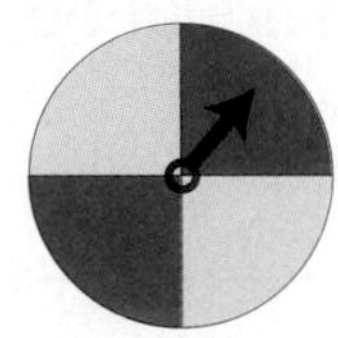

A Equally likely
B Certain
C Less likely
D More likely

12. **You toss a number cube labeled 1 through 6. Which of the following is NOT a possible outcome?**

F 6 H 3
G 9 J 5

13. **What is the probability of NOT tossing a 3 using a number cube labeled 1 through 6?**

A $\frac{1}{6}$

B $\frac{3}{6}$

C $\frac{4}{6}$

D $\frac{5}{6}$

14. **Choose a fraction to make the sentence true.**

$$\frac{3}{5} > \blacksquare$$

F $\frac{7}{10}$

G $\frac{3}{4}$

H $\frac{5}{9}$

J $\frac{2}{3}$

15. **Which of the following is NOT in simplest form?**

A $\frac{5}{8}$

B $1\frac{3}{10}$

C $1\frac{4}{10}$

D $1\frac{4}{9}$

16. **Terrence tosses a number cube labeled 1 through 6, 60 times. Predict how many times he will toss an odd number.**

F 10 times
G 30 times
H 50 times
J 60 times

Reteaching

Set A (pages 252–253)

Draw a picture to show $\frac{4}{5}$.

First, draw a simple region and divide it into 5 equal parts. Then, shade any 4 of the parts.

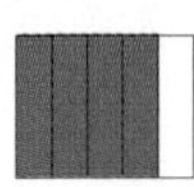

Remember the numerator is the number of shaded equal parts. The denominator is the total number of equal parts.

Draw a picture to show each fraction.

1. $\frac{3}{8}$ **2.** $\frac{3}{3}$ **3.** $\frac{4}{6}$ **4.** $\frac{2}{5}$ **5.** $\frac{3}{4}$ **6.** $\frac{1}{2}$

Set B (pages 254–256)

Write a fraction for the number of shaded parts of the set.

Number of shaded triangles ⟶ 4
Total number of triangles ⟶ 7

$\frac{4}{7}$

Remember the denominator is the total number of shapes.

Write a fraction for the shaded parts of each set.

1.

2.

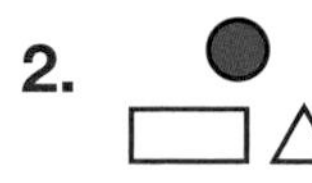

Set C (pages 257–259)

What fraction should be written at point *A*?

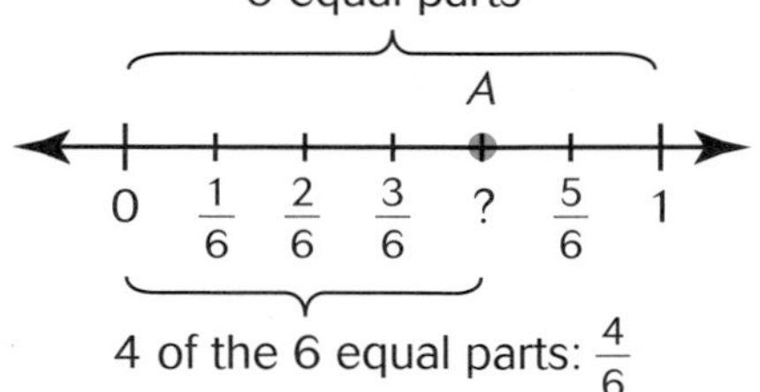

There are 6 equal parts between 0 and 1. Point *A* shows 4 of the 6 equal parts, or $\frac{4}{6}$.

Remember you can think of the distance between 0 and 1 as 1 whole.

What fractions should be written at each point?

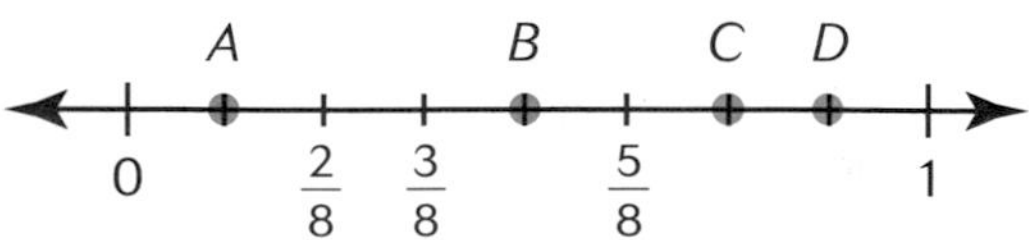

1. point *A* **2.** point *B*

3. point *C* **4.** point *D*

Set D (pages 260–262)

Write $3\frac{3}{5}$ as an improper fraction.

Multiply the denominator by the whole number and add the numerator. Write the result over the denominator.

$3\frac{3}{5} \rightarrow 5 \times 3 + 3 = 18$

$\frac{18}{5} = 3\frac{3}{5} = \frac{18}{5}$

Remember an improper fraction is a fraction that is greater than or equal to 1.

Change each mixed number to an improper fraction.

1. $1\frac{1}{6}$ **2.** $4\frac{1}{2}$ **3.** $2\frac{3}{10}$

Set E (pages 263–265)

Find 3 ÷ 4.

To find 3 ÷ 4, think about dividing 3 pizzas equally among 4 people. Divide each pizza into 4 equal parts.

Each person gets 3 slices of pizza, which is the same as $\frac{3}{4}$ of a pizza.

$3 \div 4 = \frac{3}{4}$

Remember you can draw a picture to illustrate a division problem.

Give each answer as a fraction, mixed number, or whole number.

1. 6 ÷ 4 **2.** 1 ÷ 5 **3.** 4 ÷ 3

4. 4 ÷ 12 **5.** 8 ÷ 2 **6.** 10 ÷ 7

7. 5 ÷ 9 **8.** 12 ÷ 8 **9.** 3 ÷ 11

Set F (pages 268–271)

Find the missing number.

$\frac{3}{7} = \frac{■}{14}$

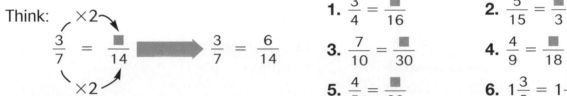

Think: $\frac{3}{7} \overset{\times 2}{=} \frac{■}{14} \rightarrow \frac{3}{7} = \frac{6}{14}$ (×2 on numerator and denominator)

Remember, when writing a mixed number in simplest form, the whole number stays the same.

1. $\frac{3}{4} = \frac{■}{16}$ **2.** $\frac{5}{15} = \frac{■}{3}$

3. $\frac{7}{10} = \frac{■}{30}$ **4.** $\frac{4}{9} = \frac{■}{18}$

5. $\frac{4}{5} = \frac{■}{20}$ **6.** $1\frac{3}{8} = 1\frac{■}{16}$

7. $3\frac{16}{24} = 3\frac{■}{3}$ **8.** $2\frac{3}{21} = 2\frac{■}{7}$

Set G (pages 272–274)

Compare: $\frac{5}{8}$ ● $\frac{2}{3}$.

Rewrite the fractions using the same denominator.

$\frac{5}{8} = \frac{15}{24}$ (×3) $\frac{2}{3} = \frac{16}{24}$ (×8)

Compare the new fractions: $\frac{15}{24} < \frac{16}{24}$.
Write the comparison using the original fractions: $\frac{5}{8} < \frac{2}{3}$.

Remember, to compare fractions that have the same denominator, compare their numerators.

Compare. Write >, <, or = for each ●.

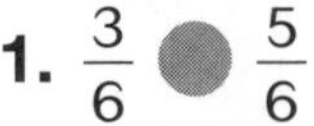

1. $\frac{3}{6}$ ● $\frac{5}{6}$ **2.** $\frac{4}{9}$ ● $\frac{4}{10}$

3. $\frac{6}{16}$ ● $\frac{3}{8}$ **4.** $\frac{5}{6}$ ● $\frac{2}{3}$

5. $\frac{3}{10}$ ● $\frac{1}{3}$ **6.** $\frac{5}{16}$ ● $\frac{4}{8}$

Reteaching (continued)

Set H (pages 278–280)

Use the words *impossible, less likely, equally likely, more likely,* or *certain* to describe how likely it is to spin green.

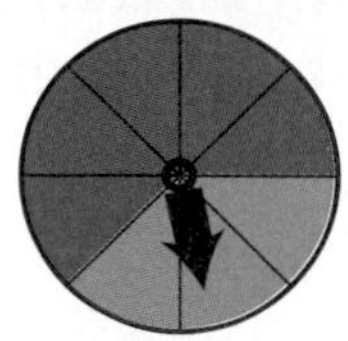

Look at the spinner. Less than $\frac{1}{2}$ of it is green. So, it is less likely that the spinner will land on green.

Remember probability tells us the chance that an event will happen.

For each spinner, use the words at the left to describe how likely it is to spin green.

1. 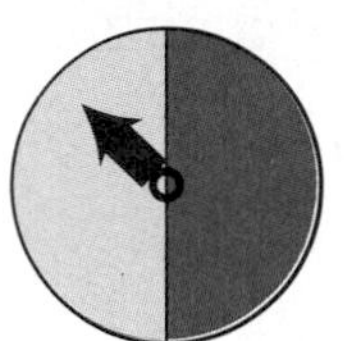

2. 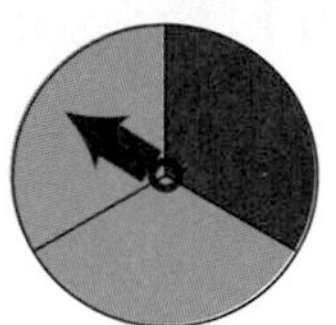

Set I (pages 282–283)

List possible outcomes for the situation.

There are 4 possible outcomes:

A, K, T, Z

Remember you can make a tree diagram or a table to find the possible outcomes.

List all possible outcomes for each situation.

1. 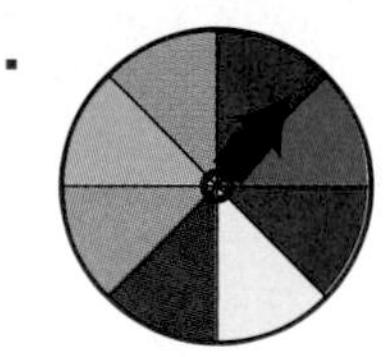

2. 

Set J (pages 284–285)

Write the probability of spinning 7.

There are 8 possible outcomes:
1, 2, 3, 4, 5, 6, 7, 8.

There is one outcome that is 7: 7.

$\frac{1}{8}$ ← number of ways to spin a 7 / ← total number of outcomes

The probability of spinning a 7 is $\frac{1}{8}$.

Remember an impossible event has a probability of 0. A certain event has a probability of 1. Any other event has a probability between 0 and 1.

Refer to the spinner in the example. Write the probability of spinning:

1. a 4

2. a number less than 9

3. a 5 or 8

4. a multiple of 2

More Practice

Set A (pages 252–253)

Write the fraction for the shaded parts of each region.

1. **2.** **3.**

Draw a picture to show each fraction.

4. $\frac{4}{6}$ **5.** $\frac{3}{8}$ **6.** $\frac{2}{3}$ **7.** $\frac{3}{4}$ **8.** $\frac{8}{9}$ **9.** $\frac{3}{12}$

10. Five eighths of a figure is shaded. How much of the figure is not shaded?

Set B (pages 254–256)

Write the fraction for the shaded parts of each set.

1. **2.** **3.**

Draw a set of shapes and shade them to show each fraction.

4. $\frac{1}{3}$ **5.** $\frac{5}{5}$ **6.** $\frac{4}{7}$ **7.** $\frac{2}{9}$ **8.** $\frac{3}{4}$ **9.** $\frac{7}{10}$

10. A train is made up of 36 cars. Of these, 12 are boxcars. What fraction of the train is made up of boxcars?

Set C (pages 257–259)

What fraction should be written at each point?

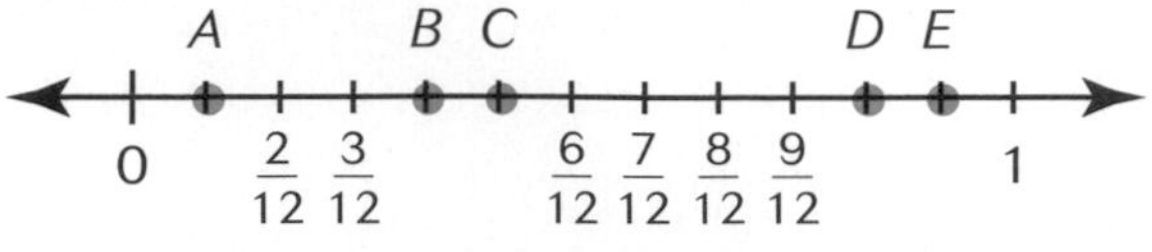

1. point *A* **2.** Point *B* **3.** point *C* **4.** point *D* **5.** point *E*

In Exercises 6 and 7, give the missing fractions.

6.
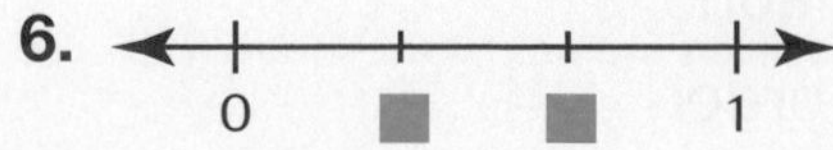

7.
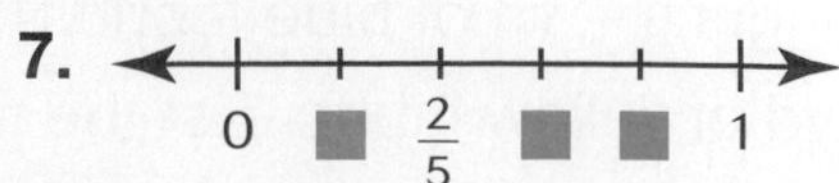

More Practice (continued)

Set D (pages 260–262)

Change each improper fraction to a mixed number or whole number.

1. $\frac{14}{7}$ 2. $\frac{11}{11}$ 3. $\frac{13}{4}$ 4. $\frac{15}{2}$ 5. $\frac{6}{5}$

Write an improper fraction as well as a mixed number or whole number for each picture.

6. 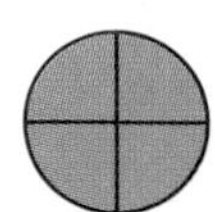

7. 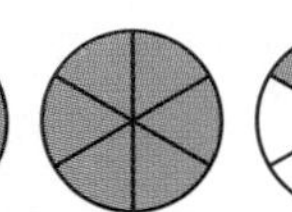

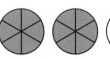

8. 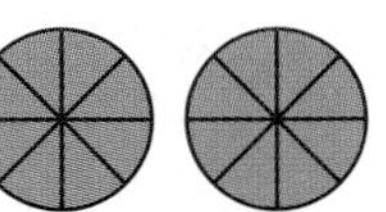 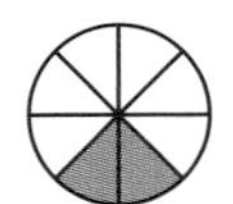

9. One and one half cups of milk is needed to make corn bread. Write this number as an improper fraction.

Set E (pages 263–265)

Give each answer as a fraction, mixed number, or whole number.

1. $1 \div 3$ 2. $7 \div 4$ 3. $30 \div 10$ 4. $3 \div 2$ 5. $10 \div 3$

6. Lori used 8 cups of flour when she baked 3 loaves of bread. Use a mixed number to tell how much flour is in each loaf.

Set F (pages 268–271)

1. $\frac{1}{2} = \frac{\blacksquare}{8}$ 2. $\frac{6}{7} = \frac{\blacksquare}{14}$ 3. $\frac{8}{20} = \frac{\blacksquare}{10}$ 4. $1\frac{4}{9} = 1\frac{\blacksquare}{27}$ 5. $\frac{3}{4} = \frac{\blacksquare}{16}$

Write each fraction or mixed number in simplest form.

6. $\frac{8}{12}$ 7. $\frac{9}{18}$ 8. $3\frac{6}{10}$ 9. $\frac{3}{27}$ 10. $\frac{5}{15}$

11. Write three equivalent fractions for $\frac{3}{8}$.

Set G (pages 272–274)

Compare. Write >, <, or = for each ●.

1. $\frac{1}{4}$ ● $\frac{2}{3}$ 2. $\frac{7}{8}$ ● $\frac{3}{4}$ 3. $\frac{6}{8}$ ● $\frac{3}{4}$ 4. $\frac{2}{10}$ ● $\frac{2}{5}$ 5. $\frac{5}{6}$ ● $\frac{9}{12}$

6. Anne bought $1\frac{3}{4}$ yd of blue fabric, $1\frac{5}{8}$ yd of green fabric, and $1\frac{1}{2}$ yd of yellow fabric. List the fabric colors in order from least amount to greatest amount.

Set H (pages 278–280)

For each bag, use the words *impossible, less likely, equally likely, more likely,* or *certain* to describe how likely it is to select a blue tile from the bag.

1.  **2.**  **3.** 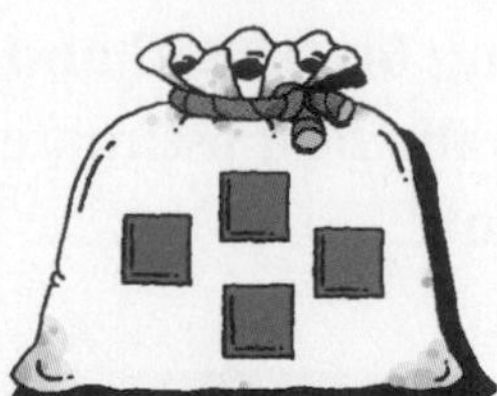 **4.** 

5. Tyler has 6 red cards and 4 black cards. If he chooses one card without looking, is it more likely he will choose a red card or a black card?

Set I (pages 282–283)

List all possible outcomes for each situation.

1. 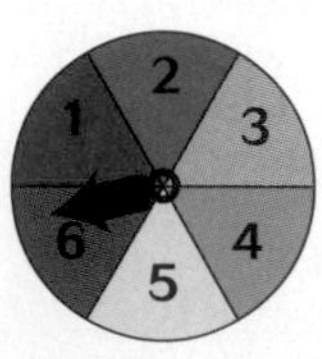

2. 

3. 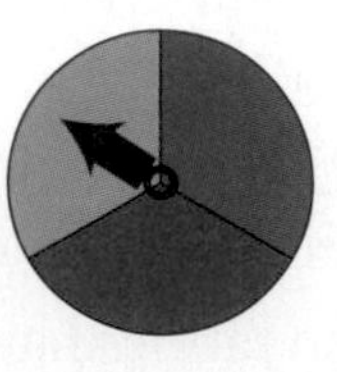

4. 

5. Claudia selects a shape from the bag in Exercise 2 and spins the spinner in Exercise 3 together. Make a tree diagram or a table to show all possible outcomes.

Set J (pages 284–285)

Refer to the spinner at the right. Write the probability of spinning:

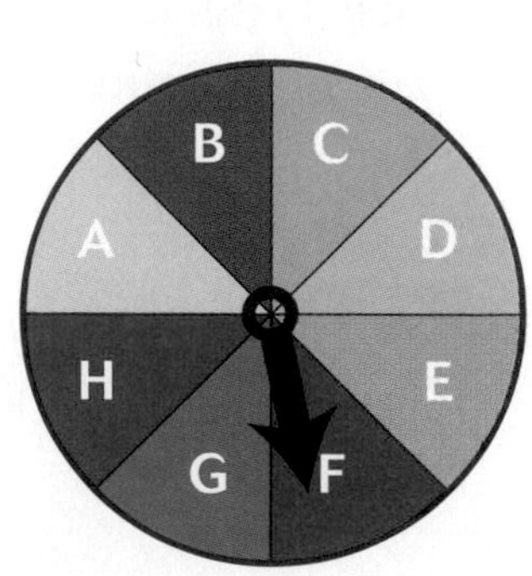

1. a B

2. a vowel

3. a consonant

4. an A, B, or C

5. an X

6. any letter except I–Z

7. Perry is playing a game with a number cube labeled 1 through 6. What is the probability that he will toss a number greater than 0?

Problem Solving: Preparing for Tests

Choose the correct letter for each answer.

1. **Ruth bought a rug for $19.87 and a lamp for $32.56. Which is the best estimate of how much money Ruth spent?**

   A $10
   B $30
   C $50
   D $60

Tip
Start by rounding each price to the nearest dollar. Then decide whether to add or subtract the rounded amounts.

2. **Li bought $\frac{3}{8}$ yard of red fabric, $\frac{7}{8}$ yard of white fabric, and $\frac{5}{8}$ yard of blue fabric. Which is a reasonable conclusion?**

   F Li bought more red fabric than blue fabric.
   G Li bought less blue fabric than red fabric.
   H Li bought less red fabric than white fabric.
   J Li bought more blue fabric than white fabric.

Tip
When you need to read the answer choices given in order to solve a problem, be sure to read all of them.

3. **Four friends wrote letters to each other. Each friend wrote 1 letter to each of the other 3 friends. How many letters did they write all together?**

   A 7
   B 12
   C 15
   D 16

Tip
Try one of these strategies to solve the problem.
- *Draw a Picture*
- *Act it Out*
- *Make a List*

4. In a survey of 2,000 people, 887 people wanted a new library and 423 people did not. Everyone else was undecided. Which number sentence could be used to find out how many people were undecided?

F $2{,}000 - 1{,}310 = ■$

G $887 - 423 = ■$

H $2{,}000 + 1{,}310 = ■$

J $887 + 423 = ■$

5. Sarah has 82 cookies to divide equally among 7 people. When she is finished, how many of the cookies will be left over?

A 1

B 5

C 12

D 13

6. Irma has 16 records, 23 tapes, and 25 CDs. How many tapes and CDs does Irma have in all?

F 2

G 39

H 48

J 64

7. On Monday a pet store sold 13 boxes of hamster food, 16 boxes of dog food, and more than 20 boxes of cat food. Which is reasonable for the number of boxes of pet food the store sold?

A Fewer than 13 boxes

B Between 13 and 20 boxes

C Between 20 and 49 boxes

D More than 49 boxes

8. Dimitri has $51.50 to spend. He buys a computer game that costs $19.95. Which is the best estimate of how much money Dimitri has left?

F $20

G $30

H $50

J $60

9. Natalie is collecting recyclable items. She finds 68 plastic bottles and 31 glass bottles. Which number sentence could be used to find the total number of bottles Natalie found?

A $31 + 31 = ■$

B $68 + 31 = ■$

C $68 - 31 = ■$

D $61 \times 31 = ■$

10. Look at the graph below. Four students worked at the library. How many more hours did Julia work than the person who worked the least?

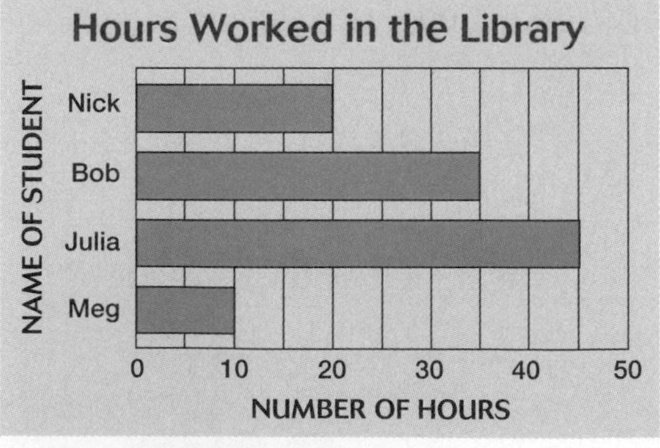

F 55 hours

G 35 hours

H 20 hours

J 10 hours

TEST PREP

Multiple-Choice Cumulative Review

Choose the correct letter for each answer.

Number Sense

1. Which street number shown below is an odd number?

   A 6111 Park Street
   B 3610 Glenview Drive
   C 1542 Lincoln Road
   D 4848 Milton Avenue

2. Mr. Goldberg flew one hundred two thousand, four hundred fifty-eight miles last year. How is this number written?

   F 100,200,458
   G 124,058
   H 102,458
   J 12,458

3. What is 3,291 rounded to the nearest thousand?

   A 2,000
   B 3,000
   C 3,500
   D 4,000

4. Which picture has $\frac{2}{5}$ shaded?

   F ○●●●○
   G ○○●●●
   H ●●○○○
   J ○●●●●

5. 345 + 678 + 99 =

   A 2,013
   B 1,122
   C 1,023
   D 922

6. Sarah wants to buy a CD that costs $13.39. She has $11.47. How much more money does she need?

   F $2.12
   G $2.06
   H $1.92
   J $1.76

7. Which is a reasonable remainder when a number is divided by 5?

   A 9
   B 6
   C 5
   D 4

8. There are 350 students and 10 teachers in a drama club. The teachers put the students into 7 groups. How many students are in each group?

   F 35
   G 45
   H 40
   J 50

Algebra and Functions

9. If 6 times a number is 72, which expression could be used to find the number?

   A $6 + 72$
   B $72 \div 6$
   C 6×72
   D $72 - 6$

---

10. Which number sentence is in the same family of facts as $4 \times 8 = 32$?

   F $32 \div 4 = 8$
   G $4 + 8 = 12$
   H $16 \times 2 = 32$
   J $32 - 8 = 24$

---

11. What is the missing number in the number pattern?

   17, 34, 51, 68, ■, 102

   A 79　　C 85
   B 82　　D 97

---

12. Annie exercised for 10 minutes on Monday, 13 minutes on Tuesday, and 16 minutes on Wednesday. If she continues to follow this pattern, how many minutes will she exercise on Sunday?

   F 7 minutes
   G 22 minutes
   H 25 minutes
   J 28 minutes

Measurement and Geometry

13. Mr. Rivera wants to build a fence around his backyard for his dog Max. How much fencing should he buy?

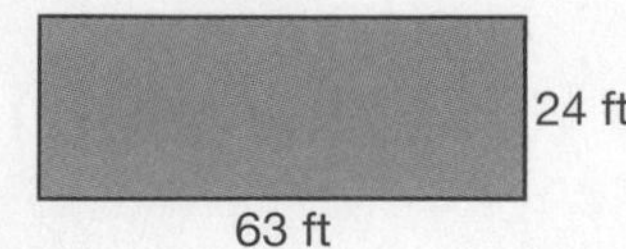

   A 39 feet　　C 174 feet
   B 87 feet　　D 1,512 feet

---

14. Mike gets up at 6:30 A.M. He leaves for school at 7:15 A.M. He gets to school at 7:30 A.M. How long does it take Mike to get ready to leave for school?

   F 1 hour
   G 45 minutes
   H 30 minutes
   J 15 minutes

---

15. What is the perimeter of the triangle below?

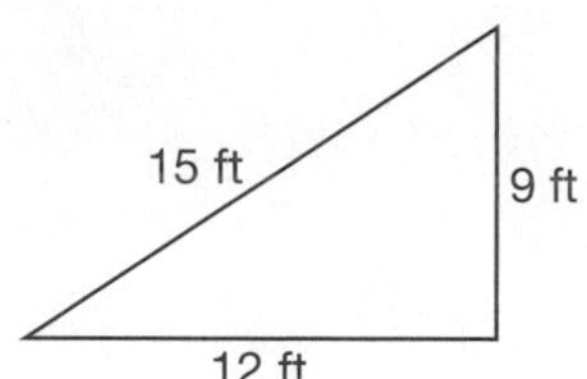

   A 36 ft　　C 26 ft
   B 32 ft　　D 25 ft

---

16. Choose the fraction that is between $\frac{2}{7}$ and $\frac{5}{7}$ on a number line.

   F $\frac{1}{7}$　　H $\frac{4}{7}$
   G $\frac{6}{7}$　　J $\frac{7}{7}$

Adding and Subtracting Fractions and Mixed Numbers

Diagnosing Readiness

In Chapter 8, you will use these skills:

Ⓐ Adding and Subtracting Whole Numbers

(pages 42–43, 47–49)

1. $\begin{array}{r} 43 \\ +\ 38 \\ \hline \end{array}$

2. $\begin{array}{r} 25 \\ +\ 67 \\ \hline \end{array}$

3. $\begin{array}{r} 124 \\ -\ 59 \\ \hline \end{array}$

4. $\begin{array}{r} 286 \\ -\ 97 \\ \hline \end{array}$

5. One movie is 129 minutes. A second movie is 147 minutes. How much longer is the second movie than the first one?

Ⓑ Factoring Numbers

(pages 223–225)

Write each number as the product of two factors in as many ways as possible.

6. 6

7. 8

8. 12

9. 16

10. 10

11. 4

12. How many different ways could you arrange 50 chairs in equal rows?

C Parts of a Region or Set

(pages 252–256)

Write the fraction for the shaded parts of each region or set.

13. 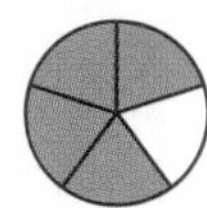

14. 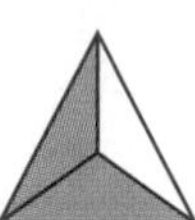

15. 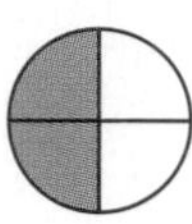

16. 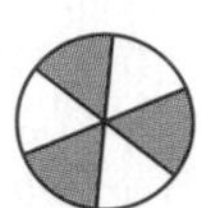

17. 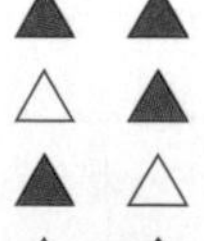

18. 

D Mixed Numbers

(pages 260–262)

Change each improper fraction to a mixed number or whole number.

19. $\frac{5}{4}$

20. $\frac{7}{3}$

21. $\frac{10}{5}$

22. $\frac{6}{4}$

Write an improper fraction as well as a mixed number or whole number for each picture.

23.

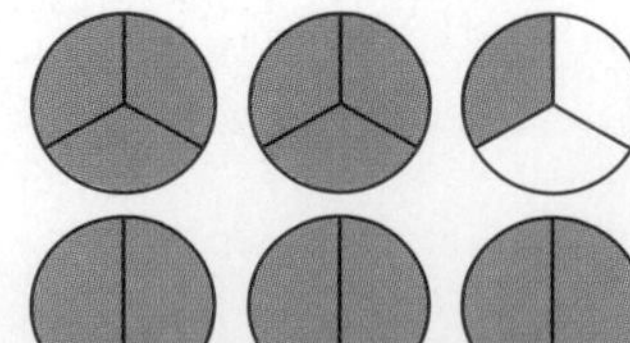

24.

E Fractions and Division

(pages 263–265)

Give each answer as a fraction, mixed number, or whole number.

25. $7 \div 8$

26. $10 \div 9$

27. $8 \div 2$

28. $9 \div 5$

29. $12 \div 5$

30. $16 \div 3$

31. The Trent family ordered 10 burritos to be shared equally by the 4 of them. How much does each person get?

F Equivalent Fractions

(pages 268–271)

32. $\frac{1}{2} = \frac{\blacksquare}{12}$

33. $\frac{3}{9} = \frac{\blacksquare}{3}$

34. $2\frac{3}{4} = 2\frac{\blacksquare}{8}$

35. $1\frac{5}{10} = 1\frac{\blacksquare}{2}$

Write each fraction or mixed number in simplest form.

36. $\frac{2}{10}$

37. $\frac{2}{12}$

38. $\frac{6}{10}$

39. $\frac{6}{8}$

40. $\frac{8}{12}$

41. $5\frac{6}{9}$

To the Family and Student

Looking Back	Chapter 8	Looking Ahead
In Grade 3, students learned how to add and subtract fractions with a common denominator. $\frac{2}{5} + \frac{1}{5}$	**Adding and Subtracting Fractions and Mixed Numbers** In this chapter, students will learn how to add and subtract fractions and mixed numbers with different denominators. $2\frac{1}{2} + 1\frac{1}{4}$	In Grade 5, students will learn how to rename mixed numbers when adding and subtracting them. $3\frac{1}{6} - 1\frac{2}{3}$

Math and Everyday Living

Opportunities to apply the concepts of Chapter 8 abound in everyday situations. During the chapter, think about how adding and subtracting fractions and mixed numbers can be used to solve a variety of real-world problems. The following examples suggest some of the many situations that could launch a discussion about adding and subtracting fractions and mixed numbers.

Math and Sewing To make one doll dress, how much material do you need in all?

Math and Fitness Katrina plans to walk $1\frac{1}{2}$ miles today. She has walked $1\frac{1}{8}$ miles. How much farther does she have to go?

Math at the Grocery Store You buy $1\frac{2}{3}$ pounds of carrots and $1\frac{1}{6}$ pounds of tomatoes. How much do your vegetables weigh in all?

What part of a carton of corn is left? What part of a carton of peas is left? How much more of the corn is left than the peas?

Math at Home How much more tomato sauce do you need to make the lasagna than to make the spaghetti casserole?

Lasagna
1 package lasagna noodles
$1\frac{3}{4}$ cup tomato sauce

Spaghetti Casserole
$\frac{2}{3}$ pound dry spaghetti
$1\frac{1}{4}$ cup tomato sauce

California Content Standards in Chapter 8 Lessons*

	Teach and Practice	Practice
Number Sense		
1.7 Write the fraction represented by a drawing of parts of a figure; represent a given fraction by using drawings; and relate a fraction to a simple decimal on a number line.		8-1, 8-3, 8-4, 8-6
2.3 (Gr. 5) ( ) Solve simple problems, including ones arising in concrete situations, involving the addition and subtraction of fractions and mixed numbers (like and unlike denominators of 20 or less), and express answers in the simplest form.	8-1, 8-2, 8-3, 8-4, 8-6, 8-8	8-5, 8-7
Algebra and Functions		
1.1 Use letters, boxes, or other symbols to stand for any number in simple expressions or equations (e.g., demonstrate an understanding and the use of the concept of a variable).		8-1, 8-6
Statistics, Data Analysis, and Probability		
1.0 Students organize, represent, and interpret numerical and categorical data and clearly communicate their findings.		8-7
1.3 Interpret one- and two-variable data graphs to answer questions about a situation.	8-9	

	Teach and Practice	Practice
Mathematical Reasoning		
1.1 Analyze problems by identifying relationships	8-5	8-8
2.0 Students use strategies, skills, and concepts in finding solutions.		8-5, 8-7
2.3 Use . . . tables . . . to explain mathematical reasoning.	8-7	8-6, 8-9
2.4 Express the solution clearly and logically by using the appropriate mathematical notation and terms and clear language; support solutions with evidence in both verbal and symbolic work.		8-9
3.2 Note the method of deriving the solution and demonstrate a conceptual understanding of the derivation by solving similar problems.		8-7, 8-9
3.3 Develop generalizations of the results obtained and apply them in other circumstances.		8-9

* The symbol ( ) indicates a key standard as designated in the Mathematics Framework for California Public Schools. Full statements of the California Content Standards are found at the beginning of this book following the Table of Contents.

Addition of Fractions

Warm-Up Review

Write in simplest form.

1. $\frac{12}{20}$
2. $\frac{6}{18}$

Write as a whole number or mixed number.

3. $\frac{7}{5}$
4. $\frac{14}{14}$
5. Joe earned \$1,260 last month and \$1,945 this month. How much did he earn in all?

California Content Standard *Number Sense 2.3 (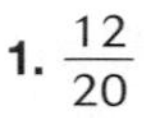) (Grade 5): Solve simple problems . . . involving the addition . . . of fractions . . . (like . . . denominators. . .) . . . and express answers in the simplest form.*

Math Link You know how to add whole numbers. Now you will learn how to add fractions with like denominators.

Example

Mr. Michaels bought $\frac{1}{8}$ pound of cheddar cheese and $\frac{3}{8}$ pound of Swiss cheese. How much cheese did he buy in all?

Find $\frac{1}{8} + \frac{3}{8}$.

Step 1 The denominators are the same, so you can add the numerators.

$$\frac{1}{8} + \frac{3}{8} = \frac{1+3}{8} = \frac{4}{8}$$

Start with one $\frac{1}{8}$ piece.

Add three $\frac{1}{8}$ pieces.

There are four $\frac{1}{8}$ pieces in all.

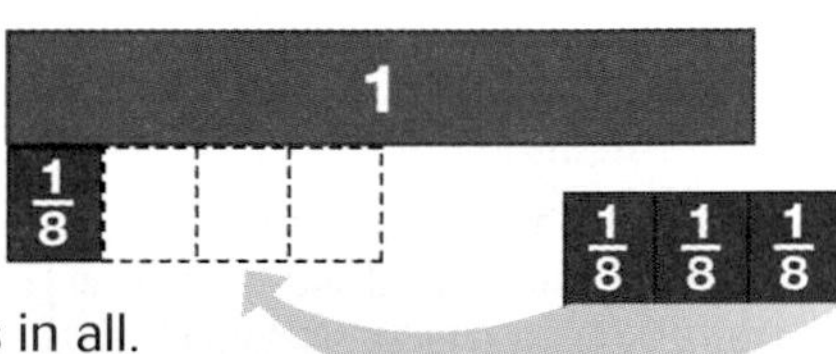

Step 2 Check to see if you can write the sum in simplest form.

$$\frac{4}{8} = \frac{1}{2} \quad (\div 4)$$

Four $\frac{1}{8}$ pieces are the same size as one $\frac{1}{2}$ piece.

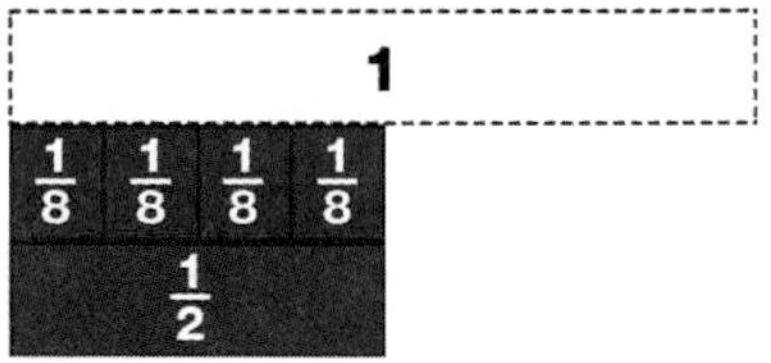

Mr. Michaels bought $\frac{1}{2}$ pound of cheese.

More Examples

A.

$$\begin{array}{r} \frac{5}{12} \\ + \frac{7}{12} \\ \hline \frac{12}{12} = 1 \end{array}$$

Rewrite $\frac{12}{12}$ as 1.

B.

$$\begin{array}{r} \frac{4}{6} \\ + \frac{4}{6} \\ \hline \frac{8}{6} = 1\frac{2}{6} = 1\frac{1}{3} \end{array} \quad (\div 2)$$

Rewrite $\frac{8}{6}$ as a mixed number.

Write $\frac{2}{6}$ in simplest form.

Additional Standards: Number Sense 1.7; Algebra and Functions 1.1 *(See p. 305.)*

Guided Practice *For another example, see Set A on p. 332.*

Write answers in simplest form. Change improper fractions to mixed numbers or whole numbers.

1. $\frac{1}{5} + \frac{3}{5}$ **2.** $\frac{1}{2} + \frac{1}{2}$ **3.** $\frac{3}{8} + \frac{3}{8}$ **4.** $\frac{9}{10} + \frac{3}{10}$ **5.** $\frac{7}{9} + \frac{3}{9} + \frac{1}{9}$

6. In the morning, Fred planted $\frac{5}{8}$ of his garden. In the afternoon, he planted another $\frac{1}{8}$ of the garden. How much of the garden has Fred planted?

Independent Practice *For more practice, see Set A on p. 334.*

Write answers in simplest form. Change improper fractions to mixed numbers or whole numbers.

7. $\frac{3}{6} + \frac{2}{6}$ **8.** $\frac{7}{8} + \frac{1}{8}$ **9.** $\frac{1}{4} + \frac{1}{4}$ **10.** $\frac{1}{9} + \frac{2}{9}$ **11.** $\frac{7}{8} + \frac{3}{8} + \frac{4}{8}$

12. $\frac{3}{5} + \frac{4}{5}$ **13.** $\frac{5}{16} + \frac{3}{16}$ **14.** $\frac{4}{12} + \frac{3}{12}$ **15.** $\frac{1}{15} + \frac{14}{15}$ **16.** $\frac{2}{9} + \frac{4}{9}$ **17.** $\frac{9}{10} + \frac{9}{10}$

18. Use the diagram at the right. Write an addition sentence with fractions to show how much pizza has been eaten.

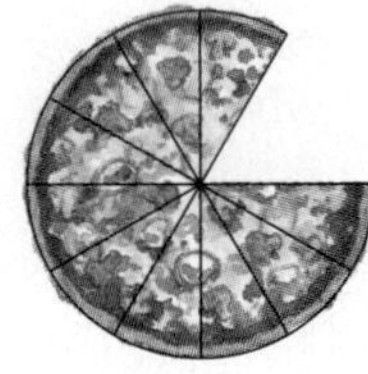
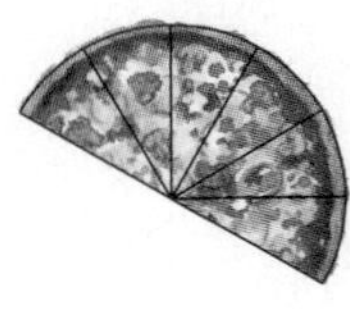

19. Algebra If $n + \frac{4}{8} = \frac{7}{8}$, then $n = $ __?__.

Mixed Review

20. Ten cards are numbered 1 through 10. If you choose one card without looking, what is the probability of drawing a prime number?

21. Suppose you draw one of the cards from Exercise 20 and toss a coin. List all possible outcomes.

22. 59 ÷ 5 **23.** 841 ÷ 9 **24.** 372 × 8 **25.** 436 × 65

Test Prep **Choose the correct letter for the answer.**

26. 2 × [(9 + 15) ÷ 3] =
(3-6)

A 28 **B** 16 **C** 11 **D** 4 **E** NH

Addition of Mixed Numbers

California Content Standard *Number Sense 2.3 (key) (Grade 5): Solve simple problems . . . involving the addition . . . of fractions and mixed numbers (like . . . denominators . . .), and express answers in the simplest form.*

Math Link You can use what you know about adding whole numbers and what you just learned about adding fractions to add mixed numbers.

Warm-Up Review

1. $\frac{5}{9} + \frac{1}{9}$
2. $\frac{1}{12} + \frac{9}{12}$

Write in simplest form.

3. $6\frac{12}{50}$
4. $9\frac{7}{14}$
5. Abby walked $\frac{5}{8}$ mile to a friend's house, and then she walked $\frac{3}{8}$ mile to the park. How far did Abby walk from her house to the park?

Example

On Monday, students watched a television documentary about dolphins that lasted $1\frac{1}{6}$ hours. On Tuesday they watched a movie about dolphins that lasted $2\frac{3}{6}$ hours. How much time did these programs take altogether?

Find $1\frac{1}{6} + 2\frac{3}{6}$.

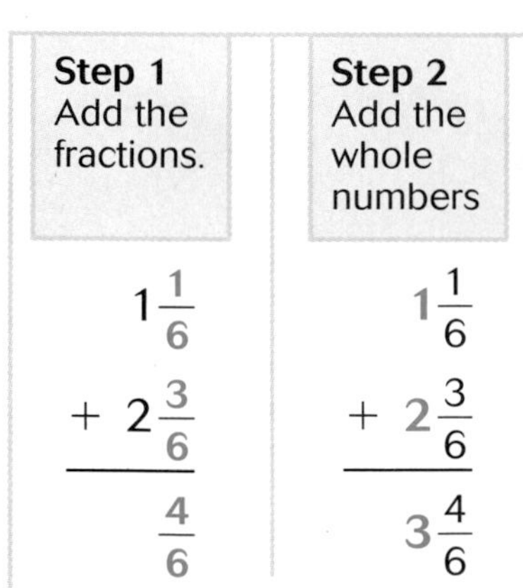

Step 1 Add the fractions.
$1\frac{1}{6} + 2\frac{3}{6} = \frac{4}{6}$
Step 2 Add the whole numbers
$1\frac{1}{6} + 2\frac{3}{6} = 3\frac{4}{6}$

Start with one whole and one $\frac{1}{6}$ piece.

Add two wholes and three $\frac{1}{6}$ pieces.

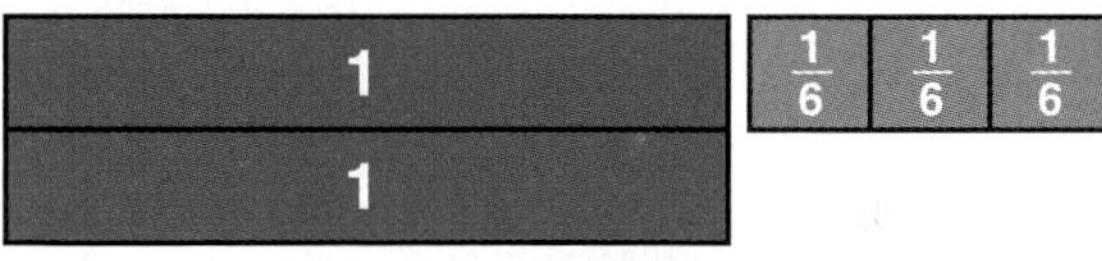

In all, there are three wholes and four $\frac{1}{6}$ pieces, or $3\frac{4}{6}$.

Step 3 Check to see if you can write the fraction in simplest form.

$$1\frac{1}{6} + 2\frac{3}{6} = 3\frac{4}{6} = 3\frac{2}{3} \quad (\div 2)$$

Four $\frac{1}{6}$ pieces are the same size as two $\frac{1}{3}$ pieces. So $3\frac{4}{6} = 3\frac{2}{3}$.

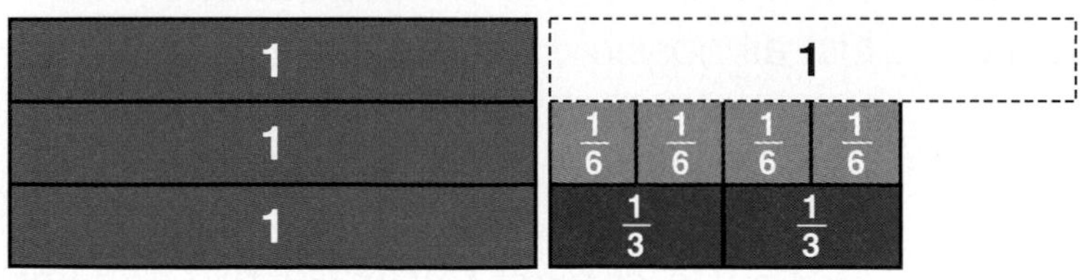

The programs took $3\frac{2}{3}$ hours altogether.

Guided Practice

For another example, see Set B on p. 332.

Write answers in simplest form.

1. $4\frac{2}{4} + 1\frac{1}{4}$ **2.** $2\frac{3}{10} + 3\frac{5}{10}$ **3.** $5\frac{4}{12} + 8\frac{2}{12}$ **4.** $7\frac{3}{8} + \frac{1}{8}$ **5.** $5\frac{1}{9} + 4\frac{2}{9}$ **6.** $2\frac{3}{20} + 2$

7. Lucille spent $2\frac{1}{4}$ hours writing a report and $1\frac{1}{4}$ hours making the cover. Altogether, how much time did she spend on the report?

Independent Practice

For more practice, see Set B on p. 334.

Write answers in simplest form.

8. $1\frac{5}{8} + 2\frac{2}{8}$ **9.** $4\frac{1}{6} + 4\frac{1}{6}$ **10.** $6 + 3\frac{7}{12}$ **11.** $5\frac{1}{3} + 6\frac{1}{3}$ **12.** $8\frac{3}{14} + \frac{4}{14}$ **13.** $2\frac{9}{16} + 7\frac{5}{16}$

14. $3\frac{1}{10} + \frac{4}{10}$ **15.** $6\frac{5}{18} + 2\frac{5}{18}$ **16.** $5\frac{2}{3} + 12$ **17.** $4\frac{3}{11} + 12\frac{5}{11}$

18. Cindy bought $2\frac{3}{8}$ pounds of grapes and $2\frac{1}{8}$ pounds of plums. How much fruit did she buy in all?

Mixed Review

Use the spinner at the right for Exercises 19–22. Find the probability of the spinner landing on:

19. 8. **20.** a multiple of 3.

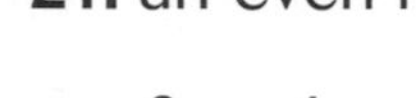

21. an even number. **22.** a multiple of 5.

23. $\frac{2}{5} + \frac{4}{5}$ **24.** $295 + 67 + 418$ **25.** $\frac{7}{12} + \frac{3}{12}$

Test Prep **Choose the correct letter for each answer.**

26. Which number is between 71,045 and 71,126? (1-3)

A 71,041
B 71,081
C 71,131
D 71,161

27. Which number is *not* between $^{-}4$ and 2? (1-6)

F $^{-}5$
G $^{-}3$
H 0
J 1

Subtraction of Fractions

Warm-Up Review

1. 15 − 8 2. 17 − 9

Write in simplest form.

3. $\frac{14}{21}$ 4. $\frac{4}{12}$

5. $\frac{20}{25}$ 6. $\frac{19}{24}$

7. Courtney is reading a 216-page book. She has already read 144 pages. How many pages does she still need to read?

California Content Standard *Number Sense 2.3 (Grade 5) (🔑): Solve simple problems . . . involving the . . . subtraction of fractions . . . (like . . . denominators . . .), and express answers in the simplest form.*

Math Link You have learned to add fractions with like denominators. Now you will learn how to subtract fractions with like denominators.

Example 1

Galina bought $\frac{5}{8}$ yard of fabric. She used $\frac{3}{8}$ yard to make doll dresses. How much fabric does Galina have left?

Find $\frac{5}{8} - \frac{3}{8}$.

Step 1 The denominators are the same, so you can subtract the numerators.

$$\frac{5}{8} - \frac{3}{8} = \frac{5-3}{8} = \frac{2}{8}$$

Start with five $\frac{1}{8}$ pieces.

Subtract three $\frac{1}{8}$ pieces.

There are two $\frac{1}{8}$ pieces left.

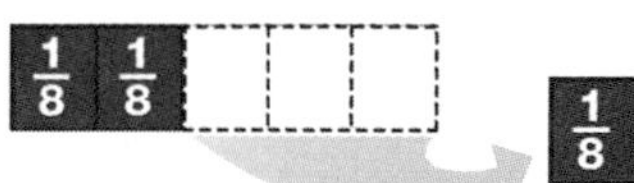

Step 2 Check to see if you can write the difference in simplest form.

$$\frac{2}{8} = \frac{1}{4} \quad (\div 2)$$

Two $\frac{1}{8}$ pieces are the same size as one $\frac{1}{4}$ piece.

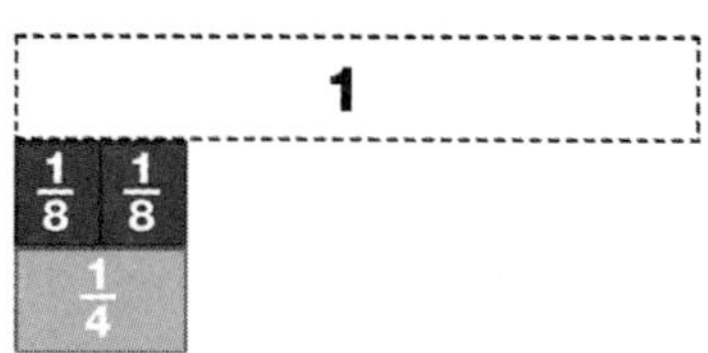

Galina has $\frac{1}{4}$ yard of fabric left.

Example 2

$$\begin{array}{r} \frac{5}{10} \\ -\ \frac{2}{10} \\ \hline \frac{3}{10} \end{array}$$

Can you rewrite $\frac{3}{10}$ in simplest form?

No, $\frac{3}{10}$ is already in simplest form.

 Additional Standard: Number Sense 1.7 (See p. 305.)

Guided Practice *For another example, see Set C on p. 332.*

Write answers in simplest form.

1. $\frac{5}{6} - \frac{4}{6}$ **2.** $\frac{7}{12} - \frac{3}{12}$ **3.** $\frac{9}{10} - \frac{5}{10}$ **4.** $\frac{3}{4} - \frac{1}{4}$ **5.** $\frac{11}{15} - \frac{1}{15}$

6. Teddy is weaving a cloth that will be $\frac{7}{8}$ of a yard long. He has finished $\frac{3}{8}$ of a yard. How much more does he need to weave?

Independent Practice *For more practice, see Set C on p. 334.*

Write answers in simplest form.

7. $\frac{2}{3} - \frac{1}{3}$ **8.** $\frac{5}{6} - \frac{1}{6}$ **9.** $\frac{11}{12} - \frac{5}{12}$ **10.** $\frac{7}{9} - \frac{2}{9}$ **11.** $\frac{7}{8} - \frac{4}{8}$

12. $\frac{3}{5} - \frac{1}{5}$ **13.** $\frac{5}{10} - \frac{3}{10}$ **14.** $\frac{11}{12} - \frac{4}{12}$ **15.** $\frac{17}{18} - \frac{9}{18}$ **16.** $\frac{9}{10} - \frac{8}{10}$ **17.** $\frac{11}{20} - \frac{3}{20}$

18. Elsa ate $\frac{6}{10}$ of a vegetable pizza. Lorna ate $\frac{4}{10}$. Who ate more? How much more?

19. Write a subtraction sentence to match the diagram shown at the right.

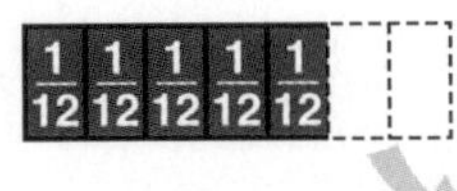

Mixed Review

20. The Boyer family is on vacation. Ms. Boyer drives for 3 hours at 55 miles per hour. How many miles has she driven?

21. Write three fractions equivalent to $\frac{3}{9}$.

22. $\frac{3}{9} + \frac{4}{9}$ **23.** $\frac{7}{12} + \frac{1}{12}$ **24.** $4\frac{1}{3} + 2\frac{1}{3}$ **25.** $5\frac{6}{10} + 1\frac{1}{10}$

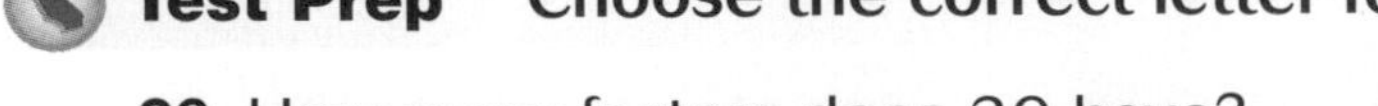

Test Prep **Choose the correct letter for each answer.**

26. How many factors does 30 have?
(6-9)

A 3

B 6

C 8

D 10

27. **Mental Math** 54,000 ÷ 9 =
(6-1)

F 60,000

G 6,000

H 600

J 60

Subtraction of Mixed Numbers

1. $\frac{9}{9} = ■$ 2. $1 = \frac{■}{5}$

Write in simplest form.

3. $3\frac{16}{20}$ 4. $8\frac{6}{24}$

5. $\frac{7}{9} - \frac{1}{9}$ 6. $\frac{8}{12} - \frac{5}{12}$

7. Eva needs $\frac{3}{4}$ cup of nuts for a recipe. She has only $\frac{1}{4}$ cup. How much more does she need?

California Content Standard *Number Sense 2.3 (🔑) (Grade 5): Solve simple problems . . . involving the . . . subtraction of fractions and mixed numbers (like . . . denominators . . .), and express answers in the simplest form.*

Math Link You know how to add mixed numbers. Now you are ready to subtract mixed numbers.

Example 1

Find $2\frac{3}{4} - 1\frac{1}{4}$.

Step 1 Subtract the fractions. The denominators are the same, so just subtract the numerators.

$$\begin{array}{r} 2\frac{3}{4} \\ -\ 1\frac{1}{4} \\ \hline \frac{2}{4} \end{array}$$

Start with two whole and three $\frac{1}{4}$ pieces.

Subtract one whole and one $\frac{1}{4}$ piece.

There are one whole and two $\frac{1}{4}$ pieces left, or $1\frac{2}{4}$.

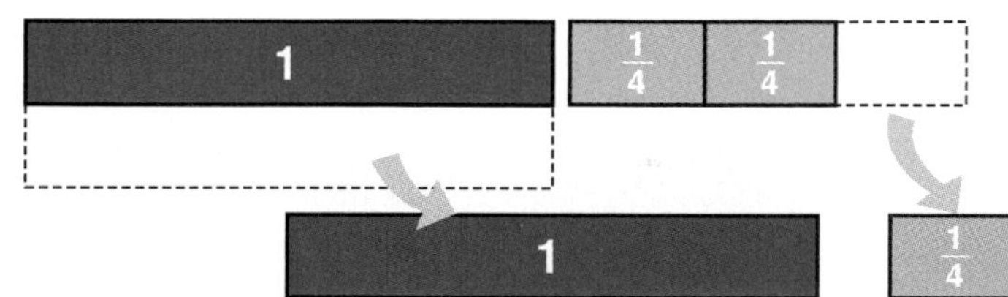

Step 2 Subtract the whole numbers.

$$\begin{array}{r} 2\frac{3}{4} \\ -\ 1\frac{1}{4} \\ \hline 1\frac{2}{4} \end{array}$$

Step 3 Check to see if you can write the fraction in simplest form.

$$\begin{array}{r} 2\frac{3}{4} \\ -\ 1\frac{1}{4} \\ \hline 1\frac{2}{4} \end{array} = 1\frac{1}{2} \quad (\div 2)$$

Two $\frac{1}{4}$ pieces are the same size as one $\frac{1}{2}$ piece.

So, $1\frac{2}{4} = 1\frac{1}{2}$.

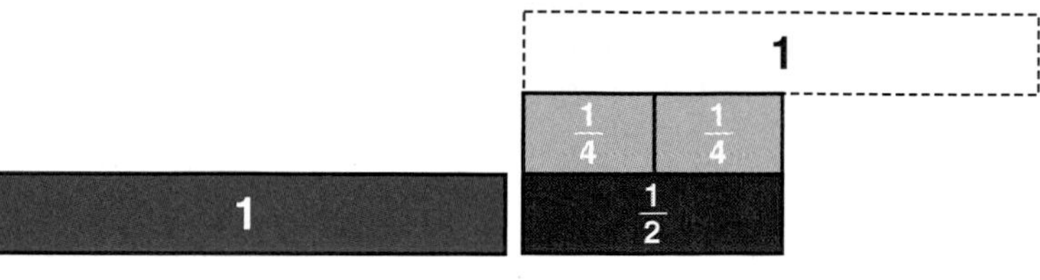

 Additional Standard: Number Sense 1.7 (See p. 305.)

When you subtract a mixed number or fraction from a whole number, you need to rename the whole number so that it looks like a mixed number. Example 2 shows you how to do this.

Example 2

Find $4 - 2\frac{1}{5}$.

Step 1 There is no fraction from which to subtract $\frac{1}{5}$.

So rename 4 as $3\frac{5}{5}$.

$$\begin{array}{rcl} 4 & = & 3\frac{5}{5} \\ -\ 2\frac{1}{5} & = & 2\frac{1}{5} \\ \hline \end{array}$$

Four wholes are the same as three wholes and five $\frac{1}{5}$ pieces.

$4 = 3 + 1 = 3 + \frac{5}{5} = 3\frac{5}{5}$

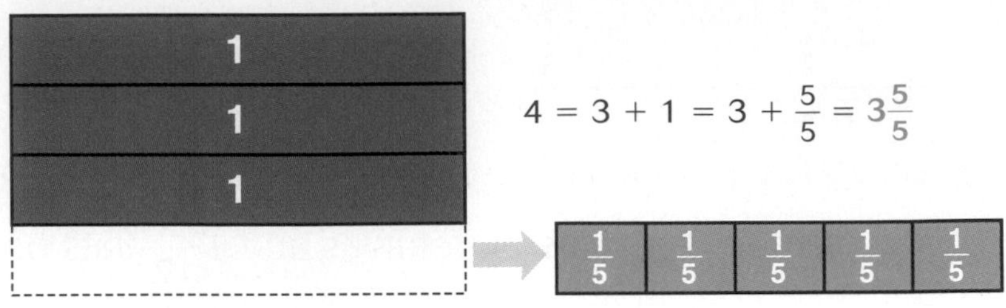

Step 2 Subtract the fractions. The denominators are the same, so just subtract the numerators. Then subtract the whole numbers.

$$\begin{array}{rcl} 4 & = & 3\frac{5}{5} \\ -\ 2\frac{1}{5} & = & 2\frac{1}{5} \\ \hline & & 1\frac{4}{5} \end{array}$$

This fraction is already in simplest form.

Subtract two wholes and one $\frac{1}{5}$ piece from three wholes and five $\frac{1}{5}$ pieces.

There are one whole and four $\frac{1}{5}$ pieces left, or $1\frac{4}{5}$.

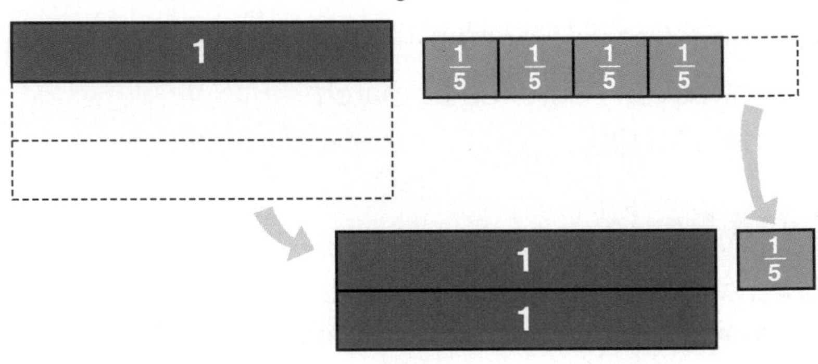

Guided Practice

For another example, see Set D on p. 333.

Write answers in simplest form.

1. $4\frac{2}{3} - 1\frac{1}{3}$

2. $5\frac{5}{6} - 3\frac{3}{6}$

3. $3 - 1\frac{1}{4}$

4. $2\frac{4}{8} - \frac{1}{8}$

5. $5\frac{2}{9} - 4\frac{1}{9}$

6. $4\frac{5}{10} - 4\frac{1}{10}$

7. Vivian lives $2\frac{3}{4}$ miles from the library. She has already bicycled $1\frac{1}{4}$ miles. How much farther does she have to go?

Independent Practice For more practice, see Set D on p. 335.

Write answers in simplest form.

8. $5\frac{3}{4} - 2\frac{1}{4}$

9. $5\frac{5}{6} - 1\frac{2}{6}$

10. $5\frac{6}{7} - 3\frac{2}{7}$

11. $5 - 3\frac{1}{2}$

12. $8\frac{7}{8} - 1\frac{6}{8}$

13. $4\frac{9}{16} - \frac{5}{16}$

14. $7\frac{5}{12} - 4\frac{5}{12}$

15. $12\frac{4}{5} - 10\frac{2}{5}$

16. $8\frac{4}{9} - 8\frac{1}{9}$

17. $9 - 6\frac{2}{5}$

18. $2 - 1\frac{2}{3}$

19. $17\frac{7}{10} - 2\frac{2}{10}$

20. Ms. Gillick bought 6 flats of flowers. In her front yard, she planted $3\frac{5}{12}$ flats of petunias and $1\frac{1}{12}$ flats of snap dragons. How many more flats of petunias did she plant than of snap dragons?

21. Refer to the fraction pieces at the right. Draw a diagram to show the result after subtracting $1\frac{1}{3}$. Write a subtraction sentence to match what you did.

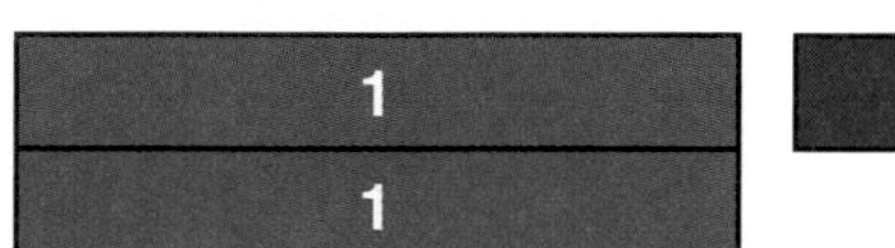

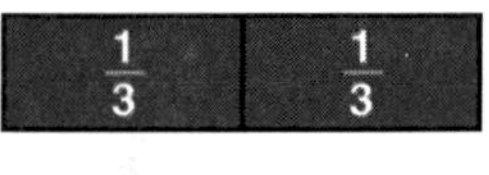

Mixed Review

22. What is the average number of tenants per floor at Shady Lane Apartments?

Shady Lane Apartments	
Floor	**Number of tenants**
1st	41
2nd	67
3rd	54
4th	54

23. **Mental Math** 64,000 ÷ 8

24. Write 54 as the product of two factors in as many ways as possible.

25. $1\frac{3}{8} + 5\frac{3}{8}$

26. $\frac{7}{12} - \frac{5}{12}$

27. $2\frac{3}{7} + 2\frac{2}{7}$

28. $\frac{9}{16} - \frac{3}{16}$

Test Prep Choose the correct letter for each answer.

29. (2-1) What is the best estimate of 23,842 + 31,059?

A 60,000
B 50,000
C 30,000
D 5,000

30. (3-8) **Algebra** If $n = 48$, then $87n =$

F 135
G 3,076
H 4,124
J 4,176
K NH

Diagnostic Checkpoint

Write answers in simplest form. Change improper fractions to mixed numbers or whole numbers.

1. (8-1) $\frac{2}{8} + \frac{3}{8}$

2. (8-1) $\frac{2}{9} + \frac{7}{9}$

3. (8-1) $\frac{3}{12} + \frac{8}{12}$

4. (8-1) $\frac{5}{12} + \frac{2}{12}$

5. (8-2) $4\frac{3}{10} + 3\frac{2}{10}$

6. (8-2) $2\frac{1}{4} + 3\frac{2}{4}$

7. (8-3) $\frac{7}{8} - \frac{3}{8}$

8. (8-3) $\frac{5}{6} - \frac{1}{6}$

9. (8-3) $\frac{8}{9} - \frac{7}{9}$

10. (8-3) $\frac{7}{10} - \frac{3}{10}$

11. (8-4) $6\frac{4}{5} - 3\frac{1}{5}$

12. (8-4) $7\frac{7}{9} - 5\frac{1}{9}$

13. (8-1) $\frac{1}{7} + \frac{4}{7}$

14. (8-1) $\frac{4}{5} + \frac{3}{5}$

15. (8-2) $3\frac{8}{15} + 1\frac{2}{15}$

16. (8-2) $8\frac{4}{11} + \frac{2}{11}$

17. (8-3) $\frac{6}{8} - \frac{5}{8}$

18. (8-3) $\frac{6}{7} - \frac{3}{7}$

19. (8-4) $6\frac{10}{12} - \frac{3}{12}$

20. (8-4) $8\frac{3}{4} - 2\frac{1}{4}$

21. (8-1) **Algebra** If $n + \frac{2}{7} = \frac{6}{7}$, find n.

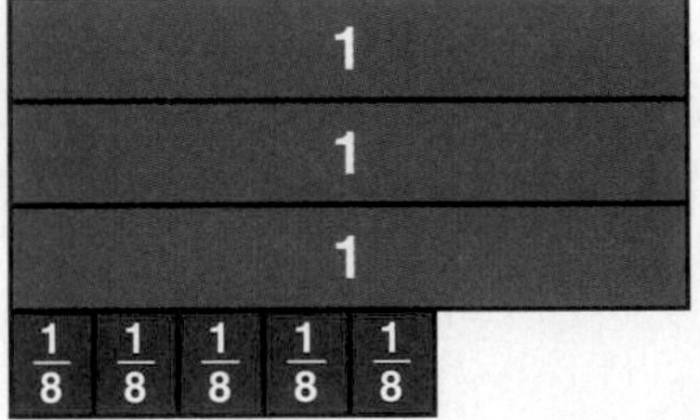

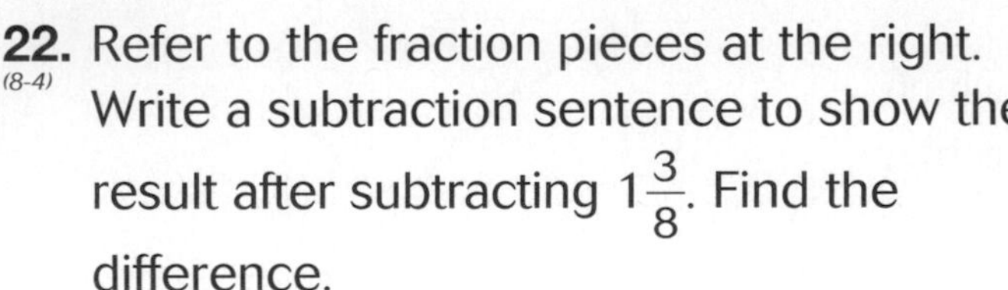

22. (8-4) Refer to the fraction pieces at the right. Write a subtraction sentence to show the result after subtracting $1\frac{3}{8}$. Find the difference.

23. (8-2) Terry bought $3\frac{1}{4}$ pounds of red sand and $1\frac{1}{4}$ pounds of yellow sand. How many pounds of sand did Terry buy in all?

24. (8-2) A bread recipe calls for $3\frac{1}{2}$ cups of wheat flour and 2 cups of rye flour. How much flour is in the recipe?

25. (8-4) Pat bought 3 pounds of grapes and ate $1\frac{1}{4}$ pounds. How many pounds are left?

26. (8-3) **Math Reasoning** The sum of two fractions is $\frac{5}{6}$. Their difference is $\frac{1}{6}$. What are the two fractions?

Problem-Solving Skill:
Choose the Operation

Warm-Up Review

1. $\frac{4}{15} + \frac{14}{15}$
2. $\frac{19}{25} - \frac{9}{25}$
3. $10\frac{2}{10} + 6\frac{3}{10}$
4. $7\frac{4}{9} - 2\frac{1}{9}$
5. Louisa bought a package of 500 sheets of paper. She has used 224 sheets. How many sheets are left?

California Content Standard *Mathematical Reasoning 1.1: Analyze problems by identifying relationships . . ..*

Read for Understanding

Jason's family is planning their vacation to McCormick's Creek State Park in Indiana. Some of the hiking trails are shown on the map to the right.

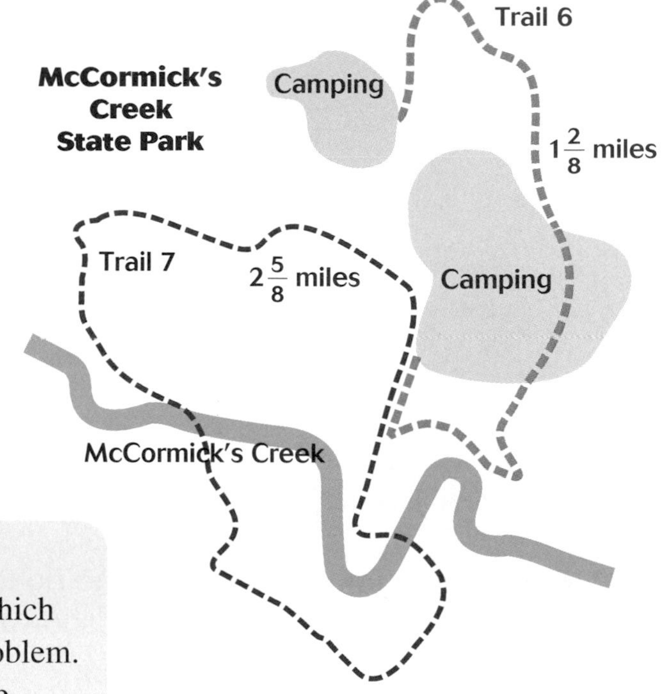

1. How long is Trail 6?
2. How long is Trail 7?

Think and Discuss

Choose the Operation

Sometimes you need to decide which operation is needed to solve a problem. Look for clues in the words of the problem to help you decide.

Look again at the map of the trails.

3. How much longer is Trail 7 than Trail 6? What operation did you use to solve the problem?
4. If Jason hikes Trail 6 in the morning and Trail 7 in the afternoon, how far will he have hiked in all? What operation did you use to solve the problem?
5. How did you decide which operation to use before solving Exercises 3 and 4?

Additional Standards: Number Sense 2.3 (key) (Grade 5); Mathematical Reasoning 2.0 *(See p. 305.)*

Guided Practice

The total driving time to McCormick's Creek State Park is $5\frac{3}{4}$ hours. After driving for $3\frac{1}{4}$ hours, Jason's family stopped for lunch.

1. Which of the following should you do to find how much longer the driving will take?

a. Add the total driving time to the number of hours the family drove before lunch.

b. Subtract the total driving time from the number of hours the family drove before lunch.

c. Subtract the number of hours the family drove before lunch from the total driving time.

2. Which number sentence shows how much longer the driving will take?

a. $5\frac{3}{4} - 3\frac{1}{4} = 2\frac{1}{2}$ hours

b. $5\frac{3}{4} + 3\frac{1}{4} = 9$ hours

c. $3\frac{1}{4} + 3\frac{1}{4} = 6\frac{1}{2}$ hours

3. Suppose lunch takes an hour. Which number sentence shows the total time for the entire trip?

a. $3\frac{1}{4} + 1 = 4\frac{1}{4}$ hours

b. $5\frac{3}{4} + 1 = 6\frac{3}{4}$ hours

c. $9 + 1 = 10$ hours

Independent Practice

Jason's backpack weighs $14\frac{4}{8}$ pounds. His father's backpack weighs $12\frac{3}{8}$ pounds.

4. Which number sentence shows how heavy the backpacks are altogether?

a. $14\frac{4}{8} + 12\frac{3}{8} = 26\frac{7}{8}$ pounds

b. $14\frac{4}{8} + 14\frac{4}{8} = 29$ pounds

c. $14\frac{4}{8} - 12\frac{3}{8} = 2\frac{1}{8}$ pounds

5. Which number sentence shows how much Jason's backpack weighs after removing $1\frac{2}{8}$ pounds of fruit?

a. $12\frac{3}{8} - 1\frac{2}{8} = 11\frac{1}{8}$ pounds

b. $14\frac{4}{8} - 12\frac{3}{8} = 2\frac{1}{8}$ pounds

c. $14\frac{4}{8} - 1\frac{2}{8} = 13\frac{1}{4}$ pounds

6. Math Reasoning Look back at your answer for Exercise 4. What is another number sentence that shows how heavy the backpacks are altogether?

Use Homework Workbook 8-5.

Add Fractions with Unlike Denominators

California Content Standard *Number Sense 2.3 (key) (Grade 5): Solve simple problems . . . involving the addition . . . of fractions . . . (. . . unlike denominators . . .), and express answers in the simplest form.*

Math Link You know how to add fractions with like denominators. In this lesson, you will learn how to add fractions that have different denominators.

When you add fractions with unlike denominators, change the fractions to equivalent fractions that have a **common denominator.** Then add the numerators of the new fractions.

Warm-Up Review

1. $\frac{1}{6} = \frac{■}{12}$
2. $\frac{1}{2} = \frac{■}{10}$
3. $\frac{2}{9} + \frac{4}{9}$
4. $\frac{7}{12} + \frac{4}{12}$
5. List the factors of 12.
6. Use equivalent fractions to rewrite $\frac{2}{3}$ and $\frac{1}{4}$ so that the new fractions have the same denominator.
7. Jill used $\frac{1}{4}$ of a can of paint to paint the hallway ceiling and $\frac{2}{4}$ of the can for the walls. How much paint did she use in all?

Word Bank

common denominator

Example 1

Craig's family ate $\frac{1}{2}$ of a blueberry pie and $\frac{1}{3}$ of an apple pie. How much pie did they eat altogether?

Find $\frac{1}{2} + \frac{1}{3}$.

Step 1 Rewrite the fractions using a common denominator.

Think: What number has 2 and 3 as factors? 6

$\frac{1}{2} = \frac{■}{6}$

$\frac{1}{3} = \frac{■}{6}$

$$\frac{1 \times 3}{2 \times 3} = \frac{3}{6}$$

$$+\ \frac{1 \times 2}{3 \times 2} = \frac{2}{6}$$

Step 2 Add the new fractions. Write the sum in simplest form.

$$\frac{1}{2} = \frac{3}{6}$$

$$+\ \frac{1}{3} = \frac{2}{6}$$

$$\frac{5}{6}$$

$\frac{5}{6}$ is in simplest form.

Both the $\frac{1}{2}$ piece and the $\frac{1}{3}$ piece can be shown with $\frac{1}{6}$ pieces.

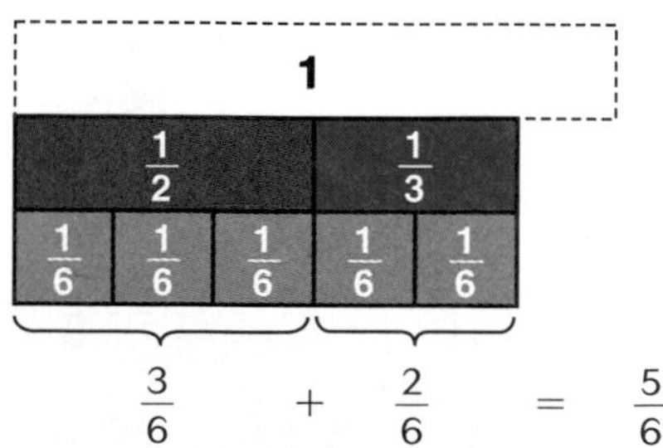

They ate $\frac{5}{6}$ of a pie altogether.

Additional Standards: Number Sense 1.7; Algebra and Functions 1.1; Mathematical Reasoning 2.3 (See p. 305.)

Sometimes you only have to rewrite one of the fractions. Example 2 shows you how.

Example 2

Find $\frac{1}{4} + \frac{3}{8}$.

Step 1 Rewrite the fractions using a common denominator.	**Step 2** Add the new fractions.
Think: Since 4 is a factor of 8, $\frac{1}{4}$ can be rewritten with 8 in the denominator. So just rewrite $\frac{1}{4}$ and leave $\frac{3}{8}$ alone. $\frac{1}{4} \overset{\times 2}{=} \frac{2}{8}$; $+\frac{3}{8} = \frac{3}{8}$	$\frac{1}{4} = \frac{2}{8}$; $+\frac{3}{8} = \frac{3}{8}$; $\frac{5}{8}$. $\frac{5}{8}$ is in simplest form.

The $\frac{1}{4}$ piece is the same size as two $\frac{1}{8}$ pieces.

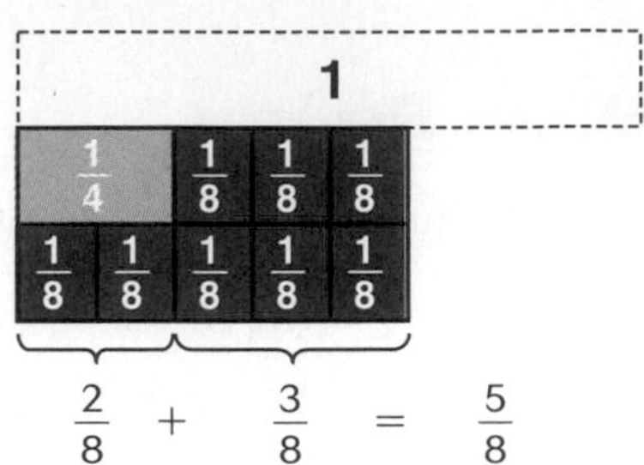

Guided Practice *For another example, see Set E on p. 333.*

Write answers in simplest form.

1. $\frac{1}{5} + \frac{1}{2}$ **2.** $\frac{1}{2} + \frac{1}{4}$ **3.** $\frac{1}{6} + \frac{2}{3}$ **4.** $\frac{1}{4} + \frac{5}{12}$ **5.** $\frac{1}{8} + \frac{1}{4}$

6. Ben ate $\frac{1}{3}$ of a raisin granola bar and $\frac{1}{4}$ of a peanut butter granola bar. How much did he eat altogether?

Independent Practice *For more practice, see Set E on p. 335.*

Write answers in simplest form.

7. $\frac{1}{3} + \frac{1}{6}$ **8.** $\frac{1}{2} + \frac{3}{8}$ **9.** $\frac{1}{2} + \frac{2}{5}$ **10.** $\frac{4}{5} + \frac{1}{10}$ **11.** $\frac{1}{12} + \frac{3}{4}$

12. $\frac{2}{4} + \frac{3}{8}$ **13.** $\frac{1}{10} + \frac{2}{5}$ **14.** $\frac{1}{3} + \frac{1}{12}$ **15.** $\frac{1}{8} + \frac{1}{4}$ **16.** $\frac{1}{6} + \frac{3}{4}$ **17.** $\frac{7}{10} + \frac{1}{5}$

18. Use the diagram at the right. How much pizza has been eaten? How much is left?

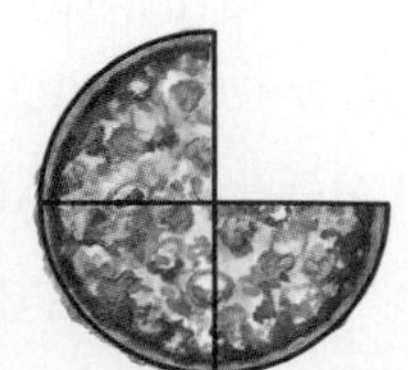
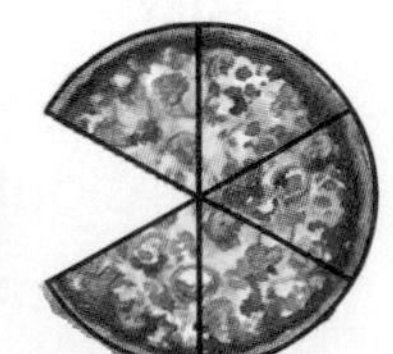

19. Terri earns $2.15 for each pizza delivery she makes. On Friday she drove $7\frac{1}{2}$ miles and made 23 deliveries. How much money did she earn?

20. Use fractions with unlike denominators to write an addition sentence modeled by the diagram.

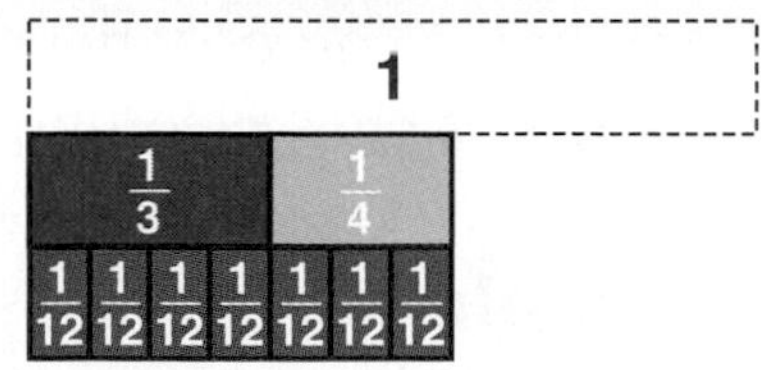

21. **Math Reasoning** Gillian and Cheryl added $\frac{1}{3} + \frac{1}{2}$. Gillian's answer was $\frac{5}{6}$. Cheryl's answer was $\frac{10}{12}$. Are they both correct? Why?

22. **Algebra** If $n = \frac{5}{12}$, then $n + \frac{1}{6} =$ __?__.

Mixed Review

23. Micky used $3\frac{3}{4}$ feet of lumber to make a mailbox and $2\frac{1}{4}$ feet of lumber to make a flower planter. How much more lumber was used for the mailbox?

24. What two equivalent fractions are illustrated by the shaded part of the diagram at the right?

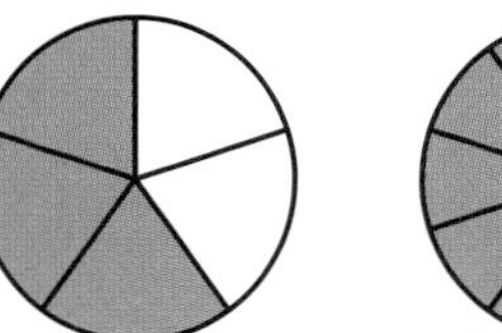

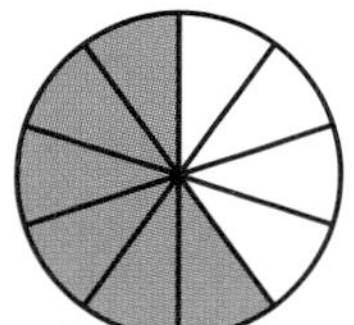

25. Earl earns $3.50 per hour for baby-sitting. If he baby-sits 12 hours next month, will he earn enough to buy a bike helmet for $39.00? Explain.

26. $5 - 3\frac{1}{3}$

27. $18 - [2 \times (6 + 3)]$

28. $\frac{7}{15} - \frac{2}{15}$

29. $11{,}025 \times 31$

30. $16{,}754 + 219{,}859$

31. $6{,}058 - 3{,}872$

32. $\frac{7}{10} - \frac{1}{10}$

Test Prep Choose the correct letter for each answer.

33. $56 \times 20 =$
(5-4)

A 76 B 112 C 1,122 D 11,200 E NH

34. The table at the right shows the results of a survey of 40 students. How many students out of 800 would you predict to choose winter?
(7-13)

F About 80
G About 100
H About 200
J About 400

Favorite Season	
Spring	8
Summer	16
Fall	6
Winter	10

Understand
Plan
Solve
Look Back

Problem-Solving Strategy:

Make a Table

California Content Standard *Mathematical Reasoning 2.3: Use . . . tables . . . to explain mathematical reasoning.*

Warm-Up Review

1. $\frac{2}{3} + \frac{1}{3}$
2. $\frac{7}{10} + \frac{7}{10}$
3. $3\frac{1}{5} + 3\frac{2}{5}$
4. $\frac{1}{6} + \frac{1}{2}$
5. A restaurant offers regular or pink lemonade in small, medium, or large cups. List all the choices.

Example 1

At a craft fair, children can make plastic monsters. There is a choice of two heads and two bodies. How tall is each possible monster?

$2\frac{1}{8}$ in.

$2\frac{3}{8}$ in.

$4\frac{3}{8}$ in.

$5\frac{2}{8}$ in.

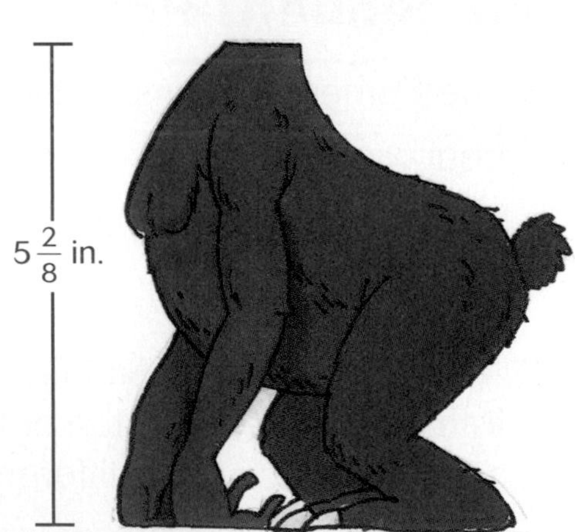

Understand

What do you need to find?

You need to find the height of each possible monster.

Plan

How can you solve the problem?

First **make a table** to show all the different possible monsters. Then for each one add the head and body heights.

Solve

Head	Body	Total Height
green	purple	$2\frac{1}{8} + 4\frac{3}{8} = 6\frac{4}{8} = 6\frac{1}{2}$ inches
green	red	$2\frac{1}{8} + 5\frac{2}{8} = 7\frac{3}{8}$ inches
orange	purple	$2\frac{3}{8} + 4\frac{3}{8} = 6\frac{6}{8} = 6\frac{3}{4}$ inches
orange	red	$2\frac{3}{8} + 5\frac{2}{8} = 7\frac{5}{8}$ inches

Look Back

Which monster is tallest? Which monster is shortest?

Additional Standards: Number Sense 2.3 (key) (Grade 5); Statistics, Data Analysis, and Probability 1.0; Mathematical Reasoning 2.0, 3.2 (See p. 305.)

Example 2

Lanie wants to buy colored beads to make bracelets. At the craft fair, red beads are sold in packages of 100, blue beads are sold in packages of 125, and yellow beads are sold in packages of 150. Lanie bought 2 packages in different colors. What are the possibilities for the number of beads she bought?

Package 1	Package 2	Total Number of Beads
Red	Blue	100 + 125 = 225 beads
Red	Yellow	100 + 150 = 250 beads
Blue	Yellow	125 + 150 = 275 beads

Guided Practice

Make a table to help you solve each exercise.

1. A cantaloupe weighs $2\frac{1}{8}$ pounds, a honeydew melon weighs $4\frac{1}{8}$ pounds, and a watermelon weighs $10\frac{3}{8}$ pounds. What are the possible total weights of any two of these melons?

2. Gordon School is ordering new gym uniforms. Their choice of T-shirts is a white one for $7.50 or a blue one for $8.25. Their choice of shorts is a black pair for $11.00 or a gray pair for $12.35. What are the prices of the different possible gym uniforms?

Independent Practice

3. The Cameron Township Library has 3 cartoons that are $\frac{1}{4}$ hour long, $\frac{1}{3}$ hour long and $\frac{1}{2}$ hour long. Two cartoons will be shown for a children's matinee. How long are the possible matinees?

4. A souvenir stand in San Francisco sells framed pictures as listed at the right. What are the prices of the different print-and-frame combinations?

San Francisco Memories	
Skyline photo	$25.00
Oceanfront watercolor	$32.50
Zoo photo	$20.00
Brass frame	$15.00
Oak frame	$18.00

5. The map at the right shows the bike paths in a state park. What are the total distances of the different routes from the camp store to the beach?

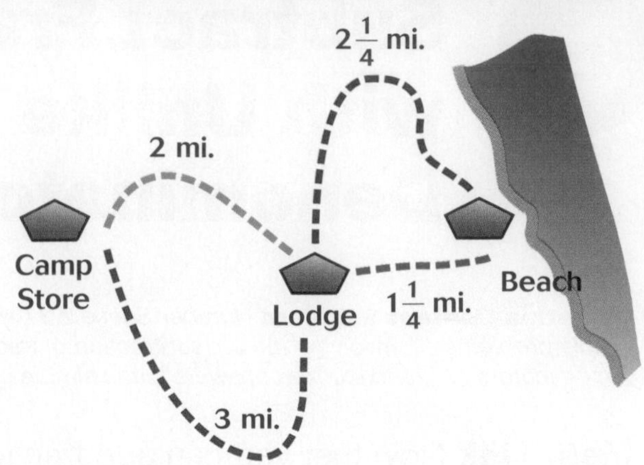

6. Kathryn is buying a friendship necklace. The chain costs $7.00, and each letter costs $2.50. Give the different costs of a necklace with 1, 2, 3, 4, 5, 6, or 7 initials.

Mixed Review

Try these or other strategies to solve each exercise. Tell which strategy you used.

Problem-Solving Strategies

- *Write a Number Sentence*
- *Work Backward*
- *Make a Table*
- *Find a Pattern*

7. Theater seats in one row are marked 101C, 103C, 105C, 107C, and so on. How is the eighth seat marked?

8. Rick has a third as many baseball cards as Susanna. Susanna has twice as many baseball cards as Luis. Luis has 18 baseball cards. How many baseball cards does Rick have?

9. Movie tickets cost $8.50 for adults and $5.75 for children. Kurt bought 3 tickets. What is the cost of each possible combination of 3 tickets?

10. The Ecology Club ordered Earth Day sweatshirts. They paid $35 to have the design created and $22 for each shirt. They ordered 47 shirts. What was their total bill?

11. Nick is making a row of attached pens for his baby farm animals. He sets a post in each corner. How many posts will he need for 7 pens?

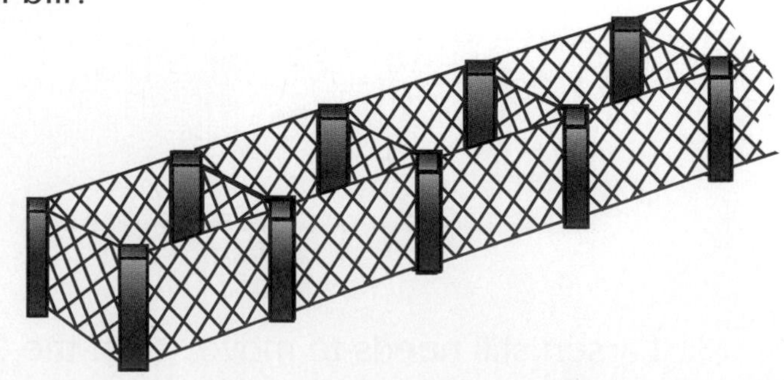

Use Homework Workbook 8-7.

Subtract Fractions with Unlike Denominators

California Content Standard *Number Sense 2.3 (🔑) (Grade 5): Solve simple problems . . . involving the . . . subtraction of fractions . . . (. . . unlike denominators . . .), and express answers in the simplest form.*

Warm-Up Review

1. $\frac{1}{2} = \frac{■}{6}$
2. $\frac{3}{5} = \frac{■}{10}$
3. $\frac{2}{3} + \frac{1}{6}$
4. $\frac{1}{5} + \frac{1}{2}$
5. List the factors of 20.
6. Connie bought $\frac{7}{8}$ pound of chicken salad and ate $\frac{3}{8}$ pound. How much is left?

Math Link Now that you can add fractions with unlike denominators, you will use a similar method to subtract fractions with unlike denominators.

Example

Mr. Larsen needs to move half of the library books into the library's new addition. Yesterday he moved $\frac{1}{5}$ of the books. What fraction of the books does he still need to move?

Find $\frac{1}{2} - \frac{1}{5}$.

Step 1 Rewrite the fractions using a common denominator.

Think: What number has 2 and 5 as factors? 10

$\frac{1}{2} = \frac{■}{10}$

$\frac{1}{5} = \frac{■}{10}$

$$\frac{1}{2} \underset{\times 5}{\overset{\times 5}{=}} \frac{5}{10}$$

$$-\ \frac{1}{5} \underset{\times 2}{\overset{\times 2}{=}} \frac{2}{10}$$

The $\frac{1}{2}$ piece and the $\frac{1}{5}$ piece can both be shown with $\frac{1}{10}$ pieces.

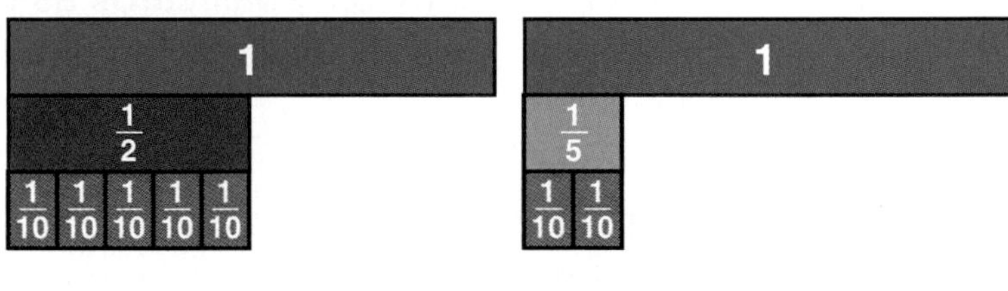

Step 2 Subtract the new fractions. Write the sum in simplest form.

$$\frac{1}{2} = \frac{5}{10}$$

$$-\ \frac{1}{5} = \frac{2}{10}$$

$$\frac{3}{10}$$

$\frac{3}{10}$ is in simplest form.

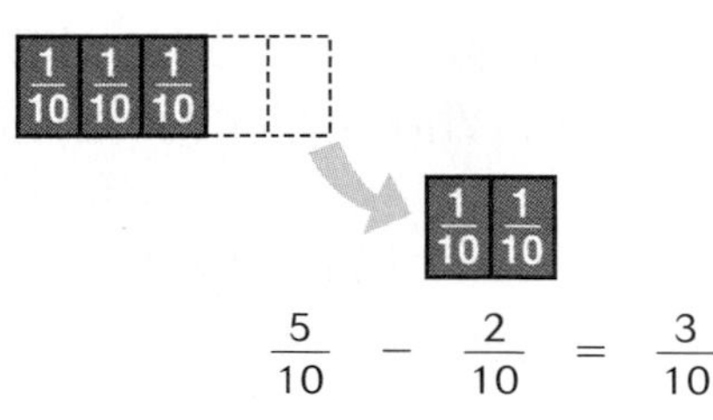

$\frac{5}{10} - \frac{2}{10} = \frac{3}{10}$

Mr. Larsen still needs to move $\frac{3}{10}$ of the books.

 Additional Standards: Mathematical Reasoning 1.1 (See p. 305.)

Guided Practice *For another example, see Set F on p. 333.*

Write answers in simplest form.

1. $\frac{2}{3} - \frac{1}{2}$ **2.** $\frac{5}{8} - \frac{1}{4}$ **3.** $\frac{2}{3} - \frac{1}{6}$ **4.** $\frac{1}{2} - \frac{2}{5}$ **5.** $\frac{7}{12} - \frac{1}{4}$

6. A muffin recipe calls for $\frac{1}{2}$ cup of oil. A nut bread mix recipe calls for $\frac{1}{4}$ cup of oil. How much more oil is needed for the muffins?

Independent Practice *For more practice, see Set F on p. 335.*

Write answers in simplest form.

7. $\frac{1}{2} - \frac{3}{8}$ **8.** $\frac{1}{3} - \frac{1}{6}$ **9.** $\frac{1}{2} - \frac{1}{6}$ **10.** $\frac{2}{5} - \frac{1}{10}$ **11.** $\frac{3}{4} - \frac{1}{2}$

12. $\frac{1}{4} - \frac{1}{8}$ **13.** $\frac{7}{10} - \frac{2}{5}$ **14.** $\frac{3}{4} - \frac{2}{3}$ **15.** $\frac{11}{12} - \frac{5}{6}$ **16.** $\frac{3}{4} - \frac{3}{8}$ **17.** $\frac{7}{10} - \frac{1}{5}$

18. Takashi lives $\frac{1}{2}$ mile from school. Jonathan lives $\frac{7}{8}$ mile from school. How much farther is Jonathan from school than Takashi?

19. Math Reasoning What is the value of $1 - \frac{1}{2}$? $1 - \frac{1}{3}$? $1 - \frac{1}{4}$? $1 - \frac{1}{5}$? $1 - \frac{1}{6}$? What pattern do you see?

Mixed Review

20. Myra bought $\frac{2}{3}$ yard of blue fabric and $\frac{1}{4}$ yard of yellow fabric. How much fabric did she buy altogether?

21. $876 \div 8$ **22.** $\frac{4}{5} + \frac{1}{10}$ **23.** $6\frac{7}{8} - 2\frac{3}{8}$ **24.** $\frac{3}{8}$ ● $\frac{1}{4}$

Test Prep Choose the correct letter for each answer.

25. $\frac{1}{12} + \frac{8}{12} =$
(8-1)

A $\frac{9}{24}$ B $\frac{3}{8}$ C $\frac{2}{3}$ D $\frac{3}{4}$ E NH

26. Algebra Find the missing number. ■ + 29 = 75.
(2-11)

F 45 G 46 H 47 J 104 K NH

Understand
Plan
Solve
Look Back

Problem-Solving Application:

Using Circle Graphs

California Content Standard *Statistics, Data, and Probability 1.3: Interpret one- and two-variable data graphs to answer questions about a situation.*

Warm-Up Review

1. $\frac{1}{3} \bullet \frac{1}{4}$
2. $\frac{3}{8} \bullet \frac{1}{2}$
3. $\frac{3}{4} + \frac{1}{4}$
4. $\frac{5}{8} + \frac{1}{4}$
5. $\frac{1}{6} + \frac{2}{6} + \frac{3}{6}$
6. Mary has 12 posters in her bedroom. $\frac{1}{4}$ of them feature animals. How many posters feature animals?

Example

The High Flying Kite Company makes 600 kites per week. The circle graph shows what fraction of their kites are red, blue, green, or yellow. How many yellow kites are made each week?

Kite Colors

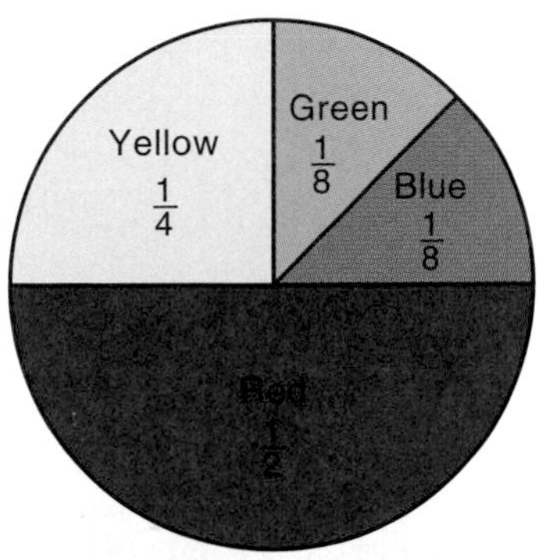

Understand

What do you need to find?

You need to find how many yellow kites are made each week.

Plan

How can you solve the problem?

You can use the fraction for yellow on the circle graph to find how many of the 600 kites are yellow.

Solve

The graph shows that $\frac{1}{4}$ of the kites are yellow.

$\frac{1}{4}$ of $600 = 600 \div 4 = 150$

Each week 150 yellow kites are made.

Look Back

Suppose the fractions were not on the circle. How could you tell which color is used the most?

Additional Standards: Mathematical Reasoning 2.3, 2.4, 3.2, 3.3 *(See p. 305.)*

Guided Practice

Use the circle graph on page 326 for Exercises 1 and 2.

1. How many green kites are made each week?

2. How many more red kites than blue kites are made each week?

Independent Practice

Elliot spent $12 on materials to make a kite. The circle graph at the right shows what part of the money he spent on each item. Use the circle graph for Exercises 3–5.

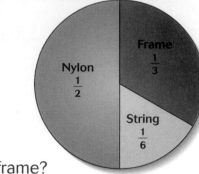

Costs of Materials

Nylon $\frac{1}{2}$

Frame $\frac{1}{3}$

String $\frac{1}{6}$

3. How much money did Elliot spend on the string?

4. How much more did the nylon fabric cost than the frame?

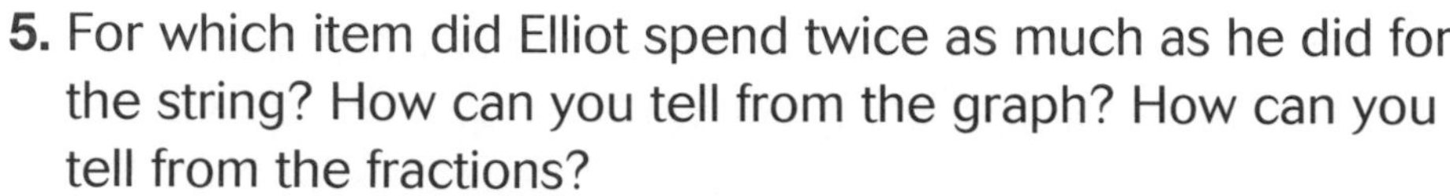

5. For which item did Elliot spend twice as much as he did for the string? How can you tell from the graph? How can you tell from the fractions?

6. What number must the fractions in a circle graph add up to? Explain why.

7. Altogether, the children in Mr. Sorensen's class have 32 pets. Arlene is making a circle graph to show what part of the pets are birds, fish, cats, or dogs. If 8 of the pets are birds, what fraction of the circle graph should show birds?

Mixed Review

8. Suppose Ralph tosses a number cube labeled 1 through 6, 120 times. Predict how many times he will get a number greater than 4.

9. The table at the right shows how much newspaper some students collected for recycling. What was the average amount collected?

Newspaper Collection	
Mercedes	84 pounds
Nadine	65 pounds
Kenji	71 pounds
Anthony	92 pounds

10. Harry's food bill at a restaurant was $11.40. The tax was $0.68, and he left a tip of $1.75. How much did he spend at the restaurant altogether?

Use Homework Workbook 8-9.

Diagnostic Checkpoint

Complete. For Exercises 1–3, use the words from the Word Bank.

Word Bank
common denominator
equivalent fractions
improper fractions
mixed numbers
simplest form

1. (7-7) $\frac{2}{6}$ and $\frac{3}{9}$ are ______________.

2. (7-4) $\frac{11}{4}$ and $\frac{10}{5}$ are ______________.

3. (8-6) $\frac{5}{12}$ and $\frac{7}{12}$ have a ______________.

Write answers in simplest form.

4. (8-6) $\frac{2}{8} + \frac{2}{4}$ **5.** (8-6) $\frac{3}{12} + \frac{1}{4}$ **6.** (8-6) $\frac{1}{2} + \frac{1}{4}$ **7.** (8-6) $\frac{2}{5} + \frac{6}{10}$

8. (8-8) $\frac{6}{12} - \frac{1}{3}$ **9.** (8-8) $\frac{7}{8} - \frac{1}{2}$ **10.** (8-8) $\frac{7}{10} - \frac{1}{5}$ **11.** (8-8) $\frac{7}{8} - \frac{1}{4}$

12. (8-5) A farmer has a field that is $\frac{7}{8}$ of an acre. He planted $\frac{3}{8}$ of an acre in corn. How much of the field is left? What operation did you use to solve the problem?

13. (8-5) Trisha drank $\frac{2}{8}$ of a quart of juice. Brittany drank $\frac{1}{8}$ of a quart of juice. How much juice did they drink together? What operation did you use to solve the problem?

14. (8-7) A statue comes in heights of $3\frac{5}{12}$ feet and $2\frac{7}{12}$ feet. Bases come in heights of $1\frac{1}{12}$ feet and $1\frac{5}{12}$ feet. Each statue can be placed on either base. What are the heights of each possible statue with a base?

Use the circle graph at the right for Exercises 15 and 16.

15. (8-9) The fourth-grade class spent $400 to organize the school carnival. The circle graph at the right shows what fraction of the money they spent on prizes, food, and to rent a ride. How much did they spend to rent the ride?

Carnival Expenses

16. (8-9) What two carnival expenses make up $\frac{4}{5}$ of the total?

Chapter 8 Test

Write answers in simplest form. Change improper fractions to mixed numbers or whole numbers.

1. $\frac{5}{8} + \frac{1}{8}$

2. $\frac{7}{8} - \frac{5}{8}$

3. $3\frac{3}{5} + 4\frac{1}{5}$

4. $6\frac{11}{12} - 2\frac{5}{12}$

5. $\frac{5}{6} + \frac{1}{6}$

6. $\frac{3}{5} - \frac{2}{5}$

7. $9\frac{1}{8} + 1\frac{2}{8}$

8. $\frac{5}{8} - \frac{3}{8}$

9. $7 - 2\frac{1}{4}$

10. $3\frac{4}{6} + 6\frac{1}{6}$

11. $6\frac{6}{10} - 5\frac{3}{10}$

12. $4\frac{5}{12} + 6\frac{5}{12}$

13. $\frac{7}{12} + \frac{1}{3}$

14. $\frac{2}{5} + \frac{4}{15}$

15. $\frac{4}{5} - \frac{1}{10}$

16. $\frac{2}{3} - \frac{2}{5}$

17. Cora's family spent a total of $1\frac{1}{4}$ hours traveling to and from a fair. They spent $3\frac{1}{4}$ hours at the fair. How much time did they spend away from home? What operation did you use to solve this problem?

18. Steven has mowed $\frac{2}{3}$ of his yard. His neighbor Kristen has a yard that is the same size. She has mowed $\frac{1}{2}$ of her yard. How much more has Steven mowed than Kristen? What operation did you use to solve this problem?

19. A bag of apples weighs $2\frac{1}{8}$ pounds, a bag of grapes weighs $1\frac{3}{8}$ pounds, and a bag of oranges weighs $4\frac{3}{8}$ pounds. What are the possible total weights for any two of these bags of fruits?

20. Shannon and Kobe made 30 beaded necklaces to sell. The circle graph at the right shows what fraction of the necklaces were each color. How many red necklaces did they make?

Necklace Colors

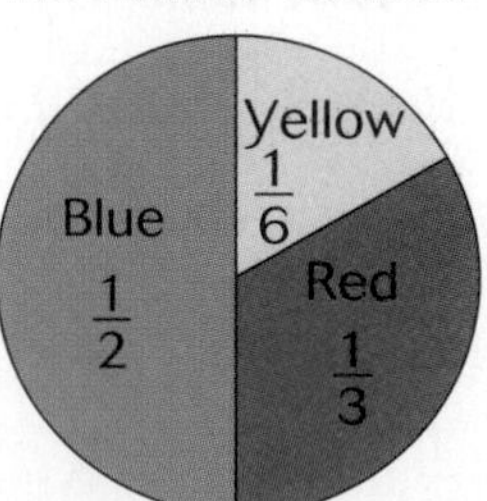

Multiple-Choice Chapter 8 Test

Choose the correct letter for each answer.

1. The Thompson family bought a dozen oranges. Marcus ate $\frac{5}{12}$ of the oranges, and his sister Marsha ate $\frac{3}{12}$. What part of the oranges did they eat together?

A $\frac{1}{6}$ | D $\frac{3}{4}$
B $\frac{7}{12}$ | E NH
C $\frac{2}{3}$

2. Find $3\frac{2}{9} + 1\frac{4}{9}$.

F $4\frac{5}{9}$ | J 5
G $4\frac{2}{3}$ | K NH
H $4\frac{7}{9}$

3. How much more is $\frac{9}{10}$ than $\frac{4}{10}$?

A $\frac{1}{5}$ | D $\frac{1}{2}$
B $\frac{1}{4}$ | E NH
C $\frac{2}{5}$

4. Penny wants to rent one of two movies. One lasts $1\frac{1}{4}$ hours and the other lasts $2\frac{3}{4}$ hours. How much longer is one than the other?

F 1 hour | J $1\frac{1}{2}$ hours
G $1\frac{1}{8}$ hours | K NH
H $1\frac{1}{4}$ hours

5. To make applesauce, Mr. Johnson needs $8\frac{2}{3}$ cups of sliced apples. He has already cut $5\frac{1}{3}$ cups. Which number sentence shows how many more cups he needs?

A $8\frac{2}{3} - 5\frac{1}{3} = 3\frac{1}{3}$
B $8\frac{2}{3} - 8\frac{2}{3} = 0$
C $5\frac{1}{3} + 8\frac{2}{3} = 14$
D $5\frac{1}{3} + 5\frac{1}{3} = 10\frac{2}{3}$

6. Find $8 - 2\frac{2}{5}$.

F $6\frac{3}{5}$
G $6\frac{2}{5}$
H $5\frac{4}{5}$
J $5\frac{3}{5}$
K NH

7. Find $\frac{2}{7} + \frac{1}{2}$.

A $\frac{3}{14}$
B $\frac{9}{14}$
C $\frac{6}{7}$
D $\frac{13}{14}$
E NH

8. **Branden is trying to choose two out of three songs to play during intermission of the school play. The songs last $2\frac{1}{6}$ minutes, $2\frac{3}{6}$ minutes, and $1\frac{2}{6}$ minutes. Which of the following is *not* a possible length of any two songs played back-to-back?**

F $3\frac{1}{2}$ minutes

G $3\frac{2}{3}$ minutes

H $3\frac{5}{6}$ minutes

J $4\frac{2}{3}$ minutes

---

9. **Find $\frac{2}{9} - \frac{1}{6}$.**

A $\frac{1}{18}$

B $\frac{1}{9}$

C $\frac{1}{6}$

D $\frac{1}{3}$

E NH

---

10. **Colette ran $\frac{9}{10}$ mile on Monday and $\frac{1}{2}$ mile on Tuesday. How much farther did she run on Monday than Tuesday?**

F $\frac{1}{5}$ mile

G $\frac{2}{5}$ mile

H $\frac{4}{5}$ mile

J 1 mile

K NH

Use the circle graph below for Questions 11 and 12.

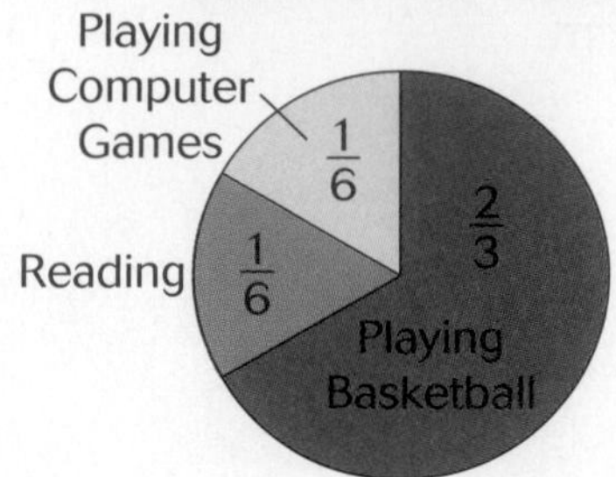

11. **Last week, Carrie had 18 hours of free time after school. How much of that time did she spend playing computer games?**

A 2 hours

B 3 hours

C 4 hours

D 6 hours

---

12. **Including after school and the weekend, Carrie had 30 hours of free time last week. How much of that time did she spend reading?**

F 3 hours

G 5 hours

H 6 hours

J 9 hours

---

13. **Find $7\frac{5}{6} - 4\frac{1}{6}$.**

A 3

B $3\frac{1}{3}$

C $3\frac{2}{3}$

D $3\frac{5}{6}$

E NH

Reteaching

Set A (pages 306–307)

Add $\frac{7}{12} + \frac{11}{12}$. Write the answer in simplest form.

$$\begin{array}{r} \frac{7}{12} \\ + \frac{11}{12} \\ \hline \end{array}$$

$$\frac{7 + 11}{12} = \frac{18}{12} = 1\frac{6}{12} = 1\frac{1}{2} \quad (\div 6)$$

Remember to add the numerators when the denominators are the same.

Write answers in simplest form. Change improper fractions to mixed numbers or whole numbers.

1. $\frac{4}{11} + \frac{5}{11}$
2. $\frac{5}{9} + \frac{7}{9}$
3. $\frac{5}{8} + \frac{7}{8}$
4. $\frac{3}{4} + \frac{3}{4}$
5. $\frac{5}{6} + \frac{4}{6}$
6. $\frac{6}{7} + \frac{5}{7}$

Set B (pages 308–309)

Add $2\frac{7}{10} + 3\frac{1}{10}$. Write the answer in simplest form.

$$\begin{array}{r} 2\frac{7}{10} \\ + 3\frac{1}{10} \\ \hline \end{array}$$

Step 1: Add the fractions
$\frac{7}{10} + \frac{1}{10} = \frac{8}{10}$

Step 2: Add the whole numbers.
$2 + 3 = 5$

Step 3: Write the fraction in simplest form.

$$5\frac{8}{10} = 5\frac{4}{5} \quad (\div 2)$$

Remember to add mixed numbers, you add the fractions, add the whole numbers and then simplify.

Write answers in simplest form.

1. $3\frac{1}{3} + 1\frac{1}{3}$
2. $4\frac{4}{8} + 2\frac{2}{8}$
3. $7\frac{5}{9} + 2\frac{1}{9}$
4. $8 + 1\frac{5}{8}$

Set C (pages 310–311)

Subtract $\frac{7}{9} - \frac{1}{9}$. Write the answer in simplest form.

$$\begin{array}{r} \frac{7}{9} \\ - \frac{1}{9} \\ \hline \end{array}$$

$$\frac{7 - 1}{9} = \frac{6}{9} = \frac{2}{3} \quad (\div 3)$$

Remember to check that the denominators are the same before you subtract the numerators.

Write answers in simplest form.

1. $\frac{4}{7} - \frac{1}{7}$
2. $\frac{7}{8} - \frac{3}{8}$
3. $\frac{9}{12} - \frac{5}{12}$
4. $\frac{9}{10} - \frac{3}{10}$

Set D (pages 312–314)

Subtract $3\frac{5}{8} - 1\frac{1}{8}$. Write the answer in simplest form.

$$\begin{array}{r} 3\frac{5}{8} \\ -1\frac{1}{8} \\ \hline 2\frac{4}{8} = 2\frac{1}{2} \end{array}$$

($\div 4$ numerator and denominator)

Step 1: Subtract the fractions.
$\frac{5}{8} - \frac{1}{8} = \frac{4}{8}$

Step 2: Subtract the whole numbers.
$3 - 1 = 2$

Step 3: Write the fraction in simplest form.

Remember to subtract mixed numbers, first subtract the fractions. Then subtract the whole numbers.

Write answers in simplest form.

1. $7\frac{9}{11} - 3\frac{3}{11}$
2. $5\frac{5}{9} - 1\frac{1}{9}$
3. $8\frac{7}{8} - 3\frac{1}{8}$
4. $6\frac{11}{12} - 2\frac{2}{12}$

Set E (pages 318–320)

Add $\frac{2}{5} + \frac{3}{10}$.

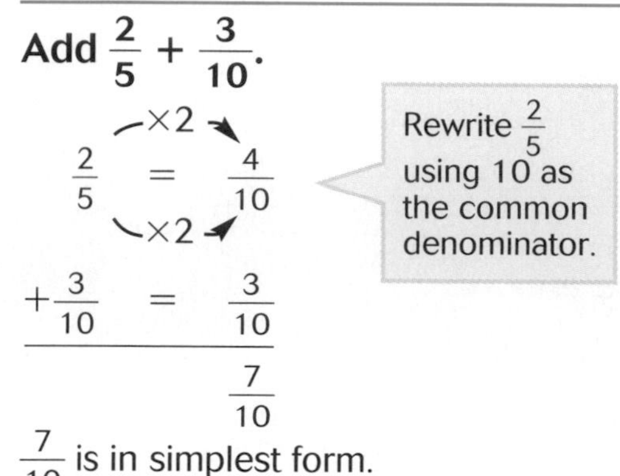

Rewrite $\frac{2}{5}$ using 10 as the common denominator.

$$\begin{array}{rcl} \frac{2}{5} & = & \frac{4}{10} \\ +\frac{3}{10} & = & \frac{3}{10} \\ \hline & & \frac{7}{10} \end{array}$$

($\times 2$ numerator and denominator)

$\frac{7}{10}$ is in simplest form.

Remember to change the fractions to equivalent fractions with a common denominator before adding.

Write answers in simplest form.

1. $\frac{1}{2} + \frac{1}{4}$
2. $\frac{1}{2} + \frac{2}{6}$
3. $\frac{2}{3} + \frac{2}{9}$
4. $\frac{1}{2} + \frac{2}{8}$

Set F (pages 324–325)

Subtract $\frac{3}{4} - \frac{1}{3}$.

$$\begin{array}{rcl} \frac{3}{4} & = & \frac{9}{12} \\ -\frac{1}{3} & = & \frac{4}{12} \\ \hline & & \frac{5}{12} \end{array}$$

($\times 3$ for $\frac{3}{4}$; $\times 4$ for $\frac{1}{3}$)

Rewrite the fractions using a common denominator of 12.

$\frac{5}{12}$ is in simplest form.

Remember that before you can subtract two fractions, both fractions must have the same denominator.

Write answers in simplest form.

1. $\frac{3}{16} - \frac{1}{8}$
2. $\frac{11}{15} - \frac{2}{3}$
3. $\frac{6}{8} - \frac{1}{2}$
4. $\frac{4}{5} - \frac{1}{2}$

More Practice

Set A (pages 306–307)

Write answers in simplest form. Change improper fractions to mixed numbers or whole numbers.

1. $\frac{1}{8} + \frac{3}{8}$ **2.** $\frac{5}{12} + \frac{4}{12}$ **3.** $\frac{1}{5} + \frac{2}{5}$ **4.** $\frac{7}{10} + \frac{2}{10}$

5. $\frac{4}{8} + \frac{0}{8}$ **6.** $\frac{2}{10} + \frac{6}{10}$ **7.** $\frac{7}{12} + \frac{10}{12}$ **8.** $\frac{7}{9} + \frac{4}{9}$

9. Carmen spent $\frac{3}{4}$ of an hour on language homework and $\frac{3}{4}$ of an hour on social studies homework. How much time did she spend in all?

Set B (pages 308–309)

Write answers in simplest form.

1. $4\frac{2}{5} + 3\frac{1}{5}$ **2.** $10\frac{1}{6} + 3\frac{2}{6}$ **3.** $3\frac{3}{5} + \frac{1}{5}$ **4.** $5\frac{3}{10} + 3\frac{2}{10}$

5. $\begin{array}{r} 4 \\ +5\frac{6}{7} \\ \hline \end{array}$ **6.** $\begin{array}{r} 5\frac{4}{9} \\ +2\frac{2}{9} \\ \hline \end{array}$ **7.** $\begin{array}{r} 1\frac{5}{12} \\ +4\frac{4}{12} \\ \hline \end{array}$ **8.** $\begin{array}{r} 2\frac{4}{15} \\ +6\frac{6}{15} \\ \hline \end{array}$

9. The Miller family has $1\frac{1}{4}$ gallons of orange juice and $2\frac{1}{4}$ gallons of apple juice. How much juice do they have in all?

Set C (pages 310–311)

Write answers in simplest form.

1. $\frac{3}{5} - \frac{2}{5}$ **2.** $\frac{7}{8} - \frac{2}{8}$ **3.** $\frac{9}{12} - \frac{2}{12}$ **4.** $\frac{9}{10} - \frac{4}{10}$

5. $\begin{array}{r} \frac{7}{6} \\ -\frac{5}{6} \\ \hline \end{array}$ **6.** $\begin{array}{r} \frac{14}{15} \\ -\frac{4}{15} \\ \hline \end{array}$ **7.** $\begin{array}{r} \frac{9}{16} \\ -\frac{3}{16} \\ \hline \end{array}$ **8.** $\begin{array}{r} \frac{19}{20} \\ -\frac{11}{20} \\ \hline \end{array}$

9. Dakota plans to run $\frac{9}{10}$ of a mile. He has run $\frac{3}{10}$ of a mile. How much farther does he have to run?

Set D (pages 312–314)

Write answers in simplest form.

1. $5\frac{8}{10} - 3\frac{1}{10}$

2. $9\frac{11}{12} - 6\frac{6}{12}$

3. $8\frac{9}{10} - 8\frac{5}{10}$

4. $6\frac{5}{5} - 1\frac{2}{5}$

5. $5\frac{4}{10} - 4\frac{1}{10}$

6. $8 - 2\frac{1}{3}$

7. $6\frac{5}{12} - 2\frac{1}{12}$

8. $17\frac{3}{8} - 6\frac{2}{8}$

9. It takes $2\frac{3}{4}$ hours to drive to Elisa's grandmother's house. Her family has been driving for $1\frac{1}{4}$ hours. How much longer will they be driving?

Set E (pages 318–320)

Write answers in simplest form.

1. $\frac{1}{8} + \frac{1}{2}$

2. $\frac{1}{3} + \frac{1}{6}$

3. $\frac{3}{10} + \frac{3}{5}$

4. $\frac{5}{12} + \frac{1}{4}$

5. $\frac{3}{8} + \frac{1}{4}$

6. $\frac{1}{3} + \frac{4}{6}$

7. $\frac{5}{12} + \frac{1}{3}$

8. $\frac{1}{2} + \frac{3}{8}$

9. It took Ramon $\frac{3}{4}$ hour to prepare dinner. The dinner lasted $\frac{1}{2}$ hour. How much time did it take to prepare and eat dinner?

Set F (pages 324–325)

Write answers in simplest form.

1. $\frac{1}{2} - \frac{1}{8}$

2. $\frac{2}{3} - \frac{5}{12}$

3. $\frac{4}{5} - \frac{3}{10}$

4. $\frac{7}{8} - \frac{1}{4}$

5. $\frac{2}{3} - \frac{7}{12}$

6. $\frac{7}{8} - \frac{3}{4}$

7. $\frac{1}{4} - \frac{1}{8}$

8. $\frac{3}{5} - \frac{1}{3}$

9. One book is $\frac{3}{8}$ inch wide. Another book is $\frac{1}{2}$ inch wide. How much wider is one book than the other?

Problem Solving: Preparing for Tests

Choose the correct letter for each answer.

---

1. Marcia wakes up at 7:00 A.M. It takes her 10 minutes to get dressed for school. Then it takes her 15 minutes to eat breakfast. After breakfast it takes her 20 minutes to walk from home to school. How long does it take Marcia to get dressed and eat breakfast?

A 5 minutes
B 10 minutes
C 25 minutes
D 45 minutes

Tip
Read the question carefully to decide what information you need to answer it.

---

2. Alan drove 55 miles per hour for 2 hours. Then he drove 45 miles per hour for 1 hour. How far did Alan drive in the 3 hours?

F 45 miles
G 110 miles
H 145 miles
J 155 miles

Tip
First find the distance Alan traveled at 55 miles per hour. Then find the distance he traveled at 45 miles per hour.

---

3. The diagram below shows a skating path in a park. John skated around the entire path one time. *About* how far did John skate?

A 500 yards
B 600 yards
C 700 yards
D 800 yards

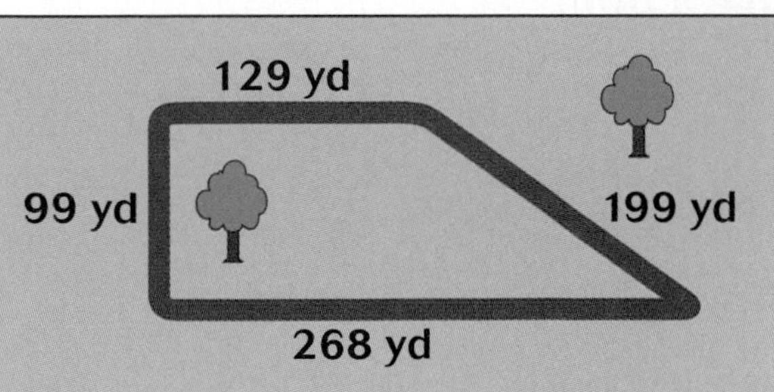

Tip
Since the problem asks for an estimate, first round each length to the nearest hundred.

4. **Tom collected 372 baseball cards. He put the same number of cards in each of 6 albums. Which number sentence can you use to find the number of cards in each album?**

- **F** $372 - 6 = \blacksquare$
- **G** $372 \times 6 = \blacksquare$
- **H** $372 + 6 = \blacksquare$
- **J** $372 \div 6 = \blacksquare$

---

5. **Martin is older than Allie. Shawn is younger than Allie. Roger is older than Martin. Which is a reasonable conclusion?**

- **A** Allie is older than Roger.
- **B** Shawn is older than Martin.
- **C** Martin is younger than Allie.
- **D** Roger is older than Allie.

---

6. **You have 48 building blocks. One fourth of the blocks are red. One third of the blocks are green. How many blocks are red?**

- **F** 8 blocks
- **G** 10 blocks
- **H** 12 blocks
- **J** 16 blocks

---

7. **On Monday the temperature was 35°F. It went up 1°F on Tuesday, 2°F more on Wednesday, and 3°F more on Thursday. If this pattern continues, what will the temperature be on Saturday?**

- **A** 47°F
- **B** 49°F
- **C** 50°F
- **D** 51°F

---

8. **Linda's school raised $4,500 by selling tickets to the school play. Ticket prices were $5 for children and $9 for adults. Which is reasonable for the number of tickets sold?**

- **F** More than 1,000
- **G** Between 500 and 900
- **H** Between 300 and 500
- **J** Fewer than 500

Use the graph for Questions 9 and 10.

This graph shows how many miles Joe rode each day during a bicycle trip.

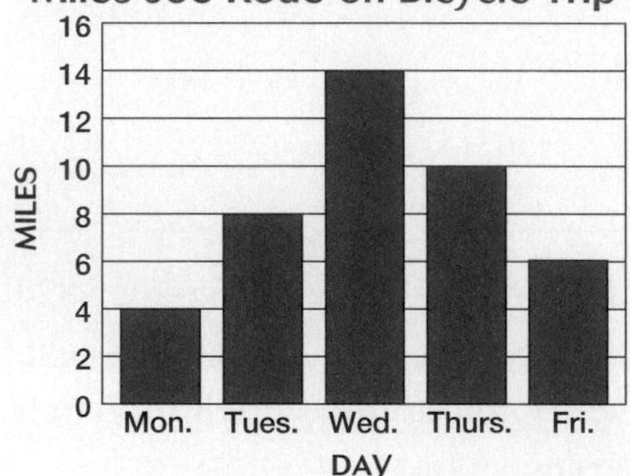

9. **How much farther did Joe ride on Thursday than on Monday?**

- **A** 6 miles
- **B** 14 miles
- **C** 18 miles
- **D** 28 miles

---

10. **Last year Joe went on a 40-mile bicycle trip. How much longer was Joe's bicycle trip this year?**

- **F** 8 miles
- **G** 6 miles
- **H** 4 miles
- **J** 2 miles

TEST PREP

Multiple-Choice Cumulative Review

Choose the correct letter for each answer.

Number Sense

1. A boat tour lasts 20 minutes. How many rides can the captain give in 4 hours? (Hint: 60 minutes equals 1 hour.)

A 8 rides
B 12 rides
C 16 rides
D 80 rides

2. 3,300 ÷ 1 =

F 1
G 33
H 330
J 3,300
K NH

3. Alex and his 3 friends spent $823 on vacation. If they split the cost evenly, *about* how much did each person spend?

A $100
B $200
C $300
D $2,000

4. Find $\frac{5}{12} + \frac{1}{4}$.

F $\frac{1}{4}$
G $\frac{1}{3}$
H $\frac{2}{3}$
J $\frac{3}{4}$
K NH

Statistics, Data Analysis, and Probability

5. There are four marbles in a bag. Two are red, one is blue, and one is yellow. How many possible outcomes are there when removing one marble?

A 1
B 2
C 3
D 5

Use the table below for Questions 6 and 7.

Adopted Animals

Kind of Animal	Week 1	Week 2	Week 3	Week 4
Dog	12	10	10	9
Cat	15	17	18	20
Bird	5	6	7	2

6. How many dogs and cats were adopted in Week 2?

F 10
G 17
H 27
J 34

7. How many dogs were adopted over the 4 weeks?

A 9
B 10
C 33
D 41

Algebra and Functions

8. **Which number is not between $^{-}5$ and 3?**

F 2

G 0

H $^{-}4$

J $^{-}6$

9. **Evaluate 17 × ■ when ■ = 35.**

A 18

B 52

C 595

D 1,735

E NH

10. **Solve ■ + 31 = 52.**

F 22

G 83

H 1,612

J 5,231

K NH

11. **The table shows how far Travis ran each day. If he continues the pattern, how far should he run on Friday?**

Day	Number of Laps
Monday	1
Tuesday	4
Wednesday	7

A 9 laps

B 10 laps

C 12 laps

D 13 laps

Measurement and Geometry

12. **Which number is inside the triangle and inside the circle?**

F 1

G 2

H 3

J 4

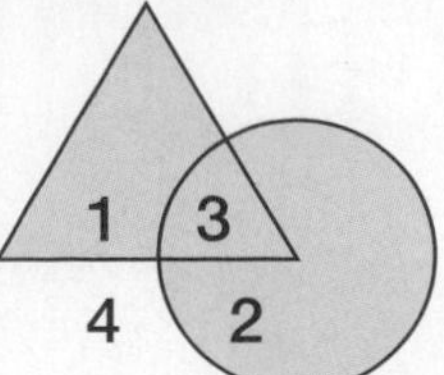

13. **How many more sides does a pentagon have than a triangle?**

A 1 more side

B 2 more sides

C 3 more sides

D 4 more sides

14. **Henry got home from school at 4:10 P.M. If Henry left school at 3:20 P.M., how long did it take him to get home?**

F 50 minutes

G 45 minutes

H 40 minutes

J 35 minutes

15. **Danny practiced skating for 2 hours 12 minutes. How many *minutes* did he practice skating? (Hint: 60 minutes equals 1 hour.)**

A 14 minutes

B 72 minutes

C 102 minutes

D 132 minutes

Decimals

Diagnosing Readiness

In Chapter 9, you will use these skills:

Ⓐ Rounding Numbers

(pages 14–16)

Round each number to the nearest ten thousand.

1. 847,263 **2.** 362,154

3. 492,084 **4.** 179,234

5. 1,305,412 **6.** 5,476,291

7. An airplane flew at an altitude of 29,560 feet. Round this number to the nearest thousand.

Ⓑ Estimating Sums and Differences

(pages 38–39)

Estimate by rounding to the greatest place value.

8. 2,947 + 3,099

9. 8,246 − 1,925

10. 1,374 + 952

11. 12,249 + 36,819

12. 45,263 − 24,895

13. Tim went mountain climbing and climbed to an elevation of 5,230 feet. Then he went down 1,968 feet. Estimate his elevation now.

C Adding Whole Numbers

(pages 42–46)

14. $\begin{array}{r} 878 \\ +418 \\ \hline \end{array}$

15. $\begin{array}{r} 941 \\ +672 \\ \hline \end{array}$

16. $\begin{array}{r} 4,571 \\ +2,031 \\ \hline \end{array}$

17. $\begin{array}{r} 8,092 \\ +3,841 \\ \hline \end{array}$

18. David burns 430 calories by playing soccer for an hour, and 260 calories by walking for another hour. How many calories does he burn altogether?

D Subtracting Whole Numbers

(pages 47–53)

19. $\begin{array}{r} 750 \\ -94 \\ \hline \end{array}$

20. $\begin{array}{r} 493 \\ -249 \\ \hline \end{array}$

21. $\begin{array}{r} 8,042 \\ -6,584 \\ \hline \end{array}$

22. $\begin{array}{r} 7,215 \\ -7,038 \\ \hline \end{array}$

23. A swimming pool can hold 520 gallons of water. It has 364 gallons in it now. How many more gallons will it take to fill it?

E Fractions on a Number Line

(pages 257–259)

Write the fraction for each point.

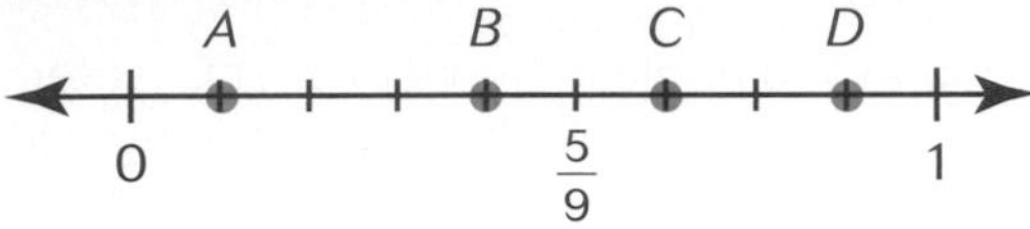

24. *A* **25.** *B*

26. *C* **27.** *D*

Which point represents each number?

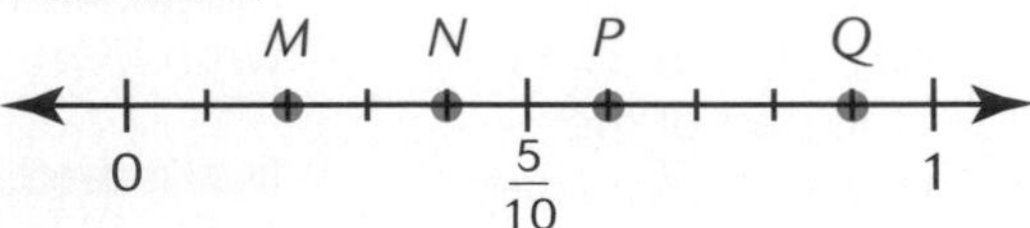

28. $\frac{9}{10}$ **29.** $\frac{2}{10}$

30. $\frac{2}{5}$ **31.** $\frac{3}{5}$

F Comparing and Ordering Fractions

(pages 272–274)

Compare. Write >, <, or = for each ●.

32. $\frac{5}{7}$ ● $\frac{2}{7}$ **33.** $\frac{8}{100}$ ● $\frac{5}{100}$

34. $\frac{7}{10}$ ● $\frac{2}{5}$ **35.** $\frac{6}{10}$ ● $\frac{60}{100}$

36. $\frac{1}{4}$ ● $\frac{3}{8}$ **37.** $\frac{75}{100}$ ● $\frac{3}{4}$

To the Family and Student

Looking Back	Chapter 9	Looking Ahead
In Grade 3, students learned to relate fractions to decimals and compare decimals to two decimal places.	**Decimals** In this chapter, students will learn how to add and subtract decimals to two decimal places.	In Grade 5, students will learn how to multiply and divide decimals by whole numbers and decimals.

Math and Everyday Living

Opportunities to apply the concepts of Chapter 9 abound in everyday situations. During the chapter, think about how adding and subtracting decimals can be used to solve a variety of real-world problems. The following examples suggest just a few of the many situations that could launch a discussion about adding and subtracting decimals.

Math and Farming The Blackburns planted ten equal rows of vegetables in a small garden. They planted three rows of corn. What decimal describes the part of the garden that has corn planted?

Math and Travel The Bradys traveled 364.3 miles by car in one day. What is this distance rounded to the nearest whole number?

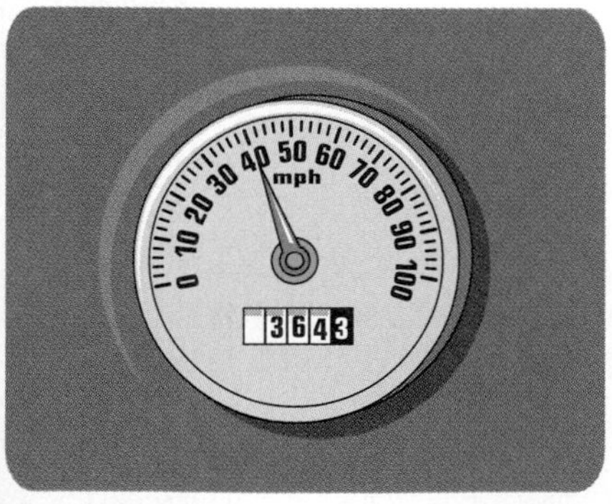

Math and Weather A meterologist said 12.45 inches of rain fell last month. Write this number in word form.

Math and Recreation Gloria rode her bike 2.7 miles before stopping for lunch. She rode another 1.4 miles to reach her destination. How many miles did she bike altogether?

Math and Sports Michael is on the track team. At the last track meet, he ran the 100 meter race 0.12 seconds faster than his previous best time of 15.39 seconds. What is his new personal best time?

Math and Exercise Mr. Matthews walked $3\frac{1}{4}$ miles. Write this mixed number as a decimal.

Math and Shopping Mrs. Cavazos bought 3 pairs of shoes. They cost $24.95, $35.30, and $55.45. How much did Mrs. Cavazos spend on shoes?

Math and Sewing Ricardo needs $6\frac{3}{4}$ yards of fabric to cover a chair. He found a fabric remnant marked 6.5 yards. Is the remnant large enough to cover the chair?

California Content Standards in Chapter 9 Lessons*

	Teach and Practice	Practice
Number Sense		
1.2 ( ) Order and compare whole numbers and decimals to two decimal places.	9-4, 9-5	
1.5 Explain different interpretations of fractions, for example, parts of a whole, parts of a set, and division of whole numbers; explain equivalents of fractions.		9-1, 9-2
1.6 Write tenths and hundredths in decimal and fraction notations and know the fraction and decimal equivalents for halves and fourths.	9-1, 9-2, 9-3	9-5
1.7 Write the fraction represented by a drawing of parts of a figure; represent a given fraction by using drawings; and relate a fraction to a simple decimal on a number line.	9-2	9-1
1.9 ( ) Identify on a number line the relative position of positive fractions, positive mixed numbers, and positive decimals to two decimal places.	9-5	9-7
2.1 Estimate and compute the sum or difference of whole numbers and positive decimals to two places.	9-9, 9-10	9-11
2.2 Round two-place decimals to one decimal or the nearest whole number and judge the reasonableness of the rounded answer.	9-7, 9-9, 9-10	
3.4 ( ) Solve problems involving division of multidigit numbers by one-digit numbers.		9-11
Algebra and Functions		
1.1 Use letters, boxes, or other symbols to stand for any number in simple expressions or equations.		9-9, 9-10
1.2 ( ) Interpret and evaluate mathematical expressions that now use parentheses.	9-11	
1.3 ( ) Use parentheses to indicate which operation to perform first when writing expressions containing more than two terms and different operations.		9-11

	Teach and Practice	Practice
Mathematical Reasoning		
1.1 Analyze problems by identifying relationships, distinguishing relevant from irrelevant information, sequencing and prioritizing information, and observing patterns.	9-8, 9-11	9-6, 9-10
1.2 Determine when and how to break a problem into simpler parts.	9-6	
2.0 Students use strategies, skills, and concepts in finding solutions.		9-6, 9-8, 9-11
2.3 Use a variety of methods, such as words, numbers, symbols, charts, graphs, tables, diagrams, and models, to explain mathematical reasoning.	9-1, 9-3, 9-8, 9-11	9-2, 9-9
2.4 Express the solution clearly and logically by using appropriate mathematical notation and terms and clear language; support solutions with evidence in both verbal and symbolic work.	9-6	9-1, 9-3, 9-11
2.5 Indicate the relative advantages of exact and approximate solutions to problems and give answers to a specified degree of accuracy.	9-7	
2.6 Make precise calculations and check the validity of the results from the context of the problem.	9-9, 9-10	9-6
3.2 Note the method of deriving the solutions and demonstrate a conceptual understanding of the derivation by solving similar problems.		9-7, 9-8
3.3 Develop generalizations of the results obtained and apply them in other circumstances.		9-3, 9-5

* The symbol ( ) indicates a key standard as designated in Mathematics Framework for California Public Schools. Full statements of the California Content Standards are found at the beginning of this book following the Table of Contents.

LESSON 9-1

Relating Fractions and Decimals

California Content Standard *Number Sense 1.6: Write tenths and hundredths in decimal and fraction notations and know the fraction and decimal equivalents for halves and fourths (e.g. $\frac{1}{2}$ = 0.5 or 0.50 . . .) Also, Mathematical Reasoning 2.3 (See p. 343.)*

Math Link You have learned how to use fractions to name part of a region or part of a set. Now you will learn how some fractions can be written as decimals.

Numbers like 0.6 and 4.97 are **decimals**. You can recognize decimals because they contain a **decimal point.** Any fraction whose denominator is 10 or 100 can be written as a decimal.

Warm-Up Review

Write the fraction for the shaded part of each region.

1. 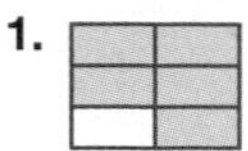
2.
3. Draw a model that shows $\frac{3}{10}$.
4. $\frac{1}{5} = \frac{■}{10}$
5. $\frac{2}{3} = \frac{■}{9}$
6. What fraction of the letters in NEIGHBOR are vowels?

Word Bank

decimal
decimal point
equivalent decimals

Fraction: $\frac{6}{10}$
Decimal: 0.6
Say: six tenths

decimal point

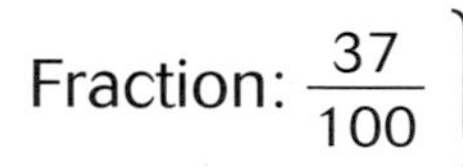

Fraction: $\frac{37}{100}$
Decimal: 0.37
Say: thirty-seven hundredths

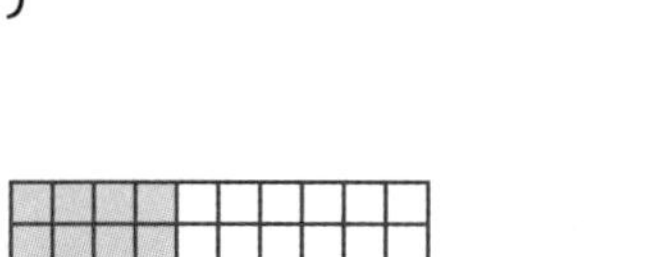

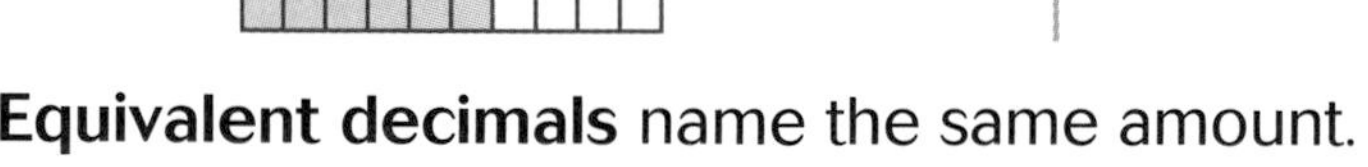

Equivalent decimals name the same amount.

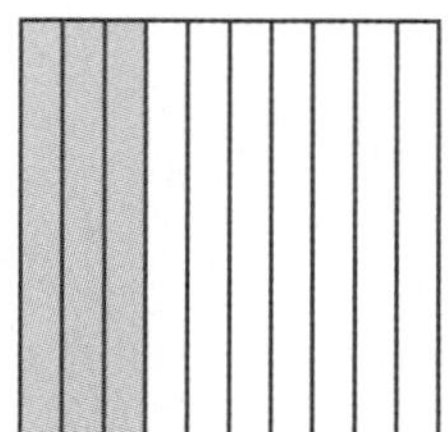

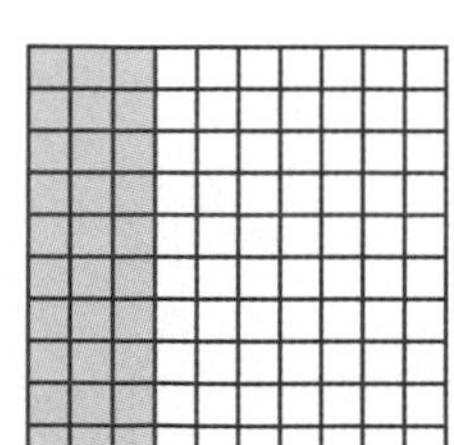

$\frac{3}{10} = \frac{30}{100}$
0.3 = 0.30
Say: three tenths equals thirty hundredths

Additional Standards: Number Sense 1.5, 1.7; Mathematical Reasoning 2.4 (See p. 343.)

Example 1

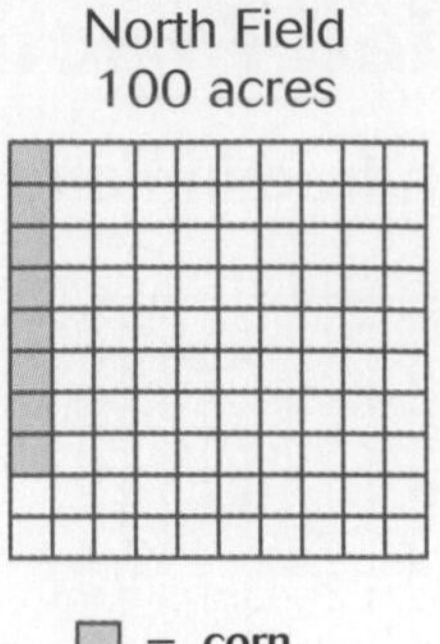

In a 100-acre field, a farmer planted corn. Write a fraction and a decimal to tell what part of this field was planted in corn.

Fraction: $\frac{8}{100}$

Decimal: 0.08

Corn was planted in $\frac{8}{100}$, or 0.08, of the field.

Notice that the number of zeros in the denominator matches the number of digits to the right of the decimal point.

Example 2

Write $\frac{1}{4}$ as a decimal.

Write an equivalent fraction with either 10 or 100 in the denominator.

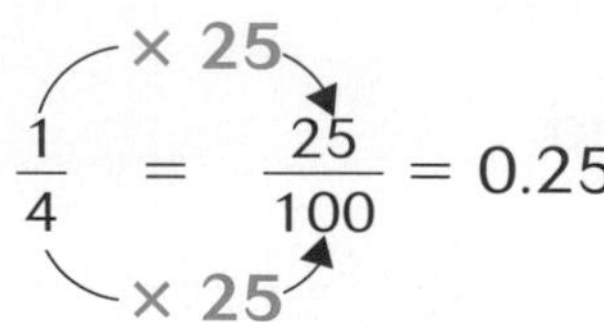

$$\frac{1}{4} = \frac{25}{100} = 0.25 \quad (\times 25)$$

Example 3

Write a decimal equivalent to 0.5.

You can write or remove a zero from the end of a decimal without changing its value.

0.5 = 0.50

Here's WHY It Works

$$0.5 = \frac{5}{10} = \frac{50}{100} = 0.50 \quad (\times 10)$$

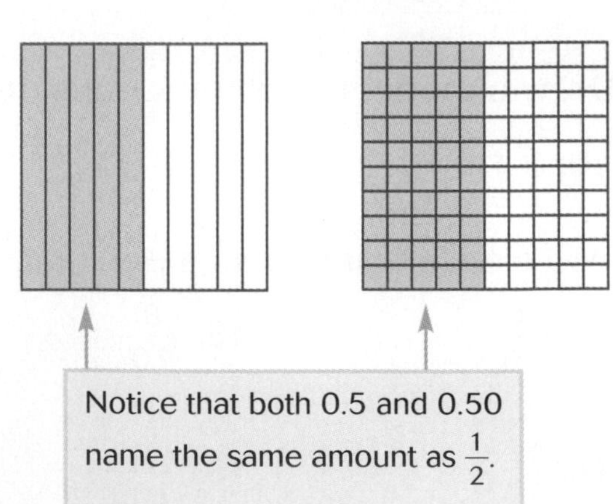

Notice that both 0.5 and 0.50 name the same amount as $\frac{1}{2}$.

Guided Practice *For another example, see Set A on p. 380.*

Write a fraction and a decimal to tell how much is shaded.

1. 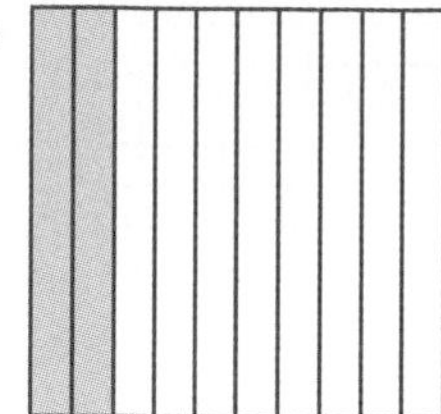

2. 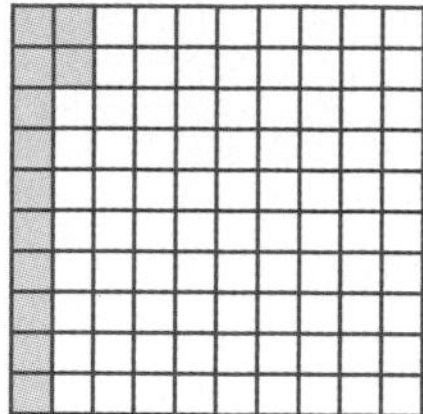

3. 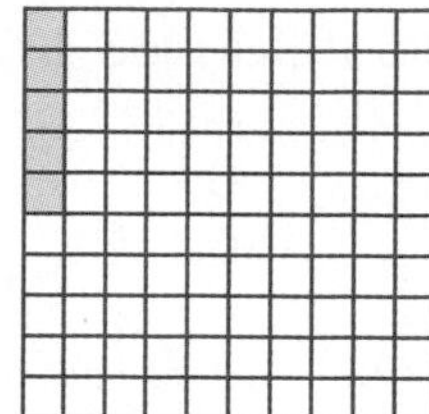

4. Write $\frac{3}{4}$ as a decimal.

5. Find a decimal equivalent to 0.9.

6. The Hall family has a large vegetable garden. They planted 10 equal rows as shown. Write a fraction and a decimal to tell what part of the garden was planted in tomatoes.

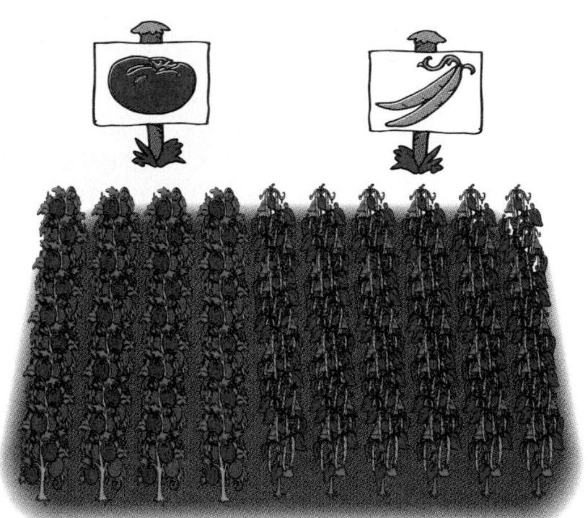

Independent Practice *For more practice, see Set A on p. 382.*

Write a fraction and a decimal to tell how much is shaded.

7. 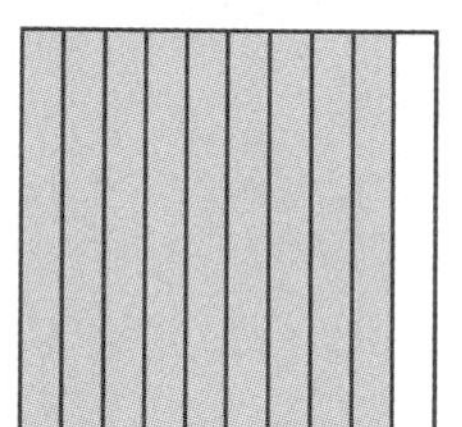

8. 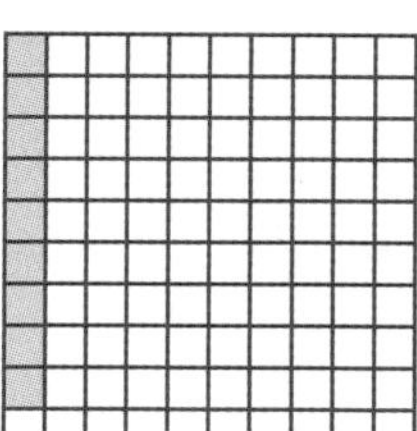

9. 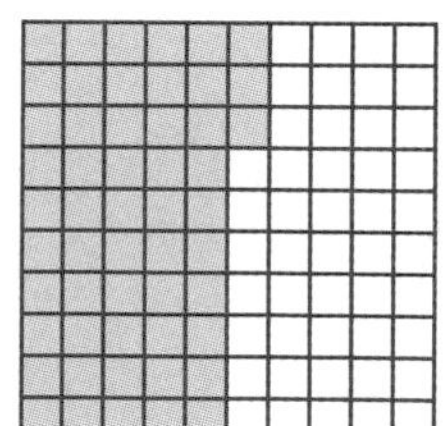

Draw a model that shows each decimal.

10. 0.1 **11.** 0.07 **12.** 0.81 **13.** 0.8

Write each fraction as a decimal.

14. $\frac{1}{10}$ **15.** $\frac{8}{10}$ **16.** $\frac{1}{100}$ **17.** $\frac{13}{100}$

18. $\frac{1}{2}$ **19.** $\frac{88}{100}$ **20.** $\frac{4}{100}$ **21.** $\frac{3}{5}$

Write an equivalent decimal.

22. 0.60 **23.** 0.1 **24.** 0.80 **25.** 0.4

26. Refer to the diagram in Exercise 6. Write a fraction and a decimal to tell what part of the garden was planted in green beans.

27. A freight train has 100 cars. Twenty-three of the cars are refrigerator cars. Write a fraction and a decimal to show what part of the train is made up of refrigerator cars.

28. Two of the pens in a package of 10 pens are red. Write a decimal to tell what part of the package is made up of red pens.

29. Math Reasoning Which, if any, of these decimals are equivalent: 0.2, 0.20, and 0.02? Draw a model of each decimal to support your answer.

Mixed Review

30. Refer to the table at the right. Are these numbers likely to be exact numbers or estimates?

Desert	Location	Area in Square Miles
Gobi	Mongolia and China	500,000
Death Valley	California and Nevada	3,300
Mojave	California	15,000
Sahara	Northern Africa	3,500,000

31. Maddie tossed a number cube, with sides numbered 1 through 6. What is the probability that she tossed an odd number?

32. Compare. 103,477 ● 122,219

33. Algebra If $x = 13$, $24x =$ _?_

34. $\frac{7}{8} - \frac{1}{2}$ **35.** $\frac{7}{12} + \frac{1}{6}$ **36.** $\frac{2}{5} + \frac{1}{2}$ **37.** $\frac{3}{4} - \frac{1}{3}$

Test Prep Choose the correct letter for each answer.

38. (8-2) $8\frac{1}{3} + 4\frac{1}{3} =$

A $4\frac{1}{3}$ C $12\frac{2}{6}$

B $12\frac{1}{3}$ D $12\frac{2}{3}$

39. (6-6) Mrs. Clayburn spent $129 to buy her triplets identical jogging shoes. How much did she spend on each pair of shoes?

F $33 H $132

G $43 J $387

Use Homework Workbook 9-1.

Relating Mixed Numbers and Decimals

California Content Standard *Number Sense 1.6. Write tenths and hundredths in decimal and fraction notations and know the fraction and decimal equivalents for halves and fourths (e.g. . . . $\frac{7}{4} = 1\frac{3}{4} = 1.75$). Also, Number Sense 1.7 (See p. 343.)*

Math Link You have seen how fractions and decimals are related. Now you will learn how to write mixed numbers as decimals.

Warm-Up Review

1. $\frac{1}{2} = \frac{■}{10}$
2. $\frac{5}{6} = \frac{■}{18}$

Write as a mixed number.

3. $\frac{11}{5}$
4. $\frac{9}{2}$

Write as a decimal.

5. $\frac{7}{10}$
6. $\frac{1}{4}$
7. Justin filled the lawnmower with 0.75 gallons of gas. Write this decimal as a fraction.

Example 1

The Guzmans had their car serviced before leaving for vacation. It is $2\frac{8}{10}$ miles from their home to the service station. Write this mixed number as a decimal.

Mixed number: $2\frac{8}{10}$

Decimal: 2.8

Say: two and eight tenths

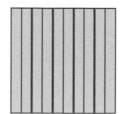

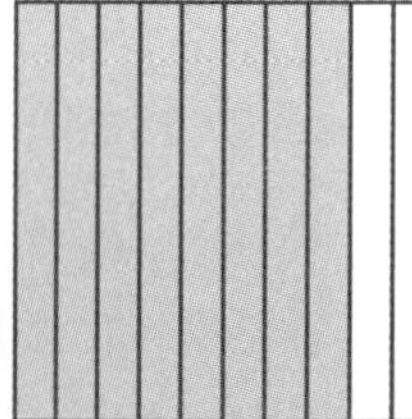

Example 2

Write $1\frac{4}{100}$ as a decimal.

Mixed number: $1\frac{4}{100}$

Decimal: 1.04

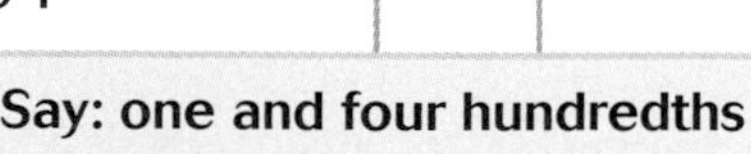
Say: one and four hundredths

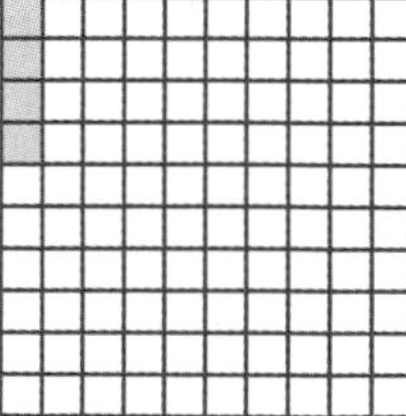

Example 3

Write $1\frac{2}{5}$ as a decimal.

Mixed number: $1\frac{2}{5} = 1\frac{4}{10}$ (× 2 numerator and denominator)

Decimal: 1.4

Say: one and four tenths

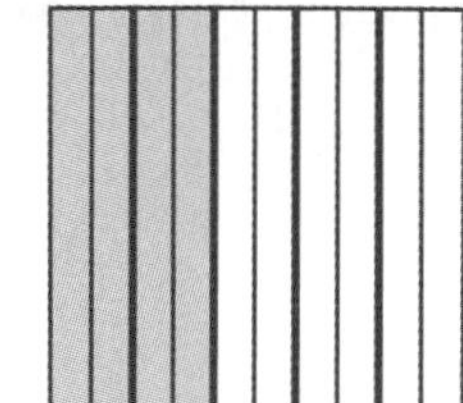

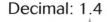

Additional Standards: Number Sense 1.5, Mathematical Reasoning 2.3 (See p. 343.)

Example 4

Write $\frac{7}{4}$ as a decimal.

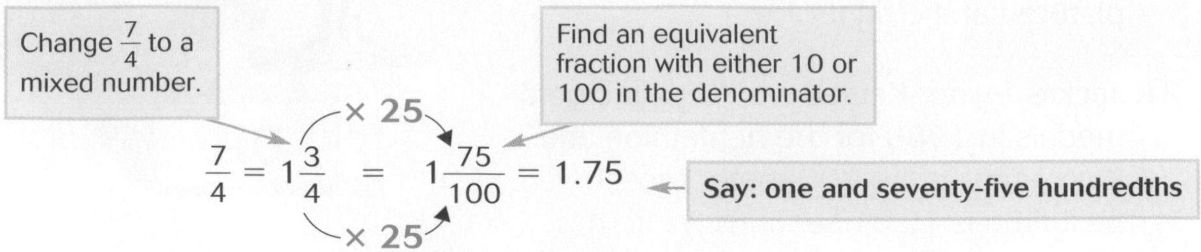

Change $\frac{7}{4}$ to a mixed number.
Find an equivalent fraction with either 10 or 100 in the denominator.
× 25
$\frac{7}{4} = 1\frac{3}{4} = 1\frac{75}{100} = 1.75$
× 25
Say: one and seventy-five hundredths

Example 5

Write 24.03 as a fraction or mixed number.

$24.03 = 24\frac{3}{100}$

Example 6

Write 0.8 as a fraction or mixed number.

$0.8 = \frac{8}{10}$

Guided Practice *For another example, see Set B on p. 380.*

Write each number as a decimal.

1. $6\frac{3}{10}$ **2.** $1\frac{47}{100}$ **3.** $4\frac{1}{2}$ **4.** $13\frac{9}{100}$ **5.** $62\frac{1}{10}$ **6.** $\frac{5}{4}$

7. Paula bought some ground turkey. The package label is shown at the right. Write the weight as a mixed number.

GROUND TURKEY	
Unit price per pound $1.69	Date 11/18
Net wt lb 4.35	Total price $7.35

Independent Practice *For more practice, see Set B on p. 382.*

Write each number as a decimal.

8. $7\frac{2}{10}$ **9.** $44\frac{4}{100}$ **10.** $\frac{13}{10}$ **11.** $3\frac{1}{4}$ **12.** $9\frac{37}{100}$ **13.** $\frac{6}{5}$

Write each decimal as a fraction or mixed number.

14. 0.4 **15.** 2.6 **16.** 92.08 **17.** 8.80 **18.** 35.32 **19.** 0.83

20. A company packages 10 quarts of oil to the case. Write a mixed number and a decimal to tell how many cases are pictured at the right.

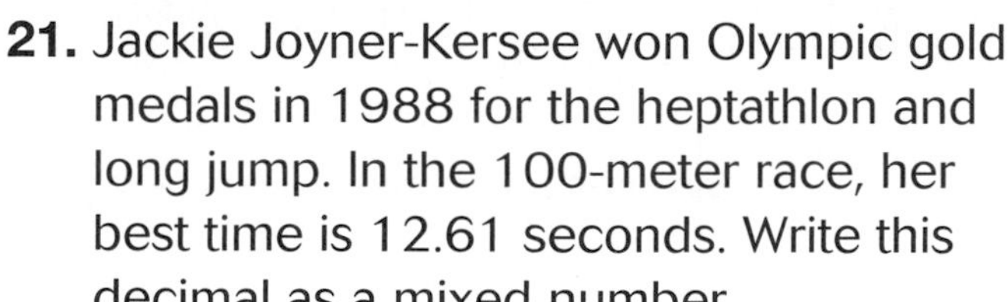

21. Jackie Joyner-Kersee won Olympic gold medals in 1988 for the heptathlon and long jump. In the 100-meter race, her best time is 12.61 seconds. Write this decimal as a mixed number.

Use the table for Exercises 22 and 23.

Average Precipitation in Inches	
Houston	46.07
Duluth	30.00
Memphis	52.10
Des Moines	33.12
San Diego	9.90

22. Write the amount of precipitation in Des Moines as a mixed number.

23. Which decimal in the table can be written as a whole number? Write the decimal and whole number.

24. **Math Reasoning** Is $5.63 the same amount as 5.63 dollars? Explain your thinking.

Mixed Review

25. Write a decimal for the shaded part of the grid.

26. Write a decimal for $\frac{9}{10}$.

27. **Algebra** If $3y = 78$, does $3y + 10 = 78 - 10$?

28. $\frac{3}{8} - \frac{1}{4}$

29. $\frac{3}{4} - \frac{1}{3}$

30. 318×44

31. $1{,}455 \div 7$

32. $5{,}970 \times 38$

33. $54{,}623 + 8{,}549$

34. $\$67.23 \times 17$

35. $82{,}935 - 2{,}008$

Test Prep **Choose the correct letter for each answer.**

36. $\frac{1}{6} + \frac{2}{3} =$ (8-6)

A $\frac{5}{6}$

B $\frac{3}{6}$

C $\frac{3}{9}$

D $\frac{3}{12}$

37. Which fraction is not equal to 1? (7-1)

F $\frac{4}{4}$

G $\frac{1}{2}$

H $\frac{18}{18}$

J $\frac{7}{7}$

 Use Homework Workbook 9-2.

TEST PREP

Multiple-Choice Cumulative Review

Choose the correct letter for each answer.

1. In a total of 25 spins, which color will the spinner probably point to the greatest number of times?

A green
B blue
C red
D yellow

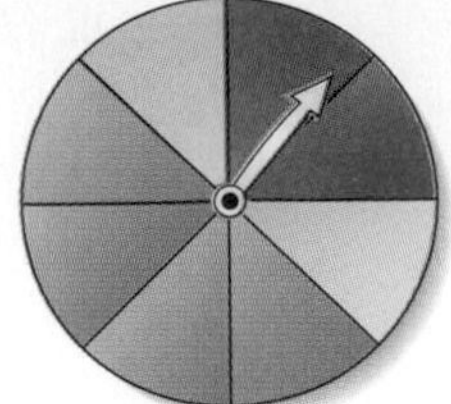

2. Weekly cassette-tape sales in November were 192 tapes, 71 tapes, 57 tapes, and 366 tapes. Which is the best estimate for the total sales in November?

F 400
G 500
H 600
J 700

3. Find 41 ÷ 2.

A 20
B 20 R1
C 21
D 21 R1
E NH

4. Which fraction is greater than $\frac{1}{3}$?

F $\frac{5}{12}$
G $\frac{1}{4}$
H $\frac{2}{12}$
J $\frac{1}{9}$

5. Abby's basketball team scored 43 points, 50 points, and 60 points in three games. What is the team's average, or mean, score?

A 51 points
B 93 points
C 110 points
D 153 points

6. Find $4\frac{2}{9} + 3\frac{4}{9}$.

F $7\frac{5}{9}$
G $7\frac{2}{3}$
H $7\frac{7}{9}$
J $8\frac{1}{9}$
K NH

7. Which number is NOT represented by the model?

A $\frac{4}{10}$
B 0.40
C $\frac{2}{5}$
D $\frac{20}{100}$

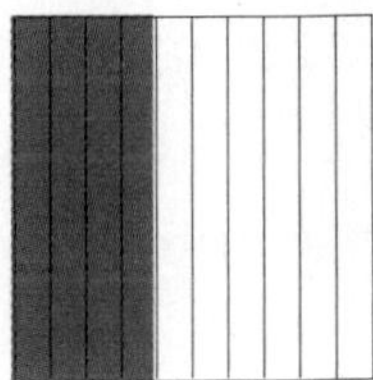

8. Solve $n + 8 = 35$.

F $n = 4\frac{3}{8}$
G $n = 24$
H $n = 27$
J $n = 43$

LESSON
9-3

Decimal Place Value

California Content Standard *Number Sense 1.6. Write tenths and hundredths in decimal notation. . . . Also, Mathematical Reasoning 2.3 (See p. 343.)*

Warm-Up Review

Give the place value of the underlined digit.

1. $2\underline{2}3$
2. $3\underline{1}8{,}709$
3. $\underline{5}{,}186$
4. $42{,}\underline{0}85$
5. Write 415,068 in word form.

Write as a decimal.

6. $\frac{1}{10}$
7. $\frac{1}{100}$
8. What is the value of 3 dollars, 4 dimes, and 2 pennies?

Math Link You have studied the place value of whole numbers. Now you will learn about the place value of decimals.

Mia filled her car's gas tank. The pump showed the amount of gasoline she purchased.

15.07 Gallons

A place-value chart helps you read and write decimals.

You can write 15.07 in different ways.

Decimal form: 15.07

Word form: fifteen and seven hundredths

Short word form: 15 and 7 hundredths

tens	ones	.	tenths	hundredths
1	5	.	0	7

Read the decimal point as "and."

Example 1

Write 0.2 in word form.

Word form: two tenths

Example 2

Write forty-seven and sixteen hundredths in decimal form.

Decimal form: 47.16

Whole numbers and money can also be written in decimal form.

Example 3

Write 6 as a decimal.

Decimal form: 6.0 or 6.00

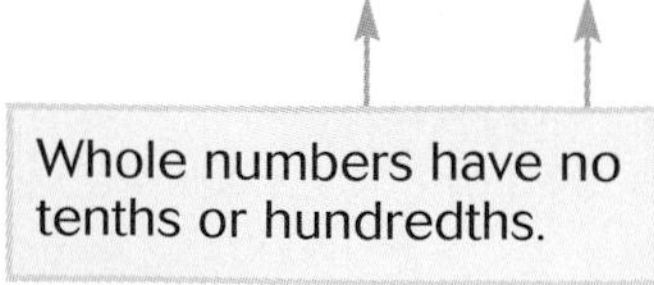
Whole numbers have no tenths or hundredths.

Example 4

Write six dollars and five cents as a decimal.

Decimal form: $6.05

Don't forget to write the dollar sign.

Since there are 100 cents in a dollar, decimals for money always show hundredths.

Additional Standards: Mathematical Reasoning 2.4, 3.3 (See p. 343.)

Guided Practice *For another example, see Set C on p. 380.*

Write the word form for each decimal.

1. 5.14 **2.** 34.8 **3.** 94.66 **4.** 461.08 **5.** 0.97

Write each as a decimal. Use a dollar sign for money.

6. seven and nine tenths **7.** seventy-four cents **8.** 4

9. A meteorologist reported that 1.7 inches of snow fell last night. What is the place value of 7 in 1.7?

Independent Practice *For more practice, see Set C on p. 382.*

Write the word form for each decimal.

10. 7.3 **11.** 12.09 **12.** 776.9 **13.** 580.14 **14.** 633.90

Write each as a decimal. Use a dollar sign for money.

15. twenty-four and three tenths **16.** 8 and 2 hundredths

17. fifty dollars and ninety cents **18.** 11

Tell the place value of the underlined digit.

19. $326.\underline{9}9$ **20.** $835.8\underline{5}$ **21.** $\underline{1}43.06$ **22.** $6\underline{0}8.92$ **23.** $42\underline{1}.64$

24. Math Reasoning Refer to the high jump data. Is the value of the digit 2 in each height the same? Explain.

High Jump	
Jack	1.02 meters
Kirk	1.2 meters

Mixed Review

25. It rained $\frac{6}{10}$ of an inch. Write $\frac{6}{10}$ in simplest form.

26. Algebra If $m = 16$, then what is the value of $3[50 - (m + 5)]$?

Write each fraction or mixed number as a decimal.

27. $\frac{2}{100}$ **28.** $\frac{1}{4}$ **29.** $5\frac{7}{10}$ **30.** $3\frac{1}{5}$ **31.** $4\frac{44}{100}$ **32.** $\frac{11}{4}$

Test Prep **Choose the correct letter for the answer.**

33. 70,006 − 10,418 =
(2-7)

A 59,588 **B** 59,592 **C** 60,698 **D** 80,424 **E** NH

Comparing and Ordering Decimals

California Content Standard *Number Sense 1.2. (🔑): Order and compare . . . decimals to two decimal places.*

Math Link You already know how to compare and order whole numbers. In this lesson, you will learn how to compare and order decimals.

Warm-Up Review

1. 518 ● 581
2. 14,672 ● 14,625
3. 6,760 ● 6,763

Order from least to greatest.

4. 167, 162, 169
5. 3,096; 3,088; 3,122
6. Write a decimal equivalent to 24.6.

Example 1

Anna bought 2 bags of seashells that were sold by the pound. They are pictured at the right. Which bag of shells weighed more?

Step 1 Line up the decimal points when you write the numbers.	**Step 2** Start at the left. Compare the digits.	**Step 3** When the digits are the same, compare the next digits to the right.
1.83 1.68	1.83 1.68 The ones digits are the same.	1.83 1.68 8 > 6, so 1.83 > 1.68.

The 1.83-pound bag weighed more than the 1.68-pound bag.

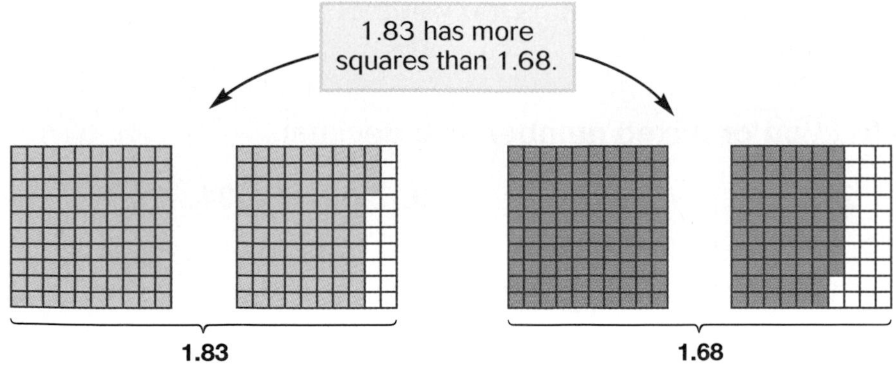

Example 2

Compare 72.58 and 72.52

Step 1 Line up the decimal points when you write the numbers.	Step 2 Start at the left. Compare the digits.	Step 3 When the digits are the same, compare the next digits to the right.
72.58 72.52	72.58 72.52	72.58 72.52 8 > 2, so 72.58 > 72.52.

You can write 72.58 > 72.52 or 72.52 < 72.58.

Example 3

Compare 13.7 and 13.74.

Step 1 Line up the decimal points. Use equivalent decimals so the digits line up.	Step 2 Start at the left. Compare the digits.	Step 3 When the digits are the same, compare the next digits to the right.
13.7 → 13.70 13.74 13.74	13.70 13.74	13.70 13.74 0 < 4, so 13.70 < 13.74

Remember, you can write zero at the end of a decimal without changing its value.

You can write 13.7 < 13.74 or 13.74 > 13.7.

Example 4

Order these numbers from greatest to least: 2.6, 2.83, and 2.69.

Step 1 Line up the decimal points. Use equivalent decimals so the digits line up.	Step 2 Start at the left. Compare the digits.	Step 3 Compare the next digits to the right.
2.6 → 2.60 2.83 2.83 2.69 2.69	2.60 2.83 2.69 8 > 6, so 2.83 is the greatest number.	2.60 2.83 2.69 9 > 0, so 2.69 > 2.60.

The numbers from greatest to least are 2.83, 2.69, 2.6.

Guided Practice *For another example, see Set D on p. 380.*

Compare. Write >, <, or = for each ●.

1. 35.77 ● 35.93 **2.** 3.15 ● 3.19 **3.** 5.80 ● 5.8 **4.** 20.86 ● 20.8

5. Use the table. Write the times for the 100-meter run in order from slowest to fastest.

Men's Summer Olympics Winning Times in Seconds		
Year	**100-Meter Run**	**400-Meter Run**
1988	9.92	43.87
1992	9.96	43.5
1996	9.84	43.49

Independent Practice *For more practice, see Set D on p. 382.*

Compare. Write >, <, or = for each ●.

6. 8.56 ● 8.59 **7.** 16.8 ● 16.08 **8.** 85.1 ● 85.10

9. 0.69 ● 0.71 **10.** 76.23 ● 76.32 **11.** 4.36 ● 0.36

Order each set of numbers from greatest to least.

12. 118.78, 118.7, 119.72 **13.** 48.03, 48.3, 48.33

14. Use the table from Exercise 5. Write the times for the 400-meter run in order from fastest to slowest.

Mixed Review

15. Lloyd ran the 50-meter dash in 8.94 seconds. What is the place value of 4 in 8.94?

For Exercises 16 and 17, write each number as a decimal.

16. three and nine hundredths **17.** $21\frac{6}{10}$

18. $6\overline{)84}$ **19.** 56×81 **20.** $7{,}951 + 4{,}136$ **21.** $645 - 273$

Test Prep **Choose the correct letter for each answer.**

22. (6-9) How many prime numbers are there between 20 and 30?

A 2 **C** 4

B 3 **D** 5

23. (1-1) Which number has no hundreds?

F 23,406 **H** 7,850

G 137,055 **J** 950,172

Fractions, Decimals and the Number Line

Warm-Up Review

Write as a decimal.

1. $\frac{7}{10}$
2. $\frac{1}{5}$
3. $1\frac{1}{2}$
4. $2\frac{3}{4}$
5. Write a decimal equivalent to 1.6.
6. Draw a number line from 0 to 3. Show $\frac{3}{4}$ and $\frac{11}{4}$.

California Content Standard *Number Sense 1.9. (🔑): Identify on a number line the relative position of positive fractions, positive mixed numbers, and positive decimals to two decimal places. Also, Number Sense 1.2 (🔑)* *(See p. 343.)*

Math Link You have worked with whole numbers and fractions on the number line. Now you will locate decimals on the number line.

If you divide the distance from 0 to 1 into 10 equal parts, you can show tenths.

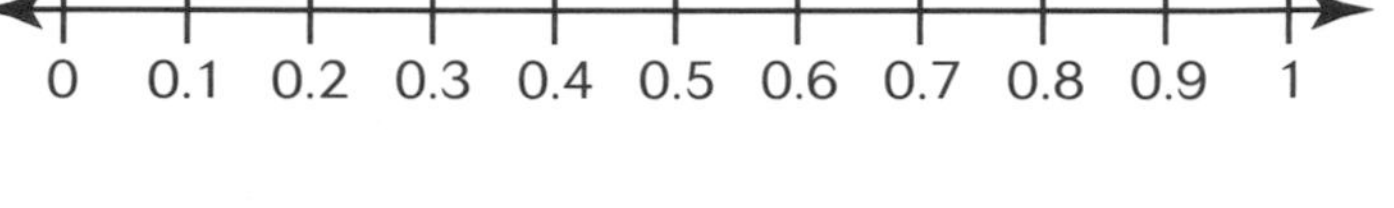

Then if you divide each tenth into 10 equal parts you can show hundredths.

You can use these ideas to place decimals all along the number line.

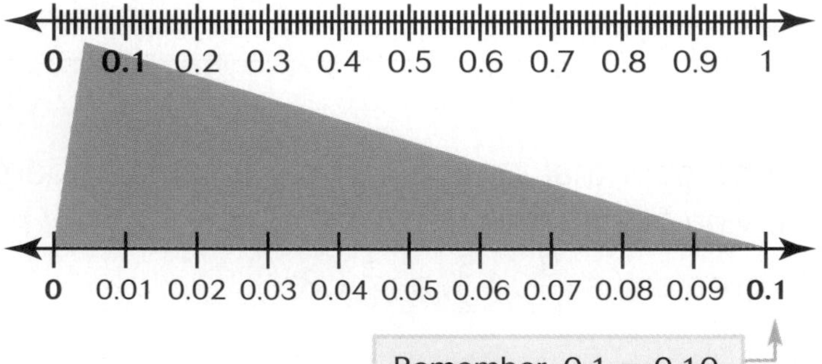

Remember, 0.1 = 0.10.

Example 1

Show 2.7 on a number line.

Place 2 and 3 on a number line. Then divide the distance from 2 to 3 into 10 equal parts.

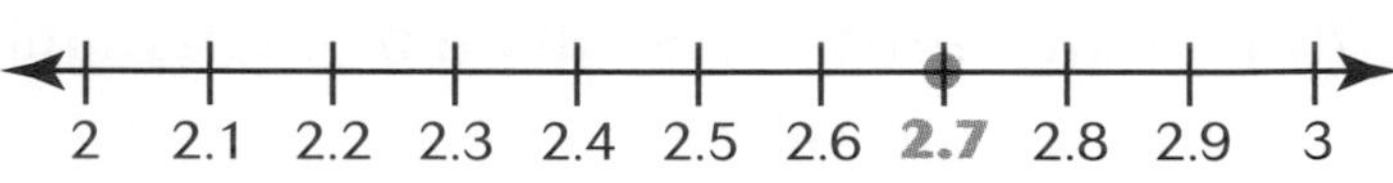

Example 2

Show 7.18 on a number line.

7.18 is between 7.10 and 7.20. So place 7.10 and 7.20 on a number line. Then divide the distance from 7.10 to 7.20 into 10 equal parts.

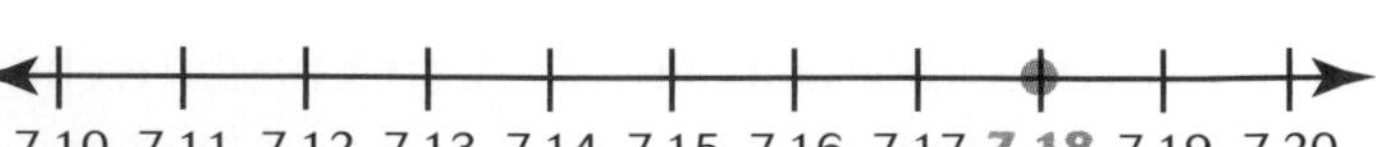

Additional Standards: Number Sense 1.6, Mathematical Reasoning 3.3 *(See p. 343.)*

Sometimes you need to estimate the position of a decimal.

Example 3

Which point is located at 4.16?

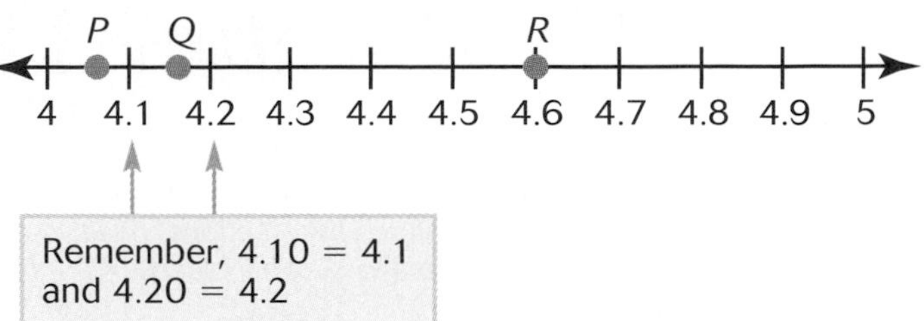

4.16 is a little more than halfway between 4.10 and 4.20.

Point Q is located at about 4.16.

Example 4

Graph $\frac{9}{10}$, 1.8, and $1\frac{3}{4}$ on a number line. Then order the numbers from least to greatest.

Use the decimal equivalents for the fractions.

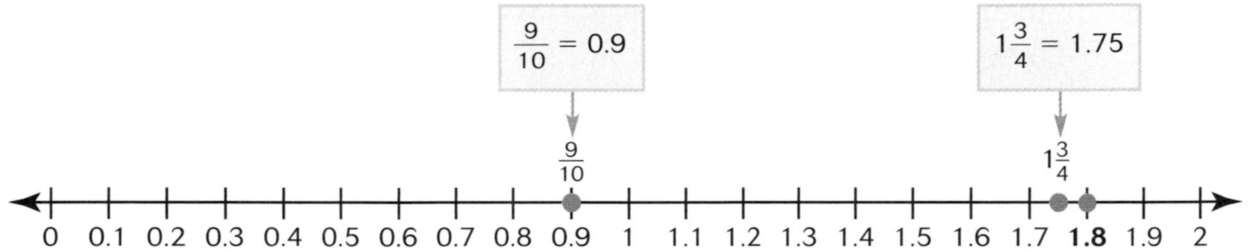

Remember that on a number line, the numbers increase when moving from left to right. So the order of the numbers from least to greatest is $\frac{9}{10}$, $1\frac{3}{4}$, and 1.8.

Guided Practice *For another example, see Set E on p. 381.*

For Exercises 1–6, use the two number lines below. What point shows the location of each number?

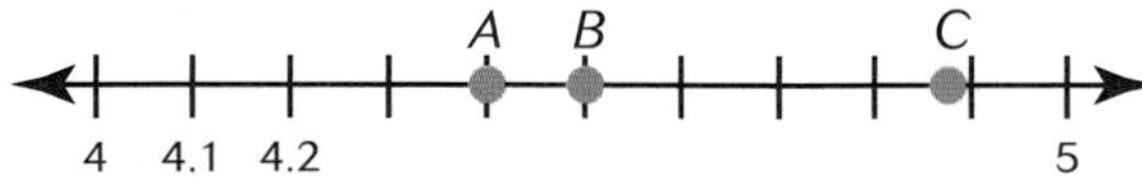

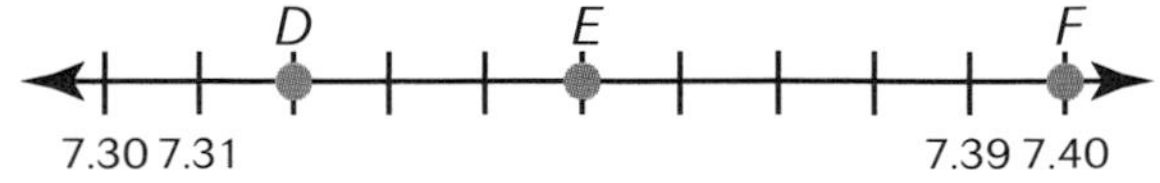

1. 4.4 **2.** 4.88 **3.** $4\frac{1}{2}$ **4.** 7.35 **5.** $7\frac{32}{100}$ **6.** 7.40

7. The thermometer below shows Julia's temperature in degrees Fahrenheit when she had the flu. What was her temperature?

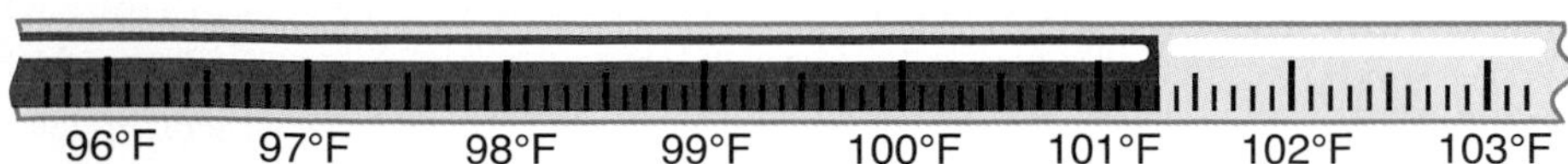

Independent Practice

For more practice, see Set E on p. 383.

For Exercises 8–13, use the two number lines below. What point shows the location of each number?

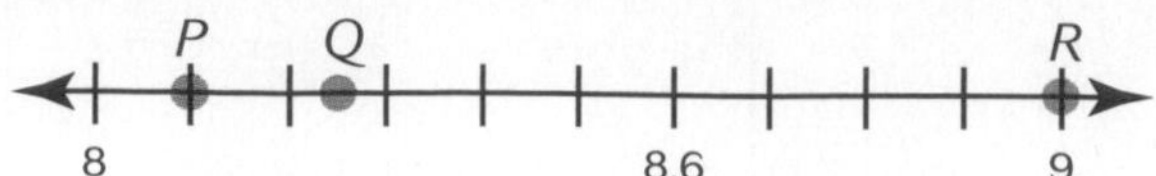

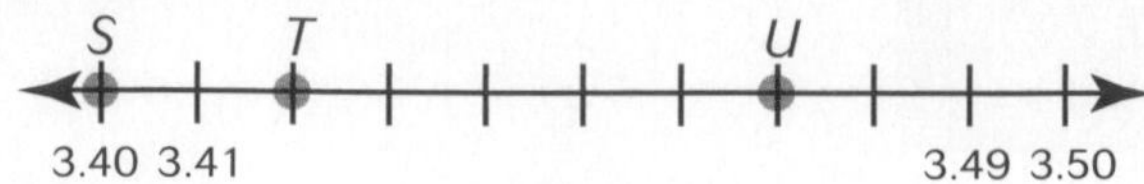

8. 8.1 **9.** 9.0 **10.** $8\frac{1}{4}$ **11.** 3.42 **12.** $3\frac{47}{100}$ **13.** 3.40

Show each set of numbers on a number line. Then order the numbers from least to greatest.

14. $1\frac{9}{10}$, $2\frac{1}{2}$, 2.3 **15.** $\frac{7}{2}$, 3.88, 3.4 **16.** 5.91, 5.2, $5\frac{1}{4}$

17. At a fishing contest, Juan's fish weighed $5\frac{1}{2}$ pounds, Samantha's weighed 6.2 pounds, and Brian's weighed 5.8 pounds. Show these numbers on a number line. Whose fish was heaviest?

Mixed Review

18. The bar graph shows the number of video tapes borrowed from the library during a one-week period. What is the average number of tapes borrowed per day?

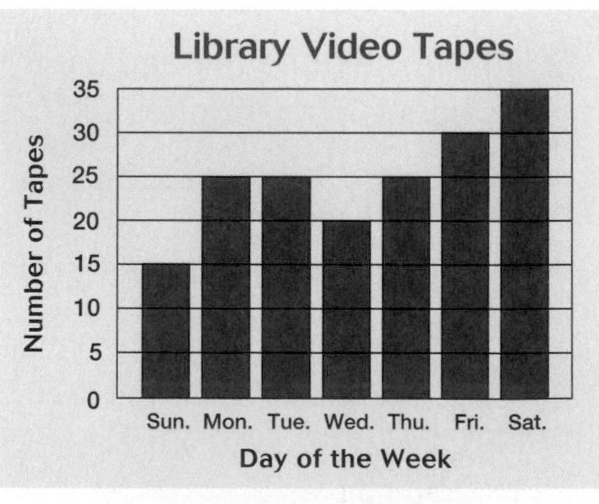

19. Frannie has two puppies. Lucky weighs 2.8 kilograms and Spot weighs 2.67 kilograms. Which puppy is heavier?

What is the place value of the underlined digit?

20. $62{,}\underline{8}14$ **21.** $77.\underline{0}5$ **22.** $\underline{1}43{,}982$ **23.** $6.7\underline{9}$

24. $\frac{7}{10} - \frac{3}{10}$ **25.** $\frac{1}{6} + \frac{5}{6}$ **26.** $1\frac{1}{8} + 2\frac{5}{8}$ **27.** $4\frac{2}{9} - 1\frac{1}{9}$

Test Prep Choose the correct letter for each answer.

28. Algebra If $r = 77$, then $\frac{r}{7} =$
(3-8)

A 11 **C** 84

B 70 **D** 539

29. What is the remainder when you divide 415 by 8?
(6-6)

F 1 **H** 7

G 6 **J** 51

LESSON 9-6
Understand
Plan
Solve
Look Back

Problem-Solving Skill: Multistep Problems

Warm-Up Review

1. 127 + 844
2. 4,918 − 733
3. 18 × 4
4. 13 × 7
5. 22 × 31
6. 655 × 74
7. Otis bought 5 photo albums that were $12 each and a camera that was $38. How much did Otis spend altogether?

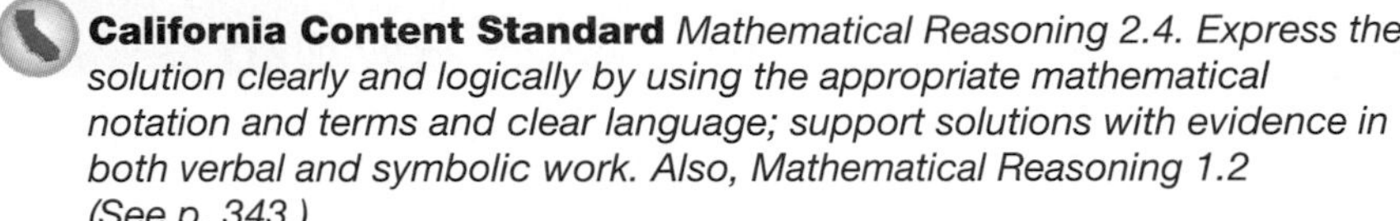
California Content Standard *Mathematical Reasoning 2.4. Express the solution clearly and logically by using the appropriate mathematical notation and terms and clear language; support solutions with evidence in both verbal and symbolic work. Also, Mathematical Reasoning 1.2* *(See p. 343.)*

Read for Understanding

The *Ferdinand Magellan* is a private railroad car that was used by several U.S. presidents. The data at the right shows how fast it traveled for two of its famous passengers.

▲ **Rate of Travel**
Franklin Roosevelt: 35 miles per hour
Harry Truman: 80 miles per hour

1. How fast did the railroad car travel when President Roosevelt rode in it?
2. How fast did the railroad car travel when President Truman rode in it?

Think and Discuss

MATH FOCUS

Multistep Problems

Sometimes it takes more than one step to solve a problem. Then you need to decide not only *what* the steps are, but in what *order* you should do them.

Reread the paragraph and the data at the top of the page.

3. How can you find how far the train car traveled in 4 hours when President Roosevelt rode in it? when President Truman rode in it?
4. How much farther could President Truman travel in 4 hours than President Roosevelt? What steps do you need to solve the problem?
5. Look back to Question 4. What operations did you use to solve the problem?

  *Additional Standards: Mathematical Reasoning 1.1, 2.0, 2.6* *(See p. 343.)*

Guided Practice

The *Ferdinand Magellan* has been at the Gold Coast Railroad Museum in Florida since 1959. It had been used by President Dwight D. Eisenhower five years earlier. Twelve years before that, it had become the official presidential railroad car.

1. What can you do to find the year that President Eisenhower used the railroad car?

a. Subtract 5 years from 1959.

b. Subtract 12 years from 1959.

c. Add 5 years to 1959.

2. How can the answer to Exercise 1 help you know when *Ferdinand Magellan* became the official car?

a. Add 12 years to 1954.

b. Subtract 5 years from 1954.

c. Subtract 12 years from 1954.

Independent Practice

The *Ferdinand Magellan* was taken out of the railroad museum in 1984 so that President Ronald Reagan could use it. He made a total of five stops with an average of 24 miles between each stop. In 1948, President Truman traveled about 250 times farther than President Reagan.

3. What number sentence shows how many miles President Reagan traveled?

a. 24 miles $\times$ 5 = 120 miles

b. 250 miles $\times$ 5 = 1,250 miles

c. 250 miles $\div$ 5 = 50 miles

4. What number sentence shows how many miles President Truman traveled?

a. 250 $\times$ 24 miles = 6,000 miles

b. 250 $\times$ 120 miles = 30,000 miles

c. 250 $\times$ 5 miles = 1,250 miles

5. Math Reasoning Look back at Exercises 3 and 4. Could you change the order of the steps to find how many miles President Truman traveled? Explain.

6. Math Reasoning What steps do you need to do to find how many miles longer President Truman's trips were than President Reagan's trip?

Rounding Decimals

California Content Standard *Number Sense 2.2: Round two-place decimals to one decimal or the nearest whole number and judge the reasonableness of the rounded answer. Also, Mathematical Reasoning 2.5* *(See p. 343.)*

Math Link You know how to round whole numbers. Now you will learn how to round decimals.

Warm-Up Review

Round to the nearest ten and nearest hundred.

1. 577 **2.** 2,350

Give the place value of 8 in each decimal.

3. 0.68 **4.** 4.82

5. Draw a number line from 2 to 3. Draw point A at 2.65.

Example 1

The odometer at the right shows how many miles the Patels drove to the first stop on their vacation. What is the distance rounded to the nearest whole number?

You can round decimals the same way you round whole numbers.

Step 1 Look at the ones place.	**Step 2** Look at the digit to the right.	**Step 3** If the digit to the right is less than 5, round down. If the digit is 5 or greater, round up.
274.3	274.3	274.3 rounds to 274.

Since $3 < 5$, keep the digit in the ones place the same.

The Patels drove about 274 miles to their first stop.

A number line shows that the rounded answer is reasonable.

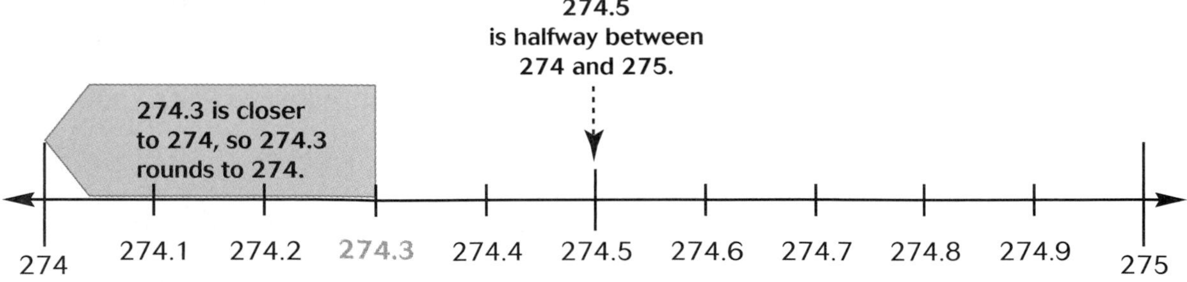

Example 2

Round 127.84 to the nearest whole number.

Step 1 Look at the ones place.	**Step 2** Look at the digit to the right.	**Step 3** If the digit to the right is less than 5, round down. If the digit is 5 or greater, round up.
127.84	127.84	127.84 rounds to 128.

Since $8 > 5$, the digit in the ones place increases by 1.

Additional Standards: Number Sense 1.9 (key); Mathematical Reasoning 3.2 *(See p. 343.)*

Example 3

Round 60.25 to the nearest tenth.

Step 1 Look at the tenths place.	**Step 2** Look at the digit to the right.	**Step 3** If the digit to the right is less than 5, round down. If the digit is 5 or greater, round up.
60.<u>2</u>5	60.2<u>5</u>	60.25 rounds to 60.3.

Since this digit is 5, the digit in the tenths place increases by 1.

Guided Practice *For another example, see Set F on p. 381.*

Round each decimal to the nearest whole number.

1. 1.24 **2.** 43.5 **3.** 26.38 **4.** 19.0 **5.** 0.75

6. The Fredricksens are planning to buy a new car. The table at the right compares their old car's mileage to that of the new car. Round each decimal to the nearest tenth.

Miles per Gallon		
Type of Car	City Driving	Highway Driving
New car	26.24	29.50
Old car	18.77	21.04

Independent Practice *For more practice, see Set F on p. 383.*

Round each decimal to the nearest whole number.

7. 46.8 **8.** 1.37 **9.** 78.2 **10.** 0.27 **11.** 50.91

Round each decimal to the nearest tenth.

12. 8.62 **13.** 17.49 **14.** 8.65 **15.** 45.03 **16.** 0.23

17. When rounded to the nearest whole number, which of these decimals round to 8?

7.4 7.7 8.29 7.09 7.82 8.08 8.6 8.3 8.71

18. When rounded to the nearest tenth, which of these decimals round to 4.7?

3.66 4.78 4.65 4.70 4.62 4.68 4.81 4.72

19. Round 5.8 to the nearest whole number. Then draw a number line to show that your answer is reasonable.

20. Math Reasoning Round 5.97 to the nearest tenth. Did the ones place change? Explain.

21. Jan needs 1.5 pounds of Swiss cheese for a fondue recipe. Round the weight of each chunk of cheese to the nearest tenth.

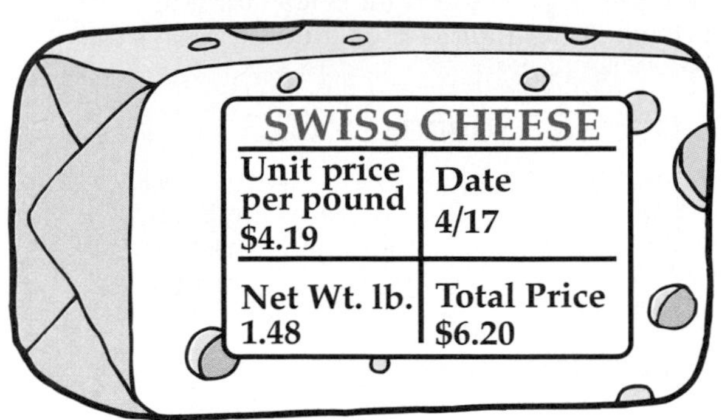

SWISS CHEESE
Unit price per pound $4.19
Date 4/17
Net Wt. lb. 1.48
Total Price $6.20

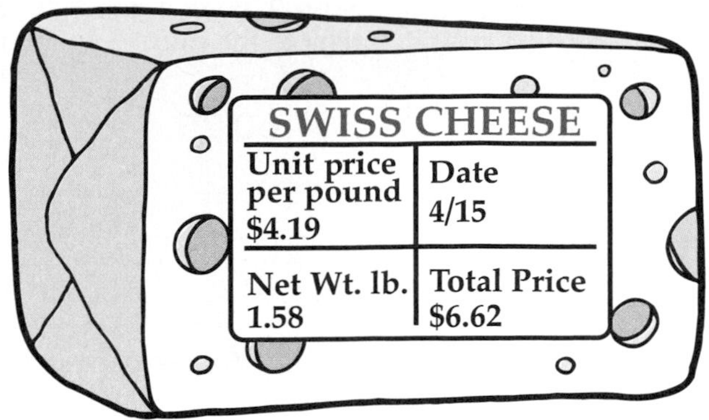

SWISS CHEESE
Unit price per pound $4.19
Date 4/15
Net Wt. lb. 1.58
Total Price $6.62

22. Refer to the total prices of the Swiss cheese in Exercise 21. Round each total price to the nearest dollar.

Mixed Review

23. Lisa bought two T-shirts for \$14 each and three sweatshirts for \$35 each. How much did Lisa spend?

For Exercises 24–27, use the number line below.

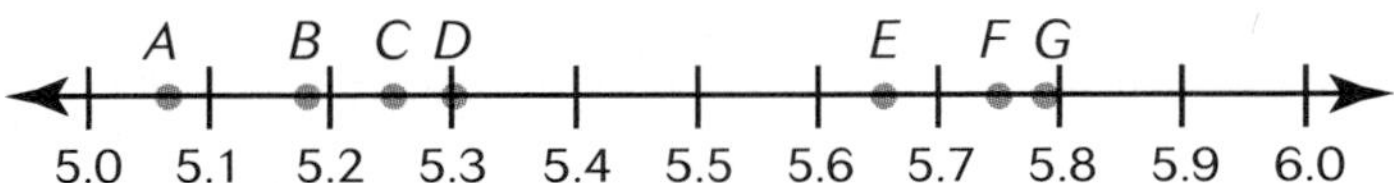

24. Which point is located at $5\frac{3}{4}$?

25. Which point is located at 5.18?

26. What number might be located at point *A*?

27. Between which two decimals named on the number line is 5.82?

28. 732 ⬤ 723

29. 19.6 ⬤ 19.8

30. $\frac{1}{2}$ ⬤ $\frac{5}{6}$

31. 14.7 ⬤ 14.76

32. $\begin{array}{r} 1{,}002 \\ \times \quad 47 \\ \hline \end{array}$

33. $\begin{array}{r} 519{,}944 \\ 67{,}318 \\ +\ 60{,}233 \\ \hline \end{array}$

34. $\begin{array}{r} 7{,}435 \\ -\ 5{,}816 \\ \hline \end{array}$

35. $6\overline{)968}$

Test Prep **Choose the correct letter for each answer.**

36. **Algebra** Which value of x makes the equation $5x = 80$ true? (3-9)

A 8
B 10
C 16
D 20

37. Which product has a value of 28? (6-9)

F $2 \times 3 \times 4$
G $3 \times 3 \times 3$
H $2 \times 4 \times 4$
J $2 \times 2 \times 7$

Diagnostic Checkpoint

Write each fraction or mixed number as a decimal.

1. (9-1) $\frac{9}{10}$ **2.** (9-1) $\frac{1}{10}$ **3.** (9-1) $\frac{92}{100}$ **4.** (9-2) $4\frac{8}{10}$ **5.** (9-2) $8\frac{11}{100}$

Tell the place value of the underlined digit.

6. (9-3) $482.\underline{3}6$ **7.** (9-3) $90\underline{5}.38$ **8.** (9-3) $\underline{2}04.91$ **9.** (9-3) $782.0\underline{8}$ **10.** (9-3) $235.\underline{2}$

Compare. Write >, <, or = for each ●.

11. (9-4) 8.3 ● 8.30 **12.** (9-4) 7.9 ● 7.09 **13.** (9-4) 3.16 ● 3.26

14. (9-4) 4.81 ● 4.72 **15.** (9-4) 1.39 ● 1.93 **16.** (9-4) 32.9 ● 32.90

What point shows the location of each number?

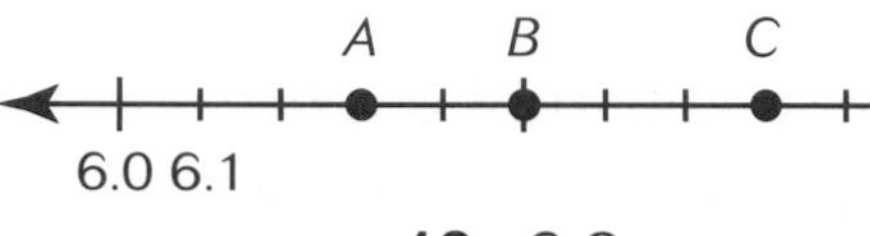

17. (9-5) 6.5 **18.** (9-5) 6.3 **19.** (9-5) 6.8

Round each decimal to the nearest tenth.

20. (9-7) 4.73 **21.** (9-7) 26.48 **22.** (9-7) 5.06 **23.** (9-7) 1.08 **24.** (9-7) 2.91

Use the figure at the right for Exercises 25 and 26.

25. (9-6) You buy 6 pounds of apples and 2 pounds of oranges. What steps do you need to do to find the change received if you pay with a $20 bill?

Oranges
$2.00 per pound

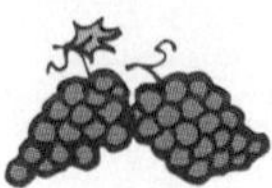

Grapes
$1.89 per pound

Apples
$1.50 per pound

26. (9-6) You buy 2 pounds of grapes and 4 pounds of oranges. How much do they cost in all?

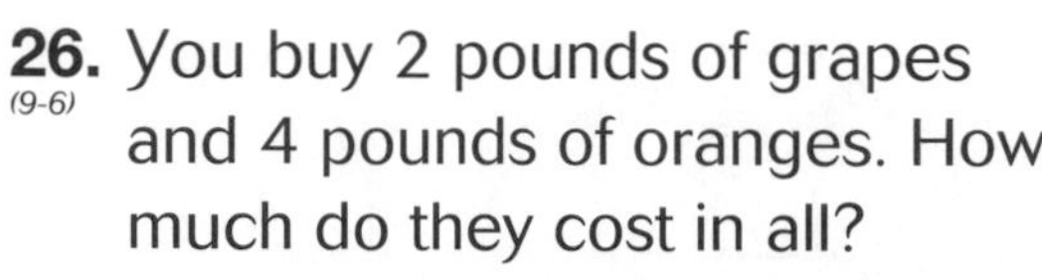

27. (9-4) A veterinarian weighed three dogs. Sport weighed 35.25 pounds, Pepper weighed 35.5 pounds, and Lefty weighed 35.75 pounds. Which dog was the heaviest? Which was the lightest?

Problem-Solving Strategy:

Draw a Picture

California Content Standard *Math Reasoning 2.3. Use a variety of methods, such as words, numbers, symbols, charts, graphs, tables, diagrams, and models, to explain mathematical reasoning. Also, Mathematical Reasoning 1.1 (See p. 343.)*

Warm-Up Review

Draw an array to model each product.

1. 5 × 8 **2.** 6 × 6

3. Draw a model for 0.7.

4. Draw all the coin combinations that have the value of 17¢.

Example

Jan, Luis, Wayne, Carmen, and Tim are horseback riding on a ranch. Use the clues at the right to figure out the order in which the friends are riding.

CLUES

1. There is a rider in front of and behind Jan.
2. Carmen is second in line.
3. The same number of riders are in front of Luis and behind him.
4. There are 2 riders between Jan and Wayne.

Understand

What do you need to find?

You need to find who is first, second, third, fourth, and fifth in line.

Plan

How can you solve the problem?

You can **draw a picture** of the 5 horses to show first, second, third, fourth, and fifth places. Then use the clues to draw the correct friend on each horse.

Solve

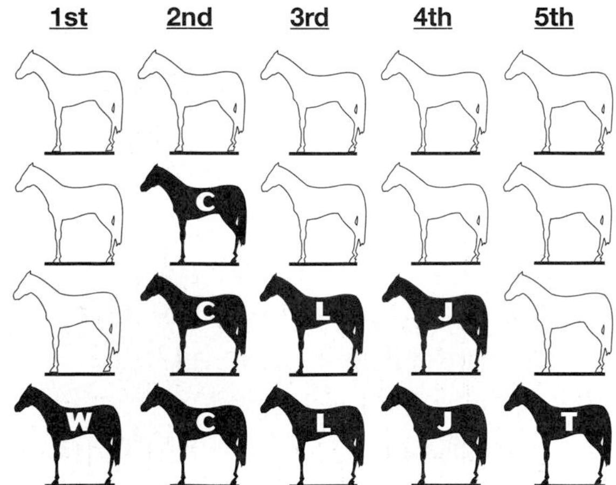

Clue 1: This tells you that Jan must be second, third, or fourth, but you can't tell which yet.

Clue 2: Carmen is second.

Clue 3: Luis is in the middle, so he is third. That means Jan must be fourth.

Clue 4: Wayne is first. There is one place left, so Tim must be fifth.

Look Back

Does the order of the friends match the clues? Explain how you know.

Additional Standards: Mathematical Reasoning 2.0, 3.2 (See p. 343.)

Guided Practice

Draw a picture to solve Exercises 1–5.

1. A barn has four horsestalls belonging to Rusty, Dusty, Gusty, and Justy. Gusty's stall is next to only one other stall. Justy is in the third stall. Dusty is not next to Justy. Which horse is in which stall?

2. The fence around a horse corral is a rectangle that is 20 yards long and 12 yards wide. There are posts every 4 yards along the fence and at every corner. How many posts are there around the entire fence?

Independent Practice

3. Ten people are going to a barbecue. Tables like the ones shown at the right are pushed together to make one long table. How many tables are needed to seat all 10 people?

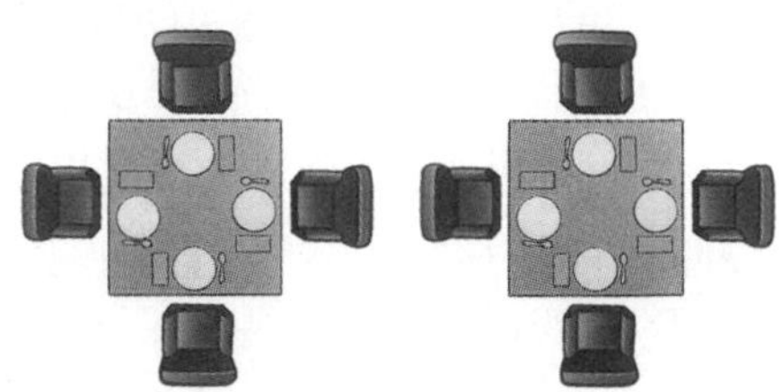

4. A fence is 15 sections long. Each section begins and ends with a post. How many posts are there?

5. Harriet is installing ceiling tiles that are 2 feet by 2 feet. How many will she need for a ceiling that is 10 feet by 12 feet?

Mixed Review

Try these or other strategies to solve each problem. Tell which strategy you used.

Problem-Solving Strategies

- *Make a List*
- *Write a Number Sentence*
- *Work Backward*
- *Make a Table*

6. Cara rode 4 miles more than Tim rode. Tim rode half as many miles as Duke. Duke rode 12 miles. How many miles did Cara and Tim each ride?

7. Troy has 3 different pairs of boots and 4 different hats. How many different outfits can he make?

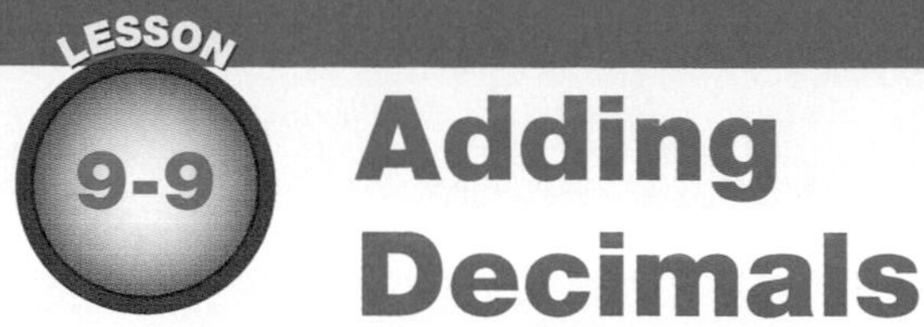

Adding Decimals

Warm-Up Review

1. 127 + 84 **2.** 53 + 266

3. Write a decimal equivalent to 5.9.

4. Write 18 as a decimal.

5. In the decimal 245.69, which digit is in the hundredths place?

Round to the nearest whole number.

6. 37.8 **7.** 9.31

8. Jodi spent $21.98 for a blouse and $28 for pants. How much did she spend on the outfit?

California Content Standard *Number Sense 2.1. Estimate and compute the sum or difference of whole numbers and positive decimals to two places. Also Number Sense 2.2; Mathematical Reasoning 2.6* *(See p. 343.)*

Math Link You know how to add whole numbers. Now you will learn how to add decimals.

Example 1

In Chaco Canyon, New Mexico, the Mannings biked 1.5 miles. Then they continued for another 0.7 mile to Pueblo Bonito. How far did they go altogether?

1.5	+	0.7	=	n
miles biked in Chaco Canyon		miles biked to Pueblo Bonito		miles biked altogether

Estimate first by rounding each decimal to the nearest whole number.

1.5 + 0.7

rounds to / rounds to

2 + 1 = 3

The estimate is reasonable because 3 miles is a realistic distance to bike.

Now add to find the actual total distance.

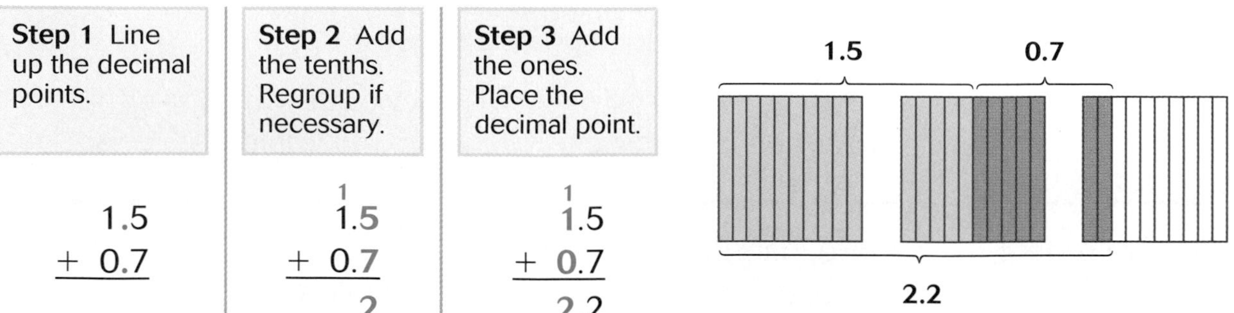

Step 1 Line up the decimal points.	**Step 2** Add the tenths. Regroup if necessary.	**Step 3** Add the ones. Place the decimal point.
$\begin{array}{r} 1.5 \\ +\ 0.7 \\ \hline \end{array}$	$\begin{array}{r} \scriptstyle 1 \\ 1.5 \\ +\ 0.7 \\ \hline 2 \end{array}$	$\begin{array}{r} \scriptstyle 1 \\ 1.5 \\ +\ 0.7 \\ \hline 2.2 \end{array}$

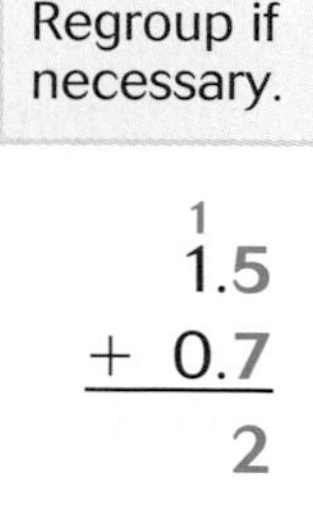

The Mannings biked 2.2 miles.

<u>*Check*</u> by comparing the answer to the estimate. The answer of 2.2 is reasonable because it is close to the estimate of 3.

Additional Standards: Algebra and Functions 1.1, Mathematical Reasoning 2.3 *(See p. 343.)*

Example 2

Find 5 + 6.76.

Estimate first by rounding each decimal to the nearest whole number.

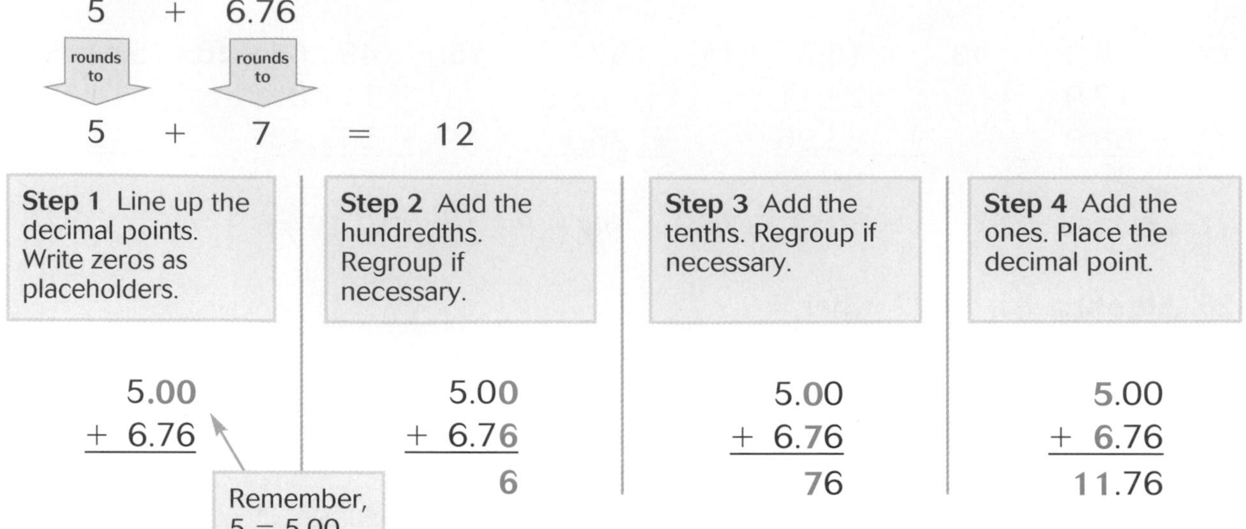
5 + 6.76
rounds to
rounds to
5 + 7 = 12
Step 1 Line up the decimal points. Write zeros as placeholders.
Step 2 Add the hundredths. Regroup if necessary.
Step 3 Add the tenths. Regroup if necessary.
Step 4 Add the ones. Place the decimal point.
5.00
+ 6.76
Remember, 5 = 5.00.
5.00
+ 6.76
6
5.00
+ 6.76
76
5.00
+ 6.76
11.76

Check by comparing the answer to the estimate. The answer of 11.76 is reasonable because it is close to the estimate of 12.

More Examples

A. Find 4.26 + 13.58.

$$\begin{array}{r} \overset{1}{4.2}6 \\ +\ 13.58 \\ \hline 17.84 \end{array}$$

Line up the decimal points.

B. Find 7.3 + 19 + 8.75.

$$\begin{array}{r} {}^{2\,1}7.30 \\ 19.00 \\ +\ 8.75 \\ \hline 35.05 \end{array}$$

Line up the decimal points. Write zeros as placeholders.

Guided Practice

For another example, see Set G on p. 381.

Estimate first. Then find each sum.

1. $\begin{array}{r} 0.5 \\ +\ 1.3 \\ \hline \end{array}$ **2.** $\begin{array}{r} 4.27 \\ +\ 0.68 \\ \hline \end{array}$ **3.** $\begin{array}{r} 4.2 \\ +\ 3.85 \\ \hline \end{array}$ **4.** $\begin{array}{r} 9 \\ +\ 7.31 \\ \hline \end{array}$ **5.** $\begin{array}{r} 24.04 \\ 1.07 \\ +\ 4.6 \\ \hline \end{array}$

6. Geri bought 2.34 pounds of nectarines and 3.71 pounds of oranges. What was the total weight of the fruit?

Independent Practice *For more practice, see Set G on p. 383.*

Estimate first. Then find each sum.

7. $3.78 + 1.49$ **8.** $6.07 + 8.94$ **9.** $5.5 + 3.86$ **10.** $8.97 + 2.85$ **11.** $7.7 + 6$

12. $8.3 + 17.9 + 58.9$ **13.** $15.3 + 527.11 + 83.96$ **14.** $157 + 38.95 + 26.1$ **15.** $492.64 + 111.8 + 537.43$ **16.** $\$12.09 + 14.60 + 12.55$

17. 24.11 + 52.4 **18.** 37.89 + 98 + 6.2 **19.** 124.5 + 7.66 + 0.31

20. Algebra If $n = 8.2$, what is the value of $7.66 + n$?

21. Mental Math Find 2.5 + 7 + 0.5.

22. Math Reasoning Refer to Example 1 on page 368. Explain why regrouping was done in Step 2.

23. The thermometer below shows Carrie's temperature in degrees Fahrenheit at 8:00 A.M. By suppertime it had risen 3.1 degrees. Estimate her temperature at suppertime. Then find her actual temperature. Do your estimate and actual temperature seem reasonable? Explain.

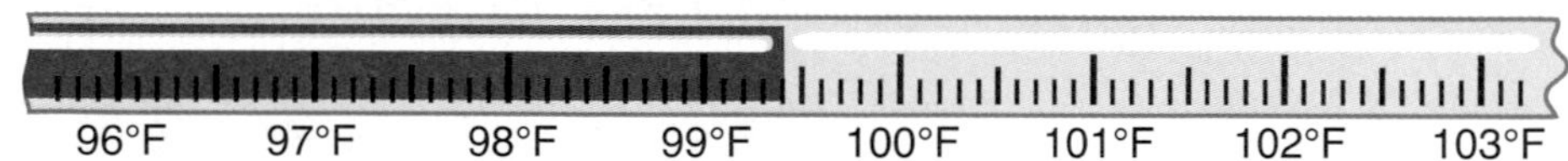

Mixed Review

24. Norio paid $54.32 for shoes. Round this amount to the nearest dollar.

25. Draw a number line and show $\frac{5}{4}$, 1.8, and 1.5.

26. $6 - 3\frac{1}{2}$ **27.** $549 \div 6$ **28.** $\$3.44 \times 13$ **29.** $\frac{1}{4} + \frac{3}{8}$

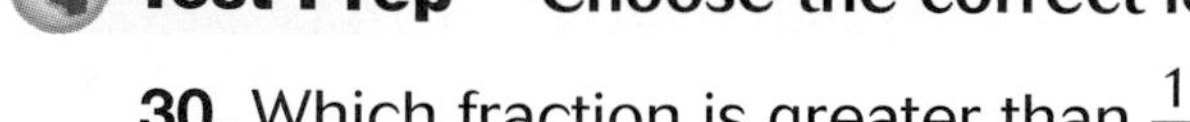

Test Prep **Choose the correct letter for each answer.**

30. (7-8) Which fraction is greater than $\frac{1}{2}$?

A $\frac{1}{4}$ **C** $\frac{2}{3}$

B $\frac{3}{8}$ **D** $\frac{1}{3}$

31. (6-10) What is the average of 12, 15, 19, and 14?

F 14 **H** 17

G 15 **J** 19

Subtracting Decimals

California Content Standard *Number Sense 2.1: Estimate and compute the sum or difference of whole numbers and positive decimals to two places. Also, Number Sense 2.2, Mathematical Reasoning 2.6 (See p. 343.)*

Warm-Up Review

1. 58 − 27
2. 603 − 76
3. Write a decimal equivalent to 13.4.
4. Write 5 as a decimal.

Round to the nearest whole number.

5. 9.7
6. 43.01
7. Moira bought a backpack for $17.32 and a marker for $0.79. She gave the clerk a $20 bill. How much change did she receive?

Math Link You know how to subtract whole numbers. In this lesson, you will learn how to subtract decimals.

Example 1

Find 2.6 − 0.8.

Estimate first by rounding each decimal to the nearest whole number.

2.6 − 0.8 (rounds to) → 3 − 1 = 2

Now subtract to find the actual difference.

Step 1 Line up the decimal points.	**Step 2** Subtract the tenths. Regroup if necessary.	**Step 3** Subtract the ones. Place the decimal point.
2.6 − 0.8	1 16: 2.6 − 0.8 = 8	1 16: 2.6 − 0.8 = 1.8

2.6; 0.8; 1.8

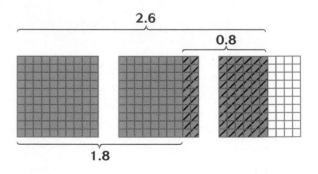

Check by comparing the answer to the estimate. The answer of 1.8 is reasonable because it is close to the estimate of 2.

Example 2

Find 7 − 5.71.

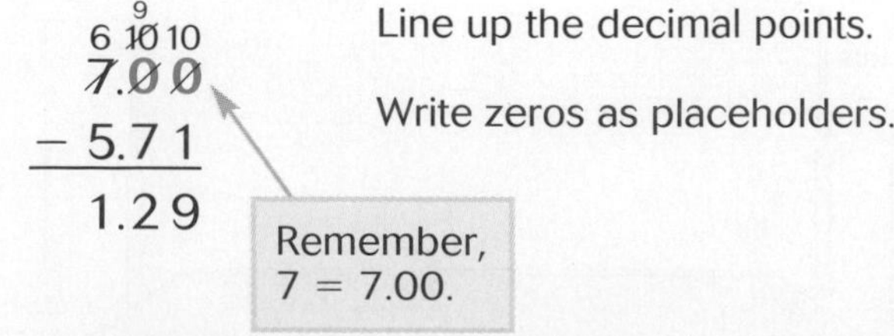

Additional Standards: Algebra and Functions 1.1; Mathematical Reasoning 1.1 (See p. 343.)

Example 3

Find 334.2 − 113.54.

$$\begin{array}{r} \overset{3\ 11\ 10}{33\not{4}.2\not{0}} \\ -\ 113.54 \\ \hline 220.66 \end{array}$$

Line up the decimal points.

Write zeros as placeholders.

Guided Practice *For another example, see Set H on p. 381.*

Estimate first. Then find each difference.

1. 1.9 − 1.2

2. 1.84 − 0.53

3. 3.6 − 1.15

4. 427.25 − 214.8

5. 56 − 34.21

6. Tracks at Dinosaur Valley State Park, in Texas, show that Acrocanthosaurus probably traveled at 5 miles per hour. If Pleurocoelus traveled at 2.7 miles per hour, how much faster could Acrocanthosaurus travel?

Independent Practice *For more practice, see Set H on p. 383.*

Estimate first. Then find each difference.

7. 29.53 − 13.85

8. 59.1 − 20.09

9. 75.58 − 19.73

10. 82.8 − 77.52

11. 90.71 − 47.83

12. 29 − 13.85

13. 509.12 − 210

14. $535.58 − 69.73

15. 812.8 − 707.52

16. 90.71 − 47.8

17. 37.2 − 14.1

18. $84.15 − $16.48

19. 17.08 − 9

20. 60 − 28.15

21. 418.9 − 5.88

22. 25.8 − 9.37

23. Algebra If $w = 77.2$, what is the value of $155 - w$?

24. Mental Math Find 36.4 − 6.4.

25. In Olympic volleyball, the top edge of the net is 2.43 meters for men's volleyball. Using the figure at the right, how much higher off the ground is the net for the men's game than for the women's?

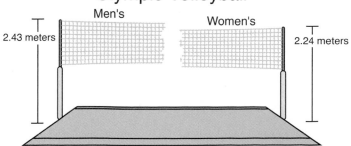

Olympic Volleyball

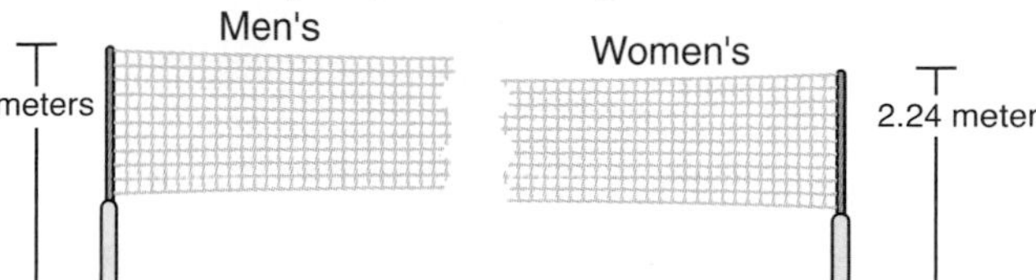

26. In 1990, a French team of four runners set a world record for the 4 × 100 meter relay. The table at the right gives each member's time. How much faster was Sangouma than Moriniére?

1990 French Relay Team	
Team Member	**Time**
Moriniére	10.58 sec
Sangouma	8.9 sec
Trouabal	9.21 sec
Marie-Rose	9.1 sec

27. The team's score in a 4 × 100 meter relay is the sum of all four runners' times. What was the French team's score?

28. **Math Reasoning** When Clint left San Antonio for a drive to Austin, his odometer read 58,453.8. Halfway between San Antonio and Austin, the odometer read 58,490.2. What was the odometer reading when Clint reached Austin?

Mixed Review

29. In 1890, an ancestor of the Venturas bought 12.8 acres of land in Texas. He bought 9 more acres in 1904. Today the Venturas own 42.4 acres. How many acres have been added to the land since 1904?

Round 3.47 to the nearest

30. whole number.

31. tenth.

32. **Algebra** Given the equation $4x = 720$, which of these numbers makes the equation true: 120, 160, 180, 360?

33. 1.5 + 9.3

34. 2.7 + 18 + 3.22

35. $11\frac{3}{5} + 6\frac{1}{5}$

36. You know that 18 × 3 = 54. Does 18 × 3 × 8 = 54 + 8? Why or why not?

Test Prep **Choose the correct letter for each answer.**

37. (9-4) One day a weather report stated that Wichita had 3.1 inches of rain, St. Louis had 3.01 inches, Chicago had 1.3 inches, and Indianapolis had 3.11 inches. Which city had the most rain?

A Wichita **B** St. Louis **C** Chicago **D** Indianapolis

38. (2-7) 10,805 − 2,918 =

F 8,987 **G** 8,113 **H** 7,887 **J** 7,913 **K** NH

Use Homework Workbook 9-10.

Problem-Solving Application:
Comparing Prices

Warm-Up Review

1. $15.18 + $2.30
2. $32.49 × 8
3. $7.32 × 26
4. 3 × (17 + 44)
5. (12 × 71) + (6 × 68)
6. Show 3 ways to make 28¢.

California Content Standard *Mathematical Reasoning 1.1 Analyze problems by identifying relationships, . . . sequencing and prioritizing information, and observing patterns. Also, Algebra and Functions 1.2 (🔑); Mathematical Reasoning 2.3 (See p. 343.)*

Example

The Harpers are visiting Carter Caves in Kentucky. What is the least expensive way they can buy 12 postcards?

Postcards
1 for $0.30
4 for $1.00
10 for $2.00

CARTER CAVES
KENTUCKY

Understand

What do you need to know?

You need to know the different ways 12 postcards can be purchased.

Plan

How can you solve the problem?

Find the costs for different ways to buy 12 postcards. Then compare the costs to see which one is the least expensive.

Solve

Here are three ways to buy 12 postcards.

12 individual cards	1 group of 10 cards and 2 individual cards	3 groups of 4 cards
12 × $0.30 = $3.60	(1 × $2.00) + (2 × $0.30) = $2.60	(3 × $1.00) = $3.00

$2.60 is the least amount of money. So, the least expensive way to buy 12 postcards is to buy one group of 10 cards and 2 individual cards.

Look Back

Are there other ways the Harpers could have purchased 12 postcards? Explain.

Additional Standards: Number Sense 2.1, 3.4 (🔑); Algebra and Functions 1.3 (🔑); Mathematical Reasoning 2.0, 2.4 (See p. 343.)

Guided Practice

1. Look at the cave tour booklet at the right. How much more does it cost for 2 adult tickets than for 2 tickets for children under 12?

2. The Jackson family has 1 adult and 4 children. But 1 of the children will turn 12 tomorrow. How much more would it cost for the family to take the cave tour next week instead of today?

Independent Practice

3. Look at the juice prices at the right. How much cheaper is it to buy a 6-pack of juice than 6 separate bottles?

4. Cave flashlights cost $12.70 without batteries, or $14.85 with 2 batteries. A pack of 2 batteries costs $2.25. Which is the cheaper way to buy a flashlight and 2 batteries?

5. Small cabins cost $37.00 a night for 2 people. There is a $5.00 charge for each extra person. Large cabins cost $50.00 for 4 people. Which is the less expensive way to rent a cabin for a family of four?

Mixed Review

6. Diane took a survey in her class and found that 10 out of the 20 students attended the county fair. Predict how many of the 480 students in Diane's school attended the fair.

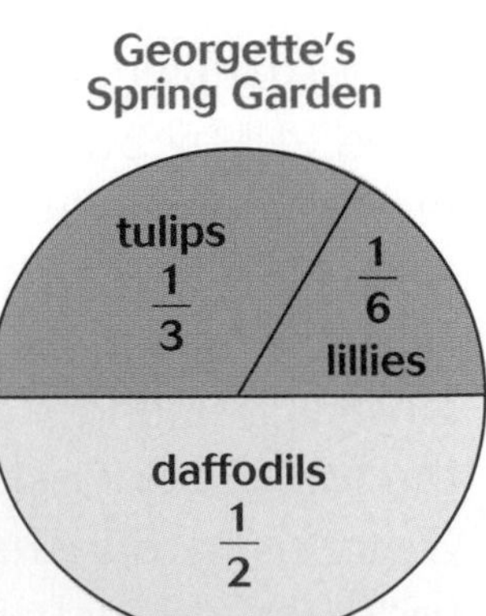

7. The circle graph at the right shows Georgette's plans for her spring garden. If she wants to have 150 flowers in all, how many will be lillies?

Diagnostic Checkpoint

Complete. For Exercises 1–3, use the words from the Word Bank.

Word Bank
decimal
decimal point
equivalent decimals
tenths
hundredths

1. (9-1) ____________________ name the same amount.

2. (9-3) The first place to the right of the decimal point is the ____________________ place.

3. (9-1) The number $\frac{7}{10}$ is in fraction form. The number 0.7 is in ____________________ form.

Estimate first. Then find each sum or difference.

4. (9-9) $85.67 + 68.10$

5. (9-9) $70.13 + 17.43$

6. (9-9) $49.88 + 12.19$

7. (9-9) $80.43 + 7.95$

8. (9-9) $24.50 + 25.81$

9. (9-10) $80.06 - 46.62$

10. (9-10) $69.59 - 59.69$

11. (9-10) $54.38 - 24.53$

12. (9-10) $74.63 - 66.96$

13. (9-10) $89.43 - 87.51$

14. (9-9) 5.95 + 5.39 + 4.67

15. (9-10) 23.5 − 2.52

16. (9-9) 0.23 + 81.2 + 85.71

17. (9-10) 9.87 − 5.3

18. (9-8) A jeweler has chains made out of gold, silver, and copper covered in gold. The silver chain is longer than the copper chain. The gold chain is not the longest or shortest. Which chain is the longest?

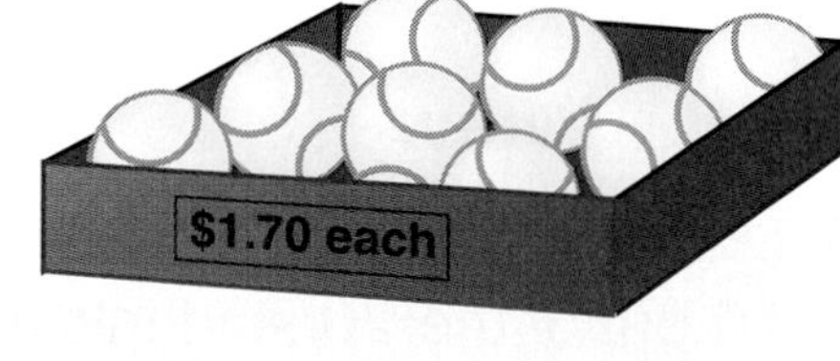

19. (9-11) The organizers of a tennis tournament need to buy 30 tennis balls. What is the least expensive way they could buy 30 balls?

20. (9-8) Silvia is painting a decorative pattern on the top of her desk. The square pattern is 6 inches by 6 inches. Her desk is 30 inches wide and 42 inches long. How many 6-inch-square patterns can she fit on her desk top?

Chapter 9 Test

Write each decimal as a fraction or mixed number. Write each fraction or mixed number as a decimal.

1. $\frac{1}{4}$ **2.** $\frac{23}{100}$ **3.** $4\frac{7}{10}$ **4.** 0.3 **5.** 0.41 **6.** 7.5

Tell the place value of the underlined digit.

7. $75.\underline{8}6$ **8.** $94\underline{3}.7$ **9.** $\underline{5}82.49$ **10.** $769.1\underline{8}$

Order each set of numbers from least to greatest.

11. 6.41; 6.14; 6.44

12. 3.5; 3.55; 3

13. Graph 0.6, $1\frac{3}{4}$, 1.8, and $1\frac{1}{5}$ on a number line. Then order the numbers from least to greatest.

14. Compare. Write $<$, $>$, or $=$ for ●. 1.47 ● 1.74

15. Find a decimal equivalent to 0.6.

16. Write 2.8 in word form.

17. Round 7.85 to the nearest tenth.

Estimate first. Then find each sum or difference.

18. 7.85 + 3.92

19. 8.12 − 5.79

20. 56.9 − 31.56

21. 29.7 + 18.44

22. Louise wants to put a fence between two trees that are 285 meters apart. She has three sections of fencing that measure 87 meters, 120 meters, and 84 meters long. Does she have enough fencing? Explain.

23. Katie made 36 copies at Kwik Kopy. Russell made 36 copies at Economy Copy. How much more did Katie pay than Russell?

ECONOMY COPY
Copies
$0.05 each

24. A fence is 11 sections long. Each section begins and ends with a post. How many posts are there?

Multiple-Choice Chapter 9 Test

Choose the correct letter for each answer.

1. **Patrick bought a sweater for \$36.42 and a pair of shoes for \$66.14. How much did he spend on the sweater and shoes?**

A \$92.00
B \$92.56
C \$102.00
D \$102.56
E NH

2. **546.15 − 213.88**

F 332.12
G 332.27
H 333.73
J 760.03
K NH

3. **Which of the following is *not* less than 35.4?**

A 35.04
B 35.39
C 35.44
D 34.16

4. **8.04 + 3.7**

F 11.74
G 11.47
H 11.07
J 11.04
K NH

5. **What is 21.14 in word form?**

A twenty-one and four tenths
B twenty-one and four hundredths
C twenty-one and fourteen hundredths
D twenty-four and four tenths

6. **Which shows 36.07 written as a mixed number?**

F $36\frac{70}{100}$
G $36\frac{7}{10}$
H $3\frac{67}{100}$
J $36\frac{7}{100}$

7. **Which shows $4\frac{3}{4}$ as a decimal?**

A 4.25
B 4.34
C 4.75
D 4.8

8. **Choose the decimal that describes the shaded area of the model.**

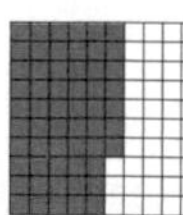

F 0.43
G 0.57
H 4.3
J 5.7

9. **Which is $\frac{35}{100}$ written as a decimal?**

A 0.10
B 0.35
C 3.05
D 3.50

10. Round 36.69 to the nearest whole number.

F 30 H 37
G 36 J 40

---

11. What point shows the location of $3\frac{1}{4}$?

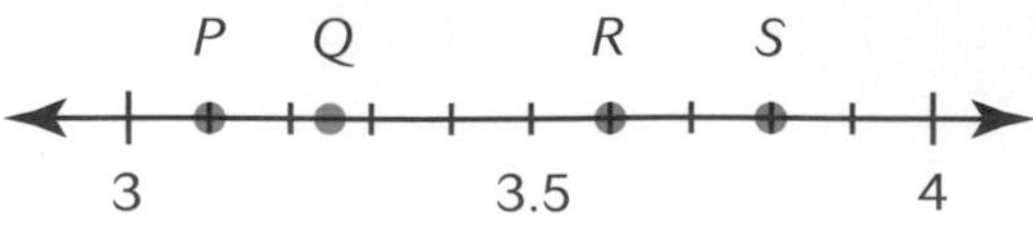

A point P C point R
B point Q D point S

---

12. Which digit is in the hundredths place in 19,346.57?

F 3
G 4
H 6
J 7

---

13. Choose the set of numbers that are in order from *least* to *greatest*.

A 43.04, 44.40, 43.34, 44.75
B 70.14, 70.11, 70.05, 69.39
C 143.60, 143.66, 144.06, 144.36
D 111.72, 112.79, 113.80, 112.84

---

14. Color copies cost $0.59 each. Black and white copies cost $0.09 each. How much will you save if you get 10 black and white copies, instead of color copies?

F $5.90 H $3.50
G $5.00 J $0.50

---

15. Claire, Tommy, Rick, Luis, and Lily are in line for movie tickets. Luis is second. Claire is in the middle and Lily is first. Tommy isn't last. Choose the correct order of friends from first to last.

A Luis, Lily, Claire, Rick, Tommy
B Lily, Luis, Claire, Tommy, Rick
C Tommy, Luis, Claire, Rick, Lily
D Rick, Tommy, Claire, Luis, Lily

---

16. Orangeton is between Bluetown and Redville. It is 43.5 miles from Bluetown to Orangeton. It is 36.7 miles from Orangeton to Redville. Estimate to the nearest whole number how far it is from Bluetown to Redville.

F 7 miles H 81 miles
G 44 miles J 121 miles

---

17. Jody is an airline flight attendant. She flew on 6 flights last month. Each flight averaged 1,600 miles. Next month she plans on flying twice as much as last month. How many miles does she plan on flying?

A 4,800 miles
B 7,200 miles
C 9,600 miles
D 19,200 miles

Reteaching

Set A (pages 344–347)

Write a fraction and a decimal for the model.

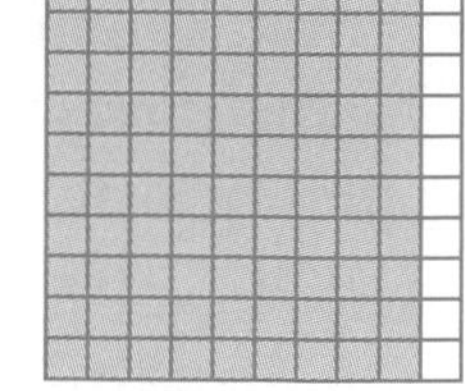

$\frac{90}{100}$ or $\frac{9}{10}$

0.90 or 0.9

Say: ninety hundredths or nine tenths.

Remember you can write or remove a zero from the end of a decimal without changing its value.

Write each fraction as a decimal.

1. $\frac{4}{10}$ **2.** $\frac{37}{100}$ **3.** $\frac{60}{100}$

Set B (pages 348–350)

Write $3\frac{3}{20}$ as a decimal.

$$3\frac{3}{20} = 3\frac{15}{100} = 3.15 \quad (\times 5)$$

Say: three and fifteen hundredths.

Remember to write an equivalent fraction with a denominator of either 10 or 100.

Write each number as a decimal.

1. $9\frac{7}{10}$ **2.** $4\frac{63}{100}$ **3.** $\frac{8}{5}$

Set C (pages 352–353)

Write nine and six hundredths in decimal form.

ones	tenths	hundredths
9.	0	6

Decimal form: 9.06

Remember that a place-value chart can help you read and write decimals.

Write each as a decimal.

1. seven and nine tenths

2. one and forty-six hundredths

3. four dollars and eight cents

Set D (pages 354–356)

Order these numbers from least to greatest: 10.15, 10.1, 10.26.

10.15
10.10
10.26

2 > 1 so 10.26 is the greatest.

10.15
10.10
10.26

5 > 0 so 10.15 > 10.1.

The numbers from least to greatest are: 10.1, 10.15, 10.26.

Remember you can use equivalent decimals so the digits line up.

Order each set of numbers from least to greatest.

1. 5.39, 5.36, 5.79

2. 8.93, 8.9, 8.33

3. 1.75, 1.7, 1.78

Set E (pages 357–359)

Graph 8.7, $8\frac{3}{10}$, and 8.45 on a number line. Then order the numbers from least to greatest.

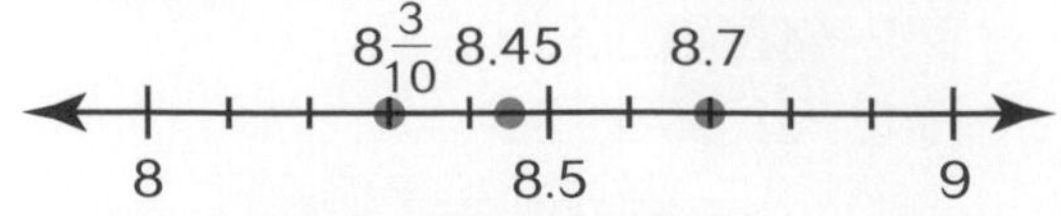

The numbers from least to greatest are: $8\frac{3}{10}$, 8.45, 8.7.

Remember that on a number line, numbers increase from left to right.

What point shows the location of each number?

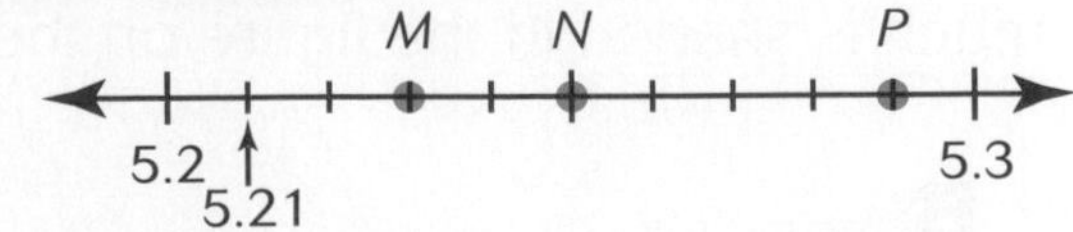

1. 5.29 **2.** 5.23 **3.** $5\frac{1}{4}$

Set F (pages 362–364)

Round 5.28 to the nearest tenth.

Look at the digit to the right of the tenths place.

5.28 Since 8 > 5, round up.

5.28 rounds to 5.3.

Remember to round up if the digit to the right is 5 or more. Round down if it is less than 5.

Round each decimal to the nearest tenth.

1. 9.68 **2.** 16.42 **3.** 12.17

Set G (pages 368–370)

Find 4.2 + 0.57.

Estimate: 4 + 1 = 5

$$\begin{array}{r} 4.20 \\ +0.57 \\ \hline 4.77 \end{array}$$

Line up the decimal points.
Write zeros as placeholders.
Add the hundredths, then the tenths, then the ones.

Place decimal point.

Remember to line up the decimal points before you add.

Estimate first. Then find each sum.

1. 1.59 + 8.02 **2.** 3.61 + 5.47

3. 6.26 + 4.4 **4.** 7.45 + 3.6

5. 1.72 + 3.15 + 6.2

Set H (pages 371–373)

Find 9 − 7.2.

$$\begin{array}{r} \scriptstyle 8\ 10 \\ \not{9}.\not{0} \\ -7.2 \\ \hline 1.8 \end{array}$$

Line up the decimal points.
Write zeros as placeholders.
Then subtract the tenths. Regroup if necessary. Subtract the ones.

Remember you can write equivalent decimals to help you line up the digits.

Estimate first. Then find each difference.

1. 98.16 − 55.46 **2.** 82.5 − 33.3

3. 8.19 − 2.5 **4.** 71.2 − 66.98

More Practice

Set A (pages 344–347)

Write each fraction as a decimal.

1. $\frac{7}{10}$
2. $\frac{3}{4}$
3. $\frac{2}{5}$
4. $\frac{29}{100}$
5. Write a fraction and a decimal to tell how much is shaded in the figure on the right.

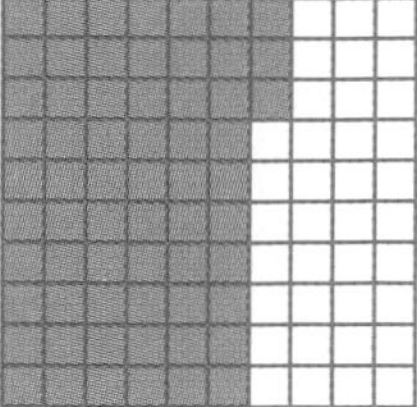

Set B (pages 348–350)

Write each number as a decimal.

1. $3\frac{9}{10}$
2. $4\frac{5}{10}$
3. $5\frac{67}{100}$
4. $7\frac{5}{100}$
5. $\frac{6}{5}$

Write each decimal as a fraction or mixed number.

6. 0.19
7. 2.25
8. 0.60
9. 16.53
10. 0.1
11. A puppy weighed 8.4 pounds. Write the weight as a mixed number.

Set C (pages 352–353)

Tell the place value of the underlined digit.

1. $863.9\underline{7}$
2. $\underline{6}06.93$
3. $233.\underline{6}0$
4. $1\underline{2}.49$

Write each as a decimal.

5. nineteen and eight tenths
6. seven and five hundredths
7. Chelsea is 126.4 centimeters tall. What is the place value of 4 in 126.4?

Set D (pages 354–356)

Order each set of numbers from greatest to least.

1. 6.14, 6.41, 6.04
2. 4.38, 4.83, 8.34
3. 3.27, 3.37, 3.7
4. The post office charges by weight to deliver packages. If a package weighs 6.75 pounds or less, it costs $3.95 to mail. If the package weighs more than 6.75 pounds, it costs $5.54 to mail. How much would be charged for a package that weighs 6.57 pounds?

Set E (pages 357–359)

What point shows the location of each number?

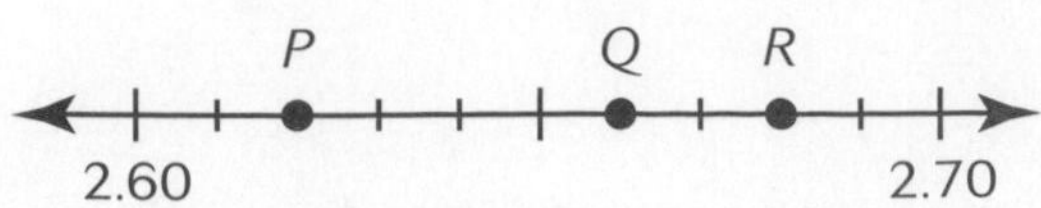

1. 2.68 **2.** 2.62 **3.** 2.66

Show each set of numbers on a number line. Then order the numbers from least to greatest.

4. $4\frac{7}{10}$, $4\frac{1}{2}$, 4.6 **5.** $9\frac{74}{100}$, 9.8, $9\frac{3}{4}$

6. What weight does the scale show?

Set F (pages 362–364)

Round each decimal to the nearest whole number.

1. 8.4 **2.** 3.9 **3.** 8.06 **4.** 1.08 **5.** 2.91

Round each decimal to the nearest tenth.

6. 7.82 **7.** 3.56 **8.** 25.35 **9.** 19.41 **10.** 16.68

11. It rained 1.78 inches. Round 1.78 to the nearest tenth.

Set G (pages 368–370)

Estimate first. Then find each sum.

1. $\begin{array}{r} 28.6 \\ +39.57 \\ \hline \end{array}$ **2.** $\begin{array}{r} 41.87 \\ +85.19 \\ \hline \end{array}$ **3.** $\begin{array}{r} 60.16 \\ +23.7 \\ \hline \end{array}$ **4.** $\begin{array}{r} 59.33 \\ +24.56 \\ \hline \end{array}$ **5.** $\begin{array}{r} 52.36 \\ +60.68 \\ \hline \end{array}$

6. Jack biked 12.5 miles on Tuesday, 15.25 miles on Friday, and 9.35 miles on Saturday. How many miles did he bike in all?

Set H (pages 371–373)

Estimate first. Then find each difference.

1. $\begin{array}{r} 67.62 \\ -58.85 \\ \hline \end{array}$ **2.** $\begin{array}{r} 91.66 \\ -87.2 \\ \hline \end{array}$ **3.** $\begin{array}{r} 79.17 \\ -46.76 \\ \hline \end{array}$ **4.** $\begin{array}{r} 94.2 \\ -58.56 \\ \hline \end{array}$ **5.** $\begin{array}{r} 81 \\ -78.66 \\ \hline \end{array}$

6. Tim ran 1.48 kilometers. Ali ran 2.3 kilometers. How much farther did Ali run than Tim?

TEST PREP

Problem-Solving: Preparing for Tests

Choose the correct letter for each answer.

---

1. **Zack had 60 inches of ribbon. He used 34 inches to decorate a present. Then he used half of the ribbon that was left to decorate another present. How much ribbon does Zack have left now?**

   A 13 inches
   B 17 inches
   C 26 inches
   D 30 inches
   E NH

Tip
Decide what steps you need to do and in what order you should do them.

---

2. **Ryan rode his bike 8 miles on Tuesday, 12 miles on Wednesday, 6 miles on Thursday, and 11 miles on Friday. How many miles did he ride on Tuesday and Thursday?**

   F 2 mi
   G 14 mi
   H 20 mi
   J 37 mi
   K NH

Tip
Read the question carefully and use only the information you need.

---

3. **Erin used a catalog to order some shirts. She noticed that the code numbers for the first 4 shirts were as follows: 00438, 00458, 00478, and 00498. If the code numbers continue in this pattern, what will be the code numbers of the next 3 shirts?**

   A 00508, 00528, 00548
   B 00508, 00518, 00528
   C 00518, 00538, 00558
   D 00518, 00528, 00538

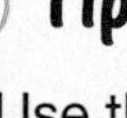

Use the *Find a Pattern* strategy to solve this problem. Start by adding to find how the numbers are increasing.

4. **Nick mailed three packages. The weights of the packages were 21 pounds, 18 pounds, and 33 pounds. About how much did the three packages weigh altogether?**

F	60 pounds	**J**	90 pounds
G	70 pounds	**K**	NH
H	80 pounds		

5. **A soccer team held a bake sale to raise money to buy 20 new uniforms. The uniforms cost $15 each. If the team made $224 from the bake sale, how much more money do they need to buy the uniforms?**

A	$76	**D**	$300
B	$176	**E**	NH
C	$239		

6. **Hal used 213 meters of fence for one of his fields and 380 meters of fence for another field. Which is the best estimate of the amount of fence Hal used in all?**

F	300 meters	**J**	700 meters
G	400 meters	**K**	NH
H	600 meters		

7. **Four people shared 3 pizzas equally. Each pizza had 8 slices. Which number sentence shows how many slices of pizza each person ate?**

A $4 \times 3 = 12$

B $4 + 3 + 8 = 15$

C $8 \div 4 = 2$

D $24 \div 4 = 6$

8. **A CD has 8 songs on it. The shortest song is 2 minutes long, and the longest song is 6 minutes long. Which is reasonable for the total time it takes to hear all 8 songs?**

F Less than 8 minutes

G Between 8 and 10 minutes

H Between 10 and 15 minutes

J More than 20 minutes

Use the graph for Questions 9 and 10.

Logan made a graph to show the favorite movies of students at his school.

Favorite Kinds of Movies

Adventure	full figure, full figure, full figure, full figure, half figure
Western	full figure, full figure
Science Fiction	full figure, full figure, half figure
Romance	full figure, full figure, full figure, full figure

Each full figure stands for 50 people.

9. **How many people chose science fiction or western movies as their favorite?**

A	25	**D**	650
B	125	**E**	NH
C	225		

10. **How many more people chose adventure movies than romance movies as their favorite?**

F	25	**J**	425
G	50	**K**	NH
H	100		

TEST PREP

Multiple-Choice Cumulative Review

Choose the correct letter for each answer.

Number Sense

1. Which is a set of even numbers?

   A 6, 12, 14, 20
   B 5, 8, 9, 11
   C 7, 13, 15, 19
   D 10, 21, 32, 43

2. An airplane flies at thirty-three thousand, five hundred fifty feet. How is this number written?

   F 3,355
   G 30,355
   H 33,550
   J 335,050
   K NH

3. Which decimal tells how much is shaded?

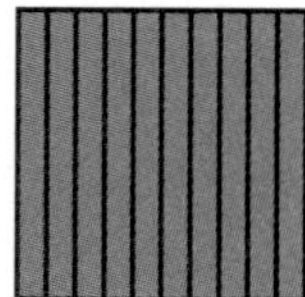
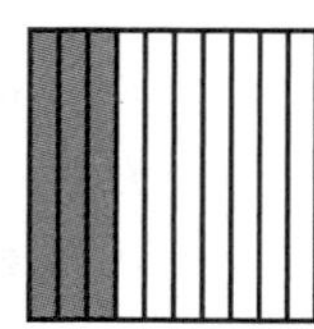

   A 20.7
   B 20.3
   C 2.7
   D 2.3
   E NH

4. Point *R* best represents what number?

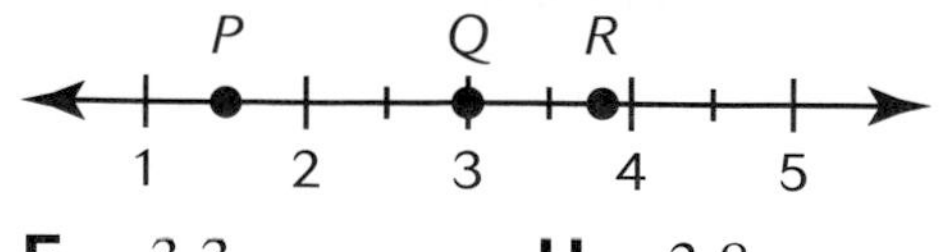

   F 3.3
   G 3.5
   H 3.8
   J 4.2

5. Brian had $20.50. He spent $3.50 on a movie ticket and $4.25 on popcorn and a drink. How much did he spend in all?

   A $17.00
   B $16.25
   C $12.75
   D $7.75
   E NH

6. Kate ordered 20 boxes of pens for her office. There are 12 pens in each box. How many pens did Kate order?

   F 2,400
   G 240
   H 144
   J 24
   K NH

7. There are 31 rows of seats on an airplane. If 6 passengers can sit in each row, *about* how many passengers can the plane hold?

   A 130
   B 150
   C 180
   D 280

8. Grant paid for a CD with a $20 bill. His change is shown below. How much did Grant spend?

   F $16
   G $14
   H $12
   J $5
   K NH

Measurement and Geometry

9. Which is the best estimate of the *area* of the shaded region?

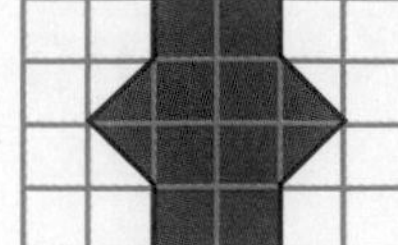

A 8 square units
B 10 square units
C 12 square units
D 24 square units
E NH

10. Samantha's fish tank holds 50 gallons of water. How many *quarts* is that? (Hint: 4 quarts equals 1 gallon.)

F 25 qt
G 54 qt
H 100 qt
J 200 qt
K NH

11. Bonnie's airplane flight took 2 hours 10 minutes. If the plane took off at 11:00 A.M., what time did it land?

A 1:10 P.M.
B 1:25 P.M.
C 2:10 P.M.
D 2:25 P.M.
E NH

12. The *perimeter* of the patio below is 34 feet. If the length is 10 feet, what is the width?

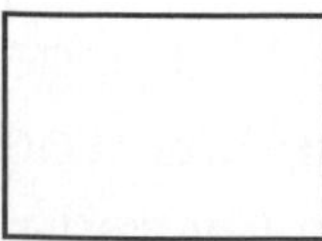

F 23 ft
G 13 ft
H $10\frac{1}{2}$ ft
J 7 ft
K NH

Statistics, Data Analysis, and Probability

Use the graph for Questions 13–16.

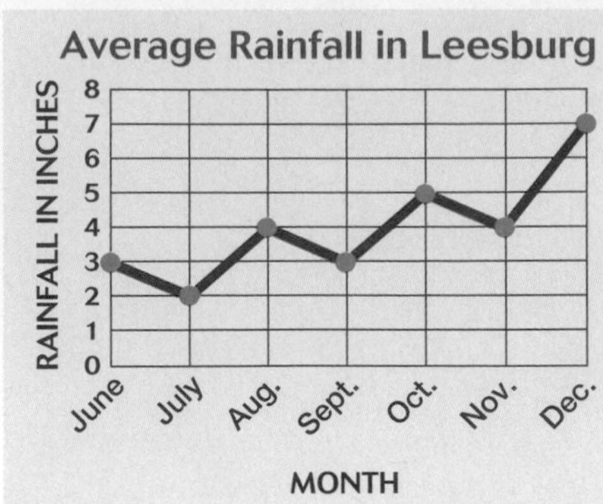

13. In which month did it rain the least?

A June
B July
C September
D November

14. How much rain did Leesburg receive in August?

F 4 in.
G $3\frac{1}{2}$ in.
H 2 in.
J 1 in.
K NH

15. How many more inches of rain were there in October than in July?

A 7 in.
B 5 in.
C 3 in.
D 2 in.
E NH

16. The largest difference in rainfall was between which 2 months?

F June and July
G August and September
H October and November
J November and December

Data and Graphs

Diagnosing Readiness

In Chapter 10, you will use these skills:

Ⓐ Using Variables

(pages 62–65)

Evaluate each expression for $n = 7$.

1. $38 + n$ **2.** $n + 35$

3. $119 - n$ **4.** $n - 2$

Solve each equation by testing values for x.

5. $x + 9 = 17$

6. $20 - x = 4$

7. $15 + x = 24$

8. $x - 6 = 11$

Ⓑ Addition and Subtraction

(pages 42–49)

9. $\begin{array}{r} 361 \\ +\ 42 \\ \hline \end{array}$ **10.** $\begin{array}{r} 5,456 \\ +1,122 \\ \hline \end{array}$

11. $\begin{array}{r} 124 \\ -\ 78 \\ \hline \end{array}$ **12.** $\begin{array}{r} 466 \\ -\ 172 \\ \hline \end{array}$

13. Cody has 2 weeks to read a 150-page book. So far he has read 54 pages. How many pages does he have left to read?

C Finding the Mean

(pages 226–227)

Find the mean of each group of numbers.

14. 3, 5, 2, 7, 8

15. 10, 20, 30, 40

16. 22, 18, 35, 12, 18

17. Last week, Sally took 3 math quizzes. Her scores were 85, 92, and 81. Find the average of her quiz scores.

D Comparing and Ordering Whole Numbers

(pages 8–9)

Order the numbers from least to greatest.

18. 3,147 3,771 3,741 3,711

19. 26,400 2,604 24,600

Compare. Use >, <, or =.

20. 6,299 ● 6,099

21. 57,008 ● 5,708

22. 3,011,110 ● 3,101,001

23. 4,576,341 ● 4,656,341

E Reading Bar Graphs

(Grade 3)

The bar graph below shows the number of fans who attended basketball games at Westlake School.

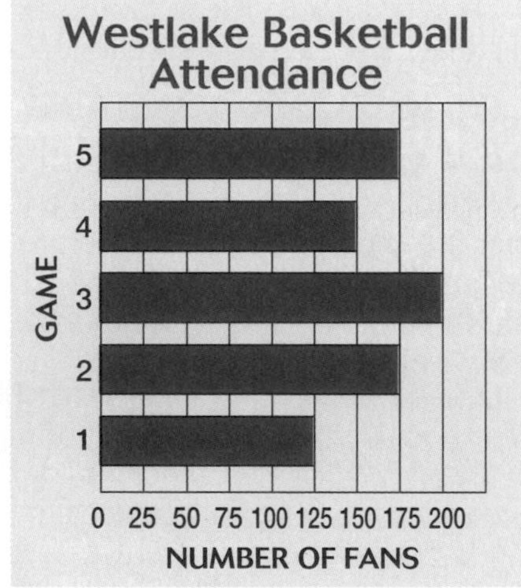

24. How many fans attended Game 2?

25. How many more fans attended Game 3 than Game 4?

26. At which two games was the attendance the same?

27. Which games were seen by more than 150 fans?

28. Which game had the greatest number of fans?

To the Family and Student

Looking Back	Chapter 10	Looking Ahead
In Grade 3, students learned how to organize data, make line plots, and graph ordered pairs.	In this chapter, students will learn how to organize data, make and read bar and line graphs, and graph equations.	In Grade 5, students will learn how to make double bar graphs, graph on the coordinate plane, and use histograms.

Math and Everyday Living

Opportunities to apply the concepts of Chapter 10 abound in everyday situations. During the chapter, think about how data and statistics can be used to solve a variety of real-world problems. The following examples suggest just a few of the many situations that could launch a discussion about data and statistics.

Math and Shopping
You are shopping for a sweater for your friend's birthday. Since you have a certain amount of money to spend, you compare the prices of sweaters at various stores. The sweaters you like cost $34, $19.50, $25, $26, and $37. Find the range of the sweater prices.

Math and Measurement
You organize the heights of your classmates in a stem-and-leaf-plot. How many students have a height greater than 50 inches? How many students have a height less than 50 inches?

Student Heights in Inches
54, 49, 48, 50, 52, 55, 56, 47, 58

Math and Pets
You want to find out the most popular pet among students in your class. Make a tally chart to organize your data.

Math and Business
You earn money feeding your neighbors' pets while they are on vacation. You want to compare your income by week for the past 4 weeks. Make a line graph for the data shown in the table below. During which week did you make the most money?

Weekly Income	
Week 1	$15
Week 2	$12
Week 3	$10
Week 4	$16

Math and Weather
You want to organize the following monthly rainfall totals in a line graph. Which month had the greatest rainfall?

Month	Rainfall Total
November	4 in.
December	5 in.
January	8 in.
February	6 in.

Math at the Library
The librarian keeps a record of the number of each type of book borrowed in one day. Make a bar graph using the data below.

Library Books Borrowed	
Mysteries	33
Science Fiction	45
Romance	12
Historical Fiction	22

California Content Standards in Chapter 10 Lessons*

	Teach and Practice	Practice
Number Sense		
1.2 (key) Order and compare whole numbers and decimals to two decimal places		10-2, 10-3
Algebra and Functions		
1.1 Use letters, boxes, or other symbols to stand for any number in simple expressions or equations (e.g., demonstrate an understanding and the use of the concept of a variable).		10-10
1.5 (key) Understand that an equation such as $y = 3x + 5$ is a prescription for determining a second number when a first number is given.	10-10	
Measurement and Geometry		
2.0 (key) Students use two-dimensional coordinate grids to represent points and graph lines and simple figures.	10-8	
2.1 (key) Draw the points corresponding to linear relationships on graph paper (e.g., draw 10 points on the graph of the equation $y = 3x$ and connect them by using a straight line).	10-10	
2.2 (key) Understand that the length of a horizontal line segment equals the difference of the x-coordinates.	10-9	
2.3 (key) Understand that the length of a vertical line segment equals the difference of the y-coordinates.	10-9	

	Teach and Practice	Practice
Statistics, Data Analysis, and Probability		
1.0 Students organize, represent, and interpret numerical and categorical data and clearly communicate their findings.	10-2, 10-3, 10-5, 10-6, 10-11	10-1, 10-4, 10-7
1.1 Formulate survey questions; systematically collect and represent data on a number line; and coordinate graphs, tables, and charts.	10-1, 10-3, 10-4	
1.2 Identify the mode(s) for sets of categorical data and the mode(s), median, and any apparent outliers for numerical data sets.	10-1, 10-3, 10-4	
1.3 Interpret one- and two-variable data graphs to answer questions about a situation.	10-2, 10-5, 10-6, 10-11	10-4, 10-7
Mathematical Reasoning		
1.0 Students make decisions about how to approach problems.		10-7
1.1 Analyze problems by identifying relationships, distinguishing relevant from irrelevant information, sequencing and prioritizing information, and observing patterns.		10-5
2.0 Students use strategies, skills, and concepts in finding solutions.		10-5, 10-7, 10-9, 10-11
2.3 Use a variety of methods, such as words, numbers, symbols, charts, graphs, tables, diagrams, and models, to explain mathematical reasoning	10-7	10-1, 10-2, 10-8, 10-10
2.4 Express the solution clearly and logically by using the appropriate mathematical notation and terms and clear language; support solutions with evidence in both verbal and symbolic work.		10-1, 10-2
3.2 Note the method of deriving the solution and demonstrate a conceptual understanding of the derivation by solving similar problems.		10-7

* The symbol (key) indicates a key standard as designated in the Mathematics Framework for California Public Schools. Full statements of the California Content Standards are found at the beginning of this book following the Table of Contents.

Collecting and Organizing Data

California Content Standards *Statistics, Data Analysis, and Probability 1.1: Formulate survey questions; systematically collect and represent data . . . [in] tables and charts. Also, Statistics, Data Analysis, and Probability 1.2* *(See p. 391.)*

Math Link You know how to compare and order numbers. Now you will learn to collect, organize, and analyze numbers of a data set.

Warm-Up Review

1. 23 − 18
2. 105 − 48

Order each set of numbers from least to greatest.

3. 21, 17, 12, 15, 22, 18
4. 98, 103, 87, 88, 94, 79
5. Peter earned $5.50 for each driveway he shoveled. He worked for 4 hours and shoveled 6 driveways. How much did he earn?

Example 1

Mr. Chang asked his fifteen students the survey question, "How many pets do you have?" The class collected pieces of information, or **data**, and organized them in a **tally chart**, which is shown at the right.

Mr. Chang's Class Survey

Number of Pets	Number of Students
0	||
1	~~||||~~
2	||||
3	||
4	|
5	
6	|

The mode is 1.

The **range** is the difference between the greatest number and the least number: 6 − 0 = 6. The range is 6 for these data.

The **mode** is the number that occurs most often. The mode is 1 for these data. Some data sets have no mode. Some have more than one mode.

The **median** is a middle value. To find the median, first list the data in order. For an odd number of numbers, the median is the number in the middle. For these data, the median is 2.

0, 0, 1, 1, 1, 1, 1, 2, 2, 2, 2, 3, 3, 4, 6

The median is 2.

Word Bank

- data
- tally chart
- range
- mode
- median

Example 2

Find the median for this set of data: 56, 17, 50, 22, 40, 61.

First list the data in order. When there are an even number of numbers, the median is the number halfway between the two middle numbers.

17, 22, 40, 50, 56, 61

The median is 45.

Additional Standards: Statistics, Data Analysis, and Probability 1.0; Mathematical Reasoning 2.3, 2.4 *(See p. 391.)*

Guided Practice *For another example, see Set A on p. 422.*

Find the range, mode, and median of each data set.

1. 2, 5, 8, 4, 3, 9, 3 **2.** 18, 22, 23, 22, 14, 22, 17 **3.** 78, 63, 84, 76

4. Write a survey question to ask all the students in your class. Organize the data in a tally chart. Find the range, mode, and median for your class data.

Independent Practice *For more practice, see Set A on p. 426.*

Find the range, mode(s), and median of each data set.

5. 7, 3, 2, 7, 6, 7, 1, 4 **6.** 45, 44, 49, 47, 41 **7.** 20, 11, 13, 15, 11, 25, 20

Use the given data about cats' weights for Exercises 8–11.

8. Organize the data in a tally chart.

9. Find the range of weights.

10. Find the mode of the weights.

11. Find the median weight.

12. An automobile company asked its customers the survey question "What is your favorite automobile color?" The results are given in the table at the right. What is the mode of the colors?

Favorite Automobile Color	
Black	58
Blue	87
Green	43
Red	34
White	55

13. Math Reasoning Can the median and mode of a data set be the same number? Explain.

Mixed Review

14. Raffle tickets sell for $2 each or 3 tickets for $5. You need 9 tickets. How much money can you save if you buy them in sets of 3?

15. 18.6 − 13.8 **16.** 12.5 + 97 + 3.4 **17.** 50.09 − 38.17

Test Prep Choose the correct letter for each answer.

18. Which is a multiple of 6? (3-1)

A 16 C 62
B 30 D 40

19. Which has a remainder of 4? (6-3)

F 64 ÷ 4 H 82 ÷ 5
G 29 ÷ 6 J 67 ÷ 7

Making a Bar Graph

California Content Standards *Statistics, Data Analysis, and Probability 1.0: Students organize, represent, and interpret numerical and categorical data and clearly communicate their findings. Also, Statistics, Data Analysis, and Probability 1.3 (See p. 391.)*

Math Link You know how to organize data in a tally chart. In this lesson you will learn to make a bar graph to display data.

Example

Some students voted for their favorite type of pet. The results are given in the table at the right. Make a **bar graph** to show the data.

You can organize the data in a vertical bar graph. First draw and label the side and the bottom of the graph. Use a scale that begins at 0 and goes beyond the highest number in the data. Draw bars on the graph that show the number of students who voted for each type of pet. Choose a title for your graph.

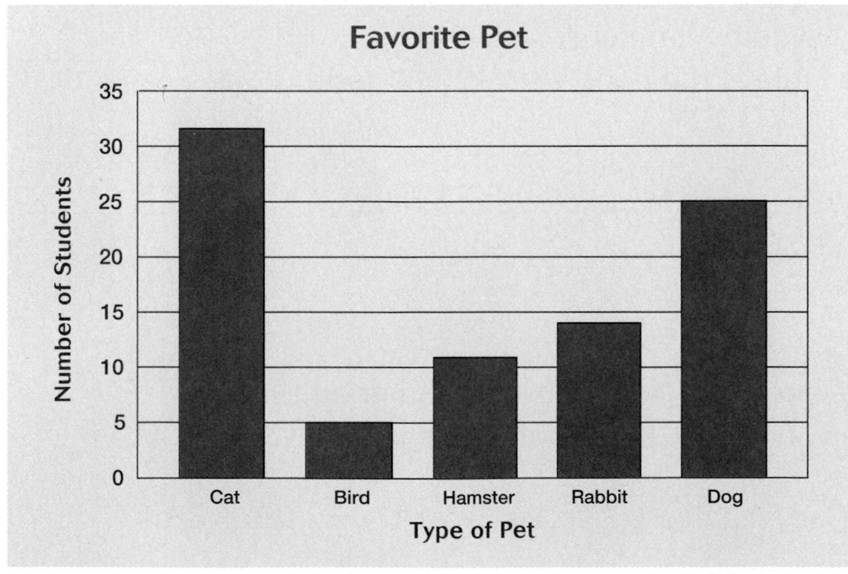

In the bar graph above, the longest bar shows that cat received the most votes as the favorite type of pet. The shortest bar shows that bird received the least number of votes as the favorite type of pet.

Warm-Up Review

Name the two tens each number is between.

1. 67 **2.** 81 **3.** 43

Find the next three numbers in each pattern:

4. 0, 15, 30, 45, ■, ■, ■

5. 250, 225, 200, 175, ■, ■, ■

6. Jeff checked out 4 books from the library on Monday, 2 books on Tuesday, and 7 books on Wednesday. How many more books did he check out on Wednesday than on Monday?

Favorite Pet

Type of Pet	Number of Students
Cat	32
Bird	5
Hamster	11
Rabbit	14
Dog	25

Word Bank

bar graph

Additional Standards: Number Sense 1.2 (key); Mathematical Reasoning 2.3, 2.4 (See p. 391.)

Guided Practice *For another example, see Set B on p. 422.*

Use the horizontal bar graph shown at the right.

1. Who has the longest arm span?
2. About how much longer is Nora's arm span than Mario's?
3. Do any students have the same arm span? How can you tell?
4. What makes a horizontal bar graph different from a vertical bar graph? How are they the same?

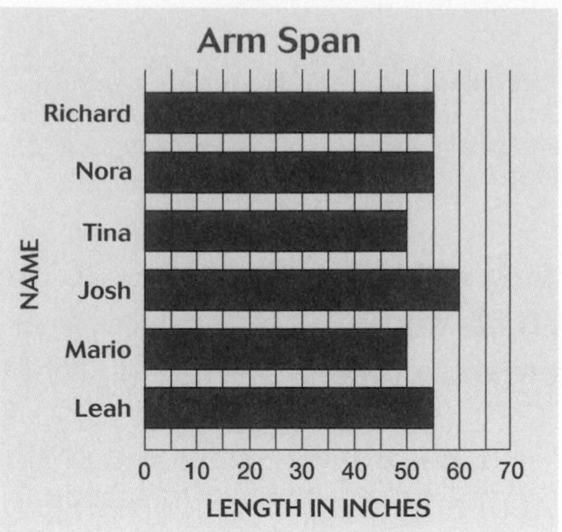

Independent Practice *For more practice, see Set B on p. 426.*

5. Make a bar graph to display the data in the table.

Animal	Number of Teeth
Dog	42
Human	32
Hyena	34
Walrus	18

Use the bar graph you made in Exercise 5.

6. Which animal has the most teeth?
7. Which animal has about the same number of teeth as a human?
8. **Math Reasoning** How does a bar graph help you compare data?

Mixed Review

9. Sarah needs 6 party invitations. They cost \$0.75 each or a box of 6 for \$3.95. How should she buy 6 invitations? Why?
10. Find the median, mode, and range of 18, 12, 14, 19, 23, 16, 21.

11. 2.8 + 3.5 **12.** 16.7 − 13.8 **13.** 4.52 + 7.9 **14.** 9.46 − 2.99

Test Prep **Choose the correct letter for the answer.**

15. (10-1) Which survey question would you use if you wanted to know how students spend their free time?

A Do you like to play computer games?
B How many hours a day do you study?
C What do you like to do in your free time?
D What is your favorite sport?

Stem-and-Leaf Plots

California Content Standards *Statistics, Data Analysis, and Probability 1.0: Students organize, represent, and interpret numerical and categorical data and clearly communicate their findings. Also, Statistics, Data Analysis, and Probability 1.2 (See p. 391.)*

Math Link You know how to organize data in tally charts and bar graphs. Now you will learn how to organize data in stem-and-leaf plots.

You can organize data in a **stem-and-leaf plot**. A stem-and-leaf plot is a graph that uses place value to organize data.

Warm-Up Review

Write the value of 7 in each number.

1. 712
2. 79
3. 5,807
4. 7,511
5. Name the tens digit in 84.
6. Name the ones digit in 29.
7. There are 24 students in your class. Ten are boys. What fraction of the students in your class are girls? Write the fraction in simplest form.

Word Bank

stem-and-leaf plot
stem
leaf

Example

The heights of nine fourth-grade students are 56, 61, 61, 57, 58, 57, 62, 61, and 58 inches. Organize this data in a stem-and-leaf plot. Find the mean, median, mode, and range of the heights.

Height in Inches

Stem	Leaves
5	6, 7, 7, 8, 8
6	1, 1, 1, 2

Each **stem** stands for the first digit of each number.

Record the tens digits in order from least to greatest.

Each **leaf** stands for the second digit of each number.

Record the ones digits in order from least to greatest.

A stem of 5 and a leaf of 7 represents 57 inches.

Mean
Find the sum of all the numbers in the set of data: 56 + 57 + 57 + 58 + 58 + 61 + 61 + 61 + 62 = 531. Then divide by the number of addends: 531 ÷ 9 = 59. The mean height is 59 inches.

Median
Find the middle number of these odd number of data.

56, 57, 57, 58, **58**, 61, 61, 61, 62

The median height is 58 inches.

Mode
Find the number that occurs most often in the set of data. The mode is 61 inches.

Range
Find the difference between the greatest number and the least number in the set of data:
62 − 56 = 6. The range is 6 inches.

 Additional Standard: Number Sense 1.2 (key) (See p. 391.)

Guided Practice *For another example, see Set C on p. 423.*

1. Copy and complete the stem-and-leaf plot at the right for the lengths, in feet, of some species of whales: 20, 32, 50, 50, 58, 60, 61, 64, 82.

Stem	Leaves
2	
3	
4	
5	
6	
7	
8	

2. Find the mean.

3. Find the range.

4. Find the mode.

5. Find the median.

Independent Practice *For more practice, see Set C on p. 427.*

Use the data in the table for Exercises 6–8.

Test Scores		
85	88	76
83	79	80
89	75	83

6. Organize the test scores in a stem-and-leaf plot.

7. Find the mean, median, and mode of the test scores.

8. Keith says his score has an even number as a leaf and 7 as a stem. Find Keith's test score.

Use the data at the right for Exercises 9–13.

9. How many raccoon weights are recorded in the stem-and-leaf plot?

10. Find the greatest weight. Find the least weight.

11. How many raccoons weighed less than 30 pounds? How many weighed more than 30 pounds?

12. What is the range of the weights?

Raccoon Weights (lb)

Stem	Leaf
0	6, 9, 9
1	0, 5, 5, 7, 9
2	0, 1, 6, 6, 9
3	3, 4, 8, 8, 8, 9
4	2, 2, 3, 3, 3, 4, 7

Mixed Review

13. Suppose you want to organize the raccoon weights in a bar graph. Which bar would be the longest? Explain.

14. 324×50 **15.** $865 \div 5$ **16.** $715 + 854$ **17.** $8760 - 24$

Test Prep **Choose the correct letter for each answer.**

18. How many tens are in 800? (1-1)

A 8 **C** 800

B 80 **D** 8000

19. Which is a prime number? (6-9)

F 19 **H** 21

G 20 **J** 22

Line Plots and Outliers

California Content Standards *Statistics, Data Analysis, and Probability 1.2: Identify . . . any apparent outliers for numerical data sets. Also, Statistics, Data Analysis, and Probability 1.1 (See p. 391.)*

Warm-Up Review

1. Draw a number line from 0 to 10.
2. Write all the whole numbers from 15 to 22.
3. Use the data about the class survey on page 392. Make a table of numbers (no tally marks) for this data.
4. Use the data about favorite pets on page 394. How many students were in the survey?

Word Bank

line plot
outlier

Math Link You have organized data using tally charts, bar graphs, and stem-and-leaf plots. Now you will learn to organize data in line plots.

A **line plot** shows data along a number line. Each X represents one number in the data set.

Example

The table below gives running speeds of some animals. Make a line plot to organize the data. Identify any outliers.

Animal	Speed (miles per hour)
Cat	30
Cheetah	70
Deer	30
Grizzly bear	30
Wart hog	30
Giraffe	32
Reindeer	32
Jackal	35
Mule deer	35
Rabbit	35

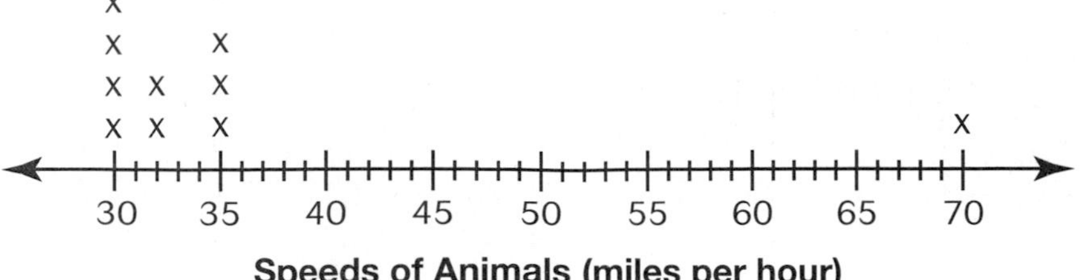

An **outlier** is a number in a data set that is very different from the rest of the numbers. In the data set above, the running speed of a cheetah, 70 miles per hour, is an outlier. Notice how far away 70 is from the rest of the numbers on the line plot.

Additional Standards: Statistics, Data Analysis, and Probability 1.0, 1.3 (See p. 391.)

Guided Practice *For another example, see Set D on p. 423.*

Use the line plot at the right.

1. How many puppies weighed 16 pounds?

2. What is the range of weights?

3. Is there an outlier in this data set? Explain.

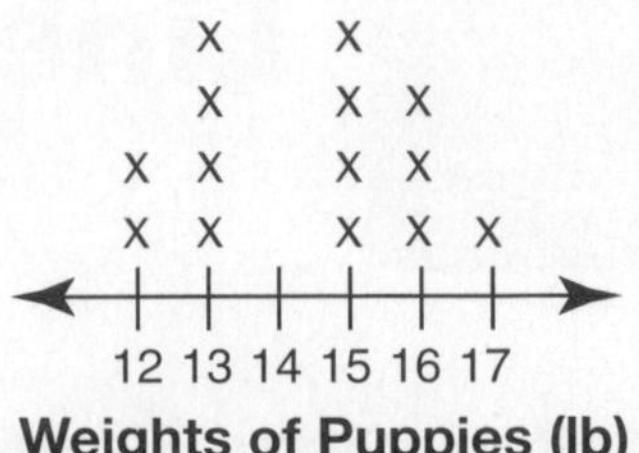

Independent Practice *For more practice, see Set D on p. 427.*

Identify the outlier in each data set.

4. 5, 8, 2, 10, 25
5. 14, 17, 19, 2, 24
6. 30, 20, 31, 31, 30
7. 8, 7, 1, 5, 19, 4, 6

Animal	Life Span (years)
Dog	11
Kangaroo	5
Giraffe	10
Cow	15
Pig	10
Lion	12
Black bear	32
Cat	11
Zebra	15

Use the table at the right for Exercises 8–10.

8. Organize the data using a line plot.

9. Name any outliers in the data set.

10. Find the range of the life spans.

Mixed Review

11. Organize the data in the table above in a stem-and-leaf plot.

12. Make a bar graph to display the Animal Speeds data from page 398. Do not include the outlier. How did the line plot help you?

13. $\frac{1}{4} + \frac{3}{4}$ 14. $\frac{1}{2} + \frac{3}{8}$ 15. $\frac{2}{3} - \frac{1}{3}$ 16. $\frac{5}{8} - \frac{1}{4}$ 17. $\frac{1}{3} + \frac{1}{2}$

Test Prep **Choose the correct letter for each answer.**

18. (7-9) Mrs. Wagner took half the markers out of the supply cabinet. She gave each of 4 groups of students a set of 8 markers. How many markers were originally in the cabinet?

 A 8 markers **C** 32 markers
 B 16 markers **D** 64 markers

19. (6-10) In one week Peter practiced the piano the following number of minutes each day: 20, 15, 0, 20, 10, 25, 15. Find his mean daily practice time.

 F 10 min **H** 20 min
 G 15 min **J** 25 min

Problem-Solving Skill:

Understanding Line Graphs

Warm-Up Review

1. 10 × 20
2. 450 × 10
3. 60 ÷ 3
4. 810 ÷ 9
5. 10 × 10
6. 1000 ÷ 5
7. Four friends are in line to ride a roller coaster. Patty is between Heidi and Amy. Lori is not by Heidi. Heidi is not first in line. List the line of friends in order.

California Content Standards *Statistics, Data Analysis, and Probability 1.3: Interpret one- and two-variable data graphs to answer questions about a situation. Also, Statistics, Data Analysis, and Probability 1.0* *(See p. 391.)*

Read for Understanding

You can look at line graphs as pictures that tell a story. Even when there are no numbers on a line graph, you can still tell what the story is. The graph at the right tells the story of a soccer ball that has been kicked.

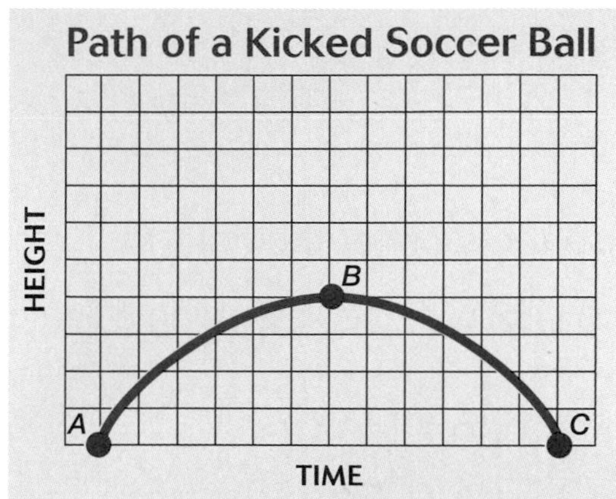

1. What is the graph about?
2. What are the two labels on the graph?

Think and Discuss

Understanding Line Graphs

Line graphs tell a story by showing a relationship. For example, the line graph above shows the relationship between time and the height of the ball.

Look back at the graph.

3. Which point shows when the ball was kicked?
4. At which point was the ball the highest?
5. What happened to the ball from Point *A* to Point *B*?
6. What happened to the ball from Point *B* to Point *C*?
7. Do you think it would be easier to understand the graph if numbers were on it? Why or why not?

 Additional Standards: Mathematical Reasoning 1.1, 2.0 *(See p. 391.)*

For Exercises 1–5, use Graphs A, B, and C. You can use a graph more than once.

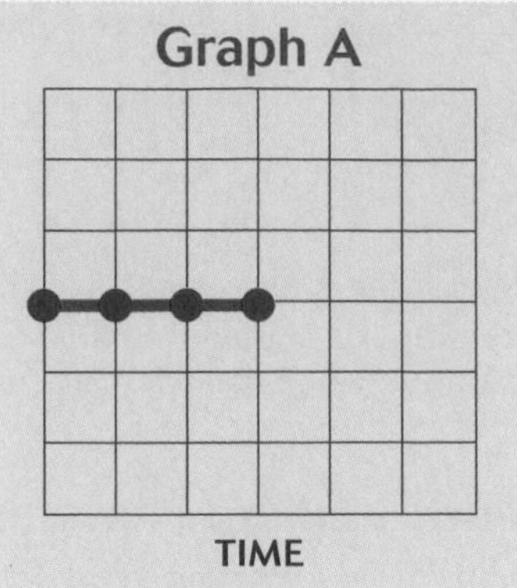

Guided Practice

1. Which graph might tell a story about a barrel filling with rainwater during a storm?
   a. Graph A
   b. Graph B
   c. Graph C

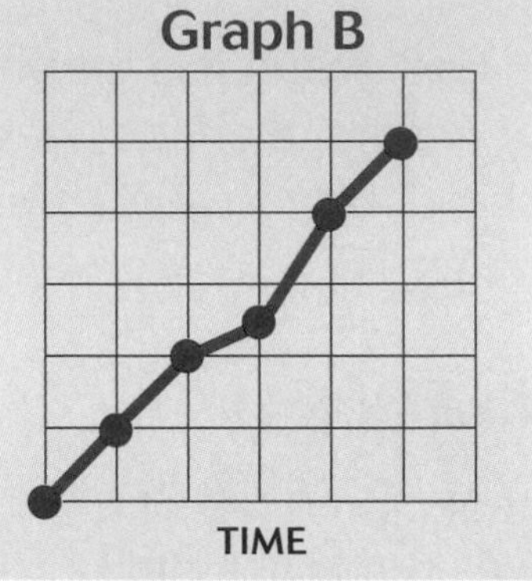

Independent Practice

2. Which graph might show what happens to the size of a beach ball when it gets a leak?
   a. Graph A
   b. Graph B
   c. Graph C

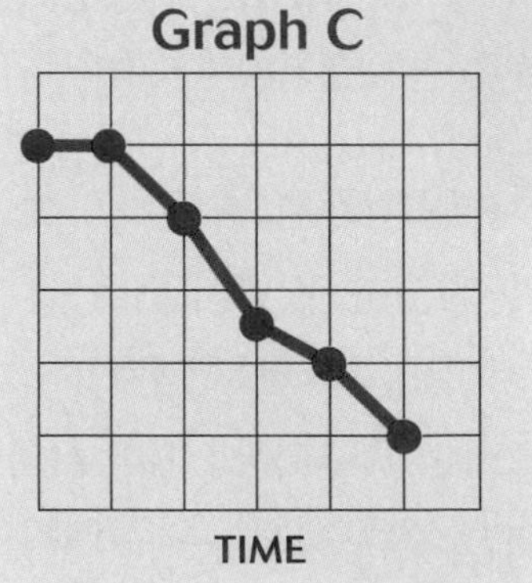

3. Which graph might tell a story about a car stopped at a red light?
   a. Graph A
   b. Graph B
   c. Graph C

4. Which graph might tell the story of a girl who puts money into her piggy bank each week?
   a. Graph A
   b. Graph B
   c. Graph C

5. Which graph might tell the story of a bathtub filled with water that is draining?
   a. Graph A
   b. Graph B
   c. Graph C

6. **Math Reasoning** Look at Graph D. Use the graph to write a story of your own.

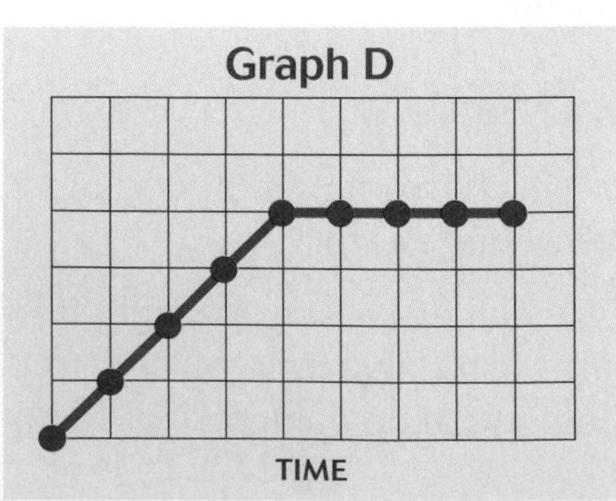

LESSON 10-6

Reading Line Graphs

California Content Standards *Statistics, Data Analysis, and Probability 1.3: Interpret one-and two-variable data graphs to answer questions about a situation. Also, Statistics, Data Analysis, and Probability 1.0 (See p. 391.)*

Math Link You have learned how to get information from line graphs that have no numbers. In this lesson you will learn how to read line graphs with numbers.

A **line graph** is a graph that connects points to show how data changes over time. The line graph below shows Billy's weight during the first twelve months of his life.

Warm-Up Review

1. 34 + 81
2. 44 − 29
3. 52 + 38
4. 28 − 15
5. 66 + 27
6. 90 − 46
7. Carson put a penny in his bank on Monday. On Tuesday he put in two pennies. Each day he doubled the number of pennies he put in. How many pennies were in his bank after 7 days?

Word Bank

line graph

Example 1

How much did Billy weigh when he was 6 months old?

Point *D* shows that at 6 months Billy weighed 18 pounds.

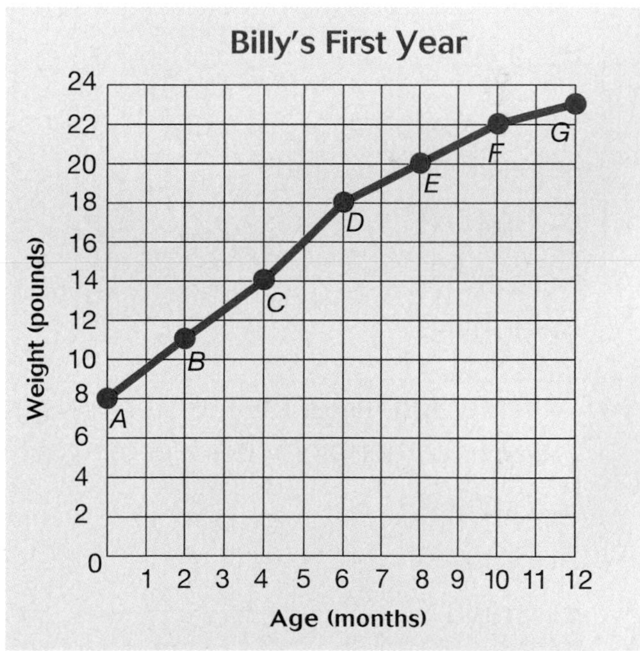

Example 2

How much weight did Billy gain during his first year?

Point *G* shows that at 12 months Billy weighed 23 pounds. Point *A* shows that at birth Billy weighed 8 pounds. Subtract to find how much he gained: 23 − 8 = 15. Billy gained 15 pounds during his first year.

Example 3

In which two-month period did Billy gain the most weight? How can you tell?

Billy gained the most weight from 4 months to 6 months. The line is steepest from point *C* to point *D*. You can subtract to find how much he gained: 18 − 14 = 4 pounds.

Guided Practice For another example, see Set E on p. 424.

Use the line graph given on page 402.

1. What does point *B* on the graph tell you?
2. About how much did Billy weigh at 9 months?
3. When did Billy double his birth weight?
4. Does a line graph give more information than a table? Explain.

Independent Practice For more practice, see Set E on p. 428.

Use the line graph to answer Exercises 5–9.

5. How tall was Catey at age 4?
6. How many inches did Catey grow from age 1 to age 2?
7. How old was Catey when she doubled her birth height?
8. During which year did Catey grow the most in height?
9. Make a table of Catey's ages (0, 1, 2, 3, 4, 5, 6) and heights.

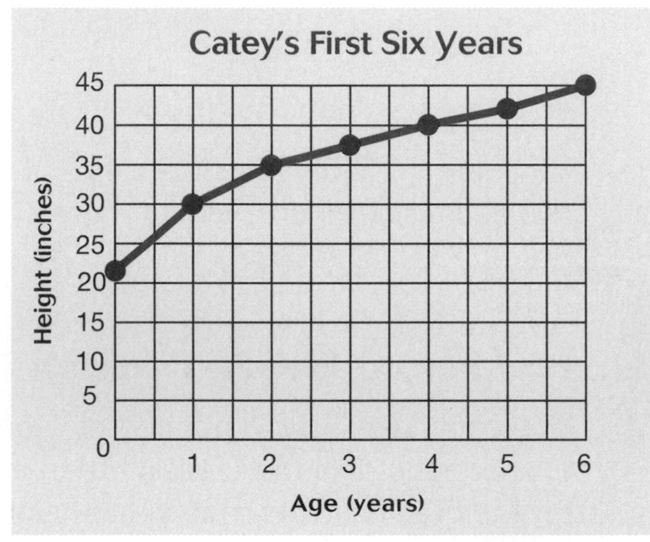

Mixed Review

10. Make a stem-and-leaf plot for Jenny's spelling grades given in the table at the right. Find the mode.

Jenny's Spelling Grades		
85	78	88
90	75	95
77	95	83

11. Draw a line plot of the data and identify the outlier: 23, 14, 15, 15, 16, 13, 15.

12. 34.07 + 58.12 **13.** 8.2 + 0.6 + 5 **14.** 812.5 − 0.3 **15.** 19.7 − 6.25

Test Prep **Choose the correct letter for each answer.**

16. Estimate 31 × 48.
(5-2)

A 1,500 **C** 800
B 1,200 **D** 700
E NH

17. Find the product of 5 and 1,004.
(4-6)

F 1,009 **H** 5,200
G 5,002 **J** 50,020
K NH

LESSON 10-7

Understand
Plan
Solve
Look Back

Problem-Solving Strategy:
Make a Graph

California Content Standard *Mathematical Reasoning 2.3: Use a variety of methods, such as words, numbers, charts, graphs, tables, . . . to explain mathematical reasoning.*

Warm-Up Review

1. $\frac{1}{2} + \frac{1}{8}$
2. $\frac{3}{4} + \frac{3}{4}$
3. $\frac{7}{8} - \frac{1}{2}$
4. $\frac{2}{3} - \frac{1}{6}$
5. Bob invites 15 friends to his party. He wants to buy a party hat and a balloon for each person. If there are 6 party hats in a package, how many packages should Bob buy?

Example

An in-line skate company made a table to show how many skates it sold each year for six years. Between which two consecutive years did skate sales increase the most?

In-Line Skates Sold

Year	Sales (in millions)
1994	10
1995	25
1996	50
1997	60
1998	95
1999	103

Understand

What do you need to find?

You need to find between which two years sales increased the most.

Plan

How can you solve the problem?

You can make a bar graph to help you examine the data more easily. Then look for the greatest difference in the heights of the bars from one year to the next year.

Solve

Make the bar graph and compare the heights of the bars. The greatest difference is between the bars for 1997 and 1998.

Skate sales increased the most between 1997 and 1998.

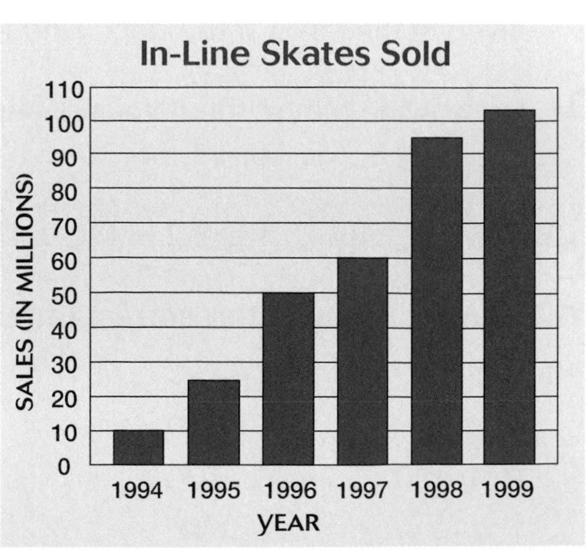

Look Back

How does the bar graph help you?

Additional Standards: Statistics, Data Analysis, and Probability 1.0, 1.3; Mathematical Reasoning 1.0, 2.0, 3.2 *(See p. 391.)*

Guided Practice

Use the information given on page 404.

1. Between which 2 years did sales increase the least?

2. Between which 2 years did sales double?

Independent Practice

Members of a skate club were asked what type of in-line skates they have used. Their answers are shown in the tally chart at the right.

Type of Skate	Number of Skaters
Multipurpose	𝍸 𝍸
Speed	𝍸
Hockey	||||
Aggressive	𝍸

3. Make a bar graph to display the data.

4. Which type of skate has been used the most?

5. Which type of skate has been used the least?

6. Which has been used more, speed skates or hockey skates?

7. How many more people have used multipurpose skates than aggressive skates?

Mixed Review

Try these or other strategies to solve each problem. Tell which strategy you used.

Problem-Solving Strategies

- *Make a List*
- *Solve a Simpler Problem*
- *Find a Pattern*
- *Draw a Picture*

8. In an in-line skating tournament, each team will play every other team once. If there are 6 teams, how many games will there be?

9. Four friends are skating in a line. Nick is in front of Kelsey. Olivia is fourth. Nobody is in front of Matt. How are the friends lined up?

10. Skate-club shirts are available in sizes S, M, L, and XL. You can get a sweatshirt or a T-shirt. List all the possible skate-club shirts.

11. Susie skates daily in this pattern: 15 min, 20 min, 25 min, day off. If she starts on a Monday, what day of the week will be her 5th day off?

Use Homework Workbook 10-7.

Diagnostic Checkpoint

Use the data below for Exercises 1–3.

Number of goals scored in 11 soccer games:
0, 3, 1, 2, 3, 1, 1, 0, 7, 2, 1

1. Organize the data in a tally chart. (10-1)

2. Find the median and the mode of the goals scored. (10-1)

3. Make a line plot of the data and identify any outliers. (10-4)

Use the table at the right for Exercises 4–6.

Game	Travel Time
3	20 min
4	30 min
6	60 min
9	20 min
10	50 min

4. Make a bar graph. (10-2)

5. What was the greatest amount of time spent traveling to a game? (10-7)

6. How many minutes were spent traveling to games in all? (10-7)

Use the stem-and-leaf plot for Exercises 7–9.

Number of Volunteers at Track Meets

Stem	Leaves
1	3, 4, 5, 6, 8, 9
2	0, 0, 0

7. How many track meets were there in all? (10-3)

8. What was the greatest number of volunteers at a meet? the least? (10-3)

9. Find the range, mode, and median of the data. (10-3)

Use the line graph for Exercises 10 and 11.

10. What was the baby's weight at 6 months? (10-6)

11. What do you think will happen to the weight of the baby as she gets older? (10-5)

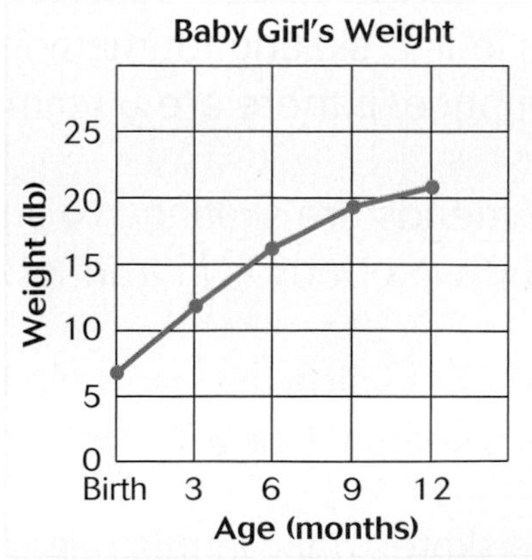

Graphing Ordered Pairs

California Content Standard *Measurement and Geometry 2.0 (🔑): Students use two-dimensional coordinate grids to represent points and graph . . . simple figures.*

Warm-Up Review

Name the value of each point marked on the number line.

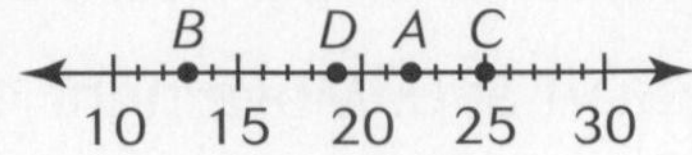

1. *A* 2. *B* 3. *C* 4. *D*

5. Paul's first draft of a story had 415 words. When he edited the story, he crossed out 37 words and added 43 new ones. How many words does his story have now?

Math Link You know how to read line graphs on a coordinate grid. Now you will learn to identify and plot points on a coordinate grid.

Word Bank

x-axis
y-axis
ordered pair
coordinates
x-coordinate
y-coordinate
plot

You can think of a coordinate grid as a kind of map. A coordinate grid has a horizontal ***x*-axis** and a vertical ***y*-axis** that meet at 0. To find the location of points on a grid, use **ordered pairs** of numbers (x, y) such as (5, 2), as shown on the first coordinate grid at the right below.

The numbers in an ordered pair are called **coordinates.** The first number in an ordered pair is the ***x*-coordinate,** and it tells you how far to move right when you start at 0. The second number in an ordered pair is the ***y*-coordinate,** and it tells you how far to move up after moving right. When you **plot** a point on a grid, you are graphing it by using the ordered pair for that point.

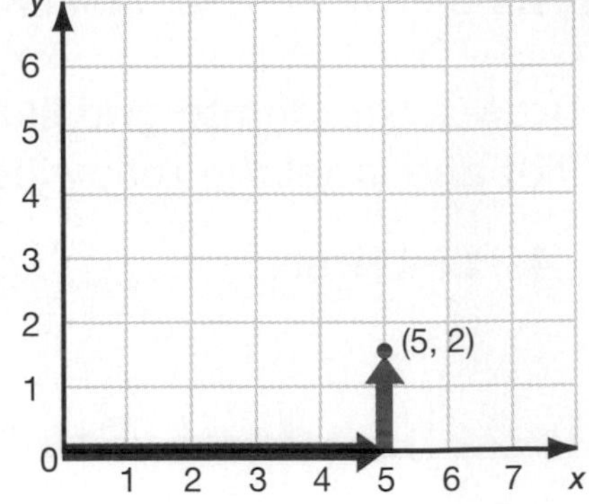

Example 1

A baseball infield is graphed at the right below. The four bases are located at points *A*, *B*, *C*, and *D*. The pitcher's mound is at point *F*. What ordered pair gives the location of first base, point *A*?

Follow the arrows to find the ordered pair for point *A*.

- Start at 0. Move right 7 units. This gives you the first number, or *x*-coordinate, in the ordered pair.
- Then move up 3 units. This gives you the second number, or *y*-coordinate, in the ordered pair.

The ordered pair for point *A* is (7, 3).

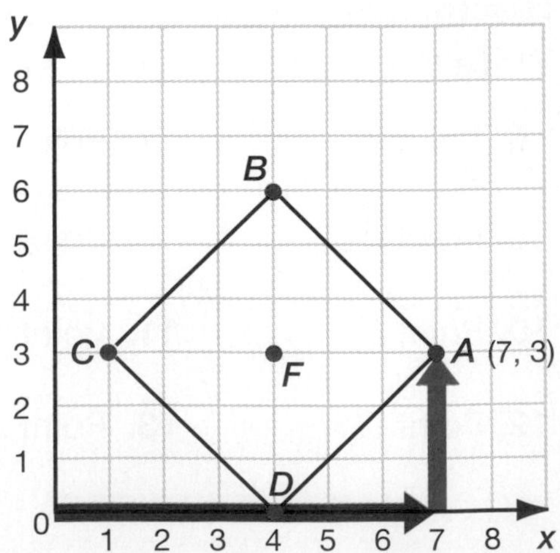

Additional Standard: Mathematical Reasoning 2.3 (See p. 391.)

Example 2

Use the coordinate grid in Example 1. What is the ordered pair for home plate, point *D*?

- Start at 0. Move right 4 units. This gives you the *x*-coordinate.
- Since D is on the *x*-axis, you do not move up. So, 0 is the *y*-coordinate.

The ordered pair for point *D* is (4, 0).

Example 3

Use the coordinate grid at the right. Plot point *E* for shortstop at (2, 5).

- Start at 0. Move right 2 units.
- Move up 5 units and draw a point. Label the point *E*.

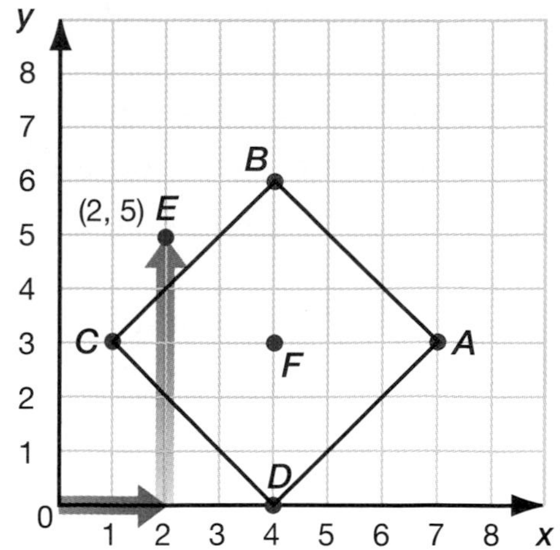

Guided Practice *For another example, see Set F on p. 424.*

Use the coordinate grid at the right. Write the ordered pair for each point.

1. Point *J* **2.** Point *K* **3.** Point *L*

Draw a coordinate grid like the one at the right. Plot and label the following points.

4. Point *W* at (1, 4) **5.** Point *X* at (0, 6)

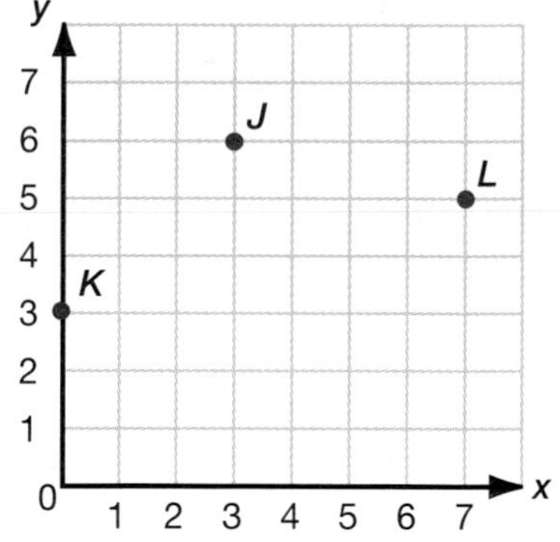

Independent Practice *For more practice, see Set F on p. 428.*

Use the coordinate grid at the right. Write the ordered pair for each point.

6. Point *A* **7.** Point *B*

8. Point *C* **9.** Point *D*

10. Point *E* **11.** Point *F*

12. Point *G* **13.** Point *H*

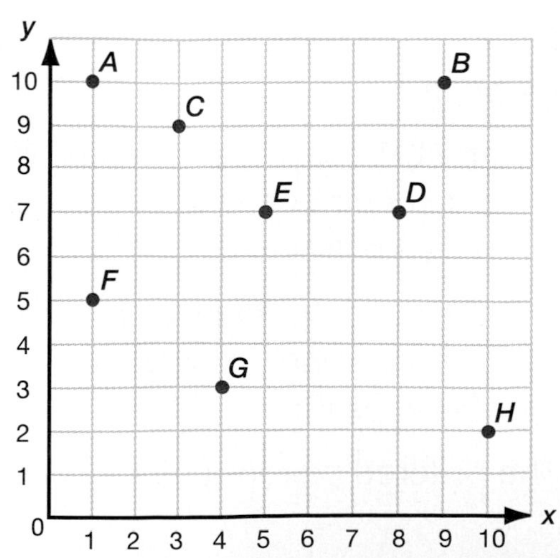

Draw a coordinate grid like the one in Exercises 6–13. Plot and label each point.

14. Point *I* at (5, 0) **15.** Point *J* at (10, 6)

16. Point *K* at (6, 10) **17.** Point *L* at (0, 2)

18. Plot four points on a grid: *A* at (2, 1), *B* at (8, 4), *C* at (7, 6), and *D* at (1, 3). Draw line segments to connect *A* to *B*, *B* to *C*, *C* to *D*, and *D* to *A*. What shape did you draw?

19. Math Reasoning Is the point (3, 5) the same as the point (5, 3)? Why do you think these pairs are called ordered pairs?

20. Algebra Copy and complete the table of ordered pairs at the right.

x	*y*	(*x*, *y*)
1	2	(1, 2)
3	8	■
4	4	■
0	6	■
5	1	■
7	0	■

Mixed Review

Use the line graph for Exercises 21–23.

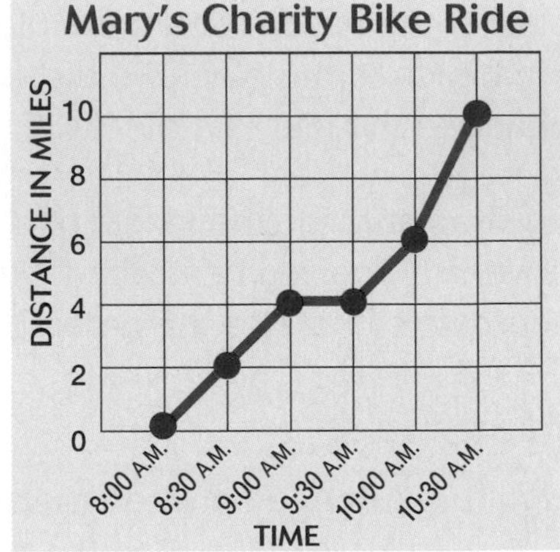

21. What story does the graph tell?

22. During which 30-minute period did Mary bicycle the farthest?

23. When did Mary take a break from bicycling?

24. $(4 + 2) \times 3$ **25.** $18 - (6 + 7)$

Identify the outlier, if any, in each data set.

26. 78, 75, 77, 18, 79, 82 **27.** 44, 42, 38, 35, 45

Test Prep **Choose the correct letter for each answer.**

28. Which is the rule for the table?
(3-8)

In	3	5	2	4	8
Out	9	15	6	12	24

A Add 6.

B Divide by 3.

C Multiply by 6.

D Multiply by 3.

29. Find the fraction for the shaded part.
(7-1)

F 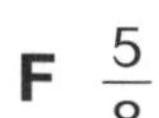 $\frac{5}{8}$ **H** 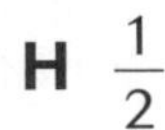 $\frac{1}{2}$

G $\frac{3}{8}$ **J** $\frac{1}{3}$

Distances on Coordinate Grids

California Content Standards *Measurement and Geometry 2.2 (🔑): Understand that the length of a horizontal segment equals the difference of the x-coordinates. Also, Measurement and Geometry 2.3 (🔑)* *(See p. 391.)*

Warm-Up Review

Write the letter for each ordered pair.

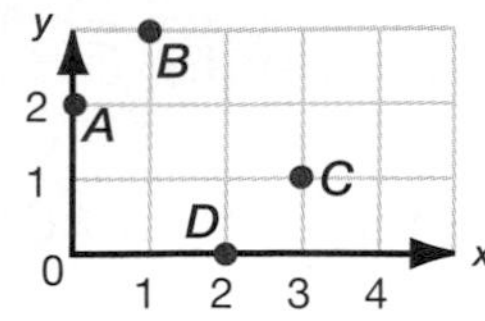

1. (1, 3)
2. (0, 2)
3. On a summer vacation, a family drove about 250 miles each day for a week. How many miles did they drive in all?

Math Link You know how to plot ordered pairs on a coordinate grid. Now you will learn how to find the distance between two points on a coordinate grid.

The map at the right below is drawn on a coordinate grid. On this map, one square represents one city block.

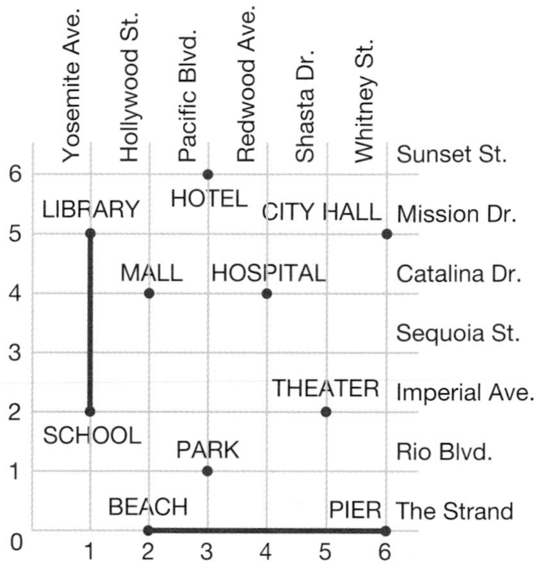

Example 1

Find the distance between the beach and the pier.

Start at the beach. Count the blocks from the beach to the pier. The distance from the beach to the pier is 4 blocks.

You can also find the length of a horizontal or vertical line segment without using a coordinate grid. Use the ordered pairs instead.

Example 2

Find the distance between the school and the library.

The school is at (1, 2). The library is at (1, 5). The *x*-coordinates are the same. Subtract the *y*-coordinates to find the length of the vertical line segment joining the two points: $5 - 2 = 3$. The distance between the school and the library is 3 blocks.

More Examples

A. What is the length of the horizontal line segment joining (18, 3) and (26, 3)?

The *y*-coordinates are the same. Subtract the *x*-coordinates.
$26 - 18 = 8$ units

B. What is the length of the vertical line segment joining (35, 49) and (35, 68)?

The *x*-coordinates are the same. Subtract the *y*-coordinates.
$68 - 49 = 19$ units

 Additional Standard: Mathematical Reasoning 2.0 *(See p. 391.)*

Guided Practice *For another example, see Set G on p. 425.*

Use the map on page 410. Find the distance between the locations.

1. School and theater **2.** Pier and city hall **3.** Hospital and mall

4. What is the length of a line segment joining (4, 13) and (4, 21)?

5. What is the length of a line segment joining (29, 8) and (35, 8)?

Independent Practice *For more practice, see Set G on p. 429.*

Use the map on page 410. Find the distance between the locations.

6. Park and hotel **7.** Library and city hall **8.** Beach and mall

Find the length of the line segment joining the points.

9. (0, 5) and (0, 8) **10.** (7, 1) and (12, 1) **11.** (8, 19) and (8, 32)

12. (31, 4) and (31, 10) **13.** (57, 15) and (70, 15) **14.** (23, 65) and (67, 65)

15. Use the map on page 410. Marsha was at school. She walked 8 blocks along Imperial Avenue to get home. She passed the theater. Write the ordered pair for Marsha's house.

16. Math Reasoning The length of a vertical line segment joining two points is 5 units. One point is (2, 14). Find the coordinates of the other point. Give all possibilities.

Mixed Review

17. You know 14 + 8 = 22.
Does 14 + 8 + 3 = 22 + 3? Explain.

18. Use the line graph at the right. Find the stopping distance at 30 miles per hour.

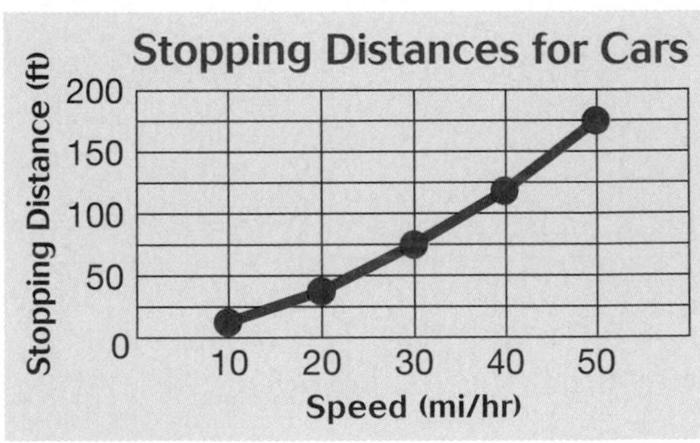

Draw a coordinate grid. Plot and label each ordered pair.

19. *X* at (5, 1) **20.** *P* at (2, 4) **21.** *Q* at (0, 3) **22.** *R* at (4, 0)

Test Prep Choose the correct letter for each answer.

23. What is $\frac{1}{4}$ of 24?
(7-2)

A 3 **C** 6
B 4 **D** 8

24. 810 ÷ 6 =
(6-6)

F 130 **H** 145
G 135 **J** 150

Graphing Equations

California Content Standards *Measurement and Geometry 2.1 (🔑): Draw the points corresponding to linear relationships on graph paper (e.g., draw 10 points on the graph of the equation y = 3x and connect them by using a straight line.) Also, Algebra and Functions 1.5 (🔑) (See p. 391.)*

Warm-Up Review

Plot the points on a coordinate grid.

1. P at (6, 3) 2. Q at (0, 0)
3. R at (1, 4) 4. S at (3, 3)
5. T at (0, 2) 6. V at (5, 0)
7. A triathlon is a three-part athletic event. This year there are 165 athletes who will swim 1.5 km, bicycle 40 km, and run 10 km. What is the total distance the athletes will cover?

Math Link You know how to graph points on a coordinate grid. In this lesson you will learn to graph equations on a coordinate grid.

Example 1

The table at the right shows how Abby's and Charlie's ages change as they grow older. Find a rule for the table. Then write an equation.

Charlie's Age (x)	Abby's Age (y)
0	2
1	3
2	4
3	5
4	6

The table shows that Abby is 2 years older than her brother Charlie. The rule for the table is *add 2*. Use the rule to write an equation that shows the relationship of their ages.

$$\text{Abby's age} = \text{Charlie's age} + 2$$
$$y = x + 2$$

How old will Abby be when Charlie is 10 years old?

You can use the equation above to find Abby's age when Charlie is 10 years old.

$$\text{Abby's age} = \text{Charlie's age} + 2$$
$$y = x + 2$$
$$= 10 + 2$$
$$= 12$$

When Charlie is 10 years old, Abby will be 12 years old.

Graph the equation $y = x + 2$.

Use the numbers in the table above to write ordered pairs. Connect the ordered pairs (0, 2), (1, 3), (2, 4), (3, 5), and (4, 6).

The graph of the equation $y = x + 2$ is a straight line.

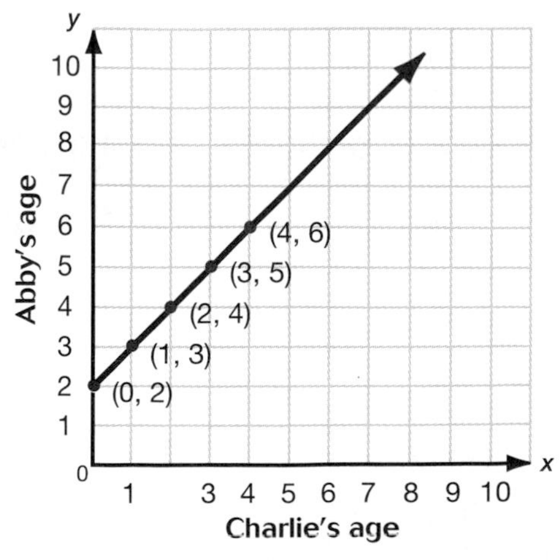

Additional Standards: Algebra and Functions 1.1; Mathematical Reasoning 2.3 (See p. 391.)

Example 2

Graph the equation $y = 2x$.

Make a table of ordered pairs. Graph the ordered pairs and draw a line.

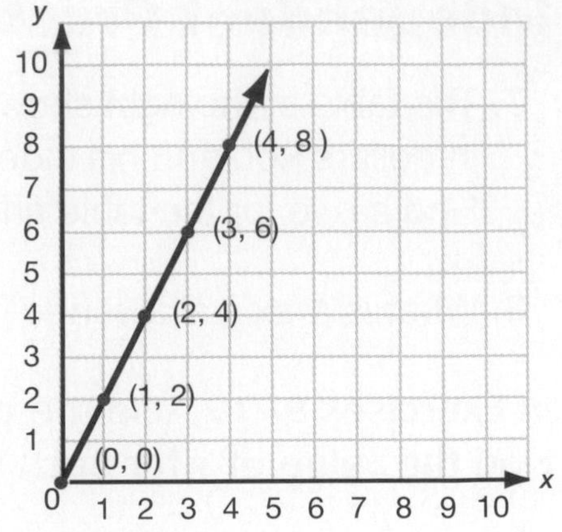

x	y = 2x	(x, y)
0	$y = 2 \times 0 = 0$	(0, 0)
1	$y = 2 \times 1 = 2$	(1, 2)
2	$y = 2 \times 2 = 4$	(2, 4)
3	$y = 2 \times 3 = 6$	(3, 6)
4	$y = 2 \times 4 = 8$	(4, 8)

In the table you can see that every x-value determines a y-value. Every ordered pair in the table is on the graph of the equation $y = 2x$.

Example 3

Find five ordered pairs on the graph of the equation $y = 3x + 7$.

Make a table for the equation $y = 3x + 7$.

x	y = 3x + 7	(x, y)
1	$y = (3 \times 1) + 7 = 3 + 7 = 10$	(1, 10)
2	$y = (3 \times 2) + 7 = 6 + 7 = 13$	(2, 13)
3	$y = (3 \times 3) + 7 = 9 + 7 = 16$	(3, 16)
4	$y = (3 \times 4) + 7 = 12 + 7 = 19$	(4, 19)
5	$y = (3 \times 5) + 7 = 15 + 7 = 22$	(5, 22)

The ordered pairs (1, 10), (2, 13), (3, 16), (4, 19), and (5, 22) are on the graph of $y = 3x + 7$.

Guided Practice *For another example, see Set H on p. 425.*

In Exercises 1 and 2, use the information from page 412.

1. How old will Abby be when Charlie is 26 years old?

2. Name two more ordered pairs on the graph of the equation $y = x + 2$.

In Exercises 3–6, use the equation $y = 6x$. Find the value of y for each value of x.

3. $x = 3$ **4.** $x = 6$ **5.** $x = 12$ **6.** $x = 23$

Independent Practice *For more practice, see Set H on p. 429.*

7. The table at the right shows the amount of allowance in dollars Rob and his older brother Max receive. Find a rule for the table and write an equation.

Rob's Allowance (x)	Max's Allowance (y)
1	5
2	6
3	7
4	8

8. What is Max's allowance if Rob's allowance is $8?

In Exercises 9–12, use the equation $y = 4x + 2$. Find the value of y for each value of x.

9. $x = 2$
10. $x = 5$
11. $x = 10$
12. $x = 13$

In Exercises 13–16, graph each equation on a separate coordinate grid.

13. $y = 3x$
14. $y = x + 1$
15. $y = 2x + 3$
16. $y = 3x + 5$

In Exercises 17–20, find five ordered pairs on the graph of each equation.

17. $y = x + 8$
18. $y = 5x$
19. $y = 6x + 1$
20. $y = 10x + 2$

21. **Math Reasoning** How do you know if a point is on the graph of a line?

Mixed Review

22. The parking lot at a conference center can hold 450 cars in nine rows. How many cars can be parked in each row to fill the lot?

23. Write a fraction equivalent to $\frac{3}{4}$.

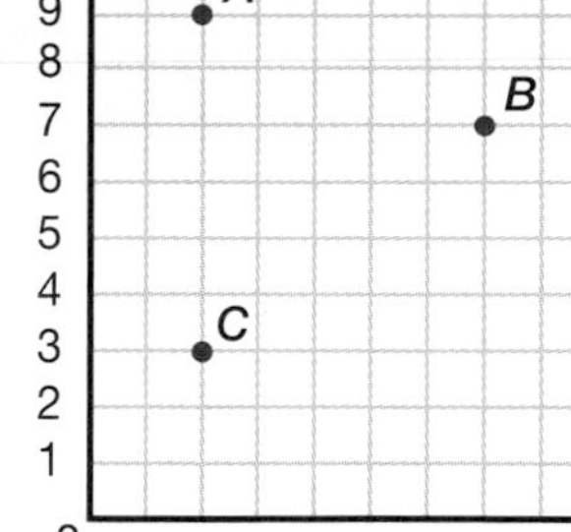

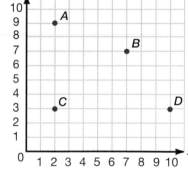

Use the coordinate grid at the right above for Exercises 24–27. Write the ordered pair for each point.

24. Point *A*
25. Point *B*
26. Point *C*
27. Point *D*

28. Find the distance between points *C* and *D*.

Test Prep **Choose the correct letter for each answer.**

29. (9-3) Tell the place value of the underlined digit in 126.<u>7</u>4.

A Ones
B Tens
C Tenths
D Hundredths
E NH

30. (7-8) Which set of fractions is listed in order from least to greatest?

F $\frac{3}{8}, \frac{7}{8}, \frac{5}{8}$
G $\frac{1}{2}, \frac{2}{3}, \frac{3}{4}$
H $\frac{4}{5}, \frac{3}{5}, \frac{2}{5}$
J $\frac{5}{6}, \frac{1}{3}, \frac{1}{2}$

 Use Homework Workbook 10-10.

Multiple-Choice Cumulative Review

Choose the correct letter for each answer.

1. Which of the following does not represent the amount shaded?

A $\frac{18}{8}$

B $2\frac{2}{8}$

C $\frac{18}{4}$

D $2\frac{1}{4}$

2. Mr. Lee bought a sweatshirt and a cap. How much change should he get back from $50.00?

Cost of Gifts	
Item	**Cost**
Sweatshirt	$39.99
Statue	$49.95
Cap	$7.29

F $2.72 H $13.82
G $3.72 J $47.28

3. $6\frac{1}{4} + 8\frac{3}{4}$

A 14

B $14\frac{1}{4}$

C $14\frac{3}{4}$

D 15

4. Find the mean of the data set.

9, 7, 6, 4, 9

F 6 H 8
G 7 J 9

5. Find the range of the data set in Question 4.

A 5 C 7
B 6 D 9

6. 1.7 + 0.5 =

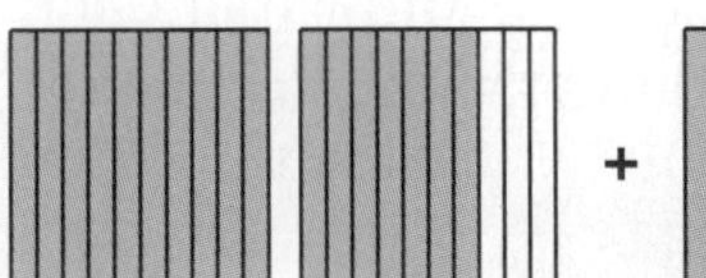

F 2.2
G 2.75
H 3.12
J 3.2
K NH

7. What is the length of the vertical line segment joining (17, 24) and (17, 32)?

A 5 units
B 6 units
C 8 units
D 17 units

Problem-Solving Application:

Ways to Represent Data

Warm-Up Review

1. 276 + 39 **2.** 419 × 5
3. 90 ÷ 6
4. 8,699 − 232
5. 15 × 23 **6.** 480 ÷ 8
7. Kevin has two jobs. On Saturday he works as a bank teller for 8 hours and earns $8 an hour. On Sunday he works at a hardware store for 10 hours and earns $6 an hour. Which job earns him more money per day?

California Content Standards *Statistics, Data Analysis and Probability 1.3: Interpret one- and two-variable data graphs to answer questions about a situation. Also, Statistics, Data Analysis, and Probability 1.0 (See p. 391.)*

Example

The graphs at the right both show the number of people who went to a county fair. Which graph would be easier to use to find how many more people there were on Day 5 than on Day 2?

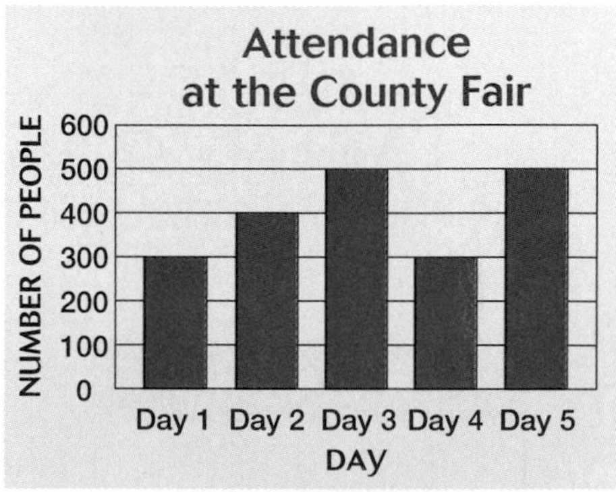

Understand

What do you need to know?

You need to know that each graph shows the same information.

Plan

How can you solve the problem?

Look at how the data has been shown in each graph. Then decide which graph is easier to use to find the difference.

Solve

To use the bar graph, count up from the top of the bar for Day 2 until you get to the top of the bar for Day 5. The number you count is the difference.

To use the pictograph, compare the rows of for Day 2 and Day 5. Day 5 has 1 more than Day 2. The difference is the value of the .

Both graphs show the difference to be 100 people.

Do you think the bar graph or the pictograph is easier to use? Why?

Look Back

What is another way you could show the County Fair data?

Additional Standard: Mathematical Reasoning 2.0 (See p. 391.)

Guided Practice

Use the graphs from page 416 for Exercises 1 and 2.

1. On which days was the attendance at the county fair the same?

2. Find the average number of people who attended the county fair during the five days.

Independent Practice

Use the table or bar graph shown below for Exercises 3–7. Explain which you used and why.

Swimming Competitions	
Month	Number
March	5
April	13
May	21
June	17
July	11

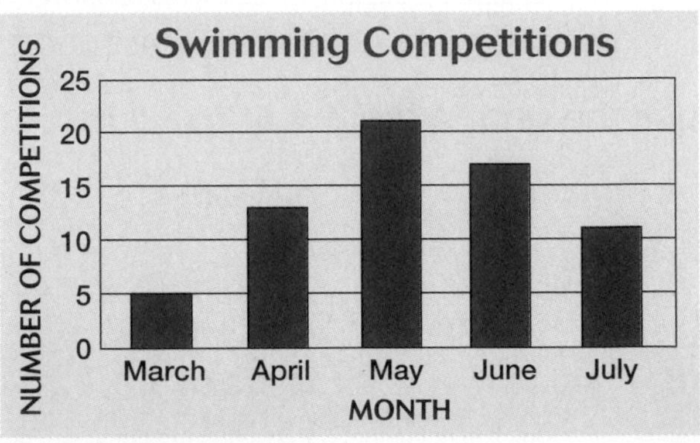

3. During which months were there swimming competitions?

4. During which month were the most swimming competitions held?

5. During how many months were there fewer than 15 swimming competitions?

6. Exactly how many swimming competitions were held in June?

7. **Math Reasoning** Which month had about twice as many swimming competitions as March?

Mixed Review

8. Suppose you toss a coin 60 times. Predict how many times the coin will land on heads.

9. Nancy earns $400 a month. The circle graph at the right shows what she plans to do with the money she earns each month. How much does Nancy plan on spending on tuition each month?

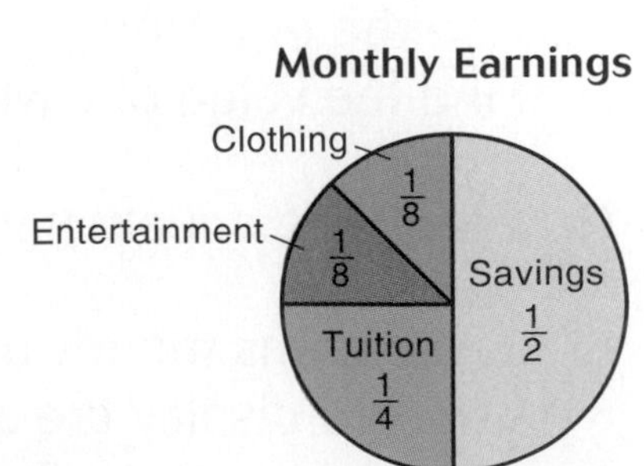

Diagnostic Checkpoint

Complete. For Exercises 1–3, use the words from the Word Bank.

Word Bank

coordinates
data
leaf
median
mode
ordered pair
outlier
range
stem

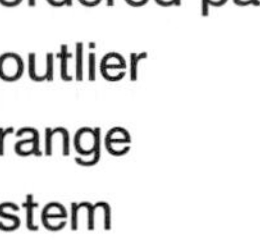

1. (10-4) A number in a data set that is very different from the rest of the numbers is called a(n) ______________.

2. (10-1) The ______________ is the middle number when items in a data set are listed in order.

3. (10–1) The ______________ is the difference between the greatest number and the least number in a data set.

Use the grid. Write the ordered pair for each point.

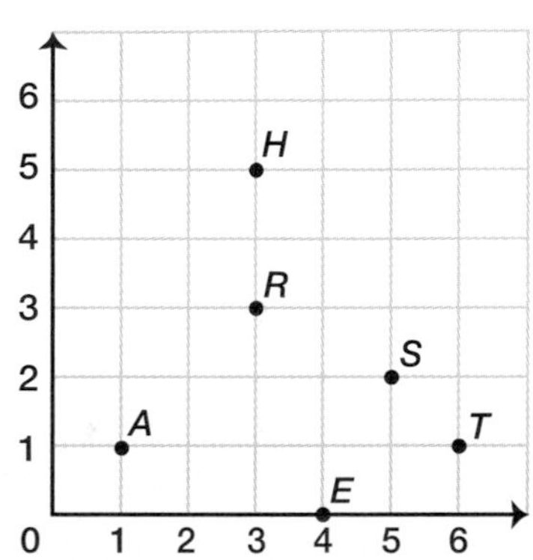

4. (10-8) Point H

5. (10-8) Point E

6. (10-8) Point A

7. (10-8) Point R

8. (10-8) Point T

9. (10-8) Point S

Find the length of the line segment joining the points.

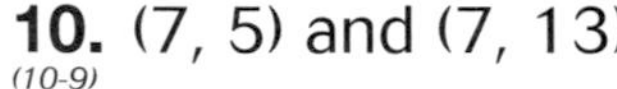

10. (10-9) (7, 5) and (7, 13)

11. (10-9) (10, 2) and (6, 2)

Use the map at the right. Find the distance between the locations.

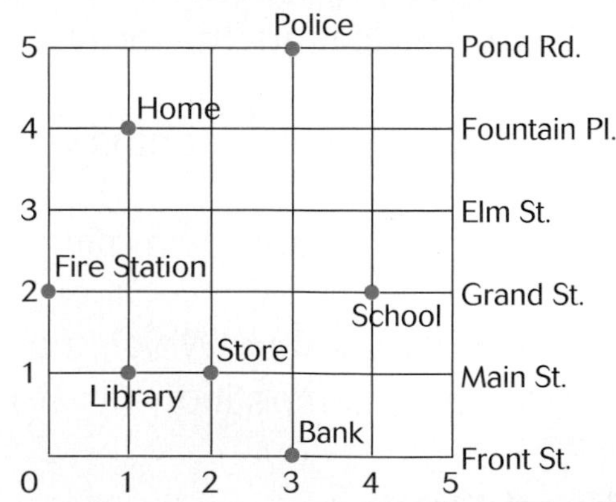

12. (10-9) Home and library

13. (10-9) Fire station and school

14. (10-10) Use the equation $y = 2x + 1$. Find the value of y when $x = 8$.

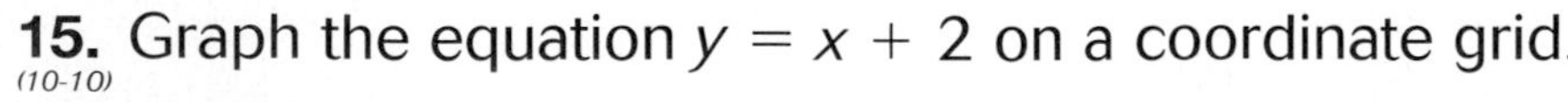

15. (10-10) Graph the equation $y = x + 2$ on a coordinate grid.

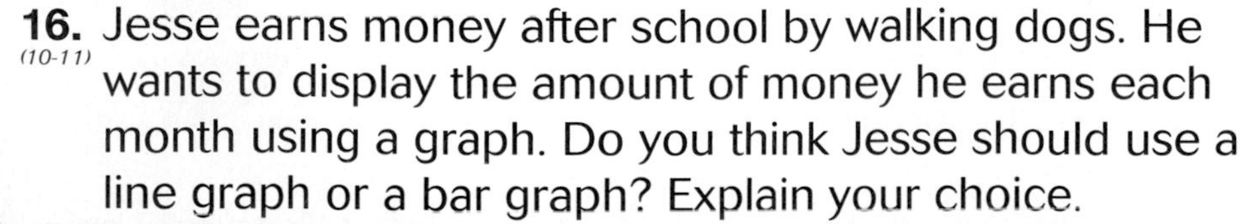

16. (10-11) Jesse earns money after school by walking dogs. He wants to display the amount of money he earns each month using a graph. Do you think Jesse should use a line graph or a bar graph? Explain your choice.

Chapter 10 Test

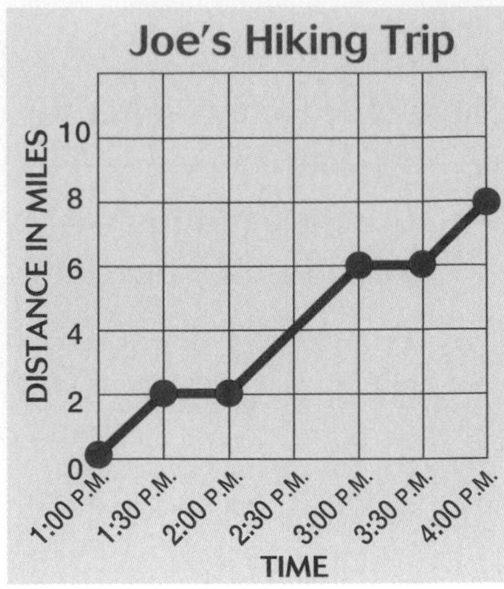

Use the line graph for Questions 1–4.

1. What does the graph show?

2. How many breaks did Joe take?

3. How far did Joe hike between 2:00 P.M. and 3:00 P.M.?

4. How many total miles did Joe hike?

Use the coordinate grid for Questions 5–9. Write the ordered pair for each point.

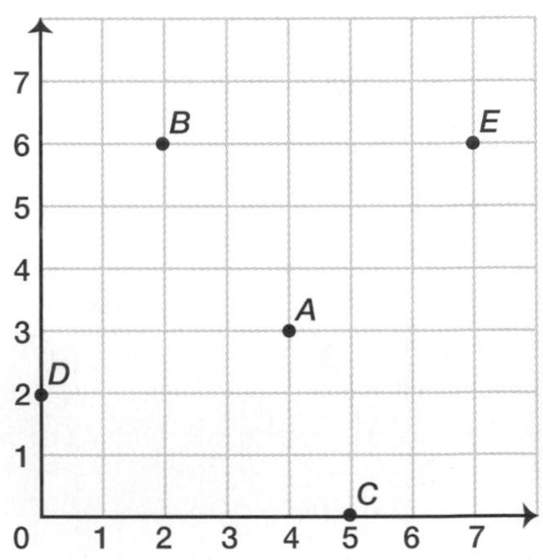

5. Point *B* **6.** Point *C*

7. Point *A* **8.** Point *D*

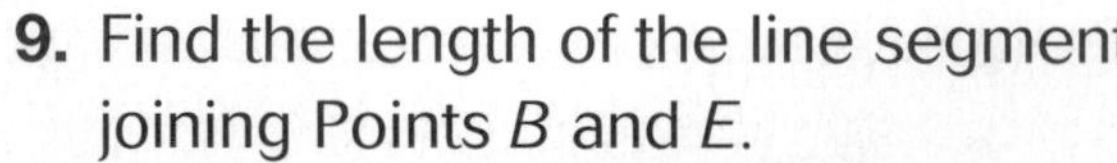

9. Find the length of the line segment joining Points *B* and *E*.

In Questions 10–13, use the equation $y = 5x + 3$. Find the value of y for each value of x.

10. $x = 1$ **11.** $x = 3$ **12.** $x = 10$ **13.** $x = 7$

14. On a separate coordinate grid, graph the equation $y = 2x$.

Use the data at the right for Questions 15–18.

15. Organize the test scores in a stem-and-leaf plot.

16. Find the range, median, and mode of the test scores.

17. Organize the data using a line plot.

18. Identify the outlier in the data set.

Test Scores			
77	82	87	93
79	96	82	37
85	84	88	78
83	82	87	

Multiple-Choice Chapter 10 Test

Choose the correct letter for each answer.

1. **Use the equation $y = 3x + 4$. Find the value of y for $x = 6$.**

A $y = 13$
B $y = 18$
C $y = 22$
D $y = 40$

2. **Which of the ordered pairs below is on the graph of $y = 2x + 2$?**

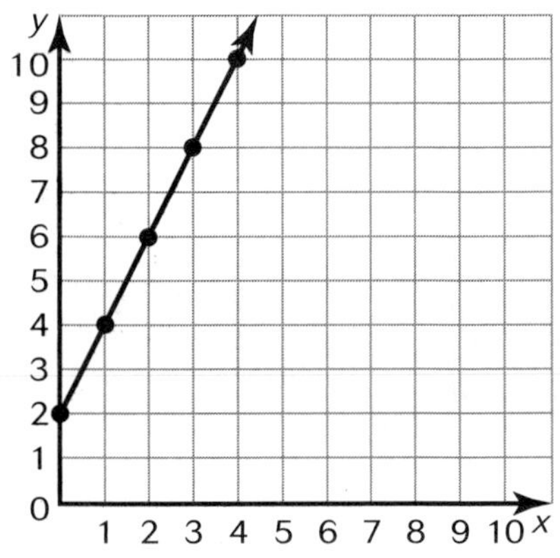

F (2, 3)
G (1, 2)
H (2, 1)
J (2, 6)

3. **Identify the outlier in the data set.**

19, 15, 15, 4, 29, 26, 18

A 25
B 18
C 15
D 4

Ginny made a coordinate grid for her garden. Use the grid for Questions 4–6.

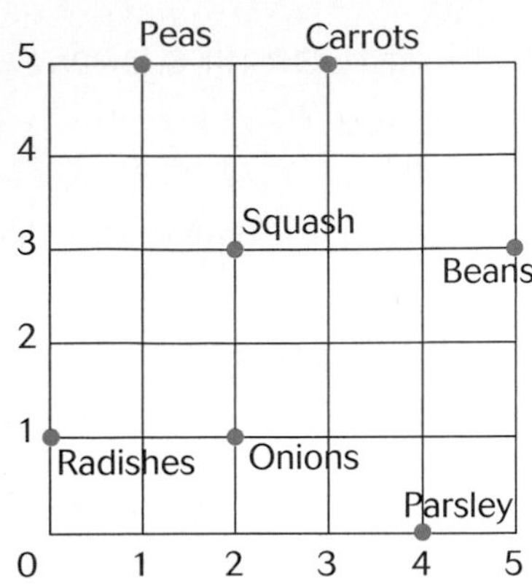

4. **What kind of seed is located at (3, 5)?**

F Carrot
G Bean
H Squash
J Pea

5. **What is the distance between the squash and the beans?**

A 0 units
B 1 unit
C 2 units
D 3 units
E NH

6. **Which is the ordered pair for parsley?**

F (0, 4)
G (4, 0)
H (3, 0)
J (4, 1)

Use the stem-and-leaf plot below for Questions 7–9.

Stem	Leaves
3	0, 3, 4, 4, 4
4	3, 3, 4, 5, 6, 7

7. Find the range of the data.

   A 17 C 30
   B 34 D 47

8. Find the mode of the data.

   F 30 H 34
   G 43 J 47

9. Find the median of the data.

   A 47 C 43
   B 34 D 30

Use the bar graph below for Questions 10 and 11.

10. On which day was 25 minutes spent on homework?

    F Monday
    G Wednesday
    H Thursday
    J Friday

11. How much more time was spent doing homework on Tuesday than on Thursday?

    A 10 minutes
    B 15 minutes
    C 20 minutes
    D 25 minutes

Use the line graph below for Questions 12 and 13.

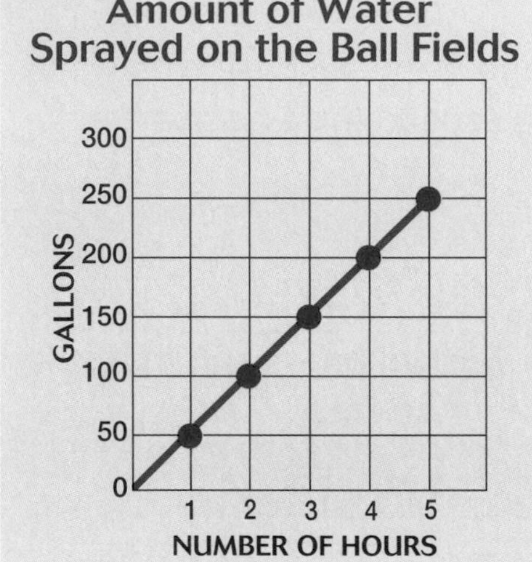

12. How many gallons of water are sprayed on the ball fields between hours 4 and 5?

    F 50 gallons
    G 100 gallons
    H 200 gallons
    J 250 gallons

13. How many gallons of water were used in 3 hours?

    A 50 gallons
    B 100 gallons
    C 150 gallons
    D 200 gallons

Reteaching

Set A (pages 392–393)

Find the range, mode, and median of the data set.

30, 36, 36, 39, 43, 45, 51

mode median

The **mode** is the number that occurs most often. The mode is 36.

The **median** is the middle number when the data are listed in order. The median is 39.

The **range** is the difference between the greatest and least numbers: 51 − 30 = 21.

Remember a set of data does not always have a mode or it can have more than one mode.

Find the range, mode, and median of each data set.

1. 17, 23, 35, 41, 63
2. 5, 2, 8, 4, 3, 9, 3
3. 2, 13, 7, 6, 2, 4, 2
4. 90, 63, 80, 76, 94, 92

Set B (pages 394–395)

Make a vertical bar graph to display the data in the table.

Student	Tickets Sold
Jordan	29
Darius	47
Bonita	73
Hurst	61

Draw and label the side and bottom of the graph. Draw bars to show the number of tickets each student sold. Choose a title for your graph.

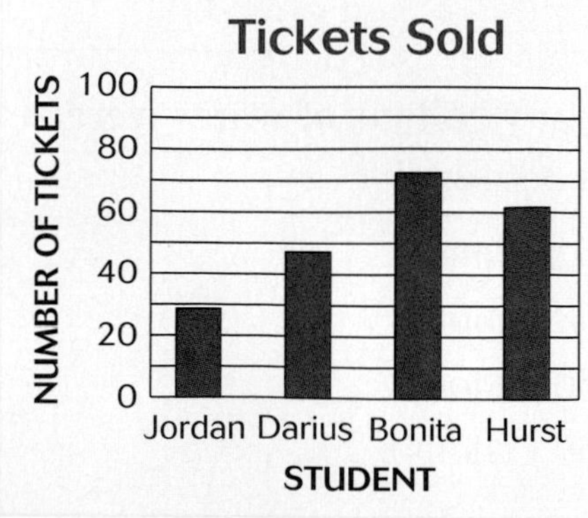

Remember to use a scale that starts at 0 and goes beyond the highest number in the data set.

Use the table and bar graph for Exercises 1–5.

1. Make a horizontal bar graph to display the data at the left.
2. Who sold the most tickets?
3. Who sold the fewest tickets?
4. How many more tickets did Bonita sell than Darius?
5. How many tickets were sold in all?

Set C (pages 396–397)

Organize the data in a stem-and-leaf plot.

Test Scores					
78	79	88	72	67	75
85	80	76	85	83	87

First, record the tens digits in order from least to greatest. Next, record the ones digits in order from least to greatest.

Stem	Leaves
6	7
7	2, 5, 6, 8, 9
8	0, 3, 5, 5, 7, 8

Remember that each stem stands for the first digit or digits of each number. Each leaf stands for the last digit of each number.

Use the data in the table for Exercises 1–3.

Plant Heights (inches)					
11	17	12	13	10	20
22	16	15	23	17	14

1. Organize the data in a stem-and-leaf plot.
2. Find the mode and range of the plant heights.
3. How many plants are taller than 15 inches?

Set D (pages 398–399)

Organize the data using a line plot. Identify any outliers.

52, 50, 55, 57, 90, 58, 55

Draw a number line and organize the data along the line.

50 55 60 65 70 75 80 85 90

You can see that 90 is far away from the other numbers on the line plot. 90 is the outlier.

Remember an outlier is a number in a data set that is very different from the rest of the numbers.

Identify the outlier, if any, in each data set.

1. 12, 9, 7, 15, 44, 18, 8
2. 37, 38, 39, 26, 25, 29
3. 45, 120, 46, 59, 54
4. 96, 89, 99, 14, 84, 93
5. 78, 79, 80, 75, 73
6. 355, 347, 350, 84, 349
7. 40, 10, 40, 45, 50, 40

Reteaching (continued)

Set E (pages 402–403)

A line graph shows how data changes over time. The graph below shows plant growth for 12 months.

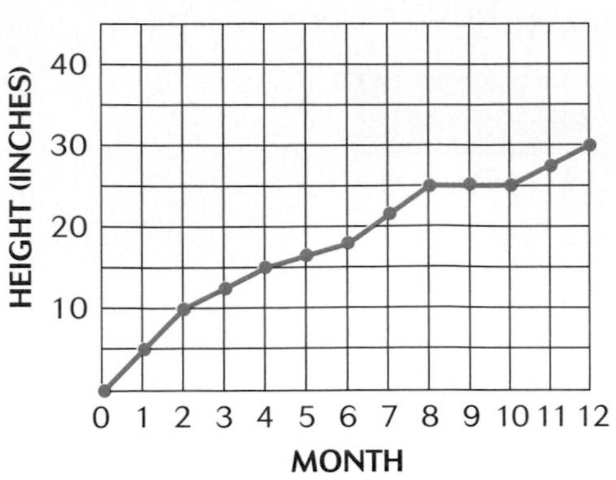

Remember that each point gives the plant height for that month.

Use the line graph at the left.

1. How tall was the plant at 2 months?
2. How tall was the plant at 4 months?
3. How many inches did the plant grow from Month 2 to Month 4?
4. During which months did the plant's height stay the same?
5. How many inches did the plant grow during the 12 months?

Set F (pages 407–409)

Using the coordinate grid below. Write the ordered pair for Point *B*.

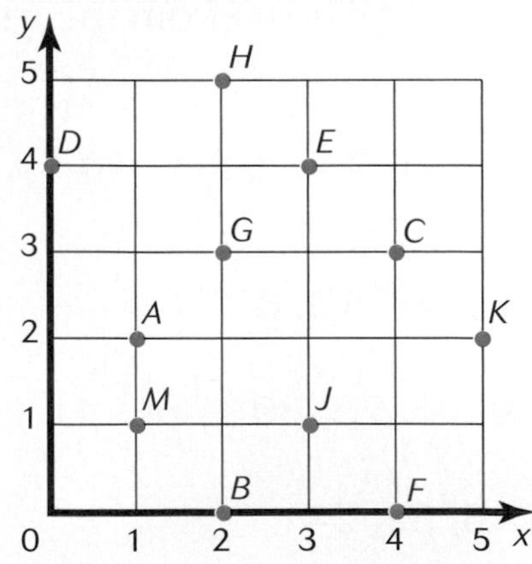

Start at 0. Move right 2 units. Do not move up. The ordered pair for Point *B* is (2, 0).

Remember the first number in an ordered pair is the *x*-coordinate, and it tells you how far to move right when you start at 0. The second number in an ordered pair is the *y*-coordinate, and it tells you how far to move up after moving right.

Use the coordinate grid at the left. Write the ordered pair for each point.

1. Point *A*
2. Point *C*
3. Point *D*
4. Point *E*
5. Point *F*
6. Point *G*
7. Point *H*
8. Point *J*
9. Point *K*
10. Point *M*

Set G (pages 410–411)

The coordinate grid shows the locations of students' desks.

Find the distance between Mark's desk and Beth's desk.

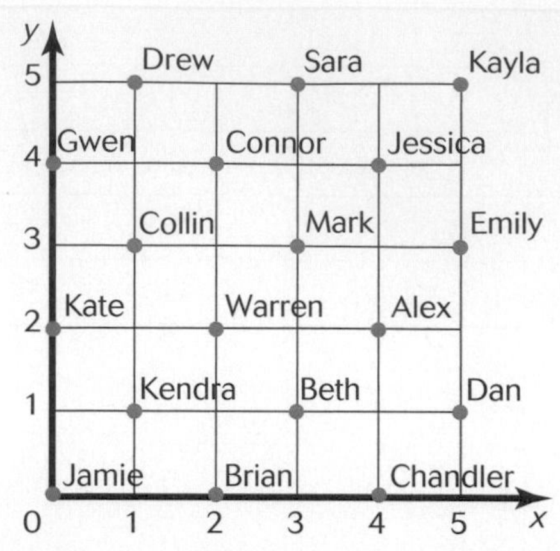

Mark's desk is at (3, 3) and Beth's desk is at (3, 1). Subtract the *y*-coordinates: $3 - 1 = 2$.

The distance between Mark's desk and Beth's desk is 2 units.

Remember you can use ordered pairs to find the distance between two points.

Use the map at the left. Find the distance between the students' desks.

1. Kate and Alex
2. Collin and Emily
3. Brian and Warren

Find the length of the line segment joining the points.

4. (3, 7) and (12, 7)
5. (5, 8) and (5, 2)
6. (21, 18) and (34, 18)

Set H (pages 412–414)

Find the value of $y = 3x + 1$ for each value of x in the table.

x	$y = 3x + 1$	(x, y)
0	$y = (3 \times 0) + 1 = 0 + 1 = 1$	(0, 1)
1	$y = (3 \times 1) + 1 = 3 + 1 = 4$	(1, 4)
2	$y = (3 \times 2) + 1 = 6 + 1 = 7$	(2, 7)
3	$y = (3 \times 3) + 1 = 9 + 1 = 10$	(3, 10)
4	$y = (3 \times 4) + 1 = 12 + 1 = 13$	(4, 13)

The ordered pairs can be used to graph the equation $y = 3x + 1$, which is a straight line.

Remember that every *x*-value determines a *y*-value.

1. On a separate coordinate grid, graph the ordered pairs at the left and draw the line.

Use the equation $y = 5x + 3$. Find the value of y for each value of x.

2. $x = 0$ **3.** $x = 4$ **4.** $x = 6$

5. $x = 7$ **6.** $x = 12$ **7.** $x = 23$

8. $x = 30$ **9.** $x = 45$ **10.** $x = 52$

More Practice

Set A (pages 392–393)

Use the table at the right for Exercises 1–5.

Minutes Played in Game 1	
Minutes	**Number of Players**
4	II
5	I
6	I
7	III
8	I
9	~~IIII~~

1. What does each tally mark represent?
2. How many players are shown in the tally chart?
3. How many players played for 7 or more minutes?
4. How many players played for less than 7 minutes?
5. Find the range of the number of minutes played.

Find the mode, median, and range of each data set.

6. 90, 88, 98, 94, 82
7. 17, 13, 12, 17, 16, 17, 10

Set B (pages 394–395)

Use the table at the right for Exercises 1–5.

Number of Error-Free Innings Played	
Game	**Innings**
1	7
2	5
3	7
4	8
5	7

1. Make a vertical bar graph for the data in the table.
2. For which game did you draw the shortest bar?
3. Which game had the greatest number of error-free innings?
4. Which games had the same number of error-free innings?
5. How many more error-free innings were there in Game 4 than in Game 2?

Set C (pages 396–397)

Student athletes at Meadow School were asked to name as many sports teams as they could. The results are shown in the stem-and-leaf plot at the right.

Number of Teams Named

Stem	Leaves
0	4, 7, 7, 8
1	2, 3, 5, 7, 7, 7
2	1, 1, 4
3	2, 2

1. What was the least number of teams named? the greatest?
2. How many student athletes responded to the question?
3. Find the median and the mode of the number of teams named.
4. Find the range of the data.
5. How many student athletes were able to name more than 20 teams?

Set D (pages 398–399)

Use the table at the right for Exercises 1–4.

Number of Players in Each Game

Game	Players
1	5
2	7
3	8
4	5

1. Organize the data using a line plot.
2. Find the mode of the data.
3. Which game had the most players?
4. Is there an outlier in this data set? Explain.

Identify the outlier in each data set.

5. 6, 3, 37, 8, 7, 4, 9, 3, 6
6. 45, 12, 36, 39, 42, 34
7. 138, 125, 136, 127, 55, 140
8. 31, 32, 7, 41, 39, 33, 43
9. 17, 19, 14, 12, 11, 18
10. 78, 93, 91, 85, 77, 26, 88, 86, 94
11. Find the range of the data set in Exercise 7.

More Practice (continued)

Set E (pages 402–403)

The line graph shows the number of babies born each month at a local hospital.

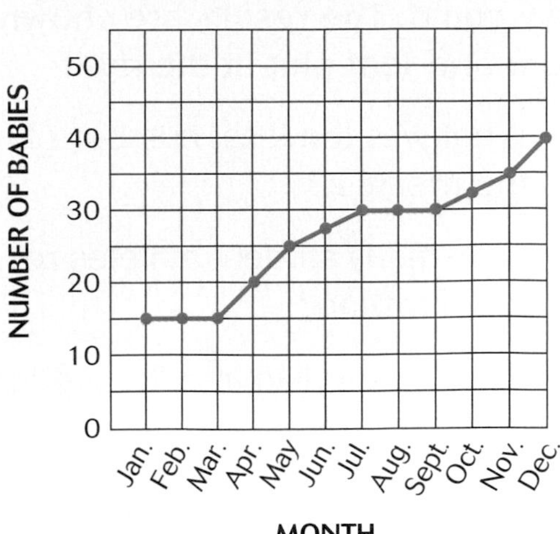

1. How many babies were born in May?
2. How many more babies were born in November than in September?
3. How many babies were born in December?
4. During which months was the number of babies born the same?
5. How many more babies were born in December than in January?

Set F (pages 407–409)

Use the coordinate grid at the right. Write the ordered pair for each point.

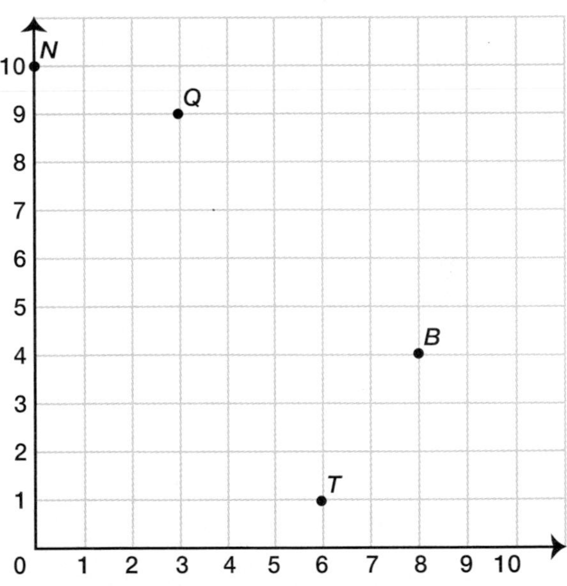

1. Point *B*
2. Point *N*
3. Point *Q*
4. Point *T*

Draw a coordinate grid. Plot and label each point.

5. Point *C* at (2, 4)
6. Point *X* at (9, 0)
7. Point *Y* at (4, 3)
8. Point *Z* at (10, 5)
9. Point *J* at (3, 1)
10. Point *R* at (7, 8)
11. Point *W* at (0, 7)
12. Point *K* at (4, 6)
13. Point *D* at (3, 0)
14. Point *E* at (2, 2)

Set G (pages 410–411)

Use the map at the right for Exercises 1–3. Find the distance between the locations.

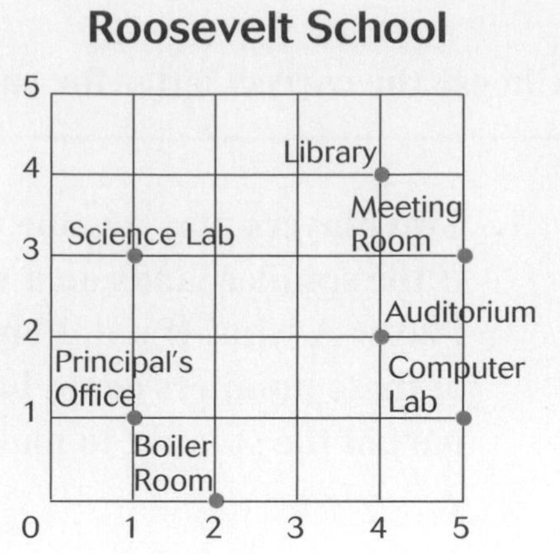

1. Library and auditorium
2. Computer lab and principal's office
3. Science lab and meeting room

Find the length of the line segment joining the points.

4. (3, 4) and (3, 10)
5. (6, 0) and (0, 0)
6. (7, 7) and (7, 2)
7. (19, 3) and (24, 3)
8. (40, 25) and (40, 18)
9. (26, 7) and (15, 7)

Set H (pages 412–414)

The table at the right shows the number of tickets sold by Kara and Tony. Use the table for Exercises 1–4.

Tony's Tickets (x)	Kara's Tickets (y)
1	2
2	4
3	6
4	
5	

1. Complete the table.
2. Find a rule for the table and write an equation.
3. Graph the equation for Exercise 2 on a coordinate grid.
4. If Tony sells 7 tickets, how many tickets does Kara sell?

In Exercises 5–12, use the equation $y = 6x + 3$. Find the value of y for each value of x.

5. $x = 4$
6. $x = 2$
7. $x = 0$
8. $x = 10$
9. $x = 13$
10. $x = 20$
11. $x = 36$
12. $x = 42$
13. Find five ordered pairs on the graph of the equation $y = x + 9$.

TEST PREP

Problem Solving Preparing for Tests

Choose the correct letter for each answer.

---

1. **Two players play a game using this spinner. If the spinner lands on a number less than 10, Player A wins. If not, Player B wins. Which of these numbers could be put in the empty part of the spinner to make the game fair?**

   A 2
   B 4
   C 7
   D 14

Tip

Which are the winning numbers for Player A? Now choose a number so that Player B has the same number of winning numbers.

---

2. **Three friends ran in a road race. It took Scott 24 minutes to finish. It took Marty 29 minutes to finish. Fred finished after Scott but before Marty. Which is reasonable for the amount of time it took Fred to finish the race?**

   F 22 minutes
   G 27 minutes
   H 29 minutes
   J 32 minutes

Tip

You can use the Make a List strategy to help you solve the problem. Make a list of all the possible number of minutes it could have taken Fred to finish the race.

---

3. **A landscaper planted 3 trees on each even-numbered street and 5 trees on each odd-numbered street. How many trees did he plant altogether on Fourth, Fifth, Sixth, and Seventh avenues?**

   A 12 trees
   B 15 trees
   C 16 trees
   D 20 trees

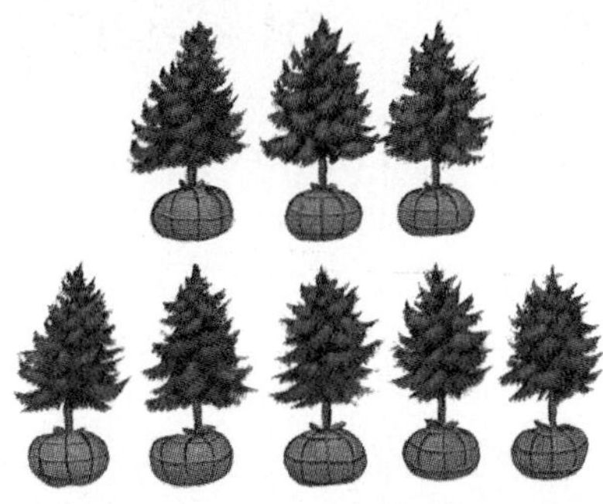

Tip

Try making a list to show the pattern in this problem. Then add to find the total number of trees.

4. **Mike made a square using square tiles. Which could be the number of tiles he used?**

   F 2
   G 5
   H 9
   J 10

5. **Susie bought 3 books that cost between \$6 and \$14. Which of these is reasonable for the total cost of the 3 books?**

   A Less than \$14
   B Between \$14 and \$17
   C Between \$18 and \$42
   D More than \$42

6. **Which is the best estimate of the total cost of 4 toys with prices of \$14.56, \$21.89, \$25.95, and \$19.20?**

   F About \$50
   G About \$60
   H About \$70
   J About \$80

7. **Four friends are sharing a box of 24 cookies equally. Which number sentence could NOT be used to show this situation?**

   A $24 \div 4 = 6$
   B $24 \div 3 = 8$
   C $6 + 6 + 6 + 6 = 24$
   D $4 \times 6 = 24$

8. **A set of 60 building blocks has an equal number of blocks in red, green, blue, and yellow. Which method could be used to find the number of red blocks?**

   F Add 60 and 4.
   G Multiply 60 times 4.
   H Divide 60 by 4.
   J Subtract 4 from 60.

The table below shows the number of marbles Jeff has in his collection.

Jeff's Marbles

Color	Number
Green	47
Blue	38
Red	22
Yellow	32

9. ***About* how many green marbles and red marbles does Jeff have?**

   A 50
   B 70
   C 80
   D 90

10. **One day a music store sold 28 classical music CDs and 57 country music CDs. Which expression shows how many classical and country music CDs the store sold that day?**

    F $28 + 28$
    G $57 - 28$
    H $28 + 57$
    J $57 + 57$

Multiple-Choice Cumulative Review

Choose the correct letter for each answer.

Number Sense

1. What is the value of the 7 in 971,234?

   A 7 thousand
   B 70 thousand
   C 700 thousand
   D 7 million

2. Which group of numbers is in order from *least* to *greatest*?

   F 6,808 6,088 6,008 6,880
   G 6,880 6,808 6,088 6,008
   H 6,008 6,088 6,808 6,880
   J 6,808 6,008 6,088 6,880

3. Which number has a 9 in the thousands place and an 8 in the hundreds place?

   A 49,850
   B 94,508
   C 459,580
   D 495,850

4. Which circle has *less than* $\frac{1}{3}$ shaded?

   F 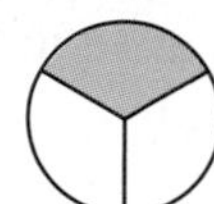
   H 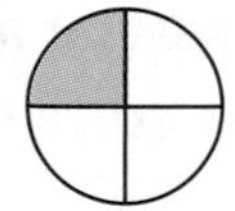
   G 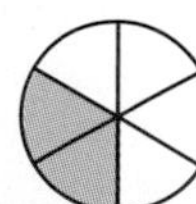
   J 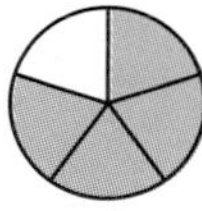

Measurement and Geometry

5. How many sides does a pentagon have?

   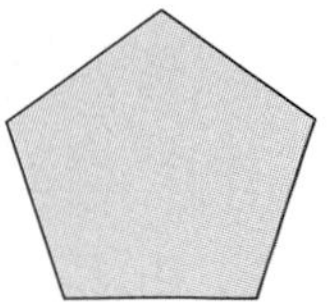

   A 4   C 6
   B 5   D 7

6. Jill has a banner that measures 20 inches by 55 inches. She wants to put ribbon around the edges. How much ribbon does she need?

   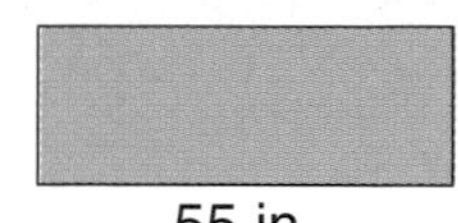

   F 35 inches   J 1,100 inches
   G 75 inches   K NH
   H 150 inches

7. How many minutes are there in 2 hours 5 minutes? (Hint: 60 minutes equals 1 hour.)

   A 25 min   D 125 min
   B 65 min   E NH
   C 120 min

8. Lisa biked 2 kilometers on Saturday and 3 kilometers on Sunday. How many *meters* did she bike? (Hint: 1 kilometer equals 1,000 meters.)

   F 5 meters   H 500 meters
   G 6 meters   J 5,000 meters

Algebra and Functions

9. Which is the rule for the table?

In	2	6	5	3	4
Out	8	24	20	12	16

A Add 6.
B Multiply by 4.
C Divide by 4.
D Multiply by 6.
E NH

10. Find the value of $y = 2x + 2$ when $x = 3$.

F $y = 3$
G $y = 7$
H $y = 8$
J $y = 9$
K NH

11. Which of the following ordered pairs is a solution to the equation $y = 4x - 1$.

A (2, 9)
B (9, 2)
C (3, 11)
D (11, 3)
E NH

12. What is the length of a line segment joining the points (3, 6) and (7, 6)?

F 1 units
G 2 units
H 3 units
J 5 units
K NH

Statistics, Data Analysis, and Probability

13. Look at the bag. How many possible outcomes are there?

A 3
B 4
C 6
D 10

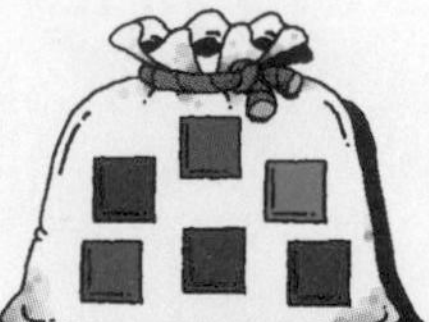

Use the graph for Questions 14–16.

The graph shows the heights of four fourth graders.

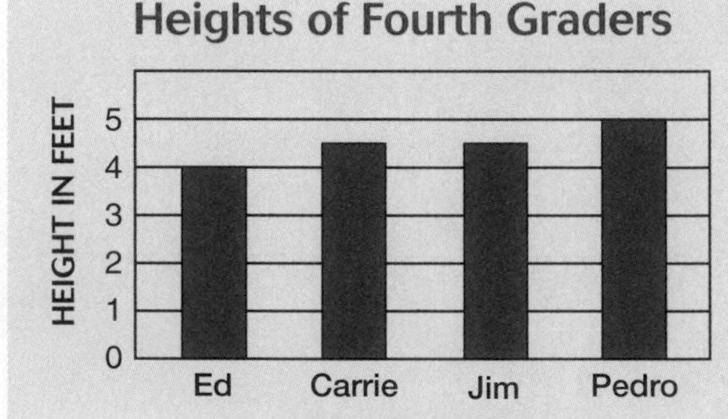

14. Which student is the shortest?

F Carrie
G Ed
H Jim
J Pedro

15. Which student is closest in height to Carrie?

A Ed
B Jim
C Carrie
D Pedro

16. How much taller is Jim than Ed? (Hint: 1 foot equals 12 inches.)

F 1 inch
G 3 inches
H 6 inches
J 10 inches
K NH

Geometry

Diagnosing Readiness

In Chapter 11, you will use these skills:

A Lines, Segments, Rays, and Angles

(Grade 3)

Tell whether each figure shows a *line, segment, ray,* or *angle.*

1. M N

2. O P

3.

4. E F

B Classifying Angles

(Grade 3)

Tell whether each angle is a *right angle, greater than a right angle,* or *less than a right angle.*

5. 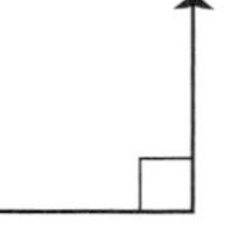

6. 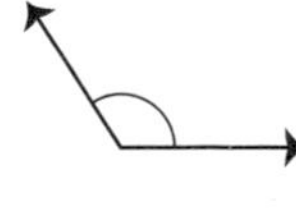

7. 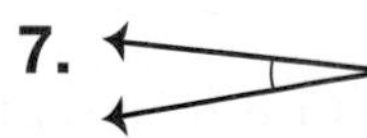

8. 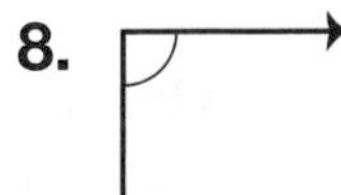

C Plane Figures

(Grade 3)

Tell how many sides each figure has.

9. 

10. 

11. 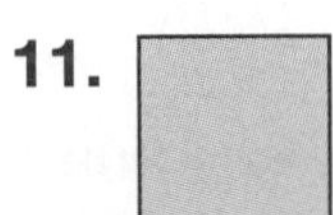

12. 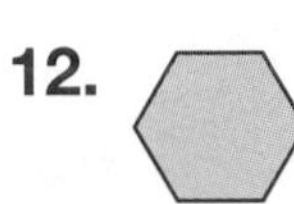

13. 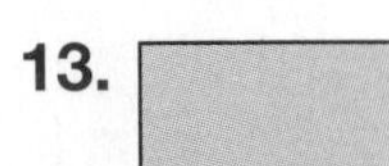

14. 

D Classifying Triangles Using Sides

(Grade 3)

Tell whether each triangle is *equilateral, isosceles,* or *scalene.*

15. 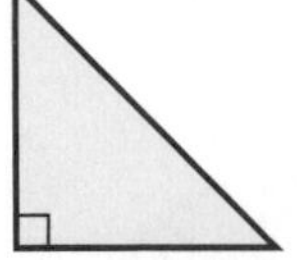

16. 

17. 

18. 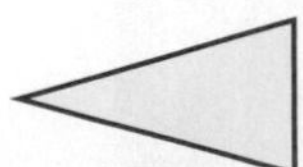

E Quadrilaterals

(Grade 3)

Write *yes* or *no.*

19. Does a square always have parallel sides?

20. Does a square always have right angles?

21. Does a square always have all 4 sides congruent?

22. Does a parallelogram always have opposite sides parallel?

23. Does a parallelogram always have right angles?

F Multiplying Two-Digit Numbers

(pages 134–136)

24. 3×12

25. 3×25

26. 3×19

27. 3×47

28. 3×78

29. 3×99

30. Tina ran about 3 times as far as Thomas. Thomas ran 35 meters. About how far did Tina run?

To the Family and Student

Looking Back

In Grade 3, students learned how to classify geometric shapes.

Chapter 11

Geometry

In this chapter, students will learn how to identify plane and solid geometric figures and relationships between them.

Looking Ahead

In Chapter 12, students will learn how to find the perimeter and area of different geometric shapes.

Math and Everyday Living

Opportunities to apply the concepts of Chapter 11 abound in everyday situations. During the chapter, think about how geometry can be used to solve a variety of real-world problems. The following examples suggest just several of the many situations that could launch a discussion about geometry.

Math in Architecture What kinds of polygons are shown? How many sides and vertices does each polygon have?

Math and Sports What are the shapes of first, second, and third bases on a baseball field? What is the shape of home plate?

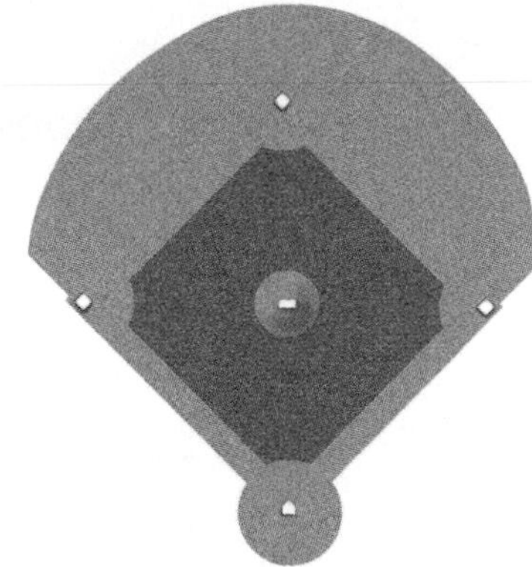

How many rectangles are in a soccer field?

Math at the Grocery Store Which solid figure does each object look like?

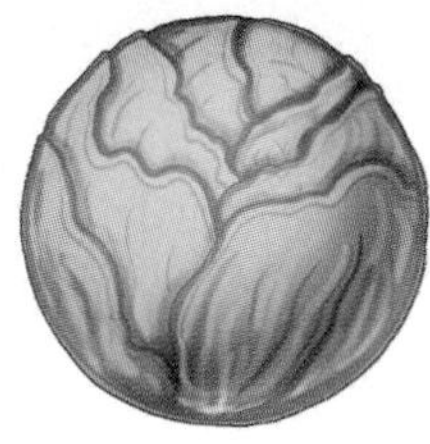

California Content Standards in Chapter 11 Lessons*

	Teach and Practice	Practice
Algebra and Functions		
1.1 Use letters, boxes, or other symbols to stand for any number in simple expressions or equations		11-3
Measurement and Geometry		
2.0 (🔑) Students use two-dimensional coordinate grids to represent points and graph lines and simple figures:		11-4, 11-8
3.0 Students demonstrate an understanding of plane . . . geometric objects and use this knowledge to show relationships and solve problems:	11-2, 11-10	
3.1 Identify lines that are parallel and perpendicular.	11-1	
3.2 Identify the radius and diameter of a circle.	11-6	
3.3 Identify congruent figures.	11-7	11-14
3.4 Identify figures that have bilateral and rotational symmetry.	11-9, 11-11	
3.5 Know the definitions of a right angle, an acute angle, and an obtuse angle. Understand that 90°, 180°, 270°, and 360° are associated with $\frac{1}{4}$, $\frac{1}{2}$, $\frac{3}{4}$, and full turns.	11-1, 11-11	
3.6 Visualize, describe, and make models of geometric solids (e.g., prisms, pyramids) in terms of the number and shape of faces, edges, and vertices; interpret two-dimensional representations of three-dimensional objects; and draw patterns (of faces) for a solid that, when cut and folded, will make a model of the solid.	11-12, 11-13	
3.7 Know the definitions of different triangles (e.g., equilateral, isosceles, scalene) and identify their attributes.	11-3	11-5
3.8 Know the definitions of different quadrilaterals (e.g., rhombus, square, rectangle, parallelogram, trapezoid).	11-4	11-5

	Teach and Practice	Practice
Mathematical Reasoning		
1.1 Analyze problems by identifying relationships . . . sequencing and prioritizing information, and observing patterns.	11-5, 11-8, 11-14	
2.0 Students use strategies, skills, and concepts in finding solutions:		11-5, 11-14
2.2 Apply strategies and results from simpler problems to more complex problems.	11-14	11-5
2.3 Use a variety of methods such as words, numbers, symbols, . . . diagrams, . . . to explain mathematical reasoning.		11-3
3.2 Note the method of deriving the solution and demonstrate a conceptual understanding of the derivation by solving similar problems.		11-8

* The symbol (🔑) indicates a key standard as designated in the Mathematics Framework for California Public Schools. Full statements of the California Content Standards are found at the beginning of this book following the Table of Contents.

Points, Lines, Segments, Rays, and Angles

California Content Standards *Measurement and Geometry 3.1: Identify lines that are parallel and perpendicular. Also Measurement and Geometry 3.5* *(See page 437.)*

Math Link You already know some geometric words, such as *line*. In this lesson, you will learn about parts of lines, special pairs of lines, and types of angles.

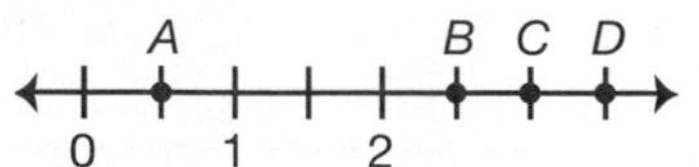

Warm-Up Review

Name the point that gives the location of each number.

A B C D
0 1 2

1. 3 **2.** 2.5

3. 0.5 **4.** 3.5

5. Sean baby-sits regularly for two different families. Sean earns about $35 a month babysitting. About how much will Sean earn babysitting in one year?

The table below lists common geometric terms.

Term	Example	Say
A **point** is an exact location in space.	A •	point *A*
A **line** is a set of points that go on and on in both directions.	B C (line)	line *BC*
A **line segment** is part of a line. It has two endpoints.	D E (segment)	line segment *DE*
A **ray** is part of a line. It has one endpoint and continues on and on in one direction.	E F (ray)	ray *EF*
An **angle** is formed when two rays meet at their endpoints. The common endpoint is the **vertex**.	P Q R, vertex	angle *Q* or angle *PQR* or angle *RQP*

Use the angle symbol (∠) to write the name of an angle. The angle shown in the chart can be represented as ∠*Q*, ∠*PQR*, or ∠*RQP*. When three letters are used, the middle letter always names the vertex.

Example 1

The size of an angle depends on the opening between its rays. Here are four different types of angles.

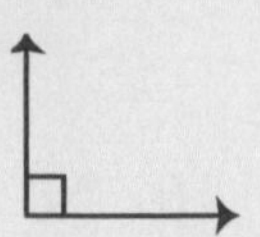

A **right angle** is an angle that forms a square corner.

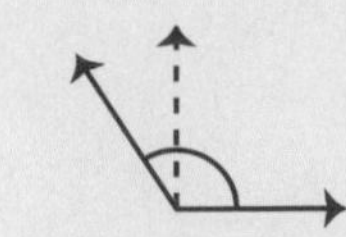

An **obtuse angle** is greater than a right angle.

An **acute angle** is less than a right angle.

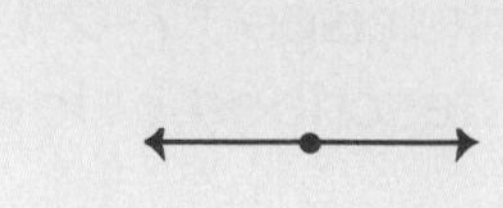

A **straight angle** forms a straight line.

Word Bank
- point
- line
- line segment
- ray
- angle
- vertex
- right angle
- obtuse angle
- acute angle
- straight angle
- intersecting lines
- parallel lines
- perpendicular lines

Example 2

Here are three ways that two different lines can be related.

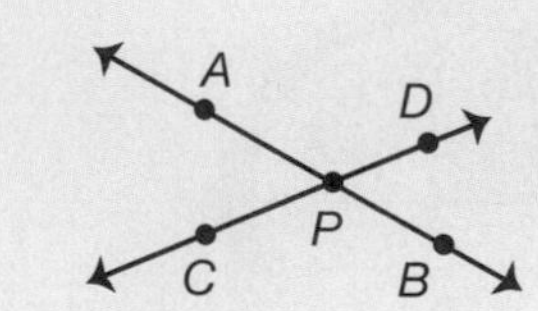

Intersecting lines pass through the same point. Line *AB* intersects line *CD* at point *P*.

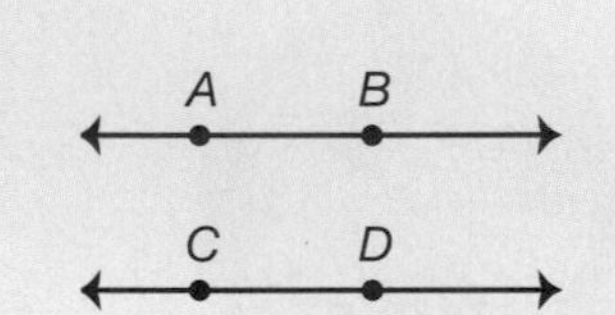

Parallel lines never intersect. Line *AB* is parallel to line *CD*.

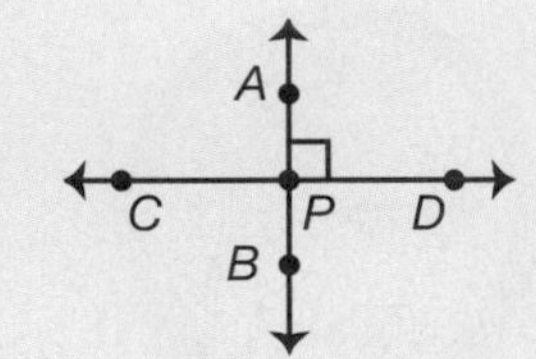

Perpendicular lines intersect to form right angles. If $\angle APD$ is a right angle, then line *AB* is perpendicular to line *CD*.

You can use the perpendicular symbol ($\perp$) when you name perpendicular lines. In the last diagram above, you can write line $AB \perp$ line *CD*.

Guided Practice *For another example, see Set A on p. 478.*

Tell what type of figure is shown.

1.  **2.** **3.** 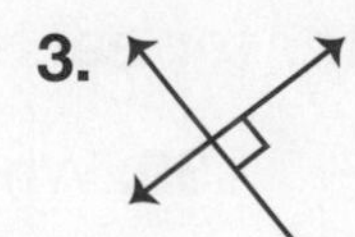 **4.** **5.** 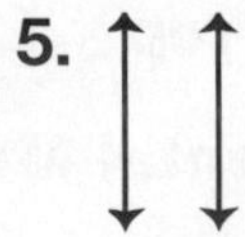

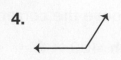

6. Draw and label $\angle FGH$, an acute angle.

Independent Practice *For more practice, see Set A on p. 481.*

Tell what type of figure is shown.

7. **8.** **9.** **10.** **11.**

12.

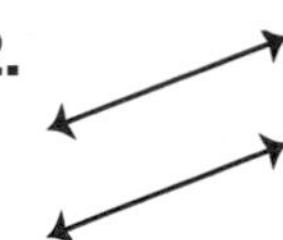

13. **14.** **15.**

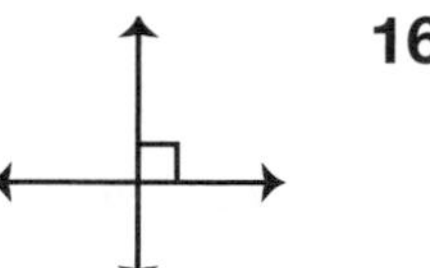

16.

Use the drawing at the right for Exercises 17–24. Name an example of each figure described below.

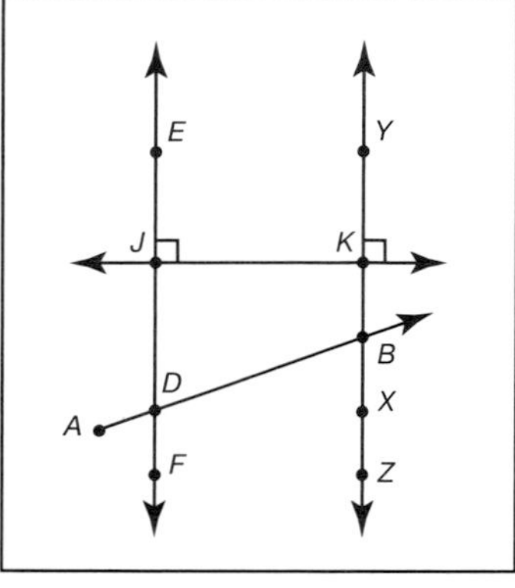

17. point **18.** line **19.** line segment

20. ray **21.** right angle **22.** acute angle

23. parallel lines **24.** perpendicular lines

Name the type of shaded angle formed by each clock's hands.

25.

26.

27.

Mixed Review

28. Algebra Find five ordered pairs on the graph of the equation $y = 2x + 1$.

29. Algebra Find the length of the line segment joining (3, 2) and (13, 2).

30. 43.25 + 16.09 **31.** 83.2 − 47.63 **32.** 3,602 × 7 **33.** 945 ÷ 5

34. 439 + 618 **35.** 574 − 229 **36.** 6 × (17 + 8) **37.** 499 × 13

Test Prep **Choose the correct letter for each answer.**

38. Mental Math 400 × 8 =
(4-1)

A 32 **C** 3,200

B 320 **D** 32,000

39. Which number is less than 5,000?
(1-3)

F 4,925 **H** 5,002

G 5,000 **J** 5,999

Polygons

Warm-Up Review

How many sides does each shape have?

1. triangle **2.** rectangle

3. square **4.** circle

5. Jill is installing a fence around a square garden. Each side of fencing costs $21.80. How much will the entire fence cost?

California Content Standard *Measurement and Geometry 3.0: Students demonstrate an understanding of plane . . . geometric objects and use this knowledge to show relationships and solve problems.*

Math Link You already know about different shapes, such as triangles, circles, and squares. In this lesson you will learn about a family of shapes called polygons.

Word Bank

plane figure
polygon
sides
vertex (vertices)
triangle
quadrilateral
pentagon
hexagon
octagon

The world around you is filled with flat shapes called **plane figures**. A **polygon** is a closed plane figure made up of three or more line segments that intersect only at their endpoints. The line segments that form a polygon are called **sides**. A point where two sides of the polygon meet is called a **vertex**. We use **vertices** when referring to more than one vertex.

Here are some examples of polygons.

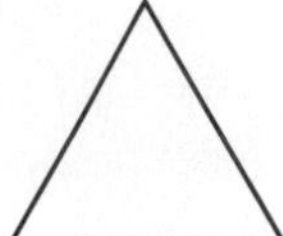

Triangle
3 sides

Quadrilateral
4 sides

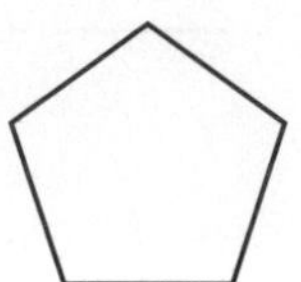

Pentagon
5 sides

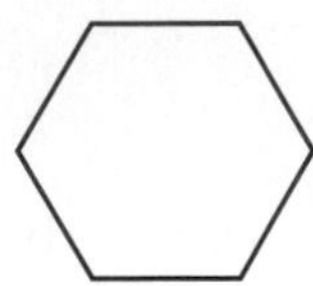

Hexagon
6 sides

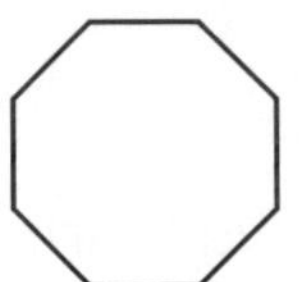

Octagon
8 sides

Here are some examples of plane figures that are *not* polygons.

a.

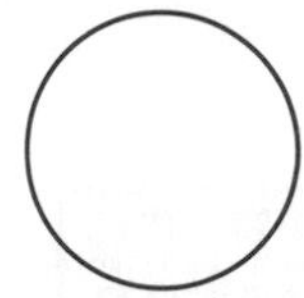

A circle is not a polygon because it is not made up of line segments. It is curved.

b.

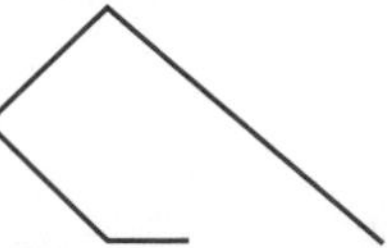

This figure is not a polygon because it is not closed.

c.

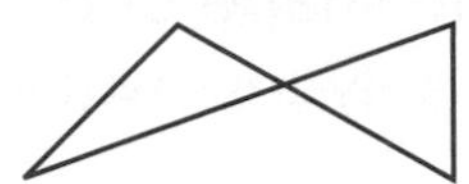

This figure is not a polygon because the line segments do not intersect only at their endpoints.

Example

Tell if each Figure is a polygon. If it is a polygon write its name.

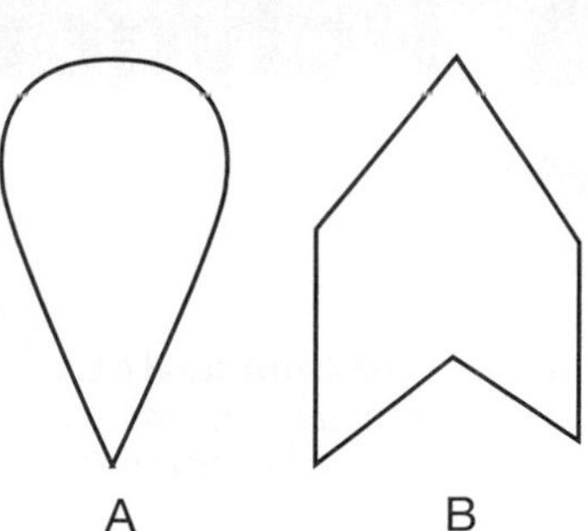

Figure A is not a polygon. The top of the Figure is curved.

Figure B is a polygon. It has 6 sides, so it is a hexagon.

Guided Practice

For another example, see Set B on p. 478.

Identify each polygon.

1. 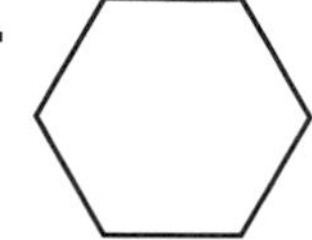

2. 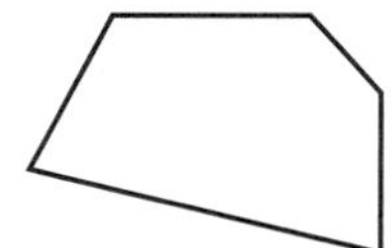

3. 

4. 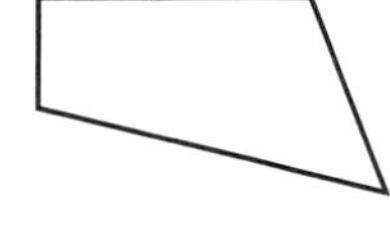

Tell if the plane figure is a polygon. Write *yes* or *no*.

5. 

6. 

7. 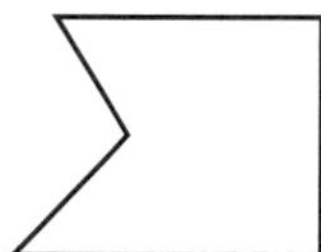

8. 

9. Trace the polygon from Exercise 1 two times. Draw a line segment that divides the polygon into two quadrilaterals. Then draw a line segment that divides the polygon into two pentagons.

Independent Practice

For more practice, see Set B on p. 481.

Tell if the shape of each figure is a polygon. Write *yes* or *no*. If it is a polygon, write its name.

10. 

11. 

12. 

13. 

Tell if the plane figure is a polygon. Write *yes* or *no*.

14. 

15. 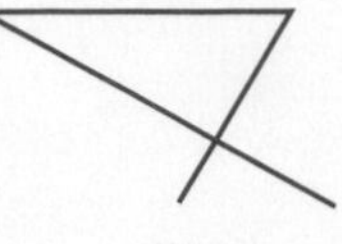

16. 

17. 

18. Copy and complete the table at the right.

Name of Polygon	Number of Sides	Number of Vertices
Triangle		
	4	
		5
Hexagon		
		8

Math Reasoning **Refer to the names of the polygons to help you answer Exercises 19–21.**

19. A pentagram is a star. How many points do you think it has?

20. A mother gave birth to quadruplets. How many babies were born?

21. Explain how the words *octagon* and *octopus* are related.

Mixed Review

22. Algebra Given the equation $y = 4x - 9$. What is the value of y when $x = 8$?

23. Draw an acute angle.

24. Draw a pair of parallel lines.

25. $\frac{1}{4} + \frac{3}{4}$ **26.** $\frac{1}{2} + \frac{3}{8}$ **27.** $\frac{2}{3} - \frac{1}{3}$ **28.** $\frac{5}{8} - \frac{1}{4}$ **29.** $5\frac{1}{9} + 6\frac{5}{9}$

Test Prep **Choose the correct letter for each answer.**

30. (7-12) What is the probability of spinning a 3 on the spinner shown below?

A $\frac{1}{8}$ **C** $\frac{3}{8}$

B $\frac{1}{4}$ **D** $\frac{3}{4}$

31. (5-6) Bonnie's sister is buying sheets and a blanket for her dormitory room at college. She can choose blue, green, or yellow sheets and a striped or plaid blanket. How many sheet-and-blanket combinations are there in all?

F 2 **H** 5

G 3 **J** 6

Triangles

Warm-Up Review

1. Draw a triangle that has a right angle.
2. Draw a triangle that has an obtuse angle.
3. Draw a triangle that has 3 acute angles.
4. Draw a triangle with all 3 sides about 1 in. long.

California Content Standard *Measurement and Geometry 3.7: Know the definitions of different triangles (e.g., equilateral, isosceles, scalene) and identify their attributes.*

Math Link You know that a triangle is a polygon with three sides. Now you will learn about different types of triangles.

You can classify triangles if you know the lengths of their sides.

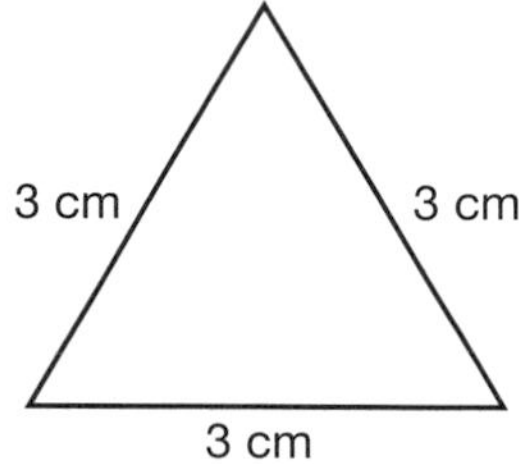

An **equilateral triangle** has all three sides that are the same length.

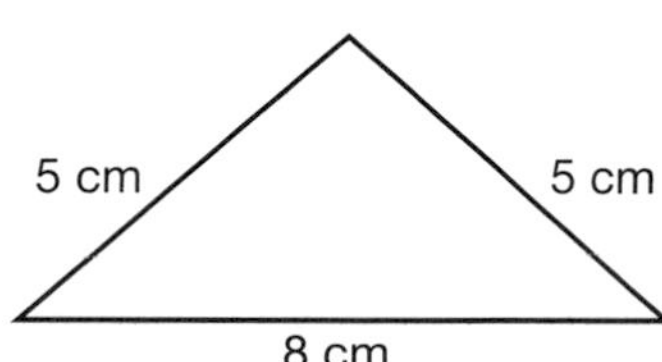

An **isosceles triangle** has two sides that are the same length.

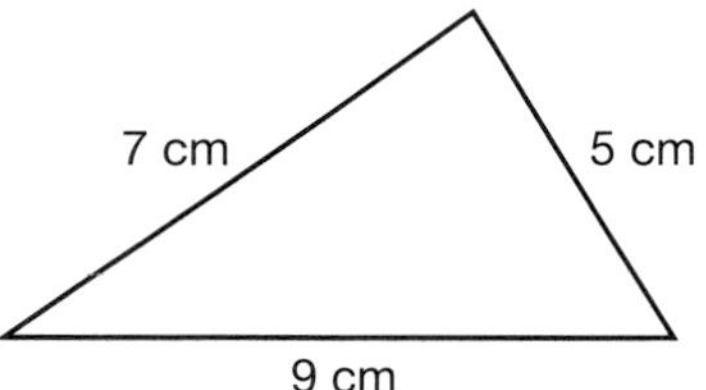

A **scalene triangle** has no two sides that are the same length.

You can also classify triangles by their angles.

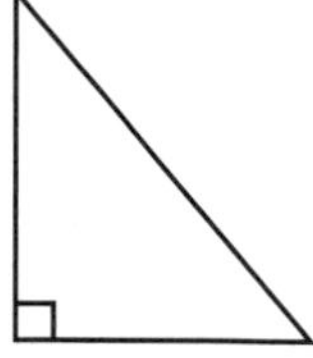

A **right triangle** has one right angle.

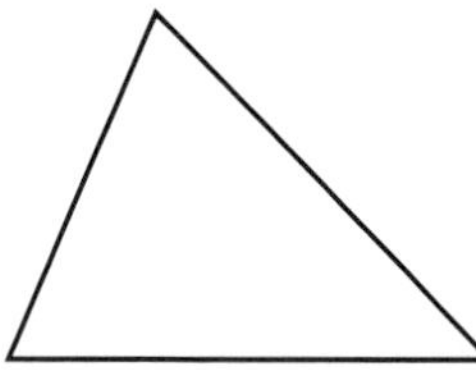

An **acute triangle** has three acute angles.

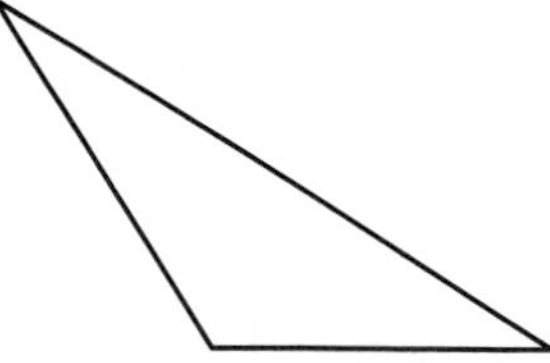

An **obtuse triangle** has one obtuse angle.

Example

Classify the triangle shown at the right by its sides and its angles.

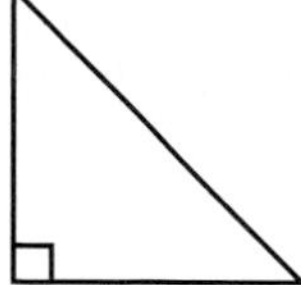

The triangle is a right triangle because it has a right angle. The triangle is also isosceles because it has two sides that are the same length.

Word Bank

- equilateral triangle
- isosceles triangle
- scalene triangle
- right triangle
- acute triangle
- obtuse triangle

 Additional Standard: Mathematical Reasoning 2.3 (See page 437.)

Guided Practice *For another example, see Set C on p. 478.*

Classify each triangle by its sides and its angles.

1. 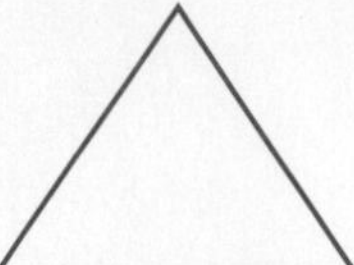

2. 

3. 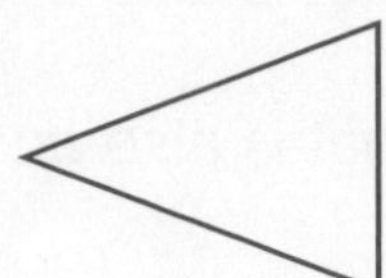

4. 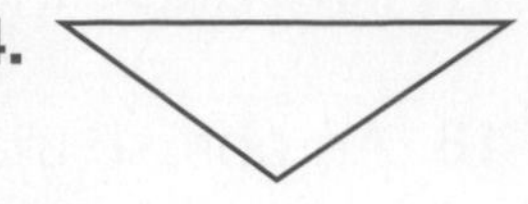

5. Math Reasoning Two sides of an isosceles triangle measure 2 inches and 3 inches. How long is the third side? Explain.

Independent Practice *For more practice, see Set C on p. 481.*

Classify each triangle by its sides and its angles.

6. 

7. 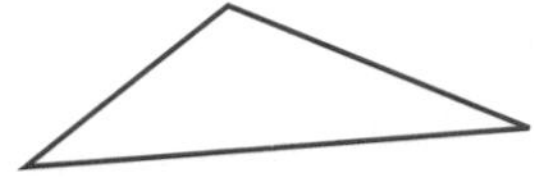

8. 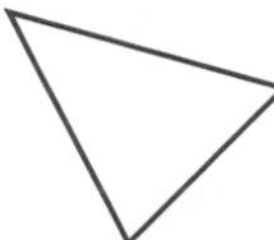

The lengths of the sides of a triangle are given. Classify each triangle.

9. 5 in., 6 in., 5 in.

10. 10 ft, 10 ft, 10 ft

11. 8 cm, 4 cm, 7 cm

In each flag below, a triangle is labeled with a letter. Classify each lettered triangle by the length of its sides.

12. 

Papua New Guinea

13. 

Guyana

14. 

São Tomé and Príncipe

15. A triangle has two sides that are each 4 cm. What kind of triangle would it be if the third side was 2 cm? 4cm? 6 cm? Classify each triangle by the length of its sides.

16. The New City Auto Supply uses an equilateral triangle as its symbol. One side of the New City symbol measures 15 inches. How long are the other two sides?

Draw each figure described. If it is not possible, write *not possible*.

17. An obtuse triangle that is also a scalene triangle

18. An obtuse triangle that is also an isosceles triangle

19. An obtuse triangle that is also an equilateral triangle

20. Trace the rectangle at the right. Draw line segment *AC*. Look at the two triangles formed. Describe them by their sides. Then describe them by their angles.

21. Trace the rectangle at the right again. This time draw line segment *AC* and line segment *BD*. Look at the four triangles formed. Describe them by their sides. Then describe them by their angles.

Mixed Review

22. Draw an acute angle, a right angle, an obtuse angle, and a straight angle.

23. Math Reasoning Can you draw a triangle with two sides that are parallel? Explain.

24. A polygon has five vertices. How many sides does it have?

25. What type of polygon has eight sides? Draw an example.

26. Algebra Copy and complete the table at the right.

x	$x + 37$
5	
21	
146	

Use division rules to find each missing number. If it is not possible to divide, explain why.

27. $0 \div 7 = n$ **28.** $5 \div 0 = n$ **29.** $6 \div 6 = n$ **30.** $3 \div n = 3$

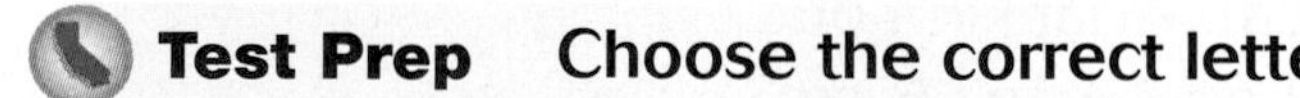

Test Prep **Choose the correct letter for each answer.**

31. (5-5) Sue's dance team lined up in 15 rows for a parade, with 12 dancers in each row. How many dancers lined up for the parade in all?

A 27 dancers **C** 170 dancers

B 45 dancers **D** 180 dancers

32. (6-3) Scott baked 40 cookies. He wants to distribute them equally to 6 friends. How many cookies will he have left over?

F 6 cookies **H** 3 cookies

G 5 cookies **J** 2 cookies

K NH

Quadrilaterals

California Content Standard *Measurement and Geometry 3.8: Know the definitions of different quadrilaterals (e.g., rhombus, square, rectangle, parallelogram, trapezoid).*

Math Link You know that a quadrilateral is a polygon with four sides. Now you will learn about different types of quadrilaterals.

You can identify quadrilaterals by the lengths of their sides and the sizes of their angles.

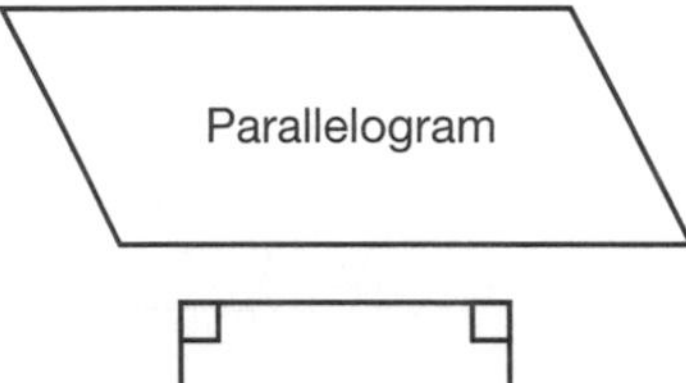

Both pairs of opposite sides are parallel.

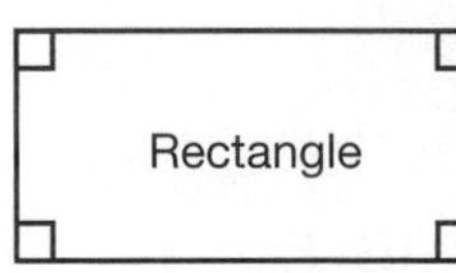

All sides are the same length. There are four right angles.

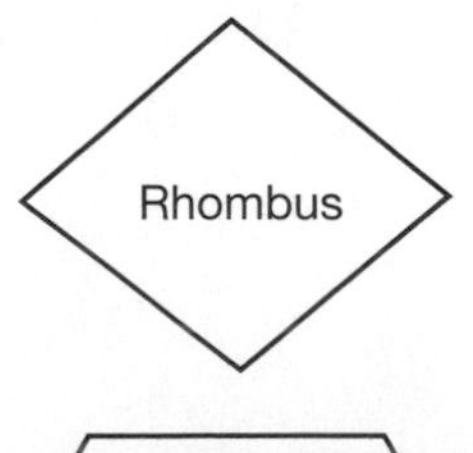

Both pairs of opposite sides are parallel. There are four right angles.

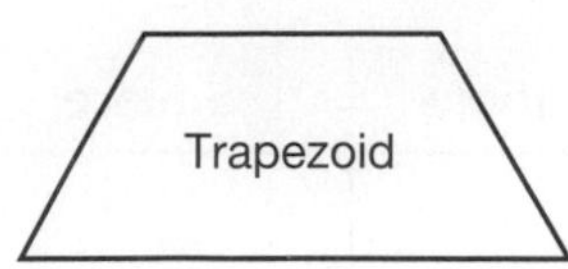

Both pairs of opposite sides are parallel. All sides are the same length.

Trapezoid

There is only one pair of parallel sides.

Warm-Up Review

Identify each polygon.

1.
2. 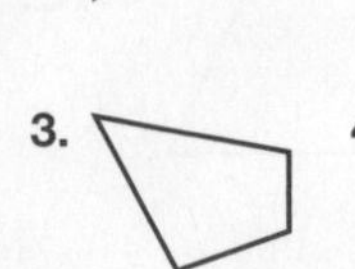
3.
4.

5. The telephone bill for the Hale family was $48.26 in April and $37.27 in May. How much more was the phone bill in April than May?

Word Bank

parallelogram
square
rectangle
rhombus
trapezoid

Example

What type of quadrilateral is shown at the right?

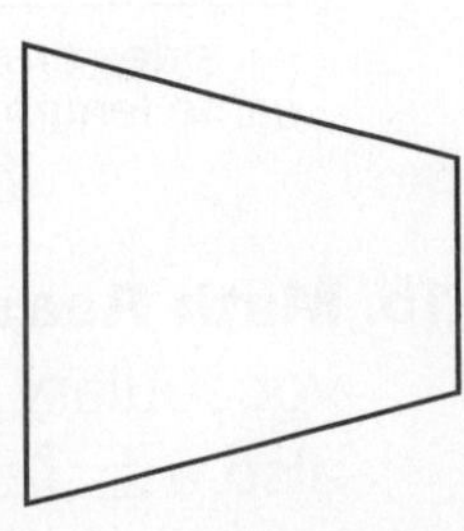

You can use the diagrams and definitions to help you decide. Look for parallel sides, right angles, and sides that have the same length.

The figure only has one pair of parallel sides, so it is a trapezoid.

Additional Standard: Measurement and Geometry 2.0 (See page 437.)

Guided Practice *For another example, see Set D on p. 478.*

What type of quadrilateral is shown?

1.

2. 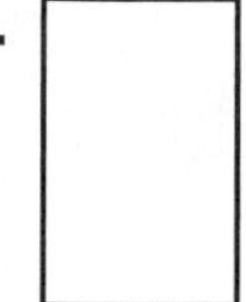

3. 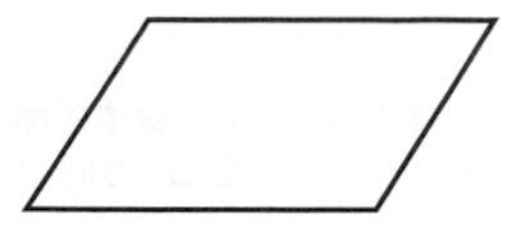

4. 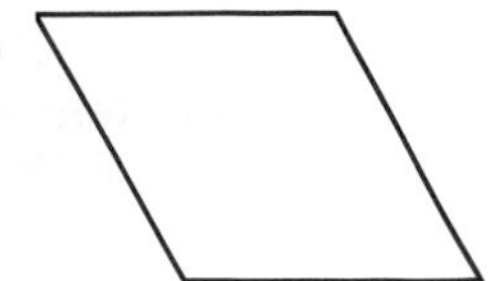

5. Draw a quadrilateral that is not a square, a rectangle, a parallelogram, a rhombus, or a trapezoid.

Independent Practice *For more practice, see Set D on p. 481.*

What type of quadrilateral is shown?

6. 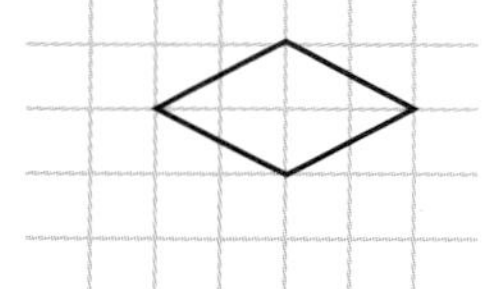

7. 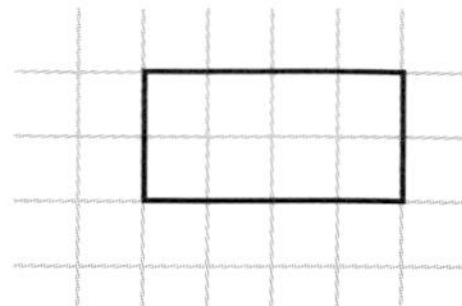

8. 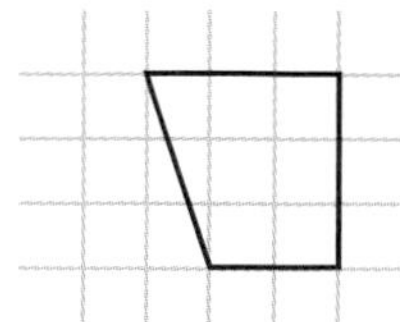

9. 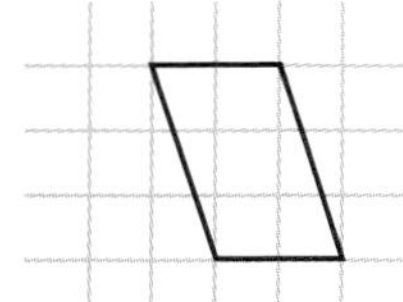

Plot each set of ordered pairs. Draw line segments to connect them in order. Then connect the last ordered pair to the first. Tell what type of quadrilateral is formed. You may use the same grid for Exercises 10–13.

10. (0, 0), (5, 0), (4, 3), (1, 3)

11. (6, 1), (8, 1), (8, 6), (6, 6)

12. (0, 5), (3, 5), (3, 8) (0, 8)

13. (4, 7), (8, 7), (10, 10), (6, 10)

14. Copy and complete the table. Mark an X in the box if the statement is true for that type of quadrilateral.

	Parallelogram	Rhombus	Rectangle	Square
Both pairs of opposite sides are parallel.				
There are four right angles.				
All sides are the same length.				

15. Math Reasoning Complete this sentence with as many vocabulary words from this chapter as you can. A square is also a __?__.

True or False.

16. All parallelograms are quadrilaterals.

17. All rectangles are squares.

18. All squares are rectangles.

19. Some quadrilaterals are trapezoids.

20. All parallelograms are rectangles.

Mixed Review

21. Sasha wants to buy hats and prizes for everyone at her birthday party. She has $15 and wants to invite 15 friends. Does she have enough money?

Party Hats	6 for $2.49
Prizes	10 for $3.49

Identify each polygon. Be as specific as you can be.

22. 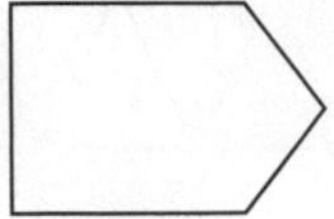

23. 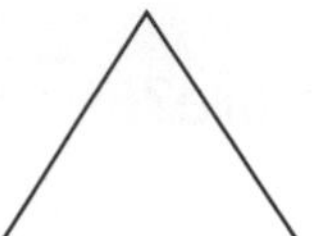

24. 

25. 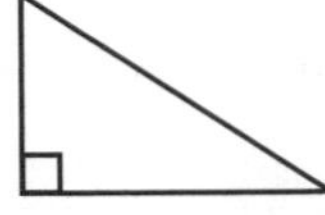

26. 452×16

27. $971 - 805$

28. $268 \div 7$

29. $814 + 59$

 **Test Prep** **Choose the correct letter for each answer.**

30. **Algebra** Which of the ordered pairs below is on the graph of the equation $y = 2x$? (10-10)

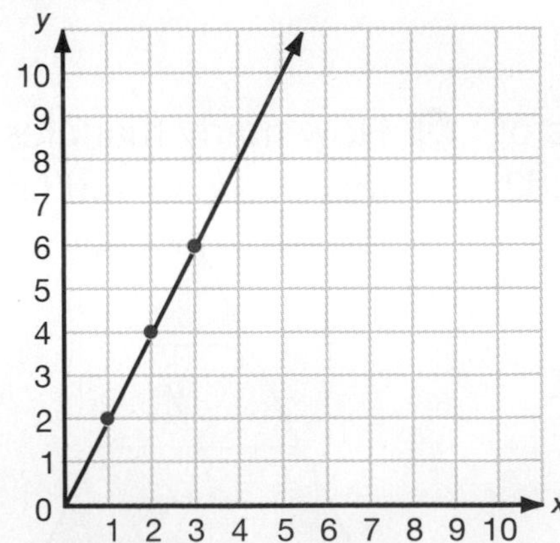

A (3, 6)

B (1, 3)

C (2, 1)

D (5, 3)

31. Randa made the following design. Which decimal describes the part of the design that is shaded? (9-1)

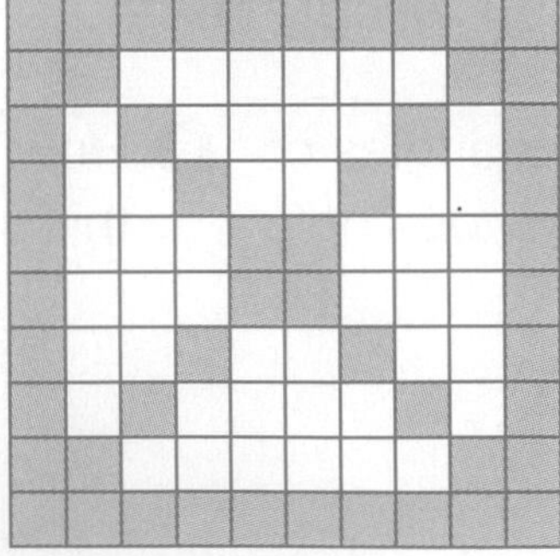

F 0.48

G 0.50

H 0.52

J 0.56

Problem-Solving Skill:

Spatial Reasoning

Warm-Up Review

1. 1 + 2 + 4 + 8 +16
2. 1 + 10 + 100 + 1000
3. 3 + 6 + 9 + 12 + 15
4. 12 + 22 + 32 + 42
5. Draw the next shape in the pattern.

 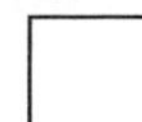 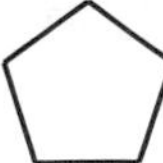

 **California Content Standard** *Mathematical Reasoning 1.1: Analyze problems by identifying relationships, . . . sequencing and prioritizing information, and observing patterns.*

Read for Understanding

Becky counted 16 triangles in the figure at the right. Robin thinks she can find more than 16 triangles.

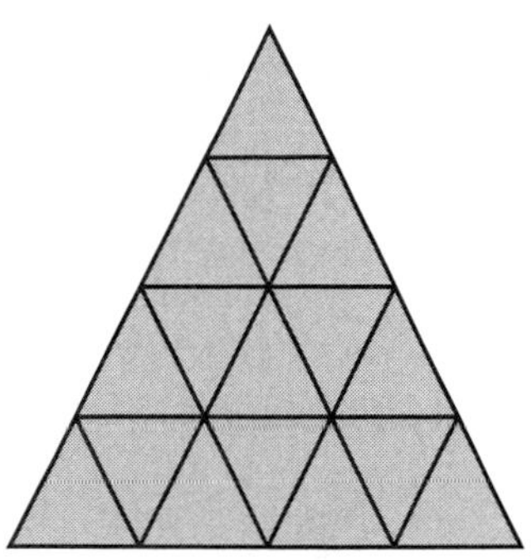

1. What geometric shape did Becky see in the figure?
2. How many of these shapes did Becky count?
3. How many triangles does Robin think there are?

Think and Discuss

Spatial Reasoning

If you look at a figure carefully, sometimes you can find geometric shapes and patterns in it. Finding these shapes and patterns can help you solve problems.

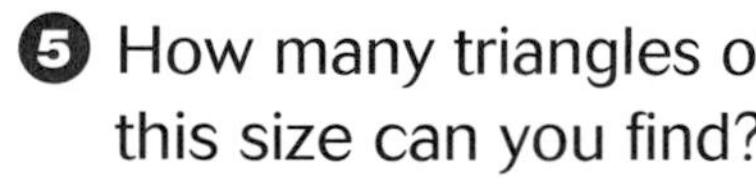

Look again at the given figure.

4. How many triangles of this size can you find?

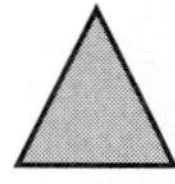

5. How many triangles of this size can you find?

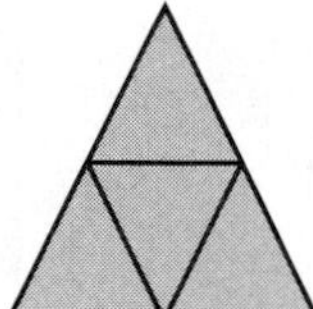

6. How many triangles of this size can you find?

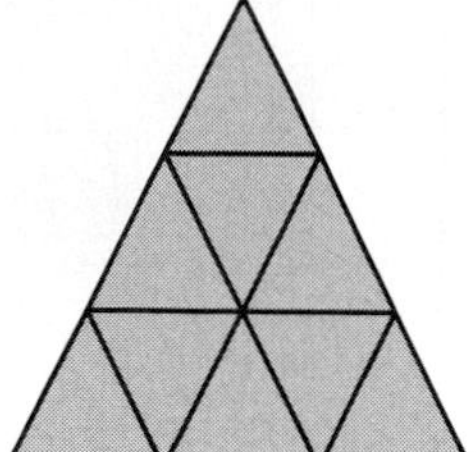

7. What is the biggest triangle in the figure?
8. How many triangles can you find in the figure?

 Additional Standards: Measurement and Geometry 3.7, 3.8; Mathematical Reasoning 2.0, 2.2 *(See p. 437.)*

Guided Practice

1. How many different sizes of squares are in the figure at the right?

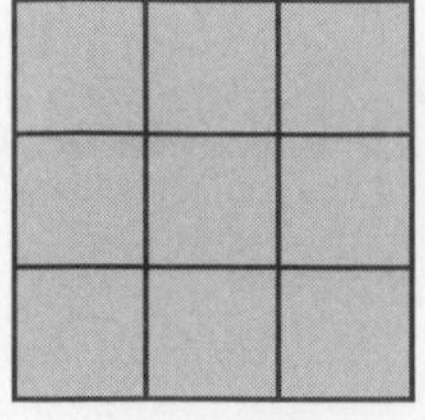

   a. 1 size

   b. 2 sizes

   c. 3 sizes

2. How many squares in all are in the figure?

   a. 9 squares

   b. 13 squares

   c. 14 squares

3. How many quadrilaterals that are *not* squares are in the figure?

   a. more than 10

   b. less than 10

   c. exactly 10

Independent Practice

4. Which group of three shapes below could be put together to make the shaded rectangle shown at the right? The shapes may be turned.

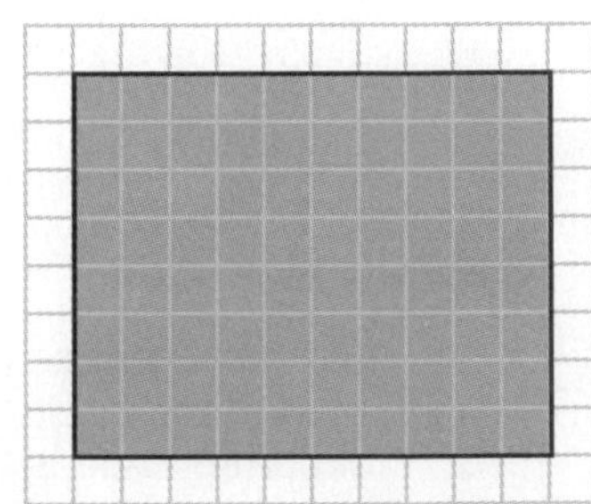

a.

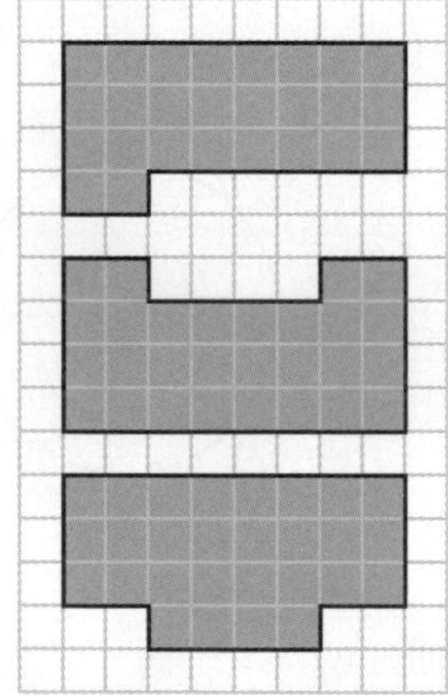

b.

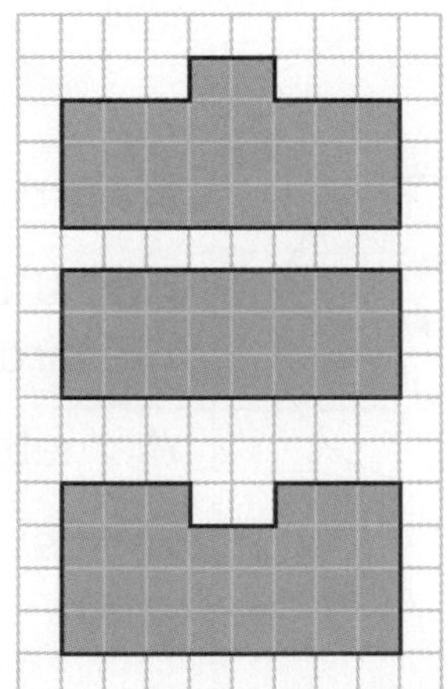

c.

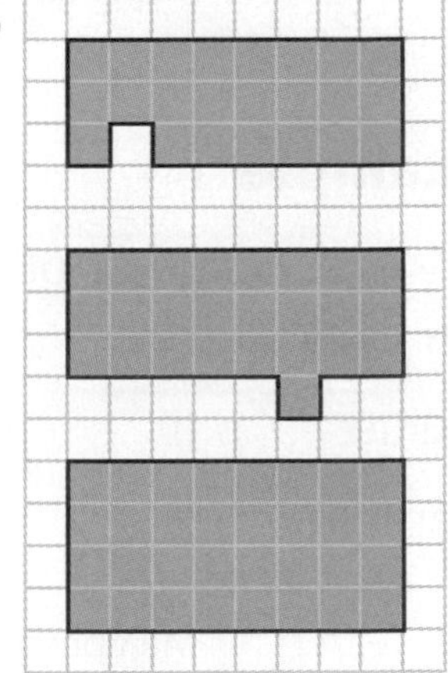

5. **Math Reasoning** Which 3 line segments could you remove from the figure at the right so that there would be only 2 quadrilaterals left?

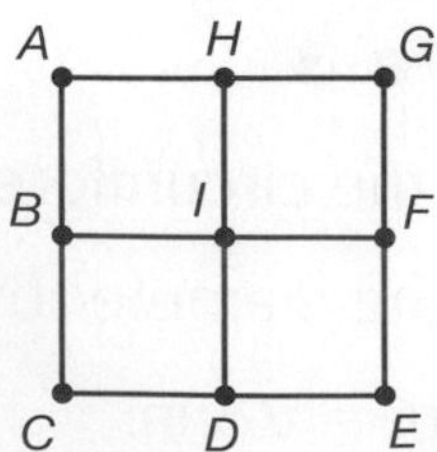

Circles

California Content Standard *Measurement and Geometry 3.2: Identify the radius and diameter of a circle.*

Warm-Up Review

Write the fraction for the shaded parts of each circle.

1. 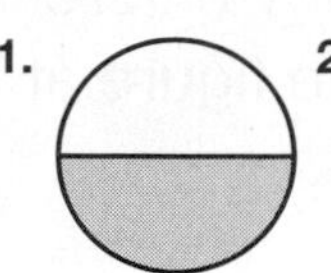
2. 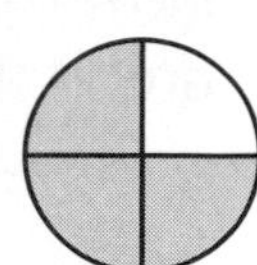
3. Fred had 48 marbles. He gave 9 of them to his sister and shared the remaining marbles equally with his two brothers. How many marbles do each of the 3 boys have?

Math Link You have learned about many different types of polygons. Now you will study circles and parts of a circle.

A **circle** is a closed curve that is made up of points that are the same distance from a point called the center.

Word Bank

circle
radius
diameter
circumference

Some Parts of a Circle

Radius—any line segment that connects the center to a point on the circle.

Circumference—distance around the circle. The circumference is a little more than three times as long as the diameter.

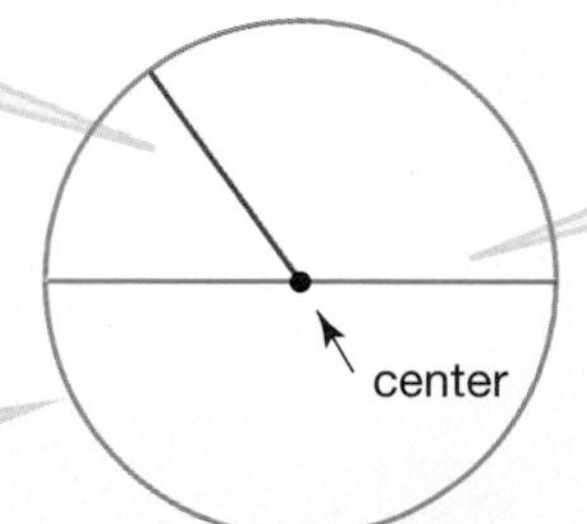

Diameter—any line segment that passes through the center of the circle, connecting two points on the circle.

The diameter is twice as long as the radius.

Example 1

Find the diameter of the circle.

radius: 5 ft

diameter: 5 ft × 2 = 10 ft

Multiply by 2.

Example 2

Find the radius of the circle.

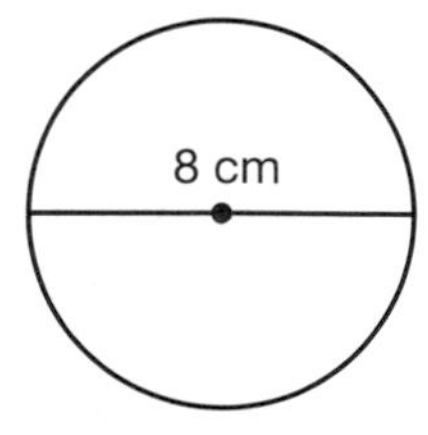

diameter: 8 cm

radius: 8 cm ÷ 2 = 4 cm

Divide by 2.

Example 3

Estimate the circumference of the bicycle wheel.

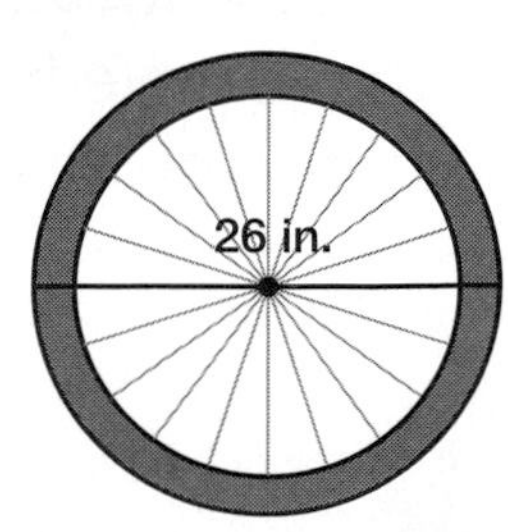

Multiply the diameter by 3.

3 × 26 in. = 78 in.

The circumference of the wheel is about 78 inches.

Guided Practice *For another example, see Set E on p. 479.*

Identify the part of each circle shown in blue.

1. 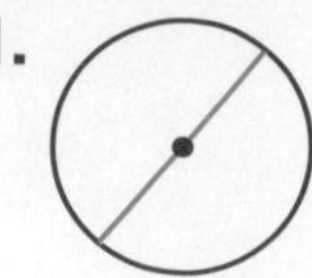

2. 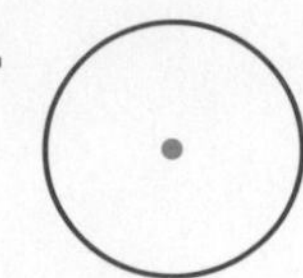

3. 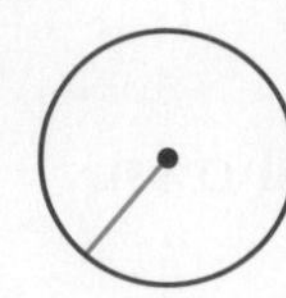

4. 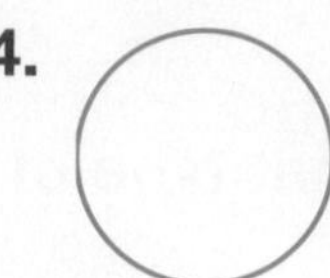

5. The diameter of a circular table top is 4 feet. Estimate the circumference of the table top.

Independent Practice *For more practice, see Set E on p. 482.*

Find the radius or diameter of each circle. Estimate the circumference.

6. 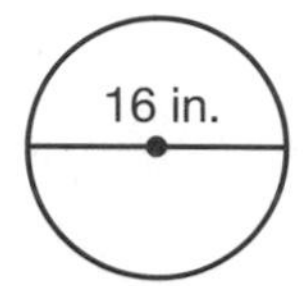

7. 

8. 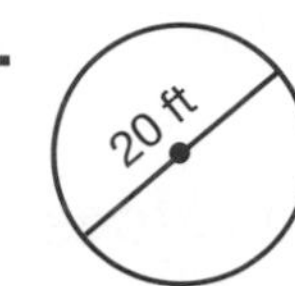

9. 

10. Mental Math The circumference of a pizza pan is 120 centimeters. Estimate the length of its diameter.

11. Math Reasoning Draw a circle. Draw a line segment that connects two points of the circle but does not pass through the center. Does this line segment seem to be shorter than, longer than, or the same length as the diameter?

Mixed Review

12. Write forty-three hundredths as a decimal.

Draw an example of each figure.

13. trapezoid **14.** obtuse triangle **15.** rhombus **16.** scalene triangle

17. 14.24 + 16.09 **18.** 13.72 − 8.88 **19.** 2.4 + 1.1 + 7.6 **20.** 9.8 − 2.94

Test Prep **Choose the correct letter for each answer.**

21. Which is a prime number?
(6-9)

A 21 **C** 31
B 30 **D** 39

22. 238 × 26 =
(5-7)

F 5,188 **H** 6,098
G 6,088 **J** 6,188
K NH

Diagnostic Checkpoint

Tell what type of figure is shown.

1. (11-1) 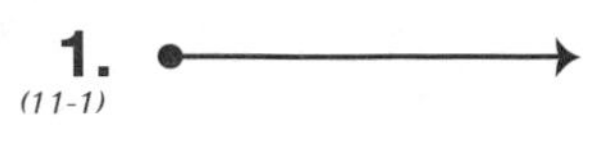

2. (11-1) 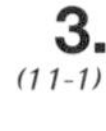

3. (11-1) 

4. (11-1) 

Tell if the shape of each figure is a polygon. Write *yes* or *no*. If it is a polygon, write its name.

5. (11-2) 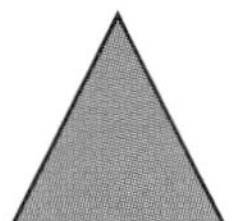

6. (11-2) 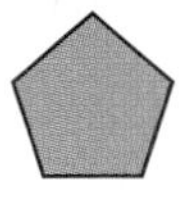

7. (11-2) 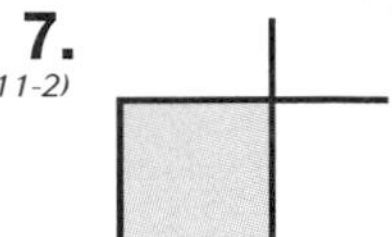

8. (11-2) 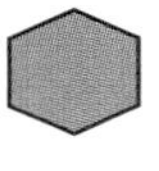

Describe each triangle by its sides. Then describe it by its angles.

9. (11-3) 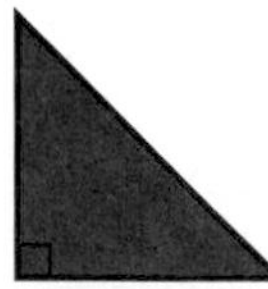

10. (11-3) 

11. (11-3) 

12. (11-4) What type of quadrilateral is shown at the right?

Find the radius of each circle. Estimate the circumference.

13. (11-6) 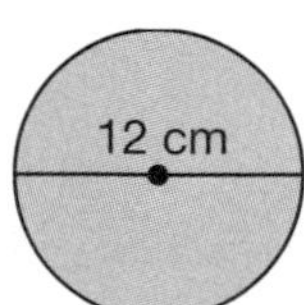

14. (11-6) 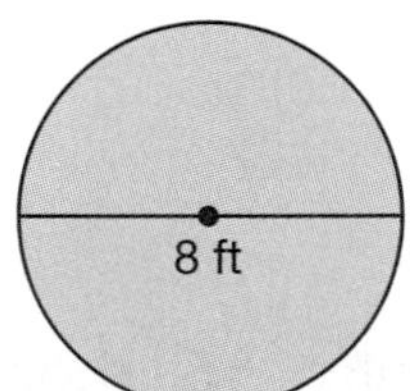

15. (11-6) 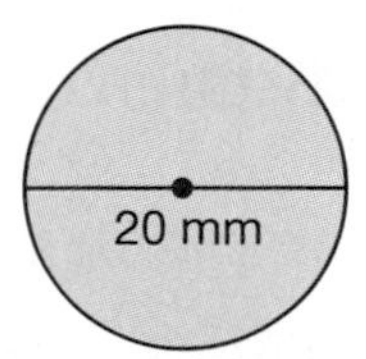

16. (11-5) How many squares in all are in the figure at the right?

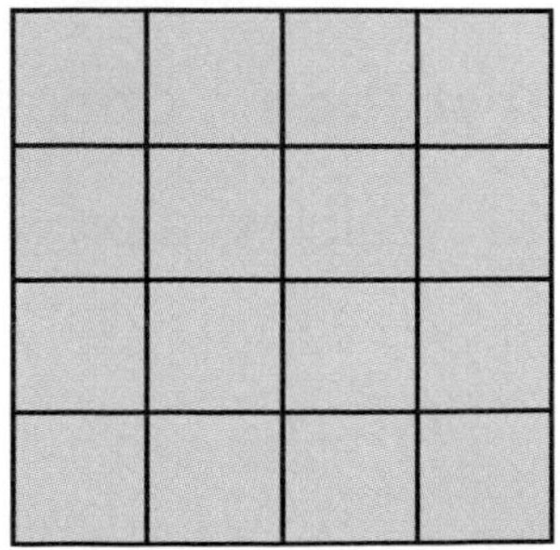

Multiple-Choice Cumulative Review

Choose the correct letter for each answer.

1. Which figure has 8 sides?

- **A** pentagon
- **B** square
- **C** octagon
- **D** hexagon

2. Which is a set of even numbers?

F	2	8	12	16
G	3	9	12	20
H	4	6	7	14
J	2	5	8	13

3. The parents at Smith School are having a bake sale. At the end of the day, they decide to round all their prices to the nearest 10¢. If an item originally cost 75¢, what will it cost now?

- **A** 60¢
- **B** 70¢
- **C** 80¢
- **D** $1.00

4. Which number sentence is in the same family of facts as $8 \times 3 = 24$?

- **F** $3 + 8 = 11$
- **G** $24 \div 3 = 8$
- **H** $8 - 3 = 5$
- **J** $24 \div 6 = 4$

5. What is the value of $31 - n$ when $n = 12$?

- **A** 43 **C** 29
- **B** 31 **D** 19

Use the graph for Questions 6–8.

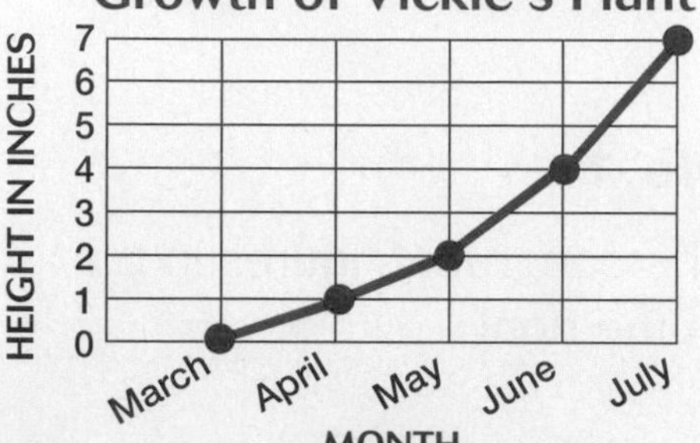

6. When did Vickie's plant grow the most?

- **F** March to April
- **G** April to May
- **H** May to June
- **J** June to July

7. How many inches did the plant grow between June and July?

- **A** 1 in. **C** 3 in.
- **B** 2 in. **D** 4 in.

8. How much did the plant grow from April to July?

- **F** 3 in. **H** 6 in.
- **G** 4 in. **J** 7 in.

Congruent Figures

California Content Standard *Measurement and Geometry 3.3: Identify congruent figures.*

Math Link You can already identify different types of plane figures. Now you will learn to identify figures that have the same size and shape.

Warm-Up Review

Draw each figure.

1. square
2. rectangle
3. circle
4. pentagon
5. parallelogram
6. equilateral triangle
7. Kelly bought a book for \$19.95. The tax was \$1.35. How much change did she receive from \$25.00?

Word Bank

congruent

Two figures that have the same size and shape are **congruent**. If a figure can be moved so that it fits exactly on another figure, the figures are congruent.

Example 1

Identify the congruent figures in the mobile at the right.

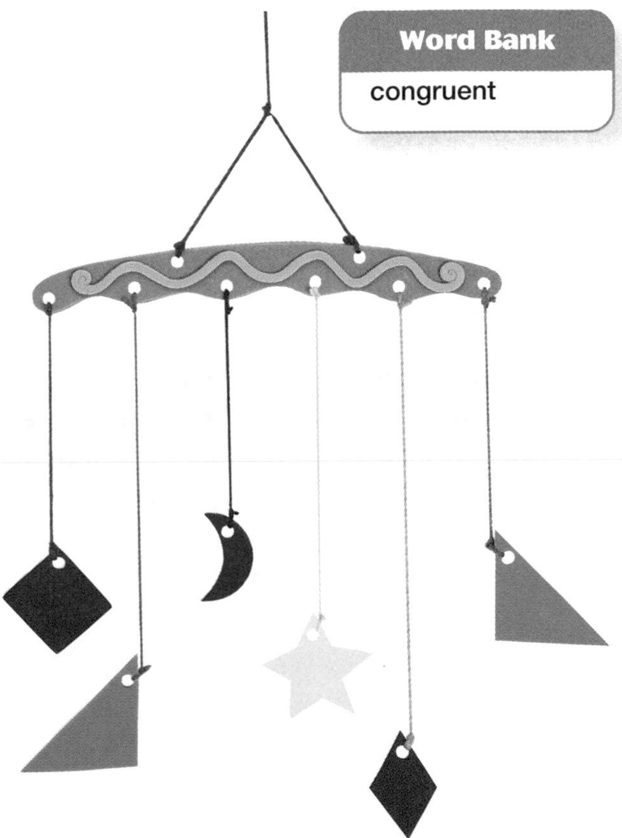

The only two figures with the same shape are the green triangles. Try to tell if they are congruent by tracing one of the green triangles. Then place the tracing on top of the other figure. If they match exactly, they are congruent.

The green triangles are also the same size, so they are congruent.

Example 2

Show some ways to divide a square into congruent parts.

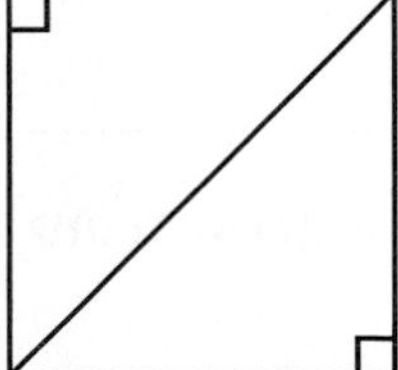

2 congruent right triangles

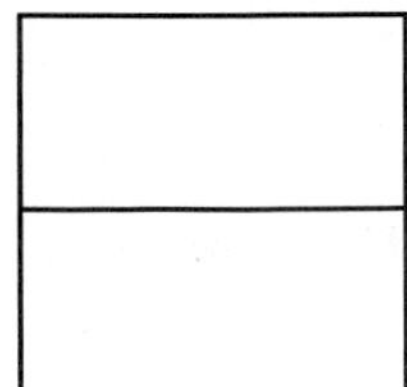

2 congruent rectangles

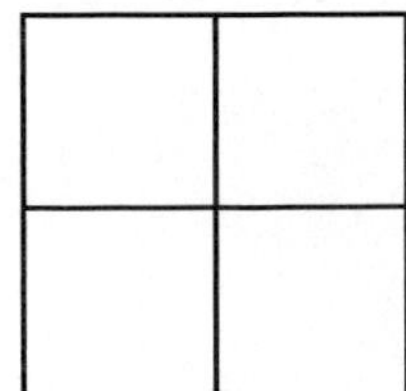

4 congruent squares

2 congruent pentagons

Guided Practice

For another example, see Set F on p. 479.

Tell if the two figures are congruent. Write *yes* or *no*.

1. 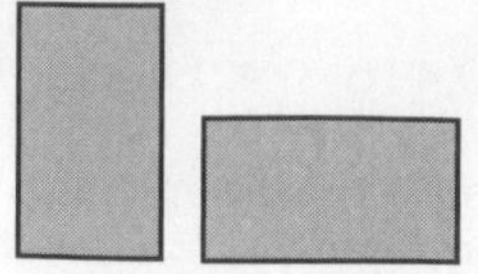

2. 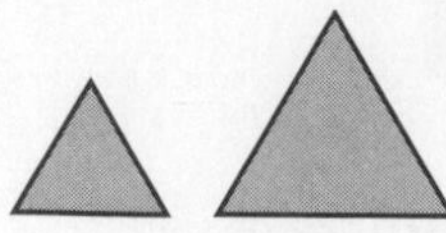

3. 

4. Draw a rectangle. Draw a line segment that divides it into two congruent triangles.

Independent Practice

For more practice, see Set F on p. 482.

Tell if the two figures are congruent. Write *yes* or *no*.

5. 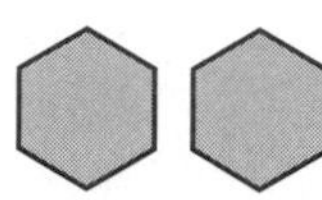

6. 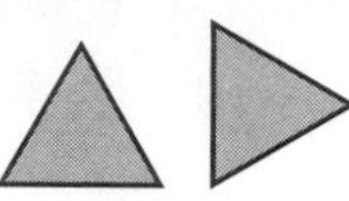

7. 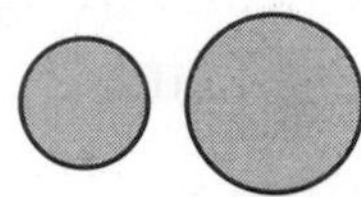

8. 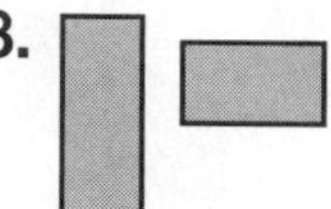

9. 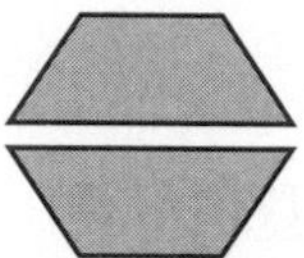

10. 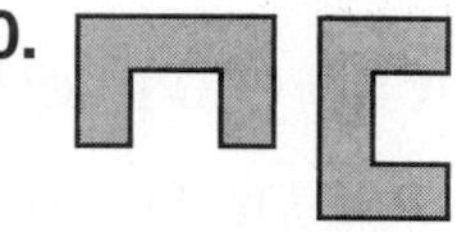

11. Draw a square. Divide it into four congruent triangles.

12. Draw an equilateral triangle. Divide it into two congruent right triangles.

13. Draw a parallelogram. Divide it into two congruent triangles.

Mixed Review

14. Math Reasoning Draw a circle. Draw 2 diameters that divide the circle into 4 congruent parts. Does your drawing also show a radius? Explain.

15. Which quadrilaterals have opposite sides that are parallel?

16. $7 \times (26 - 4)$ **17.** $(38 - 26) \times 2$ **18.** $(27 + 9) \div 4$ **19.** $42 \div (19 - 13)$

Test Prep Choose the correct letter for each answer.

20. Which has a quotient with 3 digits?
(6-6)

A $396 \div 6$ **C** $384 \div 8$

B $784 \div 7$ **D** $828 \div 9$

21. $\frac{3}{4} =$
(9-1)

F 0.25 **H** 0.5

G 0.34 **J** 0.75

LESSON 11-8

Understand
Plan
Solve
Look Back

Problem-Solving Strategy:

Use Logical Reasoning

 **California Content Standard** *Mathematical Reasoning 1.1: Analyze problems by identifying relationships, distinguishing relevant from irrelevant information, sequencing and prioritizing information, and observing patterns.*

Warm-Up Review

Write the value of each underlined digit.

1. $1{,}3\underline{7}2$ **2.** $\underline{5}{,}621$

3. $29{,}\underline{4}15$ **4.** $\underline{8}63{,}009$

5. Four boys are playing together. Brandon is the youngest. Andy is Matt's younger brother. Andy is older than Lance. List the four boys from oldest to youngest.

Example

Andrew needs to arrange the figures shown at the right in a line. Each figure has one more or one less side than the figure beside it. Each figure is next to a different-colored figure. The first figure is the square. How are the figures arranged?

Understand

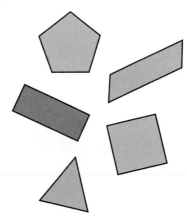

What do you need to find?

You need to find the order of the figures.

Plan

How can you solve the problem?

Use logical reasoning to organize what you know about the figures. Draw a picture to help you.

Solve

- Draw 5 lines. Put the square first.
- The 2nd figure must have 3 or 5 sides. It cannot be blue. Only the triangle works.
- The 3rd figure must have 2 or 4 sides. It cannot be green. Only the rectangle works.
- The 4th figure must have 3 or 5 sides. It cannot be pink. Only the pentagon works.
- The 5th figure is the parallelogram.

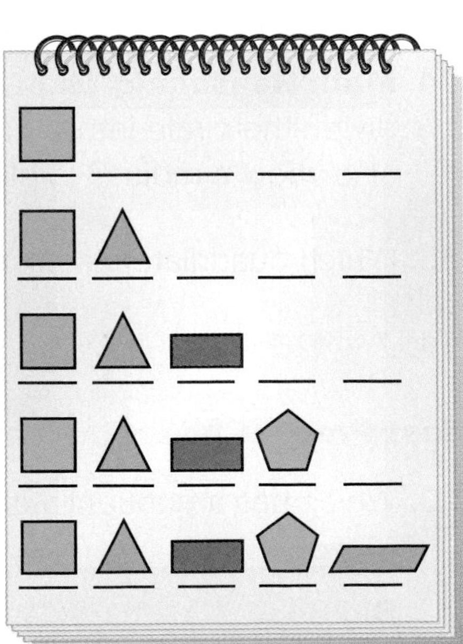

Look Back

If you were not told that the square was first, could you still solve the problem? Explain.

 *Additional Standards: Mathematical Reasoning 2.0, 3.2* *(See p. 437.)*

Guided Practice

1. Solve the problem given in the example, but replace the last clue with this sentence: The first figure is the parallelogram.

2. What is the mystery number? It is less than 30. If you divide it by 2, 3, 4, or 6, the remainder is 1. If you divide it by 5, the remainder is 0.

Independent Practice

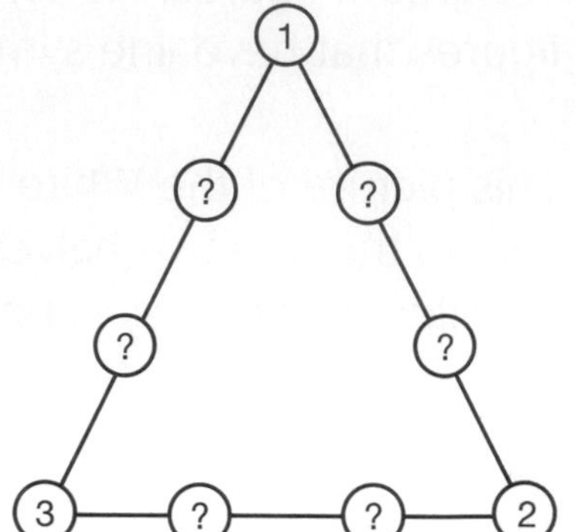

3. Use the numbers 4 through 9 to fill the circles in the triangle. Write each number only once. The four numbers on each side must have a sum of 17.

4. Lin's age is between 10 and 20. The sum of the digits is even. If divided by 5, the remainder is 1. Find Lin's age.

5. Each person gets off an elevator at a different floor. Who gets off where?
   - The elevator stops at the 5th, 6th, 8th, and 10th floors.
   - When Gary gets off, he says goodbye to Sam.
   - Jenna is the last person to get off.
   - Sue gets off one floor after Gary.

Mixed Review

Try these or other strategies to solve each problem. Tell which strategy you used.

Problem-Solving Strategies

- *Use Logical Reasoning*
- *Draw a Picture*
- *Find a Pattern*
- *Make a Table*

6. How many different ways can Julie arrange 12 photos in equal rows on a large bulletin board?

7. Pens come in packages of 2, 3, or 8. Spencer bought 29 pens in exactly 5 packages. Which packages did he buy?

Use Homework Workbook 11-8.

Line Symmetry

California Content Standard *Measurement and Geometry 3.4: Identify figures that have bilateral . . . symmetry.*

Math Link You have learned how to recognize congruent figures. Now you will learn to recognize figures that have line symmetry.

This picture of the White House can be folded along a line so that the two halves match exactly. The fold line is called a **line of symmetry**.

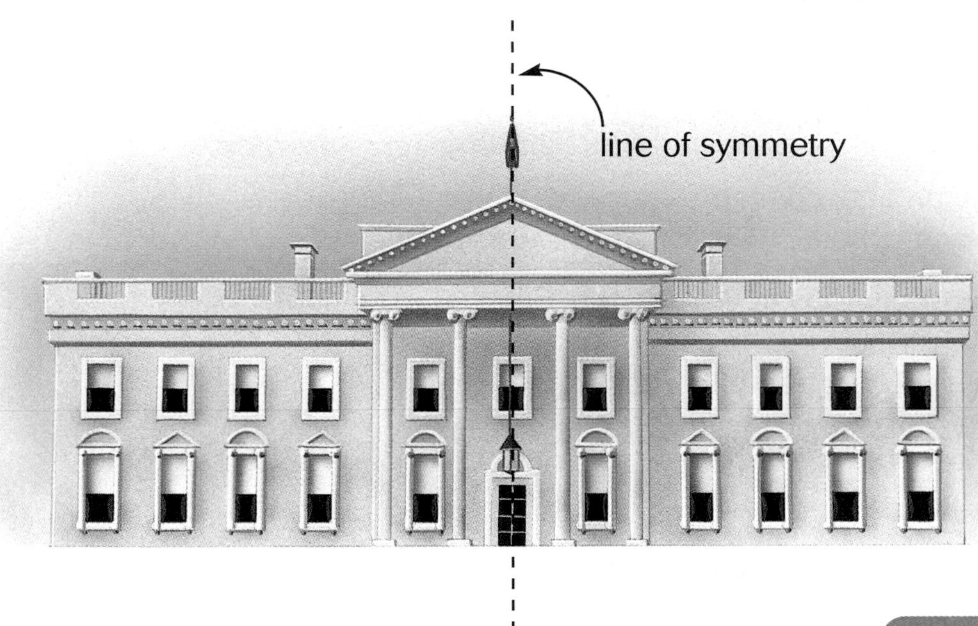

A figure with **line symmetry** has at least one line of symmetry. Some figures have more than one line of symmetry.

Warm-Up Review

Draw a square. Divide it into the given parts.

1. 2 congruent triangles
2. 4 congruent triangles
3. 2 congruent rectangles
4. 4 congruent squares
5. The Hobson family is working on a 2,000-piece puzzle. Sue has joined 175 pieces. Nick has joined 287 pieces. How many pieces are left to finish the puzzle?

Word Bank

line of symmetry
line symmetry

Example

Trace the square shown at the right several times. Draw all possible lines of symmetry.

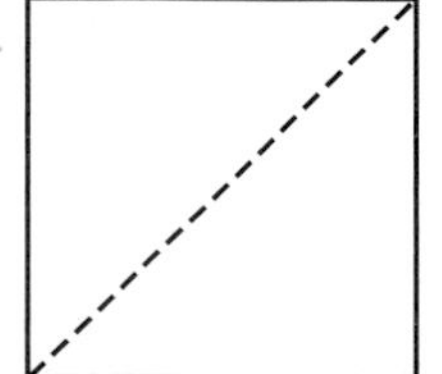

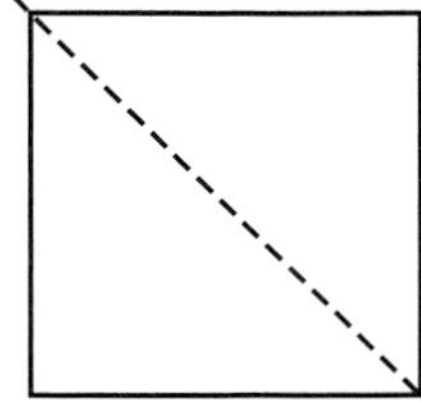

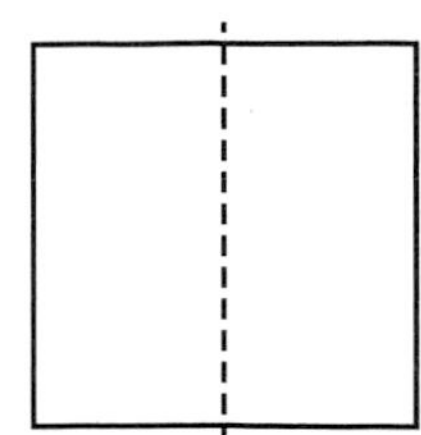

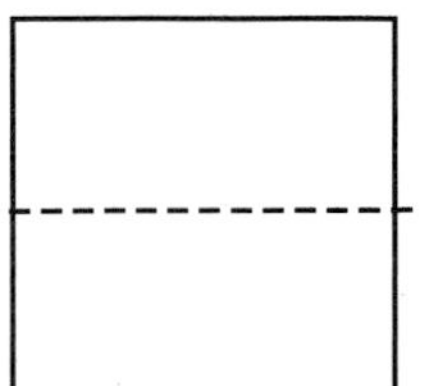

Guided Practice *For another example, see Set G on p. 479.*

Is the dashed line a line of symmetry? Write *yes* or *no*.

1. 

2. 

3. 

4. Does a circle have line symmetry? Explain.

Independent Practice *For more practice, see Set G on p. 482.*

Is the dashed line a line of symmetry? Write *yes* or *no*.

5. 

6. 

7. 

8. 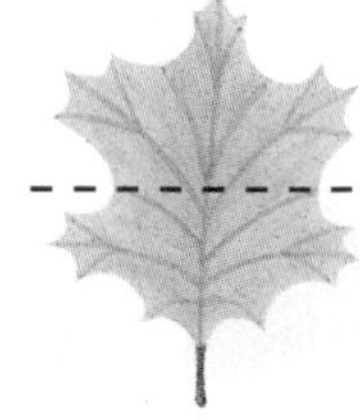

Trace each figure. Draw lines of symmetry if you can.

9. 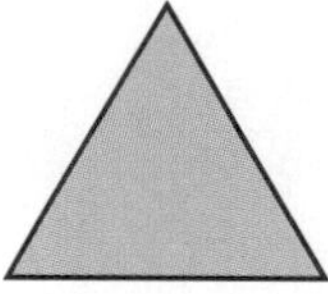

10. 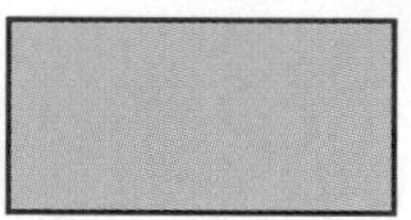

11. 

12. 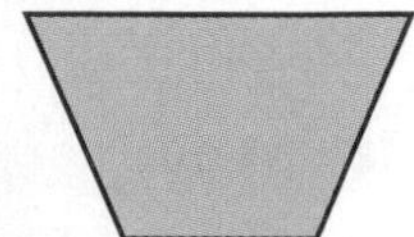

13. Math Reasoning Look at the three photos at the right. The top photo shows an actual face. The bottom photos were created by "doubling" the images of first the left half of the face and then the right half. Does the actual face have line symmetry? Explain.

Actual face

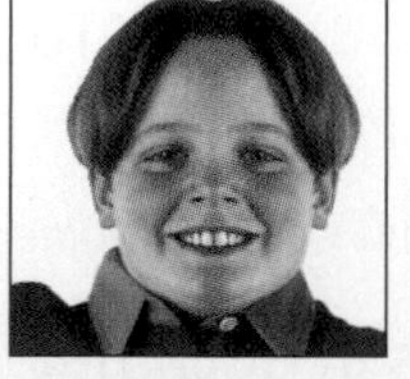

Left half doubled

Right half doubled

Mixed Review

14. A circle's diameter is 6 cm. Find its radius.

15. Draw two congruent pentagons.

16. Draw two congruent triangles.

 **Test Prep** Choose the correct letter for the answer.

17. $8.5 + 4.15 + 6.08 =$
(9-9)

A 11.08 **B** 18.28 **C** 18.63 **D** 18.83 **E** NH

Slides, Flips, and Turns

California Content Standard *Measurement and Geometry 3.0: Students demonstrate an understanding of plane . . . geometric objects and use this knowledge to show relationships and solve problems.*

Warm-Up Review

1. 26×4 2. 89×3

3. A recipe calls for $\frac{1}{2}$ cup of pecans and $\frac{3}{4}$ cup of walnuts. How many cups of nuts are needed in all?

Math Link You have worked with congruent polygons. In this lesson you will learn about slides, flips, and turns.

Word Bank

slide (translation)
flip (reflection)
turn (rotation)

Here are three different ways to move a figure. Notice that the new figure is congruent to the original figure.

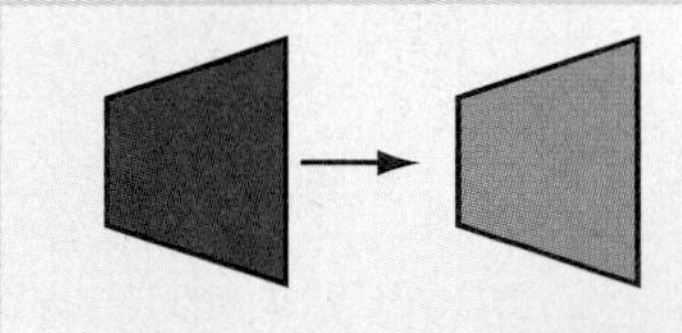

A **slide (or translation)** moves a figure up, down, or over.

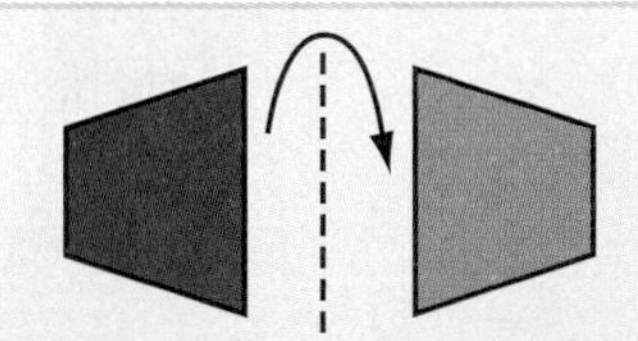

A **flip (or reflection)** gives a mirror image of the figure.

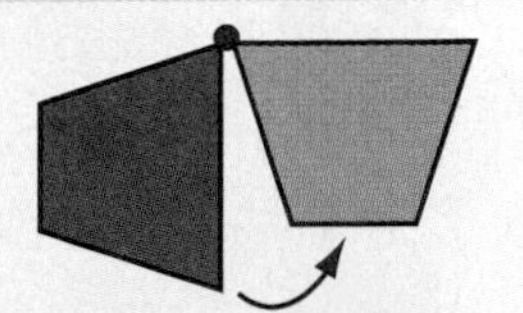

A **turn (or rotation)** moves a figure about a point.

Example

Tell how the white triangle was moved to the position of the red triangle. Write *slide*, *flip*, or *turn*.

a. 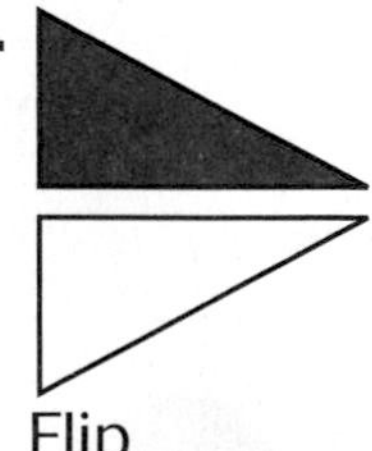

Flip

b. 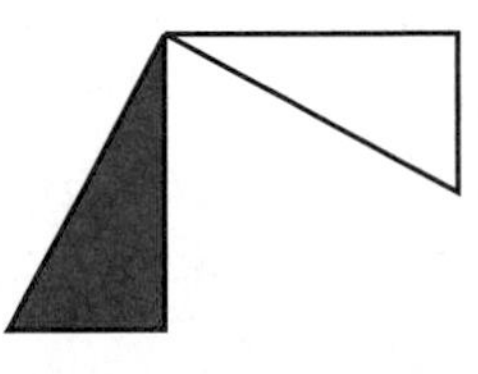

Turn

c. 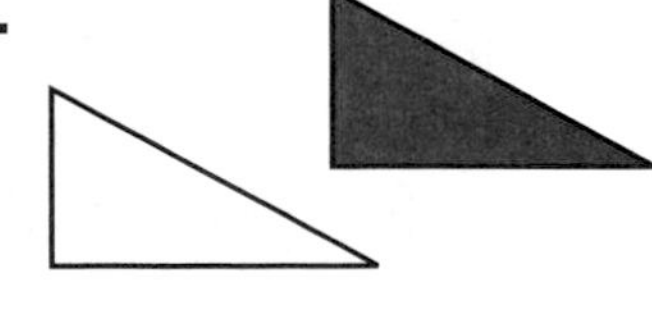

Slide

Guided Practice

For another example, see Set H on p. 479.

Tell whether the flags in each pair are related by a slide, flip, or turn.

1. 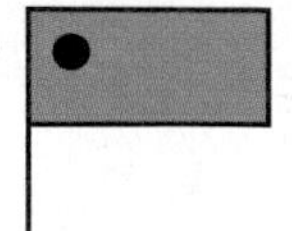

2. 

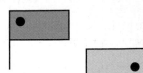

3. 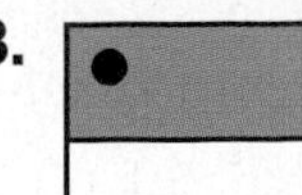 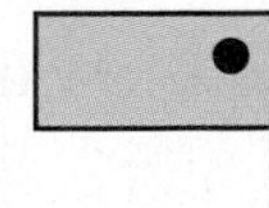

4. A message was reflected. Here is the result. What did the original message say?

.WAЯᗡ OT ƎKI⅃ I

Independent Practice *For more practice, see Set H on p.482.*

Tell whether the figures in each pair are related by a slide, flip, or turn.

5. 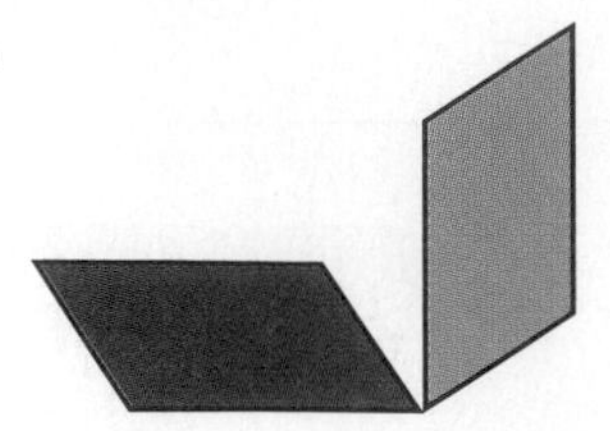

6. 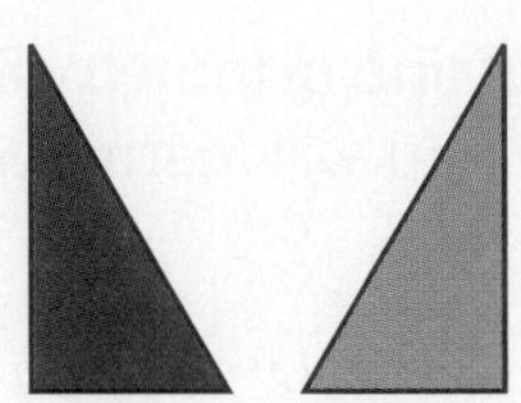

7. 

8. 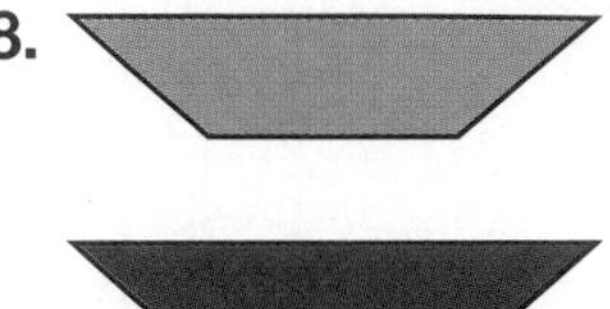

9. 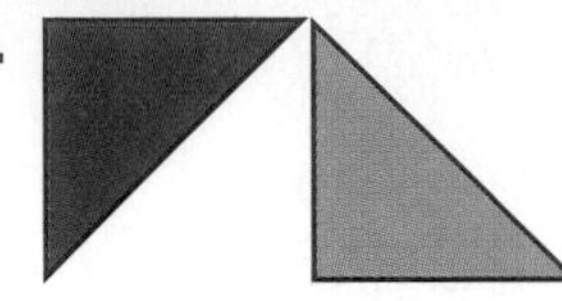

10. 

11. 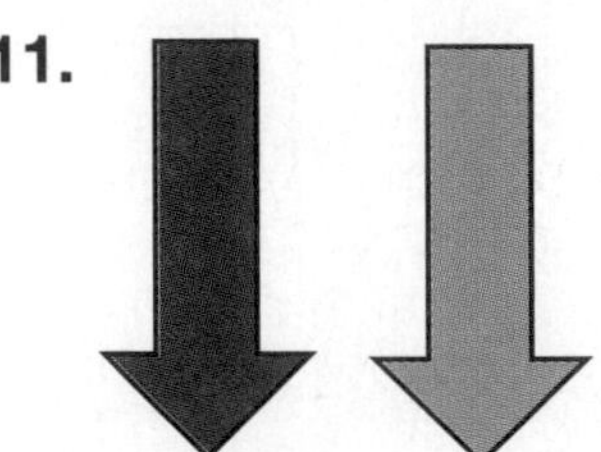

12. 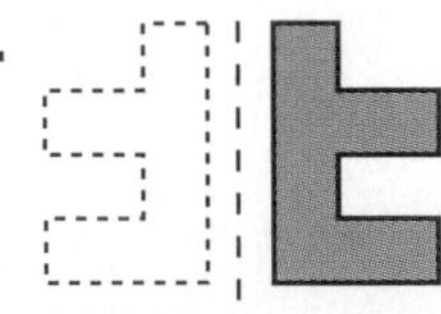

13. 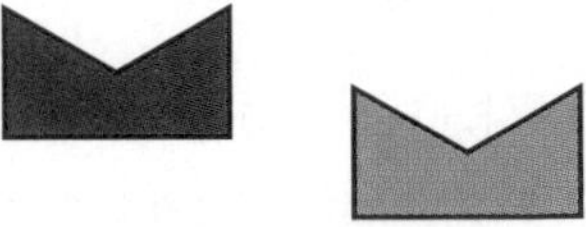

14. Math Reasoning Name a figure that looks exactly the same after a slide, a flip, or a turn?

Mixed Review

15. Draw a parallelogram. Divide it into two congruent parallelograms.

16. Draw a number that has two lines of symmetry.

17. Draw a quadrilateral that does not have line symmetry.

18. 6.23 + 1.7 **19.** 72.8 − 0.16 **20.** 10.53 − 6.2 **21.** 4.81 + 3.09

Test Prep **Choose the correct letter for each answer.**

22. Algebra Evaluate $20x$ for $x = 32$.
(3-8)

A 12 **C** 64
B 52 **D** 640

23. Algebra Evaluate $x - 27$ for $x = 45$.
(2-10)

F 18 **H** 38
G 28 **J** 72

Rotational Symmetry

Warm-Up Review

Tell whether the figures in each pair are related by a slide, flip, or turn.

1. J J
2. F

3. Draw a circle. Shade $\frac{1}{4}$ of it.

California Content Standard *Measurement and Geometry 3.4: Identify figures that have . . . rotational symmetry. Also, Measurement and Geometry 3.5. (See page 437.)*

Math Link You have learned about line symmetry as well as slides, flips, and turns. Now you will learn about rotational symmetry.

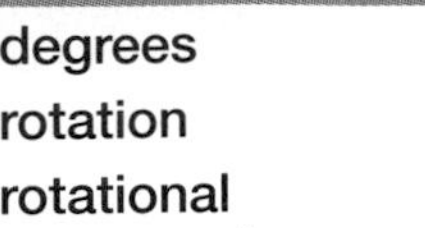

Word Bank

degrees
rotation
rotational symmetry

An angle is measured in **degrees** (°).
The measure of a right angle is 90°.
The measure of a straight angle is 180°.

A turn, or **rotation**, of a figure around a point can be described using an angle measure or fraction.

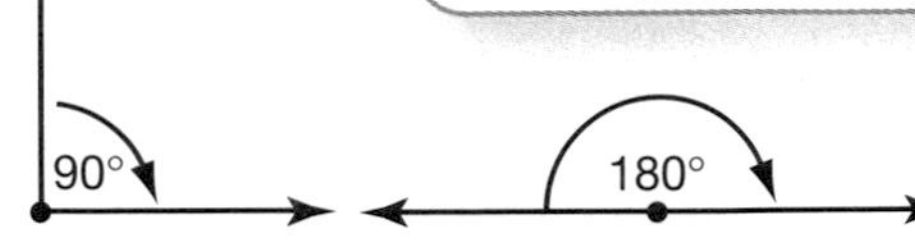

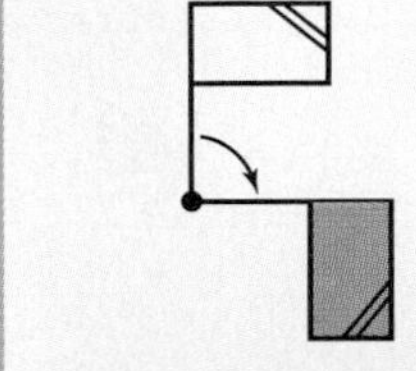	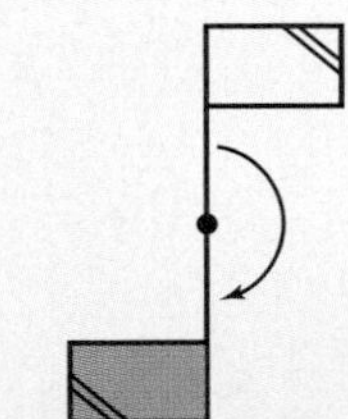	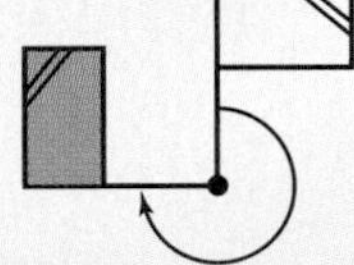	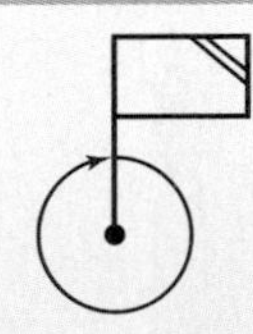
The figure has been rotated 90°, or $\frac{1}{4}$ turn.	The figure has been rotated 180°, or $\frac{1}{2}$ turn.	The figure has been rotated 270°, or $\frac{3}{4}$ turn.	The figure has been rotated 360°, or a full turn.

When a figure rotates onto itself in less than a full turn, the figure has **rotational symmetry**.

Example

Does each figure have rotational symmetry? Give the least angle measure and turn that will rotate the figure onto itself.

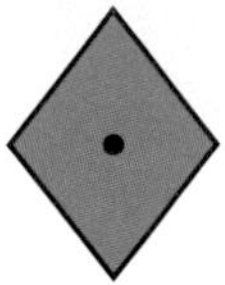

The figure has rotational symmetry. It must be rotated 180° or a $\frac{1}{2}$ turn, to land on itself.

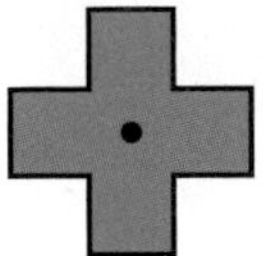

The figure has rotational symmetry. It must be rotated 90°, or a $\frac{1}{4}$ turn, to land on itself.

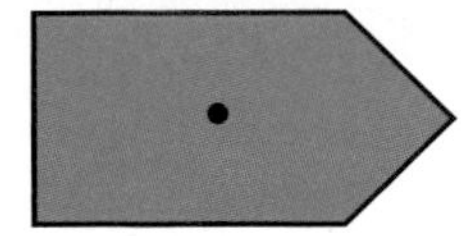

The figure does *not* have rotational symmetry. It must be rotated 360°, or a full turn, to land on itself.

Guided Practice *For another example, see Set I on p. 480.*

Give the angle measure of each rotation. Tell whether it is a $\frac{1}{4}$, $\frac{1}{2}$, $\frac{3}{4}$, or full turn.

1. 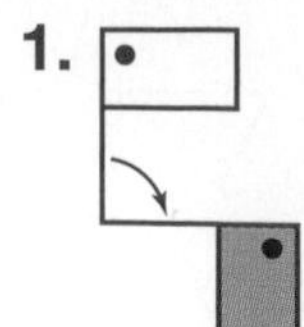

2. 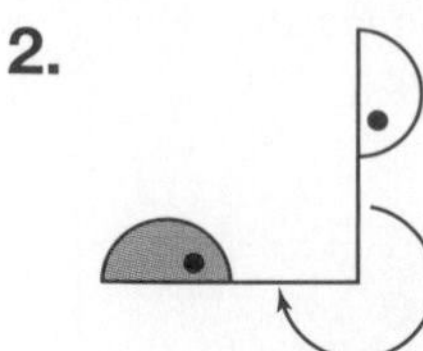

3. 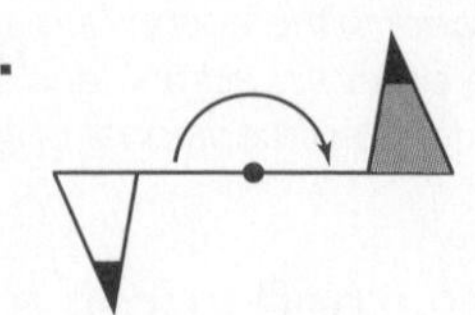

4. 

5. The letter **S** has rotational symmetry. Find another letter with rotational symmetry.

Independent Practice *For more practice, see Set I on p. 483.*

Give the angle measure of each rotation. Tell whether it is a $\frac{1}{4}$, $\frac{1}{2}$, $\frac{3}{4}$, or full turn.

6. 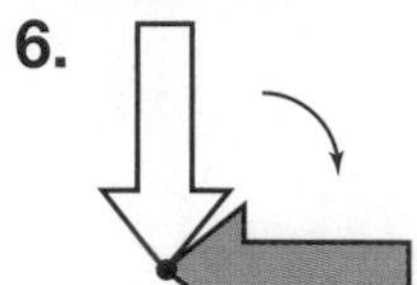

7. 

8. 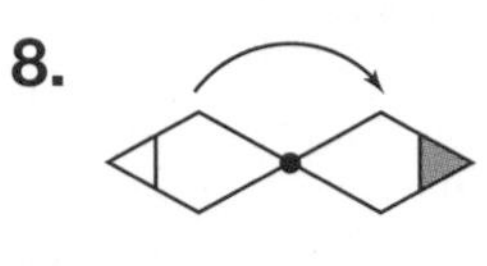

9. 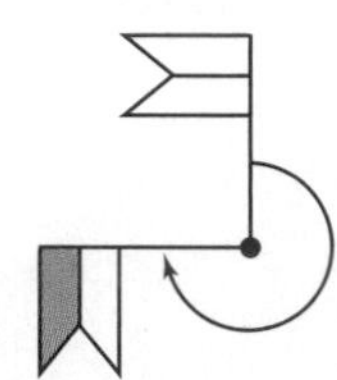

Does the figure have rotational symmetry? Write *yes* or *no*. Give the least angle measure and turn that will rotate the figure onto itself.

10. 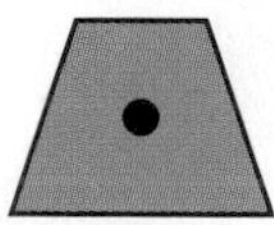

11. 

12. 

13. 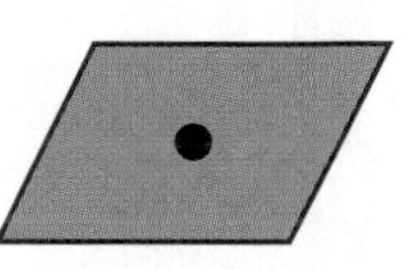

14. Math Reasoning What happens if you rotate a figure 180° and then rotate it 180° again?

Mixed Review

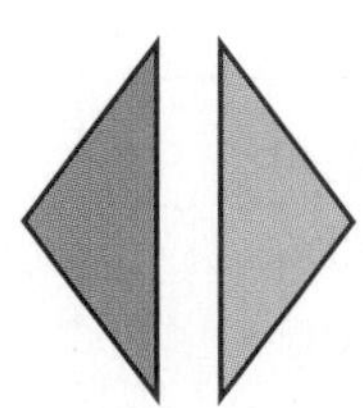

15. Are these figures related by a slide, flip, or turn?

16. Draw a figure that has two lines of symmetry.

 **Test Prep** **Choose the correct letter for the answer.**

17. Which is not a polygon?
(11-2)

F triangle **G** octagon **H** circle **J** square

Solid Figures

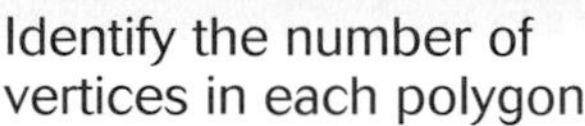

Identify the number of vertices in each polygon.

1. 
2. 
3. 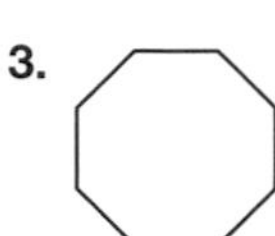
4. 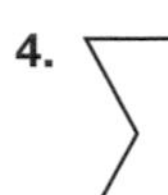
5. Jeff has 8 library books that are seven days overdue. The fine for overdue books is $0.05 per day for each book. How much does Jeff owe?

California Content Standard *Measurement and Geometry 3.6: Visualize, describe, and make models of geometric solids (e.g., prisms, pyramids) in terms of the number and shape of faces, edges, and vertices; interpret two-dimensional representations of three-dimensional objects. . ..*

Math Link You have learned about many plane figures. Now you will learn about solid figures.

The world around you is filled with three-dimensional objects called **solid figures**. A square has length and width, so it has two dimensions. But a cube has length, width, and height, so it has three dimensions.

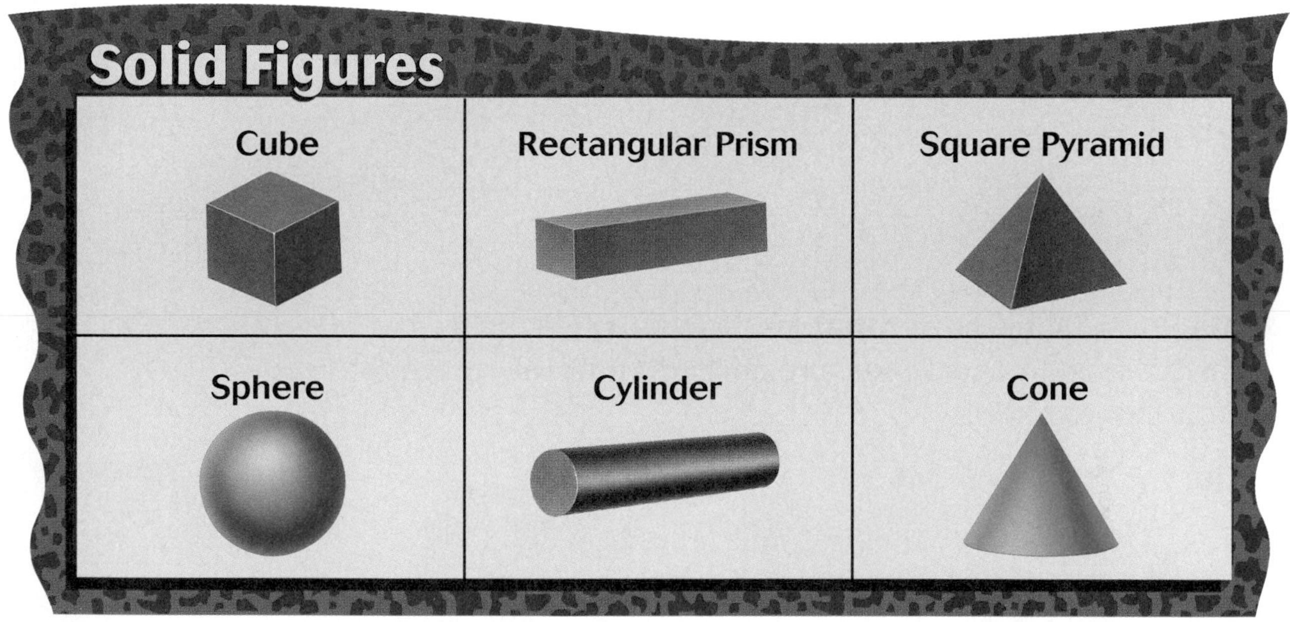

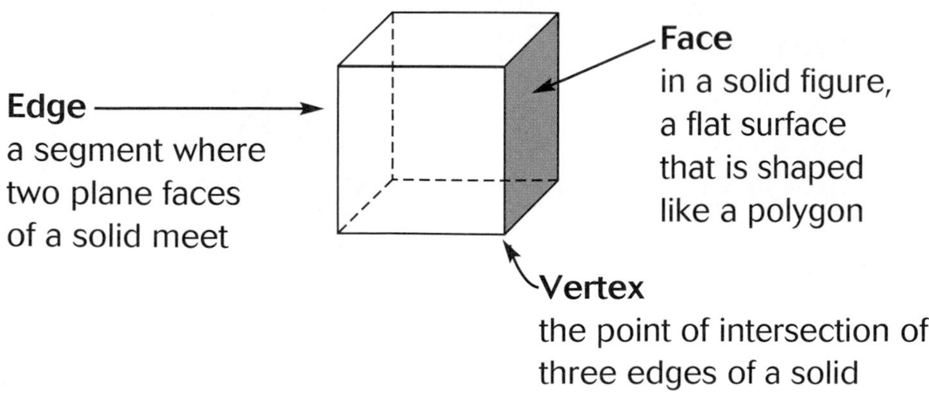

Word Bank

- solid figure
- cube
- rectangular prism
- square pyramid
- sphere
- cylinder
- cone
- edge
- face
- vertex (vertices)

Example

Describe the solid figure shown at the right.

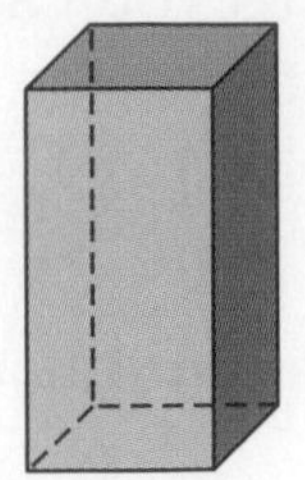

The solid figure is a rectangular prism. It has 6 faces. Each face is shaped like a rectangle. There are 8 vertices and 12 edges.

Guided Practice *For another example, see Set J on p. 480.*

Tell which solid figure each object looks like.

1. 

2. 

3. 

4. 

5. What are the shapes of the faces of a square pyramid?

Independent Practice *For more practice, see Set J on p. 483.*

Tell which solid figure each object looks like.

6. 

7. 

8. 

9. 

10. 

11. 

12. 

13. 

14. soup can

15. a sugar cube

16. box of crayons

17. a planet

18. Copy and complete the table.

Solid Figure	Number of Faces	Number of Edges	Number of Vertices
Cube			
Rectangular prism			
Square pyramid			
Sphere			

Math Reasoning Name as many solid figures as you can that fit each description.

19. There is at least one circular flat surface.

20. It has at least one square-shaped face.

21. It has a curved surface.

22. It has no flat surfaces.

23. Refer to the photo at the right. What solid figure does this sculpture look like? What part of that solid figure is the sculpture standing on?

Mixed Review

Decide if the figures in each pair are related by a slide, flip, or turn.

24. 

25. 

26. 

Does the figure have rotational symmetry? Write *yes* or *no*. Give the least angle measure and turn that will rotate each figure onto itself.

27. 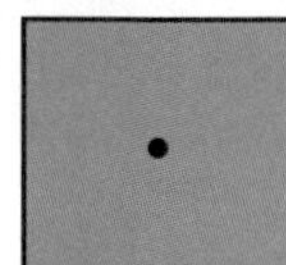

28. 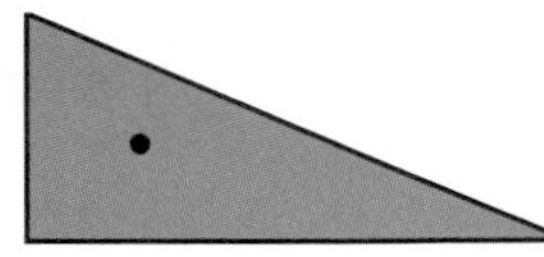

29. 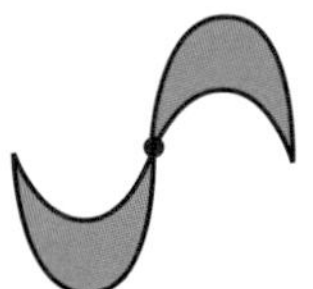

30. 14,443 − 1,987

31. $4 - 2\frac{1}{3}$

32. Find $\frac{1}{5}$ of 30.

Test Prep Choose the correct letter for each answer.

33. (9-3) Which decimal has a 4 in the hundredths place?

A 142.73 **C** 412.37

B 312.47 **D** 712.34

34. (3-6) **Algebra** If $n = 9$, then $(63 \div n) \times (8 + 6) =$

F 21 **H** 98

G 55 **J** 112

K NH

 Use Homework Workbook 11-12.

Drawing Patterns for Solids

Warm-Up Review

Identify the number of faces in each solid figure.

1. rectangular prism
2. cube
3. square pyramid
4. Name three solid figures that have curved surfaces.

California Content Standard *Measurement and Geometry 3.6: Visualize, describe, and make models of geometric solids (e.g., prism, pyramids) . . . and draw patterns (of faces) for a solid that, when cut and folded, will make a model of the solid.*

Word Bank

net

Math Link You have learned about solid figures. Now you will learn how to identify and draw a net for a solid.

Marguerita and Thomas are building a castle out of cardboard. First they make a tower by putting a pyramid on top of a rectangular prism.

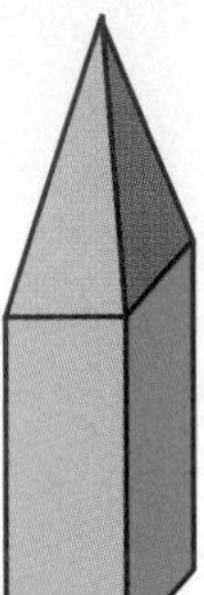

Marguerita cuts and folds a shape to make the prism. Thomas cuts and folds another shape to make the pyramid. These shapes are nets. A **net** is a pattern that can be used to make a solid. The solid line segments in a net show where to cut, and the dashed line segments show where to fold.

When drawing a net for a solid, it is helpful to try and imagine what the solid would look like if it were opened up and flattened out.

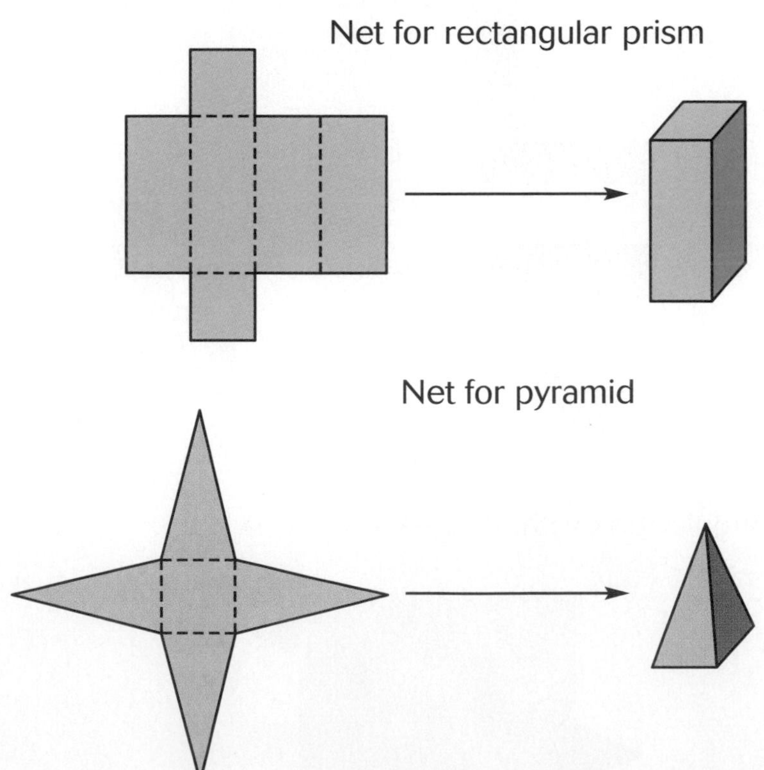

Example 1

Draw another net for Marguerita's prism.

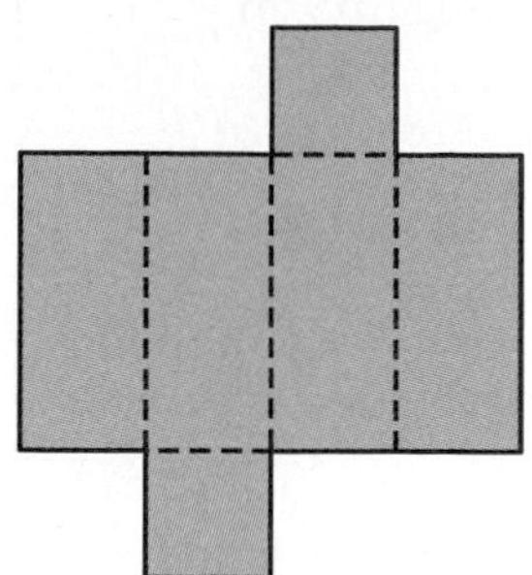

Notice that the net is similar to the one on page 469. The top and bottom are in different positions.

Example 2

Which solid figure can be made from the net shown at the right?

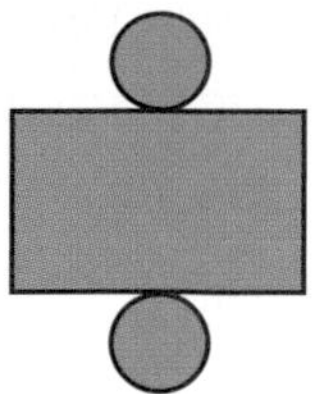

A cylinder can be made from the net.

Guided Practice *For another example, see Set K on p. 480.*

Tell which solid figure can be made from the net.

1. 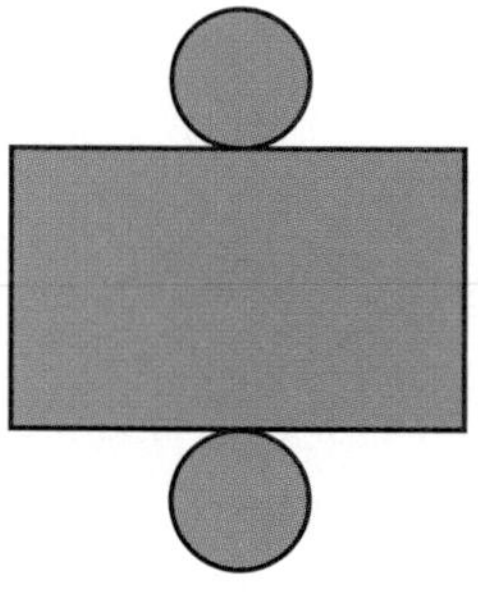

2. 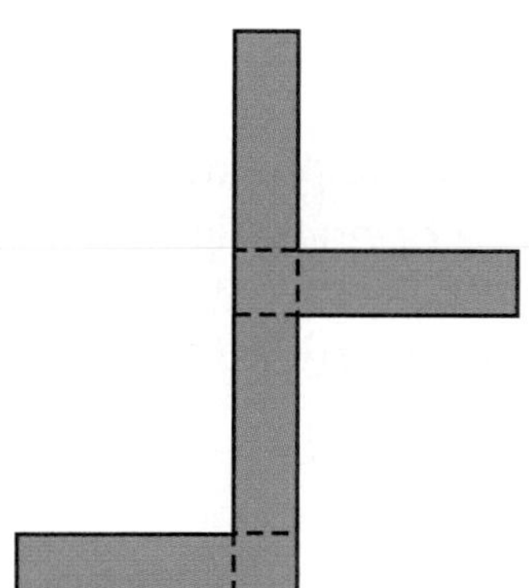

3. 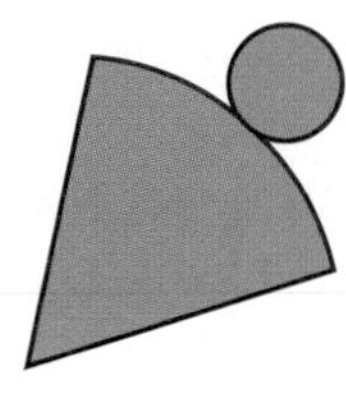

4. 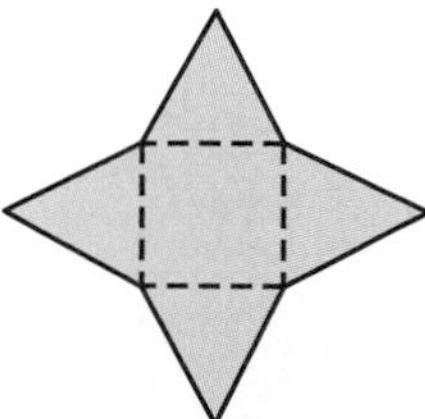

5. 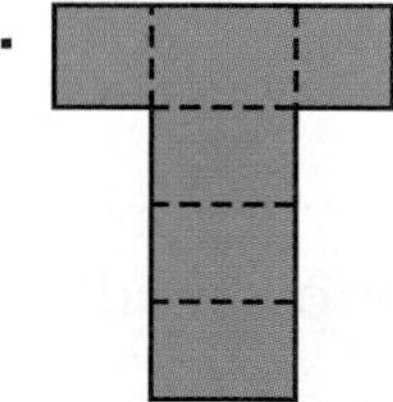

6. 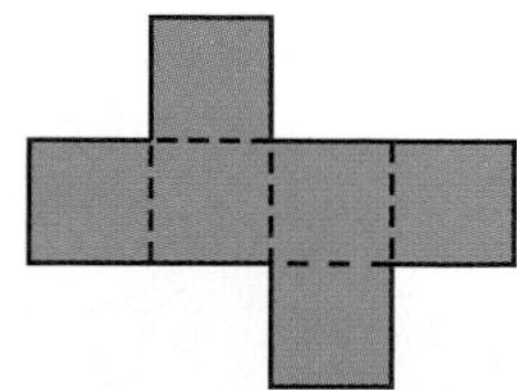

7. Draw a net for a rectangular box without a lid.

8. Does this net form a prism or a pyramid?

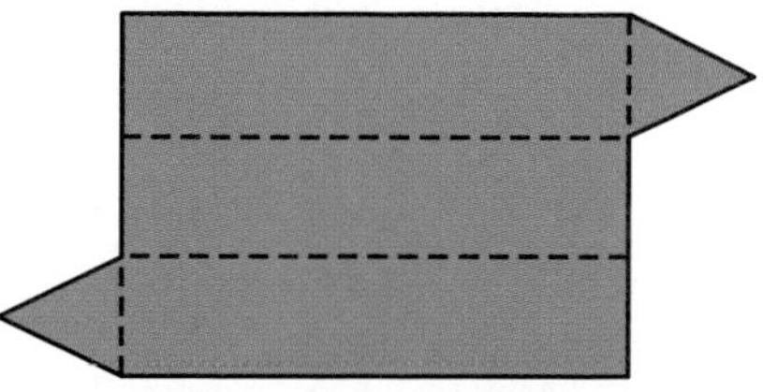

Independent Practice *For more practice, see Set K on p. 483.*

Identify the net for each solid figure.

9. cone

a. 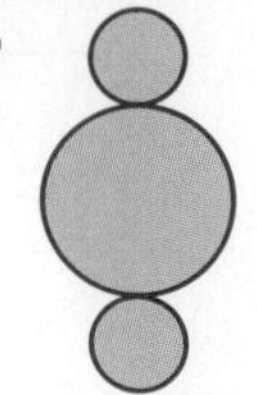 **b.**

10. rectangular prism

a. 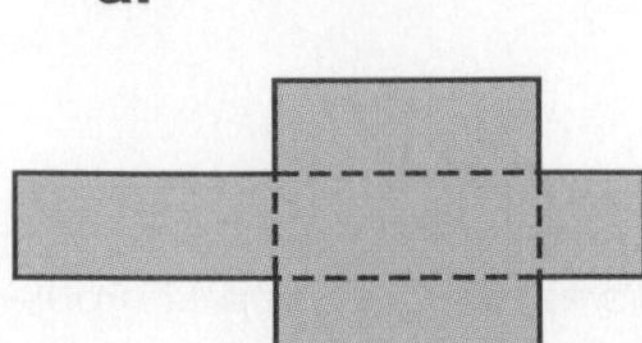 **b.** 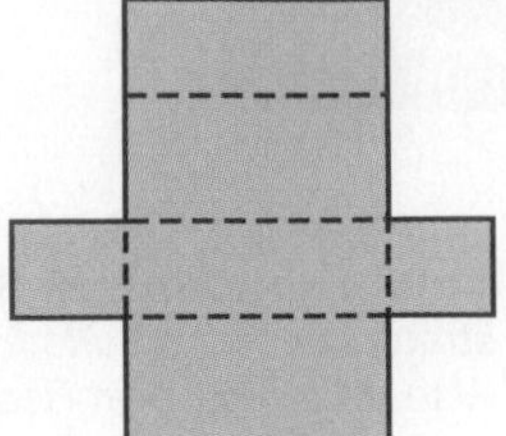

11. cylinder

 **a.** 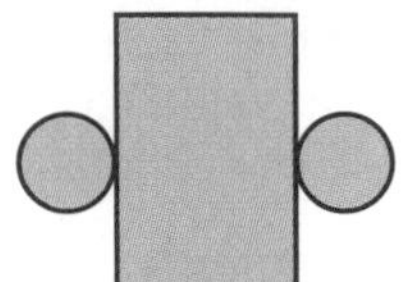 **b.** 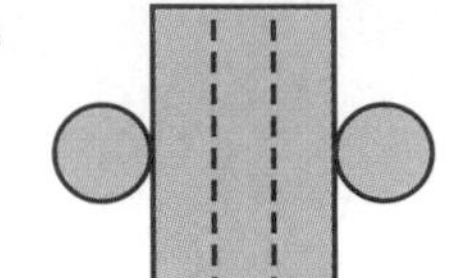

12. square pyramid

 **a.** 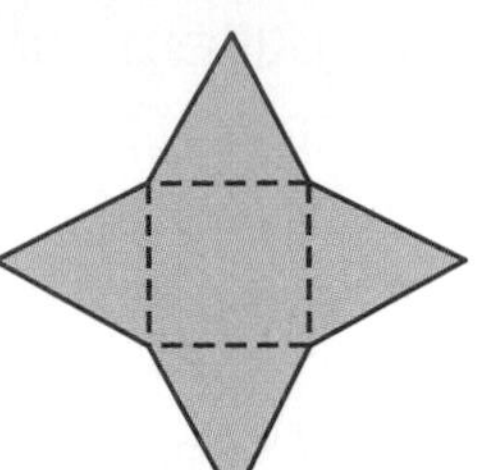 **b.** 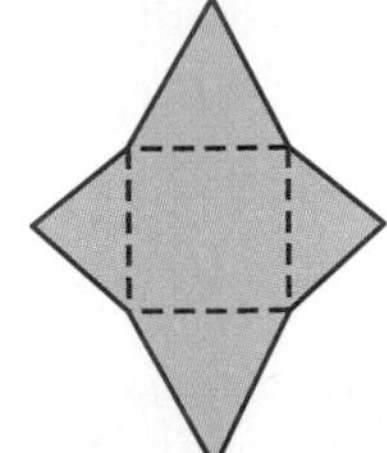

13. Math Reasoning At the right is a net that can be folded into a cube. There are 10 other nets that can be folded into a cube. Draw at least 3 of these nets.

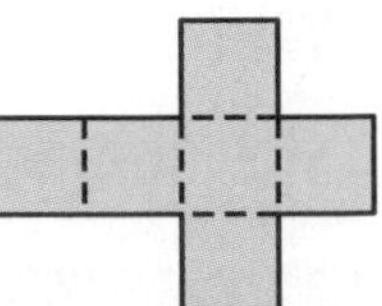

Mixed Review

14. Give the angle measure of the rotation shown at the right. Tell whether it is a $\frac{1}{4}$, $\frac{1}{2}$, $\frac{3}{4}$, or full turn.

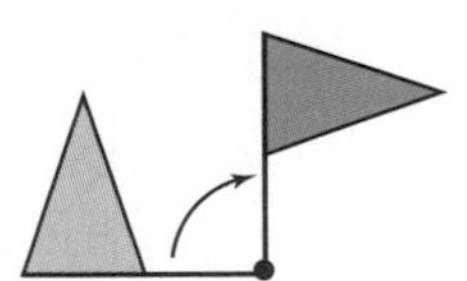

15. Name a food product you can buy in a container shaped like a cylinder.

16. Which solid figure has six congruent faces?

17. $\frac{3}{5} + \frac{4}{5}$ **18.** $0.98 × 7 **19.** $20 − $6.75 **20.** $\frac{2}{3} - \frac{1}{4}$

Test Prep **Choose the correct letter for each answer.**

21. Which is a factor of 32? (6-9)

A 3

B 4

C 5

D 6

22. How many hundreds are in 1,200? (1-1)

F 1

G 2

H 12

J 120

Problem-Solving Application:
Using Congruence

Warm-Up Review

Tell if the two figures are congruent. Write *yes* or *no*.

1.  

2.  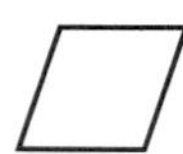

3.  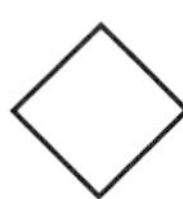

4. Parking at Ace Garage costs $3.75 for the first hour and $0.75 for each additional hour. How much would it cost to park for 4 hours?

California Content Standards *Mathematical Reasoning 2.2: Apply strategies and results from simpler problems to more complex problems. Also, Mathematical Reasoning 1.1 (See page 437.)*

Example

Jane will use the quilt pattern shown at the right to make a quilt. She will sew 12 quilt squares like this one together. How many pieces of each shape does she need to cut from the fabric?

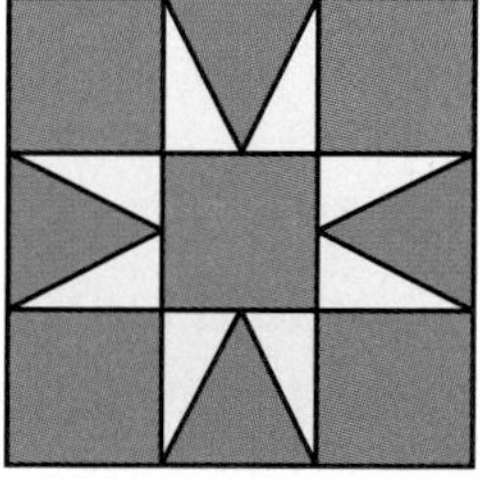

Understand

What do you need to find?

The number of pieces of each shape in the quilt pattern

Plan

How can you solve the problem?

Identify and count the congruent shapes in the quilt pattern. Then multiply by 12. You can make a table to organize your work.

Solve

Shape	Number in one quilt square	Number in 12 quilt squares
Yellow triangle	8	$8 \times 12 = 96$
Orange square	5	$5 \times 12 = 60$
Blue triangle	4	$4 \times 12 = 48$

Look Back

Explain two different ways to find the total number of pieces of each shape in the completed quilt.

Additional Standards: Measurement and Geometry 3.3; Mathematical Reasoning 2.0 (See p. 437.)

Guided Practice

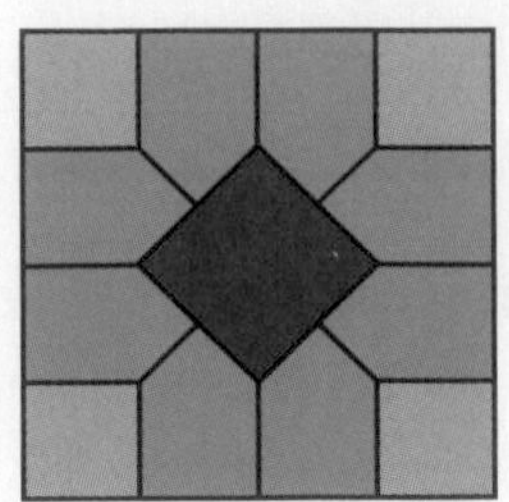

1. How many square pieces are there in the quilt pattern? How many of the squares are congruent?

2. What is the shape of each green piece? Are all the green pieces congruent?

3. How many gold squares are needed for 12 quilt patterns like the one shown?

Independent Practice

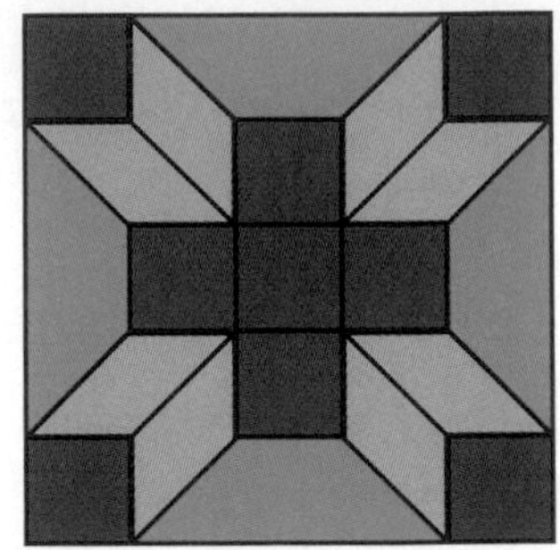

4. Copy and complete the table for the quilt pattern shown at the right.

Shape	Color	Number in 1 quilt square	Number in 12 quilt squares

5. Michael will make a quilt using 20 quilt squares like the one shown in Exercise 4. How many pieces of each shape will he use?

6. Does the quilt square have line symmetry? If so, how many lines of symmetry does it have?

7. Does the quilt square have rotational symmetry? If so, what is the least angle measure and turn that will rotate the figure onto itself?

Mixed Review

Springville Students

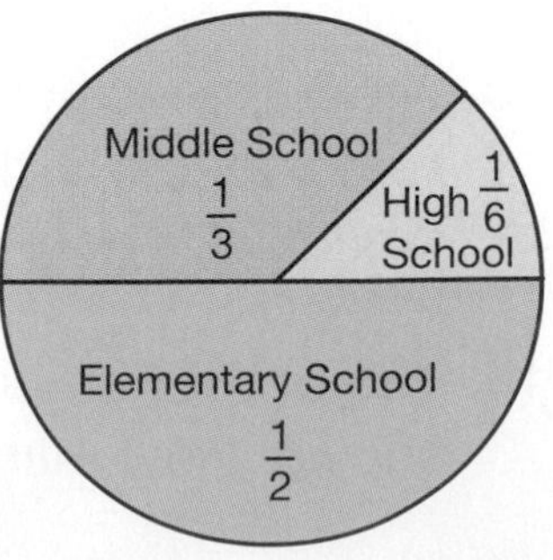

8. The graph at the right shows what fraction of the students in the Springville School District are in each school. If there are 750 students altogether, how many are in the middle school?

9. Phyllis gained 3 pounds last month. This month she lost 4 pounds. Represent each gain or loss with a positive or negative number.

Diagnostic Checkpoint

Word Bank

line
line segment
ray
angle
vertex
intersecting lines
parallel lines
perpendicular lines
polygon
sides
circle
congruent
line of symmetry
slide (translation)
flip (reflection)
turn (rotation)
degrees
solid figures

Complete. For Exercises 1–3, use the words from the Word Bank.

1. (11-10) A(n) ______________ moves a figure about a point.

2. (11-1) A(n) ______________ is part of a line with one endpoint. It continues on and on in one direction.

3. (11-7) Two figures are ______________ when they have the same size and shape.

Tell if the two figures are congruent. Write *yes* or *no*.

4. (11-7)

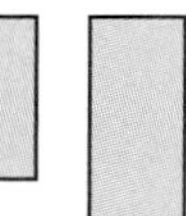

5. (11-7)

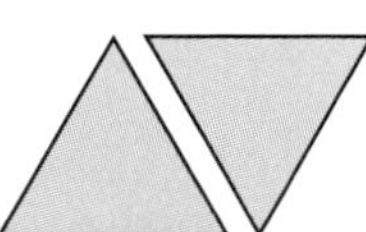

6. (11-9) Tell how many lines of symmetry the figure at the right has.

7. (11-11) Tell if the figure at the right has rotational symmetry.

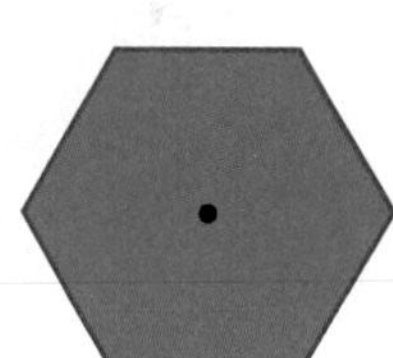

Tell whether each pair of figures are related by a *slide, flip,* or *turn*.

8. (11-10)

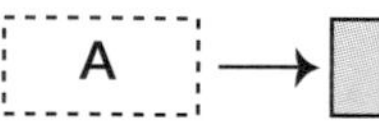

9. (11-10)

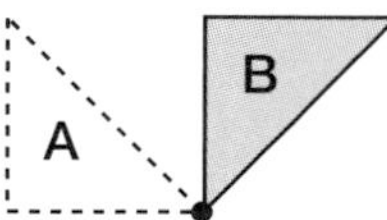

10. (11-10)

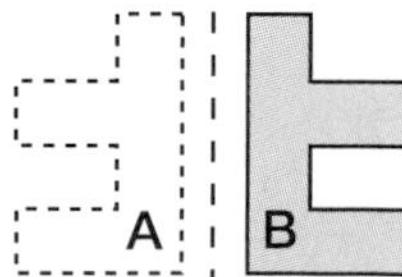

Tell which solid figure each object looks like.

11. (11-12) a juice box

12. (11-12) a globe

13. (11-12) a paper towel roll

14. (11-13) What solid figure can be made from the net at the right?

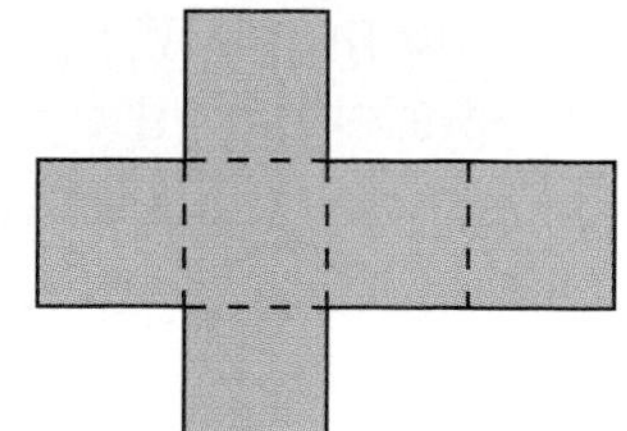

15. (11-8) Nick's age is between 5 and 15. If divided by 5, the remainder is 3. If divided by 3, the remainder is 2. Find Nick's age.

16. (11-14) The border around a room has 30 strips like the one shown. How many of each shape is in the border?

Chapter 11 Test

Tell what type of figure is shown. If the figure is a triangle, describe it by its sides and by its angles. If the figure is a quadrilateral, tell what type.

1. 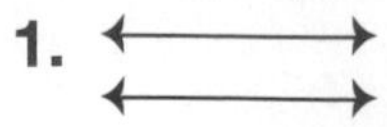

2.

3. 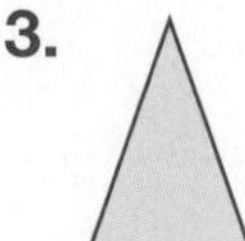

4. 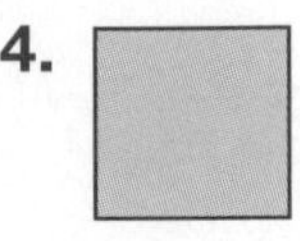

Tell if these figures are congruent. Write *yes* or *no*.

5.  

6. 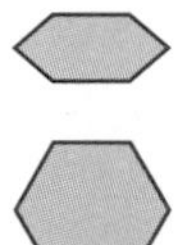

Tell whether each angle is right, obtuse, or acute.

7. 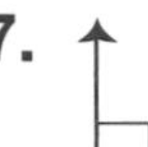

8.  

Find the diameter of each circle. Estimate the circumference.

9. 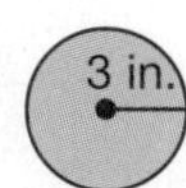

10. 

Tell whether each pair of figures are related by a *slide*, *flip*, or *turn*.

11.  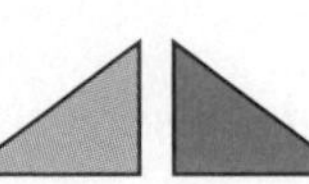

12. 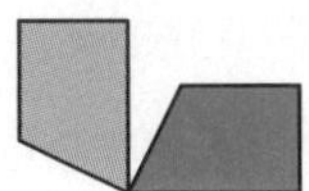

13. Tell how many lines of symmetry the figure at the right has.

14. Tell if the figure at the right has rotational symmetry.

15. Tell which solid the toy box at the right looks like.

16. Draw a net for the toy box at the right.

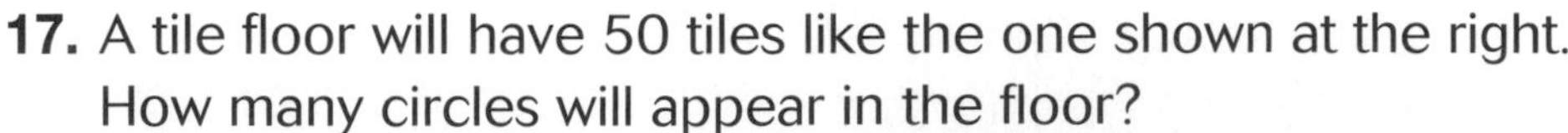

17. A tile floor will have 50 tiles like the one shown at the right. How many circles will appear in the floor?

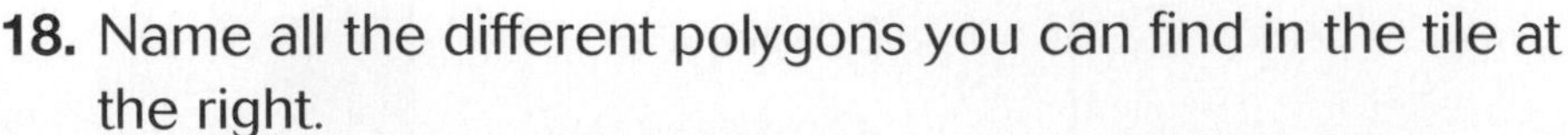

18. Name all the different polygons you can find in the tile at the right.

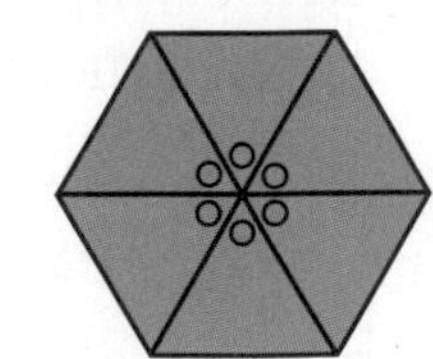

19. Kendra has arranged a triangle, square, pentagon, and hexagon so no shape is beside one with one less or one more side. The pentagon is first. How are the shapes arranged?

Multiple-Choice Chapter 11 Test

Choose the correct letter for each answer.

1. Which names the figure?

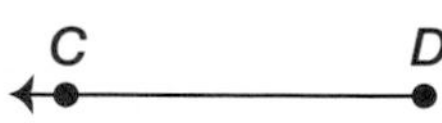

A line
B line segment
C point
D ray

2. The lengths of the sides of a triangle are 17 centimeters, 19 centimeters, and 17 centimeters. Which type of triangle is it?

F isosceles triangle
G equilateral triangle
H scalene triangle
J right triangle

3. Which of the following is NOT a name for the figure?

A rectangle
B rhombus
C parallelogram
D quadrilateral

4. A circle has a radius of 7 inches. Estimate the circle's circumference.

F 14 in.
G 21 in.
H 28 in.
J 42 in.

5. How many corners does an octagon have?

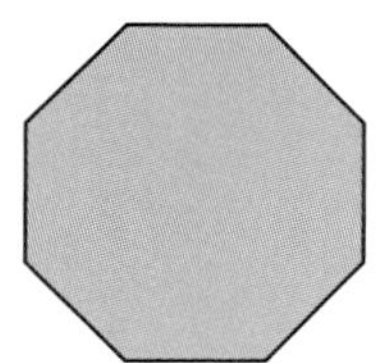

A 4
B 6
C 8
D 12

6. How many triangles are in the figure below?

F 3
G 4
H 8
J 9

7. Tell how the pair of figures are related.

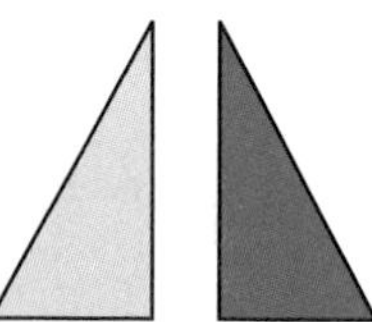

A slide
B flip
C turn
D NH

8. Which is the angle measure of the rotation?

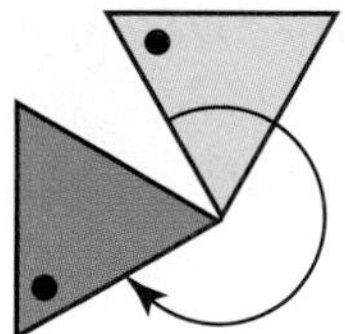

F 90°
G 180°
H 270°
J 360°

9. Which numeral has two lines of symmetry?

A 3 C 6

B 5 D 8

10. Which numeral has rotational symmetry?

F  H 

G 5 J 8

11. Look at the shape of the mobile below.

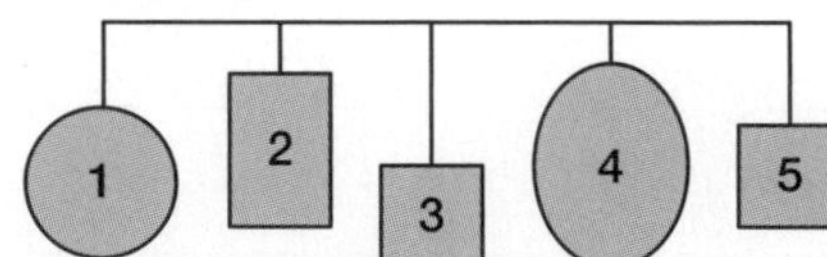

Which shapes are congruent (same size, same shape)?

A 1 and 3
B 2 and 4
C 3 and 5
D 4 and 1

12. Rick is older than Mary but younger than Jerome. Sarah is younger than Rick. Which of the following is a reasonable conclusion?

F Jerome is younger than Sarah.
G Jerome is older than Sarah.
H Sarah is older than Mary.
J Mary is older than Sarah.

13. How many edges does a square pyramid have?

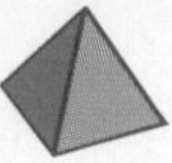

A 4 C 8
B 5 D 10

14. Which solid figure can be made from the net?

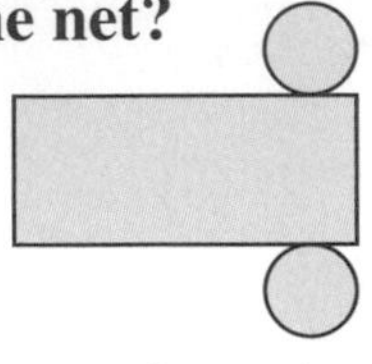

F rectangular prism
G cylinder
H cone
J cube

15. A tile floor will have 15 squares like the one shown. How many purple triangles will be in the floor?

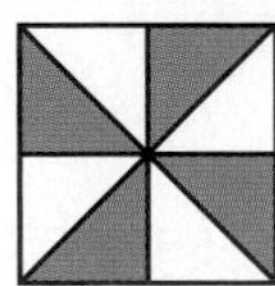

A 4 C 19
B 15 D 60

16. Which best describes the lines shown?

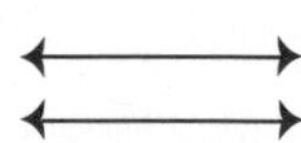

F intersecting lines
G perpendicular lines
H parallel lines
J NH

Reteaching

Set A (pages 438–440)

Tell what type of figure is shown.

The figure shows two rays that meet at their endpoints. It is an angle. It is less than a right angle, so it is an acute angle.

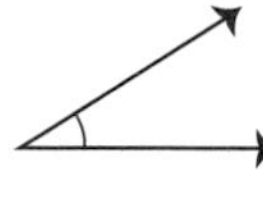

Remember that a line segment has two endpoints.

Tell what type of figure is shown.

1.

2. E F

Set B (pages 441–443)

Identify the polygon.

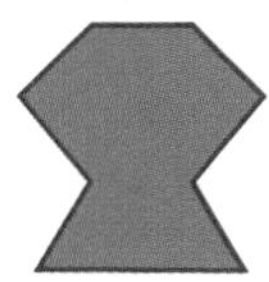

The polygon has 8 sides.
It is an octagon.

Remember that you can name a polygon by the number of sides it has.

Identify each polygon.

1. 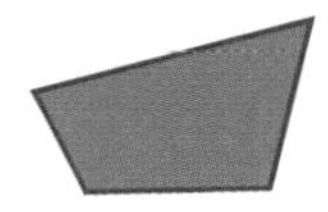

2. 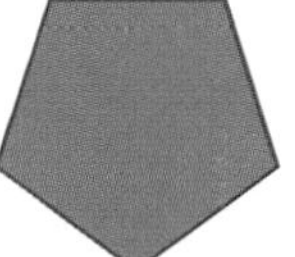

Set C (pages 444–446)

Describe the triangle by both its sides and its angles.

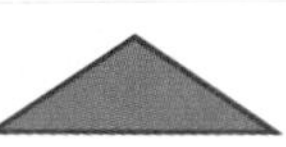

Two sides are the same length.
There is an obtuse angle.
The triangle is both an isosceles triangle and an obtuse triangle.

Remember that you can name a triangle by its sides and by its angles.

Describe each triangle by its sides. Then describe it by its angles.

1. 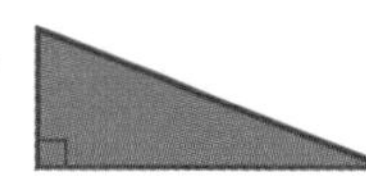

2. 

Set D (pages 447–449)

What type of quadrilateral is shown?

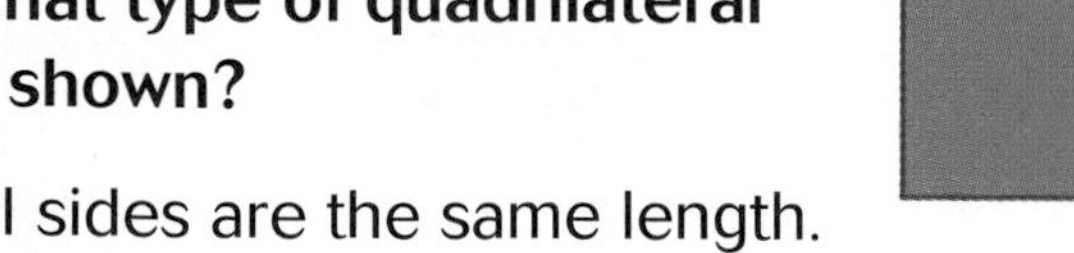

All sides are the same length.
There are four right angles.
The quadrilateral is a square.

Remember that you can identify quadrilaterals by the lengths of their sides and the sizes of their angles.

What type of quadrilateral is shown?

1. 

2. 

Set E (pages 452–453)

Find the radius of the circle. Estimate its circumference.

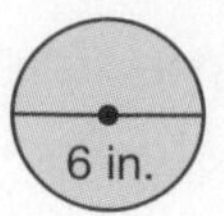

The radius is half the diameter or 3 inches. The circumference is about 3 times the diameter or about 18 inches.

Remember that the diameter of a circle is twice as long as the radius.

Find the radius of each circle. Estimate the circumference.

1. diameter: 8 centimeters

2. diameter: 22 feet

Set F (pages 456–457)

Tell if the two figures below are congruent.

The figures are not the same size, so they are not congruent.

Remember that congruent figures have the same size and shape.

Tell if the two figures are congruent. Write *yes* or *no*.

1. 

2. 

Set G (pages 460–461)

Tell how many lines of symmetry the figure at the right has.

The figure has 2 lines of symmetry, as shown.

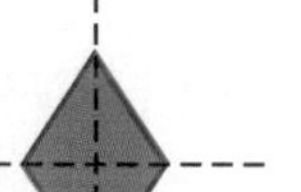

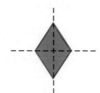

Remember that a line of symmetry divides a figure into congruent halves.

Tell how many lines of symmetry each figure has.

1. 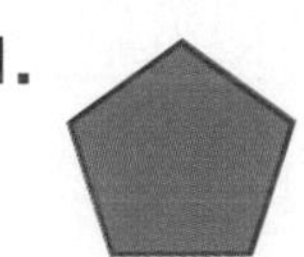

2. 

Set H (pages 462–463)

Tell whether the pair of figures are related by a *slide, flip,* or *turn.*

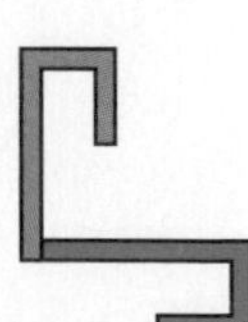

The figures at the right show a turn (or rotation).

Remember that two figures related by a slide, a flip, or a turn are congruent.

Tell whether each pair of figures are related by a slide, flip, or turn.

1. 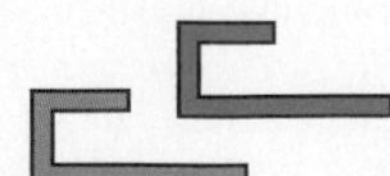

2. 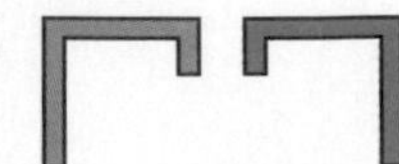

Reteaching (continued)

Set I (pages 464–465)

Give the angle measure and turn to describe the rotation.

The figure has been rotated 270° or a $\frac{3}{4}$ turn.

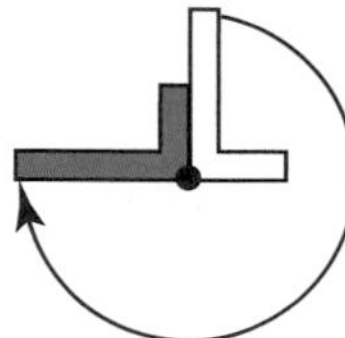

Remember that a figure rotated 90° is rotated a $\frac{1}{4}$ turn.

Give an angle measure and turn to describe each rotation.

1. 

2. 

Set J (pages 466–468)

Tell which solid figure the object below looks like.

The object looks like a square pyramid.

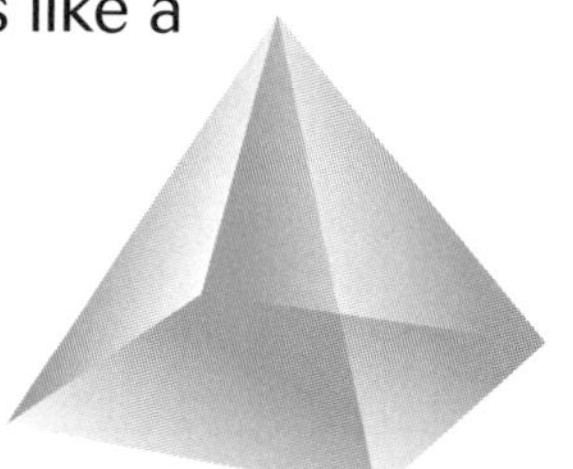

Remember that solid figures are three-dimensional shapes.

Tell which solid figure each object looks like.

1. 

2. 

Set K (pages 469–471)

Tell which solid figure can be made from the net below.

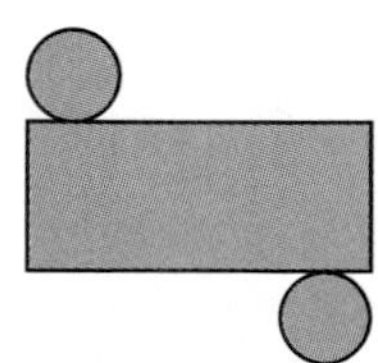

When folded and taped together, the net would form a cylinder.

Remember that a net is a pattern you can use to make a solid.

Tell which solid figure can be made from each net.

1. 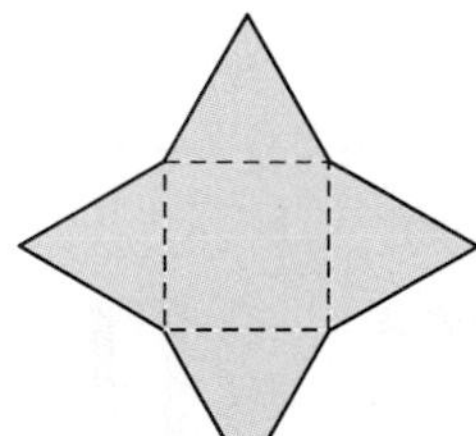

2. 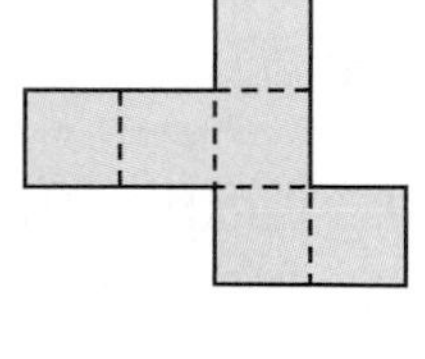

More Practice

Set A (pages 438–440)

Tell what type of figure is shown.

1. *G* *H*

2.

3.

4.

5. Suppose you are in an airplane. You look down and see these two roads on the ground. If these roads continue on, will they intersect?

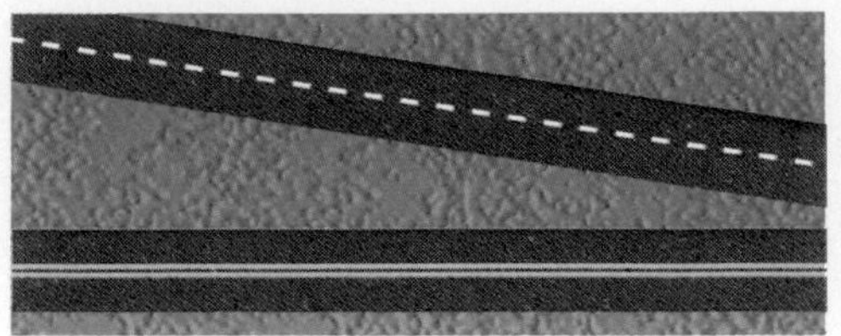

Set B (pages 441–443)

Tell if the shape of each figure is a polygon. Write *yes* or *no*. If it is a polygon, write its name.

1. 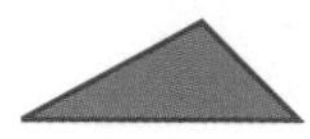

2. 

3. 

4. 

Set C (pages 444–446)

The lengths of the sides of a triangle are given. Describe each triangle by its sides.

1. 5 in., 8 in., 5 in.
2. 6 m, 7 m, 9 m
3. 2 m, 2 m, 2 m

4. A yield sign is triangular. Describe the triangle by its sides. Then describe it by its angles.

Set D (pages 447–449)

What type of quadrilateral is shown?

1.

2.

3. 

4. 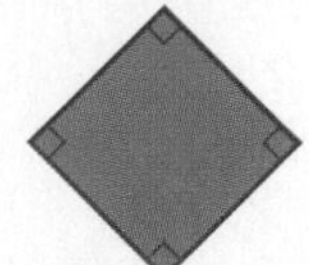

5. **Math Reasoning** Is a square a rhombus? Explain.

More Practice (continued)

Set E (pages 452–453)

Find the diameter of each circle. Estimate the circumference.

1. 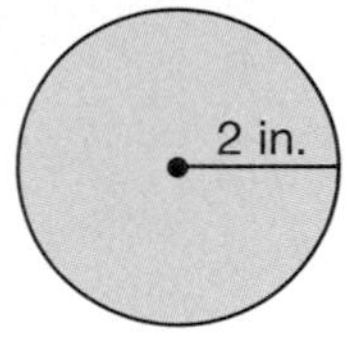

2. 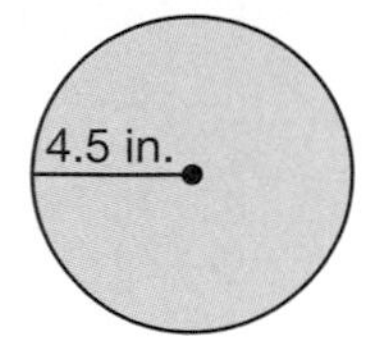

3. 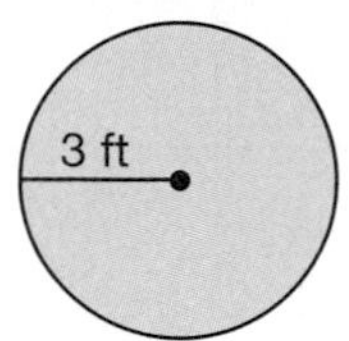

4. 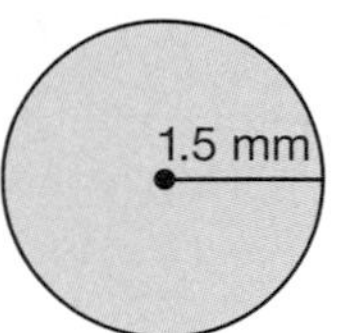

5. **Mental Math** The diameter of a wheel is 20 inches. What is the radius? About how many inches is the circumference of the wheel?

Set F (pages 456–457)

Tell if the two figures are congruent. Write *yes* or *no*.

1. 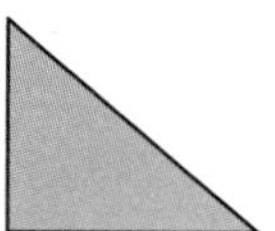

2. 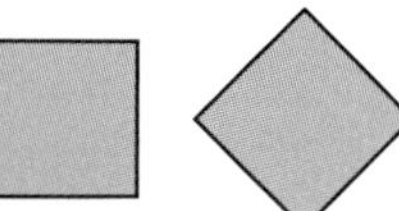

3. 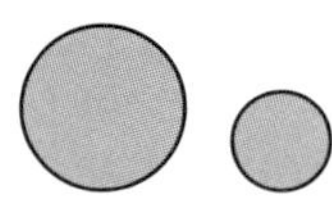

4. Kim made a tracing of a picture. Are the tracing and the picture congruent? Why or why not?

Set G (pages 460–461)

Is the dashed line a line of symmetry? Write *yes* or *no*.

1. 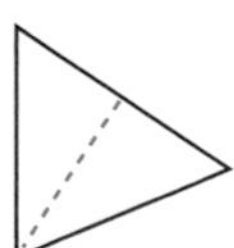

2. 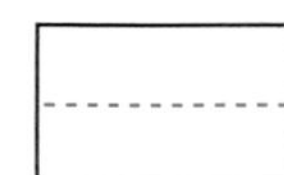

3. 

4. 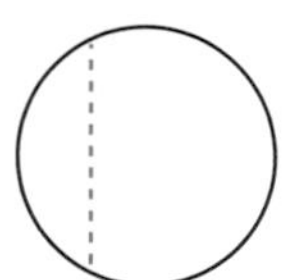

5. Does the U.S. flag have line symmetry?

Set H (pages 462–463)

Tell whether each pair of figures are related by a *slide, flip,* or *turn*.

1. 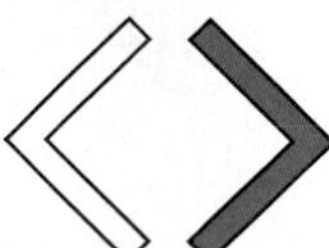

2. 

3. 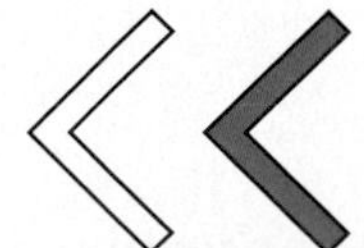

Set I (pages 464–465)

Give an angle measure and a turn to describe each rotation.

1. 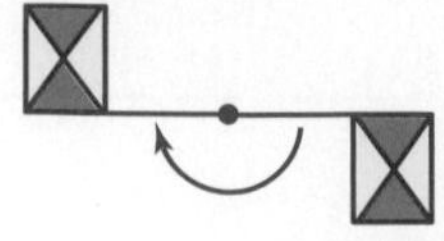

2. 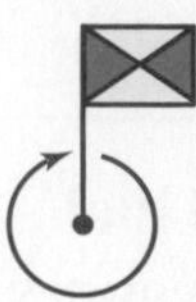

3. 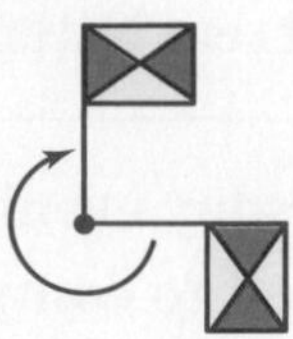

Tell if the figure has rotational symmetry. Write *yes* or *no*.

4. 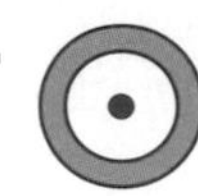

5. 

6. 

Set J (pages 466–468)

Tell which solid figure each object looks like.

1. 

2. 

3. 

4. Michael made a rectangular prism out of paper. How many faces did his rectangular prism have? How many edges and vertices?

Set K (pages 469–471)

Tell which solid figure can be made from each net.

1. 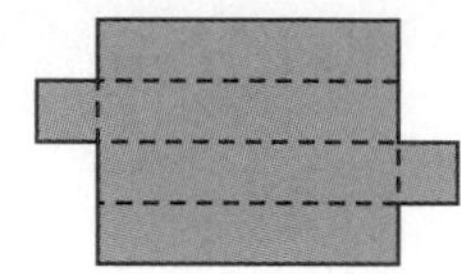

2. 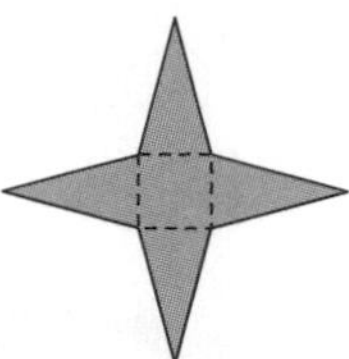

3. 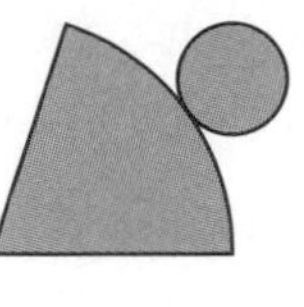

4. Draw a net for the can of soup shown in Set J above.

Problem Solving: Preparing for Tests

Choose the correct letter for each answer.

1. **On Thursday evening, January 13, Rachel had 17 days left to complete her project on volcanoes. When did Rachel have to be done with her project?**

   A Saturday, January 29
   B Sunday, January 29
   C Saturday, January 30
   D Sunday, January 30

Tip

Try making a drawing to solve this problem. Sketch a calendar with the 13th day on a Thursday. Then count ahead 17 days.

2. **Olivia had $44 in the bank. Then she earned $27.25 for each of the next 2 weeks. Which is the best estimate for the total amount of money Olivia has?**

   F $75
   G $100
   H $150
   J More than $175

Tip

Use estimation to eliminate one or more of the answer choices in this problem.

3. **Brian is choosing some computer games from a catalog. Video Rangers costs $42, Mighty Meteors costs $65, Warp Out costs $13, and Time Blaster costs $36. Which 2 games can Brian buy for $70?**

   A Video Rangers and Warp Out
   B Warp Out and Mighty Meteors
   C Time Blaster and Video Rangers
   D Mighty Meteors and Time Blaster

Tip

Sometimes a good way to solve a multiple-choice question is by trying each answer choice to see which one is correct.

4. Rebecca has a collection of 215 glass beads, 387 wooden beads, and 293 plastic beads. *About* how many glass and wooden beads does Rebecca have?

F 200 **H** 800
G 600 **J** 900

---

5. Debbie bought 4 pencils that cost 30¢ each, a pack of pens that cost \$2.50, and some erasers that cost 15¢ each. Not including tax, what other information is needed to find the total cost of Debbie's purchase?

A The number of pens in a pack
B The cost of 2 erasers
C The number of erasers Debbie bought
D The cost of 2 pencils

---

6. Sam has more pets than Pat but fewer pets than Marta. Pat has 3 pets. Which is a reasonable conclusion?

F Sam has fewer than 3 pets.
G Sam has more pets than Marta.
H Marta has more than 3 pets.
J Pat has more pets than Marta.

---

7. If 8 tickets to a ball game cost \$64.64, which is a reasonable estimate for the cost of 5 tickets?

A \$8
B \$40
C \$50
D \$56

8. This graph shows what happened when Justin rode his bike to his friend's house. Which shows a time when Justin stopped riding his bike?

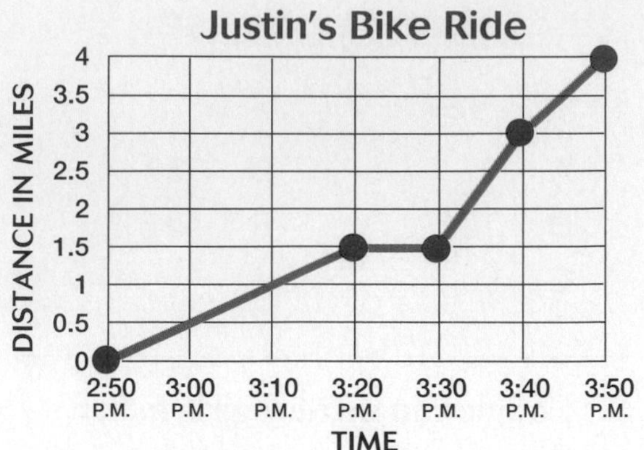

F 3:00 P.M. **H** 3:20 P.M.
G 3:10 P.M. **J** 3:40 P.M.

---

9. The Garcias filled their pool with water. On the first day they put 218 gallons of water in the pool. On the second day they added 295 more gallons of water. *About* how many gallons of water were in the pool then?

A 300 gallons **C** 500 gallons
B 350 gallons **D** 600 gallons

---

10. Ronald reads 8 to 12 pages of his book every day. Which is reasonable for the number of pages Ronald reads in a week?

F Fewer than 8 pages
G Between 8 and 56 pages
H Between 56 and 84 pages
J More than 84 pages

Multiple-Choice Cumulative Review

Choose the correct letter for each answer.

Number Sense

1. $81 \div 9 = \blacksquare$

   A 9
   B 72
   C 90
   D 729
   E NH

2. Connie can invite 9 girls to her sleepover. She made a list of 5 girls. Which number sentence shows how many more girls she can invite?

   F $5 + 9 = \blacksquare$
   G $5 - 9 = \blacksquare$
   H $9 + 5 = \blacksquare$
   J $9 - 5 = \blacksquare$

3. The school library has 485 novels, 396 adventure books, and 284 biographies. How many more adventure books are there than biographies?

   A 112
   B 201
   C 342
   D 680
   E NH

4. Mateo has 24 packages of trading cards. Each package has 11 cards in it. How many cards does Mateo have?

   F 13
   G 35
   H 48
   J 264
   K NH

Measurement and Geometry

5. Which pair of shapes appear to be congruent (same size, same shape)?

   A  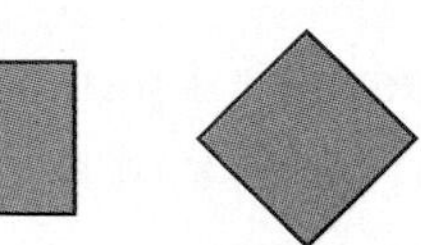

   B  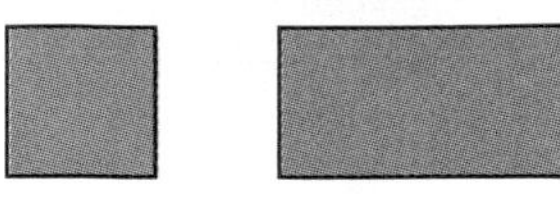

   C 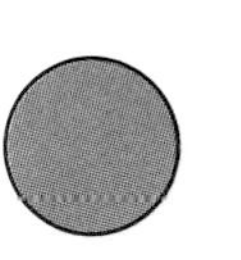 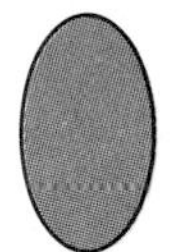

   D 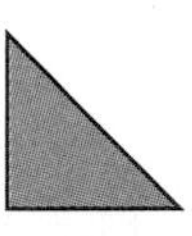 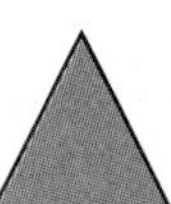

6. Which shape has 4 right angles?

   F 

   H 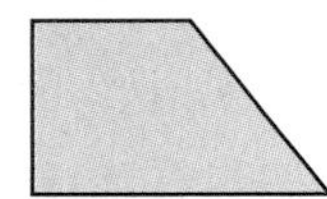

   G 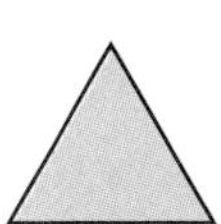

   J 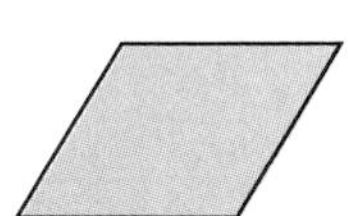

7. Which letter does **NOT** have a line of symmetry?

   A T
   B I
   C H
   D J

Algebra and Functions

8. **Solve $x - 9 = 36$.**

F $x = 4$

G $x = 27$

H $x = 45$

J $x = 324$

9. **Which letter on the graph best represents the ordered pair (3, 2)?**

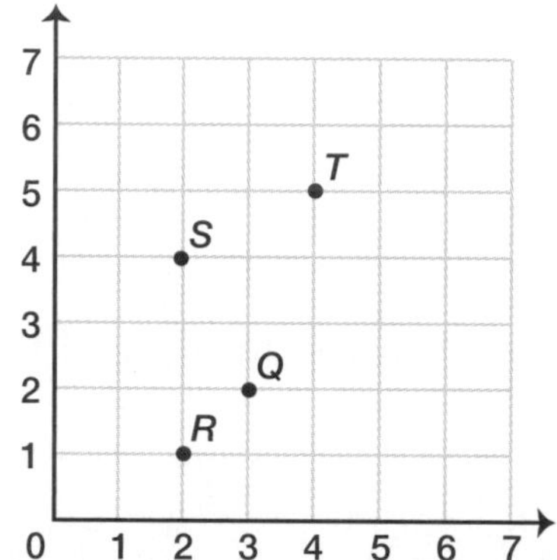

A *Q** **C** S

B *R* **D** *T*

10. **What is the missing number in the number pattern?**

16, 32, 64, ■, 256, 512

F 80

G 112

H 128

J 192

11. **Which expression could help you solve 7 × ■ = 56?**

A 7 × 56 **C** 56 − 7

B 7 + 56 **D** 56 ÷ 7

Statistics, Data Analysis, and Probability

12. **Look at the spinner. How many possible outcomes are there?**

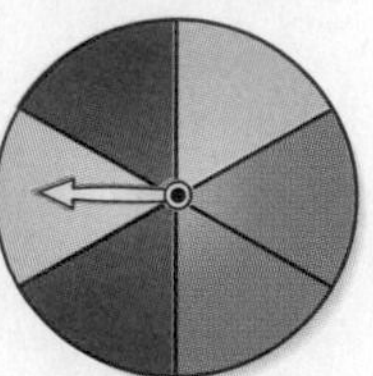

F 3

G 4

H 5

J 6

Use the graph for Questions 13–15.

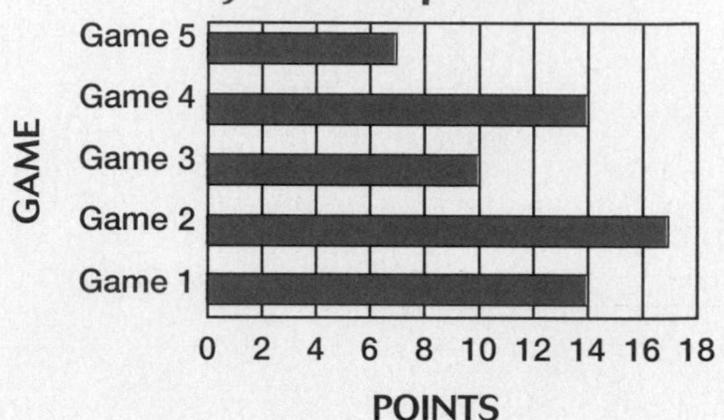

13. **In which game did the Dolphins score the fewest points?**

A Game 2 **C** Game 4

B Game 3 **D** Game 5

14. **In which games did the Dolphins score the same number of points?**

F 1 and 2 **H** 3 and 4

G 2 and 5 **J** 1 and 4

15. **How many more points did the Dolphins score in Game 4 than in Game 5?**

A 3 **C** 7

B 6 **D** 8

Measurement, Perimeter, and Area

Diagnosing Readiness

In Chapter 12, you will use these skills:

A Expressions with Multiplication and Division

(pages 104–106)

Evaluate each expression for $n = 8$.

1. $3n$ **2.** $9n$

3. $\frac{n}{4}$ **4.** $5n + 4$

5. Find the total number of bagels when $x = 6$.

B Multiplying Whole Numbers

(pages 134–136, 140–141)

6. 3×43 **7.** 2×83

8. 418×7 **9.** $3 \times 5{,}280$

10. In one section of a video rental store, 108 videos are displayed on each of the 6 shelves. How many videos are displayed on the six shelves?

G Multiplying Multiples of Ten

(pages 170–171)

11. 5×600

12. 7×90

13. $7 \times 3{,}000$

14. 4×60

15. 7×400

16. $9{,}000 \times 6$

17. 15×100

18. $26 \times 1{,}000$

19. A small theater has 60 rows with 8 seats in each row. How many people can watch a play in this theater?

D Dividing Whole Numbers

(pages 202–204, 214–216)

20. $72 \div 3$

21. $56 \div 2$

22. $120 \div 8$

23. $68 \div 4$

24. $6\overline{)192}$

25. $3\overline{)582}$

26. Todd jogs around a running track at the park. If he jogs eight laps, he knows the distance is 5,280 feet. What is the distance of one lap around the track?

E Dividing Multiples of 10, 100, and 1000

(pages 200–201)

27. $180 \div 3$

28. $210 \div 7$

29. $3{,}000 \div 6$

30. $4{,}500 \div 9$

31. $5{,}600 \div 8$

32. $1{,}600 \div 2$

33. Your friend told you that he will be 520 weeks old on his next birthday. About what age is that in years?

F Quadrilaterals

(pages 447–449)

What type of quadrilateral is shown?

34. 

35. 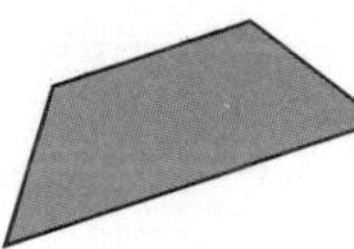

36. 

37. 

To the Family and Student

Looking Back	Chapter 12	Looking Ahead
In Grade 3, students learned how to use customary and metric units of length, weight, mass, capacity, and temperature. They also learned how to find the perimeter and area of simple figures.	**Measurement, Perimeter, and Area** In this chapter, students will learn more about using customary and metric units. They also will learn how to use formulas to find the perimeter and area of rectangles, squares, and irregular figures.	In Grade 5, students will learn how to find the area of other polygons, the circumference of a circle, and volume and surface area of solid figures.

Math and Everyday Living

Opportunitics to apply the concepts of Chapter 12 abound in everyday situations. During the chapter, think about how measurement, perimeter, and area can be used to solve a variety of real-world problems. The following examples suggest just several of the many situations that could launch a discussion about measurement, perimeter, and area.

Math at Home Your living room has the dimensions shown.

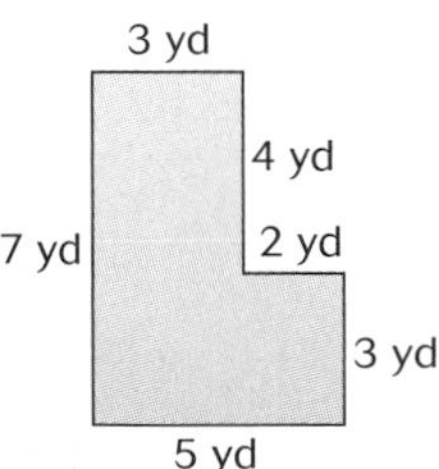

Carpet costs $55 a square yard. How much would it cost to carpet your living room?

Wood trim costs $9.50 a foot. How much would it cost to put wood trim around your living room where the wall meets the ceiling?

Math on the Farm Your uncle is a farmer. He has 360 feet of fence to make a chicken yard. He plans to make the yard in the shape of a rectangle that is 100 feet by 80 feet. What size could he make it to get more area?

Math and Sports When you hit a home run in baseball, how far do you run?

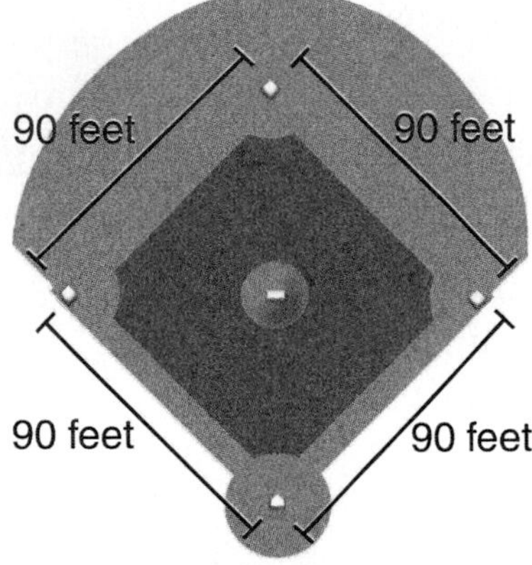

Math at the Grocery Store You pay $7.49 for a steak. What measurement must you estimate to decide if the amount charged was reasonable?

Steak
$3.79 per pound

Each of two bottles of juice costs $2.19. One holds a pint. The other holds 12 fluid ounces. Which one gives you more juice for your money?

Math and Travel You are traveling to Australia in July. You learn the average temperature is 15° Celsius. Should you take sandals or warm shoes?

California Content Standards in Chapter 12 Lessons*

	Teach and Practice	Practice
Number Sense		
1.8 (key) Use concepts of negative numbers (e.g., . . . in temperature . . .).	12-4	
Algebra and Functions		
1.1 Use letters, boxes, or other symbols to stand for any number in simple expressions or equations	12-6, 12-8	12-9, 12-10
1.4 Use and interpret formulas (e.g., area = length × width or $A = \ell w$) to answer questions about quantities and their relationships.	12-6, 12-7, 12-8	12-9, 12-10
Measurement and Geometry		
1.1 Measure the area of rectangular shapes by using appropriate units, such as square centimeter (cm^2), square meter (m^2), square (km^2), square inch ($in.^2$), square yard (yd^2), or square mile (mi^2).	12-7	12-9, 12-10
1.1 (Gr. 3) Choose the appropriate tools and units (. . . U.S.) and estimate and measure the length, liquid volume, and weight . . . of given objects.	12-1, 12-2	
1.2 Recognize that rectangles that have the same area can have different perimeters.	12-9	
1.3 Understand that rectangles that have the same perimeter can have different areas.	12-9	12-10
1.4 Understand and use formulas to solve problems involving perimeters and areas of rectangles and squares. Use those formulas to find the area of more complex figures by dividing the figures into basic shapes.	12-6, 12-7, 12-8	12-9, 12-10
1.4 (Gr. 3) Carry out simple unit conversions within a system of measurement	12-1, 12-2, 12-3	

	Teach and Practice	Practice
Mathematical Reasoning		
1.1 Analyze problems by identifying relationships, distinguishing relevant from irrelevant information, sequencing and prioritizing information, and observing patterns.		12-5
2.0 Students use strategies, skills, and concepts in finding solutions.		12-3, 12-5, 12-10
2.2 Apply strategies and results from simpler problems to more complex problems.	12-5	12-2
2.3 Use a variety of methods, such as words, numbers, symbols, charts, graphs, tables, diagrams, and models, to explain mathematical reasoning.		12-1, 12-5, 12-8
2.4 Express the solution clearly and logically by using the appropriate mathematical notation and terms and clear language; support solutions with evidence in both verbal and symbolic work.	12-10	12-4, 12-6, 12-7
3.1 Evaluate the reasonableness of the solution in the context of the original situation.	12-3	
3.2 Note the method of deriving the solution and demonstrate a conceptual understanding of the derivation by solving similar problems.		12-5

* The symbol (key) indicates a key standard as designated in the Mathematics Framework for California Public Schools. Full statements of the California Content Standards are found at the beginning of this book following the Table of Contents.

Lesson 12-1 Customary Measures

California Content Standard *Measurement and Geometry 1.4 (Gr. 3): Carry out simple unit conversions within a system of measurement . . .. Also, Measurement and Geometry 1.1 (Gr. 3) (See p. 491.)*

Math Link You have worked with customary measures. In this lesson you will use customary units of length, weight, and capacity.

You can use customary units of length to measure objects of many different sizes.

Warm-Up Review

1. 7×12
2. $84 \div 3$
3. 3×16
4. $108 \div 12$
5. 11×8
6. $64 \div 4$
7. 19×4
8. $96 \div 8$
9. For her club meeting, Teresa bought 6 boxes of cookies and 2 gallons of milk. If each box held 18 cookies, how many cookies did she bring?

Word Bank

inch
foot
yard
mile

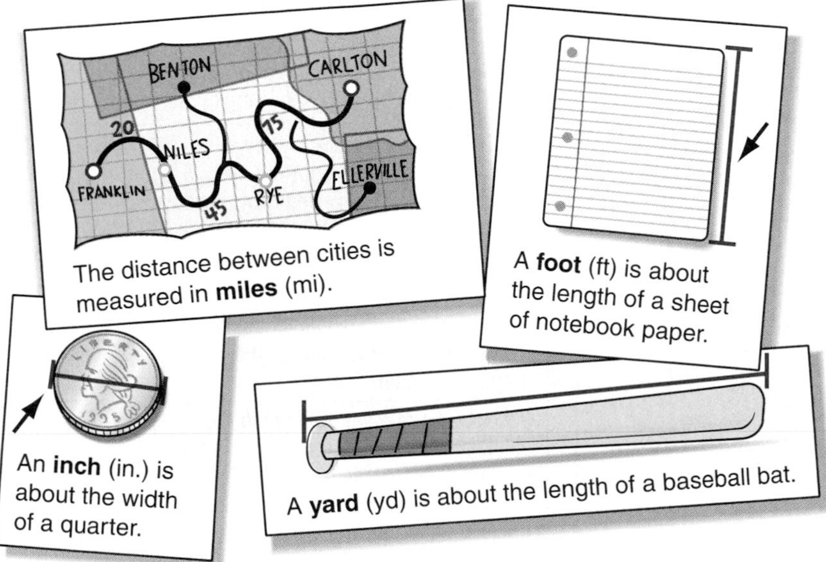

The distance between cities is measured in **miles** (mi).

A **foot** (ft) is about the length of a sheet of notebook paper.

An **inch** (in.) is about the width of a quarter.

A **yard** (yd) is about the length of a baseball bat.

The chart at the right shows the relationships between the units of length. You can use the chart to change a measurement from one unit to another unit.

Customary Units of Length
1 ft = 12 in.
1 yd = 3 ft
1 mi = 5,280 ft

Example 1

To change from a larger unit of length to a smaller unit of length, multiply.

8 feet = ■ inches

Think: 1 ft = 12 in.

$8 \times 12 = 96$

8 feet = 96 inches

Example 2

To change from a smaller unit of length to a larger unit of length, divide.

21 feet = ■ yards

Think: 3 ft = 1 yd

$21 \div 3 = 7$

21 feet = 7 yards

 Additional Standard: Mathematical Reasoning 2.3 (See p. 491.)

You can use customary units to measure weight. The weights of these common objects can be used to estimate the weights of other objects.

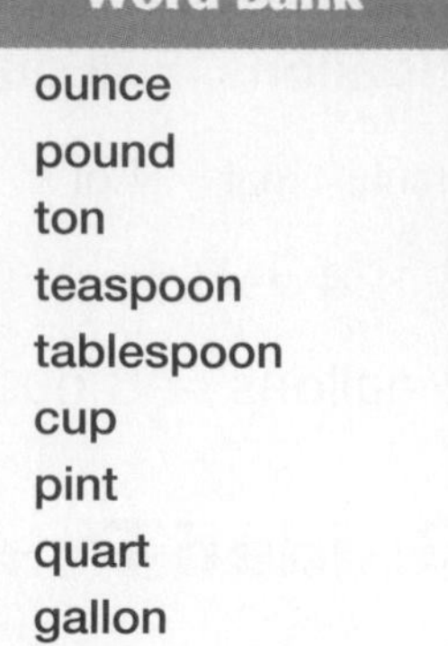

A slice of bread weighs about 1 **ounce** (oz).

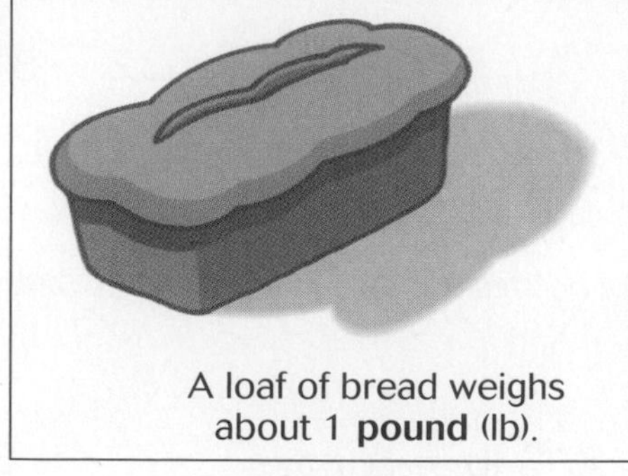
A loaf of bread weighs about 1 **pound** (lb).

A small passenger car weighs about 1 **ton** (T).

Customary Units of Weight
1 lb = 16 oz
1 T = 2,000 lb

Example 3

46 pounds 15 ounces = ■ ounces

Think: 1 lb = 16 oz

$46 \times 16 = 736$

$736 + 15 = 751$

There are 751 ounces in 46 pounds 15 ounces.

Example 4

6 tons = ■ pounds

Think: 1 T = 2,000 lb

$6 \times 2{,}000 = 12{,}000$

There are 12,000 pounds in 6 tons.

You can use customary units to measure capacity.

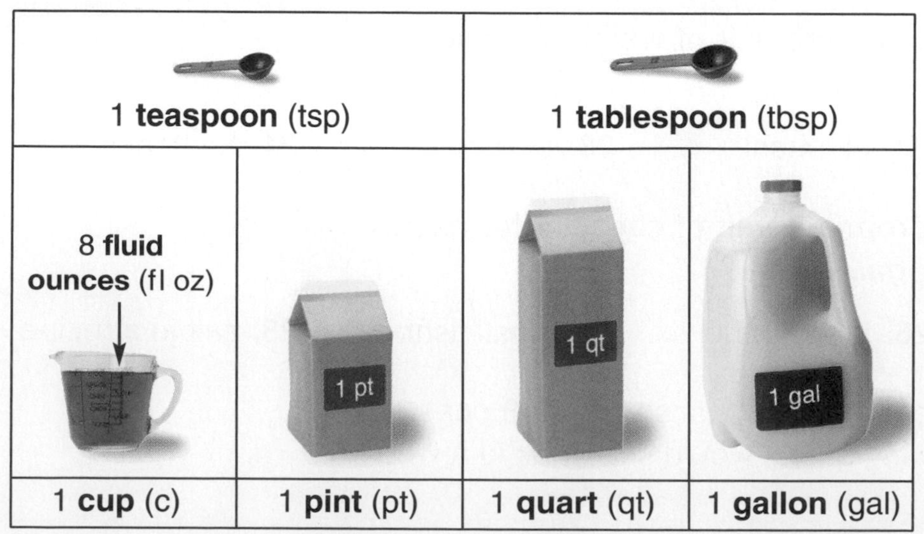

Customary Units of Capacity
1 tbsp = 3 tsp
1 fl oz = 2 tbsp
1 c = 8 fl oz
1 pt = 2c
1 qt = 2 pt
1 gal = 4 qt

Example 5

2 gallons = ■ quarts

Think: 1 gal = 4 qt

2 × 4 = 8

2 gallons = 8 quarts

Example 6

32 fluid ounces = ■ cups

Think: 8 fl oz = 1 c

32 ÷ 8 = 4

32 fluid ounces = 4 cups

Guided Practice *For another example, see Set A on p. 524.*

Find each missing number.

1. 4 yd = ■ ft
2. 3 lb = ■ oz
3. 8 gal = ■ qt
4. 8 qt = ■ gal
5. 10 c = ■ pt
6. 8 fl oz = ■ tbsp
7. Kyle swam 300 feet in 1 minute 42 seconds. How many yards did he swim?

Independent Practice *For more practice, see Set A on p. 526.*

Find each missing number.

8. 5 ft = ■ in.
9. 3 mi = ■ ft
10. 24 ft = ■ yd
11. 2 T = ■ lb
12. 16 oz = ■ lb
13. 5 lb = ■ oz
14. 4 pt = ■ qt
15. 6 tbsp = ■ tsp
16. 16 fl oz = ■ c

Choose the most appropriate unit of length for each. Write *in., ft, yd,* or *mi.*

17. car
18. pencil
19. river
20. classroom

Choose the most appropriate unit of weight for each. Write *oz, lb,* or *T.*

21. computer
22. elephant
23. bird
24. teenager

Choose the most appropriate unit of capacity for each. Write *tsp, c, pt, qt,* or *gal.*

25. bowl of soup
26. full bathtub
27. small fishbowl
28. salt in a recipe
29. Martha's doctor recommends that she drink 8 cups of water every day. How many quarts would she drink in a week?

Estimate and measure to the nearest $\frac{1}{4}$ inch.

30.

31.

32.

33.

Compare. Write >, <, or = for each ●.

34. 1 qt ● 1 pt

35. 1 lb ● 1 oz

36. 1 tsp ● 1 tbsp

37. 1 yd ● 36 in.

38. 1,500 yd ● 1 mi

39. 1 c ● 16 tbsp

Use the table at the right for Exercises 40 and 41.

40. How many ounces of food does 1 otter eat at each feeding? Is this about 1 pound, 2 pounds, or 3 pounds of food?

41. Otters at an aquarium in California eat 4 times per day. About how many pounds of food does 1 otter eat each day?

An Otter's Meal	
10 oz of rock cod	
5 oz of shrimp	
10 oz of surf clam	
4 oz of squid	
2 oz of white smelt	

42. Which weighs more: 3 pounds of apples or 50 ounces of feathers?

43. **Math Reasoning** If two grocery products are in packages of the same size, must they weigh the same? Explain.

Mixed Review

44. Identify the number of faces, edges, and vertices in the rectangular prism shown at the right.

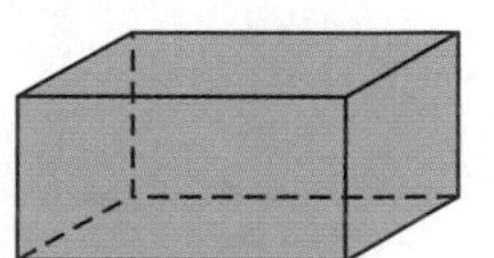

45. (117 − 84) × 3

46. 2 × (144 + 62)

47. 65 ÷ (19 − 14)

Test Prep Choose the correct letter for each answer.

48. Which is not a net for a cube?
(11-13)

A
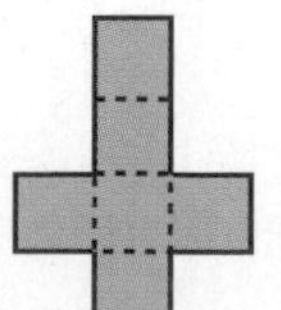

B
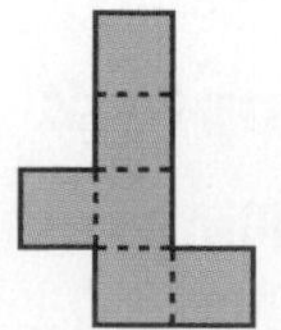

C
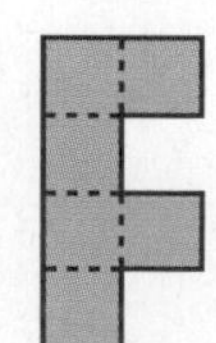

D

Metric Measures

Warm-Up Review

1. 20 × 10 2. 250 ÷ 10

3. 6 × 100 4. 300 ÷ 100

5. 2 × 1,000 6. 80 ÷ 10

7. 90 × 100 8. 1,000 ÷ 10

9. Admission to a fair is $3.00 per adult and $1.50 per child. How much would it cost for a family of 3 children and 2 adults?

California Content Standard *Measurement and Geometry 1.4 (Gr. 3): Carry out simple unit conversions within a system of measurement (e.g., centimeters and meters . . .). Also, Measurement and Geometry 1.1 (Gr. 3)* *(See p. 491.)*

Math Link You have learned about customary measures. Now you will learn about metric measures.

You can use metric units to measure length.

A **millimeter** (mm) is about the width of a pin.
A **centimeter** (cm) is about the width of a crayon.
A **decimeter** (dm) is about the width of an adult's hand.
A **meter** (m) is about the width of a door.
A **kilometer** (km) is about the length of 100 school buses lined up end to end.
BUS
BUS

Word Bank

millimeter
centimeter
decimeter
meter
kilometer

Metric Units of Length

1 cm = 10 mm
1 dm = 10 cm
1 m = 100 cm
1 km = 1,000 m

You can use the chart at the right to change a measurement from one unit to another unit.

Example 1

8 kilometers = ■ meters

Think: 1 km = 1,000 m

8 × 1,000 = 8,000

8 kilometers = 8,000 meters

Example 2

60 millimeters = ■ centimeters

Think: 1 cm = 10 mm

60 ÷ 10 = 6

60 millimeters = 6 centimeters

Additional Standard: Mathematical Reasoning 2.2 *(See p. 491.)*

A **kilogram** (kg) is a metric unit used to measure the mass of objects. Mass is the amount of matter in an object.

A **gram** (g) is a metric unit used to measure the mass of lighter objects.

The mass of each object to the right can be measured by using metric units.

Metric Units of Mass
1 kg = 1,000 g

Example 3

482 kilograms = ■ grams

Think: 1 kg = 1,000 g

482 × 1,000 = 482,000

482 kilograms = 482,000 grams

Word Bank
kilogram
gram
milliliter
liter

A **milliliter** (mL) is a metric unit used to measure the capacities of small containers.

A **liter** (L) is a metric unit used to measure larger containers.

Metric Units of Capacity
1 L = 1,000 mL

Example 4

How many milliliters are in a 2-liter bottle?

2 liters = ■ milliliters

Think: 1 L = 1,000 mL

2 × 1,000 = 2,000

There are 2,000 milliliters in a 2-liter bottle.

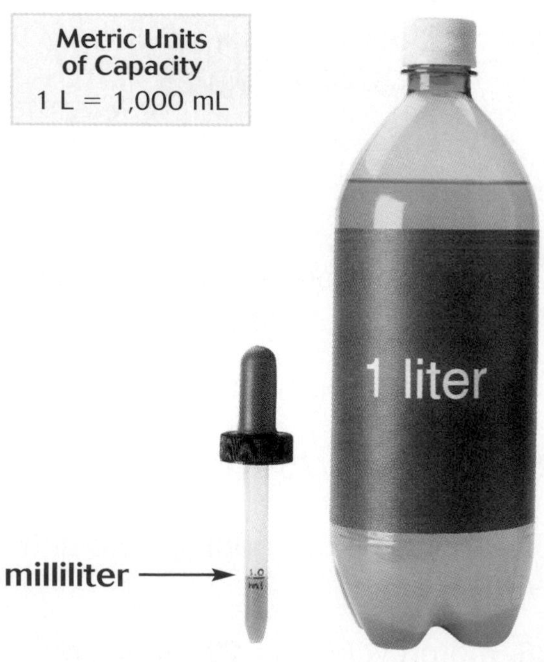

Guided Practice *For another example, see Set B on p. 524.*

Tell whether the unit measures *length, mass,* or *capacity.*

1. gram **2.** centimeter **3.** millimeter **4.** liter

Find each missing number.

5. 20 mm = ■ cm **6.** 3 kg = ■ g **7.** 1 L = ■ mL

8. How much longer is a 10-kilometer race than a 1,000-meter race?

Independent Practice *For more practice, see Set B on p. 526.*

Tell whether the unit measures *length, mass,* or *capacity.*

9. meter **10.** milliliter **11.** kilogram **12.** kilometer

Find each missing number.

13. 5 km = ■ m **14.** 4 L = ■ mL **15.** 30 mm = ■ cm

16. 1,000 g = ■ kg **17.** 40 cm = ■ dm **18.** 25 kg = ■ g

19. 6 m = ■ cm **20.** 16 cm = ■ mm **21.** 12 L = ■ mL

Estimate and then find each length to the nearest centimeter.

22.

23.

Choose the most appropriate unit of length for each. Write *cm, dm, m,* or *km.*

24. My jump rope is 3 ■ long. **25.** My thumb is 1 ■ wide.

26. The road is 75 ■ long. **27.** An in-line skate is 3 ■ long.

Choose the more appropriate unit of mass for each. Write g or kg.

28. motorcycle **29.** envelope **30.** person **31.** watermelon

Choose the more appropriate unit of capacity for each. Write *L* or *mL*.

32. perfume bottle **33.** water bucket **34.** bathtub **35.** spoonful of salad oil

Compare. Write >, <, or = for each ●.

36. 1 kg ● 1 g **37.** 1,000 mL ● 1 L **38.** 9 cm ● 1 dm

39. 3,000 m ● 1 km **40.** 10 cm ● 10 mm **41.** 2 kg ● 2,000 g

42. The length of the longest Olympic walking event was 50 kilometers. How many meters was this?

43. A racer finished a liter bottle of water during a 10-kilometer bike race. He also stopped at the 5,000-meter mark to drink a 400-milliliter cup of water. How many milliliters of water did he drink in all?

44. Math Reasoning There are about 5 milliliters in a teaspoon. There are 3 teaspoons in a tablespoon. About how many milliliters are there in a tablespoon?

45. The mass of 5 tomatoes is about 1 kilogram. Estimate the mass of 1 tomato in grams.

Mixed Review

46. What solid does the net shown at the right make?

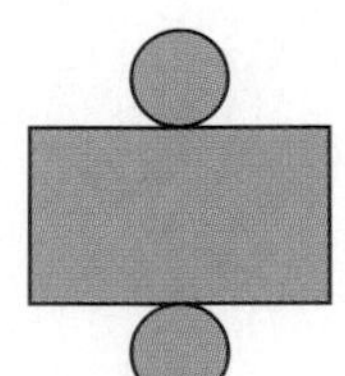

47. Lauren cut 1 yard of rope into 6 pieces of equal length. How long is each piece in inches?

48. \$62 + \$5.98 **49.** 8 × \$1.09 **50.** \$10 − \$4.95 **51.** 7)\$19.18

52. Write 36 as a product of its prime factors.

Test Prep **Choose the correct letter for each answer.**

53. Which is the word name for 2,020,000? (1-1)

A two thousand, twenty

B two hundred thousand, twenty

C two million, twenty

D two million, twenty thousand

54. Algebra What is the value of $y = 4x - 6$ if $x = 8$? (10-10)

F 6

G 8

H 26

J 38

K NH

Problem-Solving Skill:
Reasonable Answers

Warm-Up Review

Compare. Write >, <, or = for each ●.

1. 10 cm ● 10 mm
2. 8 qt ● 16 c
3. 12 oz ● 1 lb
4. 5,000 mL ● 5L
5. Amy made 72 ounces of strawberry jam and 84 ounces of peach jam. How many 6-ounce jars can she fill with strawberry jam?

California Content Standard *Mathematical Reasoning 3.1: Evaluate the reasonableness of the solution in the context of the original situation. Also, Measurement and Geometry 1.4 (Gr. 3) (See p. 491.)*

Read For Understanding

A walk-a-thon course is pictured at the right. Luis estimates that it will take him about 40 minutes to walk around the course 3 times. Is his estimate reasonable?

Walk-a-Thon Map

Start → 400 yd → Fountain; 400 yd → Picnic area; 250 yd → Playground; 100 yd → Start

❶ What is the total distance of the course in yards?

❷ What is the total distance in yards Luis plans to walk?

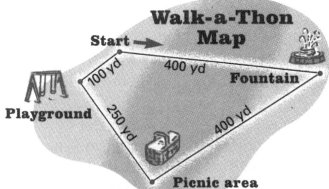

Think and Discuss

Reasonable Answers

Sometimes you can decide if an answer is reasonable by making comparisons to facts or measures you already know.

Reread the paragraph at the top of the page.

❸ Occasionally Luis walks to town, which is 2 miles from his house. How many feet is this? (Remember, 1 mi = 5,280 ft.)

❹ What is the total distance in feet Luis plans to walk in the walk-a-thon?

❺ How does the distance Luis is planning to walk in the walk-a-thon compare to the distance to town?

❻ It takes Luis about 40 minutes to walk to town. Use this information to decide if his estimated time for the walk-a-thon is reasonable.

 Additional Standard: Mathematical Reasoning 2.0 (See p. 491.)

Guided Practice

When Marie visited her aunt in Paris, she used French francs to shop. Her aunt told her that 7 French francs are nearly equivalent to one U.S. dollar. What is a reasonable price in French francs for a pair of shoes?

1. What is the most reasonable price in U.S. dollars for a pair of shoes?

a. 4 U.S. dollars

b. 40 U.S. dollars

c. 400 U.S. dollars

2. Use your answer to Exercise 1 to help you choose the most reasonable price in French francs for a pair of shoes.

a. 28 French francs

b. 280 French francs

c. 2,800 French francs

Independent Practice

You want to estimate the weight of a large orange. You notice in the refrigerator a 3-pound bag of apples. It contains 8 large apples. You think that the orange might weigh about the same amount as one of the apples.

3. How many ounces are in 3 pounds?

a. 8 ounces

b. 16 ounces

c. 48 ounces

4. Choose the best estimate for the weight of the orange.

a. 6 ounces

b. 24 ounces

c. 1 pound

You have noticed that your 12-inch ruler has centimeter markings up to about 30 cm.

5. How does the length of your shoe compare to the length of the ruler?

a. My shoe is shorter than the ruler.

b. My shoe is as long as the ruler.

c. My shoe is longer than the ruler.

6. Choose the best estimate for the length of your shoe.

a. 25 mm

b. 25 cm

c. 60 cm

7. Math Reasoning Your mother often buys beverages for the family in 2-liter bottles. How can you use that information to decide if 35 mL is a reasonable estimate for the amount of juice in a single-serving bottle?

Use Homework Workbook 12-3.

Temperature

California Content Standard *Number Sense 1.8: (🔑) Use concepts of negative numbers (e.g., . . . in temperature . . .).*

Warm-Up Review

Use > or< for each ●.

1. −5 ● 0 **2.** 12 ● −12

3. 3 ● −6 **4.** 0 ● −8

5. −6 ● 6 **6.** −4 ● −1

7. Use a negative number to represent 1,312 ft below sea level.

Math Link You have learned about some customary and metric units. Now you will learn to use customary and metric units to measure temperature.

You can measure temperature in **degrees Fahrenheit** (°F) or **degrees Celsius** (°C). Degrees Fahrenheit are customary units of temperature. Degrees Celsius are metric units of temperature.

Word Bank

degrees Fahrenheit
degrees Celsius

The thermometer at the right shows both customary and metric units. The scale of the thermometer is 2°. Freezing point is 32°F or 0°C. We read temperatures that go below 0° as negative.

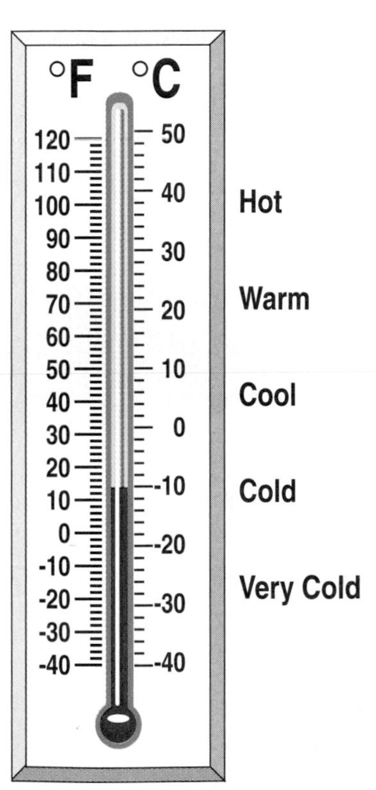

Example

Find the temperature shown on the thermometer in degrees Fahrenheit and degrees Celsius.

Using customary units, the temperature is fourteen degrees Fahrenheit or 14°F.

Using metric units, the temperature is negative ten degrees Celsius or ten degrees Celsius below zero. This is written as $^{-}10$°C.

Guided Practice *For another example, see Set C on p. 524.*

Use the thermometer above. Write the equivalent temperature in degrees Fahrenheit or degrees Celsius.

1. 20°C **2.** $^{-}20$°C **3.** 54°F **4.** $^{-}22$°F

5. Which is a better estimate for a mild spring day, 60°F or 60°C? Which temperature is warmer?

 Additional Standard: Mathematical Reasoning 2.4 (See p. 491.)

Independent Practice *For more practice, see Set C on p. 526.*

Use the thermometer on page 502. Write the equivalent temperature in degrees Fahrenheit or degrees Celsius.

6. 10°C **7.** ⁻12°C **8.** 90°F **9.** ⁻30°F

Choose the most appropriate temperature in Exercises 10–13. The table at the right provides some information that may be helpful.

	°F	°C
Water boils	212	100
Normal body temperature	98.6	37
Room temperature	68	20
Water freezes	32	0

10. child with a fever
100°F or 100°C

11. frozen banana
40°C or ⁻5°C

12. building a snowman
⁻3°C or 25°C

13. swimming outdoors
81°F or 32°F

Read each thermometer. Write the temperature in °F or °C.

14. 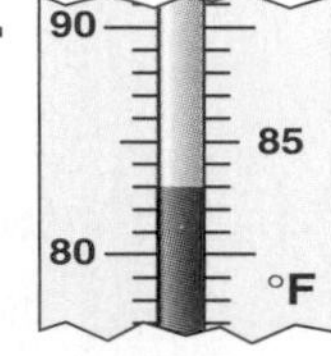

15. 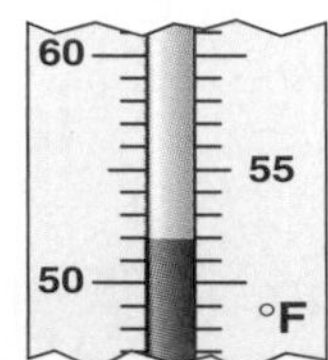

16. 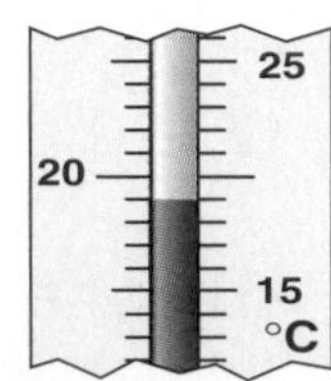

17. 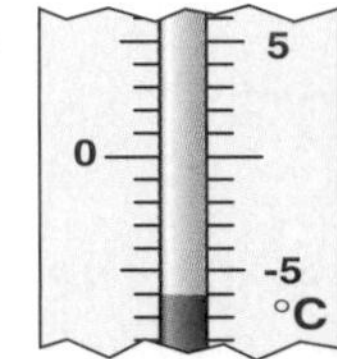

18. Early one day a thermometer read ⁻5°F. By noon it read 8°F. How much did the temperature rise?

19. Math Reasoning Do you think the air temperature on Earth could be 100°C? Explain why or why not.

Mixed Review

20. For the past 3 months, Joe spent \$155, \$248, and \$320 on computer equipment. What was the average amount he spent?

Find each missing number.

21. 3 lb = ■ oz **22.** 5 yd = ■ ft **23.** 4 kg = ■ g **24.** 1 L = ■ mL

Test Prep **Choose the correct letter for each answer.**

25. (1-1) What is the value of 5 in 27,059,000

A 50 **C** 50,000
B 5,000 **D** 500,000

26. Algebra (2-11) Solve $99 + x = 122$.

F $x = 221$ **J** $x = 24$
G $x = 199$ **K** NH
H $x = 25$

Diagnostic Checkpoint

Find each missing number.

1. (12-1) 2 gal = ■ qt
2. (12-1) 27 ft = ■ yd
3. (12-1) 2 mi = ■ ft
4. (12-1) 2 lb = ■ oz
5. (12-1) 3 T = ■ lb
6. (12-1) 5 tbsp = ■ tsp
7. (12-2) 3 cm = ■ mm
8. (12-2) 4 L = ■ mL
9. (12-2) 4 m = ■ cm
10. (12-2) 2 km = ■ m
11. (12-2) 3 kg = ■ g
12. (12-2) 60 dm = ■ cm
13. (12-2) 1,000 cm = ■ m
14. (12-2) 5 dm = ■ cm
15. (12-2) 6 L = ■ mL

Use the thermometer at the right. Write the equivalent temperature in degrees Fahrenheit or degrees Celsius.

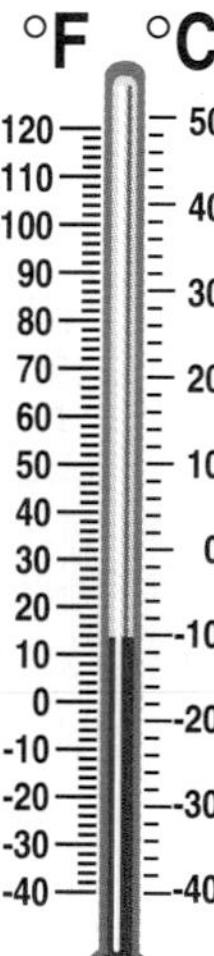

16. (12-4) 50°F
17. (12-4) 20°C
18. (12-4) $^-23$°C

Read each thermometer. Write the temperature in °F or °C.

19. (12-4) 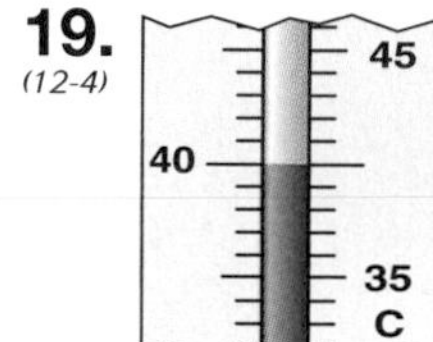

20. (12-4) 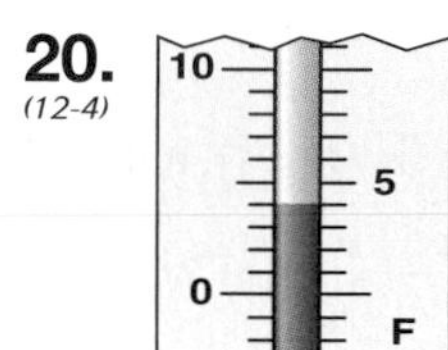

21. (12-3) You spend $3.25 making a gallon of lemonade. You charge 25¢ for a paper cup of lemonade. Which measure must you estimate to decide if this is a reasonable amount of money to charge?

22. (12-1) Choose the most appropriate customary unit of weight for a large truck. Write *ounces, pounds,* or *tons.*

23. (12-2) A long-distance swimmer swims 50 laps. Each lap is 25 meters. How many kilometers did the swimmer swim?

24. (12-4) In August, the normal high temperature for San Diego is 78°F, and the normal high temperature for San Francisco is 66°F. What is the difference in the normal high temperatures for San Diego and San Francisco in August?

Multiple-Choice Cumulative Review

TEST PREP

Choose the correct letter for each answer.

1. $92 \div 8 =$

   A 11
   B 11R4
   C 10R2
   D 10R4
   E NH

2. There are 22 lanes at a bowling alley. Six people can bowl at each lane. What is the greatest number of people who can bowl at one time?

   F 22
   G 122
   H 132
   J 142
   K NH

3. $1.7 - 0.8 =$

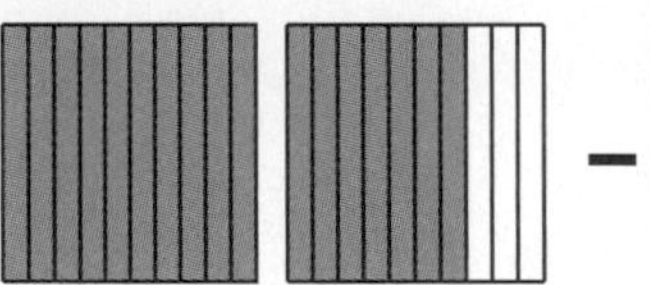

   A 2.5
   B 1.9
   C 1.5
   D 0.9
   E NH

4. In a school election, Pam got 74 votes, Amy got 67 votes, and Zora got 119 votes. How many votes did Amy and Pam receive?

   F 141
   G 186
   H 193
   J 260
   K NH

5. What is the missing number in this number pattern?

   3, 6, 9, 12, ■, 18, 21

   A 13
   B 15
   C 16
   D 23

6. If 3 times a number is 27, which expression could be used to find the number?

   F 3×27
   G $27 \div 3$
   H $3 + 27$
   J $27 - 3$

7. Look at the spinner. How many possible outcomes are there?

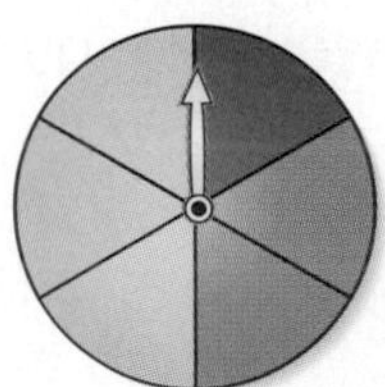

   A 2
   B 3
   C 4
   D 6

8. Which figure is shown?

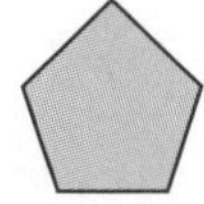

   F quadrilateral
   G pentagon
   H hexagon
   J octagon

Problem-Solving Strategy:
Choose a Strategy

Warm-Up Review

1. 35 × 20
2. 68 + 92
3. 87 − 18
4. 70 ÷ 14
5. 30 + 45
6. 18 × 18
7. Paul used a $5 bill to pay for lemonade at a movie theater. He got $2.75 in change. How much did the lemonade cost?

California Content Standard *Mathematical Reasoning 2.2: Apply strategies and results from simpler problems to more complex problems.*

Example

Kristen drives a go-cart 5 miles in 15 minutes around a track. If she continues at the same speed, how many miles can she travel in 1 hour?

Understand

What do you need to find?

You need to find the number of miles Kristen can travel in 1 hour.

Plan

How can you solve the problem?

You can **make a table** or **write a number sentence.** Your table will show distance traveled in 15, 30, 45, and 60 minutes. Your number sentence will show distance traveled in four 15-minute periods.

Solve

Make a Table

Distance Traveled				
Time in minutes	15	30	45	60
Distance in miles	5	10	15	20

Write a Number Sentence

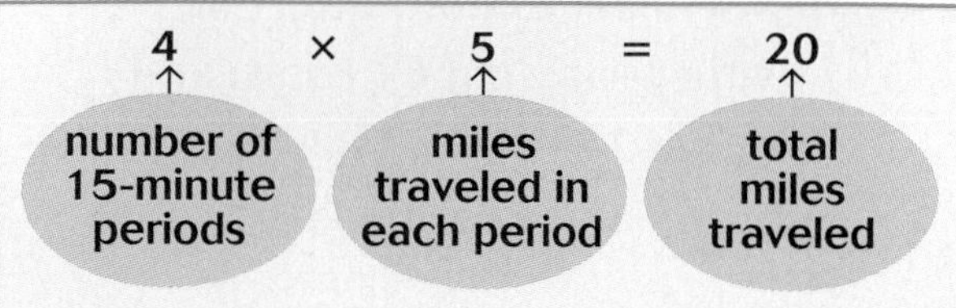

Kristen can travel 20 miles in 1 hour.

Look Back

What other strategies could you choose?

Additional Standards: Mathematical Reasoning 1.1, 2.0, 2.3, 3.2 *(See p. 491.)*

Try these or other strategies to solve each problem. Tell which strategy you used.

Problem-Solving Strategies

- *Find a Pattern*
- *Make a Table*
- *Make a List*
- *Write a Number Sentence*
- *Work Backward*
- *Draw a Picture*

Guided Practice

1. Draw the next figure in the pattern at the right.

2. Describe the 10th figure.

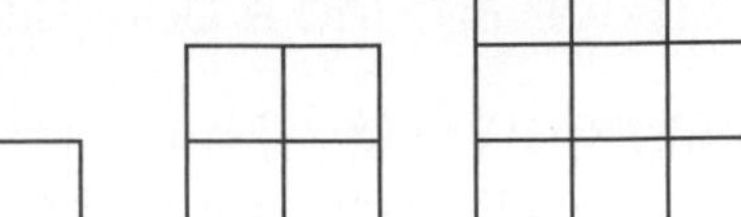

Independent Practice

3. A bus to the airport makes a stop downtown at 7:40 A.M., 9:25 A.M., 11:10 A.M., and so on, until the last stop at 7:55 P.M. At what time does the bus make its sixth stop downtown?

4. On a field trip, each student paid \$3 for admission to the museum. Half of the students also spent \$4 each in the gift shop. If 10 students went on the field trip, how much did they spend in all?

5. Darlene must be at school by 8:30 A.M. It takes her 20 minutes to dress and eat breakfast. The walk to school takes 15 minutes. She wants to plan an extra 10 minutes. At what time should she set her alarm clock to get ready for school?

6. Four friends play different string instruments in an orchestra. Tim does not play viola or bass. Anna does not play violin or cello. Kathleen does not play cello or bass. James does not play viola. A girl plays violin. Who plays which instrument?

7. The choices for a sandwich at a restaurant are roast beef, turkey, ham, and vegetarian. The bread choices are sourdough and whole wheat. List all the possible choices for a sandwich.

8. Les has 8 coins that total 73¢. How many pennies, nickels, dimes, and quarters does he have?

9. How many different ways can three friends stand in a line for a photograph?

Use Homework Workbook 12-5.

Perimeter

California Content Standard *Algebra and Functions 1.4: Use and interpret formulas (e.g., area = length × width or A = lw) to answer questions about quantities and their relationships. Also, Algebra and Functions 1.1, Measurement and Geometry 1.4* *(See p. 491.)*

Warm-Up Review

Draw each figure.

1. square
2. rectangle
3. rhombus
4. equilateral triangle
5. Is (2, 8) a solution to the equation $y = 3x + 2$?

Math Link You already know about circumference, the distance around a circle. Now you will learn about the distance around a polygon.

Word Bank

perimeter

The **perimeter** of a figure is the distance around the outside. You can find the perimeter of a polygon by adding the lengths of the sides.

Example 1

Find the perimeter of the figure shown at the right. The figure has 6 sides. Add all the side lengths.

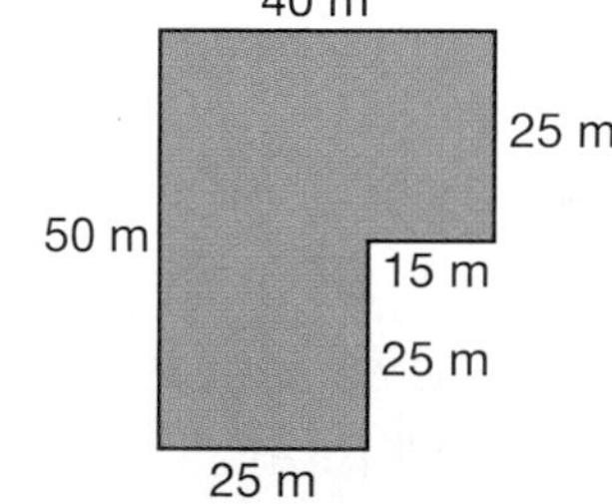

$$\text{Perimeter} = 50 + 25 + 25 + 15 + 25 + 40$$
$$= 180$$

The perimeter of the figure is 180 meters.

You can use a formula to find the perimeter of a rectangle.

A rectangle has two dimensions, length and width. In a rectangle, both pairs of opposite sides have equal length. So the perimeter of a rectangle is the sum of 2 equal lengths and 2 equal widths.

Formula for Perimeter of a Rectangle

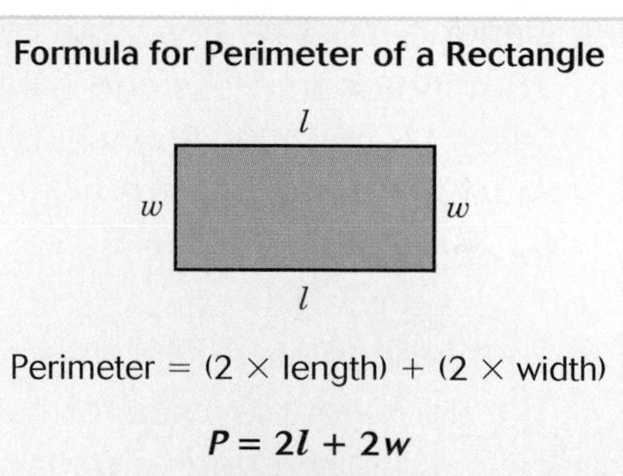

Perimeter = (2 × length) + (2 × width)

$$P = 2l + 2w$$

Example 2

Use the formula to find the perimeter of the rectangle at the right.

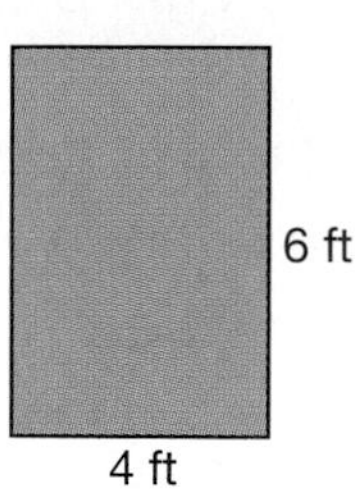

$P = 2l + 2w$ ← Formula
$P = (2 \times 4) + (2 \times 6)$ ← $l = 4, w = 6$
$= 8 + 12$
$= 20$

The perimeter of the rectangle is 20 feet.

 Additional Standard: Mathematical Reasoning 2.4 *(See p. 491.)*

You can also use a formula to find the perimeter of a square.

In a square, all sides are the same length. So the perimeter of a square is the sum of 4 equal side lengths.

Formula for Perimeter of a Square

s s s s

Perimeter = 4 × (side length)

$P = 4s$

Example 3

Use the formula to find the perimeter of a square with side length 8 inches.

$P = 4s$ ⟵ Formula

$P = (4 \times 8)$ ⟵ $s = 8$

$= 32$

The perimeter of the square is 32 inches.

Guided Practice *For another example, see Set D on p. 524.*

Find the perimeter of each figure.

1. 15 in. 6.5 in. 6.5 in. 15 in.

2. 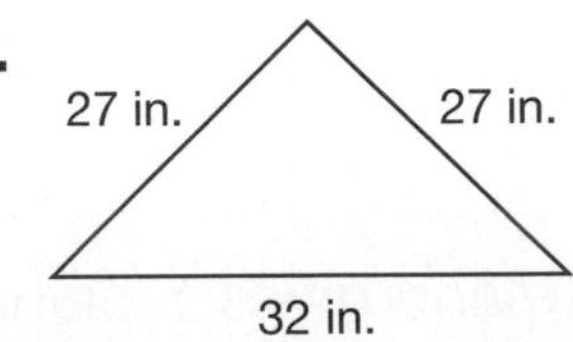

3. 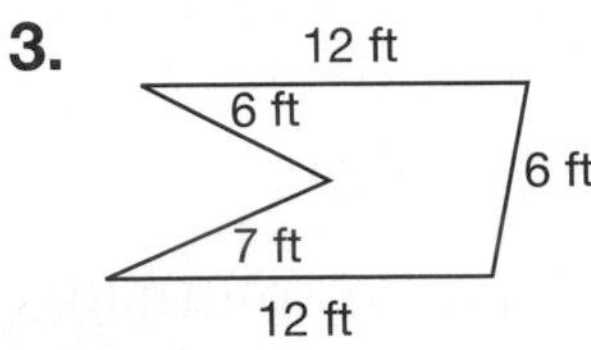

4. Find the perimeter of a rectangle with length 8 centimeters and width 3 centimeters.

5. One side of a square measures 12 meters long. Find the perimeter of the square.

Independent Practice *For more practice, see Set D on p. 526.*

Find the perimeter of each figure.

6. 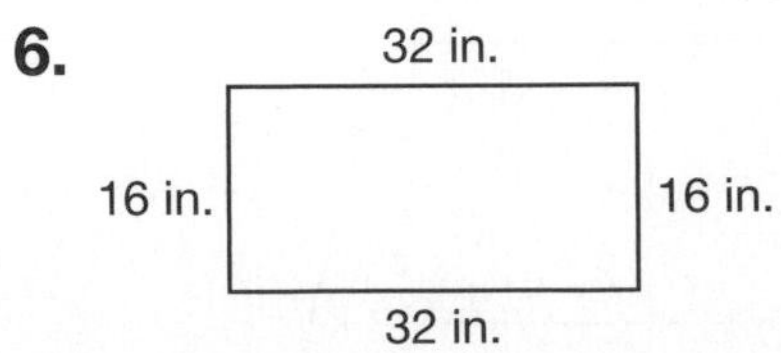

7. 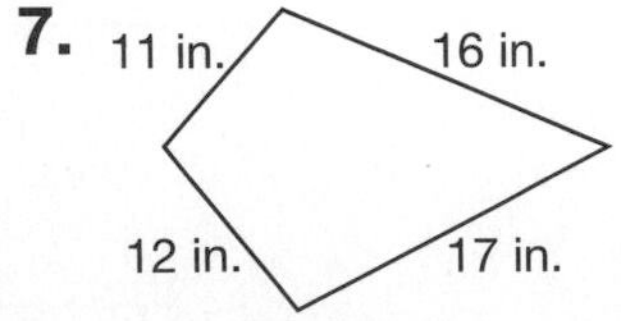

8. 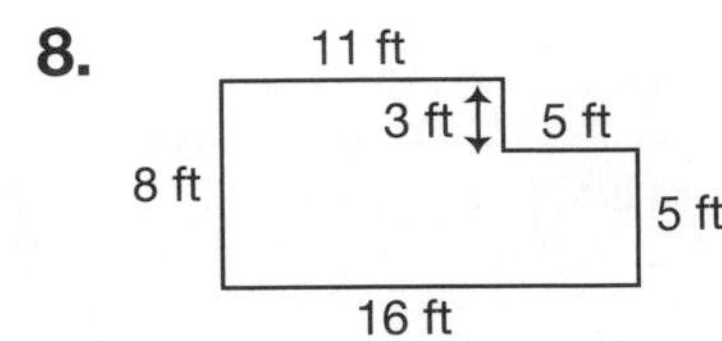

9. 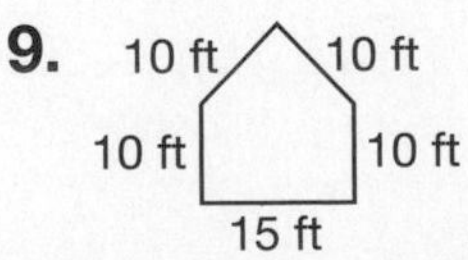

10. 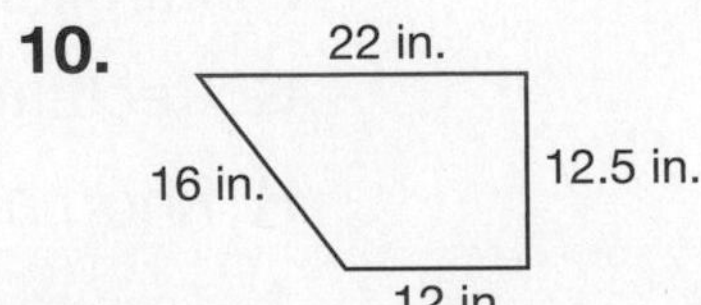

11. 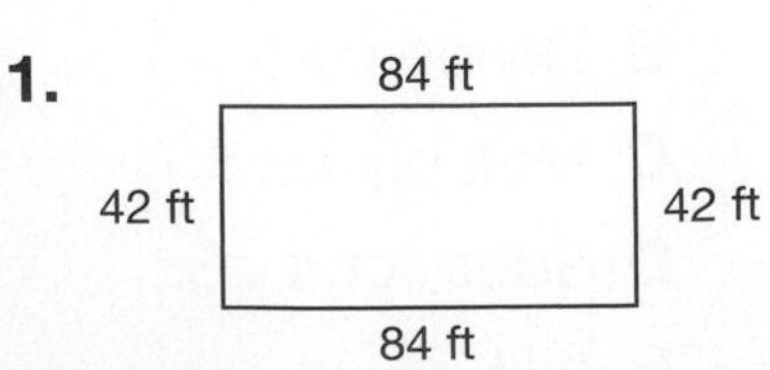

Find the perimeter of the rectangle with the given dimensions.

12. $l = 5$ dm, $w = 8$ dm **13.** $l = 14$ m, $w = 16$ m **14.** $l = 19$ mm, $w = 6$ mm

Find the perimeter of the square with the given side length.

15. $s = 5$ m **16.** $s = 7$ cm **17.** $s = 3$ yd **18.** $s = 20$ ft

19. One side of a rhombus is 18 mm. Find its perimeter.

20. The perimeter of a square is 100 ft. What is the length of each side?

21. An equilateral triangle has a perimeter of 21 inches. What is the length of each side?

22. A rectangle has a perimeter of 90 m. It is twice as long as it is wide. Find the rectangle's dimensions.

23. Math Reasoning How are perimeter and circumference alike? How are they different?

Mixed Review

24. On Saturday mornings, Mrs. Stefano gives 5 piano lessons. She starts at 9:15 A.M. and finishes at 12:55 P.M. If she takes a 5-minute break between lessons, how long is each lesson?

25. Which is a better estimate for the temperature on a cold winter morning, $^{-}30°C$ or $30°C$?

26. $\frac{1}{4} + \frac{1}{2}$ **27.** $\frac{1}{6} + \frac{5}{6}$ **28.** $\frac{5}{8} - \frac{1}{2}$ **29.** $\frac{2}{3} - \frac{1}{3}$ **30.** $\frac{3}{8} + \frac{3}{8}$

Test Prep Choose the correct letter for each answer.

31. Which is the rule for the table?
(10-10)

In	5	10	15	20	25
Out	1	2	3	4	5

A Add 5.

B Divide by 5.

C Multiply by 5.

D Subtract 4.

E NH

32. Which is the name of this shape?
(11-4)

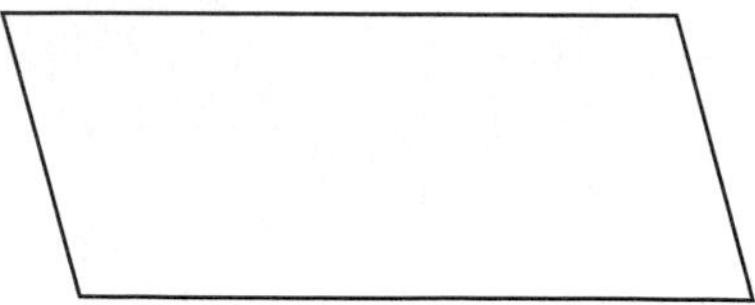

F Parallelogram

G Rectangle

H Rhombus

J Trapezoid

K NH

 Use Homework Workbook 12-6.

Area

Warm-Up Review

1. 5×5
2. 8×4
3. 12×6
4. 5×11
5. 9×9
6. 7×8
7. 8×8
8. 13×3
9. Draw a square that has a perimeter of 16 inches. Label each side length.

California Content Standard *Algebra and Functions 1.4: Use and interpret formulas (e.g., area = length x width or A = lw to answer questions about quantities and their relationships. Also, Measurement and Geometry 1.1, 1.4 (See page 491.)*

Math Link You have learned how to use formulas to find perimeter. In this lesson you will use formulas to find area.

The **area** of a flat surface is the number of square units needed to cover the surface. The area of the shaded rectangle at the right is 20 square units.

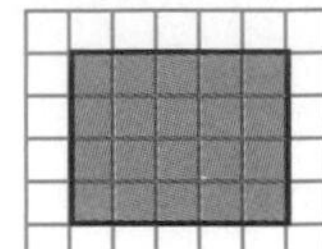

Example 1

In Mexico, colorful tiles can be seen in many places. Each square tile shown below is 1 foot by 1 foot, or 1 square foot. What is the area of the rectangle covered by the tiles?

Word Bank

area

To find the area of the rectangle, you can count the number of square feet, or you can use a formula.

$A = l \times w$ ← Formula

$A = 7 \times 3$ ← $l = 7, w = 3$

$= 21$

The area of the rectangle is 21 square feet.

Another way to write square feet is ft^2.
So, the area is 21 ft^2.

Formula for Area of a Rectangle

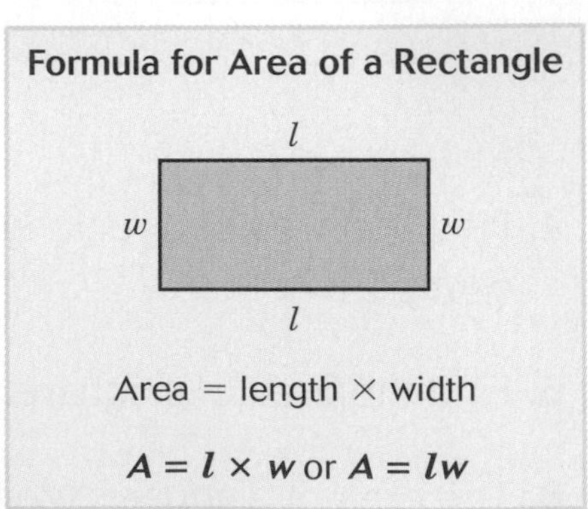

Area = length × width

$A = l \times w$ or $A = lw$

Additional Standard: Mathematical Reasoning 2.4 (See p. 491.)

Example 2

One side of a square measures 6 meters long. What is the area of the square?

You can use a formula to find the area of a square.

$A = s \times s$ ← Formula
$A = 6 \times 6$ ← $s = 6$
$A = 36$

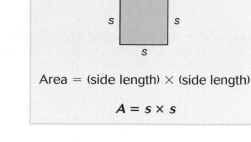

Formula for Area of a Square

Area = (side length) × (side length)

$A = s \times s$

The area of the square is 36 square meters.

Another way to write square meters is m^2. So, the area is 36 m^2.

Example 3

The area of a rectangle is 24 square inches (in^2). The width of the rectangle is 3 inches. Find the length.

Use the formula for the area of a rectangle.

$A = l \times w$ ← Formula
$24 = l \times 3$ ← $A = 24, w = 3$
$8 = l$

The length of the rectangle is 8 inches.

Guided Practice *For another example, see Set E on p. 525.*

Find the area of each figure.

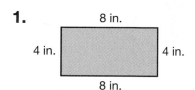

1. 8 in. / 4 in. / 4 in. / 8 in.

2.

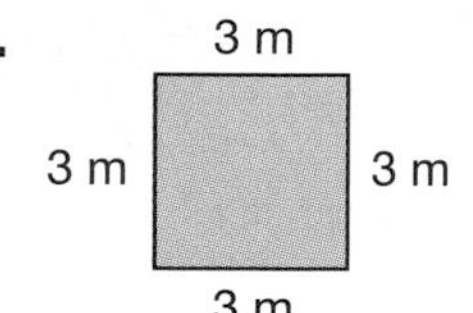

3.

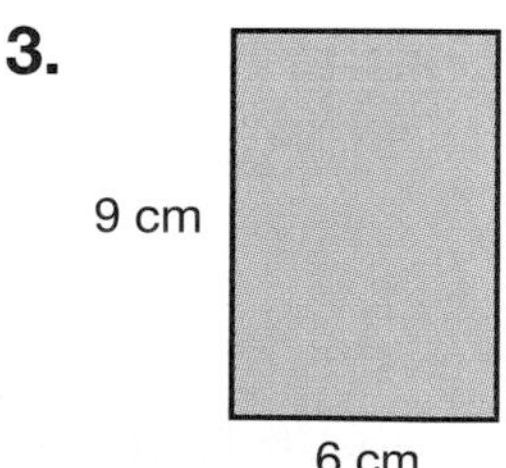

4. Find the area of a rectangle with length 7 feet and width 5 feet.

5. Find the area of a square with side length 10 meters.

6. The area of a square floor tile is 81 in^2. What is the length of each side?

Independent Practice *For more practice, see Set E on p. 527.*

Find the area of each figure.

7. 6 ft, 6 ft

8. 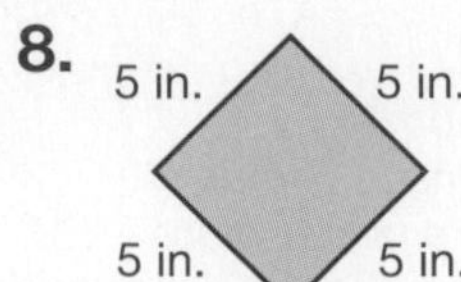

9. 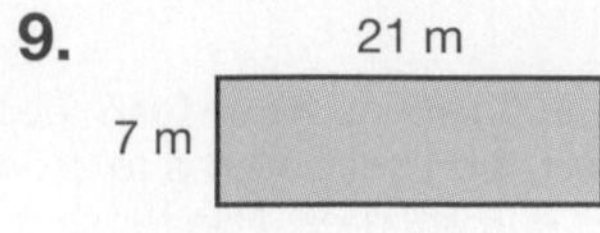

10. 7 cm, 6 cm

11. 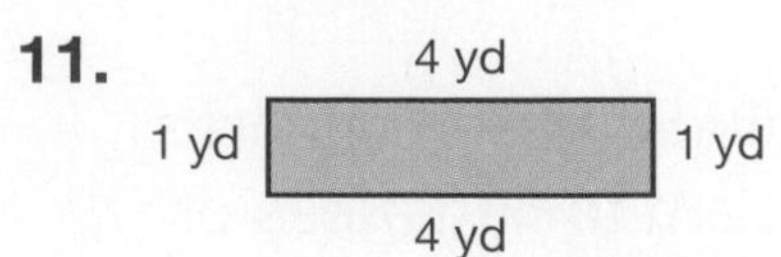

12. 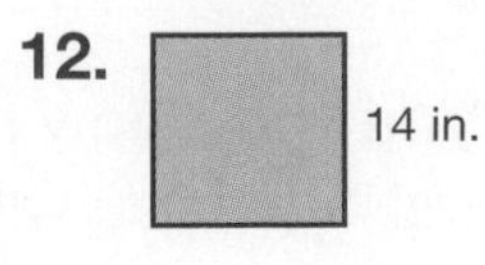

13. The area of a square is 49 cm^2. What is the length of each side?

14. The area of a rectangular garden is 60 ft^2. The length is 10 feet. Find the width.

15. Math Reasoning Is the area of an 8 inch by 12 inch rectangle greater than or less than that of a square with the same perimeter?

Mixed Review

16. Which is a better estimate for a hot summer day, 40°F or 90°F?

17. Find the perimeter of a rectangle with length 25 inches and width 13 inches.

18. Use the figure at the right. Give the total area of all 6 faces in square inches. Give the volume in cubic inches.

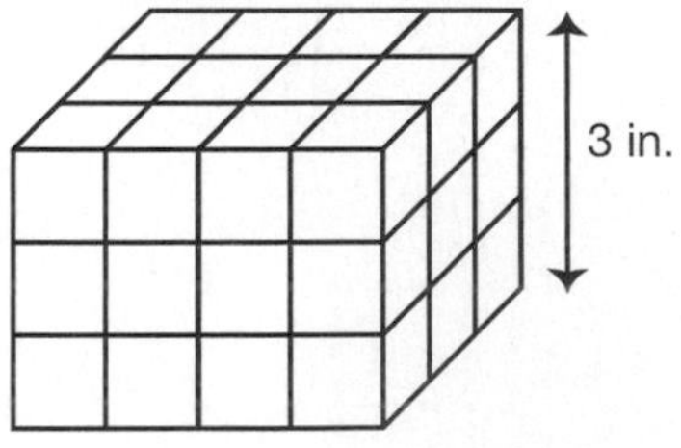

19. 18.4 + 0.62 **20.** \$4.71 ÷ 3 **21.** 87.52 − 16.3 **22.** 94.6 − 5.77

Test Prep **Choose the correct letter for the answer.**

23. Which circle has 0.75 of it shaded?
(9-1)

A 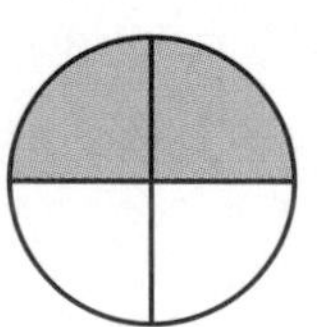

B 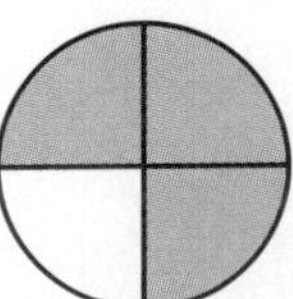

C 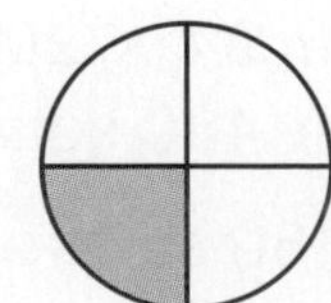

D

Areas of Irregular Figures

Algebra

California Content Standard *Measurement and Geometry 1.4: Understand and use formulas to solve problems involving . . . areas of rectangles and squares. Use those formulas to find the areas of more complex figures by dividing the figures into basic shapes. Also, Algebra and Functions 1.1, 1.4 (See p. 491.)*

Math Link You know how to find areas of squares and rectangles. Now you will learn to find areas of irregular figures.

Warm-Up Review

Find the area and perimeter of each figure.

1.

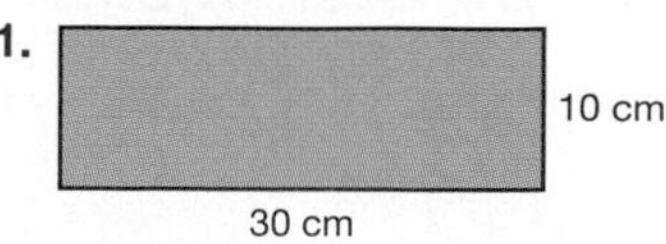

2.

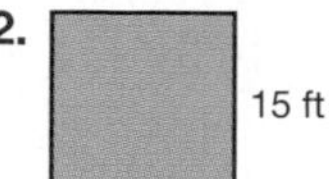

3. An airplane holds 246 passengers. How many passengers can the airplane carry in 6 trips?

Example

Mrs. Sherman, an interior decorator, needs to order carpeting for an office. The floor plan is shown at the right.

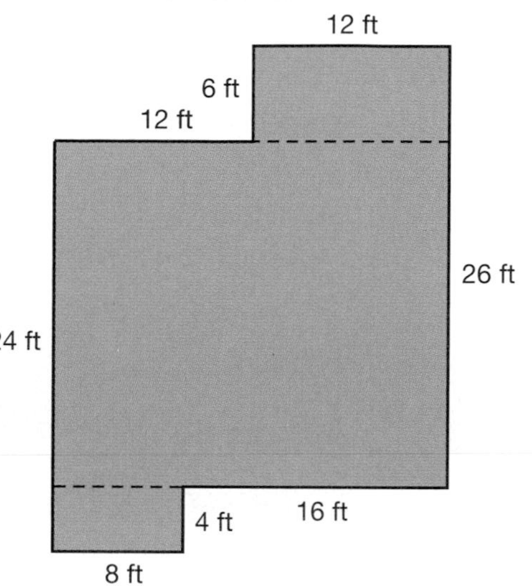

Mrs. Sherman wants to find the area of the floor. The dashed line segments show how she divides the floor into three rectangles. She will find the area of each rectangle, and then add the areas together.

To find the area of each rectangle, use the formula $A = l \times w$.

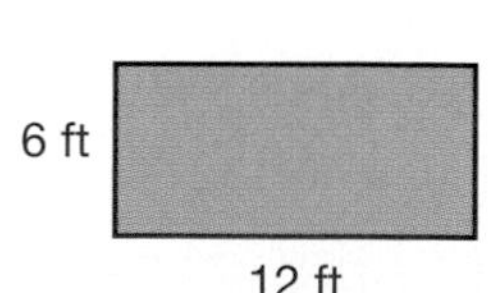

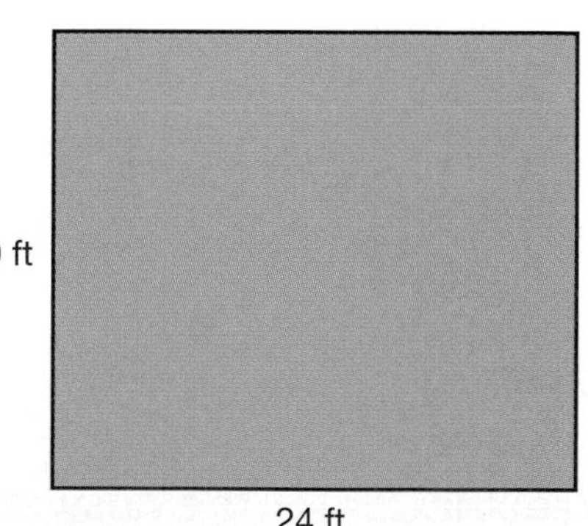

4 ft
8 ft

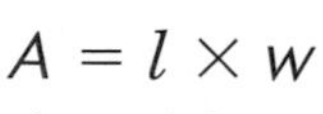

$A = l \times w$
$A = 12 \times 6$
$A = 72$ square feet

$A = l \times w$
$A = 24 \times 20$
$A = 480$ square feet

$A = l \times w$
$A = 8 \times 4$
$A = 32$ square feet

Total area = 72 square feet + 480 square feet + 32 square feet
= 584 square feet

The total area is 584 ft^2.

Remember, ft^2 means square feet.

 Additional Standard: Mathematical Reasoning 2.3 (See p. 491.)

Guided Practice *For another example, see Set F on p. 525.*

Find the area of each irregular figure.

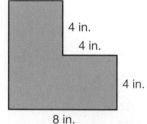

1. **2.** **3.**

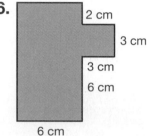

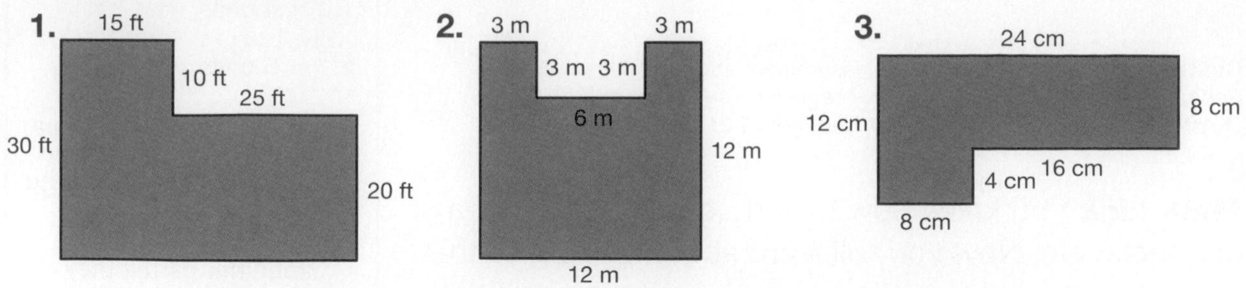

4. A hopscotch game has nine squares, each 2 feet on a side. What is the total area of the hopscotch game?

Independent Practice *For more practice, see Set F on p. 527.*

Find the area of each irregular figure.

5.

4 in.
4 in.
4 in.
8 in.

6.

2 cm
3 cm
3 cm
6 cm
6 cm

7.

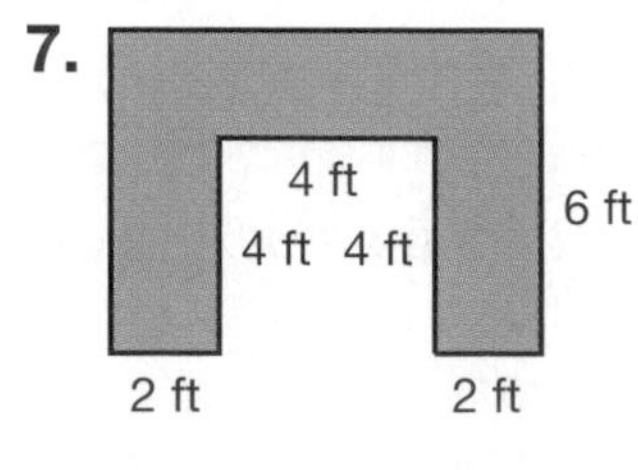

8. Robert and his father plan to tile the floor of their utility room, pictured at the right. If the tile costs $8.95 per square foot, how much will it cost to tile the utility room floor?

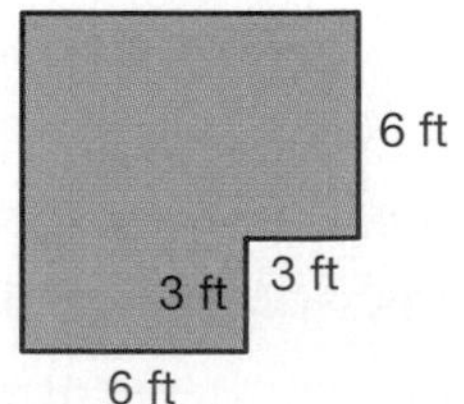

9. Math Reasoning How could you use subtraction to find the area of the figure in Exercise 7?

Mixed Review

10. Is the area of a rectangle that measures 15 cm by 25 cm greater than or less than the area of a square with the same perimeter?

11. 918 + 337 **12.** 854 − 608 **13.** 1,135 + 253 **14.** 6,000 − 514

Test Prep **Choose the correct letter for each answer.**

15. Given the length and width, which rectangle has the greatest area?
(12-6)

A 4m by 7m **B** 3m by 8m **C** 6m by 5m **D** 9m by 2m

Rectangles that are Related

California Content Standard *Measurement and Geometry 1.2: Recognize that rectangles that have the same area can have different perimeters. Also Measurement and Geometry 1.3. (See page 491.)*

Warm-Up Review

Draw a rectangle with the given dimensions. Find its area and perimeter.

1. $l = 4$ units, $w = 3$ units
2. $l = 6$ units, $w = 6$ units
3. Jessica earns \$3 an hour delivering papers. Ethan earns \$2 an hour walking a dog. How much can Jessica and Ethan altogether earn if they both work 5 hours?

Math Link You know how to find perimeter and area of a rectangle. Now you will learn about rectangles that have the same area or the same perimeter.

Rectangles that have the same area can have different perimeters. Rectangles that have the same perimeter can have different areas.

Example 1

Gary wants to fence in an area of 12 square feet for his rabbit. Draw some rectangular shapes with an area of 12 square feet that Gary can make. Then find the amount of fencing Gary would need for each rectangular region.

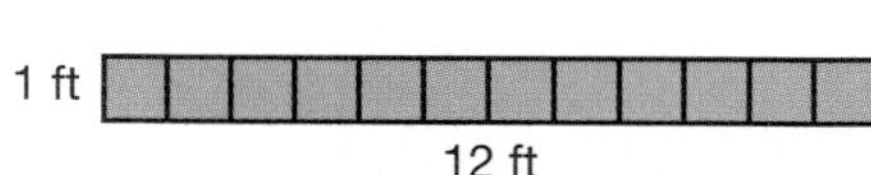

$A = 12 \times 1 = 12 \text{ ft}^2$
$P = (2 \times 12) + (2 \times 1) = 26 \text{ ft}$

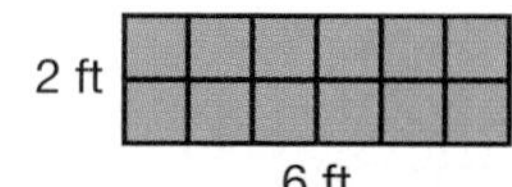

$A = 6 \times 2 = 12 \text{ ft}^2$
$P = (2 \times 6) + (2 \times 2) = 16 \text{ ft}$

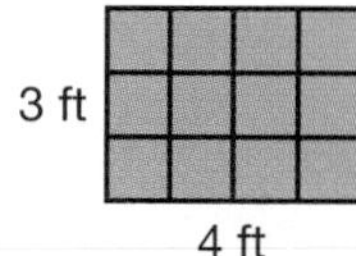

$A = 4 \times 3 = 12 \text{ ft}^2$
$P = (2 \times 4) + (2 \times 3) = 14 \text{ ft}$

Gary can use any of the rectangular regions shown above. Each has an area of 12 square feet. The perimeter of each rectangle shows the amount of fencing needed.

Example 2

Draw some different rectangles that each have a perimeter of 14 centimeters. Then find the area of each.

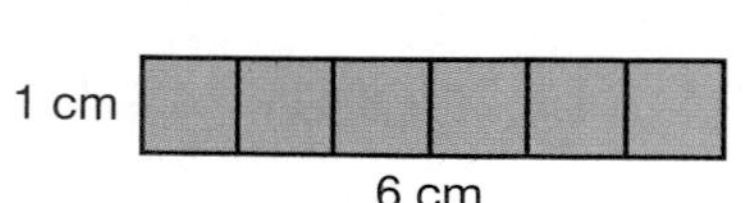

$P = (2 \times 6) + (2 \times 1) = 14 \text{ cm}$
$A = 6 \times 1 = 6 \text{ cm}^2$

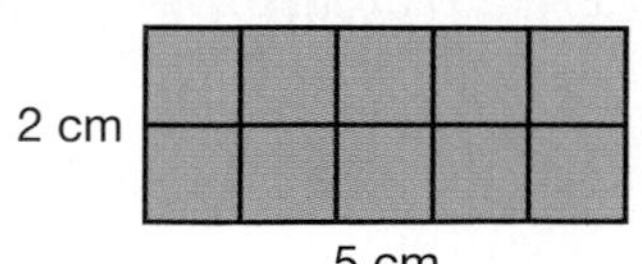

$P = (2 \times 5) + (2 \times 2) = 14 \text{ cm}$
$A = 5 \times 2 = 10 \text{ cm}^2$

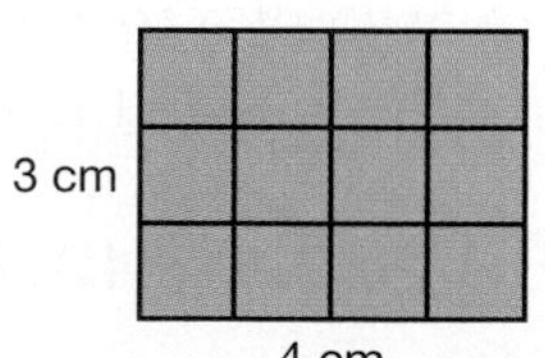

$P = (2 \times 4) + (2 \times 3) = 14 \text{ cm}$
$A = 4 \times 3 = 12 \text{ cm}^2$

Additional Standards: Algebra and Functions 1.1, 1.4; Measurement and Geometry 1.1, 1.4 (See p. 491.)

Guided Practice *For another example, see Set G on p. 525.*

3 in. 6 in.

4 ft 4 ft

1. Draw a different rectangle with the same area as the rectangle shown at the right. Then find the perimeter of each.

2. Draw a different rectangle with the same perimeter as the rectangle shown at the right. Then find the area of each.

Independent Practice *For more practice, see Set G on p. 527.*

Draw a different rectangle with the same area as the one shown. Then find the perimeter of each.

3.

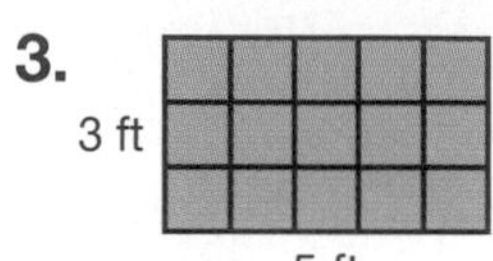

4.

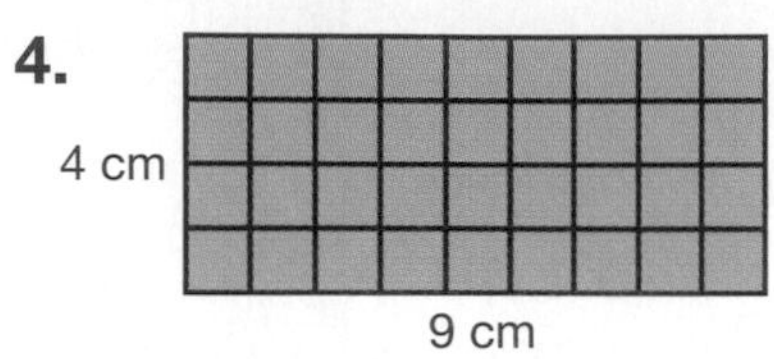

5.

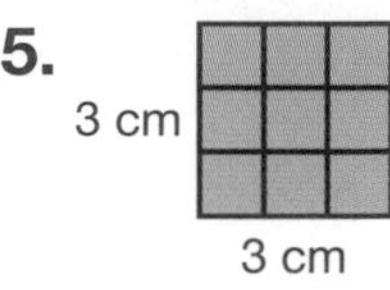

Draw a different rectangle with the same perimeter as the one shown. Then find the area of each.

6.

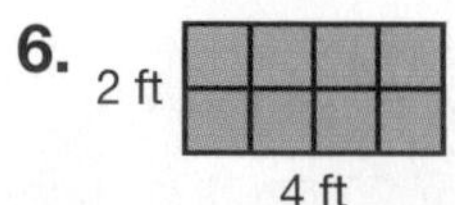

7.

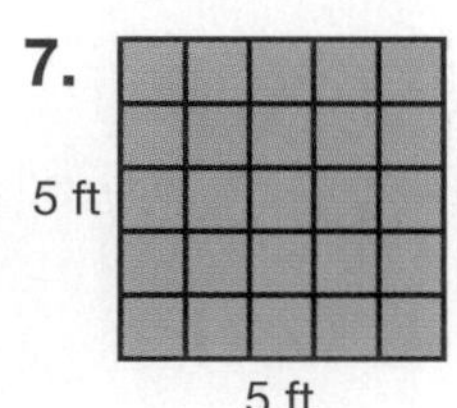

8.

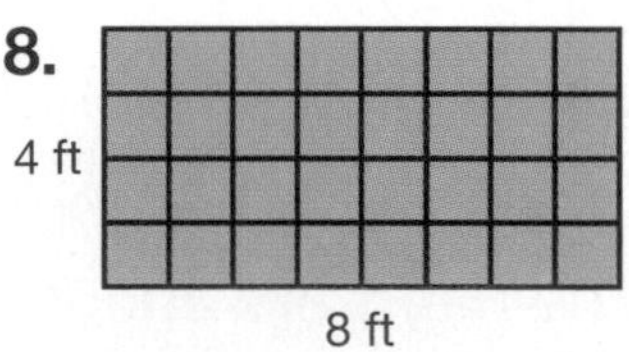

9. How can you arrange 24 square tiles to form a rectangle? List all possible answers. Then find the perimeter of each.

Mixed Review

10. What is the length of a line segment joining the points (8, 12) and (14, 12)?

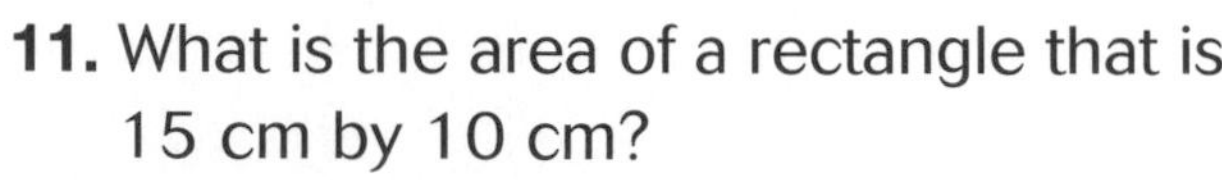

11. What is the area of a rectangle that is 15 cm by 10 cm?

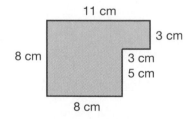

12. Find the area of the figure at the right.

11 cm, 3 cm, 8 cm, 3 cm, 5 cm, 8 cm

Test Prep **Choose the correct letter for the answer.**

13. Sam did three 20-minute sets of exercises with a 5-minute rest between sets. He started at 4:30 P.M. When did he finish?
(12-5)

A 5:35 P.M. **B** 5:40 P.M. **C** 5:45 P.M. **D** 5:50 P.M. **E** NH

Problem-Solving Application:

Using Perimeter and Area

Algebra

Warm-Up Review

1. Write the formula for the perimeter of a rectangle.
2. Write the formula for the area of a rectangle.
3. The area of a square is 81 square units. What is its perimeter?
4. The perimeter of a square is 24 units. What is its area?

California Content Standard *Mathematical Reasoning 2.4: Express the solution clearly and logically by using the appropriate mathematical notation and terms and clear language; support solutions with evidence in both verbal and symbolic work.* *(See p. 491.)*

Example

There are two parks in Katie's neighborhood. She thinks that North Park has about the same area as Central Park because their perimeters are about the same. Is she correct?

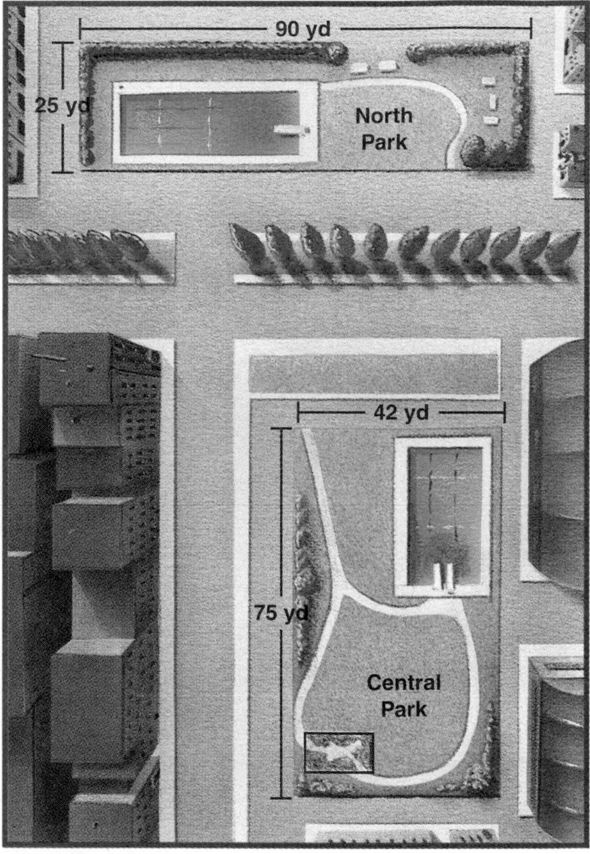

Understand

What do you need to find?

You need to find out if the areas of the parks are about the same or not.

Plan

How can you solve the problem?

Use $A = l \times w$ to find the area of each park. Then compare the two areas.

Solve

North Park: $A = 90 \times 25 = 2{,}250$ square yd

Central Park: $A = 75 \times 42 = 3{,}150$ square yd

Since 3,150 square yd is much greater than 2,250 square yd, Katie is not correct.

Look Back

Was Katie correct about the two perimeters?

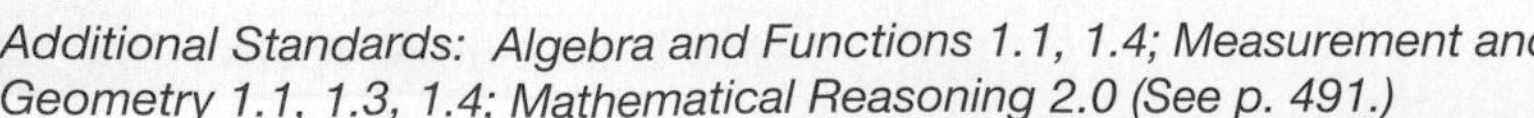

Additional Standards: Algebra and Functions 1.1, 1.4; Measurement and Geometry 1.1, 1.3, 1.4; Mathematical Reasoning 2.0 *(See p. 491.)*

Guided Practice

Use the rock garden pictured below for Exercises 1–3.

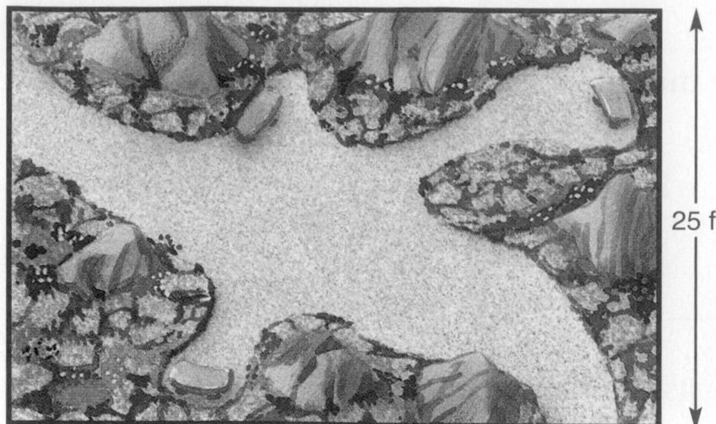

1. The perimeter of the rock garden is 130 feet. Find the length of the rock garden.

2. What is the area of the rock garden?

3. About 400 square feet of the rock garden is used for pathways. What is the area of the rock garden that is not used for pathways?

Independent Practice

Use the chart at the right for Exercises 4–8.

Size of Park Pools		
Pool	**Length**	**Width**
Central Park	85 ft	45 ft
North Park	110 ft	35 ft
West Beach	100 ft	40 ft
East Wading Pool	20 ft	40 ft

4. Alex says the area of Central Park Pool is almost the same as the area of North Park Pool. Is he correct? Explain.

5. How many times greater is the area of the West Beach Pool than the area of the East Wading Pool?

6. **Math Reasoning** If the length of the East Wading Pool were doubled, would the area double? Explain.

Mixed Review

7. Make a bar graph to display the perimeters of the four pools. Write a sentence about the perimeters.

8. Make a bar graph to display the areas of the four pools. Compare with the bar graph in Exercise 7.

Diagnostic Checkpoint

Complete. For Exercises 1–4, use the words from the Word Bank.

Word Bank
degrees Fahrenheit
degrees Celsius
perimeter
area
gram
liter
meter

1. (12-6) The _______________ of a figure is the distance around the outside.

2. (12-2) A metric unit of capacity is a _______________.

3. (12-4) _______________ are metric units of temperature.

4. (12-7) The _______________ of a flat surface is the number of square units needed to cover the surface.

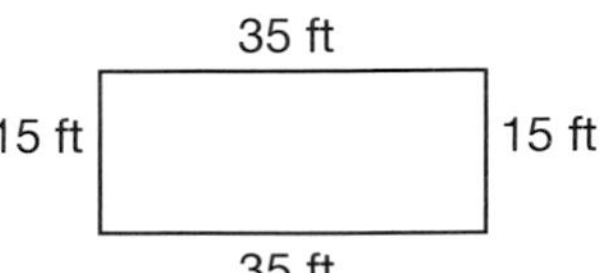

5. (12-6) Find the perimeter of the rectangle at the right.

6. (12-7) Find the area of the rectangle at the right.

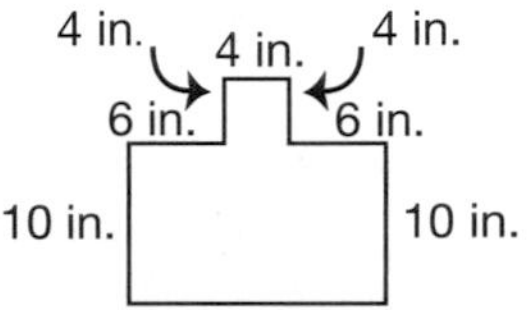

7. (12-6) Find the perimeter of the figure at the right.

8. (12-8) Find the area of the irregular figure at the right.

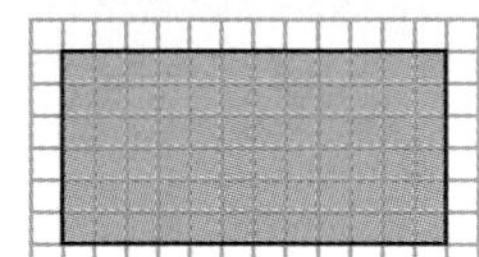

9. (12-9) Draw a different rectangle with the same area as the shaded rectangle at the right. Then find the perimeter of each.

10. (12-5) It usually takes Katrina 1 hour and 45 minutes to mow grass. What time should she start if she wants to finish by 1:15 P.M.?

11. (12-10) A baseball infield is a square that is 90 feet on each side. The dirt area is 2,700 square feet. The rest is grass. What is the area of the grass?

12. (12-9) Kelly is setting up a rectangular seating arrangement using 12 chairs. In how many different ways could she do this?

13. (12-7) The area of a room is 108 square feet. The length is 9 feet. Find the width.

Chapter 12 Test

Write each missing number.

1. 3 lb = ■ oz **2.** 5 ft = ■ in. **3.** 2 T = ■ lb **4.** 16 qt = ■ gal

5. 2 m = ■ cm **6.** 8 L = ■ mL **7.** 2,300 cm = ■ m **8.** 9,000 g = ■ kg

Compare. Write >, <, or = for each ●.

9. 1 fl oz ● 1 c **10.** 10 mm ● 1 cm **11.** 2 cm ● 2,000 mm

12. Read the thermometer at the right. Write the temperature in °F and °C.

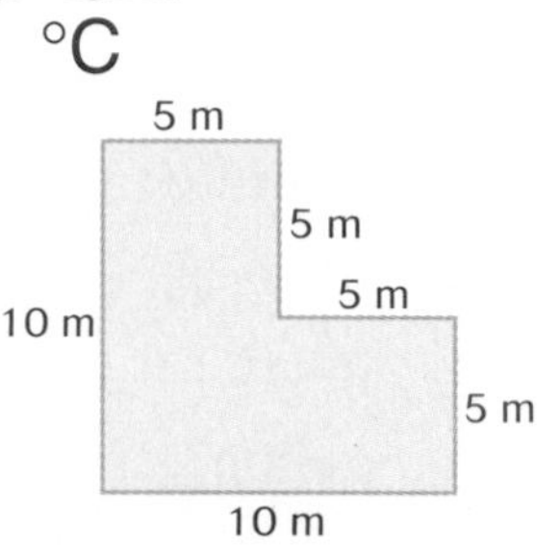

Find the perimeter and area of each figure.

13.

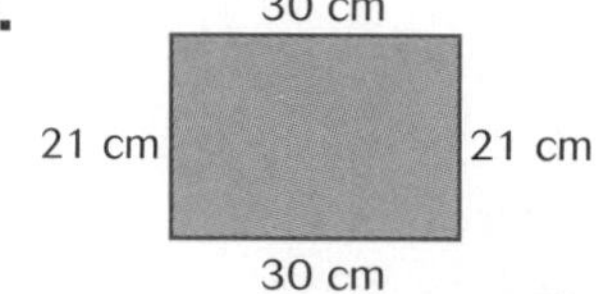

14.

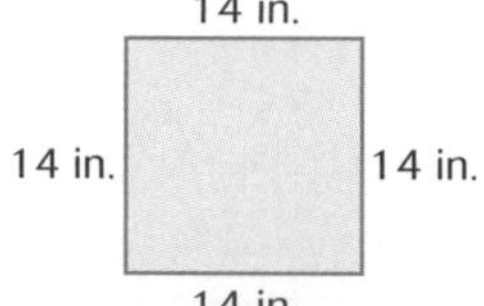

15.

5 m
5 m
5 m
10 m
5 m
10 m

Choose the most appropriate unit of measure. Write *m, km, cm, g, kg, gal, pt,* or *tsp.*

16. length of a train **17.** liquid soap in a bottle **18.** mass of a watermelon

19. Kara and Karl's mother paid $26.13 for a tank of gasoline. Which measure must you estimate to decide if the amount of money charged was reasonable?

Gasoline
$2.09
per gallon

20. Steven practiced the piano 2 days last week for a total of one and a half hours. If he practices the same amount each day but practices 6 days next week, how many hours will he practice?

21. Draw a different rectangle with the same perimeter as the rectangle shown at the right. Then find the area of each.

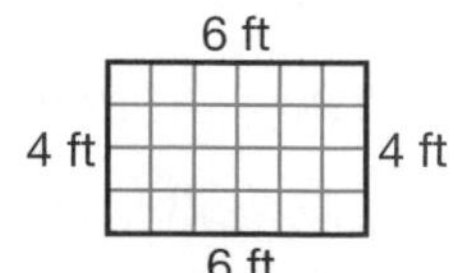

22. A rancher has 300 feet of fencing to make a corral shaped like a rectangle. She can make a 50 foot by 100 foot corral or a square corral 75 feet on a side. Which corral has the greater area? Explain.

Multiple-Choice Chapter 12 Test

Choose the correct letter for each answer.

1. **Choose the most appropriate unit of measure for the weight of a dump truck.**

   A ounce
   B pound
   C ton
   D kilogram

2. **Choose the most appropriate unit of measure for the medicine in a spoon.**

   F milliliter
   G liter
   H quart
   J gallon

3. **12 feet = ■ yards**

   A 3 **C** 36
   B 4 **D** 48

4. **20 centimeters = ■ millimeters**

   F 2 **H** 200
   G 20 **J** 2,000

5. **Which is more than 2 meters?**

   A 20 decimeters
   B 200 centimeters
   C 2,000 millimeters
   D 2,000 centimeters

6. **Which is the most reasonable estimate for the water in a bathtub?**

   F 150 mL
   G 1,500 mL
   H 150 L
   J 1,500 L

7. **Use the thermometer to find the temperature equivalent to 59°F in degrees Celsius.**

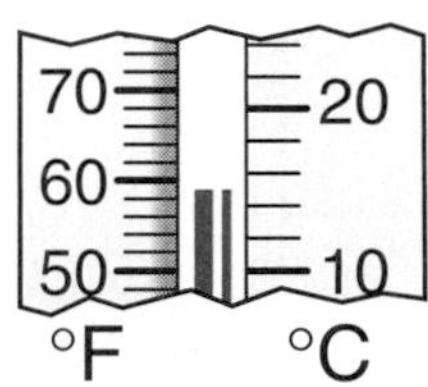

   A 15°C
   B 18°C
   C 20°C
   D 21°C

8. **Marcus rode his bike 6 miles in 20 minutes. If he continues at the same speed, how many miles can he travel in 1 hour?**

   F 2 miles
   G 3 miles
   H 12 miles
   J 18 miles

9. The area of a rectangle is 40 square centimeters. The width is 5 centimeters. Find the length.

A 8 cm
B 35 cm
C 45 cm
D 200 cm

Use the rectangle for Questions 10 and 11.

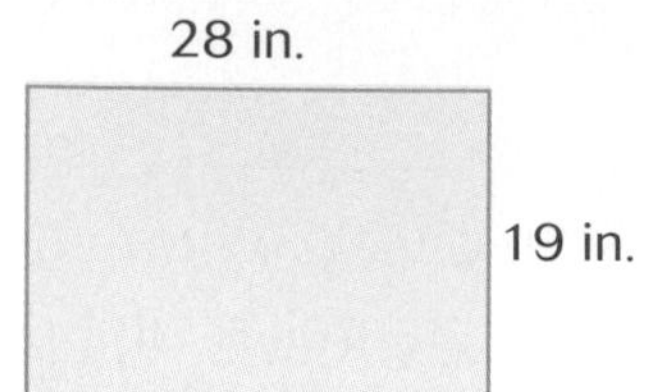

10. Find the perimeter of the rectangle.

F 47 inches
G 94 inches
H 188 inches
J 532 inches

11. Find the area of the rectangle.

A 47 in^2
B 94 in^2
C 188 in^2
D 532 in^2

12. You ran 2 km during a school competition. Your friend ran 2,800 meters. Which of the following is true?

F You ran 200 meters farther than your friend.
G Your friend ran 200 meters farther than you.
H You ran 800 meters farther than your friend.
J Your friend ran 800 meters farther than you.

Use the figure for Questions 13 and 14.

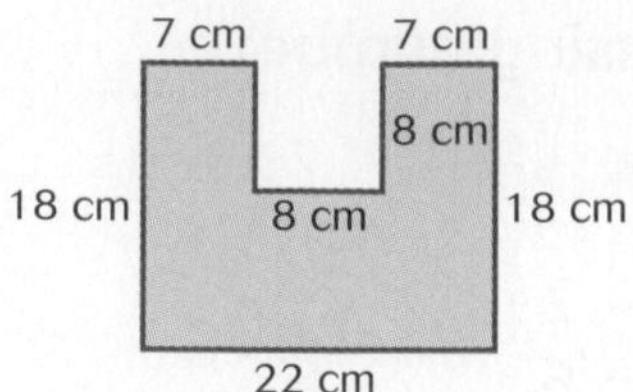

13. Find the perimeter of the figure.

A 80 cm
B 96 cm
C 332 cm
D 396 cm

14. Find the area of the figure.

F 80 cm^2
G 96 cm^2
H 332 cm^2
J 396 cm^2

15. A rectangle has a length of 7 feet and a width of 4 feet. Which of the following gives the dimensions of a rectangle with the same perimeter but a greater area?

A 2 feet by 15 feet
B 3 feet by 8 feet
C 4 feet by 9 feet
D 5 feet by 6 feet

16. Shauna's bedroom is 12 feet by 11 feet. Her brother Kobe's room is 9 feet by 15 feet. How much larger is Kobe's room than Shauna's room?

F 3 ft^2
G 5 ft^2
H 9 ft^2
J 10 ft^2

Reteaching

Set A (pages 492–495)

Find the missing number.

3 quarts = ■ pints

Think: 1 qt = 2 pt
$3 \times 2 = 6$

3 quarts = 6 pints

Remember to multiply when you are changing from a larger unit of measure to a smaller unit of measure.

Find each missing number.

1. 6 yd = ■ ft **2.** 8 lb = ■ oz

Set B (pages 496–499)

Find the missing number.

4,000 centimeters = ■ meters

Think: 100 cm = 1 meter
$4{,}000 \div 100 = 40$

4,000 centimeters = 40 meters

Remember to divide when you are changing from a smaller unit of measure to a larger unit of measure.

Find each missing number.

1. 5,000 m = ■ km **2.** 6,000 mm = ■ m

Set C (pages 502–503)

Find the temperature in degrees Fahrenheit and degrees Celsius.

The temperature is 7°C or about 45°F.

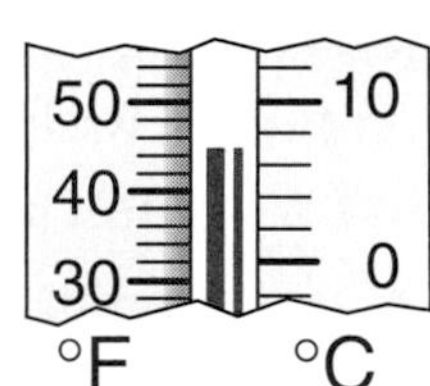

Remember that degrees Fahrenheit are customary units and degrees Celsius are metric units of temperature.

Find the temperature in degrees Fahrenheit and degrees Celsius.

1.

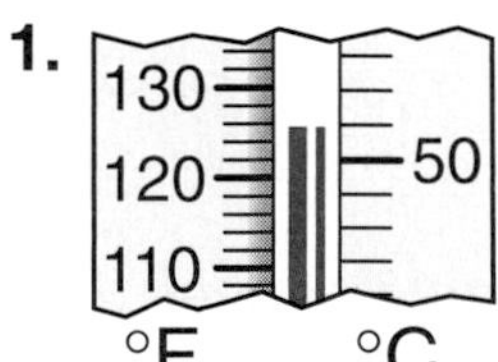

2.

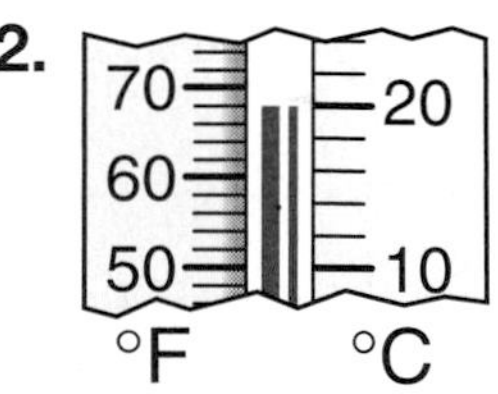

Set D (pages 508–510)

Find the perimeter of the figure.

$P = 2\ell + 2w$

$P = (2 \times 6) + (2 \times 5)$
$= 12 + 10$
$= 22$

6 ft
5 ft 5 ft
6 ft

The perimeter is 22 feet.

Remember that the perimeter of a figure is the distance around the outside.

Find the perimeter of each figure.

1. **2.**

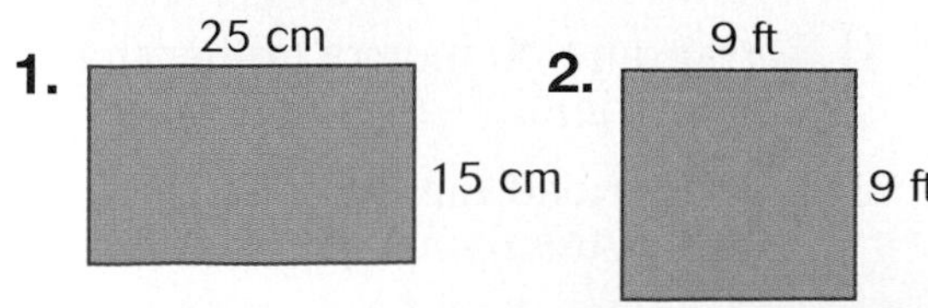

Set E (pages 511–513)

Find the area of the rectangle.

Area = length × width

$A = \ell \times w$

$A = 14 \text{ in.} \times 8 \text{ in.}$

$= 112$ square inches or 112 in^2

Remember that you can find the area of a rectangle either by counting squares or by using a formula.

Find the area of each figure.

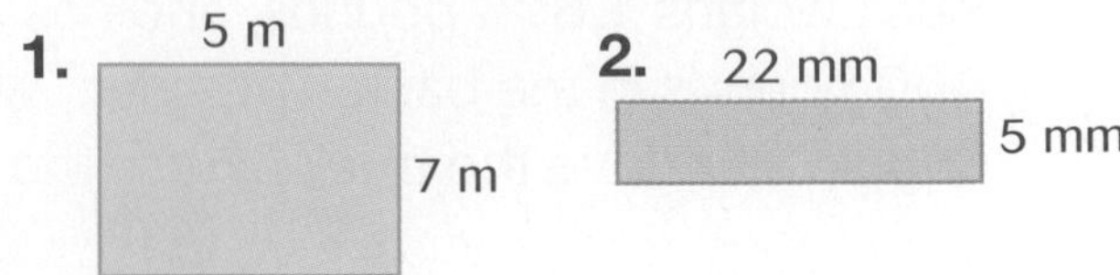

Set F (pages 514–515)

Find the area of the irregular figure.

Divide the area into three rectangles and find the area of each.

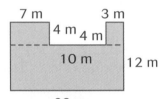

$A = 7 \text{ m} \times 4 \text{ m}$
$= 28 \text{ m}^2$

$A = 20 \text{ m} \times 8 \text{ m}$
$= 160 \text{ m}^2$

$A = 4 \text{ m} \times 3 \text{ m}$
$= 12 \text{ m}^2$

Total area $= 28 \text{ m}^2 + 160 \text{ m}^2 + 12 \text{ m}^2$
$= 200 \text{ m}^2$

Remember that you can divide many irregular figures into rectangles and find the area of each rectangle. The sum of the areas of the rectangles equals the area of the figure.

Find the area of each irregular figure.

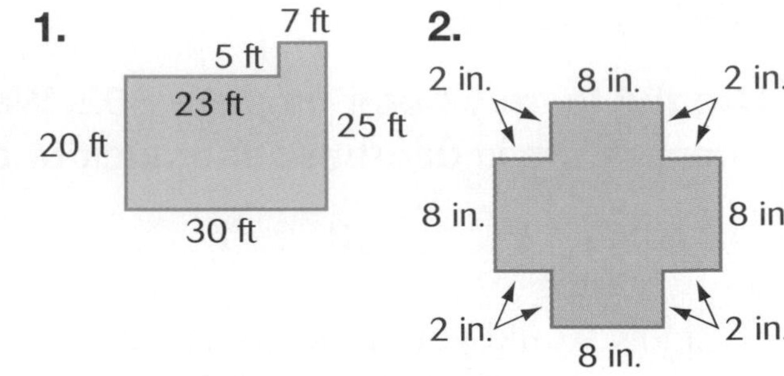

Set G (pages 516–517)

Draw a different rectangle with the same area as the one shown. Then find the perimeter of each.

$A = \ell \times w$

$A = 5 \text{ cm} \times 4 \text{ cm}$
$= 20 \text{ cm}^2$

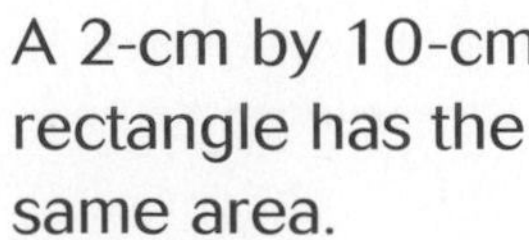

$P = (2 \times 5) \text{ cm} + (2 \times 4) \text{ cm}$
$= 10 \text{ cm} + 8 \text{ cm} = 18 \text{ cm}$

A 2-cm by 10-cm rectangle has the same area.

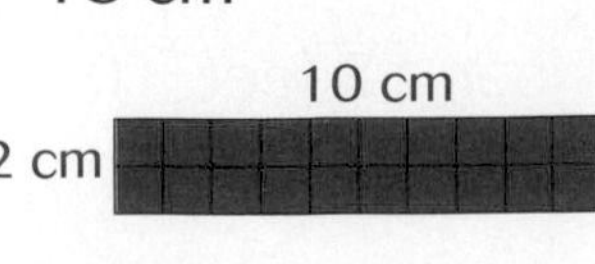

$P = (2 \times 10) \text{ cm} + (2 \times 2) \text{ cm}$
$= 20 \text{ cm} + 4 \text{ cm} = 24 \text{ cm}$

Remember that two rectangles can have the same area and different perimeters.

Use the figure at the right to answer the questions.

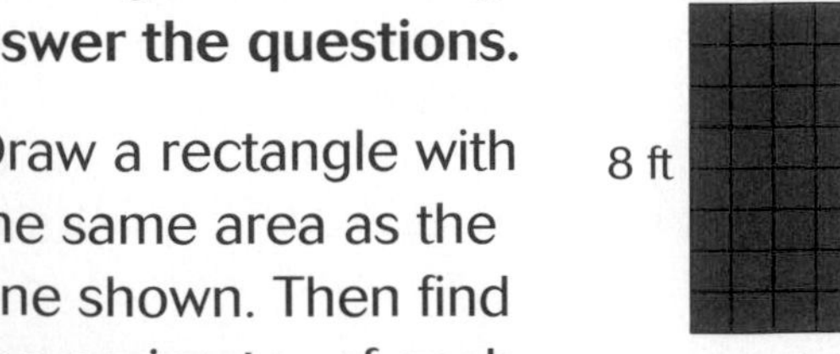

1. Draw a rectangle with the same area as the one shown. Then find the perimeter of each.
2. Draw a different rectangle with the same perimeter as the one shown. Then find the area of each.

More Practice

Set A *(pages 492–495)*

Find each missing number.

1. 2 pt = ■ c
2. 4 T = ■ lb
3. 14 yd = ■ ft
4. 2 mi = ■ ft
5. A sign before a bridge says "Weight Limit 2 Tons." The pickup truck weighs 1,675 pounds, and has a bag of sand that weighs 400 pounds in the back. The driver weighs 135 pounds. Should she drive the truck across the bridge?

Set B *(pages 496–499)*

Find each missing number.

1. 5 kg = ■ g
2. 2 L = ■ mL
3. 340 mm = ■ cm
4. 4 dm = ■ cm
5. The library is 856 meters from school. How much less than 1 kilometer is this?

Set C *(pages 502–503)*

Use the thermometer on page 502. Write the equivalent temperature in degrees Fahrenheit or degrees Celsius.

1. 10°C
2. 59°F
3. 113°F
4. $^{-}15$°C
5. How would you dress to go outdoors if the temperature were 15°C? 35°C? $^{-}10$°C?

Set D *(pages 508–510)*

Find the perimeter of each figure.

1. 10 in. 20 in. 16 in.

2. 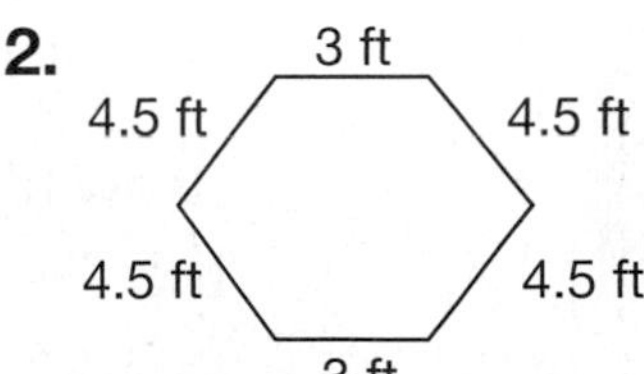

3. 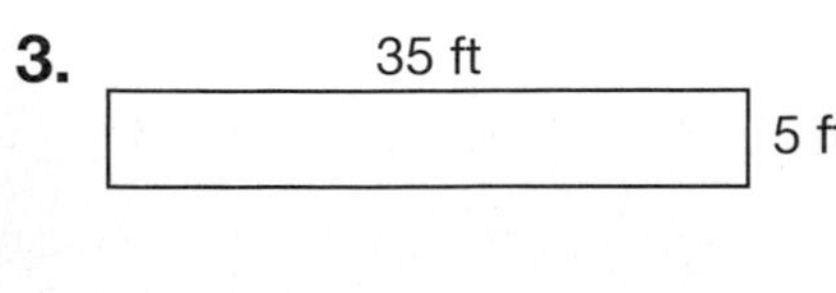

4. The four sides of a garden measure 4 feet, 12 feet, 10 feet, and 6 feet. What is the perimeter of the garden?

Set E (pages 511–513)

Find the area of each figure.

1. 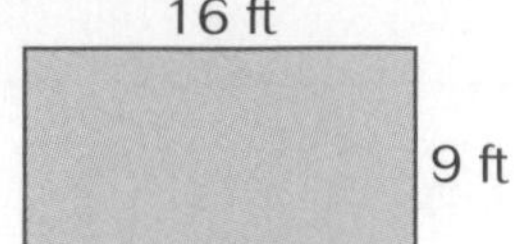

2. 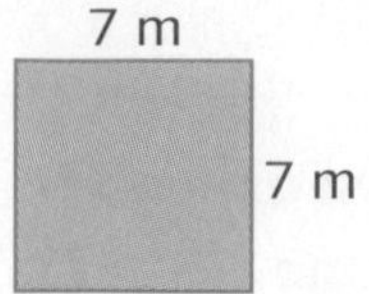

3. 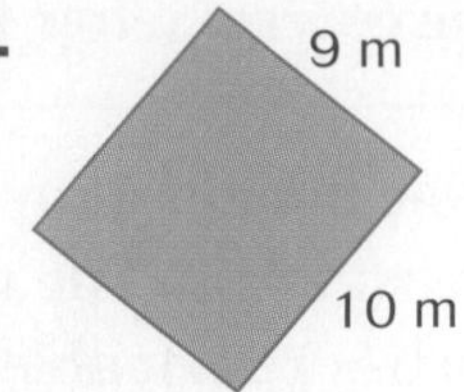

4. Suppose you want to tile a surface with 1-inch square tiles. The surface is 36 inches long and 12 inches wide. How many tiles will you need?

5. The area of a square is 25 square feet. What is the length of each side?

Set F (pages 514–515)

Find the area of each irregular figure.

1. 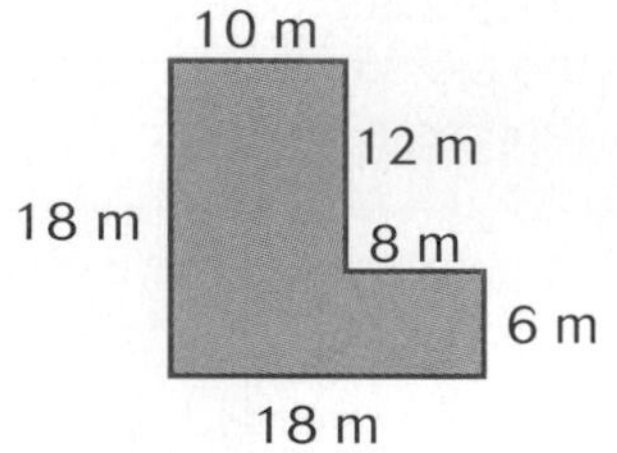

2. 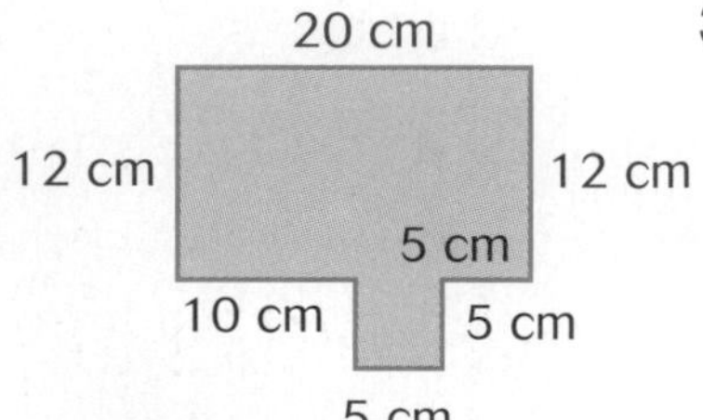

3. 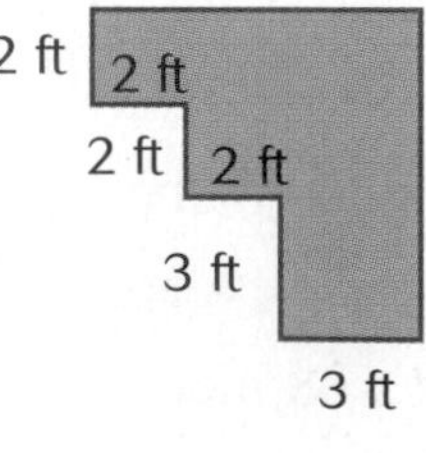

4. How many square yards of carpet would it take to cover the floor of the living room pictured at the right?

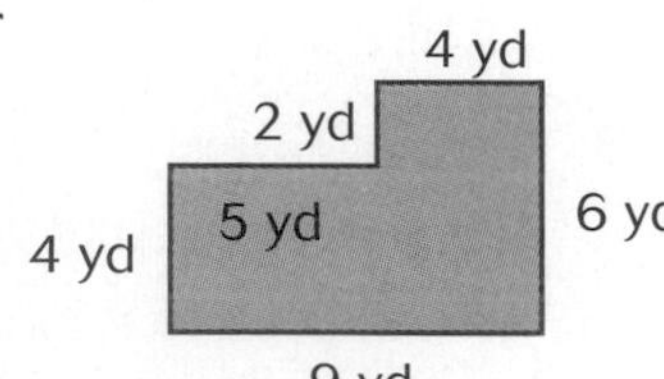

Set G (pages 516–517)

Draw a different rectangle with the same perimeter as the one shown. Then find the area of each.

1. 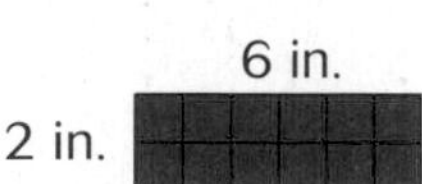

2. 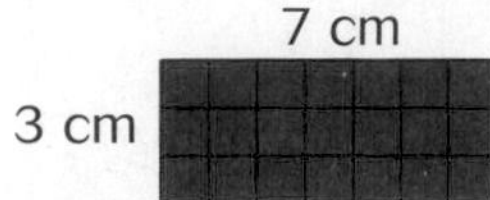

3. 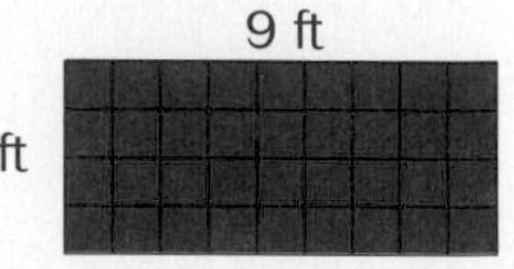

4. How can you arrange 18 square tiles to form a rectangle? List all possible answers. Then find the perimeter of each.

Problem Solving: Preparing for Tests

Choose the correct letter for each answer.

1. Debbie bought 4 toy robots. The least expensive one cost $4.89. The most expensive one cost $12.73. Which is reasonable for the total amount of money Debbie paid for the toys?

A Less than $16

B Between $16 and $20

C Between $20 and $52

D More than $52

Tip

Use estimation to help you solve this problem. Start by rounding each price to the nearest dollar.

2. Pete wants to make a frame for a picture that is 4 inches by 6 inches. He plans to make the frame 1-inch wide. What will the *perimeter* of the outside of the frame be?

F 20 inches

G 24 inches

H 28 inches

J 48 inches

Tip

Draw a Picture to help you solve this problem. Sketch the picture, then sketch the frame around it.

3. It took Sherry 15 minutes to get ready for swim team practice, 10 minutes to walk to the pool, and 10 minutes to warm up before getting in the water. If Sherry got in the water at 1:15 P.M., at what time did she begin to get ready for practice?

A 12:30 P.M.

B 12:40 P.M.

C 12:45 P.M.

D 12:55 P.M.

Tip

Try *Working Backward* to solve this problem. Start with the time Sherry got into the pool.

4. **Yesterday, Frank, Oliver, and Dave each made $42 raking leaves. Which is the best estimate of the amount of money they earned altogether?**

F $40
G $80
H $120
J $150

5. **A flower shop has 37 red roses, 51 pink roses, and 23 yellow roses. *About* how many red and pink roses does the shop have?**

A 70
B 80
C 90
D 110

6. **In this diagram the green area is a garden. The white area is a stone walk. How could you find the area of the walk in square centimeters?**

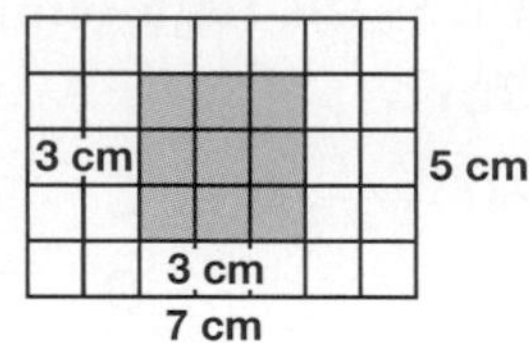

F Subtract 6 from 12.
G Subtract 9 from 12.
H Subtract 6 from 35.
J Subtract 9 from 35.

7. **Bill is following a recipe to make punch. He wants to know how many quarts there are in 18 pints. Which could Bill use to solve this problem? (Hint: There are 2 pints in a quart.)**

A $18 \div 2 = \blacksquare$
B $18 \times 2 = \blacksquare$
C $18 + 2 = \blacksquare$
D $18 - 2 = \blacksquare$

8. **Choose the method Lee Ann could use to change 3 feet 8 inches to inches. (Hint: There are 12 inches in 1 foot.)**

F Add 3 to 8, then multiply by 12.
G Multiply 8 times 12, then add 3.
H Multiply 3 times 8, then add 12.
J Multiply 3 times 12, then add 8.

Use the graph for Questions 9 and 10.

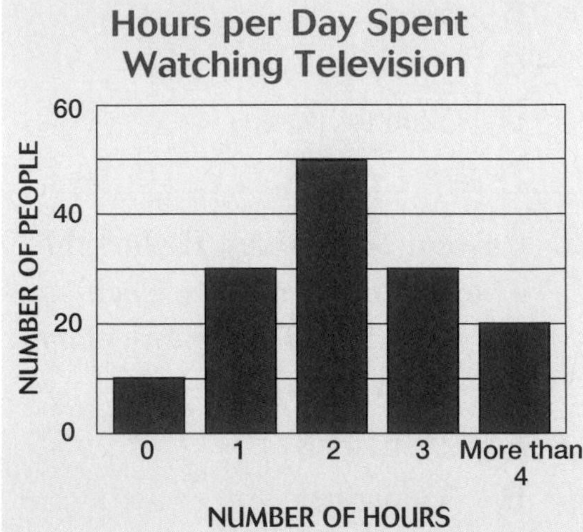

9. **How many more people watch 2 hours of television a day than watch no television at all?**

A 30 people
B 40 people
C 50 people
D 60 people

10. **How many people watch less than 3 hours of television per day?**

F 45 people
G 90 people
H 100 people
J 120 people

TEST PREP

Multiple-Choice Cumulative Review

Choose the correct letter for each answer.

Number Sense

1. What is the value of the 5 in 4,251,768?

A 5 ones
B 5 tens
C 5 thousands
D 5 ten thousands

2. Cal had 24 marbles. He bought 4 bags of new marbles. Each bag has 8 marbles. How many marbles does he have now?

F 24 marbles
G 32 marbles
H 40 marbles
J 56 marbles

3. Inez has 4 pairs of socks. If she buys one more pair, how many socks in all will she have?

A 12 socks
B 10 socks
C 8 socks
D 5 socks

4. What is the quotient of 45 ÷ 9?

F 9
G 8
H 6
J 5

Statistics, Data Analysis, and Probability

Use the graph for Questions 5–7.

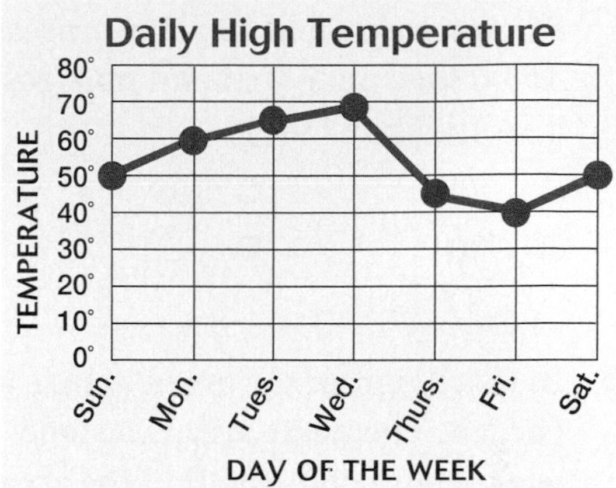

5. What was the high temperature on Monday?

A 60° **C** 70°
B 63° **D** 75°

6. Which day had the highest temperature?

F Tuesday **H** Thursday
G Wednesday **J** Friday

7. Which two days had the same high temperature?

A Sunday and Monday
B Tuesday and Wednesday
C Sunday and Saturday
D Thursday and Friday

Measurement and Geometry

8. Which figure appears to be congruent (same size, same shape) to the figure at the right?

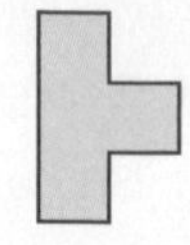

F 

H 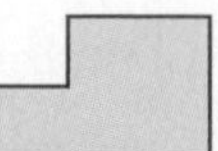

G 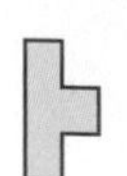

J

---

9. Abdul drank 1.5 liters of water after track practice. How many *milliliters* was that? (Hint: 1 liter equals 1,000 milliliters.)

A 15,000 milliliters
B 1,500 milliliters
C 150 milliliters
D 15 milliliters

---

10. Peg boiled an egg for 4 minutes. How many seconds is that? (Hint: 60 seconds equal 1 minute.)

F 56 seconds **H** 100 seconds
G 64 seconds **J** 240 seconds

---

11. Name the figure.

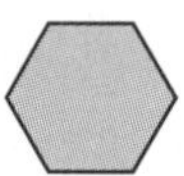

A quadrilateral
B pentagon
C hexagon
D octagon

12. What is the *area* of the shaded region?

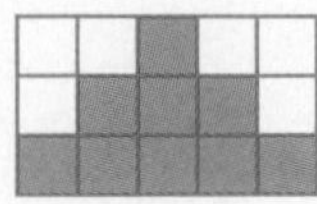

F 6 square units
G 9 square units
H 15 square units
J 16 square units

---

13. Jordan's dog, Rex, weighs 25 pounds 5 ounces. Ray's dog, Lady, weighs 42 pounds 10 ounces. How much more does Lady weigh than Rex?

A 7 lb **C** 17 lb 5 oz
B 7 lb 15 oz **D** 23 lb 5 oz

---

14. Which is the best estimate of the *area* of the shaded region?

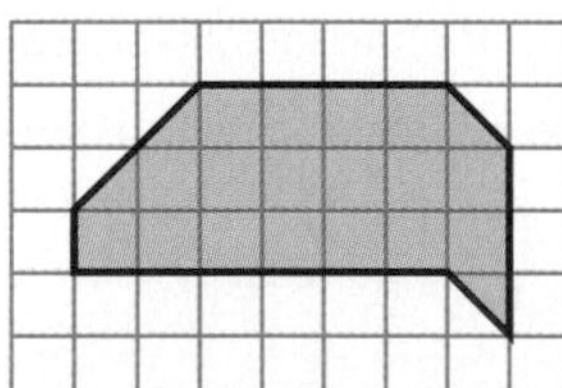

F 17 square units
G 19 square units
H 21 square units
J 28 square units

---

15. What kind of angle is shown?

A acute **C** obtuse
B right **D** scalene

Credits

Photographs

All photographs owned by Scott Foresman unless listed here.

Front Cover and Back Inset: Carr Clifton; Front and Back Cover Background: Bruce McNitt/Panoramic Images

6: David Ball/Stone

163: Art Wolfe/Stone

181: Harvey Barnett/Peter Arnold, Inc.

182: D. Holden Bailey/TOM STACK & ASSOCIATES

205: ©Will & Deni McIntyre/Photo Researchers, Inc.

221(L): Global Directions Incorporated

221(R): Global Directions Incorporated

226: Courtesy, June Kwak

360: AP/Wide World

397: Barbara Gerlach/Visuals Unlimited

398: Mitsuaki Iwago/Minden Pictures

404: Lawrence Migdale/Stock Boston

436(T): David Young-Wolff/PhotoEdit

436(B): Bill Banaszewski/Visuals Unlimited

468: Richard B. Levine

498(L): ©Rod Planck/Photo Researchers, Inc.

498(R): ©Richard Parker/Photo Researchers, Inc.

Illustrations

5: Linda Howard

14: Chris Pappas

16: Linda Howard

17: Carla Kiwior

46: Mike Dammer

59: George Hamblin

62: Reggie Holladay

63: George Hamblin

96: Burgandy Beam

105: Chris Pappas

109: Carla Kiwior

130: Gary Krejca

131: Reggie Holladay

143: Burgandy Beam

144, 145, 160: George Hamblin

165: Mike Dammer

166: George Hamblin

214: Chris Pappas

219: Burgandy Beam

230: George Hamblin

231, 233: Carla Kiwior

252: Burgandy Beam

253, 258, 261, 262: George Hamblin

263, 265, 268: Burgandy Beam

279, 280, 285, 304: George Hamblin

316: Chris Pappas

321: Reggie Holladay

323: Chris Pappas

342, 346, 358, 364: George Hamblin

365: Gary Krejca

370, 372: George Hamblin

376, 377: Carla Kiwior

397, 461: Chris Pappas

495: Burgandy Beam

502, 504: George Hamblin

504: George Hamblin

Additional Resources

Tables

Measures—*Customary*

Length

1 foot (ft) = 12 inches (in)
1 yard (yd) = 3 feet, or 36 inches
1 mile = 5,280 feet, or 1,760 yards

Weight

1 pound (lb) = 16 ounces (oz)
1 ton (T) = 2,000 pounds

Capacity

1 cup (c) = 8 fluid ounces (fl oz) or 16 tablespoons (tbsp)
1 tablespoon (tbsp) = 3 teaspoons (tsp)
1 pint (pt) = 2 cups
1 quart (qt) = 2 pints
1 half-gallon = 2 quarts
1 gallon (gal) = 4 quarts

Time

1 minute (min) = 60 seconds (s)
1 hour (hr) = 60 minutes
1 day (d) = 24 hours
1 week (wk) = 7 days
1 year (yr) = 12 months (mo), or 52 weeks, or 365 days
1 leap year = 366 days (adds one day to February)
1 decade = 10 years
1 century (c) = 100 years
1 millennium = 1,000 years

Measures—*Metric*

Length

1 centimeter (cm) = 10 millimeters (mm)
1 decimeter (dm) = 10 centimeters
1 meter (m) = 100 centimeters
1 kilometer (km) = 1,000 meters

Mass/Weight

1 kilogram (kg) = 1,000 grams (g)

Capacity

1 liter (L) = 1,000 milliliters (mL)

Symbols

$=$	is equal to
$>$	is greater than
$<$	is less than
$^\circ$	degree
°C	degree Celsius
°F	degree Fahrenheit
$\perp$	is perpendicular
$\overleftrightarrow{AB}$	line *AB*
$\overline{AB}$	line segment *AB*
$\overrightarrow{AB}$	ray *AB*
$\angle ABC$	angle *ABC*
(3, 4)	ordered pair 3, 4

Formulas

$P = (2\ell) + (2w)$	Perimeter of a rectangle
$P = 4s$	Perimeter of a square
$A = \ell \times w$	Area of a rectangle
$A = s \times s$	Area of a square
$V = \ell \times w \times h$	Volume of a rectangular prism

Test-Taking Tips

Follow Instructions

- Listen carefully as your teacher explains the test.

Budget Your Time

- Do the questions in order if you can.
- If a question seems very hard, skip it and go back to it later.

Read Carefully

- Watch for extra information in a problem.
- Watch for words like *not.*
- Be sure to answer the question asked.

Make Smart Choices

- **Estimate** when you can so that you have a better idea what the answer might be.
- **Eliminate** answer choices that are not reasonable or are clearly wrong.
- **Check** an answer that you *think* is correct by working backward.

Mark Answers Correctly

- If you are using a "bubble" answer sheet or a gridded response form, be careful to match each question number with the correct number of the answer row.
- If you skip a question, be sure to leave that question's answer space blank.

Glossary

acute angle An angle that is less than a right angle. (p. 439)
Example:

acute triangle A triangle that has three acute angles. (p. 444)

addends The numbers that are added. (p. 48)

algebraic expression An expression with variables. (p. 61)

angle A figure formed when two rays meet at their endpoints. The common endpoint is the vertex. (p. 438)
Example:

area The number of square units needed to cover the surface. (p. 511)

array An arrangement of objects or numbers in rows and columns. (p. 84)

associative property Grouping property of multiplication or addition. (p. 87)

average (or mean) is a number that gives a good idea about the sizes of the numbers in the group. It is the sum of the addends divided by the number of addends. (p. 226)

B

bar graph A graph with bars of different lengths to show information. (p. 394)

brackets [ ] grouping symbols. (p. 98)

breaking apart A mental math method in which a sum or difference is found by rewriting numbers so they are easier to work with. (p. 58)

C

certain Sure. (p. 279)

centimeter (cm) A metric unit used to measure length. 100 centimeters equal 1 meter. (p. 496)

circle A closed plane figure in which all points are the same distance from a point called the center. (p. 452)
Example:

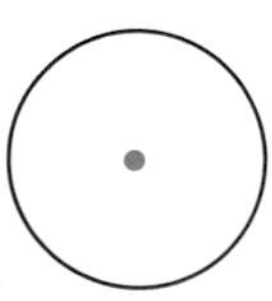

circumference Distance around a circle. (p. 452)

common denominator A common multiple of two or more denominators. (p. 318)

commutative property Order property of multiplication and addition. (p. 87)

compatible numbers Numbers that are easy to compute with mentally. (p. 212)

compensation A mental math method in which a sum or difference is changed into an equivalent sum or difference to make it easier to add or subtract. (p. 59)

composite number A whole number greater than 1 with more than two factors. (p. 223)

congruent Having the same size and shape. (p. 456)
Example:

coordinates The numbers in an ordered pair. (p. 407)

cube A space figure with six congruent square faces. (p. 466)
Example:

cylinder A space figure with two bases that are congruent circles. (p. 466)
Example:

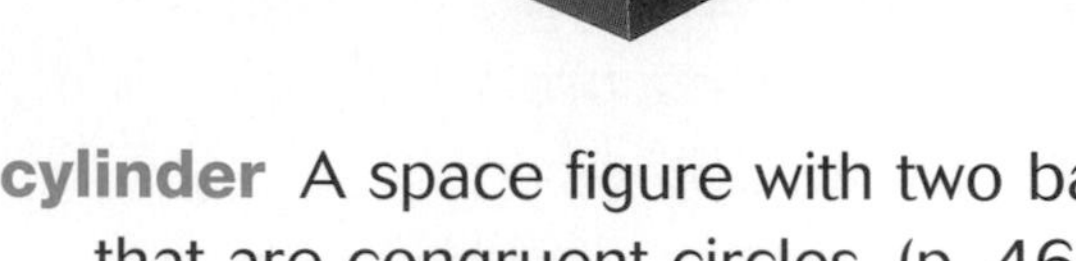

D

data Collected pieces of information. (p. 392)

decimal A number with one or more places to the right of the decimal point. (p. 344)

decimeter (dm) A metric unit used to measure length. 1 decimeter equals 10 centimeters. (p. 496)

degree A unit of measure for an angle. (p. 464)

denominator The number below the fraction bar in a fraction. (p. 252)

decimal point The mark used to separate dollars from cents and ones from tenths. (p. 344)

diameter Any line segment that passes through the center of the circle connecting two points on the circle. (p. 452)

difference The answer in subtraction. (p. 38)

digit Any of the ten symbols: 0, 1, 2, 3, 4, 5, 6, 7, 8, and 9. (p. 4)

dividend The number to be divided. (p. 90)

divisible A number is divisible by another number if the remainder is 0 after dividing. (p. 223)

divisor The number by which another number is divided. (p. 90)

doubles Facts in which the same number is added to itself or multiplied by 2. (p. 84)

Glossary

edge A segment where two plane faces of a space figure meet. (p. 466)
Example:

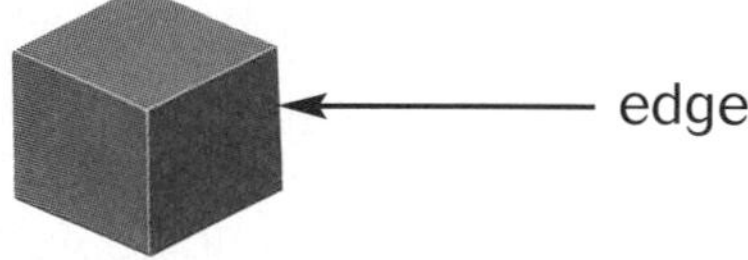

equilateral triangle A triangle with all three sides the same length. (p. 444)

equally likely Two events are equally likely to happen if they have the same probability. (p. 278)

equation A number sentence stating that two expressions are equal. (p. 64)

equivalent decimals Decimals that name the same number. (p. 344)

equivalent fractions Fractions that name the same amount. (p. 278)

estimate An approximate rather than an exact answer. (p. 6, p. 164)

expanded form A number written as the sum of the value of its digits. (p. 4)

face In a solid figure, a flat surface that is shaped like a polygon. (p. 466)
Example:

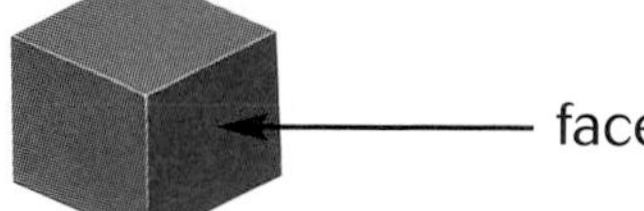

fact family Related facts using the same numbers. (p. 90)

factors The numbers that are multiplied to give a product. (p. 84)

flip A reflection of a figure that gives a mirror image of the figure. (p. 462)

foot (ft) A customary unit used to measure length. 1 foot equals 12 inches. (p. 492)

fraction A number that names part of a set or part of a region. (p. 252)
Example:

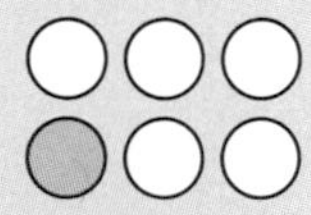

$\frac{1}{6}$ of the set is shaded. $\frac{5}{8}$ of the region is shaded.

front-end digit The digit in the place with the greatest value, used for front-end estimation. (p. 38)

front-end estimation A method using only the front-end digits to estimate sums, differences, products, or quotients. (p. 38)

G

gallon (gal) A customary unit used to measure capacity. 1 gallon equals 4 quarts. (p. 494)

gram (g) A metric unit used to measure the mass of lighter objects. (p. 497)

graph A drawing used to show information. (p. 412)

greater than (>) The symbol used to compare two numbers when the greater number is on the left. (p. 8)

grouping symbols ( ) parentheses, [ ] brackets, and { } braces. (p. 98)

hexagon A polygon with six sides and six vertices. (p. 441)

hundredths One or more of one hundred equal parts of a whole. (p. 344)

impossible Cannot occur. (p. 279)

improper fraction A fraction in which the numerator is greater than or equal to the denominator. Its value is greater than or equal to 1. (p. 260)

inch (in.) A customary unit used to measure length. 12 inches equal 1 foot. (p. 492)

intersecting lines Lines that pass through the same point. (p. 439)
Example:

isosceles triangle A triangle that has two sides that are the same length. (p. 444)

kilogram (kg) A metric unit used to measure mass. 1 kilogram equals 1,000 grams. (p. 497)

kilometer (km) A metric unit used to measure length. 1 kilometer equals 1,000 meters. (p. 496)

leaf The second digit of each number in a stem-and-leaf plot. (p. 396)

less likely An event is less likely to happen if it has a smaller probability of happening than another event. (p. 278)

less than (<) The symbol used to compare two numbers when the lesser number is on the left. (p. 8)

line A set of points that go on and on in both directions. (p. 438)

line graph A graph that connects points to show how data changes over time. (p. 402)

line plot A graph that shows data along a number line. Each **x** represents one number in the data set. (p. 398)

line segment Part of a line. It has two endpoints. (p. 438)

line of symmetry A line on which a figure can be folded so that both sides match. (p. 460)
Example:

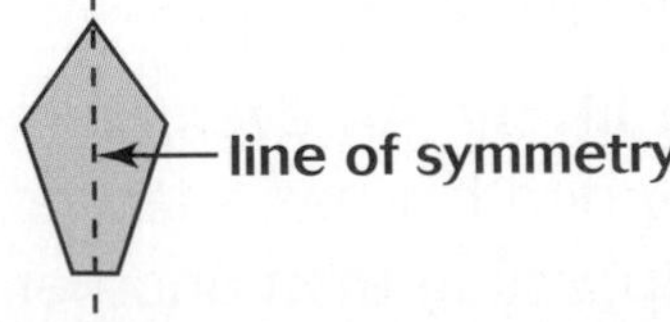

Glossary

liter A metric unit used to measure the capacities of larger containers. (p. 497)

mean (an average) A number that gives a general idea about the sizes of the numbers in the group. (p. 226)

median The middle number or average of the two middle numbers in a set of data when the data are arranged in order from least to greatest. (p. 392)

meter (m) A metric unit used to measure length. 1 meter equals 100 centimeters. (p. 496)

mile (mi.) A customary unit used to measure length. 1 mile equals 5,280 feet. (p. 492)

milliliter (mL) A metric unit used to measure the capacities of small containers. (p. 497)

millimeter (mm) A metric unit used to measure length. 10 millimeters equal 1 centimeter. (p. 496)

mixed number A number containing a whole number part and a fraction part. (p. 260)

mode The number or numbers that occur most often in a collection of data. (p. 392)

more likely An event is more likely to happen if it has a larger probability of happening than another event. (p. 278)

multiple The product of a whole number and any other whole number. (p. 128)

multiplication An operation on two or more numbers, called factors, to find a product. (p. 84)

multiplication table A table that organizes multiplication facts. (p. 84)

negative number Any number less than zero. (p. 17)

net A pattern that can be used to make a solid. (p. 469)

number line A line that shows numbers in order. (p. 17)
Example:

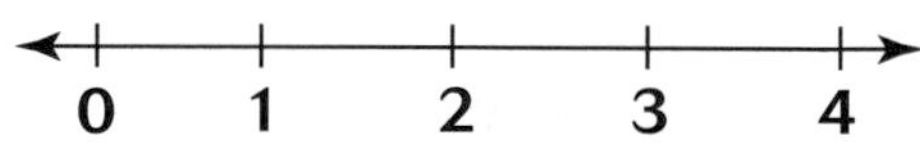

number sentence A fact about numbers written in horizontal form. (p. 181)

numerator The number above the fraction bar in a fraction. (p. 252)

obtuse angle An angle that is greater than a right angle. (p. 439)
Example:

obtuse triangle A triangle that has one obtuse angle. (p. 444)

octagon A polygon with eight sides and 8 vertices. (p. 441)

ordered pair A pair of numbers that give the location of points on a coordinate grid. (p. 407)

ounce (oz) A customary unit used to measure weight. 16 ounces equal 1 pound. (p. 493)

outcome A result of a probability experiment. (p. 282)

outlier A number in a data set that is very different from the rest of the numbers. (p. 398)

P

parallel lines Lines that never intersect. (p. 439)
Example:

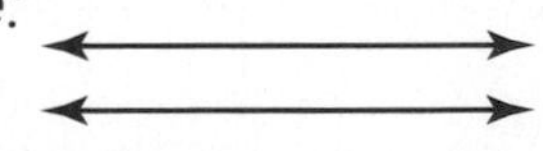

parallelogram A quadrilateral with opposite sides parallel. (p. 447)

parentheses ( ) Grouping symbols. They can show which operation should be done first. (p. 98)

pentagon A polygon with five sides and five vertices. (p. 441)

perimeter The distance around the outside of a figure. (p. 508)

period A group of three digits separated from other digits of a number by a comma. (p. 4)

perpendicular lines Lines that intersect to form right angles. (p. 439)
Example:

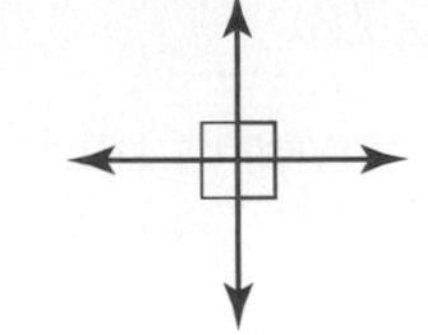

pictograph A graph that shows information by using pictures. (p. 110)

pint (pt) A customary unit used to measure capacity. 1 pint equals 2 cups. (p. 493)

place value The value determined by the position of a digit in a number. (p. 4)

place value chart A chart used to show the values of each digit in a number. (p. 4)

plane figure A geometric figure whose points are all in one plane. (p. 441)

plot To locate and mark the point named by an ordered pair on a grid. (p. 407)

point An exact location in space. (p. 407)

polygon A closed plane figure made up of three or more line segments that intersect only at their endpoints. (p. 441)

positive number Any number greater than zero. (p. 17)

pound (lb) A customary unit used to measure weight. 1 pound equals 16 ounces. (p. 494)

Glossary

prime number Any whole number greater than 1 that has exactly two factors, the number itself and 1. (p. 223)

probability The chance that an event will happen. (p. 278)

product The answer in multiplication. (p. 84)

properties of equality Equals added to equals are equal. Equals subtracted from equals are equal. Equals multiplied by equals are equal. Equals divided by equals are equal. (p. 231)

property of one for division Any number divided by 1 is that number. Any number except 0 divided by itself is 1. (p. 94)

property of one for multiplication The product of any number and 1 is that number. (p. 87)

quadrilateral A polygon with 4 sides and 4 vertices. (p. 441)

quart (qt) A customary unit used to measure capacity. 1 quart equals 4 cups. (p. 493)

quotient The answer in division. (p. 90)

radius Any line segment that connects the center of a circle to a point on the circle. (p. 452)

range The difference between the greatest number and the least number in a set of data. (p. 132)

ray A part of a line. It has one endpoint and continues on and on in one direction. (p. 438)

rectangle A quadrilateral with both pairs of opposite sides parallel. There are four right angles. (p. 447)

rectangular prism A space figure whose faces are all rectangles. (p. 466)
Example:

regroup To use 1 ten to form 10 ones; 1 hundred to form 10 tens; 12 tens to form 1 hundred and 2 tens; and so on. (p. 42)

remainder The number that is left over after dividing. (p. 205)

rhombus A quadrilateral with both pairs of opposite sides parallel and all sides the same length. (p. 447)

right angle An angle that forms a square corner. (p. 439)
Example:

right triangle A triangle with one right angle. (p. 444)

rotation A turn of a figure around a point. (p. 464)

rotational symmetry A figure that rotates onto itself in less than a full turn has rotational symmetry. (p. 464)

rounding Expressing a number to the nearest ten, hundred, thousand, and so on. (p. 14)

S

scalene triangle A triangle that has no two sides that are the same length. (p. 444)

short word form A number written with words naming the periods. (p. 4)

sides Line segments that form a polygon. (p. 441)

simplest form A fraction in which the only common factor of the numerator and denominator is one. (p. 269)

slide A translation of a figure up, down, or over. (p. 462)

solid figure A three-dimensional object. (p. 466)

solution The value of the variable that makes an equation true. (p. 64)

sphere A space figure shaped like a round ball. (p. 466)
Example:

square A quadrilateral in which all sides are the same length. There are four right angles. (p. 447)

square pyramid A space figure with a square base and faces that are triangles with a common vertex. (p. 466)
Example:

standard form A number written with commas separating groups of three digits. (p. 4)

stem A part that stands for the first digit of each number in a stem-and-leaf plot. (p. 396)

stem-and-leaf plot A display that shows data in order of place value. The leaves are the last digits of the numbers, and the stems are the digits to the left of the leaves. (p. 396)

straight angle An angle that forms a straight line. (p. 439)

subtraction An operation on two numbers to find the difference. (p. 38)

sum The answer in addition. (p. 38)

Glossary

tally chart A table used to organize data. Each tally mark represents one piece of data. (p. 392)

tenths One or more of ten equal parts of a whole. (p. 344)

tree diagram A list of all of the choices available in a problem. (p. 175)

triangle A polygon with 3 sides and 3 vertices. (p. 441)

trapezoid A quadrilateral with only one pair of parallel sides. (p. 447)

turn (or rotation) Movement of a figure about a point. (p. 462)

variable A symbol that stands for a number. (p. 61)

vertex The point where two rays meet. The point of intersection of two sides of a polygon. The point of intersection of three edges of a space figure. (p. 438)
Example:

vertex

vertices More than one vertex. (p. 441)

word form A number written as words, such as two hundred twelve. (p. 4)

***x*-axis** The horizontal axis in a coordinate grid. (p. 407)

***x*-coordinate** The first number in an ordered pair. (p. 407)

yard (yd) A customary unit used to measure length. 1 yard equals 3 feet. (p. 492)

***y*-axis** The vertical axis in a coordinate grid. (p. 407)

***y*-coordinate** The second number in an ordered pair. (p. 407)

zero property of division Zero divided by any number except zero is zero. You cannot divide a number by zero. (p. 94)

zero property of multiplication The product of any number and zero is zero. (p. 87)

Index

Index

D

Index

Index

Index

G

Index

Index

Index

N

Index

O

P

Index

Index

Q

R

Index

Index

Index